Children's Literature
An Issues Approach

Children's Literature
—An Issues Approach—

Masha Kabakow Rudman
University of Massachusetts, Amherst

D. C. HEATH AND COMPANY
Lexington, Massachusetts   Toronto   London

This book is dedicated

To my parents, Gussie and Ben Kabakow
   my husband, Sy
   my daughters, Rachel, Reva, and Debbie

With deep love and gratitude

Foreword

by JANE YOLEN

Not too long ago, a friend of mine told me "I love your book *Greyling* and have read it over and over." And while I took my turn to preen and look modest at once, she added, "I changed the ending, of course."

What my erstwhile friend was doing was not just changing the ending. She was joining a long line of censors who, down through the ages, have marked stories for children with their own brand. Francis James Childs, the collector of the Child ballads, called such people the "blind beggar, the nursery maid, and the clerk."

Certainly I can understand the desire to tamper with a tale for morality's sake. But I wish my friend had not told me of her change. After all, the story had not been written in a vacuum, moral or otherwise.

All art is moral, a striving for the light. But unlike earlier moralities which were consistent in their demands on men and women and, hence artists, the moralities of today are shifting and changing by decades rather than slowly, over centuries. Communications are swift today, the speed of light. And minorities which could previously be ignored, are eloquent in their demands for redress, for justice. They are heard and reheard, and they cannot be denied.

Artists are aware, are made aware, of injustices. As individuals in an individual age, they create out of an idiosyncratic sense of what is right. This is not to say that writers and other artists should try to be moralists and create propaganda. Propaganda is bad art. And, as Isaac Beshevis Singer reminds us, "In art, a truth that is boring is not true."

But the best writers write from the heart. As Harlan Ellison, the science fiction writer, has said, "I write what I am. There is no way to create literature."

And if all art is moral, then all art becomes morality. What I write out of my own needs and ideas and ideals becomes a statement. That statement can be accepted or rejected by the reader. If the reader is an adult, the acceptance or rejection is probably a fairly conscious choice.

The child does not read that way. A child reader reads with the heart. And so, if I write for children, I must be aware that children are going to accept what I write with their hearts. My morality becomes their morality. Heart to heart, body to body, blood to blood, a kind of literary eucharist.

The changing of the ending can change the morality of a tale, but it changes the author's intent also. That is not consistent with the idea of literature.

However, there are times when the morality of a book, even a fine literary work, is inconsistent with that of the teacher, the librarian, the parent. The answer then is not to force a change of endings, or the more extreme version of that—burn books. As a teaching device changing the ending or the characters or sex, and so on can be most productive. But arbitrarily changing an ending, without letting the child know that such a thing is happening, is direct censorship and *does* change the author's intent, whether the intent was an overt or covert one.

Dr. Rudman offers many ways in which an educator can help to structure the reading and aid young readers in sorting out conflicting or inconsistent moralities. She does not necessarily throw out a book because its morality is outdated or its characters mouth inhumane statements. Rather, she suggests methods of dealing with these problems within the classroom or home. She does not necessarily recommend a book even though it is correct in its preaching, if preaching is all the book does. She is concerned with human relationships, with understandings, with morality. But she is concerned with literature, too. In a field which is all too often crowded with didactic moralists, Dr. Rudman is literature's champion.

As a writer, I thank Dr. Rudman for that concern. However, I must also point out that what she is offering is the second step in a two-step process. The first step, of course, lies with the authors and illustrators who create the materials with which children dream. We are the myth-makers.

We must write from the heart. Write from the heart and you write your own truth. And if we have changed and grown inside, the truth we write will change and grow, too.

Then the children will be touched. Touch and pass it on. It is the only way.

Preface

HOW TO USE THIS BOOK

The book need not be read from cover to cover, nor must any particular sequence of chapters be followed. It is meant as a reference and guide to critical evaluation of the treatment of issues in children's books. Each chapter can be used independently from the others. If there are specific issues that readers are more concerned with than others, the chapters handling those topics may be treated as entities apart from the rest of the book.

Each chapter contains

1. A discussion of an issue.
2. A section relating particular books to the topic as exemplars of how that topic is handled in children's literature.
3. Two or more suggestions for activities that future teachers or other concerned adults may try in order to personalize and extend the discussion.
4. Several activities for young readers to attempt in order to expand their critical reading skills.
5. An annotated reference list of sources relating the topic to children and books.

6. An annotated bibliography of children's books pertaining to the topic.

Some readers may find the annotated bibliographies useful as a basis for building a library. These lists may also be used as book selection aids. This author has read all the books and references included on the lists. The opinions expressed in the annotations reflect this one person's ideas and reactions; therefore, readers should not hesitate to differ, argue, reject, or concur with any or all of the remarks attached to the books. The age levels attached to the books are suggested by the publishers, but readers are urged to use their own judgment as to the appropriateness of any book to any age level.

Some readers may wish to repeat the activities recommended for children for use with other topics or situations. The subject index, therefore, lists the locations of all the activities with and without reference to subject. The *Try This* sections are also noted in the subject index.

Prices of resources have not been included in the reference listings because they have changed so rapidly over the past few years. It is recommended that readers send all queries to the addresses listed; they should assume that there will be a fee for all listed materials.

This author welcomes any comments, suggestions, and additions from all readers. Useful information will be compiled and circulated to those readers who respond to this request.

MASHA K. RUDMAN
Amherst, Massachusetts

Acknowledgments

In an effort of this magnitude, spanning four years, and thousands of books, many people have been involved. The idea for the text arose from the format of my seminar in children's literature. My students wanted references to consult for a thematic approach to children's books. Few existed. Therefore, it is on their instigation that I wrote this book. Their comments, their support, and their enthusiasm have sustained me.

Other critics have been very responsive and helpful. My husband, Sy Rudman, is my first reader. His comments, from a psychological perspective, and as a jargon-detector, have aided greatly. Jane Yolen's careful and constructive readings of initial drafts have been of enormous value. My daughters Rachel, Reva, and Debbie read many of the children's books. Their comments and perceptions were invaluable.

Research for this text also involved the efforts of a number of students and friends. People kept findings new articles and sources they thought I might be interested in using. Particularly helpful in this respect and in verifying the accuracy of the entries, were Sondra Radosh and the staff of the Jones Library in Amherst. Muriel Parsisson of the Forbes Library in Northampton, and the entire staff of the reference room of the University of Massachusetts Library were patient and cooperative beyond the call of duty. Students such as Martha Cohen, Nancy Hellman, Barbara Murphy, and Linda Reeves spent long hours checking on information to be included in the text, and helping to organize the bibliographies.

The typing and other organizational work was managed over the years by Kathy Boron. In the final stages, Kathy was joined by Teri Chyz, Linda Allen, Tudor Cushman, and my daughter Debbie.

The text could not have been completed without the loving support of my entire family. Kathy Boron's endurance and good nature at coping with all of the changes and additions were extraordinary. Finally, the enthusiasm of my editor, Lane Akers, his clarifying comments and suggestions, and his steady encouragement contributed to the joys of the entire project.

To all of these, and more, I acknowledge my debt and tender my thanks.

Thanks to the Council on Interracial Books for Children, Inc., for permission to reprint "Ten Quick Ways to Analyze Books for Racism and Sexism." Thanks to the Council, also, for all of the information and materials they contributed.

Thanks are also due to McGraw-Hill Book Company for permission to reproduce sections of "Guidelines for Equal Treatment of the Sexes" in McGraw-Hill Book Company Publications.

Thanks to all of the publishers who so generously sent materials for the text.

Contents

Foreword by Jane Yolen   vii
Preface: How to Use This Book   xi
Acknowledgments   xiii

1   Introduction   1

References   8

2   Siblings   12

Suggested Criteria   14
Discussion of Children's Books   15
    The New Baby   15
    Sibling Rivalry   18
    Cooperation and Love   20
    Facing Responsibility   21
    Special Problems   22
References   23
Bibliography   25

3   *Divorce*   44

Suggested Criteria   46
Discussion of Children's Books   48
    Breaking Up   *48*
    Aftermath of the Divorce   *52*
    Managing   *54*
References   57
Bibliography   59

4   *Death and Old Age*   69

Factual Books   72
Some Questions to Explore   75
Suggested Criteria   76
Discussion of Children's Books   77
    Books for Young Children   *77*
      Funerals   *77*
      Immortality   *79*
      Old Age   *80*
      Reacting to Death   *83*
    Books for Older Children   *84*
      Reacting to Death   *84*
      Suicide   *87*
      Old Age   *88*
      Books in which Death is
      Incidental   *90*
References   93
Bibliography   96

5   *War*   113

Suggested Criteria   114
Discussion of Children's Books   115
    Books for Young Children   *115*
      General Books   *115*
      Historical Books   *121*
      Poetry   *122*

Books for Older Children   122
    Historical Fiction   123
    Revolutionary War   123
    Civil War   124
    World War II   125
    Korean War   127
    Vietnam War   127
    Poetry   127
    Nonfiction   128
References   129
Bibliography   131

6   *Sex*   145

Suggested Criteria   151
Discussion of Children's Books   152
    Books for Young Children   152
    Books for Older Children   154
        Nonfiction   154
        Fiction   156
References   158
Bibliography   161

7   *The Black*   172

Suggested Criteria   178
Discussion of Children's Books   183
    Visible at Last   184
    Urban Life   184
    Rural Life   188
    Family Life   190
    Friends   193
    Self-Image   194
    Folk Tales   195
    History   197
References   208
Black Organizations and Publishers   215
Bibliography   217

8   The Native American   253

Historical Overview   255
Suggested Criteria   260
Discussion of Children's Books   262
    Folklore   262
    History   263
    Customs   265
    Contemporary Life   266
References   269
Native American Publishers   273
Bibliography   274

9   The Female   290

Suggested Criteria   296
Discussion of Children's Books   302
    Folk and Fairy Tales   302
    Classics   305
    Nonfiction   307
    Biographies   309
    Girls as Main Characters   311
    Women in Children's Books   313
References   315
Feminist Organizations and Publishers   322
Bibliography   323

10   Using Children's Books in a Reading Program   358

Principles of This Reading Program   362
    Self-Selection   363
    Self-Evaluation   366
Implementing the Program   366
    Kinds of Groups   366
    Scheduling   367
    Room Arrangement   368
    Record-Keeping   368
Activities   369
References   374

APPENDIX A: *Publishers' Addresses*   377

APPENDIX B: *Selected Children's Book Awards*   383

APPENDIX C: *Other References for Children's*
             Literature   398

INDEXES: Author/Illustrator Index   405
          Title Index   415
          Subject Index   429

Children's Literature
An Issues Approach

1

An Overview

EDUCATORS are an audacious group. We have within our power the means to inculcate values, develop skills, influence attitudes, and affect the physical, social, emotional, intellectual, and moral development of today's youth and tomorrow's adults. We accept this responsibility when we decide to be parents, teachers, counselors, librarians, or to be in any position in which we influence children. We hope that our instruction will produce positive attitudes, values, and behaviors. In order to build a healthy society, we are continuously searching for additional and better means to transmit what we believe is positive and to change what we perceive is wrong.

The aims of education also include the appropriate acquisition of skills in such basic areas as reading, writing, and computation. Skills taught in isolation, however, or placed in meaning-less context become inoperable; people need to have real situations in which to practice their skills. Knowing how to read is useless, unless one reads. Recognizing this principle, contemporary education provides as many opportunities as possible within the environment of the schools for children to practice the basic skills meaningfully.

It has also been recognized that society needs responsible decision-makers. There is no magic age when this ability suddenly appears; it must be carefully developed. It is not useful or necessary to wait until a child has reached college, high school, or even junior high school to begin. The process should begin as soon as the child begins to reason; decision-making skills need not be reserved for important, long-range matters. The skills are developed whenever choices are available; a person weighs the options and makes a decision.

Even preschool children have the opportunity to decide about many things. They select clothing, food, activities, and playmates. Though their choices may be very limited, they should be encouraged to evaluate the success of their decisions. Was that sweater warm enough? Did the ice cream taste better than the pudding? Whose house will you play at today? Young children negotiate with each other over what game to play, what the rules will be, and when to begin and end their play. Their choices are usually accepted when they request that favorite stories be read to them, when they ask to see a specific show on television, or when they select what they want to receive as gifts.

Then, in first grade, some of these choice-making, evaluating chil-dren are too often not considered capable of making responsible choices about their use of time, selection of activity, or preference in literature. In keeping with the philosophy governing many classrooms, they are told when and where to sit and stand, and, sometimes even when to be thirsty and when to have to go to the bathroom. Schools too often have valued conformity over individual decision-making.

The current emphasis in education is on basic skills, individualized instruction, and values clarification. The structure of the conventional classroom has changed and continues to change. Means are being sought to enable children to maintain and improve their choice-making and evaluative skills. Students are being encouraged to explore their environment and to extract from it that which is meaningful to them. Reading, one of the most important areas of instruction in the schools, has emerged as a critical tool for the development of the skills of inde-pendent and responsible critical thinking and behavior.

In the past, reading programs concentrated on the mechanical as-pects of skills. Though concerned publishers and educators attempted to address comprehension and critical reading, the important part of read-ing instruction pertained to simple decoding, or word calling. These initial mechanical skills are still recognized as important, but most reading programs now also take into consideration the more complex and advanced requirements for competence in reading. Children's textbooks have undergone a marked transformation: they are, in general, more colorful, more diverse, and more calculated to attract and interest the young reader. No longer is the assumption made that children will automatically read whatever they are told to. Teachers consistently use supplemental materials and recognize the importance of a class library. The low cost and plentiful supply of paperback books for young readers enables reading programs to expand their general educational impact.

The field of children's literature has kept pace with the trends in education as a whole. Adults who study children's books today do so for a great variety of reasons. The study of children's literature for the purpose of acquiring a historical background remains valid, as a historical perspective is valuable no matter what the subject matter is. Courses directed toward this approach provide insights into how and why we have reached the point where we are. A genre approach — examining the different literary categories of children's books — is probably the most widespread way of learning about children's books. There are many excellent sources and texts guiding students in this approach, which has the advantage of providing the adult with an overview of the field. It also attempts to assist the reader in developing a set of literary criteria for use in selecting children's books. A careful reading and consideration of these criteria are helpful, even to the adult who is primarily concerned with issues.

In keeping with contemporary aims of education, directions in publishing for children, and societal needs, this author recommends an additional approach to the study of children's literature. A critical examination of the books in the light of how they treat contemporary social problems and conditions is as essential as are the historical and literary perspectives. Books are important influences on their readers' minds. They can either help or hinder us when we attempt to construct suitable bases for attitudes and behaviors. A critical, or issues, approach should, therefore, be included in the repertoire of courses and texts available to adult learners.

This text will present discussions, analyses, controversies, and arguments about the issues of sibling relations, divorce, death and old age, war, sex education, treatment of minorities such as the Black and the Native American, and the role of the female as they are handled in children's books. The discussion will pertain to children only up to age twelve. After age twelve, readers are considered to be young adults and are treated almost as adults by publishers. The expectation has been that books for children over twelve will contain issues that relate to life's problems; but, until fairly recently, books for young children attempted to shield their audience from problems, dissension, and dilemmas of social import.

That situation has drastically changed over the past ten years. There is almost no topic that is unmentionable in a child's book. Young children are encouraged to read and think about all the issues mentioned above, and more. The practice of bibliotherapy — the use of books to help children solve their personal problems — has become accepted as an important teaching competence. Librarians and counselors, as well as parents, search for books that mirror a problem they wish to help a child overcome. Reality in children's books has become the topic of many discussions in journals and at conferences. More and more articles comment on the various aspects of one issue or another.

Concerned adults who work with children should have a background and knowledge of as many as possible of the concerns that children have. They should also be able to use books as resources to help children work out the concerns and deal responsibly with the issues. Children and adults, looking critically at the way these topics are handled, should judge for themselves whether or not the authors are presenting accurate pictures. Those books that attempt to teach lessons should be analyzed for their effectiveness as well as for their intent. Often books that are not obviously didactic are the most potent.

Sometimes books teach negative lessons without their authors' recognition of the fact. An interesting exchange occurred between Roald Dahl and Eleanor Cameron regarding this matter (*Horn Book*, October 1972; February and April 1973). Cameron criticizes the popular book *Charlie and the Chocolate Factory*, by Dahl. She presents arguments demonstrating that the book promotes sadism and hypocrisy and wonders whether the book will harm its young readers. Dahl, in his reply, accuses Cameron of vicious personal attack and effrontery. He says that he dedicated *Charlie* to his son Theo, whom he adores. He protests that it is ghastly to imagine that he would write anything that would harm his son or any other child. He feels that he is contributing to children's happiness and entertainment, which cannot possibly be harmful. Cameron, in responding, reminds us that children must be helped to think about what they are reading as well as to enjoy it. She also points out that Dahl avoids the issues that she has raised.

Cameron is very gentle in her condemnation of *Charlie and the Chocolate Factory*. In this author's opinion, she does not go far enough. The story is all the more dangerous because it is very imaginative and entertaining. It describes Willie Wonka, the owner of the chocolate factory, as a man who is omniscient. Not always a benevolent dictator, he requires absolute obedience to his commands. If one of our goals is to teach children to value responsible decision-making, then unquestioning obedience cannot be a virtue. The book is considered by many critics to be blatantly racist. Here again, when Dahl was questioned, he said that he was certainly not a racist (or words to that effect) and ended the matter there. *Charlie* was subsequently revised in an attempt to ameliorate its racist impact, but the damage remains.

The story line, for those readers who have not yet encountered the book, is as follows: Charlie, who is very poor, lives with his parents and two sets of grandparents. The old people do nothing but stay in bed all day. Along with four other children, Charlie wins a lucky golden ticket for a tour through the magical chocolate factory owned by Willie Wonka, genius of the candy world. The factory is run by Oompa-Loompas (in the old version, pygmies imported from Africa; in the revision, little pale people imported from a far-away jungle land). The Oompa-Loompas are happy, singing all the time. They never leave the factory, and on occasion they are used in Willie Wonka's experiments. Sometimes one of them gets destroyed, but they are joyful, nevertheless. After all, they eat all the chocolate they want, and chocolate is their favorite food.

It is interesting that the factory manufactures candy, inasmuch as Willie Wonka seems to consider obesity a sin. Other transgressions include gum-chewing, excessive viewing of television, and greed linked with wealth. The four other winners of the magic ticket commit these crimes and are graphically and harshly punished for them. The implication is that none of them will ever be the same, either physically or psychically. The happy ending occurs when Willie Wonka dubs Charlie the future ruler of the chocolate factory and transports Charlie's terrified and protesting family to the factory to live happily ever after.

Supporters of the book argue that the book is primarily a vehicle for entertainment. They also argue that the lessons learned may be constructive ones: don't chew too much gum, watch too much television, get too fat, or be greedy or disobedient. They protest that children enjoy the colorful punishments visited upon the offenders and see no implications of sadism here. They argue that the Oompa-Loompas are not real people (even when they are pygmies, because, after all, who believes in pygmies?). They ignore the internalizing of a value structure that each of us does when we are entertained or moved. Perhaps, if we do not equate Willie Wonka with slave-owners, we should look at the similarities. If we do not consider the little people to be slaves, we should examine the pre-Civil War contention that "our slaves are happy."

Charlie is by no means the only child's book about which questions have been raised. It is the intent of this text to encourage readers to ask questions about every book they read. Furthermore, this author hopes that, after using this text, readers will no longer imagine that any child's book is free of implications that bear examining. Perhaps labels should be printed for placing on the covers of books stating: CAUTION: THIS BOOK MAY BE DAMAGING TO YOUR MIND.

One of the areas of eduation rapidly gaining interest is that of values clarification. Schools are incorporating curricula dealing with values clarification into daily schedules. An issues approach to children's literature builds in an examination and clarification of values; it also fosters the development of those skills defined as critical reading, comprehension, and critical thinking. Children's books can be used to great advantage as materials for helping to achieve almost any of the aims of education. It therefore becomes important for adults working with children to become ever more knowledgeable about the scope and materials of children's literature.

The last chapter in this book describes a methodology for using children's books as the materials for a skills approach to the teaching of reading. In each of the other chapters (Chapters 2-9) a specific issue is explored. As explained in the Preface, each chapter may be read as an entity. Only books and articles actually read by this author have been included, but there are undoubtedly many more resources pertaining to each topic. It is hoped that readers will be stimulated to explore the field and to uncover more references and readings that are applicable to their needs. The following summary of each of the chapters may help the reader to decide which chapters provide the greatest source of immediate interest.

Chapter Two: Siblings.   Sibling interaction provides one of the bases for children's social behavior. Psychological theories regarding the effect of birth order on human behavior contribute to the interest in this topic. Children's books in which characters are also siblings present a range of different attitudes and behaviors. Other kinds of sibling interactions are described in books as well. Parents are depicted as behaving in a manner ranging from destructive and irresponsible to supportive and nurturing. An appreciation for ethnic differences can be found in some of these books, while others exhibit ignorance and lack of interest in presenting a balanced view of the world. Sibling relationships also contain implications for sex-role expectations and behaviors. A valuing of cooperative behavior is communicated in a number of the books.

Chapter Three: Divorce.   Divorce statistics seem to indicate that conventional marriage patterns are changing. The books for children about the topic of divorce attempt to help young readers to recognize that they are not alone in their problems and that their problems do have solutions. The range of fiction and nonfiction about this issue is widening every day. Most books respect the perception of the child; they communicate that respect. Some of the books, centering exclusively on the child, ignore the adults' reactions; others help young readers to understand the causes of their parents' dissension. Most of the books heed expert advice in refraining from making a reconciliation the happy ending to the story. The aftermath of divorce also is treated in a number of these books. Though life styles remain somewhat conventional in most of the books, occasionally a different kind of life is presented to the readers' view.

Chapter Four: Death and Old Age. Death and old age have received much attention in the literature for children. Different religious views, family reactions, problems, and joys are presented in great variety in books, some of which are extremely well written, while others will not last long in readers' memories. Stereotypes are presented and surmounted. Painful situations are experienced. Important questions are brought to the readers' attention. This chapter, in common with the others, suggests activities for both adults and children to attempt in order to increase their awareness of the issues presented.

Chapter Five: War. As with each of the other issues, war contains complexities beyond a simple discussion of right or wrong. Each war has individual characteristics differentiating it from others, but there are universal factors also to be considered. Books about war range from allegories and satires to realistic, personal accounts. Children's books tend to be less successful in conveying the complex aspects of war than they are in other issues; consequently, much careful adult guidance is needed in this area. Occasionally books can be found that help the reader become aware of the ambiguity of morality and the ambivalence of justice surrounding this topic. As with the other issues, criteria for analysis of the books are suggested. As with the other issues, readers are invited and encouraged to disagree with this author. Critical thinking is valued on the part of all students.

Chapter Six: Sex. Sex education arouses much controversy among educators and other members of any community. Not all educators agree with one another on this topic, but then not all experts of any profession agree about this topic. Although everyone agrees that sex education is necessary, the manner, materials, timing, quantity, and setting are all matters for argument. Consequently, many different presentations exist in books. Although it is more difficult for children to locate and acquire these books than any other category, they often manage to share what they do find with each other. Peer education on this topic is greater than on any other. Adults must decide if and how they wish to intervene.

Chapter Seven: The Black.   Minorities once were missing from consideration in most children's books. That error is slowly being corrected; now more and more excellent books can be found that include minority characters in significant roles. The black child can now find herself or himself in books. The most significant progress has been made with black characters, but black authors have also begun to gain recognition. The reaction to books dealing with problems of Blacks is by no means uniform; opinions range from appreciation of good intentions on the part of the author to rejection of any book that is not written by a member of the minority discussed in the book. This chapter discusses the different reactions and presents some criteria and comments for the reader's consideration.

Chapter Eight: The Native American.   The Native American is emerging as a minority group needing more of our attention. This chapter, which contains a brief history of our treatment of the Native American, also presents some of the concerns related to Native Americans today. Different perspectives are shared; suggestions are offered for further study. The books reviewed span many years, note authors' styles, and have different intentions.

Chapter Nine: The Female.   The role of the female is one that the public has been discussing actively. Different points of view are included, with an attempt made to present one that is balanced and moderate. Many annotations and references accompany the text in this and the other chapters. Readers are encouraged to seek out these resources to be able to formulate their own positions. The activities in this chapter are aimed at self-evaluation. The discussion of the books is categorized so that different aspects of the female are reviewed.

It is this author's hope to add to the already substantial body of information that pertains to children's literature. Each resource helps the reader to build a responsible basis for forming opinions and developing attitudes. The more informed that people are, the more constructive their behavior should be. Too often, people act out of ignorance. Education is the key to positive action. In this author's opinion, it is the hope of the world.

REFERENCES

Biskin, Donald, and Hoskisson, Kenneth. "Moral Development Through Children's Literature," *Elementary School Journal*, Vol. 75, No. 3 (December 1974), 153–57.

Describes levels of moral development as identified by Kohlberg. Locates moral issues in several children's books and analyzes them according to their stage. Suggests that books can be used to help develop children's moral awareness.

Cameron, Eleanor. "McLuhan, Youth, and Literature," *The Horn Book Magazine*, Vol. 48, No. 5 (October 1972), 433–40.

Urges the reading of excellent-quality children's books. Criticizes McLuhan's lack of interest in values. Seriously questions *Charlie and the Chocolate Factory*. This article brought forth an exchange between Cameron and Dahl.

————. "A Reply to Roald Dahl," *The Horn Book Magazine*, Vol. 49, No. 2 (April 1973), 127–29.

Responds to Dahl, and reiterates and strengthens her criticism of *Charlie and the Chocolate Factory*.

Cianciolo, Patricia. "'Feeling Books' Develop Social and Personal Sensitivities," *Elementary English*, Vol. 52, No. 1 (January 1975), 37–42.

Confirms the importance of exposing children to books that convey and elicit feelings on the part of the readers. Cianciolo stresses the power of books to influence readers' behavior and attitudes. She describes and discusses several books from this perspective.

Cox, Mahala. "Children's Literature and Value Theory," *Elementary English*, Vol. 51, No. 3 (March 1974), 355–59.

Recommends the addition of values clarification to interpretation of children's books. Presents several books and examples of how to do this.

Cullinan, Bernice E. "Reality Reflected in Children's Literature," *Elementary English*, Vol. 51, No. 3 (March 1974), 415–19.

Responds to critics of realism in children's books by critiquing several high-quality books for children that are concerned with realistic and social issues. Praises these books and their impact.

Dahl, Roald. *"Charlie and the Chocolate Factory*: A Reply," *The Horn Book Magazine*, Vol. 49, No. 1 (February 1973), 77–78.

An indignant, personal reply to Eleanor Cameron's criticism of his book. Dahl righteously asserts that he would never write anything harmful for his or any children.

Donelson, Kenneth L. "What to Do When the Censor Comes," *Elementary English*, Vol. 51, No. 3 (March 1974), 403–9.

Lists five benefits of reading for young people: enjoyment, objective recognition of one's own problems, provision of vicarious experiences, exposure to diverse value systems, and discovery of the real world.

Hall, Elvajean. *Personal Problems of Children*. Boston: Campbell and Hall (Box 350, Boston, Mass. 02117), (May 1970).

A series of pamphlets presenting annotated bibliographies of books to use with children who have different sorts of personal problems.

Jordan, June. "Young People: Victims of Realism in Books and in Life," *Wilson Library Bulletin*, Vol. 48, No. 2 (October 1973), 142–45.

Discusses realism and its various interpretations in children's books.

Pleads for nourishing, constructive reality. Commits herself as a writer to this goal.

Keating, Charlotte Matthews. *Building Bridges of Understanding Between Cultures*. Tucson, Ariz.: Palo Verde Publishing Company, 1971.

A very personalized annotated bibliography of books for children dealing with different cultural groups. The author too easily classifies books as of interest to girls or boys, but in general, the annotations are helpful and interesting.

Keniston, Kenneth. "'Good Children' (Our Own), 'Bad Children' (Other People's), and the Horrible Work Ethic," *Yale Alumni Magazine*, April 1974, pp. 6-10.

Discusses the American practice of valuing work over almost any other ethic. Analyzes its impact on children. Suggests that our emphasis shift toward humaneness and imagination in addition to productivity. Demonstrates that books contribute to whatever society values.

Livingston, Myra C. "Children's Literature — in Chaos, a Creative Weapon," *The Reading Teacher*, Vol. 27, No. 6 (March 1974), 534-39.

Urges individualization in book selection for children. Recommends a constructive blend of fantasy and reality. Recognizes the power of children's books.

Lowry, Heath W. "Evaluative Criteria to Be Used as Guides By Writers of Children's Literature," *Elementary English*, Vol. 48, No. 8 (December 1971), 922-25.

Presents responses from editors of children's books listing criteria that they use for publishing these books. Concludes that children's books must have the same qualities of excellence as adult books.

Perry, Jean M. "The Changing Role of the Child in American Society as Reflected in Literature for Children," unpublished Master's Report, Palmer Graduate Library School, Long Island University, Brookville, N.Y., 1971.

A historical perspective of the changes in children's literature in terms of contemporary social implications. The author contends that these changes reflect society's attitudinal changes toward children. Thirty-three children's books and many adult references are examined and reviewed. The study includes the period from 1900 to 1970.

Porter, E. Jane. "Reflections of Life Through Books," *Elementary English*, Vol. 50, No. 2 (February 1973), 189-95.

Describes the latest edition of *Reading Ladders for Human Relations*. Lauds its intent and message. Makes several suggestions for implementing it with children. Uses several books as examples of how to help children "make the connection between books and life."

Riggs, Corinne W. *Bibliotherapy: An Annotated Bibliography*. Newark, Del.: International Reading Association, 1971.

A well-selected list of books, periodicals, and unpublished materials for adults concerned with the therapeutic use of books for children. Annotations are brief but informative.

Schulte, Emerita Schroer, "Today's Literature for Today's Children," *Elementary English*, Vol. 49, No. 3 (March 1972), 355-63.

Recognizes that literature should be directed toward all children, including those who do not enjoy reading. Reviews and recommends a
number of books that present reality to minority children. Includes
bibliography.

Shepard, John P. "The Treatment of Characters in Popular Children's Fiction," *Elementary English*, Vol. 39, No. 7 (November 1962), 672-76.
Conducted a study demonstrating the negative impact of many children's books. Urges adults to be aware of the subtle implications in
children's books and to intervene appropriately.

2

Siblings

MOST PEOPLE have had some experience in dealing
with siblings and have also thought about their own positions in their families. Some people wish that they had been
the eldest or the youngest or the only child. But the majority, at least eventually, seem to be satisfied with their family
position. Sibling relationships do not constitute a major
societal problem; but they are a universal phenomenon,
playing an important part in how individuals feel about
themselves and how they relate to other people. The sibling
situation is often a model for people in relating to friends, to
new acquaintances, to mates, to their own children, and to
society in general.

Siblings who grow up together learn each other's
characteristics in a way that no other people do, and they

have little room for pretense. Besides having to share their parents' time, attention, and love, they are forced to share physical space and possessions. They must develop a procedure for living together that will be acceptable most of the time. They can test out behaviors with the relative security of knowing that their siblings will not have the option of leaving them forever, as is the case with friends. They can usually rely on getting honest reactions to their behaviors. Parents influence siblings' interactions in the way that they deal with their children. No situation is perfect; still, people can attempt to be loving, supportive, and fair.

But parents cannot win. No matter how good their intentions, they are imposing problems on their children, simply by having them. If we are to believe what we read, no one seems to escape the imposition of her or his family placement. Several myths have persisted. The only child is depicted as a lonely, spoiled, self-centered individual, who is unable to get along with peers, is too adult-oriented, and in general maladjusted. The expected reactions when we hear that someone is a middle child are fairly well programmed for us. We anticipate that the person is resentful, squeezed, quick-tempered, unvalued, overly sensitive, and unhappy. The youngest is pampered, demanding, and favored. It is rare in literature that birth order does not play an important role. Psychologists such as Walter Toman have developed elaborate schema to describe the effect of birth order on relationships with others and on behavior in general. Fortunately, in real life, we know that we survive our sibling situation and get along very well despite our imposed birth order.

▶ Try This

What position do you occupy in birth order in your family? How has this position affected your relationship with your sibling(s)? How did it affect your relationship with your parents when you were growing up? Which of the books in the Bibliography at the end of this chapter most closely approximates your situation? Find a child who occupies the same birth-order position that you do. Share the book with that child to see how your perceptions match.

Most books confine themselves to the conventional family situation. In the past decade there have been books about "broken" families and one or two about communal groups, but the preponderance of literature assumes the intact nuclear family. In some cases an extended family situation is presented, but it is usually recognized as something out of the ordinary. Most of the exceptions to the conventional family are used as vehicles for presenting the problems that they generate.

Books containing siblings as characters are varied. Some of them deal with the topic of the sibling relationship as the main thrust of the story. Some of them only incidentally include the interaction between siblings within the context of the plot. But whether or not the intent is to look at this issue as a problem or as a model, the young reader, assisted by the helpful adult, can find the type of book needed.

Factors additional to birth order affect a family's interactions. The number of years between children; the sex of the children; the economic, social, and emotional circumstances of the family during the time the children are being reared; the state of each person's health; the physical environment; the influence of peers and schooling — all these are external factors contributing to how members of a family perceive themselves and one another. Children's books offer a wide range of family settings for readers to experience vicariously. Some of the books can be very helpful in assuring children that, contrary to their fears, they and their family are normal.

In the past twenty years authors have represented families as having internal struggles and problems. Permitting siblings to dislike each other, they have portrayed rivalries and unpleasant relationships. They have continued the tradition of making siblings responsible for one another in times of extreme crisis and have also begun to present useful models for parents and siblings to emulate in normal stress situations.

Suggested Criteria

In searching for books helpful to use in either a therapeutic or modeling fashion with children, one should seek out those stories that have realistic solutions to problems. How does the author resolve the problems? Fairy-tale endings are not valuable in these cases. If real issues are being presented, their impact is lessened if they come to an unlikely, though happy end. A solution that is too pat is also less valuable than one indicating the likelihood that more thought and time needs to be given to the problem. It is far better to suggest that there is no one answer than to present one that is not likely. For example, the situation of a new baby in the house is usually resolved in life only for short periods of time and needs constant reexamination and additional strategies as both the new arrival and the elder sibling(s) develop. Books that indicate this expectation are useful.

The behavior of the parents is an important element of stories concerned with sibling interaction. Models should be presented wherever possible in which parents behave humanely, responsively, and plausibly. No parents are saints. Some are cruel. If the problem in the book is that of a parental desertion, it should be described as arising from the plot; it is not believable unless some rationale for the motivation is indicated. The Victorian practice of eliminating parents through death or desertion as a literary device to release the children to be protagonists is not necessary or workable in contemporary times. And there are enough cases where children really must contend with the fact of their parents' having abandoned them to make this a subject for authors.

The illustrations in any of these books should attempt to demonstrate the universality of sibling problems. Particularly in nonfiction books, different ethnic groups and family styles should be included. In any case, stereotypes — both visual and literary — should be avoided. Parental roles and sibling roles should reflect a realistic pattern, but expectations need not be rigid or stereotypic for birth order. Sometimes a middle child should be atypical; sometimes the youngest and eldest should exchange characteristics. No matter what the behavior, it is useful to see sufficient contextual substantiation.

Readers can judge for themselves whether or not any of the siblings is being either unjustly favored or victimized. Sometimes the author purposely describes such a predicament. But unless favoritism or its opposite is necessary to the plot, the most advantageous portrayal is a balanced, fair treatment from each child's perspective.

Sibling conflict should not be judged as abnormal. Books can help to provide the context for healthy reactions and interactions on the part of the readers. Guilt should not be imposed, particularly since arguments and hostility between siblings is such an expected part of normal development.

Books are most effective when they have literary merit as well as didactic intent. The best lessons are taught unobtrusively. Too obvious a message damages a story.

Discussion of Children's Books

THE NEW BABY

The elder sibling — particularly when that child has been an only child up to the arrival of the new baby — is the subject of sympathetic concern in many books. It is generally the three- to six-year-old child to whom these books are directed, perhaps because it is these children who react most keenly to the new baby. Some of the books dealing directly with this topic are factual. They are designed to be read to the child in order to give information that will help the child to understand the process. Joan Samson's *Watching the New Baby* is one such book. It is illustrated with photographs that show not only new babies but also their brothers and sisters in pleasant activities. The book attempts to involve the elder sibling in an understanding of the baby's development, so that the child will not resent the baby's behavior. Although a very young child has little capacity for empathy, some of the explanations will probably alleviate anxiety and anger and will help the elder child feel more comfortable because of his or her greater knowledge.

Hi, New Baby, by Andry and Kratka, goes one step further by predicting situations that will arise calling for action on the part of the elder child. The authors suggest useful responses to the new baby, but above all, this book demonstrates to the elder that he or she is valued and loved. The message that every family member is important is communicated strongly in Sara Bonnett Stein's *That New Baby*. This is one of the "Open Family" books. As with the others in this series, there is a text for parents and one for children. The advice to parents is useful and psychologically sound. It helps families to recognize that jealousy and feelings of being misplaced are normal and should be dealt with in a loving, accepting way. The photographs are both in black-and-white and in color. The family represented in this book is a black family, adding to the universality of the message. In this book there are two elder siblings — a boy and a girl — and the grandmother is a permanent member of the family. This book helps to prepare parents for coping with the problems of sibling rivalry in a very realistic, direct fashion. It is also useful for other helping adults such as teachers, counselors, and librarians to read such books so that they can recommend procedures to parents and children. In addition, they can directly help children who are trying to deal with the situation of a new baby.

Many books of fiction also take up the problem of jealousy of the new baby. The books are aimed not only at the elder siblings but also at the parents. They contain modeling situations for their readers to follow. One such book, *Billy and Our New Baby*, by Helene S. Arnstein, speaks directly to the parents in a guide included in the back of the book. The story describes Billy, who is so perturbed because his mother is spending so much time with the new baby, that he wants it returned to the hospital. Even after his mother responds to him with extra affection, Billy reverts to baby behavior. But when his mother communicates that she understands and values him, he is helped to cope with the new child. One book that provides a bizarre solution to the problem of the new baby is *Elvira Everything*, by Frank Asch. In this story a remarkable doll is used as the symbol for a new sibling. The doll supplants the child in her parents' affections. Though the parents try to reassure their child that they still love her, she is not satisfied until she destroys the doll. The parents behave in a removed, unloving fashion throughout the bulk of the book; thus it is no wonder that the child resorts to desperate measures. At no time does the child interact in any way with the doll, nor is she encouraged to do so by her parents.

A number of the books on this topic emphasize the role the elder sibling can play in helping with the new baby. In Gerson's *Omoteji's Baby Brother*, Omoteji, a Nigerian boy, feels left out and useless until he decides on the perfect contribution that he can make to the festivities of his new brother's naming ceremony. In both Alexander's *Nobody Asked Me If I Wanted a Baby Sister* and Schick's *Peggy's New Brother*, the elder siblings find that their efforts to entertain the new baby are useful and appreciated. Eloise Greenfield's *She Come Bringing Me That Little Baby Girl* is another book in which the elder sibling accepts the younger one because he is permitted to help in some way. Children who read these books, or who have the books read to them, can be asked to give suggestions as to how they can help at home with their baby sisters or brothers. They can also dictate stories to their teachers or to helpful adults in the classroom or library. In these stories they can name themselves as the protagonists who have just had the experience of having a baby sibling come home to them. They can describe what they do to help with the new baby and can then illustrate their stories with either their own drawings or with photographs of themselves and their families. Their stories can be placed on the classroom or library shelves.

The best antidote to the poison of sibling rivalry is a feeling of self worth, along with the knowledge that the family still loves and needs the person who is jealous. Myra Berry Brown's *Amy and the New Baby* confirms the family's love for Amy. Mary Jarrell's *The Knee Baby* and Ann Herbert Scott's *On Mother's Lap* also help the child to overcome a feeling of displacement. In Jarrell's book, the boy takes turns with the new baby on his mother's lap. In Scott's book, the mother makes room at the same time for everyone.

Sometimes, no matter how well-intentioned the parents are, children still feel unwanted. In both Russell Hoban's *A Baby Sister for Frances* and Ezra Jack Keats's *Peter's Chair*, the elder siblings run away from home. But neither runs very far, and both feel much better when they realize that their parents want them back.

Norma Klein presents two sets of very understanding parents in her books *If I Had My Way* and *Confessions of an Only Child*. In the first book, Ellie reverts to infantile behavior, dreaming out her hostility by taking over the world and subjugating adults. The book is somewhat overdone but might prove helpful to children who are very angry about their lack of control over their families. Antonia, the heroine of *Confessions* . . . uses her friends and her parents to help her work out her unpleasant feelings.

SIBLING RIVALRY

Authors exhibit sympathy for the elder child, but also consider the younger one if the younger sibling in the story is still a toddler. In *If It Weren't for You*, by Charlotte Zolotow, an elder brother wishes that he were an only child. In the end, though, he is reconciled to his younger brother's existence, for he realizes that his younger brother's presence prevents him from having to be alone with grown-ups. This is not a very positive commentary on the quality of the adult-child relationship. Lois Duncan's *Giving Away Suzanne* describes a successful attempt on the part of an elder sister at giving away her younger sister, whom her aunt consents to take. For no explicable reason, the child misses her younger sister and wants her back. Some of the flaws in this book are the lack of consideration for the younger child's feelings and the willingness of the parents to give up the younger sibling. Admittedly, they are hoping that the elder sister will repent of her deed, but it is destructive to pretend that younger siblings can be given away.

Although authors demonstrate that they are very much aware of the problems for the elder children, they usually focus their happy solutions and understanding on the period when the younger sibling is an infant. A number of other books reflect the problem of the rivalry between siblings once the siblings have progressed beyond babyhood. But the point of view of the younger child is the one more often championed in these books. Natalie Savage Carlson's *The Half Sisters* describes Luvvy's plight as the sister caught in the middle. Understandably attempting to be considered a fit companion for her elder sisters, Luvvy wants to be seen as mature. However, she considers her youngest sister to be a pest, and acts accordingly. The author sympathizes with Luvvy's position as a younger sibling, but disapproves of Luvvy's negligent behavior toward her youngest sister. When this baby sister dies, poor Luvvy suffers from guilt for the rest of her life.

Similarly, in Norma Klein's *Naomi in the Middle*, seven-year-old Naomi is the narrator, protagonist, and favored character. Her elder sister, Bobo, is negatively portrayed. The parents are not as kind to Bobo as they are to Naomi. It is quite comprehensible to an empathic reader that Bobo dreads yet another addition to the household, but her feelings are not at all acknowledged by anyone in the book. Eloise Greenfield's *Sister* is a more complex book, but again favors the feelings of Doretha over her difficult elder sister, Alberta. Hila Colman's *Diary of a Frantic Kid Sister* is yet another story seen through the eyes of the younger sister.

The parents in this story are not as competent as they should be in handling the situation, which, at times, borders on the hysterical.

▶ Try This

Rewrite *Naomi in the Middle, The Half Sisters, Sister,* or *Diary of a Frantic Kid Sister* from the point of view of the elder sister. Rewrite any of the "new baby" books from the point of view of the new baby. Have children do the same thing. If they cannot write, have them retell the stories orally.

Other books portraying sibling rivalry include Doris Orgel's *Bartholomew, We Love You,* in which, while the reader's sympathy is expected to lie with the younger sister, the presentation is balanced enough so that the elder does not emerge as the victimizer. The happy ending is not that the younger one wins out, but that they learn to share and cooperate with each other. This book is useful in its depiction of the parents, who in addition to both being working people, are impartial, understanding, and capable.

In a somewhat different setting, John Branfield's *Why Me?* focuses on a younger sister whose behavior is complicated by the fact that she has diabetes. Very resentful because of this, she abuses her elder sister, her parents, and her friends. Although she is the principal character, she is not portrayed very sympathetically. Everyone tries to help her, although her sister is, at times, understandably angry. It does not look, even at the end of the book, as if the sibling relationship will ever be a good one, but the reader understands everyone's point of view and can accept the conclusion. Some mature readers might try to give other solutions for the family's problems or might write a different ending for this book. Two sisters who also have violent confrontations, but who manage in the end to work out their problems, are depicted in *Amy and Laura,* by Marilyn Sachs. The fact of their mother's illness complicates matters, but they help her to become an active participant in their family again. This story lends itself well to "Who was right?" debates among readers.

Twins are often considered to be two halves of the same child. A number of books usefully present twins as experiencing the rivalry that exists between ordinary brothers and sisters. Beverly Cleary's *Mitch and Amy* and Alice Bach's *The Smartest Bear and His Brother Oliver* are two that demonstrate this approach. The bear twins have understanding, responsive parents, but Mitch and Amy's parents unwittingly foster competition between the two of them.

Most books at least imply that the siblings will grow out of their bickering and rivalry. For some readers, this may be un unlikely development. They will be delighted with Beryl Epstein and Dorritt Davis's *Two Sisters and Some Hornets*. In this story the sisters are elderly women in rocking chairs, recalling their childhood. As they talk about their recollections, they adopt the same argumentative patterns that they had when they were children — and the book ends with their continuing to argue over the facts. It is comforting to know that they and their relationship have survived into old age.

COOPERATION AND LOVE

Perhaps less realistic for some children, but certainly reflective of others' experiences, are the books that describe amiable, helpful, and loving relationships among siblings. If these books are not held up to readers as perfect examples to be emulated, then they can serve as confirmation of positive feelings and can, perhaps, provide alternatives to quarrelsome behavior. *Striped Ice Cream*, by Joan Lexau, presents a situation in which the loving efforts of elder siblings to please their younger one are misunderstood until the very last moment. The children do not realize that the younger sister would rather have their attention than their gifts. But she recognizes, at the end, that their behavior toward her was meant to be generous; she, in turn, generously refrains from making them feel guilty. In *Do You Have the Time, Lydia?* by Evaline Ness, an elder sister again unwittingly hurts the feelings of her younger brother by being too preoccupied with her own adventures. She recognizes what she has done and, on her own initiative, sets it right.

There is no conflict whatsoever in some stories with siblings as the characters. In John Steptoe's *My Special Best Words*, Bweela, although she is only three years old, lovingly and competently takes care of her younger brother. They do have some verbal quarrels, but the reader recognizes this as part of the fun; the relationship remains strongly positive. The elder brother in Betsy Byars's *Go and Hush the Baby* also assumes some care-taking tasks for his young sibling and performs his job willingly and well. June Jordan contributes a delightful, coping family in *New Life: New Room*. The children are realistic, lively, and inventive, while both parents are loving to each other and to the children.

The siblings in Norma Klein's *It's Not What You Expect* are older but completely compatible. Two of them, Oliver and Carla, are twins. Everyone in this book gets along beautifully with everyone else. The conflict is between the parents, who eventually reunite; but, even when they are separated, they are respectful of each other's feelings. There are several characters outside the family who become a sort of extension; the group of characters form a community for the purpose of the story. A real commune is described somewhat idyllically in Sharron Love's *The Sunshine Family and the Pony*. This story is valuable not so much for its realistic portrayal of sibling relationships as for its recognition that there are other situations beyond the nuclear family. In this book everyone is responsible for maintaining a sense of cooperation; the feelings of all are considered. The children appear well taken care of. Readers could comment on their experiences in living with other families, in sharing summer vacations, or in traveling together. They can compare their interactions and feelings with those of the Sunshine family to judge the reality of the book. They can also add episodes of their own invention. Another book useful for this purpose, and portraying an ideally workable commune, is John Steptoe's *Birthday*.

FACING RESPONSIBILITY

Siblings are often called upon to take care of each other to varying degrees, depending on the extremes of the situation. In Lucille Clifton's *Don't You Remember?* the four-year-old girl is tended by her elder brother. He must postpone going back to school so that both parents can work and his sister can be adequately supervised. The statement is made that he will resume his schooling. The arrangement does not seem to be a hardship for him, but it is a unique one.

In somewhat less supportive circumstances, Lydia, in the Cleavers' *Me Too*, tries to nurture and educate her retarded twin sister. Their father has left them because he cannot tolerate his family. In the end Lydia fails, but she recognizes that her failure was inevitable, her goal, unachievable. She also accepts the fact that she cannot be responsible for her sister. On the other hand, Annie, in Clymer's *My Brother Stevie*, succeeds in taking charge of her brother and in changing his behavior. Her sense of responsibility to her younger sibling is a strong factor in their relationship. Their mother, who is seen as a woman who cannot face her responsibilities, has left them in the care of their grandmother. The mother assumes that Annie will manage.

Sandy, in Engebrecht's *Under the Haystack*, and Mary Call, in the Cleavers' *Where the Lilies Bloom*, take over the management of their families when their parents are gone. Mary Call's parents are both dead; Sandy's mother has abandoned them. Both girls hide the fact that they have no adult protection. Both are resented by their siblings for their imperious attitudes. Both are superhuman in their ability to earn a living, respond to emergencies, and maintain the family. Both stories end happily, with adults' stepping in and taking charge. But Karana, in *Island of the Blue Dolphins*, by O'Dell, never receives the benefit of someone to take care of her after she and her brother are marooned on an island. She is in this predicament because of her brother and her sense of responsibility for him. Unfortunately, despite her efforts, he dies, and she must manage her own survival alone.

In *The Bears' House*, by Marilyn Sachs, the children also do not fare well. After their father leaves them, their mother suffers a total mental collapse. The children, trying to sustain themselves, conceal their lack of parental supervision, but they fail at everything. Ultimately their situation is discovered, and the reader knows that they will be dispersed to different places. These children are not resentful of their elder brother's efforts, but they do not support each other. Their individual emotional problems make it impossible for them to function together.

SPECIAL PROBLEMS

In some books siblings and their relationships help to bring to the readers' attention some special situations with which they can empathize. In Paige Dixon's *May I Cross Your Golden River?* Jordan's brothers and sister play a large part in making his last year a happy one. Each of them reacts in a different but helpful way to the news that he is dying. His feelings for his family add to the poignancy of the story. Another, more common problem is explored in Barbara Corcoran's *A Trick of Light*, in which twins must begin to accept the fact that they are separate beings with individual lives to lead. In this story the boy is ready to be independent before the girl is; therein lies the conflict. It is resolved only after a series of traumas.

One of a pair of siblings suffers the most in Winthrop's *A Little Demonstration of Affection*. Jenny fears that she has incestuous feelings for her brother Charlie. Her family is a fairly happy but totally undemonstrative group. The parents never permit the children to see them touching each other or engaging in any affectionate behavior; they are equally reserved with the children. Jenny, therefore, misinterprets her response to her brother Charlie's normal show of affection. She is so moved by his hugging her, and so craves more of it, that she fears something is dreadfully wrong with her. Her father and her brother at last help her to see that her needs are normal and that the family has been at fault for not exhibiting any kind of physical affection for each other. They all resolve to amend their behavior. The ending is a somewhat uneasy but plausible one.

Many other books contain examples of different sibling relationships. In order to be helped in constructing a healthy mode of behavior, children need to see that they are normal, that they are valued, and that there are many acceptable ways of relating. Adults and children will find numerous examples of the ways that sisters and brothers are presented, in a variety of books that will provide models, test situations, and questions to explore. The greater the number and variety that are at readers' immediate disposal, the more beneficial will be the impact. Sibling rivalry will not be eliminated, but readers may learn to handle it with more comfort.

REFERENCES

Ellis, Anne W. *The Family Story in the 1960's*. Hamden, Conn.: Archon Books, 1970.
Analyzes family stories, mostly by British authors. Comments on the nature of family relationships throughout the world in the sixties. Erosion of family, emergence of lower classes as characters in books, partial reflection of real social problems.

Gruenberg, Sidonie Matsner. *The Parents' Guide to Everyday Problems of Boys and Girls*. New York: Random House, 1958.
Devotes one chapter to brothers' and sisters' relationships. Gives practical, uncomplicated advice on how to respond to sibling rivalry. Helps parents to recognize subtle interactions and to be fair in dealing with quarrels. Discusses the characteristics of the eldest, middle, and youngest children. Recommends some useful procedures for managing the family.

Ilg, Frances L., and Ames, Louise Bates. *Child Behavior*. New York: Harper & Brothers, 1955.
The authors devote an entire chapter to the topic of brothers and sisters. They advise parents to accept sibling rivalry and hostility as normal. They recommend keeping siblings apart as much as possible and describe the developmental aspects of sibling relationships.

Kircher, Clara J. *Behavior Patterns in Children's Books*. Washington, D.C.: The Catholic University of America Press, 1966.
An annotated bibliography containing several chapters pertinent to sibling relationships. Needs to be updated, but the brief comments serve to give the reader an overview of the books.

Lester, Julius. Reviews of *She Come Bringing Me That Little Baby Girl*, by Eloise Greenfield, and *My Special Best Words*, by John Steptoe, in *New York Times Book Review*, November 3, 1974, p. 48.
Lester accuses the Greenfield book of sexism and unreality. He praises the Steptoe book for enabling us "to experience poetry in the ordinary life of an ordinary home."

Mussen, Paul Henry; Conger, John Janeway; and Kagan, Jerome. *Child Development and Personality*. New York: Harper & Row, 1956.
Discusses the psychological influence of siblings on children's development. Primarily deals with traits and problems of the firstborn in dealing with siblings. Hypothesizes that ordinal position is critical in determining later social interaction.

Neisser, Edith G. *Brothers and Sisters*. New York: Harper & Brothers, 1951.
Up-to-date despite its age, this book advises parents how to best help

their children develop positive feelings about themselves and one another. The author presents useful do's and don'ts.

Puner, Helen W. *Helping Brothers and Sisters Get Along*. Chicago: Science Research Associates, 1952.

Helps adults recognize that selfishness, rivalry, and even hatred are normal aspects of sibling relationships. Also helps adults to feel more comfortable about not being perfect. Suggests tactics for handling family conflicts. The book is written simply and directly. It is remarkably up-to-date, despite its having been written in 1952.

Schnur, Gloria L. "A Content Analysis of Selected Fiction for Elementary School Children Depicting the Theme of Sibling Relationships and Rivalries," unpublished Master's Report, Palmer Graduate Library School, Long Island University, Brookville, N.Y., 1970.

Analyzes twenty-five books to see if they depict sibling relationships accurately. Finds that they do. Schnur presents a very useful discussion of sibling relationships in the introduction to her analysis of the books.

Toman, Walter. *Family Constellation*. New York: Springer Publishing Company, 1961.

Describes the "game" of understanding people's interactions with their families and with others as a result of their family placement. Defines the characteristics of siblings according to their place in the family (e.g., eldest brother of brothers is in charge; gets along well with males if they are not also elder brothers; is a good leader; can handle authority; is orderly, tough, would rather give than get help). Toman analyzes different family positions, making recommendations about the best sort of match and the most ideal arrangement for offspring. The book is fun to read, but it gives the impression of being just one step beyond astrology.

Ziman, Edmund, M.D. *Jealousy in Children: A Guide for Parents*. New York: A. A. Wyn, 1949.

Discusses the problems of sibling rivalry in different family structures. Makes useful suggestions to parents. The orientation is strongly Freudian and very sexist.

Zwack, Jean M. "The Stereotypic Family in Children's Literature," *The Reading Teacher*, Vol. 26, No. 4 (January, 1973), 389–91.

The author is concerned about the lack of alternatives to the nuclear family as presented in children's books. She recommends Rainey Bennett's *The Secret Hiding Place* as a sample of an unstereotypic situation.

Alexander, Martha. *Nobody Asked Me If I Wanted a Baby Sister.* New York: Dial Press, 1971. (Ages 3-7.)
A young boy tries to give away his baby sister. No one seems to want a baby girl. Finally, one family looks as if it will take her, but the baby cries and cannot be comforted except by Oliver, her brother. The incident persuades him to keep her, and even make plans for the future. Kind of a fun fantasy but hardly supportive of a realistic sibling relationship.

Anderson, Lonzo. *The Day the Hurricane Happened.* Illus. Ann Grifalconi. New York: Scribner's, 1973. (Ages 5-8.)
Graphic story of a family's bout with a hurricane on St. John in the Virgin Islands. Albie and his younger sister Eldra help prepare their house and their animals for the onslaught. The father, who is a constable, must warn the rest of the island. The house is destroyed, but no one is hurt; and the grandfather, mother, and children manage their own survival well. Image of a coping, capable, loving black family. Written with a light dialect, not overpowering, but enough to give a sense of the speech of the people. Brother very protective of sister.

Andry, Andrew C., and Kratka, Suzanne C. *Hi, New Baby.* Illus. Thomas Di Grazia. New York: Simon and Schuster, 1970. (Ages 2-6.)
The illustrations add tremendously to the book. The text is also excellent. Addressing elder siblings, it describes physiological facts about new babies. It also points out situations that elder siblings will have to cope with. The authors suggest activities that children can do to help themselves, their baby siblings, and the family situation in general.

Arnstein, Helene S. *Billy and Our New Baby.* Illus. M. Jane Smyth. New York: Behavioral Publications, 1973. (Ages 5-8.)
Billy is angry because mother and everyone else are busier with the new baby than with him. He wants to return the new baby to the hospital. Mother at last recognizes Billy's need verbally, and with hugs and kisses. But Billy decides he wants to be a baby again, crawls, cries, wants a baby bottle. Mother points out all the good things Billy can do that baby cannot. Billy starts enjoying helping out with baby. At the end, Billy still gets angry at the baby, but he loves him, too, and accepts him as part of family. A guide for parents and those who work with children included in back of book explains the situation and the emotions that the child goes through. Gives advice for adults' behavior.

Asch, Frank. *Elvira Everything*. New York: Harper & Row, 1970. (Ages 7–10.)
The narrator of the story is an only child. She gets a marvelous robot doll named Elvira Everything for Christmas, though she really wanted a teddy bear. Elvira Everything is the nightmare of the firstborn come true. The doll seems to take precedence over the child in her parents' affections. The doll is perfect. At last, the child destroys the doll, and things return to normal. A rather bizarre solution to sibling rivalry. The illustrations by the author constitute a brilliant commentary on modern life and the contemporary family.

Bach, Alice. *The Smartest Bear and His Brother Oliver*. Illus. Steven Kellogg. New York: Harper & Row, 1975. (Ages 5–8.)
Ronald wants to be different from his twin, Oliver. Ronald would rather read than feast. In order to demonstrate that they recognize their differences, the boys' parents give them each a different gift: to Ronald, a typewriter; to Oliver, a bakery truck. Although bears are the characters in this story, human siblings can identify with the situation.

Beim, Jerrold. *Kid Brother*. Illus. Tracy Sugarman. New York: Morrow, 1952. (Ages 4–8.)
Frankie is Buzz's younger brother. When their mother requires Buzz to look after Frankie, Buzz resents this responsibility; he also resents having to share his room. One day Frankie saves Buzz much public embarrassment, for which Buzz is grateful. But, although his attitude improves, Buzz still considers Frankie a pest when he is with his friends.

Blume, Judy. *Tales of a Fourth Grade Nothing*. Illus. Roy Doty. New York: Dutton, 1972. (Ages 9–12.)
Peter's younger brother, Fudge, is a monster. The child is spoiled, undisciplined, and favored by the foolish mother. Not only is the child permitted to run rampant, but also the parents are made to look incompetent. The father is depicted as a person ruled by his job, ineffectual, but pleasant. Both parents try to control Fudge's behavior and sometimes win out, but it is too often through trickery. A very unpleasant book, presenting a negative model.

Bonsall, Crosby. *The Day I Had to Play with My Sister*. New York: Harper & Row, 1972. (Ages 3–7.)
Elder brother tries to teach little sister to play hide-and-go-seek, but the little girl just cannot or will not follow the rules. The book takes no sides, but helps readers to understand the elder brother's point of view.

Bouchard, Lois Kalb. *The Boy Who Wouldn't Talk.* Illus. Ann Grifalconi. Garden City, N.Y.: Doubleday, 1969. (Ages 7–10.)
Carlos decides to stop talking because he is primarily Spanish-speaking and is uncomfortable with English. His younger brother, Angel, tries to help him, but Carlos accepts Angel's support without really responding. Angel, nevertheless, remains staunch, and eventually Carlos speaks again.

Branfield, John. *Why Me?* New York: Harper & Row, 1973. (Ages 12–up.)
Sarah and Jane are sisters who do not get along at all well; in fact, they seem to delight in making each other unhappy. Sarah is diabetic. The bulk of the story revolves around her adjustment to this condition. The parents seem to be unable to control their daughters' behavior. The only resolution is to wait until they grow up.

Brown, Myra Berry. *Amy and the New Baby.* New York: Franklin Watts, 1965. (Ages 4–6.)
Amy has mixed feelings about her new baby brother, who cries a great deal, takes much attention away from her, and stays longer than Amy expected. The parents handle the situation well, paying special attention to Amy, and letting her know that their love for her has not diminished, but at the same time also affirming that the baby is now a member of the family and will remain with them.

Byars, Betsy. *Go and Hush the Baby.* Illus. Emily A. McCully. New York: Viking, 1971. Also Pb. (Ages 3–8.)
The elder brother is called upon to entertain the crying baby while their mother finishes several tasks. The boy does this with imagination and good will; at last the baby falls asleep, and the brother is free to go out to play. The book conveys a warm, good feeling.

———. *The Summer of the Swans.* Illus. Ted CoConis. New York: Viking, 1970. Also Pb. (Ages 10–up.) (Newbery Medal.)
The fourteen-year-old heroine feels responsible for her younger retarded brother. She also resents him and has unpleasant feelings about herself. In the end, a friend helps her to resolve her feelings.

Caines, Jeannette, *Abby.* Illus. Steven Kellogg. New York: Harper & Row, 1973. (Ages 3–8.)
Abby is an adopted child who loves and is loved by her mother and her elder brother, Kevin, even though he upsets Abby sometimes.

Carlson, Natalie Savage. *The Half Sisters.* Illus. Thomas di Grazia. New York: Harper & Row, 1970. (Ages 8–12.)
Luvvy's family is in two distinct sections. Her father has had six daughters, the three elder ones by his first wife, the three younger ones from his current marriage. Luvvy is the eldest of the second

set. She longs to be accepted by her elder sisters and is impatient with the demands for attention made on her by her youngest sister Maudie. When Maudie dies, Luvvy is distraught.

Child Study Association of America. *Brothers and Sisters Are Like That*. Illus. Michael Hampshire. New York: Crowell, 1971. (Ages 7-10.)
A collection of stories about siblings and their relationships with each other. Most of the stories are also books on their own. They all have happy endings, with siblings accepting each other and feeling comfortable in their own roles.

Cleary, Beverly. *Mitch and Amy*. Illus. George Porter. New York: Morrow, 1967. Pb. Scholastic. (Ages 8-up.)
Mitch and Amy are fraternal twins who are always squabbling. Their parents unwittingly foster competition between them (Mitch does not read well; Amy cannot do multiplication). Still they enjoy being twins and manage to handle their arguments good-naturedly.

————. *Ramona the Brave*. Illus. Alan Tiegreen. New York: Morrow, 1975. (Ages 8-12.)
Ramona, six years old, is trying to be very brave despite the fact that she thinks her parents love her elder sister more than they love her, and despite the fact that she is unhappy in her first-grade class. Her parents eventually comfort her and persuade her that she is very loved, and her sister helps with her empathy. A loving family. An excellent book.

Cleaver, Vera and Bill. *Delpha Green & Company*. Philadelphia: Lippincott, 1972. (Ages 10-up.)
Delpha and her siblings have a cooperative but not empathic relationship with each other. Although Delpha joins her younger sister and brothers in their play, she is essentially a loner.

————. *Me Too*. Philadelphia: Lippincott, 1973. (Ages 12-up.)
Lydia assumes responsibility for the teaching and care of her retarded twin sister, Lornie. She hopes to change Lornie's behavior. She must cope with their father's departure, the mother's despair, and the neighbors' disapproval. Finally, she must accept, in the end, the impossibility of her task.

————. *Where the Lilies Bloom*. Illus. Jim Spanfeller. Philadelphia: Lippincott, 1969. Pb. New American Library. (Ages 9-up.)
Mary Call's relationships with her siblings range from protective to hostile. She takes over responsibility for all of them (including her elder sister) when their father dies.

Clifton, Lucille. *Don't You Remember?* Illus. Evaline Ness. New York: Dutton, 1973. (Ages 3–7.)
Desire Mary Tate, black, four years old, and very lively, considers herself to have the best memory in her family. She has three elder brothers, one of whom has taken a year off from school to care for her. Her parents both work, and her ambition is to grow up and work at the plant, "just like Daddy." Division of labor because it must get done, not because of sex role.

———. *Good, Says Jerome.* Illus. Stephanie Douglas. New York: Dutton, 1973. (Ages 3–7.)
Lovely series of conversations between Jerome and his elder sister, Janice Marie. He mentions all his fears and anxieties to her, and she helps him to resolve them, always causing him to end up with a good feeling. Warm relationship between these two siblings who are pictured as black, but who could be any color.

Clymer, Eleanor. *My Brother Stevie.* New York: Holt, Rinehart and Winston, 1967. (Ages 10–up.)
Annie and her brother Stevie, who have been deserted by their mother, live with their paternal grandfather. Their father is dead. Stevie gets into trouble all the time, and the girl, Annie, is worried about him. Her mother's last instructions were to take care of her brother. Finally, Miss Stover, a teacher, befriends Stevie and Annie. When Miss Stover must return to the country to tend her younger foster-sisters and brothers, Stevie reverts to delinquent behavior. They visit the family in the country and gather strength to live again in their city apartment. The children could be black or white. So could the teacher and her family. The girl, Annie, is too good to be true, but the relationship is a believable one. The teacher, too, is a perfect being. But the little boy is spoiled and self-centered.

Colman, Hila. *Diary of a Frantic Kid Sister.* New York: Crown, 1973. (Ages 8–11.)
Eleven-year-old Sarah is very jealous and resentful of her elder sister, Didi. The mother is too involved with her own problems to help. The father is supportive of her, but not of the mother and sisters. The book is a blow-by-blow description of a sibling relationship as seen through the eyes of the younger sister.

Corcoran, Barbara. *A Trick of Light.* Illus. Lydia Dabcovich. New York: Atheneum, 1973. (Ages 9–12.)
Cassandra and Paige are twins. They are growing up and Paige wants to have friends of his own. Cassandra is hurt, bitter, and jealous, wanting Paige to herself. He is her best friend. During the course of the book, their dog Bingo dies, Paige saves Cassandra's

life, and Cassandra learns to live with the idea of independence from her twin.

Dixon, Paige. *May I Cross Your Golden River?* New York: Atheneum, 1975. (Ages 12–up.)
Jordan, his brothers and sister and mother are a close, loving family. When Jordan contracts a fatal illness, the siblings cope with this fact in different ways; but all are supportive of Jordan and each other.

Duncan, Lois. *Giving Away Suzanne*. Illus. Leonard Weisgard. New York: Dodd, Mead, 1963. (Ages 5–8.)
Mary Kay is bothered by her younger sister Suzanne and tries to give her away. Yet, when Suzanne does go away with Aunt Trudy, Mary Kay is sad and wants her back.

Ellentuck, Shan. *My Brother Bernard*. New York: Abelard-Schuman, 1968. (Ages 5–8.)
The little girl adores her elder brother, Bernard, even though he is not very kind to her. They manage to resolve conflicts, though he retains his superior position. Perhaps a realistic but not very useful solution for real children.

Engebrecht, P. A. *Under the Haystack*. Nashville: Thomas Nelson, 1973. (Ages 11–up.)
Sandy serves as mother to her two younger sisters after their mother deserts them. They struggle emotionally and physically for survival. Sandy manages very well to overcome her sisters' resentment and their fear. In the end, somewhat unrealistically, the mother returns.

Epstein, Beryl, and Davis, Dorritt. *Two Sisters and Some Hornets*. Illus. Rosemary Wells. New York: Holiday House, 1972. (Ages 5–8.)
Sibling spats continue even through old age. This humorous story is about an incident recalled by two elderly sisters of their childhood, when they had an encounter with hornets. They react in old age in much the same way that they did as little children; the older sister smug and superior; the younger sister petulant.

Estes, Eleanor. *The Moffats*. Illus. Louis Slobodkin. New York: Harcourt, Brace & World, 1941. Pb. also. (Ages 8–12.)
One of a series of books about the Moffat family. The four children — two boys and two girls — are cooperative and loving. They never dream of indulging in sibling rivalry and are a veritable parents' dream. The episodes in the book take turns featuring each of the children.

Fitzhugh, Louise. *Nobody's Family Is Going to Change*. New York: Farrar, Straus, & Giroux, 1974. (Ages 10–up.)

Emma is eleven; Willie is seven. They seem to hate each other and their father, who is tense about his underprivileged childhood and his blackness. Willie wants to be a dancer; his father fears ridicule. Emma wants to be a lawyer; her father is sexist. The children finally band together against their father and manage to pull their own lives together. An unpleasant book.

Friedman, Aileen. *The Castles of the Two Brothers*. Illus. Steven Kellogg. New York: Holt, Rinehart and Winston, 1972. (Ages 4–8.)
Two brothers are left orphaned. Elder brother, Hubert, twelve, in taking care of younger brother, Klaus, does everything for his brother. Klaus cannot tolerate this arrangement, so he moves out of the castle that his brother owns and builds one for himself. His brother watches the process, and finally Klaus builds a high wall to hide himself from his brother's view. The wall topples, crumbling the castle. Hubert offers Klaus refuge, but Klaus now moves far away and is never heard from again. Moral? Don't do everything for anyone or you'll lose them.

Gerson, Mary-Joan. *Omoteji's Baby Brother*. Illus. Elzia Moon. New York: Henry Z. Walck, 1974. (Ages 4–8.)
Omoteji lives in Nigeria and is a member of the Yoruba tribe. Mother works in the market; father weaves. Omoteji feels left out when a new baby is born. There is no way he can help. Finally, he composes a song for his new brother and presents it as his gift at the naming ceremony. Everyone is very proud of him.

Gold, Sharlya. *Amelia Quackenbush*. New York: Seabury Press, 1973. (Ages 8–11.)
Amelia and her elder sisters cope with a free-spirit of a father, and a vague, escapist mother. The sisters try to help Amelia with her problems and demonstrate loving support for her. Although she is sloppy and careless, her sisters, aside from gently teasing her, are tolerant and sympathetic.

Gray, Genevieve. *Send Wendell*. Illus. Symeon Shimin. New York: McGraw-Hill, 1974. (Ages 3–9.)
Wendell has six siblings. Wendell is the one who always has to run errands; he does not have anything important of his own to do. His elder siblings are always busy; his younger ones are too small. After his Uncle Robert's visit, Wendell does have things of his own to do. Uncle Robert has recognized that he is a person in his own right and has invited him to live with him on his California farm when he is old enough. Now Wendell has letters to write to Uncle Robert.

Greenfield, Eloise. *She Come Bringing Me That Little Baby Girl*. Illus. John Steptoe. Philadelphia: Lippincott, 1974. (Ages 5–8.)

Black family includes mother, father, Kevin, and baby sister. Kevin wanted a brother. He is jealous of the attention that the new baby gets from all the relatives and neighbors, as well as from his parents. When his mother permits him to hold his new sister and to show her off to his friends, Kevin begins to feel happy again, and to plan for what he and his sister will eventually do together. The rivalry is taken care of in too pat a fashion, but it is handled lovingly on the part of the parents. Steptoe's illustrations are beautiful.

————. *Sister*. Illus. Moneta Barnett. New York: Crowell, 1974. (Ages 10–17.)
Doretha is afraid that she'll be just like her elder sister, Alberta. They look alike, and sometimes Doretha feels as resentful and rebellious as her sister. An unsympathetic teacher does not help when she assumes that Doretha will behave the same way that Alberta did. Doretha is helped to be herself by a school run by and for Afro-Americans. Well-written, interesting book.

Hill, Elizabeth Starr. *Evan's Corner*. New York: Holt, Rinehart and Winston, 1967. (Ages 4–8.)
Evan, his three elder sisters, and younger brother, Adam, live with their parents in a very small apartment. Evan fixes up a place of his own to satisfy a need, but he is not totally satisfied until he recognizes Adam's needs too. A warm, sharing relationship is described here.

Hoban, Russell. *A Baby Sister for Frances*. Illus. Lillian Hoban. New York: Harper & Row, 1964. (Ages 5–8.)
Frances is a baby badger. Her parents have a new baby sister, Gloria, who has somewhat disrupted their schedule, so that Frances decides to run away. She runs away (under the dining room table). Parents talk about how they miss her. It is really a child's dream-come-true, to hear how sorry people are that they are gone. Very loving family.

————. *Harvey's Hideout*. New York: Parents' Magazine Press, 1969. (Ages 6–10.)
Hoban deals with sibling rivalry. Harvey and Mildred fight all the time and exchange nasty comments to each other. In the end, realizing that they really love each other, they become good friends. The family's sex roles are delineated. The father is head of the family and the head disciplinarian. The children are supposed to fear their father because he is the domineering one.

Holland, Isabelle. *The Man Without a Face*. Philadelphia: Lippincott, 1972. (Ages 12–up.)

Charles is fourteen. His older sister, Gloria, is almost seventeen, beautiful, brilliant, self-centered, and cruel to him. She is their mother's favorite. Meg, the younger sister, is fat and neglected. Charles's problems are resolved by Gloria's going away and his mother's marriage to an understanding man.

Holland, Viki. *We Are Having a Baby*. New York: Scribner's, 1972. (Ages 3–6.)

Dana's baby brother's birth causes her some unpleasant feelings, but her father and mother help her to feel happier. The photographs are well done. The text accomplishes the purpose of helping very young children cope with the arrival of new siblings. One outdated comment, surprising in a book published in 1972, is that the father is not permitted into the delivery room when the baby is born.

Hunter, Kristen. *The Soul Brothers and Sister Lou*. New York: Scribners, 1968. Pb. Avon. (Ages 12–up.) (Council on Interracial Books for Children Award.)

Louretta is part of a very large family. Her relationship with her eldest brother is very close; he behaves like a father to her. She and her eldest sister do not get along at all well; there is mutual jealousy and resentment.

Hutchins, Pat. *Titch*. New York: Macmillan, 1971. (Ages 4–7.)

Titch is little and the youngest of three children. He is not persecuted but it is assumed that he cannot participate in activities to the same extent as his elder sister and brother. Everything that he does is insignificant until he plants a seed that grows to be an enormous plant.

Jarrell, Mary. *The Knee Baby*. Illus. Symeon Shimin. New York: Farrar, Straus & Giroux, 1973. (Ages 4–6.)

The little boy wants very much to be held on someone's lap, hugged, and cuddled. His mother spends much time with the new baby. The boy misses his grandmother and wishes that she were there for him. At last his mother gives him a turn on her lap and he is satisfied. The book contains many "baby-talk" pet words. But the message is probably a comforting one for children who feel supplanted by new siblings.

Jones, Adrienne. *So, Nothing Is Forever*. Illus. Richard Cuffari. Boston: Houghton Mifflin, 1974. (Ages 12–up.)

After Talene, Joey, and Adam's parents are killed in a car accident, the three run away to their maternal grandmother's ranch, hoping she will permit them to stay. Their father is black; their mother white. Though they face bigotry, resentment, and rejection, they love each other and manage very well.

Jordan, June. *New Life: New Room*. Illus. Ray Cruz. New York: Crowell, 1975. (Ages 6-9.)
A new baby is expected and Rudy, age ten, Tyrone, age nine, and Linda, age six, must adjust their lives to the fact. Sensitive portrayal reflecting every family member's feelings. Their apartment has only two bedrooms. It is up to the children to decide how to live together in one room. With their father's help, they arrive at a happy solution. This is a joyous, loving, constructive book.

Keats, Ezra Jack. *Peter's Chair*. New York: Harper & Row, 1967. (Ages 5-8.)
Peter has a new baby sister. His parents are painting all of his old furniture pink for the baby. He feels excluded and, taking his chair, "runs away." He actually remains close by. When he realizes that he has outgrown his chair, when he hears his parents' supportive words, and when he smells dinner, he returns to the family and resolves to tolerate his sister.

Klein, Norma. *Confessions of an Only Child*. Illus. Richard Cuffari. New York: Pantheon, 1974. (Ages 8-12.)
Antonia's mother is pregnant. "Toe" is happy being an only child and is fearful and resentful of the intrusion of a sibling. Her friends support her negative feelings with unpleasant stories about their younger siblings. After the baby is born prematurely and dies, Toe becomes reconciled to her parents' having another. Her parents understand her feelings and behave lovingly toward her and each other. Useful modeling in this book, although the setting is thoroughly white upper-middle class.

————. *If I Had My Way*. Illus. Ray Cruz. New York: Pantheon, 1974. (Ages 5-8.)
Ellie is about six years old; she has a baby brother. When her parents go out for the evening, she imagines how life would be if children ran the world. Her parents are very understanding and even let her suck on a bottle. After her imaginary trip, she resumes her own life, somewhat resigned to it.

————. *It's Not What You Expect*. New York: Pantheon, 1973. Pb. Avon. (Ages 12-up.)
Oliver and Carla are fourteen-year-old twins who are very friendly and loving. They admire each other and work together very well. They never fight. They also get along very well with their eighteen-year-old brother, Ralph. As a matter of fact, all the siblings in this book have ideal relationships. Unrealistic but enviable situation.

————. *Naomi in the Middle*. Illus. Leigh Grant. New York: Dial Press, 1974. (Ages 7-10.)

The story is narrated by Naomi, age seven. She and her elder sister Bobo, age nine, have a normal sibling relationship. When they hear of their mother's pregnancy, Naomi contemplates the problems of being the middle child, and Bobo is gloomy. The story is a vehicle for demonstrating how a loving family handles the problems of sibling relationships.

Konigsberg, E. L. *From the Mixed-Up Files of Mrs. Basil E. Frankweiler.* New York: Atheneum, 1967. Pb. also. (Ages 8-12.) (Newbery Medal.)
Claudia selects Jamie from among her siblings to be her companion when they run away from home. They learn from this experience to value each other more than they did before.

Kraus, Robert. *Big Brother.* New York: Parents' Magazine Press, 1973. (Ages 3-7.)
The little brother admires and envies his big brother. He despairs of ever feeling big himself until his parents produce a baby brother for him. This constitutes a happy ending in this book. A sequel might ensue called *Middle Brother*, but there is no hint of it here.

Lasker, Joe. *He's My Brother.* Chicago: Albert Whitman, 1974. (Ages 6-9).
Boy has a slow-learning younger brother, Jamie, who gets teased. Becka, the older sister, bakes brownies for him and is kind to him. Brother sometimes is impatient but then plays with him to make up for it. Jamie is good with babies and animals. The family is very good, loving, and patient with him.
    Mildred and Joe Lasker write at the end that they hope "this book will enable other Jamies and their families to identify with the experiences shown and take comfort."

Lexau, Joan. *Striped Ice Cream.* Illus. John Wilson. Philadelphia: Lippincott, 1968. Pb. Scholastic. (Ages 6-11.)
Black family, very poor. Five children live with their mother. Their father has left to free them to go on Welfare, but they do not; Mother works. Becky, the almost eight-year-old is the protagonist. Her sisters and brother work to surprise her for her birthday but in so doing, make her miserable. Family is compulsively preoccupied with cleanliness, as if to constantly prove they are not stereotypes. Illustrations excellent.

————. *The Trouble with Terry.* Illus. Irene Murray. New York: Dial Press, 1962. Pb. Scholastic. (Ages 8-12.) (Wel-Met Award.)
Terry and her elder brother Tommy are very good friends. Tommy is the perfect child; Terry is a tomboy. But Tommy helps Terry when she is in trouble and sympathizes with her problems. Terry admires, loves, and envies her brother. They both have increased

responsibilities because their mother is a widow and works full-time.

Little, Jean. *Home from Far*. Illus. Jerry Lazare. Boston: Little, Brown, 1965. (Ages 9–12.)
Jenny's relationship with her dead twin brother Michael was so close that she feels she will betray him if she permits herself to like her foster-sister and brother. Her mother helps her to work it out.

Love, Sharron. *The Sunshine Family and the Pony*. New York: Seabury Press, 1972. (Ages 3–7.)
A very simple telling of the way that a communal family handles the problem of an unhappy pony. The story indicates that communal living can work. There is no hint that interpersonal problems may occur; the message is that this sort of life is idyllic. The book is useful for communicating a life style different from the nuclear family.

Macken, Walter. *The Flight of the Doves*. New York: Macmillan, 1968. Pb. Collier. (Ages 9–11.)
Finn and his sister run away from their wicked stepfather across the Irish Sea to live with their grandmother. The boy nurtures and cares for his sister, who is, unfortunately, the stereotypic helpless, frightened female. But the sibling relationship is strong and supportive.

Mallett, Anne. *Here Comes Tagalong*. Illus. Steven Kellogg. New York: Parents' Magazine Press, 1971. (Ages 5–7.)
Steve is a five-year-old who has an elder and a younger brother. His elder brother permits him to tag along with him and his friends. Then, when Steve is permitted to go around the block by himself, he meets friends his own age, and his younger brother becomes the tagalong.

Manushkin, Fran. *Bubble Bath*. Illus. Ronald Himler. New York: Harper & Row, 1974. (Ages 3–7.)
Two sisters play together happily, get dirty, and bathe together. They help each other and thoroughly enjoy all of their play.

Mason, Miriam E. *The Middle Sister*. Illus. Wayne Blickenstaff. New York: Macmillan, 1947. Pb. Scholastic. (Ages 8–11.)
Sarah Samantha is the middle sister of three girls in a large family but behaves more like the youngest than the midle. Afraid of all sorts of things, she wants a special lion's tooth that her uncle has, to keep as a talisman for courage. Of course, she demonstrates bravery long before she gets the lion's tooth. The siblings behave in a fairly cooperative way.

Mathis, Sharon Bell. *Teacup Full of Roses*. New York: Viking, 1972. (Ages 12–up.)
Three brothers love each other, but the eldest is the mother's favorite. Only the middle brother survives at the end of this tragic story.

Matsuno, Masako. *Chie and the Sports Day*. Illus. Kazue Mizumura. Cleveland: World, 1965. (Ages 4–8.)
Chie's elder brother succumbs to peer pressure and runs off to play with his friends. They disdain playing with girls.

Mazer, Norma Fox. *A Figure of Speech*. New York: Delacorte Press, 1973. Pb. Dell. (Ages 12–up.)
Thirteen-year-old Jenny has a terrible relationship with her siblings and her parents. Her elder sister is purposely cruel to her; her eldest brother is self-centered and somewhat irresponsible; her other brother is sullen and troubled. The baby sister is not much of a factor. The book presents an example of ineffective, insensitive parents in an ugly family setting, but it is moving and powerful in its painful story.

Ness, Evaline. *Do You Have the Time, Lydia?* New York: Dutton, 1971. (Ages 5–8.) Pb. also.
Lydia and her brother live with their father, who is a florist. Their home is on a tropical island. Lydia is a well-intentioned elder sister, but is so busy with so many activities that she bitterly disappoints her younger brother. She makes up for it by determining to change her ways and to complete each task that she begins.

Neufeld, John. *Edgar Allan*. New York: S. G. Phillips, 1968. Pb. New American Library. (Ages 10–13.)
Minister and his wife adopt a black child without first informing their other four children. Child, Edgar Allan, is three years old. All of family, except for teen-age daughter, love him. Eventually, pressure from the townspeople, from the daughter, and from the members of the church makes the minister give back Edgar Allan to the adoption agency. Their lie about his being returned to his original family does not hold, and everyone eventually castigates the minister for listening to them. He is forced to resign and to begin again. All the sympathy seems to be invited for the minister and his family. Edgar Allan never emerges as a person in this book. He remains a plaything that has been discarded. Relationships among the siblings is explored, and growth and change are seen to take place.

O'Dell, Scott. *Island of the Blue Dolphins*. Boston: Houghton Mifflin, 1960. Pb. Dell. (Ages 9–14.)
This story, a modern classic of courage and survival, is based on a true story. Karana is abandoned on an island after all of her people

have left, and her brother has been killed. She manages to survive for many years, and is rescued, at last, by missionaries.

Orgel, Doris. *Bartholomew, We Love You*. Illus. Pat Grant Porter. New York: Knopf, 1973. (Ages 8–12.)
Kim is Emily's younger sister. Kim feels that Emily is prettier, smarter, more talented, and more favored. Kim finds a cat, Bartholomew, and nurtures him. At one point, she barters him away to Emily, hating herself as she does it. In the end, after an escapade in which Bartholomew gets lost and then recovered, the two sisters learn to share somewhat more happily. The parents in this story are understanding, competent people. The mother works in a laboratory; the father is a machinery designer. The book is realistic and useful.

Parish, Peggy. *Willy Is My Brother*. Illus. Shirley Hughes. New York: William R. Scott, 1963. (Ages 5–8.)
Narrator of story is a girl. She and her brother always fight, but they obviously love each other. Willy ignores her to play with a friend, but fights his friend when the friend calls her a pest. She finally has a friend come to play. They play lion tamer, and friend obeys little girl. Humorous arguments take place in this turbulent household.

Payson, Dale. *Almost Twins*. Englewood Cliffs, N.J.: Prentice-Hall, 1974. (Ages 4–8.)
Annabelle is a year younger than her sister Nellie. They live with their elderly aunt, who treats them exactly alike. Annabelle is often perturbed by the fact that Nellie is more competent than she in almost everything they do. Finally, Annabelle discovers that she can paint as well as Nellie. She enjoys this knowledge. The book emphasizes female stereotypes, and burdens both siblings with the obligation to be uniformly and consistently sweet.

Rosen, Winifred. *Henrietta, the Wild Woman of Borneo*. Illus. Kay Chorao. New York: Four Winds Press, 1975. (Ages 5–8.)
Henrietta is messy, clumsy, wild; her elder sister Evelyn is pretty, graceful, and neat. The girls' parents love them both, but Henrietta feels unloved. She tries to run away. Evelyn seems to support the idea but in the end, arranges it so that Henrietta returns home. The ending is happy but not believable.

Sachs, Marilyn. *Amy and Laura*. Illus. Tracy Sugarman. Garden City, N.Y.: Doubleday, 1966. Pb. Scholastic. (Ages 7–10.)
Amy and her elder sister are very different from each other. They must not only cope with their feelings of rivalry, they must also deal with the problems of their mother's illness. In the end, all is resolved.

———. *The Bears' House*. Illus. Louis Glanzman. Garden City, N.Y.: Doubleday, 1971. (Ages 9–12.) (National Book Award.)
Fran Ellen, her brother, and three sisters try to manage their household after their father has deserted them and their mother has suffered a nervous collapse. The relationships among the siblings are, in general, supportive, protective, and loving. But the book is more complex and much more painful than are most other stories of sibling survival.

Samson, Joan. *Watching the New Baby*. Photographs by Gard Gladstone. New York: Atheneum, 1974. (Ages 8–11.)
Describes the newborn baby in terms of physical development and relationship to the world. The book is useful for siblings who ask many "why" questions about new babies. The photographs show many happy relationships between newborns and their elder siblings.

Schick, Eleanor. *Peggy's New Brother*. New York: Macmillan, 1970. (Ages 5–7.)
Peggy would have preferred a dog or cat to a baby brother. Her mother encourages her to help, but she is not very good at it. Then Peggy discovers that she can make her baby brother laugh; their relationship is assured.

Schlein, Miriam. *Laurie's New Brother*. New York: Abelard-Schuman, 1961. (Ages 5–8.)
Laurie, sent away, comes back to find a brother. She is at first jealous, then helps. Unfortunately, the book is sexist — father does not do a thing. But children can empathize with Laurie's feelings and realize that these feelings are normal and universal.

Scott, Ann Herbert. *On Mother's Lap*. Illus. Glo Coalson. New York: McGraw-Hill, 1972. (Ages 5–8.)
Michael and his family are Eskimo, but we know that only because of the illustrations. The story is very simply told. Mother arranges it so there is room for everyone and everything, making it clear that her lap can accommodate them all. This makes Michael feel very happy. The book recognizes rivalry and models mother's gentle, nonreproaching manner of dealing with it.

———. *Sam*. Illus. Symeon Shimin. New York: McGraw-Hill, 1967. (Ages 4–8.)
Sam, the youngest of three children, is very much the baby of the family. The elder siblings are not unkind, but they do not want him touching their things. Sam's mother realizes that he needs to be permitted to do something special by himself. The rest of the family agrees and applauds when Sam is permitted to bake a raspberry tart.

Segal, Lore. *Tell Me a Mitzi*. Illus. Harriet Pincus. New York: Farrar, Straus & Giroux, 1970. (Ages 5-8.)
The three stories describe a contemporary Jewish family living in New York City. Mitzi (short for Martha) and her baby brother, Jacob, get along very well. They are both happy, pleasant children, and their parents seem to treat them with equal caring.

Sharmat, Marjorie. *Goodnight, Andrew, Goodnight, Craig*. Illus. Mary Chalmers. New York: Harper & Row, 1969. (Ages 3-8.)
Two brothers, put to bed by their father, take a long time falling asleep. They finally fall asleep after the elder brother promises the younger one he will play with him in the morning. Loving family relationship all around.

Sorenson, Virginia. *Miracles on Maple Hill*. Illus. B. and J. Krush. New York: Harcourt Brace, 1965. Pb. also. (Ages 9-12.) (Newbery Medal.)
Marly and her brother engage in constant competition. They love each other and their relationship is depicted as normally competitive.

Stein, Sara Bonnett. *That New Baby*. Illus. Dick Frank. New York: Walker, 1974. (Ages 3-8.)
This is one in the series of "Open Family Books for Parents and Children Together." It contains a text for parents which points out that most elder children are jealous of younger ones to some extent. Through beautiful photographs (this time of a black family) and an excellent text, the message comes through that every family member is valued. The advice given to parents is practical, direct, and psychologically sound.

Steptoe, John. *Birthday*. New York: Holt, Rinehart and Winston, 1972. (Ages 5-8.)
It is Javaka's eighth birthday. He is the firstborn of a community of black people. The community is represented as the ideal way of life: everyone is part of the extended, loving family.

————. *My Special Best Words*. New York: Viking, 1974. (Ages 5-8.)
Bweela, three years old, lives with her one-year-old brother Javaka and her father. The reader is not told where the mother is. Bweela is very good with Javaka. She helps him with his toilet-training, nose-blowing, and speech. They quarrel with each other, Javaka telling Bweela to TAKEABREAK, and Bweela retorting YOUADUMMY. Both children are bright and happy. Even without a mother, life seems happy and full of hope.

————. *Stevie*. New York: Harper & Row, 1969. Pb. Scholastic. (Ages 7-10.)

Robert experiences the pangs of sibling rivalry over Stevie, a young boy who stays at Robert's house. In the end, Robert misses Stevie when he leaves.

Talbot, Charlene Joy. *A Home with Aunt Florry*. New York: Atheneum, 1974. (Ages 9–12.)
Jason and Wendy, twelve-year-old orphaned twins, come to stay with their eccentric Aunt Florry in New York. Their relationship with each other is ideal. They never argue, are kind to each other, share happily, and are also very self-sufficient.
    Some of the messages in this book include a plea for tolerance of different life styles and for children's taking responsibility for themselves.

Taylor, Sydney. *All-of-a-Kind Family Downtown*. Illus. Beth and Joe Krush. Chicago: Follett, 1972. Pb. Dell. (Ages 8–12.)
Fourth in the series containing *All-of-a-Kind Family, More-All-of-a-Kind Family*, and *All-of-a-Kind Family Uptown*. The stories describe a Jewish family containing five sisters and one brother growing up in New York in the early twentieth century. The sisters do everything together and always think of one another's feelings. The family is pious, just, loving, and cooperative. Although the children occasionally do naughty things, they always confess and set it right. The stories are very well written and convey a flavor of the era.

Terris, Susan. *Amanda the Panda and the Redhead*. Illus. Emily McCully. Garden City, N.Y.: Doubleday, 1975. (Ages 3–8.)
Amanda is ignored because her parents are too busy with her brother. But they are essentially loving and responsive people and by evening, all is well.

———. *The Drowning Boy*. Garden City, N.Y.: Doubleday, 1972. (Ages 12–up.)
Jason is twelve years old and hates his life. His elder sister and his father are perfectionists. His mother is caring for her hopelessly senile mother. She has quit her job and does nothing but tend grandma and grow tomatoes. Jason has been attending a school for disturbed boys. When he spends the summer caring for a young autistic child, his success with the boy helps him. He also recognizes that he has to change. His relationship with his father will improve. He has depended on a teacher, but he will not have to any longer. Issues in this book include old age, family relationships, care of autistic children, fear, and coping with differences.

Viorst, Judith. *I'll Fix Anthony*. Illus. Arnold Lobel. New York: Harper & Row, 1969. (Ages 5–8.)

A charmingly written and illustrated book, depicting sibling rivalry. Anthony, the elder boy, is thoroughly nasty and mean to his younger sibling. The younger boy, dreaming of the day when he will become six years old, imagines all the ways that he will take his revenge. Excellent for demonstrating that younger brothers have feelings, but unsympathetic to elder siblings.

Watson, Clyde. *Tom Fox and the Apple Pie*. Illus. Wendy Watson. New York: Crowell, 1972. (Ages 5–8.)
Tom is the youngest in a very large family. Though greedy and lazy, he is the pet of the family. In this story, leaving his virtuous brothers and sisters to their work, he runs off to the fair. He does buy a balloon for his favorite sister but eats an entire apple pie without sharing a bit of it. He is mildly punished by his mother, but goes to bed happily unrepentant. Any youngest child would enjoy this story. Elder siblings would also probably appreciate the pattern it presents.

Wells, Rosemary. *Noisy Nora*. New York: Dial Press, 1973. (Ages 3–7.)
Nora's elder sister keeps telling her that she is dumb; her baby brother gets all their parents' attention. She runs away (into the closet). When they realize that she is gone, they are all sorry and welcome her back with affection. A happy but not realistic solution to the problem of sibling rivalry.

Winthrop, Elizabeth. *A Little Demonstration of Affection*. New York: Harper & Row, 1975. (Ages 12–up.)
Jenny, the youngest in a family of three, adores her eldest brother, John. She and John have had a close and happy relationship. Charlie, the middle child, has been left out. This summer John finds other friends and Jenny and Charlie become inseparable. Jenny fears that her feelings for Charlie are unnatural and evil, but at last they all recognize that they need affection and love and that they are normal.

Zolotow, Charlotte. *Big Sister and Little Sister*. New York: Harper & Row, 1966. (Ages 5–8.)
No one likes to always be the one who is "taken care of." By showing that sometime big sisters need help too, perhaps both big and little sisters can see a way to a happier relationship.

———. *If It Weren't for You*. Illus. Ben Shecter. New York: Harper & Row, 1966. (Ages 5–8.)
The fantasies of a boy thinking of all the wonderful things that he would be able to do if he were an only child. The thought that brings him back to reality is that if he had no brother, he would "have to be alone with the grown-ups."

NOTES and ADDITIONS

3

Divorce

LOVE, MARRIAGE, AND FAMILY have signaled emotional success in our society. Although men have not been considered total failures if they chose not to marry, their lives have been judged to be less than complete. Women, on the other hand, have been taught to anticipate marriage as a natural and proper part of existence. If a woman is not married, it is assumed that no one asked her; rarely is it considered that the single state is her choice. Only in recent years have arrangements other than marriage been socially available options. Some men and women are now recognizing that marriage is not necessarily a life goal for them. Their decision, in the light of society's new recognition of people's right to individuality and of changing life styles, is viewed with less disapproval than it once was.

Marriage, too, is being viewed differently. Happy marriages are now defined by criteria other than longevity: some marriages that have lasted a long time are, nevertheless, unsuccessful. People might choose to stay together for reasons other than constructive ones. Wives used to endure all kinds of hardships within marriage because they knew that life outside of this institution would be even more difficult for them. Husbands might stay with women that they no longer cared for because it was economically unfeasible to pay for the costs of divorce and its aftermath. Men were responsible for the total support of the family. What is more, the woman was almost always the injured party in a divorce. Marriages might also continue "for the sake of the children." These pressures still exist; but more and more, people are recognizing that they must work together to keep a marriage going well, and that if their efforts fail, they must work together to make the separation a mutually successful one.

Separation and divorce are not so difficult or costly to arrange as before. What used to be an ugly, painful, long drawn-out procedure has, in many states, been simplified so that the process itself is not a stumbling block when two partners decide that they will dissolve their contract. Divorce is less of a scandalous matter than it once was, though most state laws demand that there be an identified culprit and victim before a divorce can be granted.

Our social structure is in a state of transition, but the preponderant values continue to include the traditional expectations of lasting marriage. Ending a marriage other than by death is still considered by many observers to constitute failure. It is certainly a wrenching experience, not only to the partners but to any children involved as well. The adults and the children have many burdens to handle and many emotional hurdles to overcome. Just as the adults agonize over what they could have done to have saved the marriage (or bemoan having gotten themselves into it in the first place), so too the children worry that the failed marriage was their fault. They imagine that, if they had been better, the marriage would have succeeded; that is, if they had done their job as good children, their parents would still be together. They also worry about whether or not their parents will continue to love them and care for them. They worry about being deserted by the remaining parent and about never again seeing the absent parent. They worry about being supplanted in their parents' affections, and they worry about their own self-worth.

Friends and acquaintances sometimes respond as though there has been a death in the family. They may studiously avoid mentioning the child's predicament, eliminating the word *father* (or, if the child is living with the father, the word *mother*) from their vocabulary when the child is in listening distance. They apologize in nonverbal ways if their own families are intact or they hesitate to invite the child to a family gathering for fear of unduly inflicting pangs of jealousy. Sometimes they rain on the child a barrage of questions that are very difficult to answer. "What's your mother (father) doing these days?" "What's happening at your house lately?" "Is anything new?" While these probes might be kindly intended, they can confuse and hurt a child who does not really know how his or her parents are feeling or what is going on at home.

If divorce is an unusual occurrence in the community, the child's peers will sometimes avoid contact with the child, as though divorce were contagious. Even if this is not the case, it is sometimes difficult for peers to know what to say to help a child who no longer lives with both parents. In communities where divorce is less rare, children who have experienced the same situation can be very helpful in sharing feelings and offering support to each other. The sensitive adult can arrange for this kind of interaction to take place.

Although a large percentage of all divorced couples have children under eighteen, there is a surprising paucity of recent adult books advising parents how to deal with the feelings and problems that the divorce has aroused in their children. Agencies specializing in family help, as well as organizations such as Parents Without Partners, give advice and support. Books can be used as tools by parents, teachers, librarians, and children on a regular "Come to me whenever you need me" basis.

Suggested Criteria

Just as with any other sort of book, the literary quality of a written work dealing with divorce can enhance or detract from its effectiveness. If it is a work of fiction, it should have more than the issue of divorce to carry its readers' interest. If the book's intent is to convey information it must do so in a noncondescending, jargon-free fashion. The topic of divorce must be kept up to date because the statistics and state laws have been changing rapidly. On the other hand, the psychological reactions of children have changed little in response to divorce. If a book communicates children's feelings and suggests some effective ways to deal with them, it is a useful book.

Books for children should handle the topic realistically. One pitfall to avoid is the "happy" ending of the parents' being reunited as a result of the child's behavior. Many children believe that it lies within their power to save their parents' marriage. This is unrealistic and can serve the child badly. Books should also try to refrain from establishing guilt for the divorce, which is almost always a complicated situation with no clear cause. In any case, blame-fixing is not useful. If a book uses it as a constituent of the plot, then the case should be presented so that the reader senses either another side or the futility of blaming.

The most helpful books about divorce grant the child his or her feelings and are models for supportive behavior on the part of children and adults, providing options for everyone involved. Although they do not necessarily end happily, they do demonstrate that life can go on in a constructive fashion. Books on this topic should be used with children experiencing the problem, with their peers (so that empathy can be stimulated), and with parents, who often need to learn how to manage their responses.

The audience determines the use to which a book will be put. If the audience is a child whose parents have just divorced, the book will be used as therapy, as comfort, and, perhaps, as a source of information and suggestions for behavior. If the audience is a group of children who have never come in contact with the situation of divorce and are now responding inappropriately to a child who is involved in a divorce, the book may stimulate empathic and supportive behavior. Sometimes a book for children is a useful tool for reaching a parent, helping him or her deal with the child in a more constructive fashion. In reading a book to a child, a parent may also derive comfort, support, and ideas from it. An alert teacher or librarian can locate and collect those books that will be helpful in a variety of situations.

▶ Try This

Select three books from the Bibliography at the end of this chapter. If you were to recommend these books to a reader, (1) for whom would this book be most valuable? (2) for whom would this book be of no use at all? (3) what problems are left unsolved by these books? After sharing your selections with someone else, combine your perceptions.

Books containing even the briefest mention of a divorce usually communicate very clearly the attitude of the author and/or the prevailing societal point of view. Religion, upbringing, and ethical standards contribute to the building of an attitude toward people who are involved in divorce. Accurate information contributes to a healthy perspective. The helping adult must face his or her own opinions knowledgeably before attempting to work with a child who is coping with the problem at firsthand.

▶ Try This

Answer the following questions as accurately as you can. After you look at your answers, decide how your information and opinions will affect a child whose parents have been divorced. How will they affect children who are the peers of this child?

1. Who is usually to blame in a divorce?
2. What is the most prevalent cause of divorce?
3. What is the current divorce rate? Where can you find this information?
4. What organizations help parents to cope with this problem?
5. What are the specific religious regulations regarding divorce?
6. What are the legal regulations in this state regarding divorce?
7. Which local agencies provide information on this topic?
8. What could cause you to seek a divorce from your mate?
9. How do you feel about the idea of preserving a marriage for the sake of the children?
10. What are your assumptions about the behavior of children coming from broken homes?

Discussion of Children's Books

BREAKING UP

Books describing the initial divorce process hold out hope for children whose parents have separated or divorced. The pattern of these books includes the child's bewilderment and unhappiness when the parents separate, the difficult period of adjustment when the arrangements are first being worked out, the problem of living with mother only and father visiting once a week, and then the settling down to a satisfactory everyday existence with the single parent. The books do not pretend that the children's hoped-for happy ending — the reconciliation of the father and mother — will ever occur. They do recognize the fears and guilt feelings of the children, and they present realistic situations. They usually focus on only one child in the family, and, indeed, the books often describe the families with only one child.

Beth Goff's *Where Is Daddy?* follows the pattern, adding the specific trauma for the very young child who is not only experiencing the loss of her father from the household but also the partial loss of the mother who now goes out of the house to work for the first time in the child's existence. In this book, the child, Janeydear, goes with her mother and her dog to live with her maternal grandmother. The child is terrified that, if she exhibits anger or bad temper, her mother will behave as her father did and not return. She considers herself the culprit in the divorce. If only she had behaved well, her father would not have left. Her well-meaning but harassed grandmother unwittingly contributes to this feeling. The child becomes fearful, quiet, and withdrawn. At last, the adults, recognizing how Janeydear feels, take steps to make her more comfortable. The mother takes Janeydear to her place of business so that she can picture her mother there when her mother is not at home; her grandmother accompanies them, becoming a partner in the process. The grandmother begins to play with Janeydear, relaxing some of her rules about permitting the dog into the house. And Janeydear's father visits her and answers her questions somewhat more patiently.

The story is clearly and directly told. The characters are somewhat oversimplified but not stereotyped. They serve as good points of reference. They also have enough individuality so that the story can stand on its own without being used as a lesson. Commenting at the end of the book, Dr. John F. McDermott, a psychiatrist, describes the expected reactions of a young child to divorce and some of the difficulties that adults face. He suggests the use of this story as a bridge to help restore perspective to children and their parents. Young children may appreciate the opportunity to role-play this story and others like it.

Another book conveying a similar message for somewhat older children is Peggy Mann's *My Dad Lives in a Downtown Hotel*. When Joey's father leaves him and his mother and moves into a hotel, Joey is convinced that his father does not love him. Imagining that if he reforms, his father will be willing to come back home, he goes to visit his father, armed with a list of things that he will do to be a better person. Joey's mother also wants his father to come back to them. The father seems rather callous about their feelings and avoids any contact with Joey's mother, even though she invites it; he even avoids mentioning her in conversation with Joey. He inconsiderately drops in on Joey and his mother at night to collect some of his belongings. Taking their television set, he informs them that he has ordered a color T.V. for them.

The book specifically describes the child's feelings and each of the significant occurrences at this time of his life. The father has apparently never before been much of a companion for the boy. Now that he and the mother are being divorced, he pays more attention to his son, taking Joey to places that he enjoys visiting with his father. For the boy, the divorce brings all kinds of improvements in the behavior of both of his parents toward him. He also discovers that there are a number of children at school who are in his situation, and they decide to form a social club. It will probably serve as a support for these children. Life for the boy looks as if it will be comfortable, but the mother is left in a bad way. She is the bereft party. If past experience is any measure, the father will probably disappoint Joey, but there is no indication of this in the book.

The book demonstrates a realistic portrayal of a separation. The mother is not dependent or clinging or nagging; though obviously the injured party, she is not a martyr. She continues to work, cares about her appearance, and tries to devise special ways of attending to Joey's needs. She is an excellent model except for the fact that she keeps alive the hope that her husband will return. The husband, although inconsiderate, is not really a villain. It might have been a service for the book to have hinted that the father would not live up to his weekly commitment, but the author may have wanted to provide more hope to children whose parents have just separated and who need the hope of a continued close relationship with the absent parent. Children could devise a "What if?" exercise, telling how they would respond if the father did not visit regularly or if the father remarried.

When Joey's first attempt at bringing his parents back together fails, he accepts the reality of their always remaining separate. In *A Month of Sundays*, by Rose Blue, ten-year-old Jeff keeps dreaming of his parents' getting back together. He and his mother have moved from the suburbs to the city. At first Jeff feels uncomfortable there, but eventually learns to enjoy the benefits that the city has to offer. Topics other than divorce are introduced in this book. Jeff's friend Matthew is an adopted child. The warmth of the family and their sympathetic treatment of Jeff help construct an image that runs counter to the usual stereotype of a poor urban black family. The job that Jeff's mother takes is her first. Jeff is unhappy about it because he misses the attention she used to give him. She finally recognizes the reasons for his negative behavior, and, despite her tiredness, spends time and energy with him, cooking and baking what he wants, and participating in the plans for the block party to come. Children could suggest ways that Jeff can help at home, perhaps by writing an imaginary letter to Jeff, giving him advice.

Most books for children concentrate on the children's feelings. It would probably be useful if some of the books helped children to acknowledge their parents' feelings as well. Books such as those described above are useful for children who are enduring the painful beginnings of life after divorce. They help make the child aware that other people have gone through the same experience and have had the same ugly and confused feelings. They present a view of a positive way of relating to both parents and of coping with the problems.

Unlike the three books thus far described, one book for preteens and older, *Leap Before You Look*, by Mary Stolz, specifically details the cause of the marital breakdown of the parents. It signals the eventuality of the divorce by having the father's young, pretty, new assistant appear at the house well before the divorce is a certainty. But since the unhappiness of the marriage is described before this, the reader understands the father's position. The mother in this book is really the cause of the unhappiness. She is a withdrawn, selfish woman who prefers her own isolation to anyone's company. Her values are totally different from her husband's. Her daughter, Jimmie, prefers her father to her mother but becomes very angry when he leaves them. She resents it even more when, after the divorce, he marries his lover.

This book, which has a complicated plot and unusual characters, requires that the reader understand the different people and not judge them. The mother is dealt with unsympathetically, but all the other characters are multidimensional and invite our compassion. Jimmie's friends are helpful in alleviating her pain. In the end, Jimmie begins to move toward a reconciliation with her father.

One of the negative aspects of too many of the books for older readers is the assumption of guilt on the mother's part. In these books, where the mother is blamed for the breakup of the marriage, the father is almost always a pleasant, understanding, admirable person. There is too often no indication, other than that of the mother's unpleasantness, that there is any real cause for the divorce. Mary Stolz's book describes a woman who seems severely disturbed and whose withdrawal from the real world is probably pathological; but no one recognizes it as such in her family. It is she who is the cause of her husband's unhappiness; it is she who is the least sympathetic character. She totally withdraws at the end of the book, leaving to her mother the task of managing her, the children, and the household. Readers may find it an interesting exercise, in cases like this, to attempt to reconstruct the couple's courtship and marriage in order to understand how the pair came to marry in the first place.

Somewhat similarly, in Honor Arundel's *A Family Failing*, the mother carries the largest burden for the failure of the marriage. Again, it is the father whom the daughter prefers. Again, the father is a pleasant, honest, attractive person. In this story the father loses his job at the same time that the mother appears regularly on a successful television show. Both parents are journalists, but the mother is depicted as having few scruples, while the father is ethical, committed to quality and principle. He cannot accept his wife's position of being the sole wage earner in the family. Nor can he make good his intention to write a book. After manufacturing all kinds of excuses for his failure, he finally admits that he simply does not have the talent. He goes off to a rural spot in Scotland, deciding to stay there permanently rather than be subjected to the emotional hardship of Edinburgh. The mother loses her television job, but stubbornly refuses to join her husband because, she says, her pride will not let her.

No member of the family is without selfish characteristics. They impose upon the mother the entire responsibility for all the cooking and most of the cleaning in the house. The children realize that their parents have always permitted them to be independent, but they do not recognize the extent to which they have depended on their mother for their physical needs. When she becomes the only wage earner in the family, the family collapses. The son moves to a commune; the father moves to the small village in Scotland. The daughter first joins her brother, then her father. Despite the fact that it is the mother who carries the greatest responsibility for maintaining the family, they denigrate her jobs and her abilities. The implication is clear that the mother is at fault for the dissolution of the family. In the end the daughter decides that she has no right to intervene in her parents' lives and that they must do what they decide is best. She also begins to accept them as they are without trying to change them. Mature preteens can read this book to help them come to a position of not having to fix blame for their parents' separation. One caution to consider is that this book retains the idea that, because the parents love each other, they will eventually find a way of resuming their married life together.

AFTERMATH OF THE DIVORCE

Books describing the lives of people some time after the divorce vary more than those dealing mainly with the period during and immediately after the breakup. In general, more problems remain unresolved in the aftermath books. Certainly the many problems are clearly confronted, but the prospect of a blissful solution is less likely.

Sometimes the child's nightmare comes true in these books. The parents really do not want to have anything to do with their children; they even abuse the children physically and psychologically. These books may be useful in stimulating peer empathy or in encouraging discussion about the negative feelings of a child who feels, accurately or not, that he or she is being victimized. For the child who becomes upset by these books, an adult will do well to provide strong counseling, along with a variety of books presenting different aspects of the divorce situation.

A book in which the parents seemingly reject their child after the divorce is John Donovan's *I'll Get There. It Better Be Worth the Trip*. Davy has lived with his maternal grandmother since his parents' divorce. His father has remarried, and his mother is an alcoholic. When the grandmother dies, there is no one but his mother who is willing to take custody of him. She obviously sustains great anxiety about the idea, and the arrangement does not work out very well for Davy. His mother is overly taxed by the situation; his father and stepmother seem genuinely to care for the boy but not enough to provide a home for him. Not until the boy is independent of his family will he have any sort of security. And then it will have to be self-arranged.

Growing up — or at least attaining emotional independence — seems to be the only solution for a number of characters in books dealing with the aftermath of divorce. The daughter in *A Family Failing* outgrows her need for her parents' attention. Chris, one of the secondary characters in *Leap Before You Look,* is in therapy because of her mother's lack of regard for the institution of marriage. Chris believes that even now, although her mother is still married to her second husband, she is in the process of searching for a third. Each of her aunts has been married three times. Chris is disgusted by this behavior, besides being angry with her father, who has not once visited her in all the years since his divorce from her mother. But she, too, recognizes that, when she gets a little older, she will be more able to provide for herself the emotional support that she now requires from her family.

Guy, the hero of Harry Mazer's *Guy Lenny,* though only twelve years old, also comes to the realization that he must be emotionally separate from his parents in order to cope with his situation. With Guy, however, the fault is not easily assigned. Guy's mother, who left him and his father to marry another man, has only sporadically written to Guy during their long separation. Her new husband is a career officer in the army, and it was not feasible for them to take Guy with them. Meanwhile, the boy has lived with his father, an easy-going blue-collar worker. Guy loves his father and feels deeply hurt by his mother's desertion. When his father becomes involved with Emily, who then helps to take care of Guy and the house, Guy angrily resents Emily's intrusion into his and his father's relationship. Although she tries to befriend Guy, he will not permit it. He stubbornly maintains a hostile attitude toward her in hopes that his father will give her up.

Guy's parents are not villains in this book. His father becomes tired of having to cope with Guy's resentment of Emily. He is ready to marry again, and Guy is opposed to his doing so. Guy feels betrayed by his father when he learns that his father wants to marry Emily and is willing to relinquish him. Readers can discuss whether or not Guy could or should have been more responsive and pleasant to Emily. Each character's point of view is explored to some measure in this book. The book itself is not so well crafted as some of the others, but it could be a useful tool in helping children see more than a narrow view of their own situation.

Another book in which the child has an unnecessarily negative response to the parent's new life is *Chloris and the Creeps,* by Kin Platt. Chloris and her younger sister Jenny live with their mother. Their father remarries after the divorce and then, when his second marriage breaks up, commits suicide. Jenny seems to have adjusted well to her situation, but Chloris has constructed a fantasy about her father. Aided and goaded by her paternal grandmother, she resents and blames her mother for what, realistically, is her father's failing. She glorifies and romanticizes this weak, self-centered, self-destructive man. In reality he was impatient with the girls, unfaithful to his wife, and generally inconsiderate of everyone.

When the mother finally marries a man who is loving and solicitous of the children, Jenny is very happy, but Chloris cannot accept the situation. Her performance of a series of outlandish acts indicates that she is still enmeshed in her fantasy world. At last she is jolted back into reality when she discovers that her beloved father left money to her younger sister, but not to her. She is also tremendously supported by her new stepfather, who is an unusually kind and understanding man.

I, Trissy, by Norma Fox Mazer, ends with the hope that Trissy will respond to all the positive efforts on her behalf by her father, her mother, and her stepfather. Trissy's behavior, like Chloris's, is inappropriate and self-centered. But the adults' concern for her is apparent throughout the story; the reader feels that she will use their help well and will grow to recognize that she is an individual in her own right, valued apart from what her mother and father do with their personal lives.

Children who are resentful of any sort of independent life their parents want to lead may find comfort and a source of perspective in these books, which describe the divorce situation in terms of the children's negative and inappropriate behavior. An exercise that the class can do is to write a "Dear Abby" letter from the character and to devise an answer from "Dear Abby."

MANAGING

After the divorce has been made final, the problems of coping with everyday life set in. If the mother is the parent with whom the child remains, the difficulties of taking on a full-time job and providing adequate care for the child are paramount. Several books recognize this problem and explore solutions. *Mushy Eggs,* by Florence Adams, describes the relationship between two young boys and their baby-sitter. There is no problem until the sitter wants to retire and return to her native Italy; then the boys are hurt and angry that their sitter is leaving them. Their mother arranges for another sitter about whom they are cautious, but whom they will accept and, perhaps, grow to love as they did their old sitter.

Mushy Eggs is a gentle, somewhat uneventful book that contains some important unobtrusive messages. The mother is an excellent carpenter. She builds bookcases, closets, and a ship for the boys to play in. The boys maintain a close relationship with their father, who continues to visit them on Sundays and to whose apartment they sometimes go to play. The boys have responsibility for the maintenance of their house. They accept their situation calmly and constructively; their lives are not traumatic. They are unhappy when their beloved sitter leaves, but their mother wisely manages to take a week's vacation after the sitter's departure so that they will not feel too unhappy. Then she finds a new sitter who appears to be a warm, responsible person. Though the boys do not love her immediately, they accept her and have hope for the future.

Books of this sort are helpful not only to children who think that divorce means the end of the world for them, but also to parents who need good role models to emulate. The mother in this book is a comfortable, independent, caring person, who is managing the situation well. Her job, working with computers, is a daytime job. She manages to get help with the children from breakfast through dinnertime.

In *The Night Daddy*, by Maria Gripe, the mother works at night as a nurse. It is not clear whether she is divorced, widowed, or unwed, but the solution to the problem of child care pertains no matter what the actual marital status is. When she advertises for a person to care for her child at night, a young man who is a writer answers her ad and is hired. At first the child rejects the idea of a person to stay with her. But she and the sitter, whom she comes to look upon as her night daddy, enjoy each other's company. The young man and she are mutually sensitive to each other's feelings and share good experiences together. The child's peers are generally unpleasant to her, but in the end they begin to respond more positively. The child considers her night daddy to be almost as good as a full-time father.

This book is not a factual or didactic book exploring solutions to the problem of the single mother. The imagery and emotional content of the man and child's relationship are the most important factors in the book. It is not a book that will appeal to every reader — some may find the mood and the happenings too vague or tenuous for their taste. But for those who are ready to appreciate the sustaining quality of the relationship and the seemingly small but actually very important adventures that these two share, the book will provide a tender and memorable experience.

Charlotte Zolotow's *A Father Like That* is also a book that deals with the situation of a single mother. The small boy's father "went away before he was born." The child dreams of a father who always takes his side, who does not mind loud T.V., and who always agrees with the child's choice of clothing. He designs an ideal father, who obviously has some characteristics and opinions quite opposite from the mother's. The mother responds very positively to the child's dreaming. She says that she likes the father he has designed; but if he does not manage to acquire one of his own like that, she hopes that he will become that kind of father when he grows up.

The mother, caring about her son's feelings, is strong enough not to resent the negative implications that her child's wishes have for her. The child does not seem to take into consideration how his mother will react to his implied criticisms of her, but she permits him to give her these messages without animosity.

The burden in almost all of the books about divorce falls upon the mother. Joan Lexau's *Emily and the Klunky Baby and the Next-Door Dog* is no exception. Emily is a young girl whose parents are divorced. Her mother, though harried and worried, tries hard to be sympathetic and responsive to her children. Emily resents her baby brother and is unhappy that her mother cannot spend as much time with her as Emily would like. Going for a walk in the park with her brother, she decides to "run away" to her father's house. Not permitted to cross the street, however, she walks around the block and eventually returns home. The usefulness of this book lies primarily in the opportunity for the reader to empathize with both the mother and the child.

Muriel Stanek's *I Won't Go Without a Father* demonstrates helpful behavior on the part of other adults. People are kind to both Steve and his mother. His father is gone (we do not know whether the cause is death or divorce), and Steve is jealous of all of his friends who have both parents. He is reluctant to attend an Open House that his class is conducting, because he thinks he will be the only boy without a father. Eventually he does go, discovering several children there without fathers. His uncle, his grandfather, and a neighbor attend to give him and his mother support. One of Steve's problems is worrying about how things look to others. His peers and the helping adults work on this with him.

Advice can come in many forms. It can be disguised in a story or didactically administered through fiction. It can be directed at children or aimed specifically at parents. One nonfiction work, *The Boys and Girls Book About Divorce*, by Richard A. Gardner, is written for children. It is recommended by Parents Without Partners, an organization for adults who are in the situation of being single parents. The book contains an introduction for parents, guiding their behavior and describing their children's feelings.

The book is written in a direct and practical fashion. Dr. Gardner, a psychiatrist, reassures those children who feel that their parents do not love them that they are not unworthy. He tells them that, if their suspicions are true, they should not waste their time and energy looking for love where it does not exist, but to search for love in appropriate places where it can be found. He tells of the uses of anger. He gives advice on how to get along with divorced parents and with stepparents. There seem to be no problems stemming from divorce that Dr. Gardner avoids. His advice places the responsibility of healthy adjustment on the children's shoulders, but adults involved in this kind of problem would do well to read the book so that they, too, may benefit from the sound solutions.

Many sociologists and psychologists are making predictions about the future of marriage as we have known it. Almost everyone agrees that attitudes and arrangements are changing. Not many people agree on what the outcomes will be; but, in the meantime, while we are in the transitional or evolutionary stage, the situation of children and parents in the one-parent home remains. The appropriate and sensitive use of books to help deal with the resultant problems can ease the pressure, helping not only the individuals most directly involved but also those outsiders who are interested and concerned.

REFERENCES

Despert, J. Louise. *Children of Divorce*. Garden City, N.Y.: Doubleday, 1962. Pb.
> Says that children whose parents have deep conflicts with each other and do not divorce are worse off than children whose parents actually do divorce. Calls it "emotional divorce" when parents maintain an unhappy marriage. Summarizes causes for divorce and considers rising divorce rate part of the "groping progress toward a democratic way of life" (p. 5). Recommends that parents find someone to listen to them and that they listen to and aid the children. Her advice, in general, is compatible with the other experts including informing the child of the situation and reassuring the children that they are not to blame. Points out ways of safeguarding the children; advises parents; discusses problems and lists resources.

Grollman, Earl E. (ed.). *Explaining Divorce to Children*. Boston: Beacon Press, 1972. Pb.
> Compilation of articles about divorce. Includes different experts' social and religious points of view and one chapter on explaining divorce to children.

Haley, B. "The Fractured Family in Adolescent Literature," *English Journal*, Vol. 63, No. 2 (February 1974) 70–72.
> An annotated bibliography of books for adolescents concerning adolescents, one of whose parents is not living at home because of death, divorce, or separation.

Klein, Carole. *The Single Parent Experience*. New York: Walker, 1973. Pb. Avon.
> Discusses the person who is a single parent by choice. Warns potential single parents to be honest with themselves. Has a chapter on the

single father. Also encourages single parents and advises them. Has chapter about homosexual parents, treating them objectively and honestly; presents their points of view and opposing ones. Chapter on adoption includes interracial adoptions. Talks about problems and pressures of child care. Informative book that considers the situation of single parenthood objectively and realistically.

Mindey, Carol. *The Divorced Mother*. New York: McGraw-Hill, 1969.

Contends that "successful divorce requires rational preparation." Writes as a divorcee from her own experiences as well as from reading. Suggests going for psychological counseling before a divorce; asks couples to look to themselves for the source of problems rather than the marriage. Poses questions for women to consider concerning their lives after divorce; provides several sources of information and help. Gives practical advice about financial and prosaic matters. Advises on how to prepare the children. Also discusses social life after divorce. Provides specific information about many phases of life after divorce.

Queen, Gertrude Davidson. "A Content Analysis of Children's Contemporary Fiction Books That Pertain to Broken Homes and Steprelationships," unpublished Master's Report, Palmer Graduate Library School, Long Island University, Brookville, N.Y., 1970.

Twenty-one books analyzed. Background information provided on topics. Useful as a suggested format for looking at books.

Schlesinger, Benjamin. *The One-Parent Family Perspectives and Annotated Bibliography*. Toronto: University of Toronto Press, 1969.

Contains several essays on single parents and their situation. Valuable primarily because of extensive annotated bibliography.

Steinzor, Bernard. *When Parents Divorce*. New York: Pantheon, 1969. Pb. Pocket Books.

Discusses different types of marital relationships. Suggests that divorce not be a "friendly one, but a total psychologically free relationship." Talks about the advantages that divorce brings to children and makes suggestions about the separation agreement concerning the children. Believes visits should be a right, not an obligation. Makes recommendations as to how parents let their children know that they are separating. Openness in relationship is important. Suggests practical ways of carrying out the divorce agreements and gives direct advice for maintaining relationships. Advocates the working mother. In general, he sympathizes with children and parents who are divorcing.

Wolf, Anna W. M., and Stein, Lucille. *The One Parent Family*. Public Affairs Pamphlet #287. Public Affairs Committee and the Child Study Association of America, 1959.

Presents problems of the single parent in the form of questions. Then considers solutions and advice. Advice is sensible and free of guilt-laying. Useful even now, seventeen years after publication.

Bibliography

Adams, Florence. *Mushy Eggs*. Illus. Marilyn Hirsch. New York: Putnam's, 1973. (Ages 3–8.)
David and Sam live with their mother, a computer operator, and their wonderful baby-sitter, Fanny, in New York, while their father lives in New Jersey. The boys learn that Fanny is going away and are very sad, hoping that some day they will love their new baby-sitter as much as they loved Fanny. Here is a story of a family managing after a divorce. The mother functions well, and the children are cooperative and understanding.

Agle, Nan Hayden. *Susan's Magic*. Illus. Charles Robinson. New York: Seabury Press, 1973. (Ages 7–11.)
Susan's parents are divorced. Her father seems to be uncaring, but not unkind; his unwillingness to accept responsibility is tacitly given as the cause of the divorce. Susan grows from being a very immature, selfish girl to one who begins to think about others. She tries the reader's patience often. The mother is weak and overprotective.

Arundel, Honor. *A Family Failing*. Nashville: Thomas Nelson, 1972. Pb. Scholastic. (Ages 11–up.)
Joanna's parents both work, but when her father loses his job and her mother becomes a TV personality, their family life becomes difficult and the parents separate. Joanna's father moves out and makes a new life for himself. Joanna realizes that she must view her parents independently from herself. She must accept the fact that they are individuals, not just her parents.

Bawden, Nina. *The Runaway Summer*. Philadelphia: Lippincott, 1969. (Ages 9–11.)
Mary's parents are getting divorced. They do not really care about her, so they send her to live with her grandfather and aunt. Mary meets friends, is happy, and decides to live there permanently. She realizes that for her, her parents' divorce was not a calamity.

Berger, Terry. *A Friend Can Help*. Photographs by Heinz Kluetmeier. Milwaukee: Advanced Learning Concepts and Children's Press, 1974. (Ages 7–10.)
A simple book, but very helpful and reassuring. The photographs clearly reflect the characters' emotions. The main character's parents are divorced. The divorce is evidently a useful arrangement for everyone concerned. Susan, a friend, helps considerably with her understanding and companionship.

Blue, Rose. *A Month of Sundays*. Illus. Ted Lewin. New York: Franklin
Watts, 1972. (Ages 8–10.)
When Jeff's parents divorce, Jeff moves to New York with his
mother. With the help of Matthew and his adopted mother, Mrs.
Walters, Jeff begins to enjoy city life and gets used to his new
situation. A useful book for children who feel that divorce and a
change of life style signal the end of their world.

Blume, Judy. *It's Not the End of the World*. New York: Bradbury Press,
1972. Pb. Bantam. (Ages 10–12.)
Karen's parents go through a divorce, and Karen and her sister and
brother react normally. They try to get their parents back together;
they worry about whether or not their parents love them; they
worry about their welfare. A friend whose parents are also divorced
introduces Gardner's book, *The Boys and Girls Book About Divorce*, to
Karen. It helps them both. Not a very well constructed book, but
possibly helpful to readers going through the experience.

Brooks, Jerome. *Uncle Mike's Boy*. New York: Harper & Row, 1973. (Ages
10–up.)
Pudge's parents are divorced; both have personal problems. His
father's brother, Uncle Mike, takes care of Pudge, helping him to
accept his younger sister's death, his mother's remarriage, and his
father's mental breakdown. The plot is complicated but exposes the
problems many children must face when their parents divorce.

Chorao, Kay. *A Magic Eye for Ida*. New York: Seabury Press, 1973. (Ages
6–8.)
The adventure of a little girl whose mother and elder brother pay no
attention to what she says or does. There is no father present in the
house; the implication is that the parents are divorced. Ida must
learn to be self-reliant and receive her rewards from her own actions. She must also learn to value her own poetic abilities. In the
end her mother, brother, and friends begin to pay attention to her.
A somewhat contrived book.

Cleaver, Vera and Bill. *Ellen Grae*. Illus. Ellen Raskin. Philadelphia:
Lippincott, 1967. (Ages 9–11.)
Ellen Grae's parents are divorced; she lives with the McGruders
during the school year. Her parents love her, but neither one can
assume responsibility for her. In this book, it is demonstrated that
no adult completely understands Ellen Grae, but that she will endure nevertheless.

————. *Lady Ellen Grae*. Illus. Ellen Raskin. Philadelphia: Lippincott,
1968. (Ages 9–11.)

In this book Ellen Grae is sent to live with an aunt in order to acquire the social graces. Attempts at imposing conventional behavior on Ellen Grae fail, and she returns happily to the McGruders. Her parents love her (although her mother seems less concerned about her than her father does). The relationship is an unusual but operational one.

Clymer, Eleanor. *Luke Was There*. Illus. Diane de Groat. New York: Holt, Rinehart and Winston, 1973. (Ages 8–12.) (Wel-Met Award.)
Julius's mother has been married and divorced twice. He and his half-brother, Danny, are sent to an institution when their mother becomes ill. Luke, a sensitive counselor, proves to be a positive force in the boys' life.

Donovan, John. *I'll Get There. It Better Be Worth the Trip*. New York: Harper & Row, 1969. Pb. Dell. (Ages 12–up.)
After his parents' divorce, Davy lives with his grandmother until she dies, whereupon he goes to stay with his alcoholic mother, thinks about moving in with his remarried father, and gets involved in a homosexual relationship with his best friend. The involved feelings of the parents, the competition for the boy's loyalty, the difficulty of sorting out what is right, are all presented in this book. Too many traumas and the attempt to present too many issues mar this book.

Eichler, Margaret. *Martin's Father*. Illus. Beverly Maginnis. Chapel Hill, N.C.: Lollipop Power, 1971. (Ages 3–7.)
Martin and his father live together. The mother is either dead or divorced, or this was always a single-parent family. The story describes the commonplace daily activities that the two engage in together. A gentle, matter-of-fact presentation.

Eyerly, Jeannette. *The World of Ellen March*. Philadelphia: Lippincott, 1964. (Ages 12–up.)
Ellen is sixteen; her sister is six. When her parents divorce, the father stays in New York, while the rest of the family move to Cedar City. The whole thing is managed badly, and the children are totally left out of all plans. The father finds someone to marry; the mother is lonely, dependent and unoccupied. Ellen, who tries unsuccessfully to reunite her parents, is ashamed of the fact that they are divorcing. Evidently divorce is a rarity in Cedar Falls. The "happy" ending occurs when Ellen acquires a boyfriend whose parents are also divorced. Not a useful or well-constructed book.

Gardner, Richard A., M.D. *The Boys and Girls Book About Divorce*. Illus. Alfred Lowenheim. New York: Science House, 1970. Pb. Bantam. (Ages 12–up.)

Written by a psychiatrist for children, this book discusses a child's feelings toward divorce, uses of anger and love, reactions toward working mothers and stepparents, and provides many practical suggestions for adjustment to the new situation. The author faces all of the problems realistically. He does not mince words. His advice is reasonable and helpful.

Goff, Beth. *Where Is Daddy? The Story of a Divorce*. Illus. Susan Perl. Boston: Beacon Press, 1969. (Ages 4–7.) (Wel-Met Award.)
A little girl who cannot understand her parents' divorce blames herself, and she is afraid that her mother won't come back whenever she goes off to work. Gradually her mother and grandmother help her to accept the new situation and not to blame herself for the divorce. Parents will probably find this book informative and useful.

Greene, Constance C. *A Girl Called Al*. Illus. Byron Barton. New York: Viking, 1969. Pb. also. (Ages 11–up.)
Alexandra's mother and father are divorced. She puts on a show of not caring but is unhappy. The elderly janitor befriends her; after his death, her mother begins to pay more attention to her as a person. Her father sends her money but no love; she keeps looking for substitutes for him. Probably a useful book for purposes of empathy, but not a great work of literature.

Gripe, Maria. *The Night Daddy*. Illus. Harold Gripe. New York: Delacorte Press, 1971. Pb. Dell. (Ages 8–up.)
The story of the friendship between a girl and a writer who is hired to stay with her at night while her mother works as a nurse. The setting is Sweden. The action might not be as believable if it were set in the United States, but the story provides a feasible solution for some families.

Hellberg, Hans-Eric. *Grandpa's Maria*. Illus. Joan Sandin. Translated from the Swedish by Patricia Crampton. New York: Morrow, 1974. (Ages 9–11.)
Seven-year-old Maria considers her grandfather to be her daddy. Her parents are divorced. When she meets her father for the first time, their relationship is somewhat strained because his second wife disapproves of his seeing Maria. Maria adores her grandfather, who understands Maria and enjoys her company. Maria's mother goes to a mental hospital; she has obviously not weathered the divorce as well as her husband has. In the end it appears that all will be well for everyone. The author invites his readers to write to him and promises to engage in a correspondence.

Holland, Isabelle. *The Man Without a Face*. Philadelphia: Lippincott, 1972. Pb. Bantam. (Ages 12–up.)

Charles's mother has completed her fourth divorce, and he does not like his sisters. He is not very happy until he makes friends with a man with a horribly scarred face who helps him very much. The story gives mixed messages, implying that a successful marriage for his mother is Charles's only hope of long-term success. The intrusion of homosexuality as a possible problem burdens the plot unnecessarily.

Johnson, Annabel and Edgar. *The Grizzly*. Illus. Gilbert Riswald, New York: Harper & Row, 1964. Pb. Scholastic. (Ages 9–up.)
David has nightmares about his father, whom he is afraid of and has not seen for a long time. In an exciting adventure involving grizzly bears, David learns to like his father and brings his separated parents back together again. This solution is contrary to most experts' advice and may raise hopes that parents will get back together again. A more reasonable view is that everyone must learn to accept and cope with the divorce.

Kerr, M. E. *The Son of Someone Famous*. New York: Harper & Row, 1974. (Ages 12–up.)
Adam's father has been twice married unsuccessfully. The father's relationships with women are dreadful. Adam feels the burden, not only of his father's problems, but also of being the son of someone famous. Adam's friend, Brenda Belle, also has problems. Her father left her mother, then subsequently died. The two teen-agers are unhappy with themselves, confused over values, and find it difficult to have good relationships with people. Their problems are caused not by the fact of divorce, but by the problems that they and their parents have with themselves. An interesting, absorbing book, but not likely to be a literary classic.

Kindred, Wendy. *Lucky Wilma*. New York: Dial Press, 1973. (Ages 4–8.)
Wilma and her father, Charlie, spend every Saturday together. They visit museums and parks and play lovingly and happily together. At the end of each Saturday, Wilma's father returns to his own house, and Wilma goes home to her mother. The book demonstrates that children need not be miserable because of parents' divorcing.

Klein, Norma. *It's Not What You Expect*. New York: Pantheon, 1973. Pb. Avon. (Ages 11–up.)
Carla and Oliver Simons's father leaves home for the summer. There is no apparent reason for his going except that he is undergoing a personal crisis. The marriage has evidently been a strong one, and at the end of the summer, he returns. There is a hint that he has had an affair, but there is no question that his wife wants him back and accepts him without recrimination. This is a very "liberated" family.

The book is too casual and somewhat unrealistic, but perhaps true enough in its description of some contemporary upper-middle class suburban lives.

————. *Taking Sides*. New York: Pantheon, 1974. (Ages 9–up.)
After her parents' remarriage and second divorce, Nell and her brother live with their father in New York. The book consists of the observations and reflections of Nell as her life changes and progresses. This book is one of the few in which there is the recognition that the father may be better at nurturing children than the mother is. Unfortunately, the author creates circumstances that force the children to wind up with their mother. Both parents are different from the stereotype.

Lexau, Joan. *Emily and the Klunky Baby and the Next-Door Dog*. Illus. Martha Alexander. New York: Dial Press, 1972. (Ages 3–8.)
A little girl resents her little brother and is upset that her divorced mother cannot pay more attention to her, so she attempts to run away to her father's house. Her mother expects much from her, and the pressure is more than the child can tolerate. But the mother recognizes the problem and sets aside her own work to attend to her children. The message here is for parents.

————. *Me Day*. Illus. Robert Weaver. New York: Dial Press, 1971. (Ages 3–8.)
Rafer has an unhappy birthday until his divorced father comes to spend the whole day with him as a surprise. The reader gets the feeling that the father does not really care about his family, and that this day will be only a temporary oasis in Rafer's otherwise barren life.

Mann, Peggy. *My Dad Lives in a Downtown Hotel*. Illus. Richard Cuffari. Garden City, N.Y.: Doubleday, 1973. Pb. Avon. (Ages 8–12.)
Joey blames himself for his parents' divorce; but after spending time with his father, talking more with his mother, and finding a friend who also has no father living at home, Joey accepts the situation more happily. There are some very moving sections of this book; for example, Joey lists his faults and promises to reform if only his father will come home. Joey's mother is the defeated person in this story. His father seems insensitive but the winner in the situation.

Mazer, Harry. *Guy Lenny*. New York: Delacorte Press, 1971. Pb. Dell. (Ages 9–12.)
Twelve-year-old Guy feels betrayed by his father, who wants to marry another women rather than to keep him. Guy eventually must live with his mother, who has come back to get him after having deserted him about seven years before. But Guy has de-

veloped an inner strength and will not ever again be hurt by a dependency on either of his parents. Guy behaves badly in this book: he expects his father to devote time solely to him and deeply resents the intrusion of another woman in his father's life. The woman wants Guy to like her; she tries to be a surrogate mother, but Guy will not permit it. This story presents realistic dilemmas for families involved in divorce.

Mazer, Norma Fox. *I, Trissy*. New York: Delacorte Press, 1971. Pb. Dell. (Ages 9–12.)
The story of an imaginative girl who blames her mother for her parents' divorce. Eventually, she begins to be able to see herself and each of her parents in a realistic, individual light. Trissy behaves in a very self-centered manner throughout the entire book. She, not her parents, is the cause of problems in the aftermath of the divorce. Her parents' understanding provides a base for her to build a more mature and responsible way of behaving.

Newfield, Marcia. *A Book for Jodan*. Illus. Diane de Groat. New York: Atheneum, 1975. (Ages 7–11.)
Jodan is heartsick at her parents' divorce. Though they both reassure her that they love her, she is very unhappy. She and her mother move to California; her father remains in Massachusetts. At the end of a holiday visit, her father gives her a special book that he has made, just for her. It recalls their happy times together and serves as a secure reminder of her father's love. A story that demonstrates the effort going into a constructive relationship.

Norris, Gunilla. *Lillian*. New York: Atheneum, 1968. (Ages 8–12.)
Lillian's parents divorce, and she is afraid her mother will stop loving her now that she is so busy with her job. With her mother's help, Lillian grows more self-reliant, self-confident, and less fearful. Readers will find their own anxieties mirrored in this book.

Pevsner, Stella. *A Smart Kid Like You*. New York: Seabury Press, 1975. (Ages 9–up.)
Nina's parents are divorced. She discovers, when she enters junior high, that her math teacher is her father's new wife. She and her friends harass the teacher, until good sense prevails. Nina's father helps her to adjust to the new situation. Her mother, who has both a career and a boyfriend, is not as sympathetic a character. But the book as a whole presents a realistic view of the dilemmas arising from divorce.

Platt, Kin. *The Boy Who Could Make Himself Disappear*. Philadelphia: Chilton, 1968. Pb. Dell. (Ages 12–up.)
The story of Roger, a child who is abused, unloved, and unwanted

by his sadistic, selfish parents, who are divorced. Although he becomes totally out of touch with reality in the end, he at least has a friend who cares for him and who holds out hope that he can make a totally new life for himself. This book is probably too painful and too extreme to be of use to people in a divorce situation. The characters are not typical.

————. *Chloris and the Creeps*. Philadelphia: Chilton, 1973. Pb. Dell. (Ages 12–up.)
Chloris cannot accept her parents' divorce or her father's subsequent suicide. She is hateful and destructive to her mother, her mother's new husband, and their home because she thinks of her father as a kind of superman. Through therapy, sensitive response, and patience, Chloris's mother, sister, and stepfather nurture her back to a positive set of behaviors. A sudden awakening to her biological father's real nature also helps.

Sachs, Marilyn. *The Bear's House*. Illus. Louis Glanzman. Garden City, N.Y.: Doubleday, 1971. (Ages 9–12.) (National Book Award Finalist.)
When Fran Ellen's father deserts the family, her mother totally collapses. The elder brother assumes direction of the family, but it does not work. Eventually a teacher, recognizing the extremity of the situation, takes steps to salvage their lives. But the book itself is painful to read. Fran Ellen lives in two worlds and is in danger of retreating forever into her fantasies. Everyone's plight is emotionally wrenching in this story. Perhaps its usefulness lies in assuring unhappy readers that here are people in much worse straits than they.

Schick, Eleanor. *City in the Winter*. New York: Macmillan, 1970. Pb. also. (Ages 5–8.)
Schools are shut because of a blizzard, and Jimmy spends the day having fun around the house with his grandmother while his mother works. The absence of the father implies a divorce or death. The family is coping well.

Sitea, Linda. *Zachary's Divorce*, pp. 124–27 in *Free to Be You and Me*. New York: McGraw-Hill, 1974. Pb. also. (All ages.)
The aftermath of divorce is described through the eyes of Zachary, a young boy. He feels as if he has been divorced, although his mother assures him that it is his parents who divorced each other. Zachary's mother is supportive, understanding, and coping. Zachary's friend Amy lives with her father because her parents are divorced. Zachary decides that there are two kinds of divorces: the "mommy" kind and the "daddy" kind. He feels very much out of control and dominated

by the grown-up world. But time will pass, and he will recover from his bad feelings. A very useful little story.

Stanek, Muriel. *I Won't Go Without a Father*. Illus. Eleanor Mill. Chicago: Albert Whitman, 1972. (Ages 6-9.)
Steve is angry and jealous of anyone who has a father; but, with the support of his uncle and grandfather, he learns to become less defensive and more accepting of his family situation. He also recognizes that he is not alone in this situation.

Stolz, Mary. *Leap Before You Look*. New York: Harper & Row, 1972. Pb. Dell. (Ages 12-up.)
Jimmie adores her father before her parents' divorce and resents his remarriage afterward. Living with her mother, brother, grandmother, and aided by her friend Chris, who is bothered by several divorces in her family, Jimmie gradually adjusts and reconciles herself with her father.

Surowiecki, Sandra Lucas. *Joshua's Day*. Chapel Hill, N.C.: Lollipop Power, 1972. (Ages 3-6.)
Joshua, who lives with his mother, goes to a day-care center while she works. She is coping well without a husband, and Joshua seems fine.

Wagner, Jane. *J.T.* Photographs by Gordon Parks. New York: Van Nostrand Reinhold, 1969. Pb. Dell. (Ages 8-13.)
J.T. reacts very destructively to his father's departure. His mother tries to maintain the family but has difficulties. A cat, his grandmother, and the sympathetic storekeeper and his wife help set J.T. back on a constructive track.

Zolotow, Charlotte. *A Father Like That*. Illus. Ben Shecter, New York: Harper & Row, 1971. (Ages 3-8.)
A little boy tells his mother his dreams of the ideal father as his own father "went away" before he was born. His mother replies that, in case he never gets that father, he can *be* that father someday. The boy uses his fantasy to inform his mother of the things she does that bother him. His ideal father would always take his side in arguments and would permit him to do as he pleased. The mother, accepting the child's criticisms graciously, permits him to indulge in his fantasy.

NOTES and ADDITIONS

4

Death and Old Age

UNTIL VERY RECENTLY, books dealing realistically with the topic of death were categorized almost in the same realm as pornography. Americans, enamored of youth and trying to remain young forever, like to pretend that death does not exist. We have all too often avoided people when they grow old, and we have shunned the dying as though dying itself were a contagious disease. We value beauty, comfort, boundless productivity, and control over our lives. We have preferred not to confront old age and death, which are associated with ugliness, pain, the end of creative output, and fear of the unknown. For some people death appears to be a punishment; for some it is an ever-present threat. Even to those for whom death has compensations as a valid end to earthly life or as a transcendental episode in the balance of the universe, there are negative aspects.

We miss our loved ones, our great ones, our kind ones. But more and more we have come to realize that, even if we do not talk about it, death will not go away. Courses concentrating on questions, concerns, and issues associated with death and dying are being offered on campuses across the country. Parents and teachers find themselves increasingly called upon to answer children's questions, prompted not only by the children's actual experiences with death, dying, and old age but also by their having encountered these concepts in books.

Before deciding to work with children on the facts, attitudes, and problems surrounding the themes of old age, death, and dying, it is useful for an adult to decide how he or she feels about these topics. Helping others to cope with, or to understand, a situation is difficult unless we are conscious of our own feelings. Once we know what our attitudes are, we can more easily go beyond our own views and accept the ideas of others. It is important to view this understanding as an ongoing growth process. Just because we have a strong opinion today does not mean that we will have the same idea tomorrow. As we progress, we receive and assimilate more and more information that either confirms or changes our attitudes. We must recognize this potential in children as well as in adults, taking it into consideration whenever we are dealing with a topic of any significance.

▶ Try This

Design a questionnaire to discover what your attitudes are toward old age, dying, and death. After you have answered these questions, try to think of others that you can ask. Compare your questionnaire with one a friend has devised. Are there any questions which appear on both lists? If so, do your friend's answers differ from yours? Are these any questions either of you cannot and will not answer? Talk about your differences and your similarities. Now consider how you would handle these questions with children.

Some sample questions might be these:

Am I afraid to die?

Is there an afterlife?

Is death accidental, fated, or controlled?

Who should teach children about death?

If I were dying, would I want to know it?

How do I want to die?

What sort of funeral do I want?

Do I want to be buried or cremated?

What is death?

At what stage of development does an unborn child become a living person?

Who should decide that death has occurred?

What conditions should be set for defining death?

When is it right to kill?

What standards should be set for institutions for the elderly?

When should people retire?

When, if ever, is suicide an appropriate act?

Your exploration of your own attitude might take the form of a string of statements rather than a questionnaire.

▶ Try This

Respond *yes*, *no*, or *I don't know* to each of the following:

Death is final. Death is unjust. Death comes at the right time for each person. Death is usually peaceful. People are powerless to prevent their own death. Dying people know that they are dying. Heaven is a reward for the virtuous. Mostly very old people die. Death is necessary for the balance of nature. People should accept death gracefully. Old people should live with their families whenever possible. Children should be included in the rituals of death. It is natural to feel angry when someone that we love dies. Everyone is afraid to die. Only parents or ministers should talk about death to children. Children should be protected from the facts of death. I know all that I want to about death.

Read some of the materials suggested in References at the end of this chapter to see how they answer these questions. With which do you agree?

After you have begun to explore your own feelings, start to exchange ideas with children. Sometimes they will ask you questions that you cannot answer, just as you have asked yourself questions that you cannot answer. Sometimes all that they want is confirmation that others feel as they do and can accept those feelings, even when they are unpleasant. Sometimes the conversation will reveal misconceptions and contradictions ("My grandma died yesterday, but she'll come back in time for my birthday if I'm good."). Accept all statements without judgment, waiting to comment until you have a fairly coherent idea of how the child perceives death. Then you can decide on whether or not to use this information to build curriculum, to reassure the child, to correct erroneous information, or to refer to another adult for further handling. Several excellent sources of advice on how to talk to children about death can be found in libraries and bookstores and are discussed in this chapter.

An exercise for children to try could include role-playing verbal responses or written reactions to anecdotes such as the following:

> Your grandfather is very old. He lives in his own apartment. He forgets where he puts things. He forgets what you told him yesterday. Sometimes he forgets your name. You and he have always been fond of each other; he says you're his favorite. Your parents are afraid he will fall and hurt himself, or that he will set his place on fire. Your parents both work all day. They have decided to place him in a nursing home. They want your opinion. What will you say?

> Your best friend has leukemia, but doesn't know it. The parents have told you about it. They want your advice. Should they tell your friend, or not?

Factual Books

Earl Grollman has written a pamphlet for parents entitled *Talking About Death*. The aim is to present the ideas in order to help children to accept the reality of death. The conversations detailed in the text are also helpful in preventing harmful fantasizing. The pamphlet acknowledges the child's negative feelings and accepts them, while at the same time reassuring the child with positive statements. Edgar N. Jackson's *Telling a Child About Death* also contains direct advice for adults in handling this topic. Jackson points out differences among children of different ages in terms of their readiness to deal with concepts. Very young children can recognize the obvious differences between life and death; older children can understand the abstract idea of the balance of nature and a universal pattern. The author recommends, as does every authority on this subject, that children be told the truth as simply and as directly as possible. Euphemisms, such as "went to sleep" or "went away," are frowned upon. Jackson suggests that discussions of death are often prompted by something that has occurred in the children's experience, perhaps not directly related to the death of a loved one. A tree stump might prompt a conversation about death. The death of an animal, stories that people tell or read, a grandparent's death, or an accident may serve to stimulate questions and discussion. Strong feelings are healthy, and a display of emotion should be encouraged rather than controlled.

Anna W. M. Wolf's book, *Helping Your Child to Understand Death*, echoes Jackson's advice. She explains that, when we evade children's questions, we are probably trying to postpone our own confrontation with the idea of death. She points out that in our country modern science has successfully removed the act of dying from our homes. Nowadays, not many young children die; and when people are terminally ill, we usually send them to an appropriate institution. We no longer automatically invite an aged relative to live out his or her last years with us; our family is more the nuclear version than it is the extended family of years ago. Wolf's suggestions include sample answers to children's questions. She stresses inclusion of the children in funeral rituals and in all of the procedures surrounding the death of a relative. She recommends taking a step-by-step approach to helping children discover the truth without fear.

Death of parents is often seen by children as abandonment. Wolf provides some possible avenues for handling these anxieties. She stresses the advisability of recognizing the content of each question that a child asks. One child, for example, because of a semantic confusion thought that "body" referred only to the trunk of a person, and wanted to know why people get their arms and legs cut off when they are dead. Once the source of the question is recognized, it is relatively easy to answer.

Not all factual books concern themselves primarily with helping adults to answer children's questions. Some speak specifically to children. Herbert S. Zim and Sonia Bleeker have written a book called *Life and Death*, which briefly includes some of the life processes but concentrates on death. The authors describe the scientific process of maturation and dying. The book contains much anthropological and other scientific information. The writing, straightforward and clear, is directed at children nine years of age and older.

The book clarifies some misconceptions, such as the equating of death with sleep. It states: "With death, all of the life processes, such as growth, movement, awareness, and reaction, stop — finally and permanently." (p. 19) Details, including a description of a death certificate, health officers who verify and report a death, funeral arrangements and costs, different kinds of burial, historic and contemporary burial, and mourning customs are provided in a nonjudgmental, dispassionate style. The authors express their point of view in several instances, hoping that readers will come to accept death as part of life and in its larger context in terms of the rest of the world. Many readers may find this to be a valuable book for explaining death to children who have recently experienced the death of someone close to them. The book can also serve to prepare children for understanding death when they hear about it or ask about it. It can be a tool for generating questions.

Although the style and format are viewed by many people to be useful, one teacher remarked after reading this book, "I found the book disgusting. I feel that death cannot be explained in purely scientific terms. It only adds to the feeling that we are merely numbers and our life here has no significance." If you agree with this criticism, you have several possible options. You could, of course, hide the book. Or read it with a child and discuss your objections. Or acquire a number of books with different points of view and styles of approach. Or have a long discussion, first presenting your ideas, then reading the book. If you can think of other preferable courses of action, by all means use them. No single book covers all the available information. No one work includes all of the possible questions and answers. The more you can find in print, the more likely you are to find some satisfaction.

Another book that speaks directly to children about the facts of death is *Death Is a Noun*, by John Langone. The author includes discussions of critical contemporary issues. He comments on suicide; euthanasia; the problem of when to declare a person legally dead; and questions of capital punishment, murder, and abortion. He also talks about personal dilemmas of how to face death, ideas about life after death, and the weighty implications whenever a decision about life and death is made. Langone presents several viewpoints in each chapter. He includes an impressive, burdensome amount of information, usually leaving it to the reader to decide on the answer. He contends: "About all one can do is affirm the right of all to speak, to listen to the opposing views, consider both society as a whole and the individual, and then make a decision based on one's own conscience." (p. 106) The author does not abdicate responsibility; he does interject his own ideas and his sense of morality. He wants people to make life as mutually beneficial and as productive as possible. He selects his quotes and uses facts judiciously and persuasively. Young people would have to have attained a fair degree of maturity to appreciate this book thoroughly. Children approaching their teen-age years can benefit from reading it; while younger children, depending on their precocity, may have more difficulty but may, nevertheless, be able to handle the content.

Earl Grollman has edited a comprehensive text, *Explaining Death to Children*, which is intended for adult readers. The book contains chapters devoted to Protestant, Catholic, and Jewish rituals, each written by a minister of that faith. One chapter contains a cross-cultural analysis of how death is handled. The book as a whole adopts a developmental approach; that is, it describes the different behaviors that children manifest at different age levels and hypothesizes that children go through similar stages in thinking about, and responding to, death. The chapters most specifically describing these stages are clearly written. Teachers, parents, and other concerned adults can take these developmental factors into consideration.

Grollman's book includes a chapter on "Children's Books Relating to Death," by Eulalie Steimetz Ross, in which she cautions the reader that ministers are the most qualified people to recommend books on this subject to children. This author and other contemporary educators disagree, believing that teachers, parents, and peers are competent to lead the child to appropriate sources of information, comfort, or challenge. Ross describes a number of books for young children that she believes will help young readers in building a sense of security and of comfort in the family and daily surroundings. She contends — again, contrary to many others — that books should make no mention of death for the very young reader until this sense of security has been established. Ross recommends the sentimental and commercialized works of Joan Walsh Anglund as successful presentations of the abstract ideas of Love and Friendship. It is only after children have learned to read for themselves, she strongly suggests, that they should encounter death in literature. She lists and briefly describes a number of books and poems in her segment for older children. Although none bears a recent copyright, they all can provide topics for discussion and contain a variety of perspectives.

For some readers, Ross's religious emphasis may not serve their purpose; or they may reject some of her literary preferences, criticizing her for being overly simplistic or leaning toward the sentimental. The reader's role is to explore alternatives: it is possible to reject out of hand all that the author says; or, proposing some of her ideas as topics for open discussion, to find corroborating or disputing evidence, to look for other books of the same genre expressing different attitudes, and to read the books she talks about for the messages they contain. Attitudes of open-mindedness and critical inquiry are the goal. Individuals' responses to these emotionally loaded and controversial topics may differ widely yet be equally valid.

Some Questions to Explore

How can we help children to accept their feelings about the death of people they love? What do we want children to know about death? How much realism can they tolerate? How much detail should we present about the act of dying? Do we want them to believe that it is a painless process? How much should we dwell on the pain? How involved should they become in the issues of abortion, suicide, euthanasia, the controversies surrounding the definition of death, customs of mourning, funerals, the hereafter, and all the religious teachings concerning death? How protected should they be from the fact that we do not usually know in advance when we will die, and that the oldest people do not always die first? There are no right answers to any of these questions, and this list is by no means exhaustive. How can we approach the topic using books to help ourselves and children?

▶ **Try This**

Read some of the factual books about death, along with the articles listed at the end of this chapter and any others that you find listed in *Library Literature* or *Education Index* concerning death and children's books, or death and children. Then draw up a list of categories suggested by these readings. The categories might include a list of issues or attitudes as headings. Genre classes, such as myth, fantasy, folk tales, picture books, poetry, and biography could serve. After determining your categories, find children's books that contain death as an important factor; list the books under each category. Then subdivide the categories so that you can differentiate the treatment of death in each of the classifications. Some poems, for example, focus on the permanence of death; some point up death as a part of the natural cycle. If Permanence and Natural Cycle were your original categories, further subdivide those by genre, or age level or point of view. Once you have worked extensively with the categories and books that fit them, you will have a better idea of how you can use these books further with children.

Suggested Criteria

Storybooks for children include such topics as coping with old age and the aged; coming to terms with suicide; and the deaths of very young people, parents, grandparents, and animals. They describe feelings of rage, sorrow, loneliness, helplessness, and resignation. They include a look at how upper-, lower-, and middle-class families handle death. There are books containing Native American rituals and customs, Jewish and Christian procedures and beliefs, and glimpses into countries other than America. One can read about the responses of adults and children, males and females, Blacks and Whites. There are books aimed at the very young, the intermediate ages, and the older child. They contain a wide range of information and attitudes about death — the diversity is enormous. Children, perhaps with the help of a knowledgeable adult, can utilize the books most nearly corresponding to their level and needs.

The reading of these books invites many activities. Children can locate contradictory ideas and set up a debate. One point of debate might be nursing homes: Are they good or bad? Or funerals: What use do they serve? Evidence supporting different positions can be located in the literature. Children may enjoy writing stories stemming from their reading, while adopting the same or an opposing position from the one expressed in the book. It is always an excellent practice to accumulate a class or personal library containing books that, together, present a balancing of the many different aspects and facts about death. Be certain that the library includes picture books, folk tales, modern fiction, nonfiction, poetry, literary fantasy, and realistic fiction so as to reach the widest audience and present the greatest diversity. Books directly concerned with death are very useful, but also important are books that are not overtly concerned with death yet nevertheless contribute to the building of an outlook on death.

Most books written for children on this topic exhibit an understanding of a developmental point of view. They rarely convey too much abstract information to young children or attempt to mask the reality of death for older children. Books for older readers include realistic explorations into some of the major issues surrounding the theme of death. Picture books and stories for the very young recognize that most of the ideas, feelings, and questions expressed by very young children evolve from their personal experiences with death. It is not uncommon for them to have to cope with the death of a pet or a grandparent. Sometimes they must face the untimely death of a parent or sibling or friend. They do not usually ask abstract or depersonalized questions. Most books written for children at this stage, therefore, take this developmental factor into consideration. Even in these books, however, a variety of attitudes can be found. It is thus possible to locate evidence to support different points of view and multiple answers to any question.

Discussion of Children's Books

BOOKS FOR YOUNG CHILDREN (Ages Eight and Younger)

Funerals.   The death of an animal is probably the most frequently encountered death for a young child. Authors use this experience to help children cope with, and learn about, some of the rituals, practices, and beliefs surrounding death. Following the experts' advice about including children in the ceremonial aspects of death, several authors have written stories in which a funeral service is conducted by the children for a dead animal. In 1958 Margaret Wise Brown's book, *The Dead Bird*, was published. The first book of its kind to be accepted for young audiences, it specifically describes the physiological manifestations of death as well as the burial services the children accord the dead bird. The story is somewhat impersonal; the bird is not a pet but simply a dead bird found in the path. But the illustrations by Remy Charlip convey the emotions of the children in a way that the simple text does not attempt. The language is at the level of the early grades in school, or even preschool, but describes clearly what is happening. It also communicates that part of the process of mourning is also being glad to be alive. As the children conduct a funeral, they sing to the bird. They cry because it is dead, but they are glad that they can participate in this ceremony. And their tears are as much in response to the beauty of their own singing and the fragrance of the flowers as they are for the death of the bird.

When Violet Died, by Mildred Kantrowitz, also describes a funeral for a bird. But this bird is a pet, and the funeral is not the entirely satisfying experience for these children as it is for those in *The Dead Bird*. The children invite friends to the funeral, which centers around burying the bird in a box in the garden. Then entertainment is offered, and refreshments are served. During the funeral one child keeps clowning about and finds the whole affair boring, but he waits until he has eaten the refreshments before going home. After the funeral, when the two girls return home, they are reminded of their dead bird by the empty cage. The older sister is aware that nothing can last forever, and this knowledge saddens her. This funeral is a more realistic one for children who have had actual experience with a loved one's death. *The Dead Bird* serves better for children who have not been intimately involved in a death.

The Tenth Good Thing About Barney, by Judith Viorst, is another book in which a pet dies and a funeral is held. The child reacts to the death of his cat, Barney, by losing his appetite and by refusing to do anything but go to bed and cry. The mother, empathic, suggests a funeral service, which the child's parents and his friend, Annie, attend. The mother tells the child to think of ten good things about Barney to recite at the funeral. They can think of only nine, but he tells those nine. They sing a song and then return home for refreshments. Still sad, the child continues to mourn his pet's death. In this book the mourning period is portrayed realistically, with the funeral helping somewhat to relieve the acuteness of the loss, but with some of the hurt remaining afterward.

For John, the young boy in *Scat*, by Arnold Dobrin, the funeral fails to help him in coming to terms with his grandmother's death. He feels that he must remain at the cemetery after the funeral to say good-bye to his grandmother in his own way. An appropriate funeral for his grand-mother, complete with the kind of music she enjoyed, fails to accomplish a settled feeling for him. He needs to play a jazz tribute to her on his harmonica, even though he knows that she disliked jazz. One of the useful messages in this book is that it is acceptable to differ from someone you love in the outward show of your emotions. In the end the feelings themselves are what matter.

A surprisingly large number of books include descriptions of funerals, stressing their usefulness in helping children cope with emotions. For the families in Coburn's *Anne and the Sand Dobbies* and Lee's *The Magic Moth*, the funeral helps to focus their grief over the death of a young child. Ministers also help the families in these two books, both of which concentrate on how siblings react to a sister's death. Smith's *A Taste of Blackberries* also describes the death and funeral of a child and the reactions of his closest friend. Funerals represent the most commonly described ritual in children's books. Some stories recount practices such as the covering of mirrors in Jewish homes, as in Fassler's *My Grandpa Died Today*, which, unfortunately, is too didactically psychological in its approach. There will undoubtedly be more stories published in the near future dealing with ceremonial aspects of mourning.

Immortality.   Most of the experts advising us about how to talk about death with children recommend that we avoid definite statements about heaven or an afterlife; they suggest that we should say we do not know. Some books follow this advice and others do not. Discretion is needed here so that all views are respected. In *Anne and the Sand Dobbies*, the children are told that their sister is alive and well in another world and that they will all join her some day. An older brother informs the youngest child in *The Magic Moth* that their sister is going to a nice place, heaven. Another intimation of immortality occurs in this book when Maryanne dies: at the very moment of her death a white moth bursts forth from its cocoon. The family agrees that it is a magic moth. A similar idea occurs in dePaola's *Nana Upstairs and Nana Downstairs*, when a falling star is equated to a kiss from the dead great-grandmother. In most of the other books, however, the idea of a life after death is acknowledged to be a mystery. In Warburg's *Growing Time* and Miles's *Annie and the Old One*, as well as in *The Tenth Good Thing About Barney*, the cyclical nature of the universe and the concept of death's being necessary for the sustenance of new life is presented so that young children can understand and accept it.

The younger sister in *When Violet Died* creates her own system of immortality. She decides to name one kitten in each generation the same name as its mother, insuring that she will always have a cat named Blanche. She is excited by her invention, knowing all the while that nothing lasts forever, but telling herself that she has almost granted her cat eternal life. For some readers this will be a useful technique for softening a loss. For others it will not work well.

It is very useful for children to recognize as early as possible that books, just because they are in print, are not gospel. They must accept the challenge of disagreeing with an author whose ideas conflict with theirs. Adults should reward this kind of critical thinking, teaching children to evaluate authors' suggestions, investigate their claims, and use their own experience and judgment. If a child accepts the idea of acquiring immortality through the carrying on of a name, that is fine. But if a child refutes this idea, then the child should be encouraged to consider the issue further and to contribute his or her own point of view. Sometimes the conflict between a child and author can be filed for future reference; it can be compared with attitudes expressed in other books. The child who wishes to write to the author or publisher with a list of questions or comments is sure to receive a response.

In life, as well as in books, the attempt is sometimes made by well-meaning friends or family to replace the dead loved one. For example, when a child's pet dies, the parents may buy another animal immediately, hoping to assuage the child's grief and perhaps attempting to demonstrate that though death is final, life goes on. Sometimes this is an attempt to pretend, "Your dog didn't really die; you still have a dog." In *The Old Dog*, by Sarah Abbott, the boy accepts the new puppy, but not as a substitute. He is wiser than his parents. He regrets that the old dog is not there to welcome the new one, but while he will nurture the puppy, he is still thinking about the old dog. A kitten is supposed to replace the dead turtle in Stull's *My Turtle Died Today*. The cat in *Across the Meadow*, by Ben Shecter, sends his own replacement in the form of a kitten when he goes off to die.

In *Growing Time* the young boy receives and rejects a new puppy that was given to him to replace his dead dog. Though he recognizes that the puppy is meant to be a substitute, he knows that this is impossible. His father wisely leaves it up to the boy as to whether or not he will keep the puppy. At last the boy decides to let the puppy stay because it needs him. In *A Taste of Blackberries* the child offers himself as a substitute to his best friend's mother, and he is comforted by this act. The mother is touched by the offer. At the moment of bereavement it provides a measure of solace.

Old Age.   Several books have recently been published for children under eight years of age describing the problems as well as the positive characteristics of the aged. Ironically, this seems to be a more difficult topic to handle than death is. Old people vary as much as young ones do, but diversity is rarely recognized in the stories. Usually we find one old person who represents a generalized picture of all old people. In *Annie and the Old One*, the reader is tempted to assume that all old Navajo grandmothers are wise, gentle, and prepared to die graciously. The book is probably helpful to children who must anticipate the death of a grandparent. Annie tries to do all that she can to prevent her grandmother's demise, but the old woman gently explains to her that there is no possible way to avoid death. The stereotyping of the old woman is not a negative element; she is a wise and gentle person. But the idea that this is the behavior children should expect of their aging grandparents is unrealistic.

Nana Upstairs and Nana Downstairs describes a succession of very long-lived grandmothers, each a carbon copy of the one preceding. This book, however, affords the child a description of a helpless old person who must be tied into a chair to keep from falling off. The description is neither painful nor romanticized. The ninety-four-year-old great-grandmother remains a part of the family and is cherished, particularly by the four-year-old boy. His elder brother thinks Nana Upstairs looks like a witch, but the little boy disagrees. He wants to be tied into a chair, too, and keeps his great-grandmother company every Sunday. After she dies, and a long time later, Tommy's grandmother shifts to the upstairs.

It would be comforting to all of us if we could be guaranteed death only after a long and full life and only when we were ready to die. Unfortunately, old age is not always so comfortable and dignified as depicted in these books for young children; and life and death are not so neatly managed. But there are plenty of books for older children that tell of the realities of the process. The young children's stories at least afford a gentle introduction.

The old cat in *Across the Meadow* represents the negative aspects of growing old. He does not enjoy playing, eating, or even going to a party for a friend. Birthdays make him sad. He is obviously tired of living. The author describes his going to die as "going on vacation" and "going to sleep." Aside from the erroneous idea that this gives children and the frightening effect that it can have if they do indeed equate vacations with death, this book conveys several other misconceptions. The cat rescues a young kitten and sends it to his home, insuring his replacement. There is no indication that anyone loves this cat or cares whether it lives or dies.

Old age is pictured in *Across the Meadow* as an unpleasant, useless time of life. The implication here is that, when people grow old, they should have the good taste to go away and die. The cat evidently has control over his life and death; he simply crawls into a comfortable hiding place and dies without bothering anyone. The cat easily bids all of his friends good-bye, for he seems to have no emotional attachment to anyone. Perhaps this is a realistic portrayal of some old people. But here, too, as with the other more positive representations of old age, there is only one model presented, with no opportunity for young readers to compare and question. Teachers and parents should attempt to provide as great a variety of portraits of the aged as possible. Children can bring in photographs of grandparents, elderly relatives, and neighbors. They can cut out pictures of old people from magazines and newspapers. They can make a bulletin board or scrapbooks entitled "What Old People Look Like" or "What Old People Do" or, simply, "Old People."

Old Arthur, by Liesel Moak Skorpen, presents another picture of old age. This gentle, nicely understated story points out that, even though someone is of little use in one place, it is still possible to be valued in another. Old Arthur is a dog who is not useful on the farm anymore. He is slow, sleepy, and forgetful. He escapes being put to death by the farmer simply because he falls asleep and drops out of sight on the way to being killed. Picked up by the dog catcher, he is brought to the pound. At last a little boy comes who does not want a frisky puppy. Although everyone tries to talk him out of it, he wants a dog with Old Arthur's qualities. He likes the way that the dog looks at him and the way that he "almost wags his tail." The dog is good at waiting, at sitting, and at being gentle and affectionate. The boy cherishes the old dog, valuing him for what he can do and enjoying his company.

Another story of old age that presents a somewhat positive resolution of the problem of no longer being useful is Blue's *Grandma Didn't Wave Back*. Although the girl in the story is ten years old, younger children can understand the situation in this book. Debbie's grandmother, of whom the child is very fond, has been living with the family for more than five years. Debbie and her friends always enjoy grandma's cooking and her company. But now the old woman lapses in and out of senility: she has forgetful episodes, even beginning to do things that are potentially harmful to herself. The solution is her placement in a very carefully selected old-age home overlooking the ocean. At first Debbie is resentful of her parents for sending her grandmother away, but the old woman reassures her granddaughter. She will be comfortable there, and she will look forward to occasional visits from her family. She tells Debbie to visit her when she can, but not to think of her all the time because her own life is still ahead of her. The family in this book does not have to worry about the financial cost of the institution. They care about the feelings of everyone involved and can select the most appropriate institution. The story represents a good model for this kind of solution to the problem of the aged and senile, provided that material resources and physical facilities are available. Older children may raise more questions about this story than younger ones do. It can be used to stimulate comparisons and discussions of what constitutes a good institution.

A class visit to a local nursing home could be used as a follow-up to this sort of discussion or even as an introduction to the topic. Often a holiday provides a good excuse for a visit from children. If a child in the class has a grandparent in a nearby home or housing development for the elderly, the class can adopt that grandparent. The more comfortable that children begin to feel about old people and the more contact that they have with them, the more prepared they will be to deal with the issues surrounding old age when they arise. Another useful practice is to invite the old people who belong to a golden age club or who attend a local old people's meeting place to come to the classroom to read stories to the children, to help them with projects, and perhaps, even, just to sit and be available for some loving. This kind of practice permits children who live far away from their grandparents to experience some of the attention that old people often enjoy giving children. It also provides a service to the elderly community by employing them at what they can do and by demonstrating that there is a place and a function for them.

Reacting to Death.   Most books for young children stress tolerance of the reactions that children display when someone or something they love dies. Anger, withdrawal, refusal to eat, tears, confusion, all are acceptable behavior in the stories. *Growing Time* beautifully demonstrates how adults can be supportive of a young child when death has occurred. Each adult adds another perspective and another piece of information to help the boy cope with the death of his dog. The boy is permitted resentful feelings and grief. He is finally ready to accept the finality of death and the responsibility of caring for another dog.

In *A Taste of Blackberries* the boy at first denies the fact of his friend's death; he cannot face it. Gradually, with the help of supportive adults, he begins to believe and then to accept the idea. This death is a very difficult one because it is sudden, violent, and occurs while the child's friends are present. The child, Jamie, dies of bee stings. The idea of being unable to prevent an accident is a difficult one for even an adult to handle. This cause of death leaves an aftermath with which the survivors must cope for a long time to come.

Most of the story of *The Magic Moth* focuses on the responses of the youngest child, Mark-o. He creeps into his dying sister's room to see if she looks different from normal and if he can tell from her appearance that she is about to die. He tries to imagine a replacement for her, recalling a guinea pig that took the place of one that had died. He takes comfort in the myth of Prosperpine, thinking that perhaps his sister, too, will be permitted to return. He asks many questions about heaven, how it feels to be buried in the earth, and what to do with his feelings after his sister does die. The entire family is involved in the preparations for responding to her death. It is a loving family and copes well. Some elements of magic or mysticism intrude somewhat, but not damagingly. The point is made that describing death as "going away" is confusing. It is better to say it directly.

The boy, Ben, in *The Old Dog*, reacts in a typical young child's fashion. He misses all the functions that the dog performed for him. He misses the company of the dog and all the happiness that the dog gave him. For many young children it is the permanence of death that is incomprehensible, and their immediate reactions do not necessarily reflect their true feelings. The boy in *My Grandpa Died Today* is encouraged to play and behave in his normally cheerful fashion after the death of his grandfather even though his parents are mourning the death at home. Unrealistically, the grandfather in this book dies painlessly in his rocking chair after having forewarned his grandson only a couple of days previously; but there are some useful and informative parts to this book. The grandfather tells the child that he is not afraid to die and that he knows the grandson is not afraid to live. Although the story does not provide us with enough substance for empathy and despite its obvious didacticism, the reactions to death are effectively portrayed. The father and mother both cry. The child is encouraged not to feel guilty about wanting to play. The child, in his playing, knows that his grandfather's spirit is with him. The intent of the book seems to be more protective of a child's feelings than informative. But this, too, is useful in considering the materials to use for helping children understand and manage the problem of death.

BOOKS FOR OLDER CHILDREN (Ages Eight to Twelve)

Death and old age are not easy topics about which to write or talk. Many of us, even though we are in our adult years, have yet to resolve for ourselves the questions and anxieties surrounding these aspects of living. Death in the abstract is difficult enough, but real, immediate death can be so traumatic as to defy our ability to cope with our feelings and thoughts. Our religion, our upbringing, our personal experiences, and the opinions and help of those whom we respect have a great deal to do with our own attitudes and methods of handling the situation. There are many books directly concerning the topic and helpful in different ways. The books include a large quantity of fiction for children who can read for themselves. Some of these books are more suitable for the much older child because of the specificity and the magnitude of the issue involved. The reader should use judgment here in advising students to use these books. But often a child can handle a topic that adults would have judged to be far too advanced.

Reacting to Death.   The girl in *Julie of the Wolves*, by Jean Craighead George, is not very much affected at age four by the death of her mother. When she hears of the death of her adored father, she faces the fact with courage and a sense of independence because of what he had taught her when they were together. She responds differently to the death of the leader of the wolf pack, this death enraging her and causing her to change the direction of her life. She averts the danger of her own death, knowing full well that its prospect is imminent, by using all of her intelligence and ability to survive with dignity. This remarkable Newbery Medal book winner contains substance for discussion on almost any theme. The heroine is reminiscent of the girl in Scott O'Dell's *Island of the Blue Dolphins*, another Newbery Medal book, in the way that death affects her and in how she handles it. Each of these young women is stoic, heroic, and competent to manage alone, against all odds. Very different is the self-centered protagonist of Bolton's *Reunion in December*. When her father dies of a heart attack, she wants her mother to exist only for her and her brother. She resents her mother's need for male companionship. She exhibits no sense of responsibility or acceptance of the different style that she must adjust to. Part of the problem in this book is that it is not well constructed. The characters are drawn as shallow and stereotypic, and the situations are unlikely.

A better book in a literary sense is *Meet the Austins*, by Madeleine L'Engle. One of the characters is a girl who behaves unpleasantly after the death of her father. Her mother has died previously. She capitalizes on the fact that she is an orphan, using this as an excuse to throw temper tantrums, disregard the feelings of others, and make people miserable when they are near her. The Austin family, who invited her to live with them, teach her to relate to other people in a less selfish and obnoxious fashion. One of the problems with this book is that the parents are absolutely perfect — wise, understanding, and knowledgeable at all times. They always respond sympathetically and appropriately. They do, however, confess to not knowing the answer to why loved ones must die and what the plan is that governs life and death. The responses of the children in this book to the death of their close family friend and to the intrusion of the orphan are presented well. Readers will probably find at least one character with whom they can empathize in this book.

Jenny, in Jean Little's *Home from Far*, finds it very difficult to recover from the traumatic death of her twin brother, Michael, in a car accident. Her parents become foster-parents to a little girl and her older brother. There are already two other brothers in the family. The boy's name, coincidentally, is Michael. Jenny, who resents the boy bitterly, suspects that her parents are trying to replace her dead brother. Though she is angry with her mother for disposing of all of Michael's possessions, at last Jenny and her mother talk about their feelings. They realize they have both been missing Michael and that the mother has simply been trying to spare Jenny pain. The mother talks about the way that the mourning of a dead child was mishandled when she was a little girl; she has tried not to make the same mistake with Jenny. The mother uncovers all of the mementos of Michael so that she and Jenny can now begin to remember him with love and joy. Jenny can also participate in a positive relationship with the living Michael.

Where the Lilies Bloom, by the Cleavers, describes an Appalachian family, tenant farmers, whose mother has died and whose father is in the process of dying. The fourteen-year-old sister determines that she and her younger brother will bury their father secretly so that the family can remain together. Her response to death and her behavior during the time that her father is dying can be the subject of much discussion. Children can discuss what they would have done in her place. *The Whys and Wherefores of Littabelle Lee*, by the same authors, is also set in the rural mountains. Both the aunt, who is a nature doctor, and the girl, orphaned when she was an infant, handle life and death in their own individual but strong fashion.

The central character of *Admission to the Feast*, by Gunnel Beckman, must cope with her own impending death. She has just been informed that she has leukemia. An independent young woman whose mother, a physician, is away in India, she writes a letter to a friend describing her feelings and what she is going through. The character in this book is different from Ann Frank who also faces death and writes about it. *Hang Tough, Paul Mather*, by Alfred Slote, is another book in which the protagonist, this time a boy, is afflicted with leukemia. He must deal with the likelihood of his own death.

Different styles of living and dying are important to be conveyed in as many different kinds of books as possible. The inclusion of these books in a class or school library will help young readers to recognize that different people follow different, acceptable patterns, but may react in whatever way is most positive and appropriate for themselves. Two young women who react to their own detriment may be found in Windsor's *The Summer Before*, in which Alexandra literally goes mad over the death of her dear friend; and in Arundel's *The Blanket Word*, in which Jan is immature and selfish, making everyone around her suffer because of her own spoiled behavior. The authors hold out hope for both characters at the end of each book; consequently, the reader may be assured that, even if they do behave badly, there may still be another chance for them.

Global attitudes toward death on the part of different cultures may also be found in books for young readers. *The Big Wave*, by Pearl S. Buck, describes how two Japanese villages face death by natural disasters. Buck's aim in writing this book is to help young people learn, by recognizing that life is stronger than death, not to fear death.

Maia Wojciechowska tries to present the perspective of a bullfight afficionado in two of her books, *Shadow of a Bull*, a Newbery Medal book, and *The Life and Death of a Brave Bull*. She asserts that the ritual of the bullfight is the Spaniard's way of defeating death. The books in some measure try to glorify the wish to fight, kill, and die gloriously. A noble death defeats death, according to the message in these books. In another Newbery Medal book, *The Cat Who Went to Heaven*, by Elizabeth Coatsworth, the author attempts to express the Buddhist point of view. The cat in this story dies of pure joy because her owner, an artist, has defied tradition and has painted her into a picture of Buddha going to heaven. The idea of dying in ecstasy is a particularly Eastern one that may be of interest to Western readers. Research into Buddhism and other non-Western cultures can profitably ensue from a reading of this book.

There are a multiplicity of reactions possible when death has occurred. Some authors favor a resigned, accepting response. Others recognize the appropriateness of strong emotion even if that emotion is rage. Some people admire stoic silence. Edna St. Vincent Millay clearly advocates anger and resentment. In "Dirge Without Music," in response to the notion of the dead returning to earth and making it possible for other things to grow, she says: "I know. But I do not approve. And I am not resigned."* Some readers may wish to debate the different responses to the idea of the cycle of life. All these approaches provide the opportunity for demonstrating that, given the same information, and similar circumstances, we do not necessarily respond in the same way. This must be seen as valid and valuable.

Suicide.   Suicide is a form of dying that affects the living in a way different from "natural" death. *Grover*, by Vera and Bill Cleaver — who incidentally, plunge into all kinds of problems in their books — concerns the death of a boy's mother. Knowing she has a terminal illness, she shoots herself, because she cannot bear the thought of going through all the changes she knows will occur if she permits the illness to take its natural course. There is no attempt made in the book to mask or to ameliorate the situation. The authors do an excellent job of describing how adults try to shield children from the truth and, in the process, sometimes harm them more than they help. Grover, the boy, initially displays little external emotional reaction to his mother's death, but in his dealings with his friends he exhibits his grief and pain. He explodes into blind rage when a nasty, somewhat demented woman taunts him with the fact of his mother's suicide. He seems to be able, partially because of the support of his friends and somewhat because of an understanding housekeeper, to rebuild his own life and continue normally. His father, however, cannot cope, grieves constantly, and resents

---

* Edna St. Vincent Millay, "Dirge Without Music," in *The Pocket Book of Modern Verse*, edited by Oscar Williams (New York: Pocket Books, Inc., 1954), p. 368.

the boy's normalcy. The situation is realistic and disturbing. It raises some of the questions many of us have about suicide.

Suicide is the result of a long series of painful events in Norma Fox Mazer's *A Figure of Speech*. The eighty-three-year-old grandfather decides to kill himself rather than to be sent to a home for the aged. The people in this story are extremely insensitive to each other's feelings. They are especially cruel, without meaning to be, to the old man and his granddaughter, Jenny. Her love for her grandfather almost saves him, but in the end it becomes apparent that they are both powerless to prevent his being taken away to live in a place that would destroy his dignity and his sense of self. This story and *Grover* may help readers to examine their feelings that suicide is never right or that there is never an appropriate reason for someone's committing that desperate act.

Old Age.   *A Figure of Speech* deals with old age in a painful but forthright manner. The grandfather is full of aches and pains. He is forgetful, his apartment is messy, and he slobbers over his food. Most of the members of his family treat him with disrespect. He has an apartment set up in the basement of his daughter's house, and this arrangement is all right until one day his college-age grandson comes home newly married, requiring a place for himself and his wife. Eventually the old man is moved out. The family is worried about their lack of privacy, their added responsibilities, their economic burdens — a not uncommon situation in today's world. Only Jenny understands, respects, and responds warmly to the old man. Although the story is realistic, the author is somewhat heavy-handed when she describes the lack of humaneness with which every other family member confronts the grandfather. It is apparent that they wish he were dead.

The old man and Jenny run away from home when they discover that the family is about to put him into an institution that regards old people as worthless and helpless. Again, this sort of institution is, perhaps, not the rule, but the description is not unbelievable. The grandfather tries to dissuade Jenny from running away with him, but she insists on going. He carefully prepares for the venture, with the knowledge that he will be on his own helping to strengthen him. Here the author is clearly saying that many problems of old age could be alleviated if old people were permitted to be functionally self-reliant and independent.

Mazer includes some excellent dialogue in this book concerning the words that people use to describe old age and death. The grandfather tolerates no ameliorating phrases referring to his age or to his eventual death. He leaves notes taped to the refrigerator indicating his displeasure at such phrases. He announces that he has no intention of "passing away" — he will die. *A Figure of Speech* does not mince words and raises issues about old age, suicide, and death that have no easy answers. The questions of morality and responsibility are important ones for adults as well as for children to consider. Children may benefit from telling the story from the perspective of each of the characters, including the parents.

The old man in Robinson's *The Secret Life of T. K. Dearing* also is independent and resistant to coddling, though his family is far more understanding and far less pressured than the one in *A Figure of Speech*. Nevertheless, the elder daughter no longer wants to take care of her father, while the younger daughter, T. K.'s mother, is overly protective of her father. The old man has a distinct personality of his own, with idiosyncrasies that become annoying. He snores loudly, and even in the hottest weather he refuses to take off his suit jacket. Even though the old man invades the privacy of the boy's clubhouse, the boy and he finally manage to get along very well. T. K.'s friends enjoy what the old man contributes to their club, and they all get involved in a project to save another old man's home.

One of the most unusual elements of this book is that there are several old men in it, each with a personality of his own. One old man is a recluse until the boys and T. K.'s grandfather befriend him. Another is a shop owner. The old grandfather in this story demonstrates his stubbornness and independence several times. It is pointed out that he is not perfect and that his independence is not always for his own good. But none of the characters in this book is one-sided. They all make compromises in the end so that a happy arrangement can be reached.

In *Land's End*, by Mary Stolz, compromise is again demanded in order that the family can continue to exist. The father of a family, distraught by his wife's death, is incapable of caring adequately for the rest of the family. They have moved to a large ramshackle house in a new town because the father cannot bear to be reminded of his old life when his wife was still alive. There are many children and an old, senile grandfather. The grandfather's senility is tolerated by the family, but he is not adequately provided for. In the end, the family decides to return to their old town, where their relatives can help them.

There are no easy answers and no absolutes. Each old person is different from every other one. Each situation is also different. In one case, a nursing home is an excellent solution to a difficult situation; in another instance, it could be the worst option. The purpose of accumulating a variety of books is to find several alternative solutions for a given situation. Children should question, argue, set up several possible approaches for handling a dilemma, and seek out more books and articles confirming or debating their ideas.

Books in Which Death Is Incidental.   Most books for young readers concentrate on elements other than death. Death does, nevertheless, occur in many books and is important to their plots. It is usually used either as an incidental happening or as a plot strategy in all genres of literature, including folk tales, classics, romantic novels, and poetry. Sometimes death is seen in a religious light. Sometimes it occurs almost as an author's afterthought. It often conforms to some literary expectation or proves a literary truism; for example, the virtuous characters die young in many romances.

In *Little Women*, Beth, too good and kind to live long, dies as a teen-ager. The reader suspects that Beth's demise is fated because her behavior throughout the book is more saintly than human. The young heroine of *The Birds' Christmas Carol*, by Kate Douglas Wiggin, is an angel on earth while she is alive, carries out her mission of tenderness and virtue, and is gathered back to God on her tenth Christmas, the anniversary of her birth. The writing is sentimental and has the quaintness of a period piece. The attempt is made to teach children to emulate and admire this good and kind soul who was lent to us mortals for a brief period of time. One logical conclusion a child could reach, however, would be quite opposite than the one intended — to vow never to be that good in order not to die so young. The idea is not as far-fetched as it first may seem; forced didacticism often backfires. "Goodness" can be presented in such a saccharine and exaggerated fashion as to discourage its practice.

Hans Christian Andersen's stories, which almost always display a strong moralistic tone, sometimes pound home an obvious lesson. His characters often die as a reward for a good life. The Little Mermaid, for example, is permitted to enter Purgatory because of her willingness to sacrifice herself for the man that she loves. Her reward is that she will no longer be a mermaid, but will, in purgatory, be permitted to earn a human, immortal soul. The Little Match Girl also dies after long suffering in this world of woe and poverty. Death is for her a blessed, if oversentimentalized, release. Andersen's characters go to a specific place after they die; there is no question about life after death in his stories. Religion plays a very important part in his tales and, of course, figures heavily in the messages that he conveys about death. Children may be interested in studying Hans Christian Andersen's life in order to see the effect that it had on his writing.

Teachers may find it difficult to deal with this approach if they are uneasy about either offending or supporting any given religious attitude about the hereafter. One way of handling this dilemma is to suggest that students make a study of the different religious approaches to death. Additional research can include a comparison of modern beliefs to ancient ones. Other extensions of this sort of study would lead to comparative mythology, an examination of fairy tales and folk tales from around the world, and an inquiry into anthropological aspects of societies and their customs surrounding death. It is always a fruitful educational experience to acquire information about beliefs and customs other than one's own, since this knowledge makes us more inquisitive and less judgmental or narrow.

Death as punishment is even more common than death as reward. The fear of death is often used in literature as a deterrent to wickedness. In literature, as in real life, this threat is usually ineffectual: the wicked continue to be wicked and continue to be "justly" killed. All witches and dragons and ogres and giants die. So, too, do most if not all of the hero's enemies. The death is often violent and described in gory detail. The wicked usurper in the Grimm Brothers' *The Goose Girl* prescribes her own bloody end. Placed in a barrel with nails driven into it, she is drawn through the streets of the town until she is dead.

Villains, unless they repent, must die. What sort of attitude does this rule create in us? How can we help our students to move from the "eye for an eye" morality expressed so convincingly in our folklore? How much does this philosophy actually seep into our sense of social and political justice? For instance, why is it that even in cowboy films we know that if a person has committed a crime belonging to a certain category, that person will die in the end? We not only anticipate this ending; we require it. Questioning this accepted pattern may lead us to discussions of capital punishment, justice, and the cause and nature of crime. The teacher can begin asking this kind of question if only to work with the level of moral and social development the students have acquired.

When death is used as device rather than reality in a book, we may not even recognize that it exists. If the topic of death is one that a teacher and students are willing to tackle, then books in the realm of fantasy must not be ignored. In Dahl's *James and the Giant Peach*, James's parents are conveniently eaten up by an angry rhinoceros in downtown London; he cannot be encumbered by parents if he is to go on his adventures. So it is with many orphans in the literature. A literary decision has been made. Pippi Longstocking does her deeds because her mother is dead and her father is gone. What mother, even in fiction, would permit her outlandish behavior? The entire magic of *The Secret Garden* would forever have remained undiscovered had not cholera wiped out Mary's parents. In fantasy and satire, parents are expendable. An interesting conversation may ensue if this is brought up for discussion with young children.

Death continues to be used primarily as a device in many works of modern fiction. Parker Quiney, the thirteen-year-old hero of Beatty's *A Long Way to Whiskey Creek*, is an orphan who, in the company of another orphan, goes on a long and dangerous journey to dig up the body of his dead brother so that he can be buried on his land. The book deals much more specifically with values than it does with the emotional impact of death. The superstitions and prejudices of the time are very clearly conveyed, but attitude toward death is scarcely mentioned. The brother's death is required in order for Quiney and his companion to have their adventures.

John Donovan's *I'll Get There. It Better Be Worth the Trip* uses death (as well as pieces of many other problems such as divorce, alcoholism, homosexuality, adjustment to the city, and parent-child relationships) in its plot. The death of Davy's grandmother causes him to go to live with his mother, who is an alcoholic. The beginning of the book treats the effect that the death has on Davy and the other surviving family members. Later, the death of Davy's dog has even more traumatic consequences on the boy — and this is not the only crisis Davy must endure. Indeed, the book is such a compilation of problems and afflictions that many adults have difficulty using it with young readers: they are unable to develop discussion on any one issue or theme because the issues and themes do not arise naturally from the situation or characterization.

Pigman, by Paul Zindel, is another such book, although it is not nearly as frenetically concerned with piling problem upon problem. The two teen-agers in this book are troubled and unhappy, but their problems are consistent and we do not encounter more and more intricate neuroses at every turn. They do some irresponsible, harmful deeds, and they at least indirectly cause the death of a gullible and kindly old man; but the situation is dealt with in the book rather than presented for its shock value. One assumes that their behavior will change as a result of this death.

Many themes are included in the book *Fog*, by Mildred Lee. The death of Luke's father is only one incident in the story. The theme of death is not particularly well explored, but the book may appeal to teen-agers who feel that they are locked into a particular way of life with no possible chance for change. *Sounder* and *Sour Land*, two books by William Armstrong, on the other hand, contain as many if not more problems with which our society is grappling, but they do it movingly and effectively. In both books, death is handled not only as a necessary part of the plot, but also in such a way as to make the reader question and consider values, attitudes, and actions. In each of these books central characters die. Their deaths are symbols of human destruction and failure.

Although it is but one of many components, death is much more specifically dealt with in *Charlotte's Web*, by E. B. White. Wilbur is threatened with death during the first part of the book, and Charlotte dies near the end, but the book emphasizes the idea that life goes on.

Grief is not minimized. Wilbur never forgets Charlotte. Her children remain as her legacy, along with the memories of her special characteristics and talents. Friendship, love, and tolerance of those with different life styles are strong themes in this beautifully written book. The handling of death is done so sensitively that it would probably provide a measure of comfort to readers who are trying to deal with the death of someone dear to them. It also can provide the basis of an interesting discussion about life cycles, death, its function, and its aftermath for the living.

There are, of course, hundreds more books containing mention of, concentration upon, and implications of death. Some of these would be useful in helping readers cope with their own fears and problems surrounding this topic. Some may aid readers in uncovering attitudes and thoughts of which they had been unaware. Some books may, if the reader is not careful, convey ideas that may potentially be a detriment. The alert teacher will be ready to guide and respond to the child who is ready to deal with the many aspects of this theme that the literature can uncover.

REFERENCES

Arnstein, Helen S. *What to Tell Your Child About Birth, Death. . . .* Indianapolis: Bobbs-Merrill, 1960.
 Arnstein does an excellent job discussing attitudes about death and the harmful effects that can result if well-meaning parents hide death from their children. Arnstein explores how children react to the death of an animal, sibling, parent, and so on. The main point running throughout the entire article is that the subject of death should be dealt with truthfully and simply.

Butler, Francelia. "Death in Children's Literature," pp. 104–124, in *The Great Excluded: Critical Essays on Children's Literature*, Vol. I, 1972 (*Journal* of the Modern Language Association Seminar on Children's Literature and the Children's Literature Association).
 Reviews historically the treatment of death in literature for children. Recommends folk literature as the medium for introducing children through literature to the idea of death. Approves of the attitudes of acceptance and belief that death is not final, because resurrection will occur.

Carr, Robin L. "Death as Presented in Children's Books," *Elementary English*, Vol. 50, No. 5 (May 1973), 701–5.
 Quotes a poem by Merrill Moore on death. Presents a brief history, but an excellent one, of the treatment of death in children's books. Describes twenty books dealing with death in a variety of ways.

Cole, Sheila R. "Reviews," *New York Times Book Review*, September 26, 1971, p. 8.

Reviews six books for children on topic of death. Suggests that in modern books adults try to find easy answers for children; she criticizes this approach.

Crain, Henrietta. "Basic Concepts of Death in Children's Literature," *Elementary English*, Vol. 49, No. 1 (January 1972), 111–15.

Lists concepts such as "a calm acceptance of death is best" and includes names of books, with quotes supporting the concept. Feels that this approach can help to teach a child to think inductively. Crain does not comment on the concepts themselves, nor does she describe the books in any detail.

Grollman, Earl A. (ed.). *Explaining Death to Children*. Boston: Beacon Press, 1967.

This book contains chapters written by experts on various aspects of death. Religions are represented. Psychologists explain and describe children's reactions to death and their perceptions of the phenomenon. Grollman suggests how parents can talk to their children about this topic.

———. *Talking About Death*. Boston: Beacon Press, 1971.

A short book written for parents to help them talk to their children about death. Inside back cover is a guide to how to use the book. The book is a long conversation including children's questions, and the answers an understanding parent provides.

Hoyt, Howard. "For Young Readers: Introducing Death," *New York Times Book Review*, September 26, 1971, p. 8.

Satiric rap at books that pretty the process and avoid the unpleasantness of death.

Jackson, Edgar N. *Telling a Child About Death*. New York: Hawthorn, 1965.

Talks about children's misinterpretations of the process of death, and what parents can say to help clear these up. Recommends that each reader develop a sound philosophy of life in order to know how to deal with death.

Kubler-Ross, Elizabeth. *On Death and Dying*. New York: Macmillan, 1969.

This book explores the stages that a terminally ill person goes through when (s)he learns of impending death. Ross identifies these stages as follows: denial; anger; bargaining; depression; acceptance; and hope. The book is full of warmth and understanding. Ross learned the value of confronting and talking with the dying, old and young.

Langone, John. *Death Is a Noun, A View of the End of Life*. Boston: Little, Brown, 1972.

This book can be found in the science section of the library. It treats the subject objectively and at great length. Included in the book is an examination of each of the pressing issues we now must face concerning all aspects of death.

Locke, Linda A. "A Descriptive Bibliography of Selected Children's Books That Treat Death's Effect on the Child Hero (with An Essay on Death as a Theme in Children's Books)," unpublished Master's Report, Palmer Graduate Library School, Long Island University, Brookville, N.Y., 1969.

A historical account is given as to how death has been handled in children's books. Analyzes twenty books presenting a variety of ways of dealing with death. Categorizes the books well. A useful reference.

Morris, Barbara. "Young Children and Books on Death," *Elementary English*, Vol. 51, No. 3 (March 1974), 395–98.

Describes the developmental stages that a child goes through in facing the reality of death. Cites Gesell and Ilg, Russell, Piaget, and Chukovsky. Questions the appropriateness of realistic fiction about death.

Moss, Judith. "Death in Children's Literature," *Elementary English*, Vol. 49, No. 4 (April 1972), 530–32.

Comments on the need for treatment of death in children's books. Discusses seven books insightfully.

Nilsen, Alleen Pace. "Death and Dying: Facts, Fiction, Folklore," *English Journal*, Vol. 62, No. 8 (November 1973), 1187–89.

Discussion and reviews of books for adolescents dealing with death.

Swenson, Evelyn J. "The Treatment of Death in Children's Literature," *Elementary English*, Vol. 49, No. 3 (March 1972), 401–4.

Contends that contemporary literature for children ignores death. Traces a history of treatment of death in children's books. Suggests four contemporary books that do a good job: *The High Pasture*, by Ruth Harnden; *The Big Wave*, by Pearl S. Buck; *Up a Road Slowly*, by Irene Hunt; and *Meet the Austins*, by Madeleine L'Engle.

Wolf, Anna W. M. *Helping Your Child to Understand Death*. New York: Child Study Press, 1973.

Originally written in 1958, this book was revised in 1973. Many sound suggestions for telling children about death. Gives sample answers to children's questions. Also a section on parents' questions, which the author answers.

Zim, Herbert S., and Bleeker, Sonia. *Life and Death*. Illus. Rene Martin. New York: Morrow, 1970.

Extremely factual, objective explanation of the physical facts of death. Includes burial practices of different cultures as well as our own. Death is presented as final and inevitable. The accent in this book is on informed understanding.

Abbott, Sarah. *The Old Dog*. Illus. George Mocniak. New York: Coward, McCann, & Geoghegan, 1972. (Ages 8–10.)
A boy's old dog dies, but the boy does not feel the loss until he realizes that the dog is no longer around to run and play with. His father gives him a new puppy as a substitute for the old dog.

Agee, James. *A Death in the Family*. New York: Grosset & Dunlap. 1967. Pb. Bantam. (Ages 12–up.)
A portrayal of the effects of a man's death on the rest of his family, with tremendous insights into the world and emotions of children.

Alcott, Louisa May. *Little Women.* Boston: Little, Brown, 1868. Pb. Dutton. (Ages 8–up.)
Beth, one of four sisters in a loving family, dies after a long illness. Saddened, but not shocked, the family is accepting of Beth's death.

Allen, Terry (ed.). *The Whispering Wind — Poetry by Young American Indians*. Garden City, N.Y.: Doubleday, 1968. Pb. also. (Ages 10–up.)
This volume of poetry contains many kinds of responses to death.

Armstrong, William. *Sounder*. New York: Harper & Row, 1969. Pb. Scholastic. (Ages 11–up.) (Newbery Medal.)
The death of Sounder and the father of the family are presented as symbolic of the destructive nature of white society. The family members accept the deaths stoically.

————. *Sour Land*. New York: Harper & Row, 1971. (Ages 12–up.)
A black teacher, Moses Waters, is murdered by Whites in a southern town, yet he leaves behind him, in the hearts of a few people, the hope that love will eventually overcome racial hatred.

Arundel, Honor. *The Blanket Word*. Nashville: Thomas Nelson, 1973. (Ages 12–up.)
Jan begins to grow up after returning from school to observe her mother's painful death from cancer, the funeral, and the rest of her family's reactions to the whole situation.

Asinof, Eliot. *Craig and Joan: Two Lives for Peace*. New York: Viking, 1971. Pb. Dell. (Ages 12–up.)
The true story of two young people who committed suicide to point out the need for peace. Not a very effective book.

Baldwin, Anne Norris. *Sunflowers for Tina*. Illus. Ann Grifalconi. New York: Four Winds Press, 1970. Pb. Scholastic. (Ages 5–8.)

Tina is a black child living in the city with her mother, brother, and grandmother. Grandmother is silent, passive, and unresponsive until Tina brightens her day with a sunflower dance.

Bartoli, Jennifer. *Nonna*. Illus. Joan E. Drescher. New York: Harvey House, 1975. (Ages 5–8.)
When grandmother dies, everyone in the family, including father and mother, cries. The funeral is described; the extended family arrives, and everyone mourns together. The family then resumes life but remembers lovingly the happy times and pleasant feelings about both grandparents.

Beatty, Patricia. *A Long Way to Whiskey Creek*. New York: Morrow, 1971. (Ages 10–up.)
Two boys travel through rough land and danger to bring back a body. All kinds of attitudes toward life and death are discussed.

————. *The Big Wave*. Illus. Kazue Mizamura. New York: John Day, 1948. Pb. Scholastic. (Ages 8–12.)
When a Japanese boy's family dies in a tidal wave, his friend's family helps him to deal with death (and the fear of death) through an affirmation of life.

Buckley, Helen. *The Wonderful Little Boy*. Illus. Rob Howard. New York: Lothrop, Lee and Shepard, 1970. (Ages 5–6.)
The little boy's grandmother is loving, supportive, and understanding of all his needs. Further, she knows just how to behave. A portrait of the ideal grandmother, lovingly drawn.

Burch, Robert. *Simon and the Game of Chance*. Illus. Fermin Rocker. New York: Viking, 1970. (Ages 12–up.)
Simon, living in the Depression era, learns that life is a game of chance, when his mother is placed in an institution to recover from the death of her newborn baby, and his sister's fiancé is accidentally killed on the day before the wedding.

Beckman, Gunnel. *Admission to the Feast*. Translated from the Swedish by Joan Tate. New York: Holt, Rinehart and Winston, 1971. (Ages 12–up.)
This is a letter written to a friend by a girl who has accidentally discovered that she is dying of leukemia. The book takes the reader through the different emotions that the young woman experiences, from terror to rejection to acceptance.

Bennett, Jay. *Deathman Do Not Follow Me*. New York: Hawthorne, 1968. (Ages 12–up.)
Although basically a mystery, this story does deal with a boy's fears arising from his father's death.

Bierhorst, John (ed.). *The Fire Plume: Legends of the American Indians*. Illus. Aland E. Cober. New York: Dial Press, 1969. (Ages 9–11.)
Death is a major concern of many of these tales from the Algonquin family of tribes.

Blue, Rose. *Grandma Didn't Wave Back*. Illus. Ted Lewin. New York: Franklin Watts, 1972. (Ages 8–10.)
It is hard for Debbie, who loves her grandmother dearly, to understand that she is getting old and senile and is going to live in a nursing home. But in the end, the nursing home seems to provide a satisfying solution for everyone.

Bluenose, Philip, and Carpenter, Walter S. *Two Knots on a Counting Rope*. Illus. Joe Smith. New York: Holt, Rinehart and Winston, 1964. (Ages 6–9.)
This simple story centers around a young Navajo boy's respect and love for his grandfather, who teaches him how to count. The rope and its knots are symbolic of a person's life. After the last knot, one dies.

Bolton, Carole. *Reunion in December*. New York: Morrow, 1962. (Ages 12–up.)
A fifteen-year-old girl has a hard time adjusting to the sudden death of her father and to the actions of the rest of her family after his death.

Bontemps, Arna (ed.). *American Negro Poetry*. New York: Hill and Wang, 1963. Pb. also. (All ages.)
A book of poetry with several kinds of responses toward death. Sensitive, moving poetry.

Borack, Barbara. *Grandpa*. Illus. Ben Shecter. New York: Harper & Row, 1967. (Ages 5–8.)
Marilyn, a young girl, describes her grandfather and their relationship — there is no plot. The book points out similarities in behavior and attitude between very young children and very old people. Both grandparents are important to the little girl; their relationship is very loving.

———. *Someone Small*. Illus. Anita Lobel. New York: Harper & Row, 1969. (Ages 3–8.)
A girl feels neglected after the birth of her baby sister and is given a bird to keep her company. The baby grows older, the girls become friends, and the bird dies; but there is little sorrow at its death because its friendship is no longer needed.

Brooks, Jerome. *Uncle Mike's Boy*. New York: Harper & Row, 1973. (Ages 10–up.)

Pudge's parents are divorced and both of them have personal problems. His father's brother, Uncle Mike, takes care of Pudge, helping him to accept his younger sister's death, his mother's remarriage, and his father's mental breakdown.

Brown, Margaret Wise. *The Dead Bird*. Illus. Remy Charlip. New York: Young Scott Books, 1958. (Ages 3–8.)
Some children find a dead bird, conduct an elaborate funeral for the bird, and visit the bird's grave every day until they forget. One of the first books for young children on this topic.

Bruckner, Karl. *The Day of the Bomb*. Eau Claire, Wis.: E. M. Hale, 1962. (Ages 12–up.)
An account of the bombing of Hiroshima through the eyes and words of a Japanese family, whose daughter gradually dies of radiation poisoning.

Buck, Pearl S. *The Beech Tree*. Illus. Kurt Werth. New York: John Day, 1955. Pb. Dell. (Ages 7–11.)
A girl's love and understanding for her old grandfather helps her to convince her parents that the grandfather should not be sent away.

Cleaver, Vera and Bill. *Grover*. Illus. Frederic Martin. Philadelphia: Lippincott, 1970. (Ages 9–11.)
Grover's mother, who knows that she is dying of cancer, shoots herself. Grover understands and accepts his mother's action better than his father does and is able to cope with his loneliness with the help of his friends and a sympathetic housekeeper.

———. *Where the Lilies Bloom*. Illus. Jim Spanfeller. Philadephia: Lippincott, 1969. Pb. New American Library. (Ages 9–up.)
Set in Appalachia. A fourteen-year-old girl cares for her family after the sickness and death of their father, whom they bury and pretend is still alive. The story really concerns survival rather than death.

———. *The Whys and Wherefores of Littabelle Lee*. New York: Atheneum, 1973. (Ages 12–up.)
An independent, determined young woman overcomes the hardships of her rural mountain life. Her aunt blasts the feminine stereotype until her decision to discontinue her doctoring and settle down to be cared for by the man she loves. Each character, however, is an individual. Litabelle Lee's parents have died. The community deals with death in its own way.

Coatsworth, Elizabeth. *The Cat Who Went to Heaven*. Illus. Lynd Ward. New York: Macmillan, 1958. Pb. also. (Ages 9–11.) (Newbery Medal.)

Mythical Japanese story about an artist who paints the legend of Buddha in which he is spurned by a cat and the cat does not go to heaven. The artist, however, taking pity on his cat, paints it into the picture of Buddha; then the cat dies in ecstasy.

Coburn, John B. *Anne and the Sand Dobbies*. New York: Seabury Press, 1964. (Ages 11–up.)
Written by a minister, this story is about the deaths of a two-year-old girl and a dog, and about the family's explanation to the girl's eleven-year-old brother of what has happened. Religious character of the book may make it most useful to readers who are religiously inclined.

Coutant, Helen. *First Snow*. Illus. Vo-Dinh. New York: Knopf, 1974.(Ages 6–8.)
Liên and her family moved from Vietnam to New England. It is winter, and Liên's grandmother is dying. Liên asks her grandmother to explain what dying means. She understands when her grandmother directs her to experience the snow. Recognizing the cyclical nature of life, she is content.

dePaola, Tomi. *Nana Upstairs and Nana Downstairs*. New York: Putnam's, 1973. (Ages 3–8.)
Tommy's great-grandmother and grandmother gradually grow very old and die. His mother tells him that two falling stars are the grandmothers' good-bye kisses. A somewhat pat version of life and death.

Dixon, Paige. *May I Cross Your Golden River*? New York: Atheneum, 1975. (Ages 12–up.)
Jordan learns, soon after his eighteenth birthday, that he will die. The book describes his and his family's reactions. It includes many details of his illness, of his interaction with his family and friends, and of his thoughts. The loving support of his family helps him to prepare himself and them for his death. The story provides one model for readers faced with the same problem or thinking about death.

Dobrin, Arnold. *Scat*. New York: Four Winds Press, 1971. Pb. Scholastic. (Ages 5–8.)
An eight-year-old boy's grandmother grows sick and dies. The boy says good-bye to her by playing his harmonica at the cemetery; this makes him feel better. Even though he knows that his grandmother hated jazz funerals, he knows that she would understand and approve.

Donovan, John. *Good Old James*. Illus. James Stevenson. New York: Harper & Row, 1975. (All ages.)

James is elderly but neither senile nor infirm. After he retires, he sells his house and travels. Disliking every place he visits, he tries to regain a place in his old house and at his old place of employment. Turned down at both places, he finally rents a hotel room with a kitchen and acquires a housefly as a pet. Realistic story up to the acquisition of the fly. There are several issues raised in the book that invite discussion.

————. *I'll Get There. It Better Be Worth the Trip*. New York: Harper & Row, 1969. Pb. Dell. (Ages 12–up.)
Davy lives with his grandmother after his parents' divorce, until she dies, whereupon he goes to stay with his alcoholic mother, thinks about moving in with his remarried father, and gets involved in a homosexual relationship with his best friend. The involved feelings of the parents, the competition for the boy's loyalty, the difficulty of sorting out what is right, are all presented in this book. Too many traumas and the attempt to present too many issues mar this book. The contrast between the boy's reaction to his grandmother's death, and his response to his dog's death is interesting.

Eyerly, Jeannette. *The Girl Inside*. Philadelphia: Lippincott, 1968. (Ages 12–up.)
Three deaths come as blows to Christina. First her mother dies; than her father's death leaves her distraught and guilt-ridden. At last, after her guardian dies, his young son's need jolts her out of her self-pity and stimulates her to cope with life.

Farley, Carol. *The Garden Is Doing Fine*. Illus. Lynn Siveat. New York: Atheneum, 1975. (Ages 10–14.)
Corrie's father is dying of cancer. She cannot accept the fact until just before his death. Then, at last, with the help of an elderly friend, she realizes that her father's life has been an important factor in her and others' lives. She understands that his spirit and memory will be retained and that he leaves a legacy of joy and love. Corrie's feelings of selfishness, hope, superstition, despair, and anger will provide much food for discussion.

Fassler, Joan. *My Grandpa Died Today*. Illus. Stewart Kranz. New York: Behavioral Publications, 1971. (Ages 3–8.)
A boy's grandfather dies, and he feels sad and empty until he starts to play ball. Then he feels happy, knowing his grandfather would have been happy watching him. Somewhat Freudian orientation.

George, Jean Craighead. *Julie of the Wolves*. Illus. John Schoenherr. New York: Harper & Row, 1972. (Ages 12–up.) (Newbery Medal.)
An Eskimo girl runs away from an unhappy situation, lives in the frozen wilderness, and courageously makes friends with the wolves

and learns their ways of survival. She must face problems, not only of individual survival, but also of the changing ways of her people.

Gipson, Fred. *Old Yeller*. New York: Harper & Row, 1956. Pb. also. (Ages 12–up.) (Newbery Honor Book.)
A boy learns to deal with his grief over his devoted dog's death as a part of growing up.

Green, Phyllis. *The Fastest Quitter in Town*. Illus. Lorenzo Lynch. Reading, Mass.: Young Scott Books, 1972. (Ages 6–9.)
Johnny is a quitter; he loses his temper and quits when he cannot have his way. But with the help of his aged great-grandfather, he learns the value of patience and sticking to a task till it is done. The relationship between Johnny and his grandfather is a beautiful one. Incidentally, Johnny and his family are black.

Greenfield, Eloise. *Sister*. Illus. Moneta Barnett. New York: Crowell, 1974. (Ages 9–12.)
Doretha's father dies, and his whole family keeps on feeling the impact of his death. The descriptions of his sudden death and the way that it affects the family are eloquently handled.

Gunther, John. *Death Be Not Proud*. New York: Harper & Row, 1949. Pb. also. (Ages 12–up.)
The true story of a young man's hopeless but courageous fight against a brain tumor. Written by his father. A very moving story for adolescents.

Harris, Audrey. *Why Did He Die?*. Illus. Susan Salladé Dalke. Minneapolis: Lerner Publications, 1965. (Ages 5–8.)
Told in verse. A child's mother explains death to her son, using several analogies to illustrate the process of growing old and dying. Although some euphemisms are used, the comparison of people to motors is a helpful one, and the tone is generally constructive.

Heide, Florence Parry. *The Key*. Illus. Ati Forberg. New York: Atheneum, 1972. (Ages 10–12.)
The first story is about a young Native American boy who lives with his grandfather in a one-room walk-up in the city. The grandfather cares for the boy and tells him stories about his heritage. He is strong until the end of the story, when he weeps because he recognizes that the boy is caught and will probably never escape.

Hinton, S. E. *The Outsiders*. New York: Viking, 1967. Pb. Dell. (Ages 12–up.)
A story about the thoughts and actions of a group of boys who get involved in a gang war, which results in a death.

Hoff, Syd. *Barkley*. New York: Harper & Row, 1975. (Ages 4–8.)
Barkley, an old circus dog, finds a way to be useful and valued even

though he is old. The problems of old age are recognized, and a happy solution is proposed in this "Early I Can Read" book.

Holland, Isabelle. *Amanda's Choice*. Philadelphia: Lippincott, 1970. (Ages 9–11.)
A young girl has to deal with her feelings of rejection after a loved one's death.

Hunter, Molly. *A Sound of Chariots*. New York: Harper & Row, 1972. (Ages 12–up.) (Wel-Met Award.)
When a young girl's father dies, she learns to cope and to rechannel her grief into creative energy.

Kantrowitz, Mildred. *Maxie*. Illus. Emily A. McCully. New York: Parents' Magazine Press, 1970. (Ages 4–8.)
Maxie is an old woman who decides that she is unnoticed, unloved, and unnecessary. She remains in bed instead of adhering to her regular routine. The reactions of her neighbors and the other people with whom she comes into daily contact are gratifying. The book helps to put into perspective the seemingly aimless routines of the elderly.

———. *When Violet Died*. Illus. Emily A. McCully. New York: Parents' Magazine Press, 1973. (Ages 5–8.)
After their bird dies, the children have a funeral, realizing that living creatures do not last forever.

Klein, Stanley. *The Final Mystery*. Garden City, N.Y.: Doubleday, 1974. (Ages 9–up.)
An interesting account of the many different cultural and ethnic beliefs and practices regarding death. It would be a more effective book if the author documented his information. Some of it invites further investigation.

Lee, Mildred. *Fog*. New York: Seabury Press, 1972. Pb. Dell. (Ages 12–up.)
As a result of his father's death from a heart attack, Luke grows up, leaving his old life and his teen-age gang behind.

Lee, Virginia. *The Magic Moth*. Illus. Richard Cuffari. New York: Seabury Press, 1972. (Ages 8–up.)
Mark-O comes to accept his sister's long illness and death from a heart defect. He preserves her memory, after the funeral, in the symbol of a moth that comes out of its cocoon when his sister dies.

L'Engle, Madeleine. *Meet the Austins*. New York: Vanguard, 1960. (Ages 8–12.)
A friend of the family is killed in a plane accident, and the orphan daughter comes to live with the Austins, making them realize the

difficulties of dealing with the aftermath of death. The orphan is a spoiled brat, changing the conventional stereotype.

Lewis, C. S. *The Lion, the Witch and the Wardrobe*. New York: Macmillan, 1961. Pb. also. (Ages 9–11.)
This fantasy tale, like all the others in the Narnia series, is an allegory of Christian religious beliefs about death, life after death, and heaven.

Little, Jean. *Home from Far*. Illus. Jerry Lazare. Boston: Little, Brown, 1965. (Ages 10–up.)
Jenny's parents take two foster-children into their home after her brother Michael is killed in a car accident. Jenny has to deal with her sadness and her resentment of her foster-siblings.

Littledale, Freya. *Ghosts and Spirits of Many Lands*. Illus. Stefan Martin. Garden City, N.Y.: Doubleday, 1970. (Ages 12–up.)
These tales from around the world examine different centuries' beliefs about death and life after death.

Lundgren, Max. *Matt's Grandfather*. Illus. Fibben Hold. Translated by Ann Pyk. New York: Putnam's, 1970. (Ages 7–10.)
Matt's parents take him to visit his eighty-five-year-old grandfather in a nursing home. The old man is unhampered by the constraints of time, personal relationships, and doctor's orders. A somewhat strange story, in which no one seems to relate to anyone else in a close fashion. Certainly the grandfather and the father neither know nor like each other.

Mathis, Sharon Bell. *The Hundred Penny Box*. Illus. Leo and Diane Dillon. New York: Viking, 1975. (Ages 6–9.)
Michael loves his Aunt Dew. He understands her feelings. She is one hundred years old but still communicates and remembers. Michael is protective of Aunt Dew's feelings and is distressed by his mother's seeming lack of understanding.

Mazer, Norma Fox. *A Figure of Speech*. New York: Delacorte Press, 1973. Pb. Dell. (Ages 12–up.)
Jenny's parents, unable to deal with her grandfather's old age and senility, want to put him in a home. Jenny objects, and so does her grandfather, who kills himself instead. This is a powerful but upsetting story. Its realism leaves the reader reeling.

Mendoza, George. *The Hunter I Might Have Been*. New York: Astor Honor, 1968. (Ages 8–10.)
A young boy shoots and buries a sparrow. He is so affected by the death that he never touches a gun again.

Merrill, Jean. *Blue's Broken Heart*. Eau Claire, Wis.: Hale-Cadmus, 1960. (Ages 6-10.)
When a dog's friend dies, he goes to a doctor for a bandage on his broken heart. He helps the doctor to heal others and forgets about his broken heart as a result.

Miles, Miska. *Annie and the Old One*. Illus. Peter Parnell. Boston: Little, Brown, 1971. (Ages 6-8.) (Newbery Honor Book.)
A Navajo girl futilely tries to prevent the predicted death of her grandmother. But in the end, she accepts death as a necessary part of life.

Ness, Evaline. *Sam Bangs and Moonshine*. New York: Holt, Rinehart and Winston, 1966. Pb. also. (Ages 3-7.) (Caldecott Medal.)
Samantha fantasizes a mermaid mother for her real mother, who has died; but her father wants Sam to face reality instead of talking "moonshine."

NicLeodhas, Sorche. *Gaelic Ghosts*. New York: Holt, Rinehart and Winston, 1963. (Ages 9-11.)
Tales about chilling, scary ghosts and friendly, helpful ghosts who return from the dead in Scotland.

O'Dell, Scott. *Island of the Blue Dolphins*. New York: Houghton Mifflin, 1960. Pb. Dell. (Ages 9-14). (Newbery Medal, Notable Book, and Council on Literature for Children & Young People Awards.)
Karana, a young Native American girl, is alone on her home island after her tribe has left, and her brother has been killed by wild dogs. She tames two of the dogs, and manages her own survival courageously for many years until, at last, she is rescued by missionaries. She must cope with her brother's death, and the probability of her own death. Essentially, however, she must face the fact of her own isolated existence.

Orgel, Doris. *The Mulberry Music*. Illus. Dale Payson. New York: Harper & Row, 1971. (Ages 9-12.)
Libby survives the illness, the fears, the loss, and is comforted by the music at the funeral, as she remembers the death of her beloved grandmother. An extraordinary, moving story, demonstrating how effectively children can participate in the healthy response to the death of a loved one. Also demonstrates the harm of not informing children about what is happening.

Pintauro, Joseph. *The Music Box*. New York: Harper & Row, 1970. (All ages.)
A collage of statements and pictures about life and death.

Platt, Kin. *Chloris and the Creeps*. Philadelphia: Chilton, 1973. Pb. Dell. (Ages 12–up.)
Chloris cannot accept her parents' divorce or her father's subsequent suicide. She is hateful and destructive to her mother, her mother's new husband, and their home because she thinks of her father as a kind of superman. She is finally helped to remember her father realistically and to build a positive relationship with her stepfather.

Rabin, Gil. *Changes*. New York: Harper & Row, 1973. (Ages 10–up.)
After Chris's father dies, his mother, grandfather, and he move in with his aunt, who is not at all pleased to have them. The grandfather's health deteriorates to the point of blindness and senility. He is placed in a nursing home which apparently maintains less than marginal standards of cleanliness and care. Chris cannot bring himself to visit his grandfather there. The author helps readers to understand the feelings of all the characters involved. The issue of the unfairness of the infirmities of old age is clearly exposed.

Rhodin, Eric. *The Good Greenwood*. Philadelphia: Westminster Press, 1971. Pb. Archway. (Ages 12–up.)
Louis dies in an accident with a gun. Mike, his best friend, does not like what the townspeople do to destroy the memory of Louis and to make him into somebody he was not.

Robinson, Jean. *The Secret Life of T. K. Dearing*. Illus. Charles Robinson. New York: Seabury Press, 1973. (Ages 8–11.)
T. K.'s grandfather feels useless at home. He wants to play with T. K. and his friends in this story about an independent old man and a basically understanding family.

Saint-Exupéry, Antoine de. *The Little Prince*. New York: Harcourt, Brace, 1943. (All ages.)
A little prince from another planet comes down to earth to explore and, in the end, "returns to his planet" after being bitten by a poisonous snake. A mystical allegory about life and death.

Salten, Felix. *Bambi*. New York: Simon and Schuster, 1929. Pb. Grosset and Dunlap. (Ages 5–8.)
The story of a deer, whose mother is shot by a hunter, and of his life in the forest with his animal friends and human enemies. Death, in this story, is a tragic fact of life.

Shecter, Ben. *Across the Meadow*. Garden City, N.Y.: Doubleday, 1973. (Ages 6–8.)
A cat is too old to enjoy anything anymore, so he decides to go on a "vacation," sends a young kitten to take his place in the family, and

crawls into an automobile for a long sleep — a euphemism for death. Potentially a very damaging book.

Shulevitz, Uri. *Dawn*. New York: Farrar, Straus & Giroux, 1974. (Ages 5-8.)
A subtle but moving communication of the relationship between a young child and a grandfather. The illustrations beautifully convey the message.

Skorpen, Liesel Moak. *Old Arthur*. Illus. Wallace Tripp. New York: Harper & Row, 1972. (Ages 3-8.)
Arthur is too old to be a good farm dog anymore, so he runs away from the farmer who wants to kill him, gets put in a dog pound, and finally ends up a valued pet for a little boy. A beautiful story about the positive values of old age.

Slote, Alfred. *Hang Tough, Paul Mather*. Philadelphia: Lippincott, 1973. Pb. Avon. (Ages 9-12.)
Paul is twelve years old and has leukemia. The descriptions of his reactions to his medication are graphic, but the book essentially conveys a hopeful message. The boy's devotion to baseball carries him through some of the bad times with his illness.

Smith, Doris Buchanan. *A Taste of Blackberries*. Illus. Charles Robinson. New York: Crowell, 1973. (Ages 7-10.) (Wel-Met Award.)
Jamie dies of an allergic reaction to a bee sting, and his friend feels guilty, lonely and cannot believe it happened, until after the funeral, when he offers himself as a substitute son to Jamie's mother when and if she wants one.

Smith, Ivan. *The Death of a Wombat*. Illus. Clifton Pugh. New York: Scribner's, 1972. (Ages 9-up.)
An accidentally caused forest fire kills all the animals in the forest, even the wombat, who comes close to reaching safety from the blaze. The story is about his futile struggle to remain alive.

Sonneborn, Ruth A. *I Love Gram*. Illus. Leo Carty. New York: Viking, 1971. (Ages 5-8.)
Ellie loves her grandmother, gets worried and upset when her grandmother gets sick and goes to the hospital. She is afraid that she will die, although her grandmother does get better and returns in the end.

Soundburg, Helga. *Bo and the Old Donkey*. Illus. Marion Morton. New York: Dial Press, 1965. (Ages 7-10.)
A little boy is upset about his parents' decision to kill the family's old donkey. No talk of new life or activities will substitute for the donkey in the boy's life.

Steig, William. *Sylvester and the Magic Pebble*. New York: Simon and Schuster, 1969. Pb. Dutton. (Ages 6-9.) (Caldecott Medal.)
A donkey finds a magic pebble and inadvertently turns himself into a rock, which causes his parents confusion and grief. They have a tearful reunion, when he finally becomes a donkey again. His "death" is a temporary one, during which time he has the opportunity to see how his parents mourn him.

Stein, Sara Bennett. *About Dying*. Illus. Dick Frank, New York: Walker, 1974. (Ages 4-10.)
One of the Open Family series. Physical description is given of the death of a pet bird. The mother factually and supportively deals with the child's questions and needs. Then the grandfather dies, and again the child is helped by ritual, family support, and answers to questions. An excellent resource for adults and children, discussing reactions and stressing keeping pleasant memories alive.

Stolz, Mary. *The Edge of Next Year*. New York: Harper & Row, 1974. (Ages 12-up.)
A moving story of the devastating effects of a mother's death on her family. The husband becomes an alcoholic, and the two boys must try to fend for themselves. In the end there is hope that the father will recover.

——. *Lands End*. Illus. Dennis Hermanson. New York: Harper & Row, 1973. (Ages 12-up.)
This story includes a family's warm and loving treatment of a senile old grandfather, although it is not the main focus of the book.

Stull, Edith G. *My Turtle Died Today*. New York: Holt, Rinehart and Winston, 1964. (Ages 5-8.)
This story is about a boy's sadness over the death of his turtle and of his coping with the experience.

Talbot, Toby. *Away Is So Far*. Illus. Dominique Michele Strandquest. New York: Four Winds Press, 1974. (Ages 8-12.)
The setting is Spain. Pedro's mother has died, leaving him and his father totally forlorn. They leave their home to wander all over Spain and France. Pedro's father needs the time to pull himself together. He cannot tolerate the physical daily reminders of his wife's death. At last, with Pedro's loving support, he recovers, and the two of them return to their home. A gentle, well-written story describing the effects of grief.

Udry, Janice May. *Mary Jo's Grandmother*. Illus. Eleanor Mill. Chicago: Albert Whitman, 1970. (Ages 5-8.)
One snowy Christmas, Mary Jo visits her old but independent

grandmother, who lives alone in the country. When her grand-mother has an accident, Mary Jo gets help and cares for the old woman.

Viorst, Judith. *The Tenth Good Thing About Barney*. Illus. Erik Blegvad. New York: Atheneum, 1971. (Ages 5–9.)
Barney, a boy's pet cat, dies. The boy's parents encourage him to have a funeral and to think of ten good things about the cat, so that he will not feel so bad about its death. He finally recognizes that the death of the cat contributes to the cycle of life.

Warburg, Sandol Stoddard. *Growing Time*. Illus. Leonard Weisgard. Boston: Houghton Mifflin, 1969. Pb. also. (Ages 5–8.)
A little boy's beloved dog dies, and the boy's family help him to understand and accept the pet's death. Each adult that he questions adds to his store of knowledge and comfort.

Weil, Lisl. *The Funny Old Bag*. New York: Parents' Magazine Press, 1974. (Ages 3–8.)
Howie and his friends make fun of an old couple in the park who carry a funny old bag; but when Howie hurts himself badly, the old people with the old bag are there to help him.

White, E. B. *Charlotte's Web*. Illus. Garth Williams. New York: Harper & Row, 1952. Pb. Dell. (Ages 9–up.) (Newbery Honor Book.)
Charlotte, the spider, saves the life of Wilbur, the pig, and they become loving friends. When Charlotte finally dies, Wilbur treas-ures her memory, and cares for her children, grandchildren, and great-grandchildren.

Whitehead, Ruth. *The Mother Tree*. Illus. Charles Robinson. New York: Seabury Press, 1971. (Ages 8–11.)
Temple's mother has died, and, at ten years old, she must care for her father, her dependent sister, and her headstrong brother. After a time of inward rebellion and resentment, Temple accepts her responsibilities.

Wier, Ester. *The Loner*. Illus. Christine Price. New York: David McKay, 1963. (Ages 12–14.) (Newbery Honor Book.)
An orphan boy, who experiences the death of one of his only close friends, is found, helped, given a name, and befriended by a strong woman. He realizes that he is no longer a loner. Her grief over the death of her son is also resolved in a constructive manner.

Wiggin, Kate Douglas. *The Birds' Christmas Carol*. Boston: Houghton Mifflin, 1941. (Ages 9–11.)
The story of a ten-year-old girl who is born and dies on Christmas,

and the complete, loving acceptance of her death by her family as well as herself. Very sentimental, too-sweet story.

Windsor, Patricia. *The Summer Before*. New York: Harper & Row, 1973. Pb. Dell. (Ages 12–up.)
Alexandra goes crazy after her best friend and potential lover is killed in an automobile accident. The reader does not know if she will ever recover.

Wojciechowska, Maia. *The Life and Death of a Brave Bull*. Illus. John Groth. New York: Harcourt, Brace & World, 1972. (Ages 8–up.)
Written from the perspective of a bullfight afficionado, this book stresses the aim of achieving reputation and glory through fighting and killing, and the idea of defeating death by dying nobly.

———. *Shadow of a Bull*. Illus. Alvin Smith. New York: Atheneum, 1964. (Ages 9–12.) (Newbery Medal.)
Although death is feared in this book, "brave" death invites admiration. Manolo fears that he is a coward because he does not want to be a bullfighter. The plot's resolution creates a happy ending for Manolo, but maintains the concept of the "noble" death.

Wyse, Lois. *Grandfathers Are to Love*. Illus. Martha Alexander. New York: Parents' Magazine Press, 1967. (Ages 5–6.)
This book describes all the loving and useful things that grandfathers can do. Unfortunately, it includes only white people.

Young, Jim. *When the Whale Came to My Town*. Photographs by Dan Bernstein. New York: Knopf, 1974. (Ages 6–10.)
A whale washes up on the shore to die. A boy discovering the whale begins to think about life and death. Despite the Coast Guard's efforts and the presence of several doctors, the whale at last dies.

Zindel, Paul. *I Love My Mother*. Illus. John Mele. New York: Harper & Row, 1975. (Ages 4–8.)
Both the text and the illustrations in this book combine reality and dreams in a rather disconcerting fashion. The story describes the love of a young boy for his mother. The father is dead (or so it seems) and both mother and child miss him and are lonely without him. Although the book is somewhat sentimental, it is unique enough in its blend of fantasy and reality to merit examination.

———. *Pigman*. New York: Harper & Row, 1968. Pb. Dell. (Ages 12–up.)
The story of two teen-agers who discover an unhappy, lonely old man who cannot accept his wife's death; they mistreat and exploit him and then regret it after he dies of a heart attack.

Zolotow, Charlotte. *My Grandson Lew*. Illus. William Pène duBois. New York: Harper & Row, 1974. (Ages 3-8.)
A little boy and his mother share loving memories of the boy's dead grandfather. The mother helps the child to cope with his grief through these positive reflections.

NOTES and ADDITIONS

5

War

NOT MANY PEOPLE disagree that war is ugly, destructive, and frightening. War in the abstract is relatively easy to deal with; it is simply dismissed as evil. There appear to be no issues within the topic of war in children's books. The reasoning is logical: if we are to construct a peaceful society, we must instruct our children about the negative aspects of war.

Complications arise when we consider specific wars and when we move beyond the generalized realm of war as a concept. It is then that we encounter a complex set of issues including causes, individual concerns, ethical decisions, and conduct during war. Today's children, living in the era of the Indo-Chinese conflict, probably have been exposed to a wider variety of responses to war than were children who were growing up during the time of the Second World War, when there was widespread support of our participation. Those who dissented were more often than not labeled as traitors, facists, or, at the very least, unpatriotic.

Feelings about a specific war run very high, particularly at the time when the conflict is raging. National response is greatest when our own soldiers are involved, but we also react emotionally when people with whom we are concerned, even indirectly, are engaged in war. The issues become very complex, depending on the level of the relationship between us and the warring nations. During the Biafran War in Africa, the black populations of the United States responded differently depending on their affiliation. Nonblack populations were also divided in their opinions and recommendations. Similarly, during the Israeli-Arab confrontations, Americans were divided in their sympathies. So it is with every war. Sides are drawn; action is invited; arguments are presented for and against the combatants as well as the issues.

Suggested Criteria

In order to encourage the kind of constructive decision-making necessary for a healthy society, children should be exposed to the complexities of moral and political issues. Very young children may not be able to comprehend all the ramifications of specific situations, but they can understand the processes of escalation and competition. They can perceive the ambiguity of what is "right" or "fair." They must daily make decisions for themselves that, on a scaled-down level, are the same sorts of decisions that political leaders must handle for their countries. Therefore, an effective book dealing with war should present some indication of the difficulty of viewing any conflict in absolute terms. When only one side is right, the story becomes a piece of propaganda that is usually less powerful than its author intended. Propaganda should be permissible in the classroom, if only to teach children how to recognize and deal with it, but it is a detrimental factor in a literary work.

▶ Try This

Examine three books about a specific war, such as the American Civil War or the Second World War. How does the author treat the "enemy"? How human are the characters? What is set forth as the cause of the war? How many causes are given? How unanimous are the opinions of all the "good" characters? Compare the effectiveness for you of the three books. How much more insight or information do you think that you now have about the war?

Some authors fear that young children cannot understand complexity. They therefore write in oversimplified terms rather than risk confusing the young readers; unfortunately, they confuse the inability to deal with abstractions with a lack of appreciation for detail. Children can handle many ideas at one time. They can follow subplots and can sort out several characters. Another criterion, therefore, for a book about war is that it contain enough detail and depth so as to convey a sense of the many facets of war.

▶ Try This

Find several picture books about war. Read them to a four-, five-, or six-year-old child. Ask the child to tell you the reasons for the war, then to describe the events of the war. Judge for yourself from which books the child has gained understanding and perspective.

As has been stated before, a well-written book is always more powerful than is a poorly constructed work. A book about war that has an unlikely ending is less memorable than one that is constructed so as to convince the reader of its feasibility. The same is true for a presentation of the causes of the war. In some books that will be discussed in this chapter, it is apparent that the author was so concerned with discussing the war's impact that it did not seem to matter what initiated the war. Similarly, many fictitious wars end in so contrived a fashion that even four-year-olds say, "That couldn't be."

▶ Try This

Find a book telling a story about war whose ending or beginning dissatisfies you. Rewrite the portion that you question. Encourage a child to perform this exercise, but do it orally. How easy is it for the child to do this?

Discussion of Children's Books

BOOKS FOR YOUNG CHILDREN (Up to Age Eight)

General Books. Almost all the books written for young children concentrating on the theme of war are attempts at allegory. Their universal intent is to tell young children that war is meaningless, wrong, and hurtful. Unfortunately, in a preponderance of these books the construction of the plot is so absurd or untenable that the reader, no matter how young, is tempted to relegate the lesson to the ranks of often heard but seldom-heeded proverbs and wise sayings. Recognizing the truism, they nevertheless divorce it from real-life behavior.

Anita Lobel's *Potatoes, Potatoes,* for example, tells the story of two brothers who leave their mother to fight in opposing armies. They each become leaders of their chosen troops, meeting in battle at the site of their mother's farm. The war ends because the mother feigns death. She takes advantage of their concern for her to admonish the entire group to go home to their mothers. They obey her after she feeds them an excellent meal of potatoes. While the author does portray the pain and discomfort of war (and the illustrations are very well executed), there is no apparent reason for the war to have begun. We know that it has lasted a long time — this makes it all the more questionable to have the ending so pat. Other disparities in the text include the weeping of all of the soldiers over the supposed death of the mother. Is this the first death of the whole dreary war?

Lending balance to the presentation, neither army is more in the right or wrong than the other, and the land is realistically devastated by the battle. But the soldiers rebuild everything except the wall before they return to their own mothers, a very comforting, but hardly plausible happy ending. Even with its flaws, *Potatoes, Potatoes,* nevertheless, presents somewhat more depth than do a number of other allegorical picture books about war.

On the Other Side of the River, by Joanne Oppenheim, is oversimplified and moralistic. The lesson to be learned is that people need each other, but the plot consists of too many logical inconsistencies to be effective. The story is of one town separated into two parts by a river, over which is a bridge. The people on each side of the river are always squabbling with the other side. When a storm causes the bridge to collapse, all interaction is cut off between the two sides. Everyone is at first very happy; but when the only farmer, doctor, tailor, and other essential people are needed by the respective other sides, everyone decides to rebuild the bridge and to live peacefully ever after. After questioning the logic, a reader might perversely suggest that another possible solution would be to station at least one representative of every essential occupation on each side of the river and to remain enemies forever. Children will recognize that the press of conveying a message far outweighs the consideration the author gives to the details of the plot.

The Apple War, by Bernice Myers, invites questions of accuracy of detail. The plot revolves around two neighboring kings who quarrel over the rightful ownership of apples. The tree is in one kingdom; the apples fall onto the neighboring king's land. Unable to resolve the question peacefully of who owns the apples, the kings agree to wage war on June fifth. One child listening to the story being read was distracted by the date and asked if apples grow in June. A discussion ensued about when apples ripen and what kind of climate was necessary. Once the detail had been surmounted, the reading could continue. The obvious absurdity of the story can be effective once the reader recognizes that the intent is to convey the silliness and illogic of the argument. Then subsequent questions — such as how the king could forget that June fifth was his birthday — could perhaps be overlooked, as could the decision to have a birthday party on the battlefield. The averting of the war because of the success of the party is hardly a model for universal peace. An ironic message does get communicated when, at the end of the party, the two kings resume the original argument, having learned absolutely nothing during the course of the book.

The Apple War, in its nonsense, manages to convey that wars do have causes and that, unless the causes are addressed, nothing is solved. An allegory that avoids many of the traps of oversimplification is Jane Yolen's *The Minstrel and the Mountain*. The story is told poetically, lending to a willingness to suspend disbelief. The cause, although obviously not one that real nations would respond to, translates into one of jealousy, resentment, and ignorance. The solution is a happily-ever-after fantasy, but, in this case, the intervention of the magical minstrel moves the action in a satisfactory fashion. If, in reality, and despite the talents of "minstrels," such as Henry Kissinger, the lasting peace is not as readily achieved, at least this book conjures up the possibility of unusual solutions to seemingly hopeless conflicts.

The Duck in the Gun, by Joy Cowley, is an attempt at satire that fails to meet any of the criteria for success. The army in this case is about to invade a town. There is no hint whatsoever given for the attack. The unlikely army has only one gun. It cannot be fired because at the last moment it is discovered that a duck has built its nest in the gun and cannot be enticed into coming out. In this book a duck is much more important than human beings are. The soldiers decide to wait for the duck to emerge rather than to shoot the gun. Killing the duck is a strategy that never even enters anyone's mind.

The conduct of the potential combatants in this story is truly absurd. The general, frustrated at not being able to wage his war, has the audacity to ask the Prime Minister of the threatened town to lend him a gun. Although the official refuses this request, he does offer employment to the soldiers, hiring them to paint all the houses in the town. When at last the ducklings hatch, the soldiers are reluctant to ruin their paint job. Moreover, the general marries the Prime Minister's daughter. So the war is called off. The only ring of truth in this book is that people do not usually destroy their own handiwork. Otherwise the satire against war does not work. The story emerges as an exercise in silliness but hardly a lesson to be learned about war.

Kjell Ringi has designed an allegory that does its job very well indeed. The book *The Winner* has no text whatsoever; the story and lesson are told entirely through the illustrations. The plot, in which two characters trying to outdo each other finally get destroyed, communicates the dangers of escalation and competition. It demonstrates that the acquisition of powerful weapons destroys everyone. In this case, a dragon is the ultimate weapon that eventually eats its "master." Children of any age, and adults as well, can "read" this book and learn from it. The illustrations are colorfully and amusingly graphic. The arms race begins harmlessly enough and ends in disaster. Perhaps the absence of words is one of the greatest advantages of the book; it insures that each reader will insert vocabulary appropriate and manageable at that reader's level. The ending is not a happy one, even for the dragon, because now there is no one left to eat. The people do not spring magically back to life. They are dead. This book could be used as the starter for many discussions, providing the stimulus for some extensive thought and investigation of the problems inherent in waging war. Children can write their own text or dictate the words to an adult. They can construct puppets and perform the story in front of an audience.

One Sad Day, by Bernice Kohn, does not succeed in its good intentions. Although the war devastates both countries, and, as in *The Winner*, nothing and no one are left, the action leading up to this conclusion is neither as involving nor as probable. The combatants in this case are two nations, one rural and one totally industrialized. Even for purposes of fantasy, it is naive to imagine that many readers will accept the idea that a community described as idyllically bucolic would have the same war capability as a nation equipped with heavy machines. It is also difficult to accept the notion that, for no reason at all, the Stripes (the city) declare war on the Spots. Ostensibly, the Stripes want the Spots to be identical to them in every way. Perhaps the author is trying to convey the irony of prejudice and fear of difference. But as an allegory about war it does not work. The platitudes and omission of details create a book that is obviously didactic but with no new insight.

The well-intentioned failures can be effective in the classroom as vehicles of criticism for the students. It would be healthy for the children to recognize that conveying a socially acceptable message does not guarantee a book is good. If the story appeals to some children and not to others, the teacher can help them to set up a debate or panel situation. There should be no class vote or decision on whether or not the book is good or who is right. Some readers may appreciate the illustrations; some may be ready for the moral that a particular book conveys. There should, therefore, be no punishment by anyone for a difference of opinion. All substantiated opinions should be respected.

One book that lends itself very well to debate and investigation is *Drummer Hoff*, by Barbara Emberley. The colorful, bold illustrations by her husband, Ed, are essential to the book, which won the Caldecott Award in 1968. There are details and subtleties both within the illustrations and in the plot that bear repeated examination. The story is simple: A band of soldiers assembles and fires a cannon; the refrain "But Drummer Hoff fired it off" is repeated. The text describes the military preparations carried on by each of the soldiers, starting with the general. A double-page spread of the actual firing is impressive. At the end the cannon is left in a field of grass and flowers, a haven for grasshoppers, spiders, and birds.

The question can be asked whether or not this is a book that glorifies war. The refrain seems to indicate that the firing of the cannon is a glorious event and that Drummer Hoff is to be envied. But a close inspection of the soldiers reveals that the powder man has a wooden leg and that one soldier has only one eye. The text, coming as it does from an old folk rhyme, could be interpreted as nonsense, as prowar in the glorifying of the act of the drummer, or as antiwar in that all of the upper-echelon soldiers pass the burden of responsibility for the act of destruction onto the drummer.

Very young children may not notice many of the details of this intricate book. They should, however, be encouraged to talk about the story and about the characters. They can be invited to discuss why the cannon is all by itself in the field, without any people around it at the end. They might be asked how they would feel if they were the drummer. Those readers particularly interested in things military can assemble a hierarchical listing of ranks and analyze the importance of the task according to rank.

Another interesting and somewhat complicated book, which was named as one of the *New York Times*'s choice of Best Illustrated Children's Books of 1969, is *Bang Bang You're Dead*, by Louise Fitzhugh and Sandra Scoppetone. Designed for the five- to eight-year-old, the book's text and illustrations are controversial in their explicitness and violence. The authors are unmistakably attempting to discourage physical conflict, to introduce the concept of war to young children, and to teach the lesson that negotiation and friendly behavior are better. The story relates how the game of war for one group of little boys no longer remains a game when an invading group of bigger and rougher boys challenges them. They call each other names such as "puke-face" and "freak-out" and graphically inflict pain upon each other. One illustration shows the conflict, with one combatant sustaining a gushing bloody nose.

The fight ends with both sides losing. This is somewhat of a surprise because of the superior strength and size of the attackers, but all the boys are lying on the hill in various attitudes of pain after the fighting is done. At this point, after agreeing that no one had much fun, they decide to share the hill for playing make-believe war together. The controversies raised by the book go beyond the language and illustrations. Questions can be asked about the usefulness of the "happy" ending if the boys are indeed going to continue to play at war. If one side had won, what would have happened? How often do children agree to stop fighting simply because they have been hurt? How often does the logical or peaceful solution occur to groups of mutually angry children? For some readers the humor will be remembered without the intended moral.

Questions should be raised not only for purposes of criticism but also for purposes of analysis. If readers of all ages acquire the habit of actively questioning what they read and of having that process valued by people they respect, then one of the more important goals of responsible education will be accomplished.

Several authors have attempted, as Fitzhugh and Scoppetone have, to explain war to children by equating it with children's arguments. Crosby Bonsall's *Mine's the Best* is a very easy-to-read book describing an argument between two boys who are carrying identical balloons. Each believes his balloon is best and, in the process of arguing, destroys it. At that point, a girl walks by with a balloon identical to theirs. Quickly, the former enemies align with each other and say, "Ours was the best." The analogy is not unlike countries at war becoming allies when new adversaries appear. The book attempts to demonstrate realistic childish behavior rather than to be a more ambitious attempt at symbolizing war, but the extensions are possible.

Three other books — *The Hating Book*, by Charlotte Zolotow, *Let's Be Enemies*, by Janice May Udry, and *I Am Better Than You*, by Robert Lopshire — describe arguments between friends and their eventual reconciliation. These books do not intend to carry a message beyond that of children and their disagreements. But if a group of children and a teacher are talking about war and conflict among nations, then this sort of book is perfect as an introduction or even as a case in point for use when analyzing the more complex international situations. Children may even assign names of countries to the characters for the purpose of carrying out the analogy.

The Hating Book is about a misunderstanding. One child mistakes what she hears her friend say. Until the error is cleared up, the friendship is on rocky ground. The child's mother keeps suggesting that her daughter ask her friend directly why she is behaving in such an unfriendly way. When, at last, the girl takes her mother's advice, the whole misunderstanding dissolves. It would be wonderful if nations could function so directly and happily, but at least this serves as a model for unwarlike behavior for children.

Let's Be Enemies is somewhat different. Two boys are friends, but one is angry with the other because of his constant bossy behavior. John becomes so angry upon thinking of James's behavior that he goes to the other's house to declare that he is no longer James's friend, whereupon James also declares his enmity for John. Strangely enough, and upon no seeming intervention, John invites James to go roller skating, and James offers John a pretzel. Perhaps this does happen when children quarrel, but they should be encouraged to exercise judgment and recognize rational behavior. Why should they be friends if they mistreat each other?

I Am Better Than You involves two lizards who appear exactly alike to the reader. One of them, Sam, is determined to prove that he is the best lizard there is. He is very competitive and very quarrelsome. Pete, the other lizard, is a perfect model of excellent temperament and good fellowship. Finally, after proving that Sam is not the better lizard, but is, in fact, somewhat silly, Pete and Sam resume this friendship. Sam promises henceforth to be quiet. Again, this book could be used as a jumping-off point for analyzing the behavior of countries engaging in competition of various sorts. Pete's behavior could be used as an example of how to avoid wars, or at least, arguments.

Historical Books.   There are fewer books for younger children that relate to actual wars than there are books that deal with war in general. Nathaniel Benchley has contributed an easy-to-read book about the American Revolutionary War, called *Sam the Minuteman*. The young boy, Sam, helps his father fight at the Battle of Lexington. Benchley does an excellent job of communicating the fear and anger caused by the incidents of the battle. By graphically portraying Sam's reactions to his friend's being wounded, he personalizes the experience of war for young children. Sam's ideals take second place to his immediate responses. Although bravery is valued, Benchley makes it clear that raw survival sometimes has nothing to do with heroism. The book manages an excellent balance between reconizing that the war had a cause and that war itself is a gruesome experience. Nothing much is said about the British side, but there is enough in this book to start some deep conversations about the different shades of justification for warfare.

The Revolutionary War, the Civil War, and the Second World War are well represented in literature, especially for older children. But one war this author has never heard of is the subject of a book by Betty Baker, called *The Pig War*, a Harper & Row "I Can Read History" book. It describes a real war that took place in 1859 off the coast of the state of

Washington, where there was a small island whose rightful ownership was disputed. Both the British and the Americans claimed possession; American farmers lived there, as did a small detachment of British soldiers. The conflict erupted when a small display of patriotism escalated into a grand display of power. In the end, the armies who were sent to do the fighting ate up so much of the island's products that the regular inhabitants were disgusted with the intervention and sent everyone else away. They decided to live in peace with each other until at last ownership was given to the United States. The story sounds too good to be true, but the author claims to have researched it. Children can begin a correspondence with her through the publisher, can send to the State Historical Association of the state of Washington, and can really investigate the Pig War. Research skills could be practiced to good advantage by using this book as a starter.

Poetry.   Nursery rhymes and nonsense verses for young children mention war more often than is at first apparent. Usually the pageantry and excitement of war in general are mentioned in these verses. One collection, compiled by Leonard Clark, called *Drums and Trumpets*, titles its first section "Here Come Processions." Martial poems of glory comprise most of the selections, but there is a Thomas Hardy poem, "Men Who March Away," that hints at the futility of war and the lack of comprehension on the part of the people who fight the war as to why they are there.

A deeply moving book of poetry was selected from the archives of the State Jewish Museum in Prague by Hana Volavkova. *I Never Saw Another Butterfly* contains children's drawings and poems from the Terezin Concentration Camp. All the young poets represented in this book were destroyed in the war. Their camp was a way station to extermination centers, and they knew this; but their poetry speaks more to the joy of life than to a fear of, or preoccupation with, death. They express hope, love, and determination to survive. This is a powerful antiwar book, which does not preach against war and does not moralize. It conveys its strong message because of the information that the reader brings to the poetry. It is therefore a book that knowledgeable adults should share with others and should encourage children to read so that the strength of the message can be reinforced.

BOOKS FOR OLDER CHILDREN (Ages Eight to Twelve)

In contrast to the books written for the very young, most of the books written for older children about war are specific and based on fact. The bulk of the work falls under the category of historical fiction. But the entire Narnia series by C. S. Lewis contains descriptions of battles and wars that symbolize the conflict between good and evil. The message contained in the works is that violence and bloodshed are justified when the cause is a virtuous one. Lewis does not guarantee that good will triumph, but he avers that the fight is worth it.

An allegory written for children above age eight is *The Crane*, by Reiner Zimnik. The story revolves around a man whose talent lies in the ability to handle a giant crane. The best craneman in the world, he loves his work so much that it is his whole life. He lives on the crane, maintaining his post even when war ravages the town; as his companion during the war he has an eagle. At the end of the war, all the people are gone except the craneman. Various symbols are used, including that of a magical silver lion. As the piling up of symbols becomes somewhat heavy, the book is difficult to follow at times; and, as with many other allegories, this one misses conveying its point. Perhaps the fact that it is a translation from German contributes to its confusion, but the book seems to be an overly heavy attempt to convey universal truths without an accompanying clarity.

Historical Fiction.   For older children, most of the books about war involve young heroes or heroines so as to arouse interest and empathy in the readers. Some stories, such as Anne Frank's *Diary*, are true accounts, told in the first person. These books, which carry enormous impact, are generally the ones that readers remember best after a long period of time. If the intent in dealing with these books is to affect future attitude and behavior, then teachers and librarians should follow through on the children's reading with questions, discussions, and recommendations for further readings. For the purposes of this chapter, only a representative sampling of the books available on this topic will be discussed; others will be included in the annotated Bibliography. Although there are books written about every war, not every war will be mentioned here. The intent is to recognize that although certain elements of war are universal, each war has its own individual complexities and issues.

Revolutionary War.   Esther Forbes's *Johnny Tremain* has become a classic read by many children ages ten and up. This book, which won the Newbery Medal in 1944, is more the story of Johnny and his life than it is of the Revolutionary War. Yet, as with all good historical fiction, a sense of the times comes through clearly; more is learned about the war and its beginnings than from a purely factual text. The Whigs and Tories, as well as the British soldiers, are described as real people with several dimensions rather than as flat characters dwelling only in history.

The Colliers' *My Brother Sam Is Dead*, which is a Newbery Honor book and a finalist for the National Book Award, leaves the reader with the intriguing question of whether this war was absolutely necessary for the founding of our country as an independent nation. The authors help readers to view the war as a personal tragedy for some people, besides communicating that perhaps it was not the glorious and patriotic event depicted in many books and films.

Civil War.   Most of the books about the Civil War take a stance that the North was totally virtuous and that the South had no redeeming arguments. The war is usually described as a wrenching one for our country, but it is seldom explained that both sides had their villains as well as their heroes. There is a vast array of books in print for children telling about the Civil War, most describing the battles and their effects on the participants. Irene Hunt's *Across Five Aprils* handles the rarely considered issue of what happens tò the people who are not actively involved with the war but who nevertheless suffer.

This war story — more about people than it is about war — concerns a family, the Creightons, living in southern Illinois at the time of the Civil War. They are a close, loving family that has suffered much hardship. Several children have died of fever, and one daughter was killed in an accident by a drunken neighbor. One of the sons, Bill, is considered "odd" in the somewhat narrow-minded community where the Creightons live. He loves to read, dislikes drinking, carousing and roughhousing, and is gentle and soft-spoken; moreover, he is strong and a hard worker. He is clearly meant to be an admirable character.

As the book progresses, there is more conversation about the impending war and its causes. Discussions and arguments are mounted for and against all of the sides. Slavery is brought out as only one of the issues of the war; industrialization is also thought of as a great threat to the country. Two of the brothers — Bill, the kind one, and John, the unfriendly, somewhat distant one — argue about the war. Surprisingly enough, it is John who is for the Union, while Bill sides with the Southern cause. We have been led by conventions to believe that the "good guys" are always on the "right" side. The author has presented us with a dilemma. Students may enjoy arguing about these two characters and the logic of their stance.

For Jethro, another son, who is nine years old, war is an exciting idea. He believes that it will settle all problems and demonstrate the validity of the Union. He recognizes the thrill of battle and the satisfaction of overcoming an enemy. Bill is his favorite brother, and this causes him to be confused by what should be clear issues. Bill explains to Jethro that he, too, is confused. He hates slavery and the thought of the dissolution of the Union, but he cannot see how the war will settle the problems of the differences between the two parts of the country. He cannot agree with the overwhelming prejudice against the entire southern part of the nation.

At last, Bill and his brother John, despite their love for each other, have a dreadful fistfight. Bill decides that he must leave to fight, not so much for the South, but against the big money and Northern arrogance and hypocrisy. He goes unhappily, but believing that he must do this, even though he knows that no side is in the right. His reflections help the reader to understand that what the history books tell us is a clear-cut cause is not, after all, that simple.

Across Five Aprils won the Follett Award and was a Newbery Honor book in 1965. Very well written, it uncovers many levels of emotion and behavior in wartime. Some of the community people who are ostensibly on the "right" side of the war persecute the Creightons because of Bill's actions. The Creighton's nineteen-year-old son, Tom, is killed in the war. Eb, a boy whom they have brought up since he was ten and who was Tom's best friend, deserts. The father has a heart attack and remains in feeble health. Through each of these disasters the family endures, as the nation endures. The events of the war, which come through with awful clarity, are interwoven with the happenings at the farm. The book ends with the death of Lincoln and the agony and anxiety over the fate of the nation. It is important for students to compare different accounts of battles, causes of war, and issues in order to begin to construct a balanced, informed view.

World War II.   This war, almost above all others, had the support of most of the country, though it was a war that touched America only indirectly. It is no surprise, therefore, that most of the books written about the Second World War focus on the experiences of people in other countries. One, however, *The Summer of My German Soldier*, by Betty Greene, centers on a girl in a small town in Arkansas. When German prisoners of war are brought to the town, Patty becomes very much attracted to one of them. The book shatters many stereotypes. Patty is a desperately unhappy and lonely twelve-year-old Jewish girl living in a small Southern town. Her family, the only Jewish family in the town, own the department store. The parents are extremely cruel to Patty, who is the misfit of the family. Ruth, the family maid, cook, and housekeeper, who is black, is Patty's only friend. The events of the story are interesting but not quite believable because the author does not build up enough of a plausible cause for the behavior of the family. The story is tragic in its implications of what happens to people not only in time of war but in any time of stress.

The German soldier is a likeable, intelligent, nonviolent young man.

The reader hopes that he will successfully escape, but he is caught, despite Patty's help, and is killed. He does not fit the pattern of the bestial German that Americans were taught to recognize, and the Jewish family does not fit the pattern (except for being storekeepers) that most stories design for them. The book is moving despite the lack of justification for the characters' behavior. It adds to the readers' thinking about the consequences and complexities of war.

Other books about this war deal specifically with children and their lives. Judith Kerr's *When Hitler Stole Pink Rabbit* describes a family who escaped from Germany just before Hitler's election. Their father is an anti-Nazi journalist. The family is Jewish, although they have not practiced the religion actively. They go to Switzerland, where they are physically safe, but where they unhappily encounter antisemitism. They then move to France and, ultimately, to England. Not a horror story, this book details the everyday small discomforts and large fears occasioned by Hitler's takeover. It provides an interesting perspective for readers who have been exposed only to the tragic Anne Frank.

A story quite similar to Anne Frank's *Diary*, and also based on fact, is Johanna Reiss's *The Upstairs Room*. It has a happy ending, as the people hidden away from the Germans emerge alive at the end of the war. This book describes the individual actions of people who risk their own lives to save other people, not in active combat but through acts of quiet courage. Ordinary people — uncomfortable but, nevertheless, believing that they have responsibility for others — become the important heroes of this war.

Children of the Resistance, by Lore Cowan, is a book of a very different sort. It is a collection of stories about young people who actively aid in the resistance in Nazi-occupied countries. These children are heroes and heroines involved in death, violence, and destruction. While the book does not glorify war *per se*, it does glorify the resistance and the necessity for retribution and violence. Each chapter describes a young person from a different country. The author researched her book in many of the European countries after the war. The stories, told as great adventures, occasionally take the form of simulated diaries. Germany is included in the countries in which children are active in the resistance.

The book concentrates on the "rightness" of the Allied side and the bestiality of the Nazis with no conflicting issues raised. It begs the question of the moral problems of war. When is it right to kill or maim? When both sides believe that they are right, who can say where the crimes lie? This war, in particular, seems to invite only one answer. Even if, after much discussion, readers determine that there was no right on Hitler's side, what of the actions of the Allied defenders in the process of fighting the war? No matter what the conclusions, the process of inquiry and investigation are useful.

Korean War.   Pearl S. Buck's book *Matthew, Mark, Luke and John* tells of the plight of abandoned children after the Korean War. These children are all illegitimate offspring of G.I.'s and Korean women. The author explains in the book that Koreans consider these children to belong to the father and his family; therefore, unable to withstand the social pressure, some of the mothers desert their children. This book tells of four of these children — each with a distinct personality — who fortuitously band together for survival; it is thus about the aftermath of the war rather than of the battle itself. It does not deal with causes or take sides but recounts the effects that every war has on the people after the war is over. This story has a somewhat pat happy ending, for the children are all adopted. If students wish to explore further the delicate problems resulting from the impact of American military presence in foreign countries, they can research newspaper and magazine accounts to supplement this book.

Vietnam War.   In contrast to the Second World War, the conflict in Vietnam was probably the least popular of any American foreign involvement. Unfortunately, the books written about it have neglected a balance of views and thus do not prepare children to make their own decisions about this or any war. Alexander Crosby's well-intentioned *One Day for Peace* presents some interesting ideas of how children can get involved in activist protest, but it is unevenly written and lacks any depth of characterization. It is obviously a didactic tome aimed at protesting the war rather than the powerful tool for thought that it could have been.

Eliot Asinof's *Craig and Joan: Two Lives for Peace* is another work propagandizing against the war. It becomes more an accounting of the process of the reporter-author's search for information than a story that the author is trying to tell. The book is ostensibly about a confused and tragic couple who commit suicide in the vain hope that their death will rouse people to concrete thought and action against the war. The two are not portrayed as having thought or done much about the war; even the reasons for their decision remain a mystery at the end of the book. The other characters are, for the most part, portrayed unsympathetically. As a case study in reporting on a sad event, the book is interesting. As a serious attempt to examine the war and its ramifications, the book fails.

Poetry.   The poems included in the section for young readers are appropriate for older ones as well. They can respond to the writing of the doomed children of the concentration camp at an even deeper level than can the very young. Some preteens can even handle Kenneth Patchen s bitter war poetry. Henry Wadsworth Longfellow wrote many poems dealing with several different feelings about war; indeed, many of our most renowned poets have written several poems about war, most of them pointing to the eventual glory of battle. Thomas Moore's "Minstrel Boy" is one such poem, the gist of which is that the minstrel boy is courageous and proud and dies gloriously. The manner of his death seems to justify it for the poet. Julia Ward Howe's "Battle Hymn of the Republic" grew to be the most popular marching song of the Civil War.

Interestingly enough, it is in our popular music that many poems, set to song, decry war and bemoan its effect. Several describe war as bloody and meaningless. Folk songs such as "Johnny Has Gone for a Soldier," and many modern ballads speak to the agonies of war and its aftermath. A reading of *The Judy Collins Songbook* will unearth many antiwar songs, as will *The Joan Baez Songbook*. "Where Have All The Flowers Gone?," by Pete Seeger, is based on a traditional Russian folk song. The protests and the glorifications are available in verse as well as in longer works of fiction and nonfiction. How the teacher or librarian uses them can be of utmost importance.

Nonfiction.   An investigation of *Subject Guide to Children's Books in Print* reveals many books of both fiction and nonfiction written about each war. Betty Jean Lifton and Thomas Fox researched and reported on the war in Indo-China in *Children of Vietnam*. This book, illustrated by photographs, is an attempt to present the reality of war as it has affected the children of that devastated country. Although interesting, it, too, falls into the trap of succumbing to the simplest of explanations and the barest of facts. While vividly describing the living conditions in South Vietnam, it neglects the long history of the war, does not discuss any of the complexities of the situation, and relies on the sympathetic reaction of the readers to solve all the problems of war.

Albert Carr, on the other hand, in *A Matter of Life and Death*, addresses his book to the minds of young people as well as to their emotions. He makes a distinction between "death patriotism" and "life patriotism." The first requires the death of one's enemies; the other aims at improving one's own country. Using the Spanish-American War as an example of how our country has dealt with war, he describes several ways in which the war could have been averted. He also details several other wars. Although he offers no concrete ideas for avoiding war in the future, he does recommend that young people make their own opinions known to their representatives. He also suggests that they evaluate advice carefully and with an understanding of the many implications that any course of action carries. *A Matter of Life and Death* is a clearly written book, useful for the purpose of making readers aware of the complexities of international relationships and of the necessity for responsible personal and public behavior.

In looking at any factual accountings of wars, the reader is cautioned to read more than one point of view. Besides examining and evaluating history texts, students should read and compare accounts of a war from the perspective of different countries. As they watch for the author's attitude toward war in general, they should try to determine if and where that point of view intrudes. Is war considered a patriotic, glorious enterprise? Is it considered only to be evil, never with just and ample cause? Are wars differentiated one from the other? What sort of advice, if any, is given to the reader in terms of responding to the information? In short, how is the reader's decision-making ability enhanced as a result of reading the book?

War is indeed ugly; it does kill. There may always be another way — a better way — of solving the world's problems. But, as long as it continues to be a phenomenon of our time, we must try to learn as much as we can about its causes and its effects. We must try, with information rather than propaganda, to investigate its factors. Perhaps one day we will have the ability to avoid it and to resolve our conflicts in less disastrous fashion.

REFERENCES

Bostick, Christina. "The Individual and War Resistance," *School Library Journal*, Vol. 18, No. 7 (March 1972), p. 96-7.
  Reviews books with a bias toward war resistance. More than fifty books are listed. These are not children's books, but are suitable for high school students and older.

Gaillard, T. L., Jr., and Grew, J. C. "War in the Classroom," *English Journal*, Vol. 62, No. 2 (February 1973), 215-18.
  Describes a high school course on war, using literature from far in the past to contemporary times. Evaluates the effectiveness of the books used and makes recommendations for further reading.

Gerhardt, Lillian N. "Peace, a Publishers for Peace Bibliography," *School Library Journal*, Vol. 17, No. 2 (October 1970), 104-5+.
  An annotated bibliography of fifty books about war and peace. The annotations were compiled by a committee chaired by Gerhardt. A useful list, although the annotations refrain from debating the relative usefulness of each entry.

Hopkins, Lee Bennett, and Arenstein, Misha. "Nervose of the Thought: War and Peace in Children's Books," *Elementary English*, Vol. 48, No. 5 (May 1971), 460-62.
  Reviews of seven children's books about war. Brief discussion of children's responses to the topic.

Lane, Joan T. (ed.). "Resources in Educating for Conflict Resolution," *Childhood Education,* Vol. 49, No. 5 (February 1973), 251–52.

A listing of resources for adults interested in designing a curriculum for peace. Includes resources for children's books.

McAlpine, Julie Carlson, and Sullivan, Stephanie Carlson. "Seventy-five Recommended Teenage Books on War," *School Library Journal,* Vol. 20, No. 5 (January 1974), 222–23.

Annotated list of books about different wars.

Roth, Roslyn. "A Comparative Analysis of the Depiction of War in Selected Juvenile Fiction Published Prior to and Since 1960," unpublished Master's Report, Palmer Graduate Library School, Long Island University, Brookville, N.Y., 1969.

Purpose of study is to determine whether changes have occurred in depicting war in books for children since 1960. It was found there is essentially little difference, although a few more recent books introduce questions of conscience and morality.

Welch, Elizabeth H. "What Did You Write About the War, Daddy?" *Wilson Library Bulletin,* Vol. 46, No. 10 (June 1972), 912–17.

Reviews works of nonfiction about the Vietnamese War. Each book is described in great detail and is subjectively recommended by Welch.

Bibliography

Asinof, Eliot. *Craig and Joan: Two Lives for Peace*. New York: Viking, 1971. (Ages 12–up.)
War and its ramifications are not at all mentioned in this book. The story centers around two teen-agers who commit suicide as a gesture against the Indo-Chinese War. Not much rationale is provided for their act.

Baker, Betty. *The Pig War*. Illus. Robert Lopshire. New York: Harper & Row, 1969. (Ages 5–8.)
Takes place on an island off the state of Washington in 1859. Both Americans and British were stationed there because neither country knew to whom the island belonged. Some trespassing pigs threw the island into a minor turmoil, which was nonviolently settled. A very practical and peaceful solution was reached. This story is based on a historical incident.

Benchley, Nathaniel. *Sam the Minuteman*. New York: Harper & Row, 1969. (Ages 3–8.)
Sam fights with his father in the Battle of Lexington and is frightened of the war until his friend is wounded. Sam then fights wildly to revenge his friend, remembering only afterward the humane ideals he supposedly believes in.

Bogan, Louise, and Smith, William Jay. *The Golden Journey: Poems for Young People*. Chicago: Reilly and Lee, 1965. (All ages.)
An anthology containing many poems about many topics.

Bonsall, Crosby. *Mine's the Best*. New York: Harper & Row, 1973. (Ages 3–7.)
Two boys have identical balloons. In the process of the boys' arguing over whose balloon is the best, both balloons are destroyed. While arguing, they do not notice that there has been a special sale on balloons like theirs — until a girl walks by with one. Then the boys align with each other saying "Ours was the best!" A commentary on the subjective causes of conflict.

Bruckner, Karl. *The Day of the Bomb*. Eau Claire, Wisc.: E. M. Hale, 1962. (Ages 12–up.)
An account of the bombing of Hiroshima through the eyes and words of a fictionalized Japanese family. Sadako, the daughter of the family, dying of radiation poisoning, is making a thousand paper storks as a good-luck charm to ward off death.

Buck, Pearl S. *Matthew, Mark, Luke and John*. New York: John Day, 1967. (Ages 8–12.)
The story of four illegitimate Korean-born boys who have American fathers. They have been abandoned by the Koreans and fend for themselves until they meet a kindly American. A somewhat romanticized ending, but a compelling story of the aftermath of war.

Burland, C. A. *The Gods and Heroes of War*. New York: Putnam's, 1974. (Ages 11–up.)
A survey of how ancient peoples regarded war, shown through myths, legends, and archeological information. Tends to glorify battle.

Butterworth, W. E. *Orders to Vietnam: A Novel of Helicopter Warfare*. Boston: Little, Brown, 1968. (Ages 12–up.)
Bill is drafted, sent to Vietnam, and taught to fly helicopters. He is on his way to being a career army man like his father. War is a business, like every other normal enterprise.

Carr, Albert. *A Matter of Life and Death*. New York: Viking, 1966. (Ages 12–up.)
A history of many American wars, their possible prevention, and their individual and social implications. Also included is a discussion of patriotism and the necessity of careful consideration of alternatives to war.

Clark, Leonard (ed.). *Drums and Trumpets*. Illus. Heather Copley. Philadelphia: Dufour Editions, 1962. (Ages 10–up.)
Poetry for young people dealing with war — some of its glories, some of its despairs.

Collier, James Lincoln and Christopher. *My Brother Sam Is Dead*. New York: Four Winds Press, 1974. (Ages 12–up.) (Newbery Honor Book.)
Tim is the narrator of the story. His brother Sam and his father (as well as other characters in the story) are killed in the Revolutionary War. The war is presented here as neither right nor wrong; neither the Americans nor the British are favored. The authors suggest at the end that readers should consider whether or not the war was necessary. The ugliness and hardship of war are clearly presented. This book was one of the nominees for the National Book Award for 1974.

Cowan, Lore. *Children of the Resistance*. New York: Hawthorn, 1969. (Ages 12–up.)
Collection of stories about young people in eight different Nazi-

occupied countries who actively aided the resistance during World War II.

Cowley, Joy. *The Duck in the Gun*. Illus. Edward Sorel. Garden City, N.Y.: Doubleday, 1969. (Ages 5–8.)
A story about how a duck, nesting in a gun, prevents a war and brings the soldiers and enemy townspeople together. A fantasy that does not work.

Crosby, Alexander L. *One Day for Peace*. Boston: Little, Brown, 1971. Pb. also. (Ages 8–12.)
The death of a neighborhood friend in Vietnam convinces some junior high students to organize a large peace march in their town. The book is overly didactic and contrived.

DeJong, Meindert. *The House of Sixty Fathers*. Illus. Maurice Sendak. New York: Harper & Row, 1956. (Ages 10–up.) (Wel-Met Award, Newbery Medal.)
Tien Pao is a very young Chinese boy caught in the horror and dangers of the Second World War. Through a mishap, he is separated from his family. Only after many adventures — one of which locates him with sixty airmen eager to comfort and nurture him — does he at last find his own family. War is depicted as frightening but manageable. The attitude is somewhat that of "white man's burden," and the happy ending is unbelievable. The book's age shows.

Dunning, Stephen; Leuders, Edward; and Smith, Hugh. *Reflections on a Gift of Watermelon Pickle . . . And Other Modern Verses*. Glenview, Ill.: Scott, Foresman, 1967. (Ages 12–up.)
Excellent collection of poetry particularly appropriate for young adolescents.

Edmonds, Walter. *The Matchlock Gun*. Illus. Paul Lantz. New York: Dodd Mead, 1941. (Ages 9–11.)
The story takes place during the early pre-Revolutionary War days, when fighting was going on among settlers, French, and Indians. Edward, the young boy, fires an old Spanish gun. The mother instructs him how to do it, and devises a plan for destroying the attacking Indians. No reasons are given for the fighting, and no indication is shown that the Indians are anything but marauding savages.

Emberley, Barbara. *Drummer Hoff*. Illus. Ed Emberley. Englewood Cliffs, N.J.: Prentice-Hall, 1967. (Ages 3–6.) (Caldecott Medal.)
A folk rhyme about the loading and firing of a cannon. After the

cannon blast, flowers gradually surround it and birds come to nest in the gun. The illustrations depict the deformed and maimed victims of war in bright, cartoonlike images. The book can convey an antiwar message, but adults will need to help children to analyze this book in order to come to the intended conclusion.

Fenner, Phyllis R. *No Time for Glory: Stories of World War Two*. New York: Morrow, 1962. (Ages 12-up.)
Collection of World War II stories filled with killing, death, and glorified tragedy.

Fish, Helen Dean. *The Boy's Book of Verse: An Anthology*. Philadelphia: Lippincott, 1951. (Ages 12-14.)
Adults can help readers to add to the interpretation of these poems.

Fisher, Aileen. *Jeanne D'Arc*. New York: Crowell, 1970. (Ages 8-10.)
A biography of Jeanne D'Arc, the woman who led the French into victorious battle, was captured by the enemy, and was eventually burned at the stake.

Fitzhugh, Louise, and Scoppetone, Sandra. *Bang Bang You're Dead*. New York: Harper & Row, 1969. (Ages 5-8.)
Two groups of boys battle for possession of a hill as a playground for make-believe wars. They mutually agree that real violence is no fun, and settle their dispute cooperatively. The language is amusing; the violence is graphic. The story does not quite succeed.

Fletcher, Sydney. *The Big Book of Cowboys*. New York: Grosset and Dunlap, 1964. (Ages 9-11.)
Informative book on the settling of the West, explaining how people lived, explored, fought and died on the frontier. The fighting and dying are depicted as noble and useful in the settling of our country.

Forbes, Esther. *Johnny Tremain*. Illus. Lynd Ward. Boston: Houghton Mifflin, 1943. Pb. Dell. (Ages 12-14.) (Newbery Medal.)
The romanticized but well-written story of a boy living at the time of the American Revolution. Johnny's story is the main focus of the book, set against the background of the war. No questions are raised about the rightness of the war.

Foreman, Michael. *War and Peas*. New York: Crowell, 1974. (Ages 7-10.)
Another allegory couched in overly simplistic terms. A poor country approaches a wealthy one for aid. The king of the wealthy country, angered by this approach, declares war. The soldiers of the wealthy country are so fat that the poor, thin soldiers win with ease. The fat army has brought supplies; their trucks dig up the dry land; birds bring suds; the rains come to help the whole process. Ostensibly the

reader is to learn that poor people are more intelligent and more virtuous than rich ones. Also, that right wins over might. Interestingly, the war here is seen as a solution, rather than a universal evil.

Frank, Anne. *Diary of a Young Girl*. New York: Modern Library, 1952. Pb. Washington Square Press. (Ages 12–up.)
The diary of a thirteen-year-old Jewish girl who spent two years with her family hiding from the Nazis during the occupation of Holland. She describes the fear and horror of the times, before she herself is killed in a concentration camp.

Friesel, Uwe. *Tim, the Peacemaker*. Illus. Jozef Wilkon. New York: Scroll Press, 1971. (Ages 3–8.)
Tim plays a flute so beautifully that all who hear him stop whatever they are doing to listen. At first Tim stops constructive work from going on, and he regrets this. Then he stops soldiers from fighting and is glad. A pleasant fantasy, but not at all related to reality. The illustrations are impressive.

Gauch, Patricia Lee. *This Time, Tempe Wick?* Illus. Margot Tomes. New York: Coward, McCann & Geoghegan, 1974. (Ages 7–11.)
Another story of the Revolutionary War. The young heroine is unusual in size, strength, and behavior. Tempe outwits some disgruntled soldiers by hiding her horse in her bedroom. The war is made light of in this story. Tempe is highlighted as the heroine; her father's death and mother's illness are glossed over. But the book does provide a different perspective on this war.

Greene, Betty. *The Summer of My German Soldier*. New York: Dial Press, 1973. Pb. also. (Ages 12–up.)
Twelve-year-old Patty helps a German POW to escape from a prison in Arkansas. She does not have many friends, and she and the POW befriend each other. He is caught and killed; Patty is questioned and sent to reform school. A very grim story.

Gregory, Horace, and Zaturenska, Maria. *The Crystal Cabinet, An Invitation to Poetry*. New York: Holt, Rinehart and Winston, 1962. (Ages 12–up.)
Excellent selection.

Habenstreit, Barbara. *Men Against War*. Garden City, N.Y.: Doubleday, 1973. (Ages 12–up.)
The history of pacifism in the United States through all the wars to the present time.

Hall, Donald. *A Poetry Sampler*. New York: Franklin Watts, 1968. (Ages 11–up.)
Variety of topics and interest levels here.

Hoehling, Mary Utsehling. *Girl Soldier and Spy*. New York: Messner, 1960. (Ages 12–up.)
The biography of a courageous young woman who disguises herself as a male and joined the Union Army during the Civil War. It describes her struggle to survive despite the horrors of war.

Hollander, John, and Bloom, Harold. *The Wind and the Rain: An Anthology of Poems for Young People*. Garden City, N.Y.: Doubleday, 1961. (All ages.)
Some moving and impressive images are contained in these poems.

Holm, Anne. *North to Freedom*. New York: Harcourt Brace Jovanovich, 1965. Pb. also. (Ages 12–up.)
David is permitted to escape from a concentration camp. He remembers nothing aside from the camp, but he knows there is a mystery about his past. The story is less about war and its aftermath than one of David's survival and the unraveling of his mystery. The message of the illogical and cruel effects of war comes through.

Hunt, Irene. *Across Five Aprils*. Chicago: Follett, 1964. Pb. Grosset and Dunlap. (Ages 12–up.) (Newbery Honor Book.)
The story of the hardships of a family living in a border state during the Civil War. The story helps readers to understand that war is not simple. There are no easy answers to the question of which side is right. The author makes it clear that people constitute the sides and that people as individuals have good and bad characteristics, which add to the complexity of the issues.

The Joan Baez Songbook. New York: Ryerson Music Publishers, 1971. (All ages.)
Songs such as "Where Have All The Flowers Gone?" demonstrate the popular feeling about war.

Jones, Cordelia. *Nobody's Garden*. Illus. Victor Ambrus. New York: Scribner's, 1966. (Ages 10–up.)
Bridget, a new girl in school, is living with an aunt and uncle in London, having been orphaned in the war. The story describes postwar London in a very personal and vivid way. It also helps readers to understand the serious emotional aftermath of war.

The Judy Collins Songbook. New York: Grosset and Dunlap, 1969. (All ages.)
Several of the songs tell of the sorrows of war.

Kellogg, Steven. *The Wicked Kings of Bloon*. Englewood Cliffs, N.J.: Prentice-Hall, 1970. (Ages 5–8.)
Two brothers are raised in the Land of Monsters by their witch-mother. They hate each other; and, when one becomes ruler of East

Bloon and the other becomes ruler of West Bloon, they wage war on each other. In the end, both evil rulers are defeated by the townspeople.

Kerr, Judith. *When Hitler Stole Pink Rabbit*. New York: Coward, McCann, 1972. Pb. Dell. (Ages 8–up.)
Autobiographical story of a German Jewish family who escape just before Hitler came to power. They go first to Switzerland, then France, then England. The impact is somewhat softened because, although the family are refugees, they seem not to suffer unduly.

Knight, Clayton. *We Were There at the Normandy Invasion*. New York: Grosset and Dunlap, 1956. (Ages 12–up.)
An objectively told historical account of the Normandy invasion of World War II.

Kohn, Bernice. *One Sad Day*. Illus. Barbara Kohn Isaac. New York: Third Press–Joseph Okpaku, 1971. (All ages.)
The Stripes live in one place; the Spots, in another. Stripes make war on the Spots, everything and everyone on earth is killed. An allegory demonstrating the total devastation of war as well as its lack of appropriate cause.

Leichman, Seymour. *The Boy Who Could Sing Pictures*. Garden City, N.Y.: Doubleday, 1968. (Age 9.)
The king is at war, so the court jester takes his son traveling around the country to cheer people up. The boy sings happiness to the sad faces; back at the court, he sings the sadness of what he has seen to the blank faces. The king, realizing the truth, stops the war.

Lewis, C. S. *The Last Battle*. New York: Macmillan, 1956. Pb. also. (Ages 10–up.)
An account of a battle between Good and Evil in Narnia, an imaginary country of talking animals. It is an allegorical account of the end of the world, Judgment Day, and the entrance into heaven.

Lifton, Betty Jean. *Children of Vietnam*. Photographs by Thomas Fox. New York: Atheneum, 1972. (Ages 10–up.) (National Book Award.)
Interviews and pictures of children who survived the battles and massacres in Vietnam. A powerful description of individual suffering, confusion, fear, and sorrow.

———. *Return to Hiroshima*. Photographs by Eikoh Hosoe. New York: Atheneum, 1970. (Ages 10–up.)
A pictorial view of the damage and destruction of Hiroshima by the A-bomb during World War II as well as the consequent rebuilding of the city.

Lobel, Anita. *Potatoes, Potatoes*. New York: Harper & Row, 1967. (Ages 5-8.)

A woman and two sons grow potatoes. The two sons leave to become commanders of opposing armies. Eventually, both armies need food and come to mother's house for potatoes. The mother stops the war. The story is so oversimplified as to become silly; the allegory does not work.

Lopshire, Robert. *I Am Better Than You*. New York: Harper & Row, 1968. (Ages 5-8.)

A competition between two lizards who really are identical. One of them declines the battle; thus war is averted. A very useful book to teach the problems of competition, escalation, and boasts. Solutions other than violent ones are suggested here.

McGowan, Tom. *The Apple Strudel Soldier*. Illus. John E. Johnson. Chicago: Follett, 1968. (Ages 5-8.)

A baker, trying to help relieve his town's monetary crisis, accidently gets conscripted into the army. He fills the cannons with apple strudel, and everyone is so busy eating they stop fighting. Then, everyone loves strudel so much that they order a lot, and the baker saves his town from its monetary woes. The story is not really conducive to a suspension of disbelief.

Merrill, Jean. *The Pushcart War*. Illus. Ronni Solbert. New York: William R. Scott, 1964. (Ages 10-13.)

An allegory of how wars begin, are escalated, and are ultimately resolved. The story, colorfully and imaginatively told, is about a war (told as if it were history) between the trucks and the pushcarts in New York City. Causes, strategies, and battles are described in this humorous but thoughtful book.

Monjo, F. N. *The Vicksburg Veteran*. New York: Simon and Schuster, 1971. (Ages 6-10.)

Account of the capture of Vicksburg, Mississippi, by Ulysses S. Grant through the eyes of his twelve-year-old son.

Murray, Michele. *The Crystal Nights*. New York: Seabury Press, 1973. Pb. Dell. (Ages 11-up.)

An unusual story of the effects of war on the direct victims of the war and their family in the United States. Most of the characters are unpleasant and selfish. The backdrop of the war serves to complicate their reactions and helps the reader to recognize that no easy judgments can be made.

Myers, Bernice. *The Apple War*. New York: Parents' Magazine Press, 1973. (Ages 4-8.)

Two kings prepare to fight a war over who owns the apples from a tree on the border of their countries, but the war is postponed to celebrate one king's birthday. They have so much fun at the party that the war is almost forgotten. The capriciousness of the kings and the unreality of the situation invite the reader to dismiss the story. But the ending warns of the consequences of a lack of a real settlement of conflict.

Nash, Ogden. *Everybody Ought to Know*. Philadelphia: Lippincott, 1961. (Ages 12–up.)
Should be read with an open eye and critical mind.

Oppenheim, Joanne. *On the Other Side of the River*. Illus. Aliki. New York: Franklin Watts, 1972. (Ages 5–8.)
Story of quarrel between the East and the West when a storm breaks down the bridge between them. Both are glad at first, then, realizing that they need each other, they rebuild the bridge and live together peacefully. Again, hardly believable, with too many questions left unanswered.

Patchen, Kenneth. *First Will and Testament*. Forest Hills, N.Y.: Padell, 1948. (Ages 12–up.)
Passionate and angry poetry, much of it concerning war.

Reiss, Johanna. *The Upstairs Room*. New York: Crowell, 1972. Pb. Bantam. (Ages 10–12.) (Newbery Honor Book.)
Annie is six years old at the beginning of the book, which spans seven years in Holland. She and her family are Jews. The story is similar to Anne Frank's, but most of the family survive. The story tells of the courage not only of the Jews but also of the Dutch people who risked their lives to help the Jews.

Remarque, Erich Maria. *All Quiet on the Western Front*. Boston: Little, Brown, 1929. Pb. Fawcett. (Ages 12–up.)
A story of the battles of World War I through the eyes of a group of German soldiers. A classic story about the senselessness of war.

Richter, Hans P. *Friedrich*. New York: Holt, Rinehart and Winston, 1970. Pb. Dell. (Ages 10–up.)
A novel dealing with the effect of war on the friendship between a Jewish family and a non-Jewish family in Germany during World War II. The book is unusual because it is told from the perspective of the German, non-Jewish boy.

————. *I Was There*. New York: Holt, Rinehart and Winston, 1962. Pb. Dell. (Ages 10–up.)
An autobiographical story of the induction of two boys into the

youth corps in Germany in World War II. The book deals with children's confusion over many issues of war.

Ringi, Kjell. *The Stranger*. New York: Random House, 1968. (Ages 3–7.)
A giant stranger causes uneasiness in a land of tiny people. When the people make war on the giant he cries, flooding the land until the people float to his face level. There they talk easily and make friends. One would wish that face-to-face communications such as these could result in happy endings.

———. *The Winner*. New York: Harper & Row, 1969. (Ages 3–6.)
A story about escalation and competition. The story deals with the ultimate absurdity of war. Although there are no words in this book, the message is powerful and could extend to readers well beyond age six.

Roberts, Margaret. *Stephanie's Children*. London: Victor Gollancz, 1969. (Ages 12–up.)
A book dealing with the effect of the Reign of Terror on individuals and families in France during the Revolution.

Rothman, Larry; Bamy, Jan; and Paquet, Basil T. *Winning Hearts and Minds, War Poems by Vietnam Veterans*. Brooklyn, N.Y.: First Casualty Press, 1972. (Ages 12–up.)
Uneven quality, but food for discussion.

Ryan, Cheli Durán. *Paz*. Illus. Nonny Hogrogian. New York: Macmillan, 1971. (Ages 6–8.)
Paz and his family are pacifists who own a house on the French and Spanish border. If one country is at war, they move to the other side of the house. When France and Spain fight each other, Paz declares his family independent. Many problems arise from this pacifist stance, but all ends well.

Sach, Marilyn. *A Pocket Full of Seeds*. Illus. Ben F. Stahl. Garden City, N.Y.: Doubleday, 1973. (Ages 9–12.)
Nicole and her family are French Jews. She is the only one of her family to escape capture by the Nazis. Readers are left knowing that Nicole will survive, but sharing her anxiety, uncertainty, and grief over the rest of her family.

Sechrist, Elizabeth Hough. *Poems for Red-Letter Days*. Philadelphia: Macrae Smith, 1951. (All ages.)
Traditional and out of date, but useful for comparison purposes.

Seredy, Kate. *The White Stag*. New York: Viking, 1937. (Ages 12–up.) (Newbery Medal.)
A historical Hungarian tale about the journeys and exploits of many

great leaders, including Attila the Hun. War is seen as inevitable and useful.

Speare, M. E. (ed.). *Pocket Book of Verse*. New York: Pocket Books, 1948. Pb. (Ages 12–up.)
Beautiful assortment.

Steele, William O. *The Perilous Road*. New York: Harcourt, Brace & World, 1958. Pb. also. (Ages 8–12.) (Newbery Honor Book.)
Chris learns a powerful lesson about right and wrong and the ugliness of war. Although this story takes no sides in the Civil War, it is told from the point of view of Chris, a young Southern boy who feels that the Confederate side is the right one.

Steichen, Edward. *The Family of Man*. New York: Simon and Schuster, 1956. (All ages.)
A photographic essay on human emotion and humanity. The section on war and its aftermath is particularly powerful.

Steig, William. *The Bad Island*. New York: Simon and Schuster, 1969. (Ages 6–10.)
Violent and ugly creatures who inhabit a violent and ugly island are constantly at war with one another. When, suddenly, flowers start growing on the island, it drives the creatures totally berserk; then they annihilate each other. Eventually, the flowers take over and the island becomes an uninhabited paradise. The story may be meant as a warning to people, but it is an unpleasant book to read.

Suhl, Yuri. *Uncle Misha's Partisans*. New York: Four Winds Press, 1973. (Ages 10–up.)   The story, which was inspired by an actual event, describes Jewish partisans in the Ukraine. The hero is Motile, who has been orphaned by the Nazis. He plays his violin well enough to use it as a weapon for sabotage. Although the book glorifies revenge and violence, it also portrays the ugliness of war. It presents a little-known fact of war — that of the active resistance of bands of Jews.

Tibbets, Alfred B. *American Heroes All*. Boston: Little, Brown, 1966. (Ages 12–up.)
Historical fiction dealing with the courage and determination of soldiers in all the American wars.

Tunis, John R. *His Enemy His Friend*. New York: Morrow, 1967. Pb. Avon. (Ages 12–up.)
A German soldier stationed in France is friendly with the French. He must decide between loyalty to country and friendship. Hope is expressed at the end when the countries begin to have peaceful

dealings with each other again. This book is more than a surface examination of the conflict arising out of war.

————. *Silence over Dunkerque*. New York: Morrow, 1962. (Ages 12–up.)
Adventure story of a British sergeant in France who fights courageously to lead his troops through Dunkerque during World War II.

Udry, Janice May. *Let's Be Enemies*. Illus. Maurice Sendak. New York: Harper & Row, 1961. Pb. Scholastic. (Ages 5–8.)
Two boys, who were once close friends, fight and become enemies. They each think the other is wrong. They never resolve their conflict but resume their friendship, nevertheless. Discussions of this book can lead to suggestions for resolving personal conflicts.

Untermeyer, Louis (ed.). *The Golden Treasury of Poetry*. Illus. Joan Walsh Anglund. New York: Golden Press, 1959. (Ages 8–up.)
An excellent starter collection of different kinds of poems.

Van Stockum, Hilda. *The Borrowed House*. New York: Farrar, Straus & Giroux, 1975. (Ages 12–up.)
Janna is a member of the Hitler Youth. Her parents, German actors, are in Holland. When she is required to join them, she begins to learn that there are other, conflicting ideas from the ones she has been trained to believe in the Hitler Youth. A somewhat oversimplified and melodramatic story, but one that presents an interesting perspective.

Volavkova, Hana. *I Never Saw Another Butterfly (Children's Drawings and Poems from Terezin Concentration Camp, 1942–44)*. New York: McGraw-Hill, 1962. (All ages.)
Though Terezin was a way station to an extermination center, these poems deal with life, happiness, love, and freedom. A powerful indictment of war.

Wahl, Jan. *How the Children Stopped the Wars*. Illus. Mitchell Miller. New York: Farrar, Straus & Giroux, 1969. Pb. Avon. (Ages 8–12.)
An allegory of children marching to stop war. There is some unexplained mysticism in this uneven and thin book.

Whittier, John Greenleaf. "Barbara Frietchie" (poem), in *The Charge of the Light Brigade*. New York: Scholastic, 1969. Pb. (Ages 9–up.)
One person's view of history. Very useful for discussion.

Wondriska, William. *John John Twilliger*. New York: Holt, Rinehart and Winston, 1966. Pb. also. (Ages 7–9.)
A terrible dictator rules the town, forbidding any dancing, friendship, or pets. John John, through kindness and cleverness, changes

the situation for the better. The assumption in this book is that even villains and dictators are human and potentially reachable.

Yolen, Jane. *The Minstrel and the Mountain*. Illus. Anne Rockwell. Cleveland: World, 1967. (Ages 5–9.)
The story of two foolish kings who are jealous of each other because one can see the sunset from his kingdom, and the other can see the sunrise. A wise, peace-loving minstrel solves the problem and prevents a war.

Young, Rodney L. *Old Abe: The Eagle Hero*. Englewood Cliffs, N.J.: Prentice-Hall, 1965. Pb. also. (Ages 5–9.)
The story of the courage and inspiration of an eagle who is sent to help the North during the Civil War.

Zimnik, Reiner. *The Crane*. (Trans. from the German by Nina Ignatowicz and F. N. Monjo.) New York: Harper & Row, 1970. (Ages 8–up.)
A very complex allegory of war and society. Many abstract symbols are used in this book, which probably would confuse a young reader.

Zolotow, Charlotte. *The Hating Book*. Illus. Ben Shecter. New York: Harper & Row, 1969. Pb. Scholastic. (Ages 3–8.)
Two girls who are friends have a misunderstanding but settle it in a peaceful fashion. This story makes a good discussion starter on the topic of personal conflict.

NOTES and ADDITIONS

6

Sex

SEX EDUCATION has not yet become a comfortable topic in either schools or libraries. Almost everyone agrees that there should be some instruction on this topic for young children; but when it comes to specifically determining Who, What, Where, When, and How, opinions vary widely. Some parents object to having the topic mentioned at school, while others wish that the schools would totally handle the instruction. Most parents want to have a say in the manner of the instruction. Most libraries, recognizing the controversial nature of the information, either maintain shelves "by permission only" or simply do not purchase the controversial literature.

At present, children receive their sex instruction in a variety of ways. They sometimes learn about the process in a

145

totally satisfactory manner from their parents who are knowledgeable and comfortable in their beliefs and attitudes. They are sometimes helped in their search for answers by sympathetic and informed teachers, counselors, or friends. They can also acquire needed information from unembarrassed librarians who know what the resources are and how to handle them. But most of the time they acquire most of their information, both accurate and inaccurate, from their peers. They also seem to be adept at acquiring pornographic materials aimed at titillation rather than education. Much of their informal education comes from movies and television, and much comes from the fiction that they read, which is not consciously trying to instruct in matters sexual but which succeeds in imparting many lessons.

Few communities can arrive at consensus in determining the approach, set of values, and even quantity of information that they are willing to have their children exposed to. The dilemma, then, remains. How can an interested, positive, supportive adult communicate the necessary information to inquisitive young people? What information is necessary? Where can the materials be found? What steps can be taken to help young people feel comfortable about the topic and informed enough to behave responsibly? What values are valid for contemporary times? Before attempting to answer these questions, it would be useful for adults to examine their own attitudes and values.

▶ Try This

Answer the following questions as honestly as you can. Do not share the answers with anyone unless you want to.

What was the primary source of most of your information about sex? Your parents? Teachers? Books? Peers? Experience? Other?

How much time elapsed between your learning about puberty and the onset of puberty for you?

How well prepared did you consider yourself to handle the new situations and physical conditions imposed by puberty?

How did you feel about your body when you were a teen-ager?

How do you feel about your body now?

What is your opinion about premarital or extramarital sex for yourself? for an eventual (or current) spouse? for your children (if you have any or will have any)? for other people?

How linked do you think sex and love should be? for men? for women?

How "special" do you consider sexual intercourse to be in a relationship between two people?

What is your opinion of homosexuality?

What is your definition of pornography?

What, if any, are your personal rules about sex?

What are your opinions about masturbation?

What, if any, taboos do you hold for yourself?

How do you react to "dirty" jokes? to X-rated films?

How generalized or universal would you like your attitudes to be?
How do you feel about people who disagree with you?

Who do you feel should be responsible for educating children about sex?

When do you believe sex education should begin?

Attitudes play an important role in determining the quality of education, no matter what the content. In trying to teach children what we want them to know about sex, our attitudes and theirs come very strongly into play — but our feelings are colored by our knowledge and experience. Some of us are afraid that our students or children know more about sex than we do; we even suspect that some of them have a very active acquaintance with information that we are not even aware of. Further, we wonder where direct information about sexuality and sex practices should begin and where it should end. Some people believe that instruction ends with marriage. Some think that it should stop when a person has experienced intercourse. (After all, what more would anyone need to know?)

At a conference of publishers, educators, counselors, and representatives from various religious organizations, consensus was reached about several courses of action to follow. It was agreed that any material aiming to instruct about sex should stress the broad range of sexual behavior and responses in human relationships, not only those pieces of behavior labeled sex acts. Thus, sexuality rather than sex should be emphasized. Current research in physiological responses, family relations, education, and psychology should be taken into consideration in any program of instruction. But an overemphasis on physiology and too much duplication of already known facts should be avoided. The conference participants agreed that this kind of education should be perceived as a developmental program based on acknowledged human sexual conditions and needs from birth to old age. (See *Publishers Weekly* article in References.)

Mary S. Calderone, for many years the director of the Sex Information and Education Council (SIECUS), advises that we affirm the presence of sexuality in all human beings as a developing and continuing force from birth to death. She quotes Wallace Fulton, one of the founders of SIECUS, as stating that the intent of this organization is "to establish sexuality as a health entity, and to dignify it by openness of approach." (*Sex Education and the Schools*, p. 3) Most educators agree that this healthy and positive attitude toward sex is necessary in any program of sex education.

The content of sex education is important. For adolescents in particular, whose formal sex instruction is too often linked with units on drugs, crime, and other abuses, instruction on sex should be integrated into the regular curriculum. For very young children, this integration is also important. It is, indeed, an important factor to be considered, no matter what the age of the student. Adults generally manage to read and learn more about sex in the context of their normal living; they do not separate this learning into a compartment. Books that present sex in the light of normal and positive human interaction generally are regarded as the most positive influences.

Even after it is accepted that sexuality and learning about sex are appropriate to all ages, the specific question of direct, formal instruction remains. How can the questions of a very young child who cannot yet read be handled? How much information is appropriate for a nine-year-old? How can positive values and behaviors be presented in a manner acceptable to a twelve-year-old? How can we, as adults, insure that we are up to date in our information? How can we test that our values and our personal behavior are constructive?

▶ Try This

Do this activity with a group of classmates or colleagues. Without signing your name, list three questions that you still have regarding sex or sexuality. Your questions may pertain to physiological facts about your own body or that of someone of the opposite sex. Your questions may be about sensations, process, or myths. They may reflect a desire to clarify or to be initially informed.

Place your questions in a box. Draw out the questions one at a time. Who, in the group, has some answers? What sources can you find, in addition to peers, that can provide answers? Answer, or attempt to answer, every question in this box. How comfortable is the group with this procedure?

Once a procedure is established for the continued education of adults, it is easier to address the education of children. Comfort with the information as well as with the emotions is very useful and constructive.

The presentation of information about sex varies according to the developmental level of the student. Infants and very young children receive most of their ideas from experiencing the way that people interact in front of them and with them. A child who is accustomed to seeing his parents in affectionate embraces will probably feel differently about his or her own sexuality than does a child whose family is carefully undemonstrative. Children receive many messages from the way adults respond to their games of "Doctor." Adult reactions to children's masturbating also teach lessons. The pattern of how adults answer children's questions in general will guide children to what specific questions that they can risk asking about sex. Adult conversations overheard by children also form a powerful part of the informal educational system. Comments about the behavior of married couples, reactions to films and television, and responses to the way that other adults dress and behave are materials for sex instruction.

Most educators, counselors, and psychologists, as well as religious advisers, agree that it is important for the adult to help the child feel comfortable with his or her sexuality, curiosity, and behavior. A guilty or furtive feeling because of sexual activity is not helpful. The experts also advise that adults take into consideration the child's physical, intellectual, and emotional development in determining the extent of the information to be given in response to specific questions. The joke is told of young Johnny's coming home and asking his mother, "Mommy, where did I come from?" whereupon mother launches into an elaborate and detailed description from the progress of the egg to possible positions for intercourse. After a long lecture, during which time the child listens attentively, the mother asks for the child's further questions. "Well," says he, "Timothy comes from Baltimore, and I still don't know where I come from." On the other hand, when children do ask us pointed and specific questions, we should not try to evade them or give them incomplete answers. When they ask how the sperm and egg got together, they really do want to know about intercourse.

Reproduction education is not all there is to sex education. The facts of reproduction are, of course, an important element, but human beings engage in sexual activity for reasons in addition to the desire to have children. Further, not all sexual activity includes intercourse. Children want to know about their bodies, how they are constructed, and why. They want to know about the opposite sex. They want to be reassured that they are normal. And they need to grow to accept themselves, their bodies, and their functions with ease and self-liking. An era of Freudian education, which has taught that sex is at the root of all negative behavior, has done some damage. Many adults need to reexamine their own feelings about sex; they must refrain from imposing their miseducation on children.

Of primary importance in any program of education is the interaction between the learners and the teachers. Good sex education programs benefit from discussions among peer groups and adult leaders, parents, counselors, teachers, and any other interested adults. Multiaged sessions among students are not recommended because of the readiness of some children to acquire greater detail than others, and because it is generally acknowledged that the younger children are usually satisfied with briefer answers than the older ones are. William A. Block, a doctor specializing in sex education, identifies three developmental levels of sexuality: the dormant stage, the awakened period, and the active stage. He assigns age levels to these stages; but, as with any developmental concept, the ages will vary according to the group and the individual. He suggests that the first stage lasts until age nine, the second until age fourteen, and the third to age nineteen. He does not mention adults because his primary interest is in providing a public school program of sex education for its students. Block (see References) advises adults to take the stage of the child into consideration whenever questions need answering. He asserts that in the dormant stage, children are very inquisitive but have not become intensely concerned about sex. The time of greatest preoccupation is during the awareness period, when sexual curiosity and exploration are high. He believes that this is, perhaps, the most critical time for education.

Most adults draw upon books and other materials to help them in their explanations. Many children actively seek out books and other references to help guide them in their quest for information. There are many books now sold that have, as their primary intent, the proper sexual instruction of young children. There is an equally great number of books that instruct without, perhaps, intending to do so. The first category of books is usually in the realm of nonfiction; the second, of course, lies within fiction and fantasy. But all nonfiction is not necessarily successful in teaching the lessons that it purports to communicate. Values and attitudes lie close to the surface, coming through the factual information. Adults and children should be aware of these hidden messages and should respond to them knowingly.

In recent years numerous books have been directed toward a very young audience of preschool and primary school children. Authors and publishers have recognized that children become interested in matters sexual before their teen-age years. Some of the books are consciously written for the parent to serve as interpreter to the young child. The books represent a wide range of attitudes, values, and information and can be used as valuable tools for education.

Many sources exist with the specific intent of sex education. Most of these sources are nonfiction and obviously didactic. The illustrations vary from an approach that is carefully objective, with clinical diagrams unattached to human bodies, through romanticized, sweet paintings of affectionate parents and amiable babies, to explicit cartoons or photographs depicting sex play and intercourse. The written texts are equally as varied, including dry, detailed scientific descriptions, sentimental descriptions and euphemisms substituting for anatomical labels, and slyly humorous observations phrased in vernacular terminology.

How can these books be made available to a wide audience? If schools do not have copies or if the general public is unaware that a copy may be found in their municipal library, how can the books be used? One of the aims of this chapter is to acquaint concerned adults with the variety, intent, styles, and general usefulness of such books; it is thus hoped that the adults may acquire the resources to help young readers seek out the appropriate tools of instruction. Perhaps greater adult familiarity and comfort with the materials will help to remove the restrictions that are often unnecessarily imposed.

Suggested Criteria

Whether or not the intent is didactic, books communicating information about sex should take into consideration the readers' developmental level. An appropriate amount of information should be transmitted, not an overload or insufficient facts. Both conditions cause anxiety. Whatever information is included should be accurate, with carefully selected terminology. Some books consciously use vernacular terms because their intent is to eliminate some of the mystery and high-handedness that some adults communicate, while others use the vernacular to demonstrate to their readers that they, the authors, are on the young people's level. Some authors, fearing that clinical terms will confuse the child, use euphemistic language in order to romanticize or idealize sex. Too often the euphemism is confusing, instead. This author prefers accurate, dictionary terms to either the vernacular or the euphemistic. But if the vocabulary suits the presentation, then that vocabulary can be judged appropriate.

The approach should maintain dignity. Distortions in the guise of humor should be avoided. If the main intent of the authors is to alleviate the solemnity of many presentations and to inject a light-hearted attitude, the material should, nevertheless, be accurately communicated. A balanced, neither dour nor caricatured, presentation is preferable.

Values should be communicated clearly with the authors' acknowledgment of the intent. But books should indicate that there are many attitudes and sets of values towards sex and should not impart feelings of guilt if the readers disagree with the message of the book. No book can be acceptable to all people; no book should attempt to make all readers conform to its point of view. Moralizing about behavior is usually not so useful in books as indicating consequences of various behaviors. Care should be taken to avoid perpetuating myths, since values based on mythology have little chance of lasting.

Books should acknowledge and value sexuality in all human beings; sexual activity should not be relegated to young adults. Enjoyment should be presented as well as problems. Sex should be part of healthy living rather than a problem, but when problems are presented, they should be realistic. The solutions should also be feasible rather than contrived or romanticized. The "happy ending" should not always culminate in marriage.

Sex education should be more than reproduction education. If the intent is to communicate only the facts of birth, then there should at least be an indication to the reader that there is more to be learned. Care should be taken to include a discussion of the role and function of both sexes; for example, fathers should not be left out of the birth process. In books giving sexual information, both sexes should be invited to learn; boys are inquisitive about girls, and girls, about boys. In books addressed to either sex, facts about both sexes should appear.

Stereotypes about the interest, arousability, capability, and behavior of males and females should be avoided. Expectations that marriage is the aim of every girl and that all couples will want to have children should also be handled as opinion rather than rule. Care should be taken to label opinion as such; far too many books present their view of morality as the only proper way. Illustrations should take into account the injunction against stereotypes; multiethnic characters should people these books.

Prurient or demeaning humor should be avoided. Books with titillation as the intent are in danger of imparting negative and uncomfortable lessons rather than constructive ones. The aim of sex education materials should be to make each reader comfortable and informed about his or her sexuality and the processes of sex.

Discussion of Children's Books

BOOKS FOR YOUNG CHILDREN (To Age Eight)

Most books for young children concerned with sex education describe the birth process. They rarely take into consideration the other aspects of sexuality in a child's life. John Steptoe's *My Special Best Words* is one of the exceptions. In this book, three-year-old Bweela lives with her one-year-old brother and their father. Bweela tries to toilet-train her brother, and the two children romp together in the bathroom. They are comfortable with their bodies. The illustrations help to convey the sense of joy and comfort with themselves and each other. As usual, Steptoe is educational at the same time that he is disturbing the complacency of some of the reading public.

The illustrations in Sara Bonnett Stein's *Making Babies* are the most important feature of the book. They are beautiful and informative photographs, showing the universality of sexual curiosity, and reactions to pregnancy and birth. The text, directed toward parents of very young children, is useful, and the suggestions for activities that parents and children can do together to help the communication process are very helpful. The text for the children is not as good. There is the assumption conveyed that all normal boys and girls want to grow up to be parents. There is also the statement that dogs mating are "loving each other." But, despite these minor flaws, the book's intention to help the education process of children as young as three years of age is carried out reasonably well.

Another book designed for very young children, Andry and Schepp's *How Babies Are Made*, is also very useful. Although flowers and animals are discussed in addition to human beings, this information does not become confusing. The context is always in terms of the child's wanting to know. The illustrations are pleasant and attractive combinations of paper sculpture; they do not caricature or demean. The text, which is clear and nonmoralizing, uses terminology that is not complex, but it is accurate.

In direct contrast to *How Babies Are Made* is Pearl S. Buck's *Johnny Jack and His Beginnings*. Perhaps it is unfair to compare a book written in 1954 with one written in 1968. But both books are available on library shelves. *Johnny Jack and His Beginnings* is supposedly intended for children aged seven to ten, but that age group would be less likely to look at the book than younger children would. Even for younger audiences, the sentimental, obtuse explanation is inappropriate. Not only are terms presented that are confusing (the vaginal canal is called "the gate of life"), but the expectations of the roles of the family are clearly sexist. The baby is a girl, and the mother is judged to have had a successful experience because the baby is pretty.

Deliberately and successfully avoiding sexist implications is the book by Sol and Judith Gordon entitled *Did the Sun Shine Before You Were Born?* Incidentally included in the illustrations are children engaged in different kinds of activities that are not stereotypically sex-linked. Love and affection are illustrated. Options for different life styles are presented as normal and viable, with choices presented in many forms. Different ethnic groups are pictured. The entire book presents a balanced, positive, healthy view of life and sex.

Unfortunately, otherwise excellent books often miss the opportunity to educate readers to a balanced sex-role perspective. Paul Showers's *A Baby Starts to Grow* and Eva Knox Evans's *The Beginnings of Life: How Babies Are Born* both contribute accuracy and useful details, but both of them imply that the main role of the father is to stand and wait. Perhaps readers should write to the publishers suggesting that these books be revised in light of contemporary needs. Parents would do well to guide their children in the reading of these books so that questions will be encouraged and answers provided.

One book useful for the prompting of questions is supposedly designed for seven- to ten-year-olds. But *The Birth of Sunset's Kittens*, by Carla Stevens, could easily be absorbed and enjoyed by younger children, especially if interested adults are present to provide direction. The photographs help to satisfy curiosity in a socially acceptable way. The vocabulary is informative and nonthreatening. Uterus, amnion, placenta, and umbilical cord are described; but for some inexplicable reason, the vagina is described as "a special opening" without ever saying that it is a vagina. Nevertheless, the book is clear and informational enough to be useful with a wide variety of children.

BOOKS FOR OLDER CHILDREN

Nonfiction. Most of the books for children seven years of age and older recognize that the children will be interested in detail and description of the sex act as well as of the process of birth. Most of these books also take into consideration the questions of approaching puberty. The methods of presentation vary widely in the factual books: depending on the particular intent and point of view of the authors, the books range from objective, almost clinical presentations to intensely personal, free, catering-to-the-voyeur approach.

Show Me: A Picture Book of Sex for Children and Parents, by Fleischhauer-Hardt and Davies, is an oversized photographic essay containing explicit pictures of nude people engaging in several forms of sex play. The book, which originated in Germany, reflects a European approach to sex education. Recognizing the explosive potential of the book, the publishers are currently permitting its sale only on the East and West coasts of the United States. It is unlikely that libraries or public schools will purchase it, but some private schools and certainly many adults will buy the book. The authors of the book give very direct advice to parents as to how to use the book with children. They explain that if parents are troubled by the photographs or by the information conveyed in the book, something is wrong with the parents' attitude. No doubt the authors are sincere in their belief, which advocates a free and uninhibited casual approach to sex with the removal of mystery and secrecy. Those readers who agree with them will find the book very useful, while those readers who disagree would do well to see the book to decide how and why it is upsetting or distasteful to them.

This author would not use the book with young children for several reasons. Intolerant of people who disagree with them, the authors try to convey guilt feelings to those adults who hold different values. Further, their use of ridiculing humor, possibly to offset the serious topic, appears out of place and tends toward the prurient. Perhaps, most important, it is this author's opinion that too much information is conveyed through the pictures that will be threatening to young children. Activities are pictured that take place between much older people. The sex is on an advanced level. There is, however, not enough information about young children and their sexuality. While some attention is paid to prepubescent anatomy and to practices such as masturbation, the emphasis is on mature bodies and advanced sex play. The photographs imply responsibilities that may make the young intended audience overly anxious.

Peter Mayle's *Where Did I Come From?* also attempts to lighten the topic with humor. The illustrations are somewhat grotesque cartoons, displaying a fat man and woman — he with a very long penis; and she with great bulging breasts. Mayle's explanations strive for commonplace analogies, ostensibly so that children will be able to understand the concepts. Some readers may appreciate this attempt and agree that intercourse can be described by tickling and wiggling, and that an orgasm is somewhat similar to a sneeze. This author prefers more objective descriptions, with more options for individual interpretation and response. Further, Mayle implies that intercourse always ends in mutual orgasm and that it is always for the purpose of reproduction. The seemingly simplistic explanations carry with them many questions. That is fine; questions should be encouraged. But this book can be very misleading, and it is hoped that children will know how to find the questions that will provide them with useful answers.

Another book that attempts to talk to the children on a level that is not clinical or patronizing, and that sets the same tone as the above two books, is Hansen and Jensen's *The Little Red Schoolbook*. This book, written in vernacular language, helps the reader to expand his or her vocabulary of "street" terms. It does not generally explain sexual processes objectively, because it is calculated to make the reader do away with any guilt feelings. It attempts to convey a light and casual attitude toward sex. It may make the child who has not experienced the feelings and acts described in the book feel somewhat abnormal. The authors attempt to be at the children's level and, in doing so, lose some credibility. But the book is helpful in responding to questions and in demonstrating that there are different points of view about sex.

Wardell Pomeroy's books, *Boys and Sex* and *Girls and Sex*, are direct and frank. Pomeroy is addressing twelve-year-old readers and older. He is treating topics that concern them now, not those that they will have to postpone. He speaks about masturbation, sex play, homosexuality, petting, dating, and other questions, including intercourse. He expresses his opinions, but labels them as such and indicates his rationale.

Eric Johnson's book, *Love and Sex in Plain Language*, is exactly what the title promises. Dealing with personal and social values and with the pleasure of sex as well as some of the problems — it stresses personal responsibility on the part of each individual. The book is aimed at readers as young as ten years of age. It speaks frankly but in a calm and reassuring tone. It is a very helpful book.

Fiction.   As has been stated many times, works of fiction, particularly if they are well crafted, can convey lessons more effectively than can many books calculated to teach. The lessons may be unintentional on the part of the author, but they are learned, nevertheless, by impressionable readers. In recent years, fiction has included such previously taboo topics as premarital sex, sex play, homosexuality, and even incest.

The hint of incest occurs in Elizabeth Winthrop's *A Little Demonstration of Affection*. But it turns out that what Jennie fears as an abnormal, incestuous desire is, in reality, a simple craving for some physical familial affection. Jennie's family is singularly undemonstrative. A hug from her brother is enough to make Jennie react so strongly as to imagine all sorts of peculiarities about herself. Jennie is finally helped by her father to understand that her feelings are normal.

Both *I'll Get There. It Better Be Worth the Trip*, by John Donovan, and *The Man Without a Face*, by Isabelle Holland, deal briefly with homosexuality. In each case, the hero, a young teen-ager, fears that he has homosexual tendencies. In each case, an older male reassures the hero that love for another male is normal and need not develop into a homosexual relationship. Books of fiction and nonfiction maintain the attitude that homosexuality is to be avoided at almost all cost, and that homosexuals are "sick" people. The two above-mentioned books handle the situation in a fairly reasonable manner, but the societal fear comes through clearly.

Menstruation is a favorite topic in novels written for readers ten years of age and up. It is seldom that the heroine is permitted to accept and deal with the onset of menstruation in a calm and informed fashion. It becomes a competition to see who will begin menstruating first in Judy Blume's *Are You There God? It's Me, Margaret*. There is so much pressure placed on these girls to grow up that one girl actually lies about having her period in order to be "one-up" on her friends. Self-image hangs desperately on size of breasts and condition of puberty in this story.

Readers should probably be guided through this book by concerned adults. Perhaps a question box could be set up into which readers of this and any other book could place their questions. Several small-group sessions might be organized to answer the questions. It would be useful if the teacher read the questions first and came prepared with some sources of answers.

Menstruation is a fearsome and confusing experience in Lucille Clifton's *The Times They Used to Be*. When thirteen-year-old Tassie begins to menstruate, she thinks that it is "sin" breaking out of her body. She feels she must repent of she knows not what, but is convinced she is being punished. She has had no prior information about her body or anything sexual.

Judy Blume presents the problems of boys and their entry into puberty in *Then Again, Maybe I Won't*. Tony has nocturnal emissions and views a female neighbor in the nude. But the information in this book remains at a surface level. The question box may help in dealing with this book, but more likely some simple discussion groups in which young people compare their own experiences and feelings would be more helpful.

Norma Klein presents changing but still unconventional attitudes in two of her books, *Mom, the Wolf Man and Me* and *It's Not What You Expect*. Klein is always direct in her books; she does not deal in subtlety. In *Mom, the Wolf Man and Me*, the young heroine's mother has never been married and Brett does not want her to be. Brett, whose image of marriage is negative, fears that she and her mother will change and become stereotypes if her mother marries. She indicates comfort with sexual information, having learned all about it at school. She and her mother have a frank, open relationship in which her mother answers all her questions honestly.

In *It's Not What You Expect*, sex is again handled casually. One of the characters becomes pregnant and undergoes an abortion as a logical matter of course. Everyone knows about it and accepts it comfortably. The mother mentions that times have changed since she had *her* abortion, before she was married to the children's father and when she was dating another man. The father's extramarital episode is tolerated. This book can raise some questions about expected modes of behavior and different life styles. For fun, students can place the setting of this book in Victorian times to see how that would influence the behavior of the characters. Or students can take each character separately, saying how they would behave in contemporary times if they were in the character's place.

Honor Arundel also discusses controversial sexual behavior in her novels — but she presents the consequences. She also describes the motivations and situations leading up to the problems that arise. In *The*

Longest Weekend Eileen is an unwed mother. Her mother is understanding to the point of taking over the care and love of the child. The author attempts to remain nonjudgmental, but in the end Eileen marries Joel, the father of the child. A number of issues arise here for fruitful discussion. The students can discuss "Who was right?" They can decide what they would have done in Joel's or Eileen's place. They can discuss the book with their parents and ask what their parents would have done in the circumstances that the book describes.

Any discussion of sex is more valuable if parents and children can talk together. Situations can be arranged for peers to have discussions under the guidance or direction of a knowledgeable adult. But, in the long run, parents and children should understand and respect each other's points of view and come to terms with their value systems. Books can help. They can be vehicles for understanding and exploration, but they cannot take the place of close, supportive family interaction. Librarians, teachers, parents, and counselors can accumulate materials which present different approaches and convey an assortment of attitudes in order to have resources on which to base their discussions. No matter what emerges as the selected set of values, it cannot help but be more constructive if it has been influenced by accurate information and by an increased awareness and appreciation of human sexuality.

REFERENCES

Block, William A. *What Your Child Really Wants to Know About Sex and Why*. Englewood Cliffs, N.J.: Prentice-Hall, 1972.
  A straightforward presentation, stressing the importance of recognizing children's sexuality. Although the author's Freudian orientation sometimes intrudes, his advice is generally practical. He divides children's development of sexuality into three stages: the dormant period, age five to nine; the awakened period, age ten to fourteen; and the active period, age fifteen to nineteen. He recommends patterns of answers to questions about sex depending on the stage of the child. The author also suggests some useful activities for the classroom.

Breasted, Mary. "Nothing but the Facts — of Life," *New York Times Book Review*, Sept. 23, 1973, p. 8.
  Prefers good fiction to manuals for learning about sex. Reviews three books: *Where Do Babies Come From?* by Sheffield; *The True Story of How Babies Are Made*, by Knudsen; and *Where Did I Come From?*, by Mayle.

Brewer, Joan Scherer. "A Guide to Sex Education Books: Dick Active, Jane Passive," *Interracial Books for Children Bulletin*, Vol. 6. Nos. 3 and 4 (1975), 1, 12, 13.
  An excellent analysis of the general attitude that books convey about sex. Brewer criticizes the maintenance of the expectation of a passive role for females. She points out the negative way that homosexuality is

discussed and comments that bisexuality is rarely discussed. Brewer reviews fifteen sex education books; her comments are incisive and informative.

Child Study Association of America. *What To Tell Your Child About Sex*, revised edition. New York: Pocket Books, 1974. Pb.

Discusses sexual development in children up to age seventeen. Excellent explanations presented in nonjudgmental fashion. Useful annotated bibliography. Provides list of questions and answers. An excellent resource.

del Solar, Charlotte. *Parents' Answer Book*. New York: Grosset and Dunlap, 1969.

Poses questions and supplies answers. Presents myths and helps substitute reality. The questions have been asked by children; the answers indicated often provide choices, depending on the situation. A useful book.

Feingold, Maxine. "A Content Analysis of Materials for the Early Sex Education of Children," unpublished Master's Report, Palmer Graduate Library School, Long Island University, Brookville, N.Y., 1969.

Cites many authorities on developmental aspects of sex. Describes the attributes of sexual development for three stages: three- to four-year-olds, five- to eight-year-olds, and nine- to twelve-year-olds. Recommends that concerned adults make themselves knowledgeable about the stages in order to help select useful materials for helping children understand sex.

Frank, Josette. "Sexuality in Books for Children," pp. 168–70 in *Issues in Children's Book Selection*. New York: R. R. Bowker, 1973.

Questions what is the appropriate age level for fiction treating sex explicitly. Lists criteria for acceptable books as integrity of purpose, authenticity, moral and social validity, and resolutions offered. Praises several books and suggests that parents, teachers, and librarians recommend acceptable books to young readers.

Gerhardt, Lillian N. "Review of Peter Mayle's *Where Did I Come From?*," *School Library Journal*, Vol. 20, No. 5 (January 1974), 42.

The review is amusing and perceptive. Gerhardt criticizes the book as inaccurate and misleading.

Grannis, Chandler B. "Publishers Can Play a Key Role in Sex Education," *Publishers Weekly*, Vol. 203, No. 11 (March 12, 1973), 30–31.

A report of a conference combining religious leaders, SIECUS representatives, and publishers' representatives to set guidelines for publishing information about sex. Consensus was that sexuality should be stressed rather than sex. Sexuality includes "love, intimacy, fidelity, family life" and the way that people regard themselves physically.

Hilu, Virginia (ed.). *Sex Education and the Schools*, New York: Harper & Row, 1967.

Although this book is almost ten years old, it is timely and useful now. The contributors, Mary Calderone, Alan Guttmacher, Millicent McIntosh, and Richard Unesworth, engage in conversation with one another, offering their recommendations for healthy conveying of information and attitude about sex.

Mercer, Joan Bodger. "Innocence Is a Cop-Out," *Wilson Library Bulletin*, Vol. 46, No. 2 (October 1971), 144–46.

Pleads for recognition that children are reading books at a young age and understanding them, even when topics such as sex and drugs are included. Asks adults not to pretend innocence.

Minnesota Council on Family Relations. *Family Life Literature and Films: An Annotated Bibliography*, 1972.

Massive annotated bibliography containing references for adults and children on all aspects of sex education as well as other topics relating to family life.

Neufeld, John. "The Thought, Not Necessarily the Deed: Sex in Some of Today's Juvenile Novels," *Wilson Library Bulletin*, Vol 46, No. 2 (October 1971), 147–52.

Asks authors to write about the whole child, including acknowledgment of sexuality. Praises honesty in books for young people.

Powers, G. Pat, and Baskin, Wade. *Sex Education: Issues and Directions*. New York: Philosophical Library, 1969.

A book of readings including many different points of view. Representatives of many institutions, attitudes, and professions have contributed offerings. Useful sources are listed. Many options are presented.

Stanek, Lou Willett. "The Maturation of the Junior Novel: From Gestation to the Pill," pp. 174–81, in *Issues in Children's Book Selection*. New York: R. R. Bowker, 1973.

Presents the difficulties in writing about the adolescent's sexual drive. Analyzes the formula upon which most junior novels are based and criticizes most contemporary books for following the standard formula.

Uslander, Arlene S. "Everything You've Always Wanted to Know About Sex Education," *Learning*, Vol. 3, No. 2 (October 1974), 34–41.

Useful advice and discussion about how to respond to children's questions in the classroom.

Wersba, Barbara. "Sexuality in Books for Children," pp. 171–73 in *Issues in Children's Book Selection*. New York: R. R. Bowker, 1973.

Wants to see more recognition of enjoyment of sexuality in children's books from picture books to novels for young adults. Accuses books of presenting "the Old Morality disguised as the New Sex."

White, Eula T., and Friedman, Roberta. "Sex Is Not a Four-Letter Word," *Wilson Library Bulletin*, Vol. 46, No. 2 (October 1971), 153–62.

The authors discuss sex education programs in schools and recommend a long list of useful references directed at the teen-ager. A very useful article.

Wolkstein, Diane. "Old and New Sexual Messages in Fairy Tales," *Wilson Library Bulletin*, Vol. 46, No. 2 (October 1971), 163–66.

Interprets a number of fairy tales as exploring sexuality and responding to sexual needs. Recommends that new tales show sexuality and sensuality as important factors of life.

Andry, Andrew C., and Schepp, Steven. *How Babies Are Made*. Illus. Blake Hampton. New York: Time-Life Books, 1968. (Ages 3–10.)
Designed for children, this book with colorful pictures starts with flowers and animals and then discusses human reproduction. The pictures are a combination of cartoon and collage. They are not at all demeaning or tending to caricature. The text contains accurate information, gently and objectively conveyed. A widely useful book.

Arundel, Honor. *The Longest Weekend*. New York: Thomas Nelson, 1969. (Ages 12–up.)
Story of Eileen, a young, unwed mother struggling with her parents' wishes and her own feelings and desires. The author is not judgmental, but the happy ending is that Eileen and Joel (the father of the child) marry. Interesting complications and realistic dialogue make this a good book for discussion.

Bendick, Jeanne. *What Made You You?* New York: McGraw-Hill, 1971. (Ages 5–7.)
A straightforward book for small children dealing with birth, conception, and growth.

Blume, Judy. *Are You There God? It's Me, Margaret*. New York: Bradbury Press, 1970. Pb. Dell. (Ages 10–up.)
Margaret is twelve. She and her friends are preoccupied with their physical maturity. They all wish they had large breasts, and were attractive to boys. The attitudes of most of the characters are sexist. The relations between the boys and girls are awkward and strained. The text is very explicit about the physical description of menstruation. But it does not link it usefully to a more than surface explanation of the process. The book might appeal to girls and boys who are concerned about their appearance and their maturity (or lack of it).

———. *Then Again, Maybe I Won't*. New York: Bradbury Press, 1973. Pb. Dell (Ages 10–up.)
Tony is a young adolescent learning how to deal responsibly with life and with his new sexual feelings. Blume is again very explicit about young people's fears and curiosity. Her explanations and descriptions remain surface-level.

Buck, Pearl S. *Johnny Jack and His Beginnings*. Illus. Kurt Werth. New York: John Day, 1954. (Ages 7–10.)
Somewhat obtuse explanation of birth. Terms are ameliorated (the vaginal canal is called "the gate of life"). Sexist in its attitudes.

161

Clifton, Lucille. *The Times They Used to Be*. Illus. Susan Jeschler. New York: Holt, Rinehart and Winston, 1974. (Ages 10–up.)
Tassie, thirteen years old, knows nothing about sex. When she begins menstruating, she thinks that it is "sin" breaking out of her body. Her friend, Sylvia (the narrator of the story), is also ignorant. Finally, Sylvia's mother explains about menstruation to both of them. The explanation is not given in the text. The clearest point is that ignorance leads to fear and misinterpretation.

Day, Beth, and Liley, Margaret, M.D. *The Secret World of the Baby*. Photographs by Hennert Nilsson, Suzanne Szasz *et al*. New York: Random House, 1968. (Ages 10–up.)
A well-illustrated account of the physiological and psychological development of a child from conception to several years after birth.

DeSchweinitz, Karl. *Growing Up*, 4th edition. New York: Macmillan, 1965. (Ages 7–11.)
A detailed and informative book on how babies are born. Uses animals as examples, but relates these directly to humans. Photographs and drawings are used as illustrations. The terminology is accurate and not overpowering, but author communicates that reproduction is the reason for sexual intercourse. He also states that people marry those whom they wish to be the parent of their children. Aside from these statements, the book is universally useful.

Donovan, John. *I'll Get There. It Better Be Worth the Trip*. New York: Harper & Row, 1969. Pb. Dell. (Ages 12–up.)
Davy, among his other problems, fears that he has homosexual tendencies when he and his friend engage in some affectionate play. His father helps him to recognize that he is normal and he can resume his friendship.

Evans, Eva Knox. *The Beginnings of Life: How Babies Are Born*. Illus. Rob Howard. New York: Macmillan, 1969. (Ages 5–8.)
An introductory discussion of reproduction in animals and human beings. It labels contractions "pains," but the rest of the terminology is accurate. The stereotype of the pacing, nervous, passive father is presented as universal fact. Nursing is represented as the way that babies are fed unless something is wrong. But the biological facts are presented, in general, simply and in an unthreatening style.

Eyerly, Jeannette. *A Girl Like Me*. Philadelphia: Lippincott, 1966. (Ages 12–up.)
A sixteen-year-old adopted girl deals with dating a boy "from the wrong crowd" and the pregnancy of a friend. The account of Ro-

bin's search for her real mother is rather unbelievable. Shallow and preachy. Issues such as abortion and premarital sex are not confronted but simply judged to be bad.

Fisher, Aileen. *Listen Rabbit*. Illus. Symeon Shimin. New York: Crowell, 1964. (Ages 5–8.)
Story of a boy who wants a rabbit as a friend and explores the differences between rabbits and human beings.

Fitzhugh, Louise. *The Long Secret*. New York: Harper & Row, 1965. Pb. Dell. (Ages 10–up.)
Harriet is as obnoxious and as insensitive as ever in this sequel to *Harriet the Spy*. Her friends share some information about sex and clear up some fears about menstruation in this story.

Fleischhauer-Hardt, Helga, M.D., and Davies, Hilary. *Show Me: A Picture Book of Sex for Children and Parents*. Photographs by Will McBride. New York: St. Martin's Press, 1973. (Ages 7–up.)
A graphic discussion and photographic essay on sex play, sexual intercourse, and people's reactions to sex, for children seven to eleven, but many adults will buy it for themselves. This book is designed for people who believe in totally open and free sexual behavior. Its presentation is explicit and probably startling to a number of people. An overload of information for the young child. The humor does not relieve the weight of this overload.

Gendron, Lionel, M.D. *Birth: The Story of How You Came to Be*. Illus. Jack Tremblay. New York: Grosset and Dunlap, 1972. (Ages 9–up.)
Factual exploration of conception, birth, and heredity. Somewhat complex technical terms in very small print. Sexist attitudes conveyed. Discomfort of pregnancy described. But book accurately labels contractions without dwelling on pain.

Gordon, Sol. *Girls Are Girls and Boys Are Boys*. Illus. Frank C. Smith. New York: John Day, 1975. (Ages 5–8.)
This excellent book reflects the author's awareness of a multiethnic audience. It focuses on an acknowledgment of the needs and emotions of both girls and boys. The language is clear, communicating information and constructive values directly.

Gordon, Sol and Judith. *Did the Sun Shine Before You Were Born?* Illus. Vivien Cohen. New York: Third Press–Joseph Okpaku, 1974. (Ages 5–9.)
Realistic illustrations. Excellent explanations. Clear, accurate terminology. Many incidental learnings are included. There is a boy with a doll, a female doctor, loving sexual relations (rather than clinical) multiethnic representation, option not to get married

and/or have children, picturing of different kinds of families (including one-parent families) sexual organs depicted without exaggeration, distortion, or romanticizing, bottle and breast feeding, and a balanced view, in general.

Gruenberg, Sidonie M. *The Wonderful Story of How You Were Born*, revised edition. Illus. Symeon Shimin. New York: Hanover House, 1970. (Ages 3-10.)
For young children, this book deals with the facts and emotions surrounding birth and contains basic reproductive terminology. Freudian orientation and somewhat condescending tone. Pain, instead of contractions, is described as part of the birth process. But, in general, a useful book.

Hansen, Søren, and Jensen, Jesper (with Wallace Roberts). *The Little Red Schoolbook*. Translated from Danish by Berit Thornberry. New York: Pocket Books, 1971. Pb. (Ages 11-up.)
The book treats such topics as school, society, drugs, and sex, offering advice on how to manage problems. In its introduction to the section on sex, it claims that its primary intention is to give information. It offers this information in vernacular rather than standard terminology. The value structure of the authors is communicated very strongly. The book is intolerant of people who have a different value system but may be useful to readers who are feeling guilty about their sexual activities.

Herman, Charlotte. *The Three of Us*. Illus. Mia Carpenter. Chicago: J. Philip O'Hara, 1973. (Ages 9-12.)
Three fifth-grade girls form a club to talk about life and other topics. They are all incredibly naive about sex. They read whatever they can and campaign for a sex education class to be sponsored by the school. All their parents seem unwilling and unable to deal with the topic.

Hettlinger, Richard F. *Growing Up With Sex*. New York: Seabury Press, 1970. Pb. also. (Ages 12-up.)
An informative and comprehensive book dealing with all aspects of sex.

Hodges, Bruce E., M.D. *How Babies Are Born — The Story of Birth for Children*. Illus. Richard Cuffari. New York: Simon and Schuster, 1967. Pb. also. (Ages 7-up.)
Terry's mother is going to have a baby, so Terry's father, a doctor, takes the opportunity to explain the process of birth and conception through many comparisons between animals and humans.

Holland, Isabelle. *The Man Without a Face*. Philadelphia: Lippincott, 1972. (Ages 12-up.)

Charles is emotionally drained by his mother's multiple divorces and his elder sister's cruelty to him. He becomes attached to his tutor, fears he is sexually attracted to him, learns later that the tutor is a homosexual, and ultimately comes to recognize his own feelings as that of admiration and gratefulness. The tutor does not take advantage of the boy's love even though he loves the boy. Homosexuality is judged to be a fatal flaw.

Hurd, Edith. *The Mother Whale*. Illus. Clement Hurd. Boston: Little, Brown, 1973. (Ages 6-8.)
A whale is born, nursed, and weaned. The bull whale is challenged for leadership by the herd and wins. He and the baby's mother mate again. The book is not very specific about the facts of the baby's birth or its life afterward. Hurd's language is simple and pictures are pleasant, but the book's usefulness is probably more as a motivator of questions rather than a source book for answers. The incidental information about whales is interesting. The information about sex is sparse.

Iwasaki, Chihiro. *A New Baby Is Coming to My Home*. New York: McGraw-Hill, 1970. (Ages 5-8.)
The story of a three-year-old child who is waiting for her mother to come home with her new baby brother.

Jensen, Gordon, M.D. *Youth and Sex*. Chicago: Nelson-Hall, 1973. (Ages 12-up.)
Informative, contemporary book. Negative attitude toward homosexuals, but in general open and nonjudgmental.

Johnson, Eric W. *Love and Sex in Plain Language*, revised edition. Illus. Russ Hoover. Philadelphia: Lippincott, 1973. Pb. Bantam. (Ages 10-up.)
A discussion of personal and social values surrounding love, sex, birth, and sex-related problems. Talks plainly of erection, pleasurable sex relations, and the fact that humans engage in sexual activities for reasons other than reproduction. Stresses personal responsibility. A very informative, balanced presentation.

———. *Sex: Telling It Straight*. Philadelphia: Lippincott, 1970. Pb. Bantam. (Ages 12-up.)
A somewhat simplistic discussion of the roles of sex in American life, including both pleasure and reproduction.

———, and Johnson, Corinne B. *Love and Sex and Growing-Up*. Philadelphia: Lippincott, 1970. (Ages 10-12.)
A less complex, less specific volume than *Love and Sex in Plain Language*, this presentation is intended to prepare prepubescent

readers for the greater mass of information to follow. It focuses on clarification of the reproduction process, and on a tolerance for different social attitudes.

Klein, Norma. *Confessions of An Only Child*. Illus. Richard Cuffari. New York: Pantheon Books, 1974. (Ages 8-12.)
A story about a girl learning to cope with the birth of a new baby in her family. Much of the information informally presented here is inaccurate (such as the impression is given that babies grow in the stomach).

————. *If I Had My Way*. Illus. Ray Cruz. New York: Pantheon Books, 1974. (Ages 5-8.)
A girl copes with negative feelings about her baby brother and her parents. She fantasizes about selecting a baby and reversing the parent-child roles. Much confusion could result from a child's reading this book without assistance.

————. *It's Not What You Expect*. New York: Pantheon, 1973. Pb. Avon. (Ages 12-up.)
Sex is handled casually and in line with the "new" morality in this book. Abortion is the logical solution to unplanned pregnancy and is accepted without trauma by the characters; further, it is not punished. Premarital sexual intercourse is the expected mode. All the characters are comfortable in their heterosexual relationships. The father is permitted to have a summer affair and is welcomed home without recrimination. The mother was more experienced sexually before marriage than the father was. This is a book that can either generate much discussion or be judged as unrealistic because of the absence of any deep probing.

————. *Mom, the Wolf Man and Me*. New York: Pantheon, 1972. (Ages 10-up.)
More an indication of alternative life styles than informative about sex. Brett, eleven years old, is content living with her never-married mother; she is also content when her mother's male friend sleeps over. Her mother responds frankly in the affirmative when Brett asks if they have had intercourse. No one seems uncomfortable over the arrangement. But Brett is not happy when her mother decides to get married. Brett receives most of her sex education at school and is also fairly well informed about contraception; she treats all the information casually. Except for her negative concept of marriage, she handles her world well.

————. *Naomi in the Middle*. Illus. Leigh Grant. New York: Dial Press, 1974. (Ages 7–10.)
A very healthy view of a family about to have a new baby. The sex education is indirectly communicated. The primary message is that of love and sex linked happily with each other.

Knudsen, Per Holm. *The True Story of How Babies Are Made*. Chicago: Children's Press, 1973. (Ages 5–8.)
This book has been used as part of Scandinavian children's introduction to sex education. The illustrations are purposely humorous and nonrealistic so that young children will accept the book informally rather than as a didactic effort. It provides much specific information about intercourse. Its approach may be too direct for some readers, but for others it will serve their purpose admirably.

Levine, Milton I., M.D., and Seligmann, Jean H. *A Baby Is Born*. Illus. Eloise Wilkin. New York: Golden Press, 1962. (Ages 6–10.)
Somewhat vague information, with much laying-on of values about marriage, love, and the expectation that all married couples will have children. Illustrations are stereotypic and overly sweet.

Lipke, Jean C. *Conception and Contraception*. Illus. Patricia Bateman. Minneapolis: Lerner, 1971. (Ages 11–up.)
Factual discussion of intercourse, conception, and the variety of methods of contraception. Overly laden with implications of guilt. Treats birth almost as a catastrophe.

Mann, Peggy. *That New Baby*. Illus. Susan Suba. New York: Coward, McCann, 1967. (Ages 4–6.)
A concerned mother, introducing her new baby to Jenny, her elder daughter, teaches Jenny to care for the baby.

Manushkin, Fran. *Bubble Bath*. Illus. Ronald Himler. New York: Harper & Row, 1974. (Ages 3–7.)
Two sisters take a bath after playing together and getting dirty. They wash and play with each other. The conversation is mostly in babytalk. Dull, but invites the reader to accept the idea of nakedness and enjoying bathtub play, and the sensuous pleasure children receive in washing, tickling, and hugging each other.

May, Julian. *How We Are Born*. Illus. Michael Hampshire. Chicago: Follett, 1969. (Ages 8–12.)
An illustrated book about how we are born, with love being the key incentive for enjoying sex and bearing children.

————. *Living Things and Their Young.* Illus. Don Merghan. Chicago: Follett, 1969. (Ages 8–12.)
This book describes the differences and similarities between animal and human births.

————. *Man and Woman.* Illus. Tak Murakin. Chicago: Follett, 1969. (Ages 8–12.)
A book dealing simply and expressively with intercourse, love, birth, and the process of becoming an adult.

Mayle, Peter. *Where Did I Come From?* Illus. Arthur Robins. Secaucus, N.J.: Lyle Stuart, 1973. (Ages 6–9.)
Although the subtitle of this book is "the facts of life without any nonsense and with illustrations," both the text and the cartoons attempt to be humorous; at times, they are nonsensical. Sexual orgasm is directly compared to a baby's sneeze. Intercourse is depicted as tickling and wiggling. Sperm are depicted as romantic. And the intent of intercourse is implied to be reproduction. For some readers the humor is useful; for some it is not.

Neufeld, John. *Freddy's Book.* New York: Random House, 1973. Pb. Avon. (Ages 10–up.)
A young boy is growing up with many questions about sex and life. His search for answers leads him to gather much misinformation from many sources. He finally gets some accurate answers from his father.

Odenwald, Robert P., M.D. *How You Were Born.* Illus. Mary Reed Newland. New York: P. J. Kenedy, 1962. (Ages 8–12.)
This book presents the cycle of life with respect to religion and ideal family situations; it is often stereotypic and stilted.

Pomeroy, Wardell B. *Boys and Sex.* New York: Delacorte Press, 1968. Pb. Dell. (Ages 12–up.)
Speaks directly and clearly about sex play, masturbation, homosexuality, intercourse, and other questions that boys and girls would have. Girls would also benefit from reading it.

————. *Girls and Sex.* New York: Delacorte Press, 1969. Pb. Dell. (Ages 12–up.)
Speaks in an unpatronizing way to girls. Stresses positive self-concept. Expresses strong opinions on topics such as the positive value of petting and the negative consequences of dating married men.

Portal, Colette. *The Beauty of Birth*. New York: Knopf, 1971. (All ages.)
Explanation of conception, growth of the embryo, and birth. Sex is linked directly to love. There is no discussion of any other facts about sex.

Rudolph, Marguerita. *Look At Me*. Illus. Carla Kuskun. New York: McGraw-Hill, 1967. (Ages 4-6.)
An explanation, in poetry, of a child's body parts and physical features. Designed to give a child an understanding and pride in his/her body.

Sheffield, Margaret. *Where Do Babies Come From?* Illus. Sheila Bewley. New York: Knopf, 1973. (Ages 7-10.)
The illustrations in this book are a major asset. They are paintings of real-looking people — frank but not titillating. They contain no distortions and are not idealized; their realism is not frightening. The text is a reasonable companion to the pictures. It is direct and utilizes accurate terminology. The information is not so complex as to be confusing but contains enough detail to be useful with children across a wide age span.

Showers, Paul. *A Baby Starts to Grow*. Illus. Rosalind Fry. New York: Crowell, 1969. (Ages 5-8.)
Detailed account of the development of a baby inside the uterus. Clear and factual. Many illustrations. The book focuses on the baby and on the mother. Only a brief mention that sperm comes from the father gives any indication that the mother is not the only adult involved. No explanation of intercourse. The focus is solely on the development of the baby inside the uterus.

Showers, Paul and Kay. *Before You Were a Baby*. Illus. Ingrid Fetz. New York: Crowell, 1968. (Ages 6-8.)
A clear story of the process of conception and birth with illustrations of each month of pregnancy.

Stein, Sara Bonnett. *Making Babies*. Photographs by Doris Pinney. New York: Walker, 1974. (Ages 3-8.)
This is another in the Open Family Series. It is a discussion of the importance of an open atmosphere for growing up, understanding sex, love, birth, and families. The photographs and the text respond to a very beginning level of inquiry. The value system is somewhat imposed in this book; dogs are described as "loving" each other when they are mating. It is presumed that all boys and girls want to be parents. But for those who want these values conveyed, this is an excellent book.

Steptoe, John. *My Special Best Words*. New York: Viking, 1974. (Ages 3–7.)

Bweela, three years old, lives with her one-year-old brother Javaka and her father. The reader is not told where the mother is. Javaka is not yet toilet-trained, so Bweela teaches him. The book is full of "special" words, including the family's personal bathroom language. Steptoe has modified his style in this book. The faces are almost photographs. The illustrations have specific detail — and Javaka has a penis. A frank and educational book.

Stevens, Carla. *The Birth of Sunset's Kittens*. Photographs by Leonard Stevens. New York: Young Scott Books, 1969. (Ages 7–10.)

A clear and sensitive book picturing and discussing the birth of four kittens. The transition to information about humans is well made.

Strain, Frances B. *Being Born*, revised edition. New York: Appleton-Century-Crofts, 1970. (Ages 12–up.)

A book about human sexuality easy enough for very young children to understand, though somewhat stereotypic about love, families, and men and women's sexual roles.

Sucksdorff, Astrid Bergman. *The Roe Deer*. New York: Harcourt, Brace & World, 1967. (Ages 8–up.)

An explanation and description of the mating cycle of the roe deer. Illustrated by the author with photographs, this is a useful addition to a library but should not be relied upon to provide answers.

Winthrop, Elizabeth. *A Little Demonstration of Affection*. New York: Harper & Row, 1975. (Ages 12–up.)

Jenny fears that she has incestuous feelings toward her brother, Charles. Her family is undemonstrative, never showing affection outwardly. Jenny is so moved by her brother's hugging her that she fears she is abnormal. Eventually her father helps her to work out her feelings.

Zapleen, Simone. *Mommy, Where Do Babies Come From?* Illus. Tina Cacciola. New York: Platt and Munk, 1974. (Ages 5–8.)

Two children learn about many different kinds of birth on their search to discover where babies come from.

Zindel, Paul. *My Darling, My Hamburger*. New York: Harper & Row, 1969. Pb. Bantam. (Ages 12–up.)

A novel dealing with abortion, premarital sex, and interpersonal relationships.

NOTES and ADDITIONS

7

The Black

RACISTS are people whose behavior toward specific groups is based solely on the color of skin or ethnic origin. Racist practices include ostracism; economic, social, and political deprivation; social slights; educational discrimination; denial of human dignity; and, ultimately, murder. Racists create, believe, and then use stereotypic descriptions to excuse their actions; they also use these stereotypes to foster and maintain divisions between people. Racists are frightened, insecure individuals who feel threatened by those who are different from them.

This author doubts that any reader of this book considers himself or herself to be a racist. We do not persecute people different from ourselves. We respect other cultures and tolerate unconventional customs and life styles. We are all well-meaning, just, and caring. We never intentionally judge people on the basis of their racial or ethnic characteristics. We try to be open-minded about appearances and behaviors. We suffer from few, if any, damaging preconceptions about genetic inferiority or superiority. Valuing individuals, we recognize that all people, no matter what their group membership may be, are unique. Moreover, we try to act to eliminate unjust practices wherever they occur, no matter how uncomfortable the situation and despite peer pressure to remain aloof or silent.

But not always. And not consistently. Human beings are not perfect. We are well intentioned but are nevertheless products and victims of our society. And our society, in common with all modern societies, is racist. We carry within ourselves the influence of our parents' and grandparents' and teachers' and neighbors' experiences, as well as our own. We retain the teachings of the books that we have read, the lectures that we have heard, the films that we have seen. We cannot claim total objectivity about anything and should not claim to have totally accurate information. We can only hope for clearer perspective as a basis for acting in a way that we can be satisfied with ourselves.

It is not the intention of this author to impart guilt or a sense of hopelessness to the reader. Rather, recognizing that we share a common condition and affliction, we must set about remedying it to the best of our ability. We must learn to diagnose the extent of the problem within ourselves so that we may determine what next steps we may take to help ourselves grow. Then we can evaluate and diagnose ourselves again in order to develop even further. Helping each other at the same time that we are helping ourselves, we can also help children at an early stage to avoid the negative attitudes and behavior that have afflicted our society in the past. Racism is a harmful and corrosive problem for the perpetrator as well as for the victim. It is our hope that this chapter and the next (on the Native American) will provide a format for working with the issues of any minorities as they are presented in children's books.

Not a simple condition, racism consists of many different kinds of attitudes and behaviors that build into a pattern destructive to all involved. We are all tempted to say, "Not I. I behave humanely toward all people." The danger in this response, even if it is true, is that we may then absolve ourselves of the responsibility for becoming part of the solution, since we do not view ourselves as part of the problem. Especially for those of us who are involved with children, our responsibility must be actively maintained. How do we stock our homes and our classrooms? What criteria do we consider when we build a library? How do we handle racist attitudes in books? How aware are we of the connotations and innuendos in the books that our children read? How do we manage the classics? What of the popular fantasies and novels and even works of so-called nonfiction that are rife with racist ideas?

How do we manage to keep progressing with our own sense of openness and world-mindedness, and at the same time help children who are, perhaps, not at the same level of awareness that we are? How can we recognize our acts of omission?

The focus here is on books. Each of the above-mentioned questions should also be applied to all other media and, indeed, to our social behavior. Though this chapter will be concerned with the Black in children's books, it is important to remember that there are many more minorities in the United States who need to see themselves in the literature. The presentation of people of other countries, of different ethnic groups living here, of people who speak a language other than English, of the poor, leaves much to be desired. By concentrating in this chapter on the treatment of Blacks in the children's books (and in the next chapter on Native Americans), this author hopes to present a wide-enough range of responses and suggestions so that the reader may then transfer the ideas to *any* minority group. The eventual client is the child. If, in our analyses and comments we can help children to value themselves and each other, then we will have succeeded in our primary objective.

The emphasis, then, will be on influencing attitudes and developing constructive strategies for dealing with racism directed toward black people in children's books. Whites sometimes are so guilt-stricken that they wallow in their feelings of guilt, confess to being criminals, and become paralyzed (or overly comfortable), never moving from this position. Guilt may be a useful response at times to prevent recurrence of a crime, but we must learn to go beyond guilt and to build a repertoire for future behavior. We must learn to be much more than sorry.

Our first task is to cultivate awareness; to recognize how other people react to certain phrases, how they feel about themselves and their world, how their modes of response compare with ours, and what their backgrounds and values are. Even when we are uncomfortable with their differences, after we become aware of them, we must tolerate them. Tolerance is only a minimal step in the direction of nonracism. It implies a passive permission and a sense of superiority to the tolerated. If our previous inclination has been to prevent or prohibit others from dressing, speaking, or living differently from our own way, then tolerance is the next step. Cultural differences cause many people discomfort, but they are an aspect of society that is to be valued rather than to be feared.

After tolerance, acceptance and then respect should grow. The more that people are encouraged to value their own diversity, the more they should be able to value others'. Respect and admiration should lead to a sense of comfort and joy, eventually inviting the cooperation that is an ultimate aim in human relations. We must each keep taking the next steps that will lead us through these stages, continuing to examine our own reactions in order to guarantee our steady progress. And even after comfort and collegiality are reached, we must continue to learn more and more about each other. The cultivation of awareness must continue.

No person can be said to have reached a state of total awareness. Some of us may still be at the point at which culturally different people are either invisible, "strange," or frightening. The fact that books in the past excluded any but all-white characters has fostered this problem. Minority children have not been able to find themselves in children's books. They have not been able to identify with heroes or heroines or even with ordinary children who simply "belong." Nancy Larrick brought this appalling gap to the attention of the children's book publishers and the public in her important and influential article in the *Saturday Review* of September 11, 1965 (see References). In the past five years, more and more culturally diverse books have been published. One of our first steps, then, in working toward nonracist and antiracist classrooms, is to stock them with books that include a variety of people, cultures, points of view, life styles, and situations.

▶ Try This

Locate several books published before 1970 that, upon examination, include no minority characters. Rewrite the text so that the characters are black. How does this change the story? How difficult was this to do? Reexamine your assumptions. What changes will you effect in yourself? Now locate several picture books that have only white characters in them. Design new illustrations so that some or all of the characters are black. How does this change the story? How does this change the effect on the book? How could you have children perform these same exercises?

For the black reader, or for any reader who is part of a minority, the steps toward collegiality are similar. The first step, to be repeated again and again, is that of awareness. Knowledge about one's own heritage, about one's characteristics, and about the problems that society imposes are essential for learning and growth. Tolerance of oneself and of one's people is important as a temporary, but necessary, next step. That is the ability to say, "I'm not sure I'm comfortable with that behavior, but I'll recognize that it exists, that it is not abhorrent, and that I will do nothing to prevent it from occurring." Acceptance and valuing must follow in order for true self-pride to grow. Finally, the ability to make one's own decisions comfortably and a sense of independence should result.

Again, the steps must be repeated in all situations and must be practiced consistently.

Sometimes our own good intentions cause us to be less effective than we may wish to be. We want our students, our peers, and our community to progress to our level of awareness and behavior, but we recognize that we are where we are only after much searching and growing. We sometimes make the mistake of expecting others to achieve our level without that important process first occurring. We try to force people to move more quickly than they are able. We must work hard to remember that people are where they are, not where they should be. It is not the "shoulds" that we can successfully attend to; it is the reality of the present situation. We can help people to take next steps; it is not feasible to force them to take leaps. Meanwhile, we can continue to advance in our own attitudes and behaviors.

▶ Try This

Select three books for young children that you believe demonstrate a good level of awareness and valuing. List the qualities that support your judgment. Find one way each of the books could have done an even better job. Do the same with three books for older children. Compare your observations with a peer.

The practices of both publishers and authors in the past have been so lax, at best, and so malicious, at worst, that they have warped many generations of readers. Dorothy Broderick's work *Image of the Black in Children's Fiction* contributes vastly to an understanding of the dimensions of prejudice that books have conveyed. Broderick includes many references from books that today would cause any intelligent reader to react angrily. The depth of bigotry, misinformation, and degradation are impressive. Teachers and students should acquaint themselves with these abusive practices in order to equip themselves with a perspective for viewing modern works.

Broderick deals with work of literary fiction. Folk and fairy tales set in nineteenth-century Europe are also sources of problems for people who are trying to grow in racial awareness. The folk tale relies on stereotypes in order to convey its messages in a simple and symbolic fashion. Thus, in the European-based tales, the good, innocent beauty is usually blond, blue-eyed, and very fair-skinned. The only notable exception is Snow White, who escapes the stereotype only because her hair is ebony; but she makes up for it in the whiteness of her skin.

Witches, gnomes, ogres, giants, and other villains are never blond; Evil is couched in the language of blackness and darkness. The vocabulary, too, aids in the impression of what is virtuous and what is evil. Individual characteristics are discouraged; the happy ending is always the same: obedience, patience, generosity, and acceptance of one's lot are rewarded. Ambition, seeking to change one's social position, and characteristics of rebellion or dissatisfaction are punished. Beauty is rewarded; ugliness is punished. Beauty is equated with good; lack of the standard form of beauty is considered evil. Those folk tales that do reward cleverness and real courage should be shared with children.

If our children were exposed to more than the conventional European folk tales and myths and were treated to more Asian and African and Native American myths and tales, perhaps the stereotypes created by the "classical" tales would not be so pervasive. But myth can be far more powerful than realistic writing can, and the lessons learned through fantasy tend to remain longer than those conveyed through didactic literature. It is our responsibility, then, to provide ourselves and our students with a variety of folk and fairy tales and myths, as well as the modern variety of stories that we now easily have at our disposal.

▶ Try This

Select five books of fairy tales. Finding a character who is a villain, describe this character's physical appearance. Now, changing the appearance, see if it makes the story less powerful or less logical. Share your findings with the class. Compile a class list of physical characteristics of villains. Do the same for heroes and heroines.

How can we examine books knowledgeably in order to assess their usefulness in helping readers to become more aware and more valuing of other cultures and differences? What criteria can we establish that will help us, not only to locate racist inferences but also to recognize positive gains? Many individuals and groups have provided us with lists of criteria; eventually it is the reader who must compile one personally. One invaluable aid, not only to constructing criteria but also to fostering greater awareness of the situation, is the *Bulletin* published by the Council on Interracial Books for Children. This organization, located at 1841 Broadway, New York, N.Y. 10023, exerts a powerful influence on publishers, educators, authors, and readers. The publication contains an analysis of at least one current book in each of its issues. The reader is helped to look at books from different perspectives, to decide how to handle the particular books discussed, and then how to proceed with other such books.

In its Vol. 5, No. 3 (1974) issue, the Council printed in the *Bulletin* "Ten Quick Ways to Analyze Books for Racism and Sexism." The article is reprinted here, almost in its entirety. The sections on sexism are omitted from this chapter but are included in Chapter 9, *The Female*. Sections that pertain only to textbooks are deleted. Comments added by this author are italicized and bracketed. The original article is divided into two parts: criteria 1 through 5 analyze picture and story books, while criteria 6 through 10 are specifically for texts. This author, however, has included and adapted the last five criteria so that they pertain to books other than texts.

Suggested Criteria

Ten Quick Ways to Analyze Books for Racism and Sexism*

Both in school and out, your children are being exposed to many books that convey racist and sexist attitudes. These attitudes — expressed over and over by books and other media — gradually distort their perceptions until stereotypes and myths about minorities and women are accepted as reality. It is difficult for a parent or a teacher to convince their children to question society's attitudes. But if you can show a child how to detect racism and sexism in a book, the child can proceed to transfer the perception to wider areas. The ten guidelines below are a starting point. [*It is important to take the step of communicating these guidelines to the children. Adults should not confine to themselves the privilege of exercising these judgments.*]

1. Check the Illustrations.

   Look for stereotypes. A stereotype is an oversimplified generalization about a particular group, race, or sex, which generally carries derogatory implications. Some "famous" stereotypes of Blacks are the happy-go-lucky Sambo eating watermelon, or fat, old, eye-rolling mammy [*or the ignorant, physically powerful savage, or the larger-than-life "noble" savage, or the figure created to be of service to the White, or the contented slave, or the superstitious ignoramus, or the inherently rhythmic singer and dancer, with no other dimension of character, or the newly created ghetto child, whose whole*

---

* Adapted and reprinted by permission of the Council on Interracial Books for Children, Inc.

life is poverty and crime]. While you may not always find them in the forms described, look for variations which in any way demean or ridicule characters because of their race or sex.

Look for tokenism. If there are nonwhite characters, are they just like the white faces but tinted or colored in? Do all minority faces look stereotypically alike, or are they depicted as genuine individuals?

Look at the life styles. Are minority characters and their setting depicted in such a way that they contrast unfavorably with an unstated norm of white middle-class suburbia? For example, minorities are often associated with the ghetto, migrant labor, or "primitive" living. If the story does attempt to depict another culture, does it go beyond oversimplifications of reality and offer genuine insights into another life style? [*Look for appropriateness. Are minority characters "quaint" or "curious"? Are they dressed in costume? Or do the illustrations reflect reality? Are they accurate?*]

2. Check the Story Line.

Civil Rights legislation has led publishers to weed out many insulting passages and illustrations, particularly in stories with black themes, but the attitudes still find expression in less obvious ways.

Relationships. Do Whites in the story have the power and make the decisions? Do nonwhite people function in essentially subservient roles?

Standard for success. What does it take for a character to succeed? To gain acceptance, do nonwhite characters have to exhibit superior qualities — excel in sports, get A's, etc.? In friendships between white and nonwhite children ("brotherhood"), is it the nonwhite who does most of the understanding and forgiving?

Viewpoint. How are "problems" presented, conceived, and resolved in the story? Are minority people themselves considered to be "the problem"? Do solutions ultimately depend on the benevolence of a white person?

3. Consider the Effects of the Book on the Child's Self-Image and Self-Esteem.

Are norms established which limit the child's aspirations and self-concepts? What does it do to black children to be continuously bombarded with images of white as beautiful, clean, virtuous, etc., and black as evil, dirty, menacing, etc.?

4. Consider the Author's or Illustrator's Qualifications.

Read the biographical material on the jacket flap or on the back of the book. If a story deals with a minority theme, what qualifies the author or illustrator to deal with the topic? If they are not members of the minority being written about, is there anything in the author's or illustrator's background that would specifically recommend them for this book?

The above observations do not deny the ability of writers to empathize with experiences other than those of their own sex or race, but the chances of their writing as honestly and as authentically about other experiences are not as good.

5. Look at the Copyright Date.

Books on minority themes — usually hastily conceived — suddenly began appearing in the mid-1960s. There followed a growing number of "minority experience" books to meet the new market demand, but these were still written by white authors and reflected a white point of view. Only very recently, in the late 1960s and early 1970s, has the children's book world begun to even remotely reflect the realities of a multiracial society.

The copyright dates, therefore, can be a clue as to how likely the book is to be overtly racist or sexist although recent copyright date, of course, is no guarantee of a book's relevance or sensitivity. Note that the copyright date only means the year the book was published. This time lag has meant very little in the past, but in a time of rapidly changing consciousness, when children's book publishing is attempting to be "relevant," it is becoming increasingly significant.

6. Determine the Author's Perspective.

[*The description of this criterion in the article deals exclusively with textbooks and has, therefore, been rewritten. But the criterion is an important one and must be considered in looking at other kinds of books as well.*

No author is totally objective. But, since most authors of children's books have traditionally been white, the perspective has been somewhat limited. Omissions and distortions are therefore to be expected. These should be exposed and dealt with accordingly.

7. *Note the Setting. (This criterion was added by this author.)*

Many of the more recent works of fiction for children dealing with the black experience are set in the ghetto. While this may be a realistic background for some stories, it is not the only one in which black people live and work. *If the story is set in the city, but not the ghetto, are there other minorities represented, and are there Whites visible as well? Is the setting a place that confirms the identity of the characters? Does it help the reader to form a positive image of the Black? If it is a middle-class setting, does it convey a sense of individuality rather than imitativeness of a white standard?*

In rural or suburban settings, is there evidence of a multiethnic population? Again, are the characters drawn as individuals rather than as symbols or types?

8. *Note the Relationships. (This criterion was added by this author.)*

   Look at descriptions of families. Is the black mother always the domi-nant member of the family? How intact is the nuclear family? If the family is separated, are there reasons given that indicate society's responsibility? What kinds of friendships are described? Are white friends valued over black? What are the aspirations of the characters? How are these received by the others?]

9. Watch for Loaded Words.

   A word is loaded when it carries overtones of insult. Examples of loaded adjectives, usually racist, are *savage, primitive, conniv-ing, lazy, superstitious, treacherous, wily, crafty, inscrutable, docile,* and *backward*.

   [*Look, too, for inappropriate use of dialect. Dialect is often useful in conveying a sense of authenticity to a story and in permitting the readers to see in print what they hear during their daily existence. But dialect used inappropriately, and as a differentiating mechanism with negative intent, can cause readers to feel that the dialect and therefore the person who speaks it are inferior.*]

10. Note the Heroes and Heroines.

    For many years books showed only "safe" minority heroes and heroines — those who avoided serious conflict with the white establishment of their time. Minority groups today are insisting on the right to define their own heroes and heroines based on their own culture and struggles for justice.

    [*A list of figures often omitted or maligned in textbooks is included in the original article. Look at the qualities that black heroes and heroines are permitted to have in works of fiction. How varied are they? How often are their qualities not the same as those admired in white pro-tagonists? How often must they rescue white folks in order to be accepted and admired? Do they perform more than a service function? Can black characters take the lead when white ones are present?*]

The above criteria constitute a beginning. Add your own and encourage students to develop their own as well.

The article then goes on to suggest that teachers and parents can actively develop programs and take action to eliminate bias from books. These range from organizing consciousness-raising meetings, to writing to publishers, to informing all interested and influential adults about racism that has been detected in books. The Council invites all readers to inform them of their efforts and ideas.

▶ Try This

Select three children's books for young children (preschool to age eight) and three books for older children (eight to twelve). Use the Bibliography at the end of this chapter as a source if you wish. Using the above ten criteria, analyze the books for evidence of a nonracist approach to Blacks. For example, try to find specific evidence of nonstereotypic illustrations. In examining the plot, try to find examples of situations in which minority members have constructive power. List the books that you have found and the positive characteristics that you have discovered.

Very few books can be classified as totally nonracist or antiracist. It therefore becomes necessary to recognize what can be used, what must be counteracted, and what should at least come up for discussion. It is important to be able to recognize the positive as well as the negative aspects of any book. It is also necessary to filter one's observation through such qualities as literary excellence, the effectiveness of the story, the side effects of the message, and the universality of the human experiences described in the book. The mood of the story, the author's effectiveness in causing the reader to empathize with the characters — in short, the overall effect of the book — must always be considered. Then, the more knowledgeable the reader is, the more able the reader will be to determine whether or not the author has presented historical, anthropological, and emotional truth.

What steps can we expect authors to take in order to provide the reading public with fewer racist books? First, they must examine their own racial biases and fantasies before presenting them in print. Those authors who already possess advanced skills of communication must take special care, for their words are read by many children and adults and their ideas are received, internalized, and acted upon. Their power is enormous. We frequently admonish ourselves and our students not to believe all that we read, but we willingly suspend disbelief when a writer is powerful, particularly when we are confronted not with facts but with fantasy. Then the messages seep into our systems without our having weighed or recognized the information.

Authors, then, must take care to present characters in a varied and unstereotypic fashion. They should try to examine their own work with a diagnostic eye, looking for positive images for a variety of people and trying to weed out negative suggestions or artificial characters that would foster racist attitudes and responses in their readers. They should attempt to convey universality while valuing diversity.

We, on our part, can communicate to publishers and authors both our positive as well as our negative criticisms. We can examine our own perceptions, check them with others, and ask for validation. We can stop when we find ourselves so immersed in a book that we are not actively questioning the author's intent and methodology. We can learn to recognize positive factors and to keep our minds open for negative implications. Once we have reached the point of easily detecting overt negative racial attitudes, we can look for subtle indications.

Discussion of Children's Books

A wide range now exists of books at least containing black characters. Books are currently published specifically for black audiences, while others reflect an attempt to educate white readers. Some of the books are at the earliest level of fostering awareness; some attempt to inform the reader about long-neglected black history. A fairly large body of books deals with constructing and reinforcing a sense of pride and positive self-image for black children, while at the same time, helping the nonblack reader to develop awareness and appreciation of black qualities and black contributions. Differences are cherished rather than discouraged in the best of these books. African folk tales and informational books about Africa are also increasing in number. The folk and fairy tales are particularly valuable for offsetting the prevailing sense of the folk tale's coming only from Europe.

In fiction for the older child more black protagonists are appearing; moreover, there is a greater sense of this country's multiracial construct. Illustrations reflect this trend. Poetry books, too, have begun to reflect the work of black poets, and poetry anthologies have become somewhat more inclusive and contemporary in their selections. Although many gains have been made, more are needed, as the prevailing mode is still that of the exclusively white world. We have noted the exceptions, not the rule. And we must continue to criticize and analyze even the new, well-intentioned books to secure the progress that they and we have made.

This chapter will include critiques primarily of works of fiction. Nonfiction is important for children to read, but the scope of nonfiction about Blacks is too large to be confined to one chapter. Indeed, the fiction is so extensive as to permit only a sampling to be reviewed here. This author hopes, however, that a format and frame will be provided for readers to continue on their own to examine the literature critically and to make judgments of a constructive nature.

VISIBLE AT LAST

One of the chief criticisms of books before the last decade was that in stories for young children, only Whites seemed to exist in this world. All families were white; all neighborhoods had only white people living in them; all people appeared to be middle class and to live in the suburbs. This situation could not continue in a society that was interested in moving away from racism. Nonwhite, nonmiddle-class children were made to feel as if they were invisible. They were told, by omission, that they did not exist or, if they did, that they were not considered impor- tant enough to mention. They were unvalued. Even as late as 1967, two books by Lois Wyse, *Grandmothers Are to Love* and *Grandfathers Are to Love*, were published that purported to give a sense of all grandmothers and grandfathers and their diverse functions. All the people in these books, however, are white. Moreover, most of them, old and young, are fair-haired. There are a couple of black kittens, but otherwise there is no indication that the illustrator, Martha Alexander, is aware of the non- white world. Interestingly, Alexander wrote and illustrated *The Story Grandmother Told* in 1969. In this book the child and her grandmother are Blacks. It is a charming story that could be illustrated with a child and grandmother of any color. All the more important that this simple, pleasant book describing a loving relationship between a little girl and her grandmother contains a black family as its protagonists. No one insists that every book should include a representation of all peoples. But there should be some books reflecting a true picture of what the world looks like. And now there are.

URBAN LIFE

Ezra Jack Keats has, since 1963, been writing and illustrating books using black characters. Keats, who is white, grew up in New York City and must have recognized the need for black children to see themselves. His stories are more universal than ethnic. White children can easily be substituted in the pictures. *The Snowy Day*, published in 1962, and winner of the Caldecott Award in 1963, was the first book in which Peter, the black child in all of Keats's books, appeared. The story is simply that of a child playing in the snow. The mother is too heavy and dressed in gaudy colors, but the book marks a breakthrough because of its casual depiction of a black family. The story contains no trauma, few harmful stereotypes, and no condescension.

Whistle for Willie, 1964, continues the pattern. Willie, the dog, also appears in most of Keats's books. By 1967 Peter has a baby sister, and his responses are recorded in *Peter's Chair*. (See Chapter 2, *Siblings*, for further description.) Peter's setting is changed in 1969. He is older now. His locale has always been the city, but it has changed from a sunny, pleasant place; his world is no longer a secure one. In *Goggles* he is menaced by older boys who chase and threaten him in order to take away the motorcycle goggles that he found in a junk heap. Peter and his friend Archie seem none the worse for the experience, and they do escape the older bullies, but it is unfortunate that the city is depicted in such totally harsh terms. It is also unrealistic that the older boys would continue the chase as long as they did; they would more likely go after larger rewards.

Despite its negativism, *Goggles* is highly recommended in *Starting Out Right*, published in 1970. This is a booklet compiled by Bettye I. Latimer and several associate editors, listing and commenting on more than two hundred books for young children about black people; it is the most comprehensive annotated bibliography of its kind. Although some readers see Peter and Archie's strategies as ingenious and light-hearted, this author sees them as perpetuating the myth of life in the ghettos' always calling for raw survival tactics. Keats may have recognized the danger of stereotyping, because in *Apt. 3*, published in 1971, although the setting is the city, not one character in the book is black. The apartment house is appallingly run-down; the families in the apartments are obviously poor and not inviting; and the superintendent is an unpleasant person. The only hope in the book is that human relationships are formed between the two boys who are the protagonists and a blind man who can play the harmonica, and who senses more than most seeing people. Keats may, therefore, be demonstrating that slums are places where poor white people live too. But the depressing version of the city is a strong one.

John Steptoe is another illustrator whose pictures of black characters have won awards and accolades. His first book, *Stevie*, was published when he was only seventeen years old. Steptoe, a Black, says of himself, "I don't just happen to be Black." His illustrations, reminiscent of Rouault's paintings, convey a sense of black universality that is at once appealing and dramatic. Ray Shepard, in his article "Adventures in Blackland with Keats and Steptoe" (see References), claims that Keats's characters could be either white or black but that Steptoe "celebrates the ethnic differences of Blacks." He feels that the characters in Steptoe's books could not be white without drastically changing the story. Perhaps this is true in the case of *Uptown*, which is written in contemporary black urban speech. *Uptown* is the story of two boys who wonder what they will do and be when they grow up. They talk about black pride and clothing that sets them off from Whites, but their conversation about how they feel and what their options are is the same as most poor urban children growing up in less than middle-class comfort in a large city.

Stevie, Steptoe's first book, could, in this author's opinion, easily have nonblack characters as its main figures. The story is about sibling rivalry, about caring adults, and about a child and his feelings. Steptoe's illustrations combined with the text fit well. There is certainly no sense that Stevie's blackness is inappropriate, but he is not a stereotype and could therefore be a child of almost any ethnic background. He would not be rich or even middle class, but he could be any color.

In Steptoe's books, as in Keats's early ones, the city is a place that is challenging but not punitive. The colors are not pastel, but they are not brash or ugly. Keats's ghetto is littered, depressing, and to be reckoned with; Steptoe's is alive and flourishing. His book *Train Ride* again affirms the city and the children's capability of coping with it and enjoying it. This time the children live in Brooklyn, not Harlem. Again, black urban speech is used. The story is simply that of a group of young black boys who take a forbidden subway ride uptown to Times Square. They arrive home very late after having had a marvelous time. Each is punished by his parents. Though they all agree that their fathers have given them the worst beatings they ever had, they are undaunted and will probably repeat the adventures at a subsequent time.

The city is again presented here as a place in which people can enjoy life and survive adversity. The children in the story all have names; they are recognizable individuals. They all have loving, concerned families; they are not stereotypes of children from broken homes. Their parents all care about their behavior; they are not permitted to run loose. They are bright, capable children who feel good about themselves. It is this sense of positive self-image and underlying optimism that Steptoe conveys. These qualities are part of what makes his books appealing and useful.

There are many books for young children set in the city. Kathryn Hitte's *What Can You Do Without a Place to Play?* attempts a facetious approach. The children in this book, who are all nameless, are in the way of everyone else as they attempt to find a place to play in the city. They do play in the elevator, on the stairs, on the roof, in the lobby of a posh apartment house, in a laundromat, and in an alley, among other places. They are chased away from every place but the alley, and their play in all of the places but the alley is quite destructive. The point of view of the narration seems very negative, as though the reader is invited to feel superior to these young mischief-makers. The book probably is meant to convey a sense of the children's ingenuity as well, but the negative implications keep coming through. The children clearly do not appreciate their own inventiveness. The story ends with the main character sitting unhappily on a window ledge with his cat, asking, "How can you have any fun when there isn't any place to play around here?" The child is technically right: there is no place in his neighborhood set aside for active children to play. But their imaginative games in the alley prove that they can occupy themselves without getting into trouble and with enjoyment. What they and the author concentrate on is, sadly, the lack of facility, not the presence of opportunity.

In this book most of the characters are white. There is an attempt made at some integration in the illustrations, but it does not matter what color the children are. They represent an attitude toward the city child that is potentially destructive. The children in this setting are not taught to value their own ingenuity. Steptoe's children do. So, too, does Nina, Billy Jenkins's big sister in *Walk Home Tired, Billy Jenkins*, by Ianthe Thomas. She has been playing in the city playground with her little brother; now it is time for them to return home. The small boy, very tired, does not think that he can walk the long distance home; but Nina coaxes him through the streets by conjuring up a silver sailboat, a smooth riding plane, and a "train as black as midnight coal." Billy at first does not want to play her game until she points out that the alternative is to "walk home tired." At last, when he joins her in her fantasy, they glide the rest of the way home.

The illustrations of the city in this warm, helpful book are realistic, but softened by the style of the illustrator, which is in perfect keeping with the intent of the story. All the people pictured are black. It is not a fancy neighborhood, but there is a sense of well-being conveyed in the pictures. Another such book is *Adam's World: San Francisco*, by Kathleen Fraser and Miriam F. Levy. Adam is a black child who lives with his family on the top floor of a tall building on one of the hills of San Francisco. His father is a seaman. There is always a happy reunion when Adam's father comes home. When his father brings home cloth from Africa, his mother sews beautiful African-style clothes for herself, Adam, his twin sisters, and his father; they then wear the clothing to a street party. The book not only describes a loving family relationship, it also conveys a sense of the city of San Francisco within the story line. It is a beautiful book.

Other books set in the city, and conveying a positive but not complacent or subservient attitude, include *Evan's Corner*, by Elizabeth Starr

Hill; *The Boy Who Didn't Believe in Spring*, by Lucille Clifton; and *And I Must Hurry for the Sea Is Coming In*, by George Mendoza. These books have young black boys as the protagonists, each depicted as an active, thoughtful child who does something about his own life. In *Evan's Corner*, the child manages to design a space for himself, even within the crowded two-room apartment that he shares with his family. After he helps his younger brother also to obtain a similar space, he feels better for this act of brotherly affection. The child in Mendoza's book creates a special adventure for himself in his imagination. He is actually playing in the spray of a hydrant with a tiny toy sailboat. But his fantasy takes him out to sea as the captain of a beautiful big sailboat. The photographs are lovely, and the text makes it plain that the boy will not let the world destroy him. *Starting Out Right* highly recommends both books. Children could construct a list of positive qualities about the city in order to counteract some of the negative impact of some books.

In *The Boy Who Didn't Believe in Spring*, King Shavazz, a first-grader, does not believe his teacher when she describes spring. "No such thing," he says, when he hears about it. Finally, he and his friend, Tony Polito, go to search for signs of spring. After encountering many of the ordinary sights and smells of the city (all of them positive), they discover a patch of crocuses and a nest of robin's eggs. The children set out to accomplish something, and they succeed. Though the book is thin, its importance is in the sense of personal power demonstrated by the children.

Factual books about the city can also be used to help all children change their negative attitudes without romanticizing the city. Full of useful information, *The City Book*, by Lucille Corcos, explains many aspects of the city. It pictures an integrated setting in all cases. The tremendous amount of detail may be overwhelming for a child unless an adult is near to guide the young reader. The book is factual and makes no judgments. *The Other City*, by Ray Vogel, in contrast, reports only the negative, ugly, and poverty-ridden side of the city. The photographs are excellent in their detail and their artistic conveying of the message. This is not a demeaning or stereotyping book; but in its negativism and image of no hope for escape or reconstruction, it is ultimately damaging. Michael Deasy's *City ABC's* also uses photographs of the poor sections of the city, but the text and most of the photos indicate a constructive attitude that promises survival. It is preferred by this author.

RURAL LIFE

Polly Greenberg's *Oh Lord, I Wish I Was a Buzzard* is based on a childhood recollection told to the author by a black woman who grew up in Mississippi. *Starting Out Right* does not recommend this book because, they say, the father is too strict, the animals that the child wishes to be have demeaning connotations, and the black child is forced into a stereotype of laziness. To this author, these criticisms seem unjust. The children are obviously laboring steadily; the father is not harsh, but anxious about their putting forth their best effort. Although three of the five animals are a snake, a dog, and a buzzard, two are a butterfly and a partridge. The story captures the quality of a remembrance. It is slow, dreamlike, and creates an atmosphere rather than concentrating on plot.

It does seem hard and unfair that, after the children have labored so long and diligently, their only recompense should be a lollipop, but the children obviously enjoy their treat. One black librarian particularly wanted her daughter to read this book because she wanted her to empathize with the kind of existence that some black children at one time had to lead, and indeed still do. Perhaps the book does contribute to the danger of stereotyping the poor Southern black family, but gentle and informative guidance on the part of the adult can help to offset this image. As there are few books about the rural Black, this book should not be simply set aside.

Sweet Pea, by Jill Krementz, is set in the contemporary rural South and is illustrated with photographs. The descriptive text centers around Barbara, a fourth-grader, whom everyone calls Sweet Pea. All of the people in the book are Blacks, including the minister, teacher, neighbors, and students in the school. This is a segregated community. Sweet Pea is a pleasant, energetic child who lives with her mother and four brothers. There are three other daughters in the family, but they do not live at home. Her father, who comes to visit every other Thursday, helps with the family support but lives and works in another community. There is no explanation given for the family separation. Sweet Pea does not remember when he moved out, but she misses him.

The family lives in a house set in the middle of a patch of land. It has no indoor toilet or running water. It does have electricity, and the family does own a television set, but it does not work. The children bathe regularly in a galvanized steel tub. Their house is heated by fireplaces.

Sweet Pea, who narrates the story, gives the reader a specific and vivid picture of her life. She describes her summer job of cotton-chopping, her home life, her friends, her family, her aspirations, and her school. She tells in detail of one of her school lessons about the "Indians." In the lesson, one member of the tribe says "that the settlers had helped them [the Native Americans] with better ways of farming and had made the Indians richer with trade and had taught the Indian children how to read and write and the women how to keep better homes and that they shouldn't have a war." Sweet Pea seems to have no perception that the lesson she is learning is a distorted view of history. She accepts whatever exists in her life with the same calm, coping attitude. She mentions at one point that she often has nightmares, but does not bother her mother with them. She rarely has good dreams.

This book graphically demonstrates the poverty level of many rural black families. It conveys the idea that this family works hard, enjoys what is enjoyable, and cares very much for each family member and each member of the community. None is self-pitying; none is defeated. One of the daughters goes to college. The family will endure.

Children can construct books of photographs describing their own homes and families. These books can then become part of the class library, and can serve as a basis of comparison and discussion.

FAMILY LIFE

Grandmothers and mothers play a very important role in the lives of black children in books. Very often the father is simply not present, his absence sometimes explained, sometimes not. In several books the child lives only with the grandmother; there is no explanation of what happened to the parents. Two such books are Joan Lexau's *Benjie* and *The Story Grandmother Told*, by Martha Alexander, mentioned earlier. In both books the child is very ably cared for by the grandmother. In both books the mood is gentle and positive. But it would have been better for the reader if there had been some explanation of why the children have no visible parents; even one explanatory sentence would suffice. The children are, nevertheless, seen as able and self-possessed. During the course of his story, Benjie grows emotionally, overcoming his shyness in order to find his grandmother's earring. The grandmother in each of these books is a caring, competent woman who is valued by her grandchild and by the community.

In *I Love Gram*, by Ruth Sonneborn, Ellie lives with her elder sister and mother as well as her grandmother, but it is the grandmother who takes care of Ellie while her mother and sister are away working and going to school. A crisis occurs when Ellie's grandmother becomes ill and has to go to the hospital. But the story has a happy ending. Ellie's grandmother eventually recovers and returns home. Meanwhile, the teacher has been very kind to Ellie, and friends have watched over her after school. Some questions that occur to the reader of this otherwise gentle and positive book concern the whereabouts of the father and the necessity for Ellie to be walked home from school. She seems to be somewhat overprotected. Perhaps that is to counteract the stereotype of neglect of black children that the literature has conveyed in the past. The family in this story is poor but not downtrodden. Ellie and her elder sister share a bed, but that is a source of comfort to Ellie, and her sister is very kind to her. The book is also useful in demonstrating that people who become ill enough to go to the hospital do frequently recover and come home.

The Lollipop Party, also by Sonneborn, repeats the image of the very protected child. Tomas lives with his mother, sister, and cat. The child is very distressed when, one day, his mother does not come home from work at her usual time — again there is no explanation of where the father is. This helps to perpetuate the myth of the black family's consisting only of the mother and children and, sometimes, the grandmother. It is almost as if there were the expectation that there will be no father at home. Rose Blue's *How Many Blocks in the World?* perpetuates this stereotype. The story is otherwise a pleasant, if dull one. When Brian, the hero of the story, goes to Head Start for the first time, he gets interested in how many city blocks there are in the world. He grows from thinking that there are three (the number from home to school) to five (the number additional around the school) and, after a bus trip to the Children's Museum with his class, to a recognition that there are millions of blocks in the world. It is somewhat difficult to believe that Brian has never been anywhere in the city with his mother. She seems always to be around, taking him to school and home. Have they never gone shopping together? And where is the father? No mention is made of him. Again there is the assumption that, since this is a black family, the father is not at home.

Fortunately, the trend seems to be turning away from depicting unhappy black families, at least in the books written for young children. Most of the books describing family life include an intact family. Even when the family is poor, there is the indication that they are working together to build their lives. All of Steptoe's books are examples of this nonstereotypic approach to black family life. Keats's children have whole families, too. In this day of increasing divorces it is not unusual to find families of all colors and economic conditions described as severed by divorce. But there should at least be some explanation given in order to allay the assumption that black families, in general, are fatherless. An excellent book portraying a warm, intact family is June Jordan's *New Life, New Room*.

Janice May Udry's books about Mary Jo (*What Mary Jo Wanted; What Mary Jo Shared; Mary Jo's Grandmother*) all describe a middle-class black family living together in a very conventional but loving way. In *Mary Jo's Grandmother*, Mary Jo gets the opportunity to help her grandmother dramatically. An independent old woman, the grandmother lives alone in an isolated rural area. During a visit, the child must cope with a difficult situation. Her grandmother has fallen and cannot get up. Though there is no phone, Mary Jo manages very well to get help. The whole family in this story is close and loving. The characters could be of any ethnic origin; but it is useful for them to be black if only to expand white readers' views of the world and to demonstrate to black readers that the literary world includes and values them. The father is a special person in *What Mary Jo Shared*. When Mary Jo chooses him for her

"Show and Tell" in school, he manages the situation with grace. In all the books he is pictured as an intelligent, understanding, successful man. All of Mary Jo's adventures are highly recommended by *Starting Out Right*.

Don't You Remember?, by Lucille Clifton, also includes an intact family, but they are not so middle class as Mary Jo's family. Both parents work — the father at a plant, the mother at a bakery. The chief character in this book is also a little girl, but younger and livelier than Mary Jo. She is a "four-year-old person who remembered everything." Although her name is Desire Mary Tate, she enjoys being called Tate. Her ambition is to work at the plant, just like her father. She is unhappy because her family keeps making promises to her that they postpone keeping. She is afraid that they have all forgotten. The story describes how her mother and father and three older brothers make her fifth birthday very happy. They fulfill all their promises on that day: her brothers permit her to drink coffee with them; her mother gives her a cake; her father takes her to the plant with him.

Again, erasing the negative stereotype is important. The family is together and will obviously remain so. They care about each other. They are working hard, but are not doing demeaning tasks. The father and mother are both valued, as are the children. They are poor but not desperate. Adding to the appeal of the book are the illustrations by Evaline Ness.

Black families dealing with special situations are also included in the books for young children. As has already been noted, sibling rivalry is one of the themes of Ezra Jack Keats's *Peter's Chair*. That problem gets resolved when Peter recognizes that he is growing up, an idea that he likes. In Eloise Greenfield's *She Come Bringing Me That Little Baby Girl*, Kevin's jealousy of the baby is complicated by the fact that he wanted a baby brother. The story nicely demonstrates the warmth of the parents' feelings toward both of their children and toward each other. The extended family helps Kevin to cope with his negative feelings, too. But ultimately, when his mother lets him hold the baby and permits him to show her off to his friends, he loses most of his angry and hurt feelings. The ending is somewhat pat, but the book is successful in presenting the black family as a loving entity. The illustrations by John Steptoe aid immeasurably in conveying the sense of the book.

In *Abby*, Jeannette Caines describes a black family that has adopted one of their children — a little girl. A charming, lively, bright youngster, Abby adores her older brother, Kevin. The family is a close, loving unit. The illustrations help to build this image as well. The author, who is black, has a husband and two children, Kevin and Abby.

Black Is Brown Is Tan, also reflecting the author's actual life, is a book about a family with a white father and a black mother. Arnold Adoff, the author, is white; his wife, Virginia Hamilton, is black. The book describes a joyous, love-filled family experience with all the members of the family, including aunts and uncles and grandmothers. It is the only book currently available on this theme. The message of the book is one of contentment and pride at being what each person is and of respect for each other. The illustrations confirm the text's mood. The family is active, happy, and together.

FRIENDS

One of the first integrated stories for young children was Lorraine and Jerrold Beim's *Two Is a Team*, published in 1945. The story is a simple one, describing the friendship between Ted and Paul, one of whom is black, the other, white. Ted and Paul play very well together and are very much alike. After having some difficulty building a coaster wagon cooperatively, they each build one separately. When they cause some damage as they ride in their coasters, they join together to make enough money to pay for the damage. The whole neighborhood is integrated, but the integration occurs in the pictures only; any of the characters might easily be any color. The story, though a mild one, constituted a major exception in children's books at the time of its publication. Perhaps one of the reasons for its excellent illustrations is that the illustrator, Ernest Crichlow, is black and was aware of the need for including black children in books.

Gabrielle and Selena, by Peter Desbarats, is another story of friends, one of whom is white and the other, black. Although *Starting Out Right* highly recommends it, this author found the book to be contrived and ineffective. The story revolves around the girls' decision to exchange identities with each other for a while. They each go to the other's house, where the parents play identical tricks on them. They pretend that their daughters like food that they really hate, hate desserts that they really love, and enjoy doing chores that they really do not like to do at all. They also independently of each other, set the same early bedtime for their visiting "daughters." The two girls find out about their parents' duplicity when they encounter each other halfway between their houses. They share what has happened to them and enjoy a laugh together. If the girls have, as the author says, been "like sisters" for years and years, why do they not know each other's likes and dislikes? After all, they have eaten and slept at each other's homes. Why did their parents not go along with their exchange? Is it taboo for a black child to sleep in a white child's bed and vice versa? And what of the friendship? On what is it based if they know so little about each other?

Again, only the illustrations give the clue that the girls are of different races. And perhaps, because interracial friendships are so rare, the book should be accepted more readily. To this author, however, the incongruity of the plot spoils the value of the illustrations. Perhaps a useful exercise might be for some children to rewrite the story to make better sense, while retaining the very appealing illustrations.

In contrast to *Gabrielle and Selena*, Phyllis Hoffman's *Steffie and Me* describes a friendship in which the two girls share their likes, dislikes, and ambitions. They frequently visit each other's homes and also share a boyfriend named Brucie. ("Stephanie and I are going to marry him.") The illustrations again are the only means for the reader to recognize that this is a friendship between a black girl and a white one. The most dominant mood of the story is exuberance. The narrator, who is the white child, relies strongly on Steffie's family because she goes to their house when her mother has not yet returned from work. Both families seem equally poor, equally happy, equally loving. In the case of this book, this author heartily concurs with *Starting Out Right's* recommendation.

SELF-IMAGE

Many nonfiction books have been created with the express purpose of helping the black reader to improve his or her self-image, and to cause the white reader to adapt, amend, or dispel any negative preconceptions about Blacks and Blackness. Although this chapter emphasizes works of fiction, a description of at least a few of these very effective books should be useful as well.

Some of these books are very direct in their message. Ann McGovern's *Black Is Beautiful* is a compilation of very lovely photographs and very simple text. The text is didactic in intent and approach, but it is effective next to the photographs. *Brown Is a Beautiful Color*, by Jean Carey Bond, tells of the journey of a black child through the country and then back to the city, where he finds many attractive and useful objects, animals, and people that are brown. This book, like the other one, uses rhyme.

Other books have been published on the subject of emotions, and try to help readers accept themselves and their feelings no matter what their color. These books are intended to convey universal responses rather than special ones; but it is gratifying to see a minority family on these pages. *Don't Worry, Dear*, by Joan Fassler, deals with the very young child's thumb-sucking, stuttering, and need for a "security blanket." The illustrator has chosen to represent these feelings common to all children by picturing a black family. Both parents are very supportive and understanding of the child's needs, and the problems get resolved as the child grows older. Readers identify with the circumstances.

Two books by Norma Simon also concentrate on the universality of children's feelings. The texts of the two books, *How Do I Feel?* and *I Know What I Like*, are illustrated with characters of both races. The situations are realistic; the feelings are genuine. Interestingly, in *How Do I Feel?* the main characters, who are white, live with their grandparents. There is no reason given for the absence of the parents. In *Look at Your Eyes*, Paul Showers describes for children the function and parts of the eye. The explanatory text is narrated by a black child, and the pictures of the community indicate that it is integrated. This brief view of a few books is meant to direct the reader's attention to an investigation of other such books. Whenever possible, even more minorities than black should be included in a book that purports to speak to all children.

FOLK TALES

The realm of oral literature is a rich and wide one. Unfortunately, our libraries and our classrooms have acquired an unbalanced collection of literature drawn from the folk. There have been many reasons for this, not the least of which has been the assumption that most Americans draw their heritage from Europe. Too often there has been no indication of the existence of any source other than the European. Children of all races have been deprived of the imaginative, colorful, and rich heritage derived from Asia, Africa, North America, and South America. They have remained ignorant of the interrelationships throughout all of folk literature, and of the effect that societies and cultures have had upon each other. They have missed the important implications of the universality of many of the themes that folk tales and myths share, no matter what the country of origin.

Fortunately, we are gaining more insight into our previous errors. Libraries and classrooms are beginning to be stocked with more of a variety. Children are beginning to ask about their own and others' backgrounds and to value diversity in a way that was not possible before. There are many collections of African folk tales in print. Not all are well written; appallingly few are even adequately illustrated. Perhaps a constructive activity would be to search out photographs and magazine illustrations that are attractive and realistic, substituting them for the unsatisfying illustrations already contained in books of folk tales.

Folk tales appeal to readers of all ages. Some stories are too difficult for very young readers to handle by themselves, but these are almost always effective and enjoyable when read aloud; teachers would do well to read folk tales to their classes as a steady diet. The tales present a ready curriculum in almost any area. Discussion about the differences and similarities among the different countries and peoples can provide material for many research projects, lessons, and other classroom activities. They are also an informative device for learning about customs and climates of other lands.

Readers should take care before reading the folk tales to verify the author's expertise. Some of the collections are taken from other literary sources and are several steps removed from authenticity. Others are told patronizingly by white "friends" of Africa. Still others are authentic but are not very interestingly told. There are many, however, that are written with competence and flavor. Not at all recommended is Frances Carpenter's *African Wonder Tales*. The author collected the tales from other literary sources and then retold them in a very patronizing, demeaning fashion. She imposes a white perspective on the stories, making negative judgments about the customs and behavior of the people of Africa. The illustrations match the stories; they convey no sense whatever of the characteristics of the people. This book is on the "not recommended" list of the publication called *Africa: A Life of Printed Materials for Children*, published by the Information Center on Children's Cultures. This booklet contains an annotated list of printed materials about Africa in general, as well as items specifically relating to individual countries. It includes fiction, nonfiction, and folklore. It does not annotate or give reasons for the items that it does not recommend.

Very different from the Carpenter collection is Joyce Cooper Arkhurst's *The Adventures of Spider: West African Folk Tales*, a collection introducing Spider, that mischievous, magic, amusing, amazing character. The author maintains a respectful attitude toward the stories and the customs described in them. The style of the writing is clear and smooth in these tales, which abound in elements of cleverness and good humor. Spider's adventures are detailed in mythlike stories as well as in less complex folk stories. Most anthologies of African tales contain at least several episodes about Spider.

Harold Courlander, who has traveled extensively in Africa and is a folklorist, has compiled several volumes of folk tales. One of them, in association with George Herzog, is called *The Cow-Tail Switch and Other West African Stories*. This one and another, in which Courlander was assisted by Albert Kofi Prempeh, called *Hat-Shaking Dance and Other Tales from the Gold Coast*, afford the reader an excellent, entertaining, and informative view of these tales. The notes included at the end of each of these books tell where each of the stories comes from and describe more of the customs of the people.

The illustrations in books of folk tales are rarely as good as the text. But in Terry Berger's *Black Fairy Tales* the illustrations are fitting companions to the colorful and intricate stories. Elton Fax's illustrations outshine the written word in Verna Aardema's *Tales from the Story Hat*; yet the stories are well worth reading. Some of them help the reader to recognize the origin of many of the *Uncle Remus* tales. The notes here, too, are an interesting addition to the stories, as is the glossary, which serves to add to the reader's appreciation of the tales. All these stories were adapted from other literary sources, three of them from Henry M. Stanley's *My Dark Companions and Their Strange Stories*. The stories are generally well told by the author.

Most books containing African myths and stories will prove to be worthwhile. They are almost unfailingly complex but clear. Their messages are gentle but pointed. Their action is rarely violent but seldom placid. The annotated Bibliography at the end of this chapter lists more collections that the reader can enjoy. These tales will almost inevitably communicate a sense of history and culture difficult to acquire in any other way.

HISTORY

Not enough black history has been written into textbooks, but more and more publishers are moving to fill that void. The Fitzgerald Publishing Company produces a very useful series of magazines in comic-book format called *The Golden Legacy*. The magazines include the stories of black people who have made outstanding contributions to the world. Each of the magazines, in addition to retelling the life of the featured person, includes paragraphs at the end describing the work of some other contemporary black men and women. Since this chapter is focusing on nonfiction, however, the reader should consult publishers' catalogs, and the sections in *Subject Guide to Children's Books in Print* listed under "Black" and "Blacks," in addition to the published bibliographies listed at the end of the chapter, in order to obtain a more complete picture of the books available.

Several books have been written in fictionalized form but present a true history of black people in the United States. Ann McGovern and Jacob Lawrence have each produced two quite different books about Harriet Tubman. Lawrence's illustrations are so stark and dramatic in *Harriet and the Promised Land* that although *Starting Out Right* recognize their artistic quality, they do not recommend this book for young children, because they fear that children will be frightened by the pictures. The book won the Brooklyn Art Book for Children Citation and was selected by the *New York Times* as one of the best-illustrated children's books of the year. The text is by Robert Kraus, but it is the illustrations, by Lawrence, a black artist, that carry the book. McGovern's *Runaway Slave* tells the story of Harriet Tubman in a smooth narrative, sympathetically conveying the details of her incredible life. Moses, as she was called, never got caught and never lost a passenger from her Underground Railroad ventures. One of the volumes of *The Golden Legacy* series also tells of Harriet Tubman.

Stories of the Underground Railroad have been told by several authors. F. N. Monjo wrote an "I Can Read History Book" called *The Drinking Gourd*, which is based on historical fact but is a fictionalized account. It tells the story of one of the stations on the Underground Railroad, run by a minister. In this story the minister's son, Tommy, who is always in trouble, discovers and then helps a black family attain freedom. The book is written in an unpatronizing style. The young white boy is responsible for saving the lives of the black runaway slaves, but at no time do the fugitives lose their dignity or sense of self-possession. They are not passive; they are ready to fight to the death rather than to lose their freedom. At the end of the story there is a thoughtful discussion between the boy and his father about what it means to be breaking a bad law. This book is one highly recommended by *Starting Out Right*.

Black history is often presented from a white perspective. In some cases, such as the Underground Railroad, it is just as much a part of white history as it is black. *Brady*, by Jean Fritz, is the story of a young white boy whose father, a minister, is a conductor on the Underground Railroad, but no one in the family knows about it. Brady grows in the story from an immature child who cannot keep his mouth shut about anything — and who does not have an opinion about slavery — to a young man who has courage and the ability to keep silent when he should. He carries a runaway slave to the next station on the Underground Railroad and becomes his father's partner. The struggle for abolition of slavery and the deep feelings that split the country are part of this story.

It is written so that readers will understand how the white community was split over the issue of slavery. Brady's mother, a Southerner, though disapproving of her husband's views, dutifully stands by him, even when half his congregation becomes angry enough to absent themselves from his services. Though the book attempts to convey a sense of the emotional conflict, it does not succeed as well in this endeavor as it does in communicating the conflict and growth in the boy. It dramatizes the courage of white people who recognized and fought the evil of slavery.

Florence Freedman's *Two Tickets to Freedom* also demonstrates the willingness of Whites to take risks to help fight slavery. But it focuses much more on the lives of Ellen and William Craft, who ingeniously managed to escape their bondage. Overcoming enormous odds, they manage to get to England, where they raise a family. After the Civil War they return to the United States, where they establish the Woodville

Cooperative Farm School for rural black children. This book is more factual than *Brady* is. It is equally dramatic, and emphasizes the black, rather than the white, experience.

A very important book that helps readers acquire perspective is Julius Lester's *Long Journey Home, Stories from Black History*. This book dramatically demonstrates the role that black people took in maintaining the Underground Railroad. Few students know that it was not only Whites who maintained stations for fugitive slaves; many of the conductors, as well as those who received runaways in their homes, were former slaves themselves. Black people were often the source of their own freedom; many did not have to rely upon the kindness and generosity of sympathetic Whites. The book tells very well the fascinating accounts of people who did not, perhaps, make a giant mark in the history books, but who were individuals who should be known. It tells of some of the horrors of slavery without oversentimentalizing the stories.

Two other books, both also written by black authors and both very readable and useful, are Lucille Clifton's *The Black BC's* and Deloris L. Holt's *The ABC's of Black History*. Clifton's book can be read at two levels. Each letter has a simple verse helping the young reader to fill in some of the concepts of black pride and history that the longer, more complex text then expands upon. Each letter takes up only one page, but that page is filled with factual and attitudinal information. Holt's *ABC* presents a person from black history for each of the letters of the alphabet. The people that Holt selected range from contemporary figures such as Duke Ellington, Martin Luther King, Jr., Malcolm X, and Benjamin Quarles, to figures from the past, such as Deborah Sampson Gannett, Pedro Alonso Nino, Harriet Tubman, and others. Both books would be valuable additions to any library.

Contemporary history is also depicted in books for children. June Jordan's *Dry Victories* compares the time of Reconstruction and the Civil Rights era. The book is a conversation between two young black men discussing, in black speech, their perception of the history of the Black American. The book's many valuable illustrations include photographs, articles from newspapers, and reproductions of posters. The illustrations help the text to convey to the reader the author's message of no real victory for Black Americans. In her afterword the author says that she is angry "and you should be too. Then we can do something about this after-mess of aftermath, following on so much tragedy." The book ends with the comment that the Poor People's March on Washington accomplished nothing and that Blacks are still in need of proper housing, social conditions, and economic and political power.

The Poor People's March and Resurrection City play an important part in Natalie Savage Carlson's *Marchers for the Dream*. But in this book, the main characters, Bethany and her great-grandmother, believe that the march has been effective. They are encouraged by Congress's appropriation of a large sum of money to help poor families buy or rent homes. The two, along with Bethany's mother, have had to move out of their old house because of urban renewal and have not been able to find another place to rent. They have been denied several places because of their color. When they return home to Massachusetts from their time in Washington, they decide to mount their own demonstration for better housing. A white landlord, Mr. Watson, is influenced by their peaceful demonstration. He arranges for them to rent a house that he owns in a predominantly white neighborhood at a price that they can afford. Although he warns them that life will be made difficult for them by their white neighbors, they are resolved to overcome all adversity.

The author of this book, who is white, obviously has deep sympathy for the cause of black people; but the book is oversimplified. It would have readers believe that anger is an inappropriate response to persecution. Emphasizing peaceful resistance as the best and only way to effect change, it holds out the promise that this approach will work. In so doing, it places the burden of action only on the Blacks. It nowhere indicates, except for Mr. Watson's gesture, that Whites share the responsibility for action.

Another book by the same author, *The Empty Schoolhouse*, addresses the problem of school segregation. It tells of a black Southern family in which one of the girls, Lullah, is very bright. The elder sister has left school, works at a cleaning job in a motel, and has a very low self image. She will never return to school and seems not to have any ambition for herself; recognizing Lullah's abilities, however, she wants her younger sister to complete her education. She proves to be an able person, but no one in the story seems to recognize it. The plot involves the desegregation of the local Catholic school, some Whites' attempts at destroying the school, and the eventual success of integration. At one point in the story, Lullah is the only child attending the school.

The story itself is a dramatic one and could truly have taken place in many communities. In addition to some negative implications about Blacks' appearance, all of the "consequential" people are Whites: the doctor, the priest, the teachers, and Lullah's best friend. Lullah's friend treats her abominably throughout most of the book, but Lullah sets such store in their "friendship" that she forgives all cruelties and is delighted to reestablish the relationship at the end of the book. The standard here is a white one. The Blacks appear to be subservient and impressed with white society. The ambition seems to be to grow up white.

The author seems not to be conscious of conveying this message; her intentions are obviously excellent. She specifies that the church services are integrated, but "since the colored folks sit in the back of the church, they get out first." There is no comment about the segregated seating other than that. The family is drawn as a loving, mutually respectful one. The father and mother are both strong figures, although they are anxious about the times that they live in. The two daughters behave in a responsible, independent fashion — they are admirable characters. All the characters are somewhat narrowly drawn, but the reader does acquire some feeling of their identity. This is a gentle, first-step kind of book that invites much discussion about "what next?"

Another book on the same topic is *Mary Jane*, by Dorothy Sterling. A public junior high has just been integrated, but Mary Jane is the only black girl there. Her friend, Fred Jackson, also attends the school. The author graphically describes the ordeal that the two young people must endure the entire first week of school. She leads us through the semester with Mary Jane. Fred is very tall and an excellent basketball player, but Mary Jane has no outstanding talents to overcome people's prejudices. The music teacher invites her to come to choir. But after Mary Jane tells her that she cannot sing, the music teacher is incredulous; Mary Jane realizes that it is not due to kindness but to a stereotypic preconception that the music teacher has invited her.

This well-written book describes the depths of bigotry that a community contains. To some readers, the response of the Whites may seem unbelievable; to others, the lack of extreme violence may be unrealistic. The author attempts to present a realistic, sensitive, and sympathetic account of the difficulties that black students encounter when they take advantage of their legal rights. Mary Jane and Fred are well-mannered, middle-class students. Mary Jane's grandfather is a renowned agricultural biologist. They are depicted as "quality." They want no trouble; they rarely even fight back. When Mary Jane does react to taunts, she is chastised by her family for doing so.

Mary Jane, published in 1959, was for its time a frank and important book. It is somewhat less powerful for contemporary readers because of its deference to white behavior and its acceptance of cowardice on the part of white "friends." Sally, Mary Jane's only friend in school, cannot associate with her after school. Sally implies that she is Mary Jane's friend because no other girl in the junior high wants to associate with a tiny, blushing girl like her. Sally feels that she is inept at everything. There is no indication that she likes Mary Jane because of her own individual characteristics. Her liberal white parents forbid her to see Mary Jane outside of school because they have received nasty phone calls telling them that their daughter is eating lunch with a black girl, and they are scandalized. Mary Jane's family is very understanding; recognizing the necessity for moving one step at a time, they counsel Mary Jane to be patient.

At the end of the book Mary Jane has made great progress and so have a number of white students. She has two teachers as allies, the principal appreciates her qualities, and her feelings of self-worth have returned. Unfortunately, she seems no longer to have any black friends. It would be sad, indeed, if integration separated black people from each other rather than bringing them and others closer together.

Many new books for older readers contain black characters and make allusions to the problems of minorities in the United States. Readers from the ages of eight to twelve are considered to be much more sophisticated and mature now in their reading preferences than they were before. Racial violence and abuses are realistically portrayed. For the older child the plot and the characters are emphasized, since the literary quality of a long text makes a tremendous difference in books for these older readers. Whereas in a picture book, the illustrations can help to carry the message and make an impact, for the older child the words convey the bulk of the effect. Therefore, teachers, parents, and librarians must seek out books that have high literary quality as well as constructive social values.

Charlie and the Chocolate Factory was discussed in the introductory chapter as an example of a very well constructed but harmful book. Classics such as *Mary Poppins*, by P. L. Travers, and *Dr. Dolittle*, by Hugh Lofting, are also books that adults should help children to read in light of today's needs and the level of societal awareness. P. L. Travers, in an interview recorded in the Interracial Books for Children *Bulletin* (see References) admits she knows little, if anything, about Blacks but has consented to have her chapter "Bad Tuesday" revised because she realizes it troubles black readers. The illustrations, which convey the same negative stereotype as the text did, have not been changed. And the text still includes pejorative references to minorities. The desirable values in *Mary Poppins* are unmistakably the values of white and English superiority. If readers can be helped to counteract its damaging implications and its obvious air of colonialism, then the *Mary Poppins* series can be enjoyable as an imaginative fantasy. But we may not yet have powerful enough ammunition. Certainly the ugly implications of the book should be treated as such whenever adults have the opportunity to intervene.

Dr. Dolittle is far more obvious and direct in its pervasive negative view of black people. Prince Bumpo appears throughout the series as a fool. He is first introduced to us as the Black Prince who falls in love with Sleeping Beauty, awakening her only to find that she would rather sleep for another hundred years than to marry a Black Prince. Dr. Dolittle accedes to Bumpo's plea to be turned white, in return for Bumpo's freeing the doctor from captivity. Bumpo's face becomes a horrid, though temporary, chalk white, and he is happy. In subsequent books in the series he accompanies Dr. Dolittle on his voyages, serving as comic relief and as a further object of ridicule.

Other racial "jokes" abide in the series. Dr. Dolittle's animals are contemptuous of black people and constantly make snide remarks. The atmosphere is one of patronizing "White Man's Burden." The article "Doctor Dolittle — The Great White Father," by Isabelle Suhl, analyzes the series in this light (see References). Suhl points to the sections on the doctor's rule over the Indians. They are described as helpless, ignorant, superstitious, and childlike people. The Africans that he encounters are treated as savage, vain, grotesque, and stupid. All the illustrations reinforce the message of the text. Though *Dr. Dolittle* has recently been expurgated, the essence of the racism remains. Perhaps if readers have achieved the level of looking at this as a monstrous piece of historical evidence of racism and can cope with it constructively, the reading of this "classic" can be tolerated. But it should certainly be handled with much caution.

Children are always learning and growing. They need to be helped to deal with the information that they encounter in the books that they read. Their favorites are sometimes harmful to them in racial awareness. Even books that are acknowledged to be aesthetically fine can be marred by authors' lack of self-perception. The benevolence of the Whites and the contrasting dependence of the minority member is a frequent message in well-meaning but ultimately harmful books. One such book is *The Cay*, by Theodore Taylor. This book won the Jane Addams Book Award for stressing the dignity and equality of all mankind, peace, and social justice. This honor is conferred by the Women's International League for Peace and Freedom and the Jane Addams Peace Association. *The Cay* also won, among other literary awards, the Woodward School Annual Book Award for demonstrating good human relations. As Albert V. Schwartz discusses in his commentary upon the book (see References), it is really the story of a white child's inheritance of the mantle of colonialism.

The story of the white boy who is rescued and cared for by the old black sailor ends unhappily for the sailor, who gives up his life to save the child. The book is meant to impress the reader with the changes of heart that the boy experiences. He converts from being a person who fears and looks down upon black people to one who is grateful that a black person saved his life. He supposedly then becomes comfortable with all black folks forever after. This progress is seen as enormously positive by some readers. It is deemed a virtue to no longer despise and avoid the company of Blacks. But the boy's communication with Blacks is not on an equal-to-equal basis; his association with them has no other than a selfish purpose for the boy. He will never become an activist in the fight against racism. His personal experience, upon which he now bases his attitude toward all Blacks, is not an adequate foundation for aiding society. The critics are just in their attacks.

Other recent prize-winning books have also been criticized, but by no means universally, for their racist implications. The charges are not of blatant or conscious negativism; rather, they are of a far more subtle and controversial nature. Both *Sounder*, by William Armstrong, and *The Slave Dancer*, by Paula Fox, won the most coveted and prestigious award for children's book writing, the John Newbery Medal. Both books are written by white authors. No one has suggested that the books are not very well written: they demonstrate tremendous literary talent on the part of their creators. One of the chief criticisms stems from the fact of the authors' Whiteness. Some critics believe that no non-Black can legitimately write about the black experience.

In recalling the fourth criterion for a nonracist book (p. 180 of this chapter), the reader will note that direct experience is recommended over the vicarious. But in recommending that an author be a member of the group written about in the book, it is not ruled out that others may have appropriate past experience or interest to equip them for their task.

While it is true that having lived an experience adds authenticity to the recounting of it, in this author's opinion, it is a useful but not totally necessary prerequisite for success. If an artist has insight, empathy, accurate information, and talent, then the resulting work can be effective in achieving its stated goals. If any of the four ingredients is lacking, then the product will be less powerful in its positive achievement.

William Armstrong explains in an author's note at the beginning of *Sounder* that his first teacher, a black man who taught in a "one-room Negro school," told him the story that he then retells in this book. The plot is of a poor black Southern family who sharecrop on a white man's land. They are very poor and hungry. The father is a strong, vigorous man, but the mother is a passive person who believes that it is God's will that the Black is "born to lose." There are other children in the family, and there is a hound called Sounder, the only character in the book who has a name. The others are called "the boy" or "the mother" or "the father." None of the white characters is named, either.

The father steals a ham and is dragged off, seemingly unresisting, to jail. The dog, trying to interfere, is shot, crippled, and deformed as a result. The father is kept imprisoned for a number of years, during which time his son keeps searching for him to no avail. The son eventually meets a teacher (it is not clear whether he is black or white) and begins to satisfy his craving for learning. When the father does return, he, like the dog, is crippled and deformed. Both the man and the dog are feeble relics of their former selves; at the end of the story they both die. The son continues his education. The author leaves the reader with the impression that the ghosts of the man and dog remain youthful and strong and that the hope of the boy and his people will be fulfilled through quiet acceptance of one's lot and through education.

Critics of this book reprove the author for not naming any of the characters except for the dog. They claim that the lack of names dehumanizes the people, and they decry the seeming valuing of the animal over the humans. In this author's opinion, Armstrong means to use the dog as the symbol for the man. The dog's powerful voice, which is stilled by the ugliness of oppression, becomes full-bodied again after the man has regained his freedom. The dog and the man are symbolically linked in the book. When the man dies, so does the dog. Here, too, the critics resent the analogy. They point out that the man is made to go off by himself to a private place to die, just as the mother has explained that animals do. The injuries to both dog and man are almost identical. Perhaps Armstrong means to tell the reader that this is the way some human beings are treated by others.

For white readers the book presents a clear and strong indictment of an oppressive system. It does arouse a deep sense of sympathy and anger on behalf of the treatment of the Blacks. It invites questions about a country's so-called democratic system that permits these abuses to occur. But it may also cause a white reader to think, "Why didn't anyone fight back? Why didn't the family seek legal help? Why did the man steal the ham? Why didn't they attempt to hide the ham and evidence once he did steal it? Why was the mother so defeatist and so discouraging of her son's ambition?" And these questions may possibly lead the reader to feel just a little smug or superior without ever investigating the truth of the implications.

The black reader may also have some questions about the story. The analogy using the dog and other animals may be useful as a literary device, but it can also be demeaning to a black person. The total defeatism of the mother and the son's passive behavior — even in seeking out his father and then an education — may be somewhat perplexing to the reader. Nowhere in the book is it explained why the father must remain imprisoned for so long. He is supposedly let off early (after so many years?), because of his severe injuries (caused by a mine explosion). There is no mention made beforehand of the length of his sentence, only that he went to "hard labor." Is it not difficult to believe that the stealing of a ham, most of which was returned, would call down such a punishment? Why did the author choose to treat his character so very harshly? Historical investigation may corroborate the reality of this severe sentence, but it remains a puzzle in the story.

For those readers who have never been deeply moved by the plight of the Black as victim, this book can constitute an important experience of growth. For those who already understand and decry white oppression, it may possibly be an affirmation of white abuse. But it may also help to affirm some negative images in the minds of those readers who believe that black people are essentially incapable of asserting their own rights. It may confirm for some the idea that Blacks are passive, ignorant, unambitious people who cannot rise above their plight. It may salve the consciences of some readers who rest comfortably at the thought that schools are now "integrated" and that, therefore, this could not occur in today's enlightened age. There is no one correct interpretation or criticism of this book. The reader and interested adults must decide for themselves what the message is; they must also decide for themselves how to proceed. But it is helpful to be aware of the ambiguity of the text, of the ambivalence of the messages, and of the author's special past experiences in order to process fully the experience of reading the book.

The Slave Dancer, which won the 1974 Newbery Award, raised a storm of protest from black and white critics even stronger than that sparked by Sounder. (See Interracial Books for Children, Bulletin, Vol. 5, No. 5, 1974.) The criticism centers on the author's portrayal of slaves on the ship and her seeming lack of blaming the white slave traders. The critics point to the ugliness of the remarks that the white crew members make about the slaves, recognizing that, though these may not be the author's opinion, they constitute the only information that the book offers about the character of the slaves.

None of the slaves is identified by name except, at the very end, for one boy, Ras. None of the slaves has an identity other than that of a piece of the cargo on the horrible ship. The hero of the story is Jessie, a thirteen-year-old boy who has been kidnapped from his native New Orleans in order to play music on the slave ship for the slaves' exercise. The boy's reactions to the kidnapping and to the enterprise of slavery may be somewhat puzzling to the reader. It is a strange, removed experience, almost as if it takes place in another world. The characters of the white men on the ship are also out of focus and blurred. It is as if the whole venture is part of a terrible nightmare that one can awaken from and remember with dread, but have the option of not believing.

In the story the white characters keep giving Jessie all kinds of details about slavery, slaves, and the slave trade. Many of the details are false and degrading. Some are true, but only partly so. For example, one of the crew members tells Jessie that the slaves are there because African kings captured and sold them. He would have Jessie believe that all the slaves are there by the hand of their own people. Even the Portuguese slave broker is black. There is no indictment of the Whites' role in the institution of slavery. One could believe that, if the African kings refused to supply their people for the slave trade, it would stop.

As Julius Lester tells of it, in To Be a Slave, it is true that some white slave traders formed alliances with some black African tribal chiefs; but this was by no means the only method of capture. In The Slave Dancer there is never a discussion about the morality of slavery itself; it seems to be taken for granted that slavery is a viable institution. Paula Fox only once gives the reader a slight shred of evidence that the crew members' comments are not to be trusted. When Purvis, a crew member, tells Jessie that the slaves grow quite cheerful once they realize that they will be fed regularly and not eaten themselves, Jessie perceives that this does not happen at all. They remain miserable and mournful. But the weight of description remains that of the Whites' bigoted, demeaning observations.

At first Jessie is concerned about the slaves. He sees their suffering and feels for them. But by the time they have journeyed awhile, he begins to hate them and to resent them as if they, rather than the white men who kidnapped him, were the cause of his misery. He acquires the same attitude of contempt that his white partners in crime have. No adequate reason is given for this by the author. Psychologically, the response may be normal in this far-from-normal situation — studies of the behavior of prisoners in concentration camps indicate that sometimes victims despise their peers in the manner of the persecutor — but the author tells none of this. She gives us no indication that the boy gets over his hatred, except that the crew members accuse him of sympathy for the slaves. The book recounts horror after horror. And still the slaves are faceless and nameless.

One young slave is identified apart from the others from the time that the slaves board the ship. He frequently catches Jessie's eye, retrieves his fife for him, and keeps recurring, but only to be mentioned in connection with Jessie's awareness that he exists. It is this boy, Ras, who, with Jessie, survives the holocaust that hits the ship. Everyone else dies in one way or another. Jessie is instrumental in rescuing Ras, and they both wash up on shore. It turns out to be Mississippi, where they are found and cared for by an old black man, an escaped slave who helps Ras to freedom via the Underground Railroad. He permits Jessie to return home after extracting and believing Jessie's promise that he will not be betrayed. When Jessie returns home, he demonstrates that he has been affected by his experience in only two ways: he never goes to visit the slave blocks, and he cannot bear hearing music of any sort.

The author has created an ugly, probably realistic portrait of the appalling degradation of a slave ship. Her readers must be sickened by the lack of humanity of the entire venture. White readers may be moved to feelings of guilt, sympathy, or indignation. Black readers may be moved to anger, empathy, or possibly shame. Therein lies the problem of the book. If the author chose to present this situation as the central theme of her book, she should also have recognized that its impact would be of mixed value. She fails to articulate any opinions or evidence to counteract the crew's distorted view of the slaves and the slave trade.

The author has chosen to draw Jessie as a person who refrains from active intervention even after his harrowing experience. He avoids music. This deprivation of what once was important and enjoyable to him seems to be the most telling effect that the experience has had on him. Again, the nightmare quality returns; the whole affair becomes one that the reader can decide to reject as a bad dream. There is certainly no indication that any responsibility falls on Jessie or the reader to engage in any action to remedy the observed evils. Jessie even says, at the end of the book, that it is impossible for him to fulfill his resolve to avoid contact with anything connected with slavery. "But I soon discovered that everything I considered bore, somewhere along the way, the imprint of black hands." Eventually he settles in Rhode Island, although he misses the South. If the author wished to arouse consciousness in her readers, could she not have had her hero take some positive steps? Could he not, at the very least, have become actively involved in the Underground Railroad? As it is, the book remains, at best, a masterful descriptive piece. At worst, it is an apologia for white participation in the slave trade.

Julius Lester's *To Be a Slave* also graphically portrays the horrors wrought upon Blacks. But, unlike Fox, he helps the reader to see slaves as individuals. Many of them, despite all odds, maintained their selfhood and managed to overcome their specific hardships. Giving us their own words, he helps us, by adding his own comments, to understand more deeply what they signify. After offering the reader descriptions of some of the ways that some slaves managed to enjoy themselves, Lester adds, "whatever pleasure the slave was able to provide for himself was a remarkable testimony to the ability to retain humanity under the most unhuman conditions." Lester does not leave it to the inexperienced reader to draw conclusions; he helps every reader to acquire a deeper perception.

It is an author's responsibility, in this transitional time in history, to make a work that includes minorities as a part of the movement toward a better society. Good work is read and accepted by so many people that it lies in the author's power to make an impact, the results of which will be felt by future generations. It is also the parent's, the librarian's, and the teacher's responsibility to bring to the young reader's attention those ideas, attitudes, and facts that will help to construct a new and healthy community for everyone.

REFERENCES

Alexander, Rae. "What Is a Racist Book?" Interracial Books for Children, *Bulletin*, Vol. 3, No. 1 (Autumn 1970) 1, 5, 7.
    Cites research that demonstrates damaging effect of literature on black children. Recommends the exclusion of any book that may give pain to even one black child. Critiques a number of books.

Baker, Augusta. "The Changing Image of the Black in Children's Literature." *The Horn Book Magazine,* Vol. 51, No. 1 (February 1975), 79–88.
Traces the history of the Black in children's literature. Provides questions to be used as criteria for judging quality of these books. Supports the search for black authors. Supports the positive direction of contemporary books. Praises *Sounder* and *The Slave Dancer.* Hopes for a sense of universality on the part of the reading public.

Baxter, Katherine. "Combating the Influence of Black Stereotypes in Children's Books," *The Reading Teacher,* Vol. 27, No. 6 (March 1974), 540–44.
Excellent article analyzing both subtle and blatant stereotyping in children's books. Criteria presented for judging books. Recommendations made for helping children recognize racist implications.

Beck, Katy and Armin. "All They Do Is Run Away," *Civil Rights Digest,* August 1972.
Discusses impact of racial insults upon children. Recommends in-service programs so that teachers can learn how to handle this problem.

Bernstein, Joanne E. "Minorities in Fiction for Young Children," *Integrated Education,* Vol. 11, No. 3 (May–June, 1973), 34–37.
Ninety-eight stories with school settings analyzed to see how roles of minority group members are portrayed. Is optimistic about current trend toward multiethnic portrayals. Bibliography (not annotated).

Bingham, Jane. "The Pictorial Treatment of Afro-Americans in Books for Young Children 1930–1968," *Elementary English,* Vol. 48, No. 7 (November 1971), 880–86.
Investigated illustrations in forty-one recommended books, which had black characters in them. Criteria are offered for judging the impact of the illustrations. Recommendations are made, based on the findings of the study.

Birtha, Jessie. "Portrayal of the Black in Children's Literature," *Philadelphia Library Association Bulletin,* Vol. 24 (July, 1969), 187–97.
Suggests guidelines for examining books, with specific evaluative criteria. Offers her own list of notable books portraying black people. Author is a black librarian.

Britton, Jean E. *Selected Books About the Afro-American for Very Young Children, K-2.* Commonwealth of Massachusetts, Department of Education, Division of Curriculum and Instruction, Bureau of Curriculum Innovation. (182 Tremont St., Boston, Mass. 02111.)
This bibliography was compiled with the assistance of the Massachusetts Commission Against Discrimination. It includes guidelines for evaluating books and an indication of books that children in Roxbury particularly enjoyed. Its listing of other bibliographies is somewhat out of date. It also lists publishers and their addresses.

Broderick, Dorothy M. *Image of the Black in Children's Fiction.* New York: R. R. Bowker, 1973.
Excellent historical and background information for learning about, and understanding the negative treatment of Blacks in children's books. The author includes quotes from books written for children that are

demeaning to Blacks. She demonstrates the pervasive negative attitudes and behaviors specifically and powerfully.

Carlson, Ruth Kearney. *Emerging Humanity, Multi-Ethnic Literature for Children and Adolescents*. Illus. Louise Noack Gray and Ernest Jaco. Dubuque, Iowa: William C. Brown, 1972.

Excellent reference containing discussions, bibliographies, and practical suggestions for activities relating to minority groups. The two chapters specifically relating to Blacks are informative and extensive.

Citron, Abraham F. "Rightness of Whiteness." Detroit: Office of Urban Education, 1971. (College of Education, Wayne State University, Detroit, Mich. 48202.)

Discusses the impact of language, environment, and books on white and black children. Cites research; provides useful bibliography.

Clapp, Ouida H. "Language Arts — The Invisible Child," *Instructor*, Vol. 80, No.6 (February 1971), 63-65.

Pleads for inclusion of books containing black characters, particularly in order to help the black child.

Cornelius, Paul. "Interracial Children's Books: Problems and Progress," *Library Quarterly*, Vol. 41, No. 2 (April 1971), 106-27.

Reviews criticism and research leading to the awareness of the dearth of representation for minority groups in children's books. Presents a history of books dealing with black characters. Describes a number of books, organizations, and movements designed to change the system. Presents current issues about children's books containing black characters. Critiques several books. Useful overview.

Council on Interracial Books for Children. *Bulletin*.

An excellent newsletter, helping readers to analyze current children's books and keeping them abreast of current issues.

Davis, Mavis Wormley. "Black Images in Children's Literature: Revised Editions Needed," *School Library Journal*, Vol. 18, No. 5 (January 1972), 37-39.

Criticizes language and character portrayal demeaning Blacks in many children's books. Praises others for their positive treatment. Recommends revision of the negative books.

Denby, Robert V. "Literature by and about Negroes for the Elementary Level," *Elementary English*, Vol. 46, No. 7 (November 1969), 909-13.

A listing of ERIC documents including rationale, background readings for teachers, and bibliographies on Blacks in children's literature. The documents listed are through 1968, including some which are no longer in print but are still available on microfiche.

Douglass, Joseph H. "Mental Health Aspects of the Effects of Discrimination Upon Children," *Young Children*, May 1967, pp. 298-304.

Discusses effects of discrimination on children, and, by extension, on society.

Foundation for Change. "Black Women Are Proud," January 1973.

One of a series of pamphlets presenting historical information about minorities. The aim is to help minority children build and reinforce a positive self-image.

Fraser, James. "Black Publishing for Black Children," *School Library Journal*, Vol. 20, No. 3 (November 1973), 19–24.

Traces the history of black publishing; that is, enterprises "owned and operated by black people producing literature by black writers with the needs and interests of black people in mind." Gives an overview of companies and their publications. Supplies a list of publishers and their addresses.

Gast, David K. "The Dawning of the Age of Aquarius for Multiethnic Children's Literature," *Elementary English*, Vol. 47, No. 5 (May 1970), 661–65.

A very influential article, listing different approaches to beware of in children's books dealing with the black experiences.

Glancy, Barbara J. "Annotated Bibliography of Integrated and Black Books for Children," in *Black Image: Education Copes with Color*, edited by Grambs and Carr. Dubuque, Iowa: William C. Brown, 1972.

Classifies books in age groupings. Includes books with black characters with content related to racial problems, and also with content not related to racial problems in separate lists.

———. "Why Good Interracial Books Are Hard to Find," pp. 44–45 in *Black Image: Education Copes with Color*, edited by Grambs and Carr. Dubuque, Iowa: William C. Brown, 1972.

Discusses the roles of publishers, reviewers, sales, library and teacher selection tools in seeing to it that interracial books become available to children. Includes an excellent and comprehensive (though now outdated) bibliography of bibliographies.

Graham, Lorenz. "An Author Speaks," *Elementary English*, Vol. 50, No. 2 (February 1973), 185–88.

Graham, a black author, tells about his life and his decision to become a writer.

Granstrom, Jane, and Silvey, Anita. "A Call for Help: Exploring the Black Experience in Children's Books," *The Horn Book*, Vol. 48, No. 4 (August 1972), 345–404.

Reproduces a panel discussion among concerned educators and librarians concerning the black experience as negatively portrayed in children's books.

Griffin, Louise. *Multi-Ethnic Books for Young Children: An Annotated Bibliography for Parents and Teachers*. Washington, D.C.: National Association for the Education of Young Children, 1970.

Lists books available up to 1970 for minority, nonmiddle-class children. Many cultures listed. Adult books suggested for parents and teachers. Annotations are very useful.

Information Center on Children's Cultures. *Africa: A List of Printed Materials for Children*. New York: U.S. Committee for UNICEF, 1968.

An excellent annotated bibliography. Divided into sections on each country, with further subclassifications when appropriate. Also includes books that are not recommended.

Jenkins, Esther C. "Multi-Ethnic Literature: Promises and Problems," *Elementary English*, Vol. 50, No. 5 (May 1973), 693–99.

Describes goals of a multiethnic literature program and recommends ways of setting one up.

Keating, Charlotte Matthews. *Building Bridges of Understanding Between Cultures*. Tucson, Ariz.: Palo Verde Publishing Company, 1971.

Several chapters of this book pertain to books concerning Black Americans. One chapter is devoted to Black Americans, one to selections with multiethnic representation, one to Africa, and one to the Caribbean. The annotations are extensive, interesting, and very personalized. The author may not be critical or sensitive enough to the negative implications of some of the books that she recommends; but her intentions are honest, and the book is, in general, a valuable one.

Kerckfoff, Richard, and Trella, Sherry Crane. "Teaching Race Relations in The Nursery School," *Young Children*, April 1972, 240.

Describes how reading certain books to young children helped them to develop constructive racial attitudes.

Lanes, Selma G. "Black is Bountiful," in *Down the Rabbit Hole*. New York: Atheneum, 1971.

Discusses several books, including classics, in terms of their treatment of black characters and their effect on the reader. Also reviews the criticisms of some books. Presents interesting points of view for the reader to consider.

Larrick, Nancy. "The All-White World of Children's Books," *Saturday Review*, September 11, 1965, 63–85.

Presents a powerful argument against stereotypes in children's books. Helps the reader to recognize subtle negative implications in books. Expresses hope that publishers will take heed.

Latimer, Bettye I. "Children's Books and Racism," *The Black Scholar*, May–June, 1973, 21–27.

This article, excerpted from *Starting Out Right*, includes the listing of the most common flaws in books about Blacks.

———— (ed.). *Starting Out Right, Choosing Books About Black People for Young Children*. Madison, Wis.: Department of Public Instruction, 1972.

Presents sixteen criteria for judging books involving Blacks. Several chapters discuss the issues involved in books for children. The authors annotate more than two hundred books according to their established criteria. They are in alphabetical order by title. Not-recommended books are also included in the bibliography. The authors suggest several ways of effecting change. A very useful publication.

Lester, Julius. "The Kinds of Books We Give Children: Whose Nonsense?" *Publishers' Weekly*, Vol. 197, No. 8 (February 23, 1970), 86.

Recommends that we begin to acquaint our children, through books, to the real world.

————, and Woods, George. "Black and White: An Exchange," *New York Times Book Review*, May 24, 1970, 1, 34–38.

Correspondence between Julius Lester and George Woods concerning their opinions on the way books affect black and nonblack readers. Both points of view are well stated and represent two perspectives.

MacCann, Donnarae. "Overdue," *Wilson Library Bulletin*, Vol. 46, No. 9, (May 1971), 880–81.
Recommends a careful analysis of the images in children's books.
———, and Woodard, Gloria (eds.). *The Black American in Books for Children: Readings in Racism*. Metuchen, N.J.: Scarecrow Press, 1972.
A series of informative articles, all dealing with issues of minorities in children's books.
Mathis, Sharon Bell. "True/False Messages for the Black Child," *Black Books Bulletin*, Vol. 2, No. 3 and 4 (Winter 1974), 12–19.
Criticizes a number of books demeaning Blacks by their use of stereotypes and "poison-words." Illuminating article.
NAACP Education Department. *Integrated School Books*. New York: NAACP Special Contribution Fund, 1967.
A descriptive bibliography of 399 preschool and elementary school texts and story books. Out of date, but useful because of the categories included.
National Conference of Christians and Jews. *Books for Brotherhood*.
The books in this annual listing were selected "on the basis of their contribution to the search for community in a pluralistic society. . ." The children's and young people's list for 1971–72 was selected by a panel of experts. Includes books about different minorities. Notations are helpful.
Parks, Carole A. "Good-bye Black Sambo," *Ebony*, November 1972, 60–70.
Describes a number of black children's book authors and their writing. Applauds the rise in numbers of these authors and the emergence of black publishing companies.
Reid, Virginia M. (ed.). *Reading Ladders for Human Relations*, 5th edition. Washington, D.C.: American Council on Education, 1972.
Contains discussion of necessity for positive self-image. Reviews many books considered to be helpful in this area. Also includes multiethnic literature.
Rollins, Charlemae. "The Role of the Book in Combating Prejudice," *Wilson Library Bulletin*, Vol. 42, No. 2 (October 1967), 176.
Useful history of treatment of black characters in children's books. Analysis of some books included.
——— (ed.). *We Build Together*. Urbana, Ill.: National Council of Teachers of English, 1967.
Although this bibliography was reprinted in 1974, it was not revised. Somewhat out-of-date, it is still useful. It contains a discussion of the history and scope of books containing black characters, as well as an extensive categorized annotated bibliography.
Rollock, Barbara (ed.). *The Black Experience in Children's Books*, 1974. (Office of Branch Libraries, New York Public Library, 8 E. 40th St., New York, N.Y. 10016.)
The most complete listing of books relating to black people. Everything that has a black character in it is included. Annotations are very inform-

ative. The list, originally compiled by Augusta Baker, is regularly updated.

Schmidt, Nancy J. "Books by African Authors for Non-African Children," *Africana Library Journal*, Vol. 2, No. 4 (Winter 1971), 11.
Interesting reviews of several books on Africa.

Schwartz, Albert V. "*The Cay*: Racism Rewarded," Interracial Books for Children *Bulletin*, Vol. 3, No. 4 (1971), also in *Interracial Digest*, No. 1, 35-37.
Seriously criticizes *The Cay*, by Theodore Taylor. Attacks the handling of the character of Timothy, the black sailor. Schwartz discusses the negative presentations in this book and considers that some parts of it constitute an outrage.

———. "*Sounder*: a Black or a White Tale?" Interracial Books for Children *Bulletin*, Vol. 3, No. 1 (1970), also in *Interracial Digest*, No. l, 26-29.
Schwartz criticizes Armstrong's *Sounder* because of its white perspective, the anonymity of the family, and the stereotypes supported. He says that the book does not accurately reflect the black perspective and is not relevant to black children.

Shargel, Susan, and Kane, Irene. *We Can Change It*. San Francisco: Change for Children, 1974.
An excellent, though brief, annotated bibliography of nonsexist, nonracist books. Also suggests several ways of dealing with books so that children will learn to combat racist and sexist attitudes and practices.

Shepard, Ray Anthony. "Adventures in Blackland with Keats and Steptoe," Interracial Books for Children *Bulletin*, Vol. 3, No. 4 (Autumn 1971), 3.
Makes distinction between black and white illustrators. Claims that "Steptoe shows love for his people." "Of course, John Steptoe is not a liberal White, thus he has no need to show human sameness, but instead celebrates the ethnic differences of Blacks." Claims that Steptoe's stories would have to be changed if the characters were made nonblack. Claims that Keats's characters would, if turned white, not change the story. "For the Black reader, . . . the difference is simple. In Keats there is someone who looks like me, and in Steptoe there is someone who knows what is going on."

Suhl, Isabelle. "Doctor Dolittle — The Great White Father" in Interracial Books for Children *Bulletin*, Vol. 2, Nos. 1 and 2 (1969).
This article stimulated many people to reexamine not only *Doctor Dolittle*, but other classics as well for their possible racist content. The article analyzes the plot, characterization, and style of the *Doctor Dolittle* series.

Thompson, Judith, and Woodard, Gloria. "Black Perspectives in Books for Children," *Wilson Library Bulletin*, Vol. 44, No. 4 (December 1969), 416-24.
Comments on the need for writers to include a black perspective based on black experience. Criticizes books which place black characters in subsidiary roles. Lists acceptable books for young children and older children.

Walton, Jeanne. "The American Negro in Children's Literature," *Eliot-Pearson School*, February 1964. (Alumnae Office, Eliot-Pearson School, Tufts University, Medford, Mass. 02155.)
> Criticizes certain books for having defects when describing Blacks. Provides annotated bibliography.

Watt, Lois B. (ed.). *Literature for Disadvantaged Children, a Bibliography*. Washington, D.C.: Office of Education, U.S. Department of Health, Education, and Welfare, 1968.
> Somewhat out-of-date, but useful because of the categories included and information noted.

Wolfe, Ann G. *About 100 Books . . . a Gateway to Better Intergroup Understanding*. New York: American Jewish Committee, Institute of Human Relations, 1972.
> Includes books published between 1969 and 1972. Several hundred books examined; one hundred chosen. Several minorities represented. Annotations are brief but useful.

Wunderlich, Elaine. "Black Americans in Children's Books," *The Reading Teacher*, Vol. 28, No. 3 (December 1974), 282–85.
> Recalls Nancy Larrick's 1965 study on black characters in children's books. Finds that the situation has improved in the past ten years, but cautions responsibility on teachers' part to accent books that have high literary quality and that provide positive identity base for black children. List of references is useful.

Young, Jacqueline Lee. "Criteria in Selection of Black Literature for Children," *Freedomways*, Vol. 13, No. 2 (2nd quarter 1973), 107–16.
> Discusses self-image and its psychological importance. Includes a short story to exemplify necessary black-oriented themes.

BLACK ORGANIZATIONS AND PUBLISHERS

AFRO–AM PUBLISHING COMPANY. 1727 S. Indiana Ave., Chicago, Ill. 60616

AMURU PRESS, INC. 161 Madison Ave., New York, N.Y. 10016

ASSOCIATION FOR THE STUDY OF AFRO-AMERICAN LIFE AND HISTORY, INC. 1401 14th St., N.W., Washington, D.C. 20005

BROADSIDE PRESS. 12651 Old Mill Pl., Detroit, Mich. 48238

COUNCIL ON INTERRACIAL BOOKS FOR CHILDREN. 1841 Broadway, New York, N.Y. 10023

COMBINED BLACK PUBLISHERS. 7848 S. Ellis Ave., Chicago, Ill. 60619

DRUM AND SPEAR PRESS. 1902 Belmont Rd., N.W., Washington, D.C. 20009

FITZGERALD PUBLISHING CO. P. O. Box 264, St. Albans, N.Y. 11412

FOUNDATION FOR CHANGE. 1619 Broadway, New York, N.Y. 10019

EMERSON HALL PUBLISHERS, INC. 209 West 97th St., New York, N.Y. 10025

INSTITUTE OF POSITIVE EDUCATION. 7848 S. Ellis Ave., Chicago, Ill. 60619

JOHNSON PUBLISHING CO. Book Division, 820 S. Michigan Ave., Chicago, Ill. 60605

JULIAN RICHARDSON ASSOCIATES. 540 McAllister St., San Francisco, Calif.
   94102
N.A.A.C.P. 1790 Broadway, New York. N.Y. 10019
NEW DAY PRESS. c/o Karamu House, 2355 E. 89 St., Cleveland, Ohio, 44106
THIRD PRESS: JOSEPH OKPAKU PUBLISHING CO., INC. 444 Central Park, W.
   New York, N.Y. 10025
THIRD WORLD PRESS. 7850 S. Ellis Ave., Chicago, Ill. 60619
U.S. COMMITTEE FOR UNICEF. 331 East 38th St., New York, N.Y. 10016

Aardema, Verna. *Tales from the Story Hat*. Illus. Elton Fax. New York: Coward McCann, 1960. (Ages 8–10.)
All but one of these stories are based on folk tales. The book shows that the Uncle Remus stories are taken from Africa. One of the stories has a wily rabbit as the hero. Three of them are from Henry M. Stanley's *My Dark Companions and Their Strange Stories*. Notes about the stories and a glossary contain useful information. Stories are well told and illustrations are excellent.

Abdul, Raoul. *The Magic of Black Poetry*. Illus. Dane Burr. New York: Dodd, Mead, 1972. (Ages 12–up.)
Collection of poetry written by black people all over the world, some of them anonymous, across a great span of years. Many are by notable living poets. Also contains a section describing the poets.

Adoff, Arnold. *Black Is Brown Is Tan*. Illus. Emily Arnold McCully. New York: Harper & Row, 1973. (Ages 3–8.)
Interracial family. Author Adoff (who is white) is married to Virginia Hamilton (who is black). Positive feelings of warmth and energy and togetherness are conveyed. Family members each have good feelings about themselves. The story is written in a kind of verse that may require some adult help for young children, but the book is a very useful, realistic, and positive one.

———— (ed.). *Black Out Loud*. Illus. Alvin Hollingsworth. New York: Macmillan, 1969. (Ages 9–up.)
Anthology of modern poems by black Americans. Consistently high quality of poetry. Wonderful variety.

———— (ed.). *I Am the Darker Brother*. Illus. Benny Andrews. New York: Macmillan, 1968. (Ages 12–up.)
Poems about the black experience by many black poets. Notes at the end of the book explain some of the parts of the poems as well as tell about the poets. Excellent anthology.

————. *Malcolm X*. Illus. John Wilson. New York: Crowell, 1970. (Ages 7–10.)
Tells simply, and in a factual manner, the details of Malcolm X's life. Very specific in its recording of what Malcolm believed and what happened to him. The heroic quality of his life emerges clearly.

————. *My Black Me: A Beginning Book of Black Poetry*. New York: Dutton, 1974. (Ages 8–up.)

Excellent accumulation of poetry by many black poets. Poems deal largely with black identity: families, history, pride. Brief descriptions of poets included.

Alcock, Gudrun. *Turn the Next Corner*. New York: Lothrop, Lee and Shepard, 1969. (Ages 5–7.)
Ritchie's father has been convicted of embezzlement and sentenced to prison. Ritchie and his mother move to an apartment in the Near-North Side of Chicago, where Ritchie and a black boy named Slugger become close friends. Slugger's father is a detective; his family is middle class, concerned, steady. Black-white relationships are somewhat mentioned, but the central problem of the book is that of the father's imprisonment and Ritchie's coping.

Alexander, Martha. *Sabrina*. New York: Dial Press, 1971. (Ages 4–7.)
Sabrina is a very young child just starting school. She is ashamed of her name because the other children seem to consider it unusual. She decides to be called Susan, and the children begin competing to see who will win her real name. She then decides that she wants it back. Sabrina is white; several of the children in the class and the teacher are pictured as black. A mild, everyday sort of book, useful because of the integrated class.

———. *The Story Grandmother Told*. New York: Dial Press, 1969. (Ages 5–8.)
Story is about a black child and her grandmother. Lisa asks her grandmother to tell her a particular story. In describing which story she wants, she tells the whole thing herself; then her obliging grandmother retells it for her. Warm, loving relationship. Illustrations nicely done. Neighborhood is pictured as integrated. Recommended for children by *Starting Out Right*. But where are Lisa's parents? Some explanation would have helped remove a stereotype.

Alexander, Rae Pace, and Lester, Julius (eds.). *Young and Black in America*. New York: Random House, 1970. (Ages 11–up.)
Excellent collection of self-descriptive essays about eight black people whose contributions have been outstanding. Introductory notes by Julius Lester accompanying each account aid the reader.

Anderson, Lonzo. *The Day the Hurricane Happened*. Illus. Ann Grifalconi. New York: Scribner's, 1973. (Ages 5–8.)
Graphic story of a family's bout with a hurricane on St. John in the Virgin Islands. Albie and his younger sister Eldra help prepare their house and their animals for the onslaught. The father, who is a constable, must warn the rest of the island. The house is destroyed, but no one is hurt; and the grandfather, mother, and children

manage their own survival well. Image of a coping, capable, loving black family. Written with a light dialect, not overpowering, but enough to give a sense of the speech of the people.

Arkhurst, Joyce Cooper. *The Adventures of Spider: West African Folk Tales*. Illus. Jerry Pinkney. Boston: Little, Brown, 1964. Pb. Scholastic. (Ages 7–11.)
Stories from Liberia and Ghana. Spider is a mischievous character who is clever and usually outwits his foes, but sometimes he catches himself. The stories explain natural phenomena. In the telling, details of African foods, the work that the people do, and some of the customs are described. Most of the stories are good-humored; no one gets badly hurt. One of these stories is similar to the Uncle Remus "Tar Baby." This is an excellent book.

Armstrong, William. *Sounder*. Illus. James Barkley. New York: Harper & Row, 1969. Pb. Scholastic. (Ages 11–up.) (Newbery Medal.)
Black Southern family, very poor. Father is jailed for many years because he steals a ham. Dog, Sounder, is crippled and deformed as a consequence of his trying to save the father. Father also comes home crippled and deformed. Man and dog die at the same time. Son begins an education, and the hope for a better life. Very movingly written story, but criticized by many because of its depiction of the Black as a passive accepter of the white man's injustice.

———. *Sour Land*. New York: Harper & Row, 1971. (Ages 12–up.)
Sequel to *Sounder*. Intelligent, sensitive black teacher, Moses Waters, lives his life avoiding conflict and violence. One white family loves and tries to protect him, but to no avail; he is senselessly murdered at the end of the book. He is an inspiration to the white children of the family; the reader is left to assume that they will guide their lives differently because of the values Moses Waters has taught them. Same criticism for this book as for *Sounder*, but very well and movingly written.

Arnott, Kathleen. *African Myths and Legends*. Illus. Joan Kiddell-Monroe. New York: Walck, 1963. (Ages 9–12.)
Collection of tales from all over Africa. Well told, not at all patronizing or indicating a different value structure. Illustrations do nothing to enhance the book, but are not really objectionable. Useful for enriching one's background of African myths and legends.

Baldwin, Anne Norris. *Sunflowers for Tina*. Illus. Ann Grifalconi. New York: Four Winds Press, 1970. (Ages 5–8.)
Black child, Tina, lives in city and longs for a garden. Brother finds her two sunflowers, which she shares in an imaginative way with

her grandmother. Loving family but generally negative view of the future. Stereotype again of the broken home.

Bambara, Toni Cade. *Tales and Stories for Black Folks*. Garden City. N.Y.: Doubleday, 1971. (All ages.)
Collection of stories about the lives of black people, told from a black perspective.

Baron, Virginia Olsen (ed.). *Here I Am!* Illus. Emily Arnold McCully. New York: Dutton, 1969. (Ages 6–up.)
An anthology of poetry written by children in minority groups. The verse, collected from all over the United States, contains an excellent range of mood and message.

Beim, Lorraine and Jerrold. *Two Is a Team*. Illus. Ernest Crichlow. New York: Harcourt, Brace & World, 1945. (Ages 5–8.)
Ted and Paul are friends — one is black, and one is white. They play very well together and are very much alike. After having some difficulty building a coaster wagon together, they each build a separate one. They cause some damage and join together to earn the money to repay the damages. This is one of the first integrated stories. Many characters, black and white; integration is in the illustrations, not the text. Any of the characters could be either black or white. Illustrator is black.

Berger, Terry. *Black Fairy Tales*. Illus. David Omar White. New York: Atheneum, 1969. Pb. also. (Ages 8–12.)
Excellent illustrations dramatically conveying different kinds of beauty. Tales well told. All are tales from South Africa. Complex, fascinating stories. The style of the telling is such that readers will be captured by the intricacy of the plots, and will also acquire information about Swazi and Shangani and 'Msuto ways.

Blue, Rose. *Black, Black, Beautiful Black*. Illus. Emmett Wigglesworth. New York: Franklin Watts, 1969. (Ages 5–8.)
Danita is excited about going to the zoo. Text recounts all the beautiful and shiny and attractive black objects and animals that she sees. Then she sees her own reflection — black and beautiful. Nicely done for self-image.

————. *How Many Blocks in the World?* Illus. Harold James. New York: Franklin Watts, 1970. (Ages 5–8.)
Brian, who goes to Head Start, is a bright, inquisitive boy. His mother is loving and supportive and very proud of him. The style of writing is a joyful one. The story demonstrates Brian's growing awareness that the world is larger than just the few blocks around his house and school.

————. *The Preacher's Kid*. Illus. Ted Lewin. New York: Franklin Watts, 1975. (Ages 7–10.)
A heavily moralizing story of a minister and his family who stand fast for their principles of brotherhood, while the rest of the congregation objects to the busing-in of black children to their school.

————. *A Quiet Place*. Illus. Tom Feelings. New York: Franklin Watts, 1969. (Ages 9–11.)
Matthew, adopted (foster) child loves to read. He finds a special quiet place in the public library, but when the library closes to make way for a new building, Matthew is bereaved. He finds a new place at last, out of doors, and has confidence that he will find one indoors somewhere when bad weather sets in. Matthew's life is a good one now. His mother and father are loving, understanding people. His big sister has been in trouble, but now she has a fine boyfriend who helps her to stay on the right track. He also has a baby brother. All are foster children. All benefit from the warmth of the home. Whole family is black. Parents have had other adopted children and have been successful at it.

Bond, Jean Cary. *Brown Is a Beautiful Color*. Illus. Barbara Zuber. New York: Franklin Watts, 1969. (Ages 5–8.)
Black child goes to the country and finds many wonderful things that are brown. Then, back in the city, there are many more lovely and useful brown things. Many shades of brown are pictured. Child visits the U.N. and sees many brown people dressed in the traditional costumes of their countries. Book is all in rhyme. Good for self-image and expansion of concepts.

Bontemps, Arna (ed.). *American Negro Poetry*. New York: Hill and Wang, 1963. (Ages 10–up.)
Diverse selection of poetry across a span of many years. Biographical descriptions of the poets are included.

Bontemps, Arna. *Lonesome Boy*. Illus. Feliks Topolski. Boston: Houghton Mifflin, 1967. (Ages 12–up.)
Bubber loves playing his trumpet so much that he forgets everything else in the world when he is playing. Ignoring his grandfather's warning to take care, he gets trapped into playing for the Devil. He finally learns to value his grandfather's experience and to place his horn in proper perspective. This poetically written book raises many questions for the reader.

Booth, Cordelia. *The Nubie*. Illus. Larue High School students. Amherst, Mass.: Eutu Publishing, 1973. (Ages 10–up.)
Elwood, nine years old, worships his elder brother, Vernon, who is

wanted by the police. Vernon is a thief and a drug pusher. Elwood steals a statue of an elephant. Proud of his feat, he wants to share it with his brother, who is not interested. Vernon gets shot in a police raid. The elephant gets smashed. Elwood is rescued by an old derelict neighbor and is brought home. His values are somewhat clarified by this experience, but much is left ambiguous. Story is set in Washington, D.C. Maintains the stereotype of the city as a bad place and of black families as fatherless and crime-ridden.

Bothwell, Jean. *African Herdboy — A Story of the Masai.* New York: Harcourt, Brace & World, 1970. (Ages 9–11.)
Batian, an African herdboy, is anxious about the approaching coming-of-age rites. Officials arrive, criticizing the Masai for using too much water and land for their cattle. Batian sees Nairobi, the new civilization, which convinces him and his family that he should go to school and learn new ways. Interesting story of Africa in transition.

Brown, Turner, Jr. *Black Is.* Illus. Ann Weisman. New York: Grove Press, 1969. (All ages.)
A somewhat carping and bitter book of definitions of what it means to be black and done in.

Bryan, Ashley. *Walk Together Children, Black American Spirituals.* New York: Atheneum, 1974. (Ages 6–up.)
Beautiful woodcuts by Bryan, who selected the spirituals. The music is included with the words. Twenty-four songs are presented in this valuable book.

Burchard, Peter. *Bimby.* New York: Coward McCann, 1968. (Ages 8–11.)
Bimby is a young, naive slave, obedient and unquestioning. When an elderly slave, who is a friend of his, learns that all of the slaves are to be sold he kills himself. This incident causes Bimby to change into a person determined to win his freedom. He sets off after deciding "better to be dead than have your spirit cut to ribbons." Characters are not very well developed. Harshness of slavery is described, clearly showing how much at the mercy of the master the slaves were. The story is based on the historical accounts of Pierce Mease Butler who auctioned his slaves in 1859 from his Georgia plantation. Slaves are shown to be weak, foolish, and nasty to each other if they have any power at all.

Burt, Olive. *Black Women of Valor.* Illus. Paul Frame. New York: Messner, 1974. (Ages 9–11.)
Tells the stories of four black women who demonstrated their courage and ability: Juliette Derricotte, Maggie Mitchell Walker, Ida Wells Barnett, and Septima Poinsette Clark. The book also contains

a long list of other black women of valor. Valuable addition to information about black history. One would wish, however, that the author had not so facilely referred to each of the women by her first name.

————. *Negroes in the Early West*. Illus. Lorence F. Bjorklund. New York: Messner, 1969. (Ages 9–11.)
Except for some outdated terminology, this book presents a fascinating account of the role that black people played in the development of the West. Many of the names in this book will be unfamiliar to the readers. Well-told descriptions of the lives of these interesting people.

Caines, Jeannette. *Abby*. Illus. Steven Kellogg. New York: Harper & Row, 1973. (Ages 3–8.)
Abby is an adopted child who loves and is loved by her mother and father. She is also loved by her older brother, Kevin, even though he upsets her sometimes. Warm, gentle story. Family is black. Well done.

Carlson, Natalie Savage. *The Empty Schoolhouse*. Illus. John Kaufmann. New York: Harper & Row, 1965. (Ages 7–11.)
Southern family live in a town in which the parochial school has just integrated. Lullah is the bright, favored daughter; she and her white friend both go to this school. Violence causes all the students to stop attending. Lullah is very unhappy at the public black school. She finally decides to return to St. Joseph's even if she is the only student there. Finally, after more violence, the community rallies round and students return to the school. White instigators move away. Several negative factors: all consequential people are white — doctor, teachers, priest, best friend. Negative descriptions of black characteristics.

————. *Marchers for the Dream*. New York: Harper & Row, 1969. (Ages 9–12.)
Bethany Jackson and her great-grandmother participate in the Poor People's March on Washington. When they return to Massachusetts, they demonstrate for a home for their family. It works. Somewhat flawed but well-intentioned book.

Carpenter, Frances. *African Wonder Tales*. Illus. Joseph Escourido. Garden City, N.Y.: Doubleday, 1963. (Ages 7–12.)
Very patronizing, demeaning retelling of tales collected by the author from other literary sources. Judgmental and condescending.

Chambers, Bradford (ed.). *Chronicles of Negro Protest*. New York: Parents' Magazine Press, 1968. (Ages 12–up.)
Interesting and informative collection of documents and commentary related to black protest.

Clifford, Mary Louise. *Bisha of Burundi.* Illus. Trevor Stubley. New York: Crowell, 1973. (Ages 10–up.)

A somewhat biased story of the change coming to Africa. Bisha is a remarkable young woman who craves an education and a way of life different from that of her parents. The author's bias toward the white and Catholic world affects the objectivity of the story, but it still contains interesting information about politics, customs, and attitudes in Burundi.

Clifton, Lucille. *All Us Come Cross the Water.* Illus. John Steptoe. New York: Holt, Rinehart and Winston, 1973. (Ages 5–9.)

Ujamaa tries to trace his heritage; he wants to know his country of origin. His family helps, but his friend says it does not matter. "All us crossed the water." Somewhat ambiguous, uncertain ending. Characters not very well drawn.

———. *The Black BC's.* Illus. Don Miller. New York: Dutton, 1970. (Ages 3–9.)

An ABC book that presents a concept for each letter and then explains it further. There is a short verse for the letter, and then a clarification in addition to it on the same page. It is an excellent vehicle for enhancing self-image.

———. *The Boy Who Didn't Believe in Spring.* Illus. Brinton Turkle. New York: Dutton, 1973. (Ages 3–7.)

Contemporary version of an old theme. King Shavazz and his friend Tony, both young boys, go on a search for spring. King has difficulty believing in spring. After encountering many of the sights and smells of the city (all of them positive), they discover a patch of crocuses and a nest of robin's eggs. Then they know that the stories about spring are true and that it has actually arrived. The language is contemporary vernacular. The illustrations are accurate in detail, and the mood is positive. The city setting is realistically but not negatively portrayed. Pictures are of a completely integrated neighborhood, with individual ethnic characteristics pictured.

———. *Don't You Remember?* Illus. Evaline Ness. New York: Dutton, 1973. (Ages 3–7.)

Desire Mary Tate, black, four years old, and very lively, considers herself to have the best memory in her family. Her family promises her all kinds of pleasant experiences "next time." She fears that they have forgotten, but on her birthday, they all remember. Realistic, but not downtrodden family. Loving, coping.

———. *Everett Anderson's Year.* Illus. Ann Grifalconi, New York: Holt, Rinehart, and Winston, 1974. (Ages 4–8.)

Another in the series of *Everett Anderson* books, this one reinforces the loving world that Everett lives in. His mother manages well, even though the father has left them. Everett misses and still loves his father. He, too, is coping well.

————. *Good, Says Jerome*. Illus. Stephanie Douglas. New York: Dutton, 1973. (Ages 3–7.)
Lovely series of conversations between Jerome and his elder sister, Janice Marie. He mentions all his fears and anxieties to her, and she helps him to resolve them, always causing him to end up with a good feeling. Warm relationship between these two siblings who are pictured as black, but who could be any color.

————. *Some of the Days of Everett Anderson*. Illus. Evaline Ness. New York: Holt, Rinehart and Winston, 1970. (Ages 3–8.)
Energetic boy of six goes through the week in a lively manner. The charm and personality of the boy emerge through each of the short poems on the pages. The illustrations reflect the same sense of warmth and energy.

————. *The Times They Used To Be*. Illus. Susan Jeschler. New York: Holt, Rinehart and Winston, 1974. (Ages 8–12.)
Reminiscences of a black woman who grew up in the 1940s in Baltimore. Perpetuates many negative stereotypes. In talking about her uncle, she says, "He got a check from the government so he didn't have to work." Widespread ignorance, superstitions.

Cobble, Alice. *Wembi. The Singer of Stories*. Illus. Doris Hallas. St. Louis: Bethany Press, 1959. (All ages.)
Author, who was a missionary for twenty-five years in Belgian Congo, retells the stories that she heard there. Most of the tales have a moral. They are well told. A picture of life in the village is graphically drawn. Illustrations are well done.

Coles, Robert. *Dead End School*. Boston: Little, Brown, 1968. (Ages 8–12.)
Again, father is not around; he was killed in an accident. Jimmy and three brothers and sister must sleep in one room. Mother and two babies sleep in another. School is overcrowded. Busing is instituted, and parents protest because black children will simply be bused to another overcrowded, poor school. They demand that the children be bused to a less crowded, formerly all-white school. This is done. Jimmy is tremendously impressed by the white school's facilities. The teachers, principal, and children are friendly. It is a happy ending except that some of Jimmy's friends think that he is deserting them. Too pat an ending. Too one-dimensional.

Colman, Hila. *End of the Game.* Photographs by Milton Charles. New York: World, 1971. (Ages 8–12.)
Donny is a nine-year old black child who gets invited to spend three weeks with a well-to-do white family. Timmy, their son, is Donny's age. Timmy's mother treats Donny very differently from white children. She bends over backwards to be kind and never reprimands or punishes him. In the end Donny's mother berates him for behaving like a white man's fool and upbraids Timmy's mother for her racism. A useful mind-opening book.

Corcos, Lucille. *The City Book.* New York: Golden Press, 1972. (Ages 3–10.)
Full of useful information. Integrated setting in all cases. Covers many aspects of the city. Tremendous number of details. Illustrations and text somewhat overwhelming for the younger child. Probably very useful for the older child.

Courlander, Harold, and Herzog, George. *The Cow-Tail Switch and Other West African Stories.* Illus. Madye Lee Chastain. New York: Holt, Rinehart and Winston, 1962. (Ages 9–11.) (Newbery Honor Book.)
These tales are not as well told as some of the author's other collections, but are interesting, nevertheless. The illustrations are too stylized to be very informative. A useful feature is the section of Notes at the back of the book, telling where each story comes from and describing more about it to the reader. The author has traveled extensively in Africa and is a well-known and respected folklorist.

Courlander, Harold, and Prempeh, Albert Kofi. *Hat-Shaking Dance and Other Tales from the Gold Coast.* Illus. Enrico Arno. New York: Harcourt, Brace & World, 1957. (Ages 8–12.)
Stories, from the Ashanti, are very well told, and the style is not at all patronizing. Most are about Anansi. The notes at the end tell more about the background. This is a good book of tales.

Dahl, Roald. *Charlie and the Chocolate Factory.* Illus. Joseph Schindelman. New York: Knopf, 1964. Pb. Penguin. (Ages 9–up.)
Imaginative fantasy about Charlie and his adventures in the wonderful chocolate factory owned by Willie Wonka. The factory is run by little people called Oompa Loompas. In the new edition they are white, but in all the other editions, they are black pygmies imported from Africa. The story takes place in one day during which time the reader and several children take a tour through the magical chocolate factory. To some readers the book appears to tacitly support slavery.

DeAngeli, Marguerite. *Bright April.* Garden City, N.Y.: Doubleday, 1946. (Ages 8–10.)
An early attempt at presenting a black family in a positive light. Well intentioned, but out of date. Very much a white perspective. Story is simply about a young black girl, named April, who responds to bigotry with patience and good humor. Her family is middle class and very clean. *Starting Out Right* devotes a whole chapter to critiquing this book.

Deasy, Michael. *City ABC's.* Photographs by Robert Perron. New York: Walker, 1974. (Ages 5–8.)
Good photos of a variety of places in a city help change the negative image that cities have. Mixture of people pictured. No special connotations for any particular group of people. Constructive actions pictured.

Desbarats, Peter. *Gabrielle and Selena.* Illus. Nancy Grossman. New York: Harcourt Brace Jovanovich, 1968. (Ages 5–8.)
Two girls, Gabrielle (black) and Selena (white), have been friends all their lives. One day they decide to change places. The parents trick the girls into going to their own homes, by pretending that each loves what she hates. Unlikely that the girls would not know each other's likes and dislikes if they were really friends. Why couldn't the parents permit them to go on with the pretend game?

deTrevino, Elizabeth Borton. *I Juan de Pareja.* New York: Farrar, Straus & Giroux, 1965. (Ages 12–up.) (Newbery Medal.)
This is a fictionalized biography. Juan is a slave who spends most of his life serving the great painter Velasquez. He secretly and illegally becomes a competent painter on his own. When he confesses to the king, his master frees him. He is a clever, talented man who is depicted as accepting slavery too passively, but he uses his freedom well and is admirable, even as a slave.

Evans, Mari. *JD.* Illus. Jerry Pinkney. Garden City, N.Y.: Doubleday, 1973. (Ages 9–11.)
Takes place in the Midwest. JD lives with his mother — there is no father and no explanation of why not. Very poor neighborhood. Each of the four stories in the book ends with the reader left to figure out what will happen next. The book is a sad one. JD has energy and intelligence, but the reader is made to feel that life will defeat him.

Fassler, Joan. *Don't Worry, Dear.* Illus. Stewart Kranz. New York: Behavioral Publications, 1971. (Ages 3–8.)

Jenny is a small child who wets her bed, stutters occasionally, and sucks her thumb. Her mother is very understanding. The story takes the reader to the point at which Jenny outgrows all these habits — a very comforting conclusion. Jenny's father is also supportive. The illustrations show that the family is black. Useful for a book to have a black family represent the universal and understanding family.

Feelings, Muriel. *Jambo Means Hello, Swahili Alphabet Book.* Illus. Tom Feelings. New York: Dial Press, 1974. (Ages 5–10.) (Caldecott Honor Book.)
Beautiful illustrations accompany the simple text. Each of the twenty-four letters has a word and its definition, and then a more complete explanation of the customs associated with the word. For example, after defining *arusi* as a wedding, Feelings then explains how weddings are celebrated.

————. *Zamani Goes to Market.* Illus. Tom Feelings. New York: Seabury Press, 1970. (Ages 6–9.)
Zamani is the real name of the author's son. The book, inspired by the Feelings's visit with a Western Kenyan family, tells of Zamani's being at last old enough to accompany his father and brothers to market. The family is a loving, mutually sharing family, thoughtful of each other. The flavor of the place and the group are communicated as well as the universal emotions of love and family caring.

Feelings, Tom. *Black Pilgrimage.* New York: Lothrop, Lee and Shepard, 1972. (Ages 12–up.)
Autobiography of one of our most gifted black artists. Book traces his struggle as a young aspiring black artist in a white-dominated system, and his decision to leave America. Recounts his feelings about Ghana and his subsequent removal to South America. Illustrations in this book are beautiful. Text is clearly written and conveys very well a sense of self-respect and pride in being black.

Fife, Dale. *Adam's ABC's.* Illus. Don Robertson. New York: Coward, McCann and Geoghegan, 1971. (Ages 6–10.)
The book is calculated to improve and support black children's positive self-image. The ABC's are introduced through a simple narrative describing Adam's pleasant day. He lives in the city with both of his parents, an elder sister, and a baby brother. His family is comfortable and loving. Stereotypes are avoided. Useful, realistic illustrations and actions are characteristics of this book.

Fitzgerald, Bertram A., Jr. (ed.). *Golden Legacy: Illustrated History Magazine.* St. Albans, N.Y.: Fitzgerald Publishing Company, 1967. (Ages 9–up.)

Series of seventeen magazines in comic-book format depicting black people who have made historical contributions. At the end of each magazine is a series of short descriptions about other black leaders. Artists for the series are Joan Bacchus, Tom Feelings, Ezra Jackson, and L. C. Arty. Writers include Joan Bacchus, Francis Taylor, and L. C. Arty. Benjamin Quarles is consultant.

Folsom, Franklin. *The Life and Legend of George McJunkin: Black Cowboy.* Nashville: Thomas Nelson, 1973. (Ages 10–up.)
McJunkin was a competent cowboy, as well as a naturalist, meteorologist, and rancher. He undertook many responsibilities and discharged them well. Interesting account of his life, drawn from research.

Fox, Paula. *The Slave Dancer.* Illus. Eros Keith. Scarsdale, N.Y.: Bradbury Press, 1973. (Ages 11–up.) (Newbery Medal.)
Jessie, a thirteen-year old boy, is kidnapped from New Orleans and forced to serve on a slave ship. He has to play the fife so that the slaves will exercise. When the ship encounters trouble, all but Jessie and Ras, a young slave, are killed. Ras is helped to freedom by an old man, who is himself a fugitive from slavery. Jessie never wants to hear music again but otherwise seems strangely unchanged. Ugly, harrowing descriptions of the conditions of the slave ship and the cruelty of the crew. Very well written, but absolves Whites too easily.

Fraser, Kathleen, and Levy, Miriam F. *Adam's World: San Francisco.* Illus. Helen Hipshman. Chicago: Albert Whitman, 1971. (Ages 5–7.)
Adam lives with his mother, father, twin sisters, and a cat in San Francisco. The family is black. Father is a seaman. One day he brings home cloth from Africa, which the mother makes into clothes for a street party. Beautiful book describing the city and the warm, happy life of this black family.

Freedman, Florence. *Two Tickets to Freedom.* New York: Simon and Schuster, 1971. (Ages 9–12.)
Ellen and William Craft, the hero and heroine of this book, escape from slavery by using their wits. They have many adventures and meet many interesting people before they escape to England. After the Civil War, they return to the U.S., where they found a school for poor rural black children. Good book.

Fritz, Jean. *Brady.* Illus. Lynd Ward. New York: Coward McCann, 1960. (Ages 9–13.)
Brady does not know when to keep his mouth shut — he tells all that he knows about anything. He finally learns to keep a secret when he

discovers that his father is a conductor on the Underground Railroad. He also takes a young black slave to safety. Characters are
somewhat too good or too bad, but the story is an interesting one,
serving to tell about the climate of the time. Told from a white
perspective, but not condescending.

Giovanni, Nikki. *Spin a Soft Black Song: Poems for Children.* Illus. Charles
Bible. New York: Hill and Wang, 1971. (Ages 6–13.)
A book of poems by this young black poet reflecting black experi-
ences and feelings.

Glasser, Barbara, and Blustein, Ellen. *Bongo Bradley.* Illus. Bonnie
Johnson. New York: Hawthorn, 1973. (Ages 7–11.)
Bradley Clark's father is a jazz musician; his mother is a nurse.
Bradley goes to North Carolina for the summer to visit his father's
family. There he learns about his father's roots, about music, and
about more of the ways of his people.

Graham, Lorenz. *Hongry Catch the Foolish Boy.* Illus. James Brown, Jr.
New York: Crowell, 1973. (Ages 7–10.)
The Prodigal Son retold in Liberian English. Beautiful rhythm to the
words. Dramatically simple illustrations. Graham, a minister's son,
was born in New Orleans. He has retold other Bible stories in this
style: *David He No Fear* and *Every Man Heart Lay Down.* All are
excellent.

———. *Whose Town?* New York: Crowell, 1969.
David Williams, eighteen years old, is an intelligent, quiet, young
black man, who wants to go to medical school after college. A series
of tragic events deprives his father of a job, gets David into trouble
with the police, and makes everyone wonder whether they can ever
be safe and comfortable again. In the end, David does graduate from
high school, with a scholarship to college, but there is not total hope
that the future will be bright. Discussions in the book about Black
Power — and what course of action to take — are useful. This is a
sequel to *North Town* and *South Town,* which also tell about David
Williams and the struggles that his family have to endure.

Gray, Genevieve. *A Kite for Bennie.* Illus. Floyd Sowell. New York:
McGraw-Hill, 1972. (Ages 5–8.)
Bennie lives with his mother, sister, and two brothers in a poor
neighborhood; they are on welfare. Bennie sees, is fascinated by,
and desirous of, a kite. Many kind people (including his brother's
parole officer) contribute to his building a kite. Mutually helpful and
loving family. Flaw — again father is gone, with no explanation. But
quality of togetherness comes through strongly.

————. *Send Wendell.* Illus. Symeon Shimin. New York: McGraw-Hill, 1974. (Ages 3–9.)
Wendell is the one in his family always sent on errands — his elder siblings are too busy; his younger ones are too small. But he goes happily. His Uncle Robert, a successful California farmer, comes to visit. He invites Wendell to come to help on the farm when he gets big enough. After that, Wendell also has something to do when his mother needs an errand run; he writes to Uncle Robert. Good, happy family story. Uncle Robert is a great character — big, wealthy, happy, and loving.

————. *The Seven Wishes of Joanna Peabody.* Illus. Elton Fax. New York: Lothrop, Lee and Shepard, 1972. (Ages 7–11.)
Unhappy Joanna lives with her mother, baby brother, and elder sister in a run-down apartment. No father, and no indication of where he is. Joanna suddenly acquires a fairy godmother, named Aunt Thelma, who informs Joanna that she has won the right to make seven wishes. Most of the wishes backfire, but at last Joanna learns to wish for other people's happiness as well as her own; and there is a happy ending. Black urban speech is used throughout the book. The story is fun but has some flaws. People in the story are unkind and judgmental. The reader is left with the idea that the only way out of poverty and nastiness is through magic.

Greenberg, Polly. *Oh Lord, I Wish I Was a Buzzard.* Illus. Aliki. New York: Macmillan, 1968. (Ages 5–7.)
Somewhat controversial story of a young girl and her family working in the cotton fields all day sustaining herself by her wishes to be anything she sees that is not what she is. She wishes to be a dog, a buzzard, a snake, a butterfly, and a partridge. At the end of the time she walks home weary but happy with a lollipop in her mouth. Negative stereotypes may be invited. At best, the story is very sad.

Greene, Bette. *Philip Hall Likes Me, I Reckon Maybe.* Illus. Charles Lilly. New York: Dial Press, 1974. (Ages 8–11.) (Newbery Honor Book.)
Flavorful story about a black community in rural Arkansas. Beth Lambert is the eleven-year-old protagonist; Philip is the boy that she loves. Her adventures are fun. The community is social and active. The parents are proud of their children and want the best for them. Excellent illustrations.

Greenfield, Eloise. *She Come Bringing Me That Little Baby Girl.* Illus. John Steptoe. Philadelphia: Lippincott, 1974. (Ages 5–8.)
Black family includes mother, father, Kevin, and baby sister. Kevin wanted a brother. He is jealous of the attention that the new baby

gets from all the relatives and neighbors, as well as from his parents. When his mother permits him to hold his new sister and to show her off to his friends, Kevin begins to feel happy again and to plan for what they will eventually be able to do together. The rivalry is taken care of in too pat a fashion, but it is handled lovingly on the part of the parents. Steptoe's illustrations are beautiful.

————. *Sister.* Illus. Moneta Barnett. New York: Crowell, 1974. (Ages 10–up.)
Author is black. Doretha and her sister Alberta live with their mother. Father dies of a heart attack and is sorely missed by everyone. Alberta drops out of school and rebels against convention. Doretha is sensitive and perceptive but has problems in school. She is afraid that she will be like her sister. Finally a school, run by Afro-Americans, affords her some hope. Except for the sketchiness of description of the school, the book is well written and useful.

Guirma, Frederic. *Princess of the Full Moon.* New York: Macmillan, 1970. (Ages 6–8.)
Old tale, but this is the first time that it has been set down in English. The author-illustrator is from Ghana and Upper Volta. The story, set in Africa, is about a proud, beautiful princess who refuses to marry anyone who has even a small physical blemish. She eventually is captured by a dreadful dragon and rescued by an ugly shepherd. The shepherd, of course, turns into a handsome prince, and they live happily ever after. The imagery of the tale is very well done; the magic is imaginative and exciting. The moral: Never judge a book by its cover.

————. *Tales of Mogho, African Stories from Upper Volta.* New York: Macmillan, 1971. (Ages 8–10.)
Creation myth and other tales passed along by storytellers. Interlaced with words of the Mossi people in the Moré language. The words are set down here in print for the first time. A glossary is provided for the reader. Like other African tales, these are complex and rich in detail.

Guy, Rosa. *The Friends.* New York: Holt, Rinehart and Winston, 1973. (Ages 12–up.)
The Cathy family, from the West Indies, live in Harlem. The girls, Phyllisia and Ruby, are victimized at school. Mother dies of breast cancer; father is stern and harsh in his bereavement. Edith, a friend of Phyl's, is looked down upon by both Phyl and her father, but she proves to be Phyl's truest friend. At end, everyone has grown in some way, and it looks as if the family will make it. Very sad, very powerful story. Author is black.

Haley, Gail E. *A Story, a Story.* New York: Atheneum, 1970. (Ages 5-8.) (Caldecott Medal.)
Beautifully told, beautifully illustrated story of how many African folk tales come to be called Spider tales. Tells how Anansi, by his wits, caused Nyame, the sky god, to share all his stories with Anansi.

Hamilton, Virginia. *The House of Dies Drear.* Illus. Eros Keith. New York: Macmillan, 1968. (Ages 10-up.)
Mystery story. Black family (but they could be any color) purchase very large, historic old house in Ohio. Father is a college professor. House was a station on the Underground Railroad. Descendant of one of the slaves who hid there was bequeathed a fabulous underground cavern full of treasures. The cavern is under the house. Good adventure story, with message of black pride contained in it.

————. *M. C. Higgins, the Great.* New York: Macmillan, 1974. (Ages 12-up.) (Newbery Medal.)
Interesting and complex story of a black family living in the mountains of Ohio. M. C. is the unusual hero of the story. The plot involves family love and pride and the process of growing up.

————. *Paul Robeson, The Life and Times of a Free Black Man.* New York: Harper & Row, 1974. (Ages 12-up.)
Well-written account of this talented and controversial man. Hamilton, who very much sympathizes with and admires Robeson, hopes that his country will raise him to the position of esteem she feels that he deserves.

————. *The Planet of Junior Brown.* New York: Macmillan, 1971. (Ages 12-up.) (Newbery Honor Book and National Book Award Finalist.)
Junior Brown is a very fat (almost three hundred pounds), very disturbed young Black. He has one friend who is also a friend to many young black boys who live in abandoned houses all over the city. Junior's whole life is a nightmare. At the end of the story he is totally insane. Strange, complicated story of people who have been defeated by the world and who create their own planet in order to escape.

————. *Time-Ago Lost: More Tales of Jahdu.* Illus. Ray Prather. New York: Macmillan, 1973. (Ages 7-10.)
Mama Luka, the storyteller, is sad because her building will be torn down; she will have to relocate. Lee Edward is worried that she will move away too far for him to visit, but his father reassures him that it will take a very long time for the building to be torn down. Meanwhile, Mama Luka tells him more about that great character Jahdu.

————. *The Time-Ago Tales of Jahdu.* Illus. Nonny Hogragian. New York: Macmillan, 1969. (Ages 7–10.)
Lee Edward is a young black child whose baby-sitter, Mama Luka, tells him stories of Jahdu, a magical young boy. Jahdu is similar to Anansi in some ways. The stories and this book are aimed at helping black children to develop and to maintain a sense of self-pride and positive ambition. The people live "in a fine good place called Harlem." The stories are told in a very stylized but interesting fashion, and the character of the storyteller is well captured.

————. *Zeely.* Illus. Symeon Shimin. New York: Macmillan, 1967. (Ages 10–12.)
Elizabeth and John Perry go for a vacation to their uncle's farm. They are black. While they are there, they meet a strikingly beautiful black girl named Zeely. Six and a half feet tall, she is undoubtedly a descendant of the Watusi. Zeely helps Elizabeth to be herself and to be proud of it. It is a growing summer for both Elizabeth and her brother.

Harman. Humphrey. *Tales Told Near a Crocodile.* Illus. George Ford. New York: Viking, 1962. (Ages 9–11.)
Tales from Nyanza. Author lived and worked in Kenya for many years. Good collection of many tales. Told somewhat in the manner of one who is above and outside of the tales, but not really offensive.

Haskins, James. *The Creoles of Color of New Orleans.* Illus. Don Miller. New York: Crowell, 1975. (Ages 9–up.)
The author describes the Creoles in an ambivalent fashion. They have been a group that has consciously separated from other Blacks. Their practices and values are questioned in this book, but in a subtle way. Their history is interesting. Readers will have many questions after reading this book.

Haynes, Betsy. *Cowslip.* Nashville: Thomas Nelson, 1973. (Ages 10–up.)
Cowslip, a slave, is thirteen years old, ignorant, and somehow convinced that it is God's will that she be a slave. The story is undoubtedly meant to help the reader gain insight into the abuses of slavery, but none of the characters is drawn well enough to do this. The story has potential but falls short.

Hill, Elizabeth Starr. *Evan's Corner.* Illus. Nancy Grossman. New York: Holt, Rinehart and Winston, 1967. (Ages 5–8.)
Evans lives in two rooms with his parents, three sisters, and two brothers. They share a kitchen with neighbors down the hall. They are black; both parents work. When Evan wants a place of his own, his mother says that everyone can have a corner. Evan decorates

and furnishes his corner, then helps his little brother to do the same. Although the family is very poor, the mood is not depressed. All the members love, appreciate, and respect each other. They enjoy their lives, and everyone does what he or she can. They do not sit back and complain; they are active and constructive.

Hitte, Kathryn. *What Can You Do Without a Place to Play?* Illus. Cyndy Szekeres. New York: Parents' Magazine Press, 1971. (Ages 5–8.)
New child moves into somewhat integrated neighborhood. Children play on elevator, stairs, roof, firehouse, lobby, and alley, among others. In the end, the child feels that there is no place to play, and he is unhappy. Meanwhile, the ingenuity of the children has been demonstrated, but has been defeated by the child's attitude. The child, incidentally, is white.

Hoexter, Corinne. *Black Crusader, Frederick Douglass.* Chicago: Rand McNally, 1970. (Ages 10–up.)
Conveys well a sense of the man and his times. Other figures are also described in the book, making it a valuable contribution to the learning of black history. Douglass emerges as a brilliant, courageous, far-seeing man. The author respects her subject and handles it well.

Hoffman, Phyllis. *Steffie and Me.* Illus. Emily McCully. New York: Harper & Row, 1970. (Ages 6–9.)
Warm story of ordinary children, happy in their relationships. Stephanie is black; narrator is white. Children live in same neighborhood, have similar lives.

Holland, John (ed.). *The Way It Is: Fifteen Boys Describe Life in Their Neglected Urban Neighborhood.* New York: Harcourt, Brace & World, 1969. (Ages 12–up.)
The title accurately describes the contents of the book. The photographs were taken by the fifteen young men who participated in a project funded by Eastman Kodak Company. The experience was a valuable one for the students. The text is in their own words; unfortunately, the whole book emphasizes the ugly, miserable aspects of their lives. Nowhere is there hope.

Holt, Deloris. *The ABC's of Black History.* Illus. Samuel Bhang, Jr. Pasadena: Ritchie Ward Press, 1971. (Ages 9–11.)
Written by a black teacher. Each letter offers the name of a black person who achieved much and who contributed to the struggle for freedom. Contemporary as well as long-gone heroes and heroines are presented. This book contains an impressive array of people about whom more should be known and taught.

Hopkins, Lee Bennett (ed.). *On Our Way, Poems of Pride and Love.* Photographs by David Parks. New York: Knopf, 1974. (Ages 8–up.)
Twenty-two poems by black poets, singing of the special black experience. A beautiful collection, visually as well as poetically.

Hopkins, Lee Bennett. *This Street's for Me.* Illus. Ann Grifalconi. New York: Crown, 1970. (Ages 7–9.)
City poems conveying a sense of the moods and activities of the city. Nicely integrated illustrations. Poems are general: there are no specific references to any minority groups or customs. Useful for dispelling negative stereotypes about the city.

Horvath, Betty. *Hooray for Jasper.* Illus. Fermin Rocker. New York: Franklin Watts, 1966. (Ages 5–8.)
Black family in the suburbs. Warm relationship between Jasper and his grandfather. Jasper wants to be bigger. He follows his grandfather's advice, does a good deed, and feels bigger. Pleasant story.

Howard, Moses L. *The Ostrich Chase.* Illus. Barbara Seuling. New York: Holt, Rinehart and Winston, 1974. (Ages 10–up.)
Author (whose African name is Musa Nagenda) is from Uganda. The story is about Khuana, a young woman of Botswana, who rebels against the Bushman tradition. She hunts and builds fires, and in so doing, saves her grandmother's life and conquers the desert. The customs of the tribe are well described.

Howard, Vanessa. *A Screaming Whisper.* Photographs by J. Ponderhughes. New York: Holt, Rinehart and Winston, 1972. (Ages 12–up.)
Vanessa Howard is a young black poet who was born in 1955. She began writing when she was twelve. Her poem "For My Children" could be used as a guide to writers. In it, she says, "My children are unique," . . . "my children have names." Some of her poems are bitter, some despairing. All are insightful.

Howell, Ruth. *A Crack in the Pavement.* Photographs by Arline Strong. New York: Atheneum, 1970. (Ages 5–9.)
Excellent book for helping children to explore nature in the city. Good descriptions and advice about city plants and animals. Photographs illustrating the text are appropriate and well done. They include white children as well as black.

Hughes, Langston. *Black Misery.* Illus. Arouni. New York: Paul S. Eriksson, 1969. (All ages.)
Collection of short, to-the-point expansions on the definition of misery when one is black — such as learning that a slum is what you thought was home. Somewhat oversimplified but effective. Illustrations well done.

———. *Don't You Turn Back.* Ed. Lee Bennett Hopkins. Illus. Ann Grifalconi. New York: Knopf, 1969. (Ages 11–up.)
The title comes from a line in the poem called "Mother to Son." It stresses the positive determination of the black people to keep on going. The poems in this collection reflect this courage, despite the fact that "life for me ain't been no crystal stair."

Hunter, Kristin. *The Soul Brothers and Sister Lou.* New York: Scribner's, 1968. Pb. Avon. (Ages 12–up.) (Council on Interracial Books for Children Award.)
Louretta has seven brothers and sisters and mother at home, plus her sister's baby. Father has left home; sister was never married. Many things happen in the story, including a police raid that ends up with an innocent boy's getting shot. Lou sings well and achieves success singing with a group. She tries to act so that she will accomplish her goals. Her mother is fearful and discouraging of her brother's and her ambitions; she is a warm but beaten woman. The book is realistic but bitter. Even fame and fortune do not constitute a happy ending.

Jackson, Florence. *The Black Man in America, 1932–1954.* Illus. with contemporary photographs. New York: Franklin Watts, 1975. (Ages 8–12.)
Somewhat surface, but nevertheless informative account of the history and development of black people from 1932 to 1954 in America. Many questions are left unexplored in this book, but readers may use it as a starter.

Jones, Adrienne. *So, Nothing Is Forever.* Illus. Richard Cuffari. Boston: Houghton Mifflin, 1974. (Ages 12–up.)
The children in this interracial family are left to take care of themselves after their parents are killed in a car accident. Their uncle will take responsibility for them in a year, but they must first survive that year. Other than mentioning their color occasionally, there are few references to their race or to any problems they might have because of it. An engrossing story but somewhat evasive of the issues.

Jordan, June. *Dry Victories.* New York: Holt, Rinehart and Winston, 1972. (Ages 12–up.)
Black perspective, in black dialect, of Reconstruction and the Civil Rights Era. Directed at both black and white readers. Somewhat forced dialogue, but excellent illustrations and photographs. Jordan points out that at the end of each of these periods of alleged victory for Blacks, they were defeated politically, economically, and socially.

———. *New Life: New Room.* Illus. Ray Cruz. New York: Crowell, 1975. (Ages 6–9.)

A beautiful, warm story about a coping black family. The parents wisely permit the children to work out their own solution to the problem of space in their small apartment.

————. *Who Look At Me.* New York: Crowell, 1969. (Ages 9–up.)
Poem accompanies the reproduction of twenty-seven paintings. Uses the combination as a way of focusing the reader's attention on his or her perceptions. Very effective.

Kaufman, Michael. *Rooftops and Alleys: Adventures with a City Kid.* Photographs by Lee Romero and Michael Edmonds. New York: Knopf, 1973. (Ages 9–11.)
Account of several days in the life of a young man named Michael Edmonds. The book is a good idea but does not succeed. Michael survives the city by using his wits. He is imaginative and resourceful, but the text is too long and wordy. The photographs are good but do not really match the text. It is as if the photos and text were done separately and never coordinated.

Keats, Ezra Jack. *Apt. 3.* New York: Macmillan, 1971. (Ages 5–9.)
Sam and his younger brother, Ben, live in a run-down apartment house. They and everyone else in the house are Whites. Going on a search for music they hear being played on a harmonica, they finally find that the blind man in Apartment 3 has been creating the music. He is sensitive and knows everything that is going on outside his room. A friendship is formed. Perhaps Keats wants to prove that not only Blacks live in slums.

————. *Goggles.* New York: Macmillan, 1969. (Ages 5–7.) (Caldecott Honor Book.)
Setting is the city, but now it is unfriendly. Peter finds a pair of motorcycle goggles in a debris-filled lot. Big, mean boys try to get the goggles away from Archie and Peter, who finally escape from the bullies.

————. *Hi Cat.* New York: Collier, 1970. Pb. Macmillan. (Ages 5–8.)
Archie and Peter perform on the city street, but Willie, the dog, and a cat spoil their theater. A fun story, in which the pictures are even more important than usual in a Keats book.

————. *A Letter to Amy.* New York: Harper & Row, 1968. (Ages 5–8.)
Peter writes a letter to Amy inviting her to his party. Through a misunderstanding, Amy is hurt by Peter. But she shows up at his party and all is well.

————. *Peter's Chair.* New York: Harper & Row, 1967. (Ages 5–8.)
Peter has a new baby sister, and his parents are painting all his old furniture pink for the baby. He feels excluded and, taking his chair,

"runs away." He actually remains close by. When he realizes that he has outgrown his chair and when he hears his parents' supportive words and smells dinner, he returns to the family, resolving to tolerate his sister.

————. *The Snowy Day.* New York: Viking, 1962. (Ages 3–6.) (Caldecott Award.)
Peter has a lovely, joyful time in the snow. This is the reader's first introduction to Peter and his family. Only slightly flawed by the somewhat stereotypic image of the mother.

————. *Whistle for Willie.* New York: Viking, 1964. (Ages 4–6.)
City setting, but pleasant and sunny. Peter is an inventive, charming child. He tries to learn to whistle so that he can call his dog, Willie. He finally succeeds, and everyone is very proud of him. It is not at all stereotypic. Peter is a successful, excellent model.

Kirn, Ann. *Beeswax Catches a Thief.* New York: Norton, 1968. (Ages 4–8.)
Adaptation of a Congo folk tale. A version of the Tar Baby story; only here it is the tortoise who is coated with beeswax and the jackal who gets caught. Nicely told and illustrated by the author.

Konigsburg, E. L. *Jennifer, Hecate, Macbeth, William McKinley and Me, Elizabeth.* New York: Atheneum, 1967. Pb. also. (Ages 9–12.) (Newbery Honor Book.)
Elizabeth and Jennifer become friends, and Elizabeth believes Jennifer's claims that she is a witch. Both girls are imaginative and active. Jennifer is the only black child in the school, but her blackness is not a factor in the friendship. Jennifer is, however, ostracized by the other children in school. No discussion of this problem is included in the book.

Krementz, Jill. *Sweet Pea: A Black Girl Growing Up in the Rural South.* New York: Harcourt, Brace & World, 1969. (Ages 8–12.)
Very poor family in the rural South living in a segregated community. Their conditions are such that they have no indoor plumbing, no central heating. History lesson Sweet Pea learns in school is biased against Native Americans. Family and community are supportive, friendly, accepting of each other. Father has left but visits regularly. Family manages to be fairly comfortable and happy.

Larrick, Nancy (ed.). *On City Streets: An Anthology of Poetry.* Photographs by David Sagarin. Philadelphia: M. Evans, 1968. (Ages 10–up.)
One of the few books of children's poetry that does not have a rural bias. Poems by prominent poets mirror both the excitement and the bleaker aspects of city living. Photographs reflect varying facets of the city.

Lawrence, Jacob. *Harriet and the Promised Land*. Verses by Robert Kraus. New York: Simon and Schuster, 1968. (Ages 6–10.)
Jacob Lawrence is a black artist. His paintings form the book, accompanied by Kraus's verses. The combination conveys very powerfully the sense of Harriet Tubman's heroism. The paintings are stark. The book won the Brooklyn Art Book for Children award and was selected by the *New York Times* as one of the best-illustrated children's books of the year.

Lester, Julius. *Black Folktales*. Illus. Tom Feelings. New York: Grove Press, 1969. Pb. also. (Ages 10–up.)
Powerful retelling of tales from Africa, the South, and from black sections of cities. Very militant, angry, antiwhite. In all cases, the white man is the enemy. The illustrations are excellent. The book adds to each reader's store of perceptions and events.

———. *The Knee-High Man and Other Tales*. Illus. Ralph Pinto. New York: Dial Press, 1972. (Ages 3–8.)
Retelling of tales from slavery times. All are tales of trickery and competition, with one creature outwitting another. Very well told tales, each of which could be allegorical.

———. *Long Journey Home, Stories from Black History*. New York: Dial Press, 1972. Pb. Grove Press. (Ages 12–up.) (National Book Award Finalist.)
Fascinating and very well told accounts of people who did not so much make a giant mark in the history books, but were individuals who should be known. Book demonstrates that many black people were the source of their own freedom, not having to rely on the kindness and generosity of Whites. A very important book.

———. *To Be a Slave*. Illus. Tom Feelings. New York: Dial Press, 1968. Pb. Dell. (Ages 12–up.) (Newbery Honor Book.)
Accounts in slaves' own words of what it means to be a slave. Proceeds from the transportation of slaves from Africa to the time after Emancipation. Lester's comments guide the reader to a deeper understanding of the time and the people. The bibliography adds to the potential sources of information. A very powerful, well-constructed, important book.

Lewis, Richard (ed.). *Out of the Earth I Sing*. New York: Norton, 1968. (All ages.)
Well-selected collection of poems described here as from "primitive peoples of the world." The illustrations, powerful and remarkable, are photographs of original art work of the people who are represented by the poetry. The sources of the poetry are mostly other written works; the sources of the art are mostly museums.

Lexau, Joan M. *Benjie*. Illus. Don Bolognese. New York: Dial Press, 1964. (Ages 3-8.)

Benjie and his grandmother live alone — there is no explanation of where Benjie's parents are. One Sunday the grandmother loses an earring that is of great sentimental value. Benjie overcomes his shyness to find the earring. All the characters in this gentle book are black. The quality of love and caring comes across strongly.

―――. *Benjie on His Own*. Illus. Don Bolognese. New York: Dial Press, 1970. (Ages 4-8.)

Benjie's grandmother usually comes to take him home from school. One day she does not arrive, and Benjie is worried. He manages, with a number of problems, to find his way home through the hostile city streets. He discovers that his grandmother is ill. The ghetto then turns into a supportive place, and people help him in his time of need.

―――. *Me Day*. Illus. Robert Weaver. New York: Dial Press, 1971. (Ages 3-8.)

Rafer has an unhappy birthday until his divorced father spends the whole day with him as a surprise. Depressing conditions; not much hope offered.

―――. *Striped Ice Cream*. Illus. John Wilson. Philadelphia: Lippincott, 1968. (Ages 8-11.)

Black family, very poor. Five children live with their mother. Their father left to free them to go on welfare, but they do not. Mother works. Becky, the almost eight-year-old, is the protagonist. Her sisters and brother work to surprise her for her birthday but in so doing, make her miserable. Family is compulsively preoccupied with cleanliness as if to constantly prove they are not stereotypes. Illustrations excellent.

―――. *T for Tommy*. Illus. Janet Compere. Champaign, Ill.: Garrard, 1971. (Age 6.)

Fun story of Tommy, a black child who builds a house, and plays with his friend, Dolly, a white child. They are active children, playing catch, and running up and down the hill several times. The line of the illustration follows their actions, and eventually the drawing of a gigantic cat emerges from their action. The children are pictured with their arms around each other and holding hands. There is no real story here, but the book is fun and a very easy reader.

Lofting, Hugh. *The Story of Doctor Dolittle*. Philadelphia: Lippincott, 1920. Pb. Dell. (Ages 9-11.)

Classic in children's literature. This is the story of Doctor Dolittle, who is a renowned and kind animal doctor. The trouble is that this book presents black people in the worst possible stereotypes. They are either savage and wicked, or stupid. The Doctor feels sorry for them. The book is written in a patronizing, distorted manner when it comes to Blacks.

Longsworth, Polly. *I. Charlotte Forten, Black and Free.* New York: Crowell, 1970. (Ages 10–12.)
Fictionalized autobiography. Charlotte Forten's life is rich and eventful. She is active all her life in the fight for equal rights for black people. The book describes other abolitionists, such as William Lloyd Garrison, and tells the stories of such notable Blacks as Frederick Douglass, James Forten, and William Wells Brown, among others.

McGovern, Ann. *Black Is Beautiful.* Illus. Hope Warmfeld. New York: Four Winds Press, 1969. Pb. Scholastic. (Ages 5–8.)
Beautiful photographs describing the beauty of blackness. The text is poetic. Different kinds of people are pictured. This book is a good one to reinforce positive self-image or to change a once negative perspective.

———. *Runaway Slave.* Illus. R. M. Powers. New York: Four Winds Press, 1965. Pb. Scholastic. (Ages 7–9.)
Well-told story of the remarkable woman Harriet Tubman, or Moses, as she was known. The simple facts of her life are incredible. Her courage and strength were legend. She never got caught, and she never lost a passenger on her Underground Railroad.

Marshall, Catherine. *Julie's Heritage.* Illus. E. Harper Johnson. New York: Longmans, Green, 1957. Pb. Scholastic. (Ages 12–up.)
Julie, a middle-class black young woman finds that her white "friends" no longer want to associate with her once they have all entered high school. She has a beautiful voice and wins admirers through her talent. Many different reactions to bigotry are presented through the characters in this book. White friendship seems to be more important than black. Julie ostensibly accepts herself and her heritage at the end of the book. She demonstrates this by singing a spiritual in public.

Mathis, Sharon Bell. *Listen for the Fig Tree.* New York: Viking, 1974. Pb. Avon. (Ages 12–up.)
Kwanza, an African celebration, figures strongly in this complex and interesting story. Muffin Johnson, the heroine, is sixteen years old and blind. The black community is very important to Muffin and is very supportive of her. The sense of community and black identity is stressed in the book.

————. *Sidewalk Story.* Illus. Leo Carty. New York: Viking, 1971. (Ages
9–11.) (Council on Interracial Books for Children Award.)
Lilly Etta Allen is the nine-year-old protagonist. She manages to
help her friend, Tanya, overcome the effects of being evicted. She
calls the newspapers, contacts a sympathetic reporter, and saves the
day. Unfortunately, the prevailing situation in this book is that of
the fatherless black family, accepting their poor conditions.

————. *Teacup Full of Roses.* New York: Viking, 1972. (Ages 12–up.)
A very sad story about a black family. Two of the brothers are
destroyed, partly because of the mother's favoritism. Very moving.

Mendoza, George. *And I Must Hurry for the Sea Is Coming In.* Illus.
DeWayne Dalrymple. Englewood Cliffs, N.J.: Prentice-Hall, 1971.
(Ages 8–up.)
Young black child is pictured as the captain of a large, beautiful
sailboat. He handles the ship masterfully and withstands all obsta-
cles. The reader knows that this child will persevere and overcome
even though the reader sees, at the end of the book, that the child is
really sailing a toy boat in the water of a fire hydrant in the city. The
rest of the book is his fantasy. Beautifully done.

Messer, Ronald K. *Shumway.* Nashville: Thomas Nelson, 1975. (Ages
11–up.)
The South in the 1950s was an ugly place to be. The story describes
an uneasy friendship between a white boy named Shumway and a
black boy named Lyle. Shumway is ignorant and naive, but spunky.
The incidents in the story indicate the extent of the poor Whites'
hatred against Blacks.

Monjo, F. N. *The Drinking Gourd.* Illus. Fred Brenner. New York: Harper
& Row, 1970. (An "I Can Read History Book.") (Ages 5–8.)
Tommy Fuller, white child, is always in trouble and always being
punished by his parents; but he redeems himself by helping a family
of fugitive slaves continue through the Underground Railroad. Although Tommy saves the black family by using his wits to escape
detection, the family is not demeaned or depicted as weak. Each
family member is named, and Jeff, the father, helps to educate
Tommy. The family is dignified, courageous, and determined to win
their freedom.

Murgatroyd, Madeline. *Tales from the Kraals.* Illus. Joyce Ordbrown.
Capetown, South Africa: Howard Timmis, 1968. (Ages 10–up.)
Folk tales from Zululand, Basutoland, and the Lowveld. Somewhat
condescending manner of telling the tales. The stories are good
ones, but some of the language is pejorative and mars the stories.

Myers, Walter Dean. *Fast Sam, Cool Clyde and Stuff.* New York: Viking, 1975. (Ages 12–up.)
Reminiscences of the adolescent years of a young black boy in New York City. His group of friends is close-knit, and constructive. They are unusually naive despite their rough surroundings. The language is that of the city. The plot is thin, but there is much here that destroys the negative stereotype of the young Black in the city.

Nagenda, John. *Mukasa.* Iilus. Charles Lilly. New York: Macmillan, 1973. (Ages 10–12.)
Excellent story of a young Ugandan boy whose parents struggle to send him to school. Many customs very well described. His and his family's feelings and their growth are well demonstrated. Beautiful understanding of the individuality of all the students displayed in this book. Not only does this story convey some of the essence of Uganda, but it is also a good story on its own.

Neufeld, John. *Edgar Allan.* New York: S. G. Phillips, 1968. Pb. New American Library. (Ages 10–up.)
Minister and his wife adopt a black child without first consulting their other four children. Child, Edgar Allan, is three years old. All the family except for teen-age sister love him. Eventually, pressure from the townspeople, from the daughter, and from the members of the church, makes the minister give back Edgar Allan to the adoption agency. Their lie about his being returned to his original family does not hold, and everyone eventually castigates the minister for listening to them. He is forced to resign and to begin again. All the sympathy seems to be invited for the minister and his family. Edgar Allan never emerges as a person in this book. He remains a plaything that has been discarded. But some useful questions could be asked after reading this book, such as, would it have been better if they had never adopted the child? Or, what would have happened if they had kept the child? Or, how do you think Edgar Allan felt?

Ortiz, Victoria. *Sojourner Truth, A Self-Made Woman.* Philadelphia: Lippincott, 1974. (Ages 12–up.)
In reading the story of this remarkable black woman, much history is learned. The link between the feminist and abolitionist movement is described. Sojourner Truth, a pioneer for the cause of black civil rights, vigorously fought for her people until her death.

Randall, Florence Engel. *The Almost Year.* New York: Atheneum, 1971. (Ages 10–up.)
For almost a year, the narrator of this book, a sixteen-year-old black girl, lives with a white family. She is full of anger and is suspicious of all white people. The white family is well-meaning. Strange

things happen throughout the year. All finally decide that these happenings are caused by a poltergeist, or mischievous spirit. At the end, everyone recognizes his/her own part in the bad feelings, and the black young woman (we never learn her name) realizes that she must confront herself as well as the world. A somewhat confusing but interesting book.

Schick, Eleanor. *City in the Summer*. New York: Macmillan, 1969. Pb. also. (Ages 5-8.)
Many ethnic groups pictured. Positive feelings about the city come from this book. Child and old man escape the heat of the sidewalks by going to the beach.

Schraff, A. E. *Black Courage*. Illus. Len Ebert. Philadelphia: Macrae Smith, 1969. (Ages 9-up.)
Twenty-one black heroes of the American West are described here. Not all of the stories have happy endings, but all of the heroes have contributed; thus readers may take pride in their undertakings.

Scott, Ann Herbert. *Sam*. Illus. Symeon Shimin. New York: McGraw-Hill, 1967. (Ages 4-8.)
A middle-class, close-knit black family. Sam is the youngest. At first, in the story, everyone sends him off. When he weeps, in frustration and rejection, they rally to him and provide him with an enjoyable task. Beautiful illustrations.

Shearer, John. *I Wish I Had an Afro*. New York: Cowles, 1970. (Ages 8-12.)
Author is a black photographer. The book is about an eleven-year-old boy who lives with his family in a very poor section of Westchester County, New York. No story as such, but thoughts of each of the family members written in Black English. Each character is seen as an individual.

Shepard, Ray Anthony. *Conjure Tales by Charles W. Chestnutt*. Illus. John Ross and Clare Romano. New York: Dutton, 1973. (Ages 9-up.)
Retelling of the 1899 *The Conjure Woman*. Tales of slaves and their attempt to relieve their plight through the use of magic. Sometimes it worked; sometimes it did not. Tales are well told. The point is made each time about the oppressiveness of slavery.

Shotwell, Louisa R. *Roosevelt Grady*. Illus. Peter Burchard. New York: World, 1963. Pb. Scholastic. (Ages 9-11.)
Roosevelt's family are tenant farmers. The story tells of Roosevelt's desire for learning and his longing for a permanent home. It also describes his family as dignified, loving, and worthy.

Showers, Paul. *Look at Your Eyes.* Illus. Paul Galdone. New York: Crowell Company, 1962. (Ages 5–8.)
Explanations of the eye and its parts. The function of the eye as well is explained by the author, through the mouth of a black child who narrates the book. The pictures show an integrated community. It is nicely done.

Simon, Norma. *How Do I Feel?* Illus. Joe Lasker. Chicago: Albert Whitman, 1973. (Ages 8–up.)
Carl and his twin brother Eddie live with their grandparents. Each of the twins has his own personality. Pictures show that their teacher and some of their friends are black. Feelings are genuine, situations realistic.

———. *I Know What I Like.* Illus. Dora Leder. Chicago: Albert Whitman, 1971. (Ages 3–7.)
Integrated pictures. Children like all kinds of different things; unfortunately, boys and girls are pictured in somewhat stereotypic situations.

Solbert, Ronni. *I Wrote My Name on the Wall, Sidewalk Songs.* Boston: Little, Brown, 1971. (Ages 8–up.)
Remarkable photographs. Sad comments accompany almost all of them. This is not a story, but a collection of portraits and moods. Sensitive but very depressing.

Sonneborn, Ruth A. *I Love Gram.* Illus. Lee Carty. New York: Viking, 1971. (Ages 5–8.)
Ellie lives with her mother, sister, and grandmother. No father. Mother works; sister is away most of the day. Grandmother takes care of Ellie. One day grandmother becomes ill and is hospitalized. Eventually, she returns home; meanwhile, Ellie has missed her dreadfully. Story shows a concern for each other and a very warm relationship between Ellie and her grandmother. Ellie seems to be an overprotected child.

———. *The Lollipop Party.* Illus. Brinton Turkle. New York: Viking, 1967. Pb. Scholastic. (Ages 5–8.)
Tomas lives with his mother, sister, and a cat. He is usually very protected. One day when his mother does not come home on time, he is very worried and frightened. His teacher arrives unexpectedly; Tomas entertains her with lollipops. His mother returns home safely, and all is well. Perhaps reassuring for some children. Certainly blasts the stereotype of the neglected child.

Steptoe, John. *Birthday.* New York: Holt, Rinehart and Winston, 1972. (Ages 4–8.)

Idealized black community. All the people in it are loving, joyful, and productive. All have African names. Javaka is the firstborn of the community, and it is his birthday, so there is a celebration. Pictures and text combine to give the reader a strong, positive sense of the community and each person in it.

————. *Stevie*. New York: Harper & Row, 1969. Pb. Scholastic. (Ages 4–8.)
Robert's mother takes care of Stevie while his mother works. Robert resents Stevie's demanding, babyish ways. But when, after some time, Stevie and his parents move away, Robert remembers the good things about Stevie and misses him. Both families are close and caring. The illustrations are strong and appropriate. The text is written in black dialect that conveys the thoughts of the characters very well.

————. *Train Ride*. New York: Harper & Row, 1971. Pb. Scholastic. (Ages 6–10.)
This book, too, is written in Black English. The story is that of a group of black children who decide to take a train ride uptown from Brooklyn, where they live, to Times Square. They do so, have a marvelous time, and return home late, knowing that they will be severely punished. Their worried parents do punish them, but the reader knows that this intrepid band will repeat their experience. The children like themselves and each other. Their families are all intact. The illustrations are of a realistic but supportive city.

————. *Uptown*. New York: Harper & Row, 1970. (Ages 5–8.)
The entire book is a conversation between Dennis and John about what they will be when they grow up. They discuss junkies, black pride, clothing, the army, karate, and hippies. They come to no conclusions but agree that they will continue to be alert and to enjoy life. Some readers may be uncomfortable with this book because there is no glossary to help them with some of the vernacular terminology. The book, however, is worth the discomfort. It paints a realistic but not completely negative picture. Its ending indicates optimism and strength on the part of the boys. They will have a say in what happens to them in the long run.

Sterling, Dorothy. *Mary Jane*. Illus. Ernest Crichlow. Garden City, N.Y.: Doubleday, 1959. Pb. Scholastic. (Ages 9–11.)
Mary Jane is the only black female in the junior high school, which has been newly integrated. She goes through many trials, but finally emerges, proud of her blackness, but able to have white friends. Many different points of view are presented in this book. It is a mild but useful book.

Stolz, Mary. *A Wonderful, Terrible Time.* Illus. Louis S. Glanzman. New York: Harper & Row, 1967. Pb. Scholastic. (Ages 9–11).
Mady and Sue Ellen, two black children, are very close friends. Mady's father was killed in a voter registration demonstration. Her mother works hard. Sue Ellen's father serves as surrogate father to Mady. The two girls go to camp, where Mady finds herself. Story is of how the girls work out their relationship and of the difficulties of growing up black.

Taylor, Mildred D. *Song of the Trees.* Illus. Jerry Pinkney, New York: Dial Press, 1975. (Ages 7–10.) (Council on Interracial Books for Children Award.)
The setting is rural Mississippi during the Depression. The story is about a black family and their battle to protect their trees from a white lumberman. The father is the strongest figure in the story. His response to the threat is potentially violent but effective. The family is portrayed somewhat sketchily, but a sense of pride and togetherness impresses the reader.

Taylor, Theodore. *The Cay.* Garden City, N.Y.: Doubleday, 1969. Pb. Avon. (Ages 11–up.)
Phillip lives in Curacao with his mother and father. When World War II comes, his mother is worried about his safety, so she and Phillip board a ship to return to the U.S. The ship is torpedoed, and Phillip is blinded temporarily. Timothy, a black sailor, after teaching Phillip how to survive, sacrifices his life to shield Phillip from a storm. When Phillip finally returns to Curacao, his attitude toward black people has changed; he now speaks to them. This book has been much criticized for its paternalistic attitude and its white perspective.

Thomas, Ianthe. *Lordy, Aunt Hattie.* Illus. Thomas di Grazia. New York: Harper & Row. (Ages 4–8.)
A loving tone poem of growing up in the Deep South. The child, Jeppa Lee, and her Aunt Hattie engage in a conversation that demonstrates their warmth, affection, and positive sense of self.

————. *Walk Home Tired, Billy Jenkins.* Illus. Thomas di Grazia. New York: Harper & Row, 1974. (Ages 5–8.)
It is time to go home from the playground, and Billy Jenkins is very tired. His sister, Nina, lovingly and imaginatively makes the trip home a magic ride for the two of them. Illustrations of the people and the city are beautifully and gently done.

Thum, Marcella. *Exploring Black America: A History and Guide.* New York: Atheneum, 1975. (Ages 10–up.)

Combines an informative and comprehensive historical account of black people in the United States with a guide to places of historical and cultural significance for black people. An invaluable, well-constructed resource.

Travers. P. L. *Mary Poppins*. Illus. Mary Shepard. New York: Harcourt, Brace, Jovanovich, 1934, 1962. Pb. also. (Ages 9–11.)
Mary Poppins is a magical, marvelous person, whose adventures are very entertaining. Travers writes very well. This edition has been changed to avoid offending minority people. A fairly good job has been done, but the sense of English and white superiority remains.

Udry, Janice May. *Mary Jo's Grandmother*. Illus. Eleanor Mill. Chicago: Albert Whitman, 1970. (Ages 5–8.)
One snowy Christmas, Mary Jo visits her old but independent grandmother, who lives alone in the country. When her grandmother has an accident, Mary Jo gets help and cares for the old woman. Middle-class black family. Loving, caring, constructive.

———. *What Mary Jo Shared*. Illus. Eleanor Mill. Chicago: Albert Whitman, 1966. (Ages 6–9.)
Mary Jo goes to an integrated school. She is very shy and is worried because everyone else has something special to share. Finally, she shares her father. Very positive, gentle book.

Vogel, Ray. *The Other City*. Photographs by William Boyd, James Freeman, Alfonso Garcia, and Ronald McCoy. New York: David White, 1969. (Ages 8–up.)
Excellent photos. Not demeaning or stereotyped, but the text is very negative. The book presents no sense of hope.

Wagner, Jane. *J. T.* Illus. Gordon Parks, Jr. New York: Van Nostrand Reinhold 1969. Pb. Dell. (Ages 9–up.)
J. T. is an unhappy black boy. Father has left; mother poor, busy, distracted, worries about J. T. He steals a radio on impulse. Finds a hurt, stray cat, cares for it. Grandmother who is warm, loving, and understanding, comes to visit. When his cat gets run over, store owner gives him another. J. T. returns radio, gets a job — things will be all right.

Walker, Alice. *Langston Hughes, American Poet*. Illus. Don Miller. New York: Crowell, 1974. (Ages 7–9.)
One of a series of biographies including a number of black Americans. The author, who knew Hughes personally, tells simply and sympathetically of his youth. She indicates the problems that Hughes had because of his father's negative attitudes. Not much is said of his adult years, but the poet is introduced to young readers,

who may then be motivated to read more about and by Langston Hughes.

Walter, Mildred Pitts. *Lillie of Watts*. Illus. Leonore E. Prince. Pasadena, Calif.: Ward Ritchie Press, 1969. (Ages 8–up.)
The story takes the reader through two days in Lillie's life. She is eleven years old, and it is her birthday. Her teacher is black, as are all the other characters in the book. He is an excellent teacher. Lillie's family is poor, fatherless, and somewhat stereotyped. The mother is a day worker for wealthy white familites. Life is hard, but the community is a supportive one, and the family is loving.

Weik, Mary Hays. *The Jazz Man*. Illus. Ann Grifalconi. New York: Atheneum, 1967. (Ages 9–up.) (Newbery Honor Book and *N.Y. Times* Choice of Best Illustrated Children's Book Award.)
Zeke, who lives in Harlem, stays at home and dreams a lot. His life becomes a nightmare for a while — first his mother and then his father leave. He listens to the music of a jazz man in a building nearby, and that sustains him. In the end, the reader does not know if it is a dream or not, but his parents return and they will live happily again.

Weiner, Sandra. *It's Wings That Make Birds Fly*. New York: Random House (Pantheon Books), 1968. (Ages 6–9.)
Otis is a sensitive young man. He and his friends have a difficult time of it in New York. They are good boys but are destroyed by their environment. The author notes that Otis was killed by an automobile while he was playing in the street. All the text is from tape recordings made of the boys' conversation.

White, Edgar. *Omar at Christmas*. Illus. Dindga McCannon. New York: Lothrop, Lee and Shepard, 1973. (Ages 6–9.)
Omar and his mother spend the day before Christmas cleaning and serving at a wealthy white couple's apartment. Omar receives one of their books as a gift. He is an introspective, bright child. His mother is loving but tired and, at times, unresponsive. The story sensitively characterizes this child and his world.

Whitney, Phyllis. *Willow Hill*. New York: David McKay, 1947. Pb. Scholastic. (Ages 12–up.)
Teen-agers at a high school manage integration after a number of unpleasant incidents. Ends with hope for the future.

Wilson, Beth P. *The Great Minu*. Illus. Jerry Pinkney. Chicago: Follett, 1974. (Ages 5–8.)
Black author and illustrator. The story, which is very well told, is about a traveler who goes to an unfamiliar town. Everyone he meets

answers his questions with, "I don't understand" — *Minu* in their language. The traveler thinks that *Minu* is the name of a great and rich man. When he receives "Minu" as the reply to his question of who was the dead man in the coffin, he returns home glad that he is not *Minu*. A good story, not only in plot, but in message.

Yates, Elizabeth. *Amos Fortune, Free Man.* Illus. Nora S. Unwin. New York: Dutton, 1951. Pb. Dell. (Ages 10–up.) (Newbery Medal.)
Understated but well-written story of a man who could have been a king in Africa, but who became a slave in America. He emerges as a strong, able, dignified man. Some questions that readers may ask are: Why did he not accept the many offers of freedom that his first master made? Why did the author choose to describe only the kindly slave-owners? Why was the institution of slavery not more realistically described? Why was the period of thirty-five years of Amos Fortune's slavery glossed over as if it were a short time? Perhaps some of the answers have to do with the date that the book was written. In contemporary times this book does not quite suffice.

Young, Bernice Elizabeth. *Harlem, The Story of a Changing Community.* New York: Messner, 1972. (Ages 8–10.)
The history of Harlem from early Dutch times to the present. Gives a good sense of its transition. Author is a black writer.

NOTES and ADDITIONS

8

The Native American

THE NATIVE AMERICAN, or American Indian, was our first victimized ethnic group.* Although many of the first white settlers sought religious freedom and had, themselves, been oppressed for their beliefs, they were intolerant of others. Fearful and contemptuous of the people who already inhabited the country, they viewed these natives, for the most part, as less than human. Their religion was considered to be pagan and, therefore, no religion at all. Their manner of dress was an affront to the standards of the Europeans. Because of this superior feeling on the part of the colonists, their disregard for the rights of the American

* Since this author's intent is to look at those Native Americans who were displaced by the coming of the White, books about Eskimos or Hawaiians will not be included in this chapter.

Indians was not considered to be persecution. By converting the "heathens" to the true and proper religion of Christianity, they felt that they were repaying helpfulness on the part of Native Americans with the greatest kindness of all — initiation into white culture.

No recognition was paid to the life styles, beliefs, and temperaments of the native tribes. It was assumed that any response to the Whites other than gratitude would be inappropriate. So convinced were the new settlers of their righteousness that the chronologies they wrote of their times reflected their attitude — that the Indians were barbaric, naive, and in need of enlightenment. This point of view unfortunately has permeated our history books and, until now, few people have questioned its validity.

Our history books and our works of fiction have stressed the image of the intrepid pioneer, fighting valiantly against all odds to make something of the land. As Americans we have been proud of a heritage of tenacity and valor. We have not been encouraged to think about the people whose lands we usurped, and we have not been correctly informed about their customs and characteristics. It has been to our advantage to glorify our white predecessors, at the same time denigrating the Native Americans. As Americans we like to believe that justice and righteousness have always been on our side. We view ourselves as moral people who would not hurt unless we had to.

But this has not been the case with American Indians. We began, systematically, to persecute them as soon as we landed on this continent. We have not yet stopped. Up to the past ten years, very few books even hinted at the true account of our treatment of these peoples. Our storybooks have either villainized or romanticized them; our histories have distorted facts. It is, therefore, necessary that we acquaint ourselves with some of the facts.

Several books that could constitute a beginning for building background information about the history, culture, and present-day situation of Native Americans are Stan Steiner's *The New Indians*, Robert Burnette's *The Tortured Americans*, and Virgil Vogel's *The Indian in American History*. Each book discusses the treatment that the United States has given the Indians; each suggests ways to change the miserable conditions in which they still exist; and each helps the reader to build a clearer perspective and understanding of the relationship between history and the present.

Deloria's *Custer Died for Your Sins* should be required reading for anyone interested in understanding how complex, how difficult the realities are confronting the Native American. Deloria is an Oglala Sioux from the Standing Rock Reservation. He is an acknowledged, although by no means uncontroversial, leader of the movement for tribal self-determination. He criticizes other Native Americans, churches, practices of the United States government, Republicans and Democrats, and anthropologists. But his book, exceptionally well written, is laced with a wry humor that helps the reader to accept the importance of what he says without resenting it. His points of discussion enlighten the reader and raise many questions. His detailing of history sheds an enormous amount of light on fuzzy areas obscured by traditional texts. The bulk of his book helps the reader look at today's Indians; it suggests new approaches to aid them to achieve appropriate status in their own land.

Other books for young adults and older readers deal with changing White Americans' views of the historical "facts" concerning the building of the American West. James Forman's *People of the Dream* tells of the Nez Percé containment on the Colville Reservation in Washington. Forman, who is very subjective about his topic, is less than kind when describing the behavior of Chief Joseph's Indian compatriots. For example, he says, after the tribes were dispersed and settled on different reservations, "There White Bird, who had skulked in Canada, rejoined them," He also attributes the defeat of the Nez Percé to the stupidity and negative characteristics of the other chiefs and tribes. He describes Chief Joseph's daughter as having been broken by the Sioux, and he indicates that other Native Americans were almost as much to blame as the Whites were. Nevertheless, the book is interesting as the story of Chief Joseph, who is Forman's hero.

In a well-researched book, *Bury My Heart at Wounded Knee*, Dee Brown describes the history of Native American–White relations from a point of view that is sympathetic to the Indian people. His recounting of the treachery and atrocities, particularly on the part of white soldiers, is difficult for the reader to read without revulsion. His descriptions of the battles and the events leading up to them are important for modern Americans to read. This book, in combination with Deloria's, can constitute background for enlightened reading of current fiction concerning the American Indian. Of course, the more informed one becomes, and the more sources one consults, the more able one is to interpret and evaluate any work.

Historical Overview

A short chronology of United States relations with Native Americans may help the reader to assume a perspective when reading works of historical fiction or when teaching about Indians to young children.

When Columbus reached the shores of the West Indies, mistakenly thinking that he had reached India, he called the natives of the land Indians. Since most of the tribes had no specific names to call themselves, other than "the people," this misnomer remained. After the colonists had settled in, and more and more kept coming, the once helpful and friendly tribes began to recognize that they were being pushed out of their homes, and that there was no recourse from the Whites' acts of hostility.

Some tribes participated in the wars between the Whites. Although not absolutely confirmed, conjecture is that the practice of taking the scalp from one's victims was introduced to the American Indians by either the Spaniards in the seventeenth century or by the English in the eighteenth century sometime before the French and Indian War.

Before the American Revolution, Indian lands were somewhat protected by the English Crown. Even after the colonists won the war, it was considered unlawful to take land without either purchasing it or making some attempt at treaties. The new American government attempted to maintain peaceful relations with the Native Americans. But although the Northwest Territory Ordinance and the Articles of Confederation insured the rights of the American Indians to their own government and their property, the Congress was, by 1800, beginning to demand Indian loyalty to the government of the United States. Indian Affairs were administered by the United States government through the Secretary of War. The Indians, though still technically considered to be separate foreign nations existing on American soil, came more and more under American domination.

In 1804 the infamous removal of the Cherokee from their lands was made "legal" under the provisions of the Louisiana Purchase. The Cherokee nation, which had conformed in every way to white demands and expectations, was nevertheless forced to relinquish all of their lands and possessions. Soon after, other tribes were ordered removed to the West. It may come as a surprise to some readers that Andrew Jackson's attitude and behavior toward the Native Americans was totally oppressive and without regard for their legal or human rights. When the Chief Justice of the Supreme Court, John Marshall, declared the occupation of Indian land to be illegal, Jackson refused to enforce the ruling and, in effect, told Marshall to enforce it himself, if he could. Meanwhile, Congress kept appropriating funds to "civilize and educate the heathen natives." Presidents after Jackson were no less cruel when it came to destruction of Native Americans. The demand that they change their ancient ways was pressed on all tribes.

In 1824 the Bureau of Indian Affairs was established to handle the problems "caused" by the Native Americans. The Bureau was contained in the War Department until 1849, when it was transferred to the Department of the Interior. For the rest of the nineteenth century, the United States conducted a systematic and ruthless campaign of genocide against all Native American tribes. Under the most cruel conditions,

Indian nations were removed forcibly from their lands. Their possessions were confiscated, and they were forced to endure killing
marches across many miles to substandard land. Torn from their well-
established patterns of life, they were forced to try farming a land that
was almost totally barren. Some of them were set down in swamp lands,
where it was hoped they would all succumb to fever — and many of
them did. Most of the tribes were decimated on their "long marches."
The remaining people found it almost impossible to survive the hostile
conditions of the new lands to which they were sent. They were removed time and time again, whenever the Whites discovered that their
land contained lead or gold deposits or anything remotely useful. Those
people who did not die of disease or starvation were subject to constant
military harassment.

In 1887 the infamous Allotment Act was passed, permitting the
United States to divide all Indian lands into small allotments and to
make all acreage that remained after the Indians had received their
"share" available to white settlers. At this point there were only about
250,000 Native Americans remaining in the United States, where before
there were more than a million. Most of them were contained in the land
reserved for them alone (reservations) but subject to United States law.
The Bureau of Indian Affairs was, and still is, responsible for adminis-
tering the funds assigned to Native Americans and for protecting their
rights. The BIA has been prey to graft, pressures of politicians, and
mismanagement by unqualified staff. But there have been people in the
Bureau who have truly held the interests of the American Indians to be
their responsibility and who have tried to accomplish gains in Native
Americans' economic, political, and educational welfare.

In the twentieth century, the policy of the United States government
has become somewhat more responsive to Native American needs.
Laws have been enacted granting citizenship, permitting tribes to incor-
porate, and granting compensation for land lost. But schools have in
general been established and run by the government. These schools
have discouraged the practice of native religion, ancient tribal customs,
and speaking of the native tongue, and have attempted to thrust upon
the tribes the acceptance of English, Christianity, and white ways.

Termination, a government policy which became established in recent decades, has endangered many tribes. By abdicating its responsibility, that is, by withdrawing its protection to those tribes who have
achieved a measure of economic independence, the United States government has been able to purchase reservation land, in effect dispersing
the tribes. The Native Americans are forced to leave the reservation,
possessing only the amount of money that they were paid for their
land, to seek new places and new ways of life. Generally, they have
been unsuccessful in establishing a viable economic and cultural posi-

tion for themselves; indeed, some of the slums of Chicago and other Midwestern cities are testimony to the destructive impact of the termination policy. Outspoken native leaders have denounced this policy and have influenced change. The BIA and the government now recognize that tribal self-determination rather than assimilation will probably be more effective in helping Native Americans to be contributing citizens of the United States. It is to be hoped that termination will not recur as established United States policy.

An era of change has begun. Native Americans are again practicing once forbidden religious rites and speaking their ancient languages. At last a knowledge of — and respect for — the customs and beliefs of tribal ancestors are being communicated in schools and communities. No longer is the white way the accepted way. Young Indians are being encouraged to write about their heritage, and there are many tribal newspapers and publications across the country. Indian associations whose membership is comprised largely if not exclusively of Native Americans are gaining in influence. American Indian voices are being heard in Congress, in the news media, and in books. Native Americans are relying on their own abilities and leadership, as tribes more and more control their own affairs. No longer will the Indians remain silent — no longer can we imagine them as a vanishing race. We must heed their voices; we must end the oppressive and abusive practices that have continued.

▶ Try This

Find histories of American Indians in encyclopedias and history texts. Compile descriptions of their removal to "Indian Territory" from a white perspective. Then, after reading about the removal in any of the books written after 1965 from an Indian perspective, analyze the difference in factual presentation. Do the same with the Battle of Little Big Horn and with the massacre at Wounded Knee.

What kind of information are our children receiving? Because our texts have so consistently damaged or distorted information about Native Americans, it seems to be a general rule that little is taught in elementary school classrooms that is not stereotypic or inaccurate. Every child has had several units of work about the Indian. Few have any accurate notion of the history, diversity, and plight of these people. Rey Mickinock points out that even talented illustrators commit inaccuracies in their pictures. They dress characters in inappropriate and incorrect costumes and mix tribal characteristics. Mickinock goes on to describe many other errors, oversights, and misconceptions conveyed to the young reading public by authors and illustrators ignorant of such details. Mary Gloyne Byler, in her informative introduction to the selected bibliography of *American Indian Authors for Young Readers*, published by the Association on American Indian Affairs, further describes and then corrects some of the mistakes made in books for young children. After having examined hundreds of books, Byler comes to this conclusion: "Only American Indians can tell non-Indians what it is to be Indian. There is no longer any need for non-Indian writers to 'interpret' American Indians for the American public."

▶ Try This

Find a book by a Native American describing life on a reservation. (Any of Virginia Driving Hawk Sneve's books would be useful here.) Contrast the information and attitudes transmitted with a book about the same topic by a non-Indian. (Clymer's *The Spider, the Cave, and the Pottery Bowl* or Barnouw's *Dream of the Blue Heron* can be consulted.) Contrast two books in the same way on the topics of schooling, history, and folklore. Do you agree or disagree with Mary Gloyne Byler's conclusions?

The literary treatment of Native Americans has been distorted both in an idealized as well as negative manner. The Indian has been viewed either as a noble savage or as a marauder. It is seldom apparent that the Native American was threatened by the settlers and that, if tribes did not fight for their land, they would lose it. Those American Indians who are portrayed in the stories as having positive qualities usually are praised for adapting to white ways, and for helping white people. One book, *American Indian Woman*, by Marion E. Gridley, talks of famous Indian heroines such as Milly Hadjo Francis, who saved a white soldier's life at the expense of her own father's life. Too many of these so-called heroines betrayed their own people in order to help the whites. These women would not be considered favorably by their own people, but the reader is asked to admire their deeds. Not all the women are betrayers, but almost all of them were successful in white terms, married white man, and lived in white society.

Assimilation, once the government's goal, is not the goal of the "new Indian." It seems to be one of the "happy" endings in fictionalized history for children. Perhaps it is out of ignorance that authors assume that success in the white sense is a goal for Native Americans. Undoubtedly it is ignorance that has authors speaking in global terms of and for

Indians. Any investigation of the customs, life styles, and values of Native Americans demonstrates the necessity for specifying the tribe and the location. Native Americans vary as greatly as do Whites. Their commonalities are also great; but in order to do justice to them, books must demonstrate a recognition of the differences.

▶ **Try This**

Select a group of tribes, such as those belonging to the Cherokee or Sioux nations. Find as many works of fiction and nonfiction as you can that specifically describe the group you selected. (*Subject Guide to Children's Books in Print* can be of use here.) Write a summary of their major characteristics, roles of the men and women, government, means of livelihood, and history of how they came to be where they are. Compare your findings with students who have investigated other tribal confederations or groups.

Suggested Criteria

One of the signals of respect for Native Americans is the care that the author takes in detail. If the characters in a book are American Indians, with no indication of their tribe or special origin, the book is usually less than effective. Therefore, look for the name of the tribe and the setting of the story when selecting books on this topic. The adequate research that most authors attempt to do in order to validate their stories is particularly important in the case of books about the Native American. Not only should the details be accurate but also the values conveyed in the text should reflect as closely as possible the attitudes of the real-life counterparts of the characters. If the author is not a Native American, then perhaps consultants could be located to authenticate the text.

Not all American Indians agree about any given question. For example, the label *Indian* is not an accurate one, but it is less objectionable to some groups than to others. Any label is likely to be inadequate. An author who recognizes this and uses tribal names or demonstrates a sensitivity to the preference on the part of some people to be called Native Americans would be satisfying part of the criterion of treating the subject with respect.

Other signs of respect (and probably the most important criterion is this one of respect) include refraining from comparing tribal ways unfavorably with those of Whites. Any indication that manner of dress, family relationships, or religious beliefs are not beneficial to society are negative factors to be avoided. Ann McGovern, in *If You Lived with the Sioux Indians*, makes a well-intentioned attempt to acquaint readers with the customs and habits of the Sioux in the first half of the nineteenth century. She does try to maintain a respectful stance, but in pointing out the vast and somewhat alien differences between Sioux and white ways, the description can appear condescending to some readers. The book is not a bad one, but it demonstrates the difficulty of a non-Sioux in telling about a manner of life totally different from the author's.

Authors should not use such adjectives as *strange* or *savage* when describing differences. People *are* different from one another, and our differences are to be encouraged and valued. The differences should be apparent in their actual description, not in their labeling. An overly sentimental description is just as detrimental to understanding and appreciation as one that is critical. Overly idealized descriptions violate the criterion of accuracy. For example, much is made in many books of the American Indian's belief that no one can own land; but it would be false to assume that tribes had no sense of territory. They also had personal possessions. True, they were, in general, communal people, and cared for each other, but they also respected each other's belongings and had ways of indicating possession. Land is an important consideration for the contemporary Indian. One of the ways that Indian nations have been able to strengthen themselves in recent times has been through the acquisition of land. It is essential for authors and readers to recognize that although the ideas Native Americans have about personal property and administration of the law are somewhat different from those of most white societies, their sense of protocol and behavior is clear and consistent.

In considering the contemporary Native American, authors should take care to identify problems and directions from a nonwhite perspective or, if the book is to be written from an avowedly white perspective, to avoid patronizing statements. Respect and recognition of the tribal point of view is essential even through a white perspective, and assimilation should not be the goal or the happy ending. Careful research is necessary. Here again, consultation with members of the tribe would be of great value.

Historical facts should be presented in perspective. In too many books, when the Indians are victorious, the battle is called a massacre. When the whites win, it is a "victorious battle," usually "heroically" fought. As was mentioned before, the practices of scalping and mutilation of bodies are attributed only to the "savage" Indian. In reality it was encouraged by the Puritans and other settlers, when bounties were paid to Whites or mercenaries for Native American scalps. At first, the whole head of a victim was required as proof of a kill, but eventually the scalp was accepted. Only Indian scalps brought bounties. Native Americans generally retaliated in kind rather than initiating the atrocities; however, no one claims that either side was kind and generous to enemies in war. It should simply be understood that our "facts" are misconceptions, which should now be corrected. Stereotypes should be avoided both for the Native American and the white settler.

In books of folklore, the complexity of the symbols and the messages of the tales should be conveyed accurately. Some collections miss the whole point of the stories. Some of them — as with any attempt to set down in writing what has been part of the oral literature — are obscure and badly told. Here, too, the reader should search for the author's credentials, since an understanding of the background and specific meaning of the tale is necessary for its proper telling and a knowledgeable author would demonstrate this understanding.

Illustrations, very important in any book, are particularly critical when much undoing of past harm is needed. Features, dress, and environment must be depicted correctly, with all the criteria used for excellence in the writing also pertaining to the illustrations. Native American illustrators as well as writers have fortunately been recognized in recent years and have been employed by publishers who care about presenting an Indian people's perspective.

Discussion of Children's Books

FOLKLORE

Folklorists have been interested in the Indian *Pourquoi*, or explanatory tales for a long time. Recognizing the different origins of the various tales, they have appropriately labeled them according to the group from which they came. One such work is *Skunny Wundy: Seneca Indian Tales*, by Arthur C. Parker, himself a Seneca Indian. The Seneca belong to the Iroquois Nation, and these animal tales convey the special qualities attributed to them by the Iroquois. Other collections describe Zuni ways. Papago and Pima myths, Paiute, Algonquin, Hopi, Kiowa, and many other individual tribal customs and beliefs.

Some of the collections add notes informing the reader about the contemporary lives of the people, as well as some of their recent history. George Scheer's *Cherokee Animal Tales* does this. Another is Emerson Matson's *Legends of the Great Chiefs*. In this book the chiefs of the tribes from which the stories were taken are described. Unfortunately, neither the biographies nor the tales are adequately written, but the idea is an excellent one and, in conjunction with some other collections, provides interesting comparisons.

The complexity of the tales is such that it is sometimes difficult to convey the intended meaning. Alex Whitney's *Stiff Ears: Animal Folktales of the North American Indians* tries to teach a lesson with each of the stories. Sometimes, however, the moral is obscured by the way that the story is told, and the reader is left somewhat confused. In contrast are Betty Baker's stories in the collection *At the Center of the World* and Margaret Hodges's *The Fire Bringer: A Paiute Indian Legend*. Contemporary tribal education is emphasizing the continuation of the old tales. Let us hope that more members of the Indian nations will set down the tales as they have heard them so that their special qualities will be communicated in print.

HISTORY

Not much of a search needs to be made to find books that distort history, particularly that of the Native American in the eighteenth and nineteenth centuries. Contemporary writers have attempted to depict the American Indian honestly, but some have perpetuated stereotypes and misconceptions. Syd Hoff, in his book *Little Chief*, an "I Can Read" book, conveys the impression that it was to the Indians' advantage that the settlers came. He has the young Native American rescue the pioneer children, thus earning their affection and that of their parents. There is no indication whatsoever in this little book of what will happen to the Indian boy and his family as a result of the encroachment of the Whites. No attempt has been made here to portray the lives of the American Indians with any kind of reality or detail. The author probably is trying to demonstrate to the reader that there were once some good and friendly Indians who were rewarded with white goodwill and companionship. Readers should weigh the appropriateness of this message.

F. N. Monjo, an author who respectfully handles a story of the Underground Railroad, *The Drinking Gourd*, is less understanding of the need for fairness and accuracy in *Indian Summer*. He responds to Mary Gloyne Byler's criticism of his book by saying that he will try not to offend in the future, but that he is trying to present the pioneer point of view in this book. He does acknowledge that writers have an obligation to inform themselves on their topics, but he reserves the right of every author to choose any topic whatsoever. The book is the story of how a woman and children fend off cowardly maurauding Indians in pioneer times. It is only one of many of its type, which unfortunately does not provide an accurate historical description to young readers.

Alice Dalgleish wrote the now-classic *Courage of Sarah Noble* in 1954. Although no real issues are raised in the story and the tone is somewhat that of implied white superiority, the fact that the father leaves the little girl in the care of an American Indian family (no tribal name is given) and the girl is lovingly cared for is useful to counteract the otherwise negative image of Indians. The setting is Connecticut, but the two families seem to be the only ones around; thus the opportunity is missed for a description of communal life. It would have been interesting to have seen what East Coast Indians were like and how their friendly relations with the Whites affected them. But the story of Sarah and her family is, nevertheless, a positive one to use in contrast with the very negative others.

Another more recent story of the same genre is *Little Yellow Fur*, by Wilma Pitchford Hays. Again, it is told from the perspective of the white settlers, but it conveys a sympathetic attitude based on the recollections of the author's own childhood and has that sort of authenticity. Certainly it is valid to have some stories from this perspective, as long as there are others to balance it from the Indian point of view.

History for the older child has been written with a more empathic attempt in terms of the Native American. Betty Baker's *Killer-of-Death* describes how the Apache (a word meaning "enemy") came to accept that name. The ways of the tribe are included in what appears to be accurate detail. The hero of the story is well described, and the reader's sympathy is with him throughout the story; he understandably becomes the enemy of all Whites as a result of the perfidy of the white community. The book describes the white practice of scalping Native Americans, even women and children. It also indicates some of the rivalries among tribes. Treating customs without condescension, this book maintains the reader's respect as well as attention. Although it is fictionalized history, it has the ring of truth and adds to the reader's store of information and attitude.

Sing Down the Moon, by Scott O'Dell, is another story that helps illuminate history. The main character in this tale is a young Navajo woman who exhibits remarkable determination and tenacity. She has many adventures, not the least of which is the Long Walk that she and her people must endure when they are removed from their beloved Canyon de Chelly. Although she proves to be emotionally stronger than her husband, he is a fit partner for her; together they leave the unsuitable lands designated for them by the Whites and return to their own home. The book has some flaws: The unutterable hardships that the Navajo suffer are not fully described; Navajo readers have noted inaccuracies in descriptions of hair (Navajo do not wear braids, only buns and headbands) and other details. The story, nevertheless, is a moving one. The author's intention is to convey the fortitude of the people through the example of the young woman and her husband. The reader finishes the book with respect for these individuals and with some questions about United States policy regarding the Navajo.

White Shell Horse, by Jane and Paul Annixter, also tells of the successful return of the Navajo to their original homes in Arizona. The hero is a young man named Agapito who retains his faith in the old ways and in his visions. The story conveys the message that the Navajo learned to use weapons other than warfare in order to cope with their white enemies; it ends with the hope that these other weapons of faith and talk will help the Navajo to maintain their own ways and to succeed in their own terms. The story is well written and respectful.

Nathaniel Benchley's *Only Earth and Sky Last Forever* gives us a fictionalized account of the battles of Custer's last stand and Wounded Knee. It is a well-constructed novel but lacks the sense of authenticity of some of the other historical novels portraying this same set of events. Crazy Horse is an unclear figure in this story. The main character is a Cheyenne who lives among the Sioux. The plot revolves around his attempts to win the right to marry the young woman he loves. The ending is sad and hopeless, giving credence to the feeling that the Native Americans are a vanquished and vanishing race.

Other, more factual accounts of the sequence leading to the defeat in warfare of the Indian nations can be found in Dee Brown's *Wounded Knee: An Indian History of the American West*, adapted for young readers by Amy Ehrlich. This clearly written book does not for one instant permit the reader to sympathize with the acts of the United States government. It is powerful in terms of counteracting what the history texts would have had us believe in years past. Alex Bealer's *Only the Names Remain: The Cherokees and the Trail of Tears* is another informative and illuminating factual book, telling of the Cherokee Nation and its accomplishments as well as the criminal acts perpetrated against it. Peter Collier's *When Shall They Rest? The Cherokees' Long Struggle with America* continues the story to the present day, helping the reader to understand some contemporary problems.

Children can examine conventional history texts and insert extra pages adding the new information that they receive from books with a Native American perspective.

CUSTOMS

Some books of nonfiction link history and contemporary life by describing various tribes as they once lived. Ann Nolan Clark's *Circle of Seasons* is one of these. The author, who has written many books for use in the education of young Native Americans, tells in this book about the Pueblo Indians. She describes their religious customs, using as a theme the different seasons of the year, and presents the reader with many details of Pueblo life, dress, and belief. Unfortunately, although the author is a friend to the Pueblo Indians and wants her readers to respect their customs, she disparages the older people who resent and mistrust the white celebrations. She somehow conveys the impression in this book that all the Indians are somewhat childlike and inferior to Whites.

S. Carl Hirsch's *Famous American Indians of the Plains* uses excellent paintings by well-known artists to illustrate the ways of the Plains Indians. The reader is invited to respect and admire the accomplishments of the Plains Indians while at the same time learning about their customs and situation. There are many books that children can use, such as this one, as references and instruction on the differences in life styles among the diverse tribes of North America. Other titles are included in the Bibliography at the end of this chapter. It is to be hoped that the reader will seek out those books that treat the topic accurately and in a noncondescending fashion.

CONTEMPORARY LIFE

Several books giving factual descriptions of contemporary Native Americans have recently been published. Alfred Tamarin's *We Have Not Vanished* is useful in describing the several tribes of Native Americans living in the eastern part of the United States. They inhabit almost all the states from Maine to Florida. The book describes the history of each of the tribes, its customs, and its present-day political structure. *Circle of Life: The Miccosukee Indian Way*, by Nancy Henderson and Jane Dewey, a book with a similar intent, provides a close look at the modern Miccosukee Indians. It is a very optimistic story, tracing the history of the tribe to the present, when the tribe has control over governmental funds and projects. This management over their own education and economy is one of the most hopeful signs of progress for the Native Americans. It will, perhaps, serve as a model for government treatment of other tribes.

Some Native Americans left the reservation either voluntarily or because their tribes were victims of the termination policy that the United States effected in the 1950s. Books, like Carol Ann Bales's *Kevin Cloud: Chippewa Boy in the City*, describe in detail the sordid existence that some Native Americans are subjected to in urban slums. The similarity to black slums is evident, but there are important differences in the treatment contained in this book. Although the mood is one of despair, the attempt to remember old stories and customs and the loving behavior of the extended family toward one another gives the reader some cause for hope. The photographs by the author are excellent in their stark detail.

The Key, by Florence Parry Heide, contains a story called "Wild Bird," which describes the life of a young Native American and his grandfather living in the slum section of the city. The grandfather tries to keep the boy's vision alive with his tales of the old days and old ways. The boy enjoys listening to his grandfather, but the old man and the reader both know that the boy's life is doomed by the squalor and oppression of the life that they lead. This is indeed a depressing story, but it is well written and helps the reader to recognize that there is a problem for urban Indians.

Another depressing but well-constructed and truthful book is Hal Borland's *When The Legends Die*. Only mature readers could handle this book, which contains a great deal of personal violence. It is the story of a Ute, Tom Black Bull, who is orphaned as a very young child and who grows up very tough. After venting his hatred on horses and people, he returns in the end to his birthplace, determined to learn more about himself and his people.

Several recent books have been told from a white perspective, but treat contemporary Native Americans in a sympathetic fashion. One of these is Barbara Williams's *The Secret Name*, the story of a white family that becomes the foster family of a young Navajo girl. Becoming friendly with the Navajo, the daughter of the family tries to get her to reveal her secret name, but the child does not truly trust any Whites. The story is somewhat condescendingly told, in that white ways (a bed rather than a blanket on the floor to sleep in, white soap, white schools) are considered to be superior to Navajo ways. Ben, a friend of the elder brother, is a Navajo who now lives among the Whites. He is used by the author to explain Navajo ways and to enhance assimilation further. But it is done with obvious good intentions, and the reader is left to draw his or her own conclusions. Young readers can imagine a white child becoming a foster-child in a Navajo home. How would that child's life change?

In *Dakota Sons*, by Audree Distad, Tad, a white boy, comes to respect, and wants to learn more about, Indian ways because of his friend Ronnie, who is a Dakota Sioux. The reader is expected to admire Tad for maintaining a friendship with a Sioux, but the book is not terribly marred by this flaw. The story provides a vehicle for understanding between the two races and, as such, is useful.

Evelyn Lampman does not succeed as well in *The Year of Small Shadow*. Shad, as he is renamed by a white lawyer, is brought to stay with this lawyer, who has defended Shad's father. The father is guilty of the crime, but through a lie, the lawyer manages to secure a light sentence for him. Shad, through some unclear tribal action, is sent as a son to the lawyer for the year that the father is in prison. During this year Shad is a model of obedience, cleanliness, and humility, repaying unkindness and slurs with smiles and good deeds. He saves the life of his worst enemy's child. He acts to humiliate a member of his own tribe whose behavior is erratic, to say the least. Throughout the book the reader may receive the message that white ways are far superior to Indian ways, and that white standards of food, beauty, intelligence, and cleanliness, as well as white habits and customs, are admired and coveted by Native Americans. There is, at least, a happy ending when Small Shadow chooses to return to his tribe with his father rather than accept the invitation of the townspeople to stay with them.

Somewhat different is *Six Days From Sunday*, by Betty Biesterveld, who has lived among the Navajo and presents their life style lovingly. Willie Little Horse, who must go away to school, is very anxious about the prospect, though his family believes that it will be a good experience for him. He really does not want to leave his family or his well-known and loved existence. The book is optimistic about the possibility of taking advantage of new knowledge while retaining what is good about the old ways. Students may arrange to establish a pen-pal correspondence with children attending a reservation school. They will learn much to counteract the inaccuracies of many of the books and to acquire accurate information.

School is described as somewhat of a mixed situation in both *Ride the Crooked Wind*, by Dale Fife, and *Dream of the Blue Heron*, by Victor Barnouw. Both books indicate that it is difficult for the young students to adjust to school, particularly since white ways are thrust upon the students and the attempt is made to destroy old ways. But in both books the rebellious young men recognize the value of utilizing new information and skills in order to maintain what is good of the old ways. Both books emphasize the necessity for self-pride and a valuing of one's heritage.

Some of the most useful and encouraging books about the contemporary Native American have been written by Virginia Driving Hawk Sneve, a Sioux Indian. Three of her books for young readers, *Jimmy Yellow Hawk*; *High Elk's Treasure*; and *When Thunders Spoke* (all illustrated beautifully by Oren Lyons) not only authentically reflect the life of the Plains Indians but also indicate a hope for the future that is based on their actions today. Besides conveying a sense of the history of the people, the books also describe the beliefs held by some of the tribe and the problems of the conflicting new ways. All include families that are happy to be together; all tell interesting stories in a competent fashion.

Partly because it is difficult to secure many of the books written by Native Americans, and partly because of the conviction that many different points of view should be aired and considered, this author differs from Mary Gloyne Byler's conclusion* that only books by Native Americans should be presented to young readers on the topic of Native Americans. The teacher, librarian, parent, and child are cautioned to

---

* See *Introduction to American Indian Authors for Young Readers: A Selected Bibliography*, p. 11.

read all materials with care and sensitivity and to accept very little without verifying their authenticity. Questions and research stemming from this reading can be effective in counteracting the generations of misinformation and distortions and in building a new and healthy respect for the First Americans.

REFERENCES

Abel, Midge B. "American Indian Life as Portrayed in Children's Literature," *Elementary English,* Vol. 50, No. 2 (February 1973), 202–8.
Gives historical overview of the variety of children's books concerning Native Americans. Criticizes the poor quality of most illustrations. Abel is well-meaning but is not sensitive enough to the negative stereotyping in some of the books that she recommends.

American Indian Historical Society. *The Weewish Tree.* (1451 Masonic Ave., San Francisco, Calif. 94117.)
A magazine of Indian America for young people. Contains stories, poetry, articles by Native Americans.

Brown, Dee. *Bury My Heart at Wounded Knee.* New York: Holt, Rinehart and Winston, 1971.
History of U.S. relations with the Native Americans written from a point of view sympathetic to the American Indian people. Shocking details of atrocities, lies, and betrayals.

Burnette, Robert. *The Tortured Americans.* Englewood Cliffs, N.J.: Prentice-Hall, 1971.
Describes present-day political and economic situation of the Rosebud Sioux. Recommends an investigation of the entire field of Indian affairs. Also recommends the establishment of a Federal Indian Commission instead of the BIA and the passage of a new act to grant American Indians control over themselves. Burnette is a Sioux who has for a long time been involved in the battle of independence for American Indians.

Byler, Mary Gloyne (ed.). *American Indian Authors for Young Readers: A Selected Bibliography.* New York: Association on American Indian Affairs, 1973.
In her introduction to the annotated bibliography, Byler explains why she decided to include only work written by Native Americans. She eloquently criticizes most work written by non-American Indians, with specific references to several books. Her presentation is convincing. Unfortunately, many of the items in her bibliography are difficult to secure, except directly from the publisher. It is to be hoped that libraries, schools, and bookstores across the country will take the trouble to purchase these books.

Byler, Mary Gloyne. "The Image of American Indians Projected by Non-Indian Writers," *School Library Journal,* Vol. 20, No. 6 (February 1974), 36–39. Excerpt taken from pamphlet *American Indian Authors for Young Readers: A Selected Bibliography* (see above).

Builds a powerful case for more accurate and well-informed books on the American Indian.

Cane, Suzanne S.; Chatfield, Carol A.; Holmes, Margaret C.; and Peterson, Christine C. (eds.). *Selected Media About the American Indian for Young Children.* Boston: Commonwealth of Massachusetts, Department of Education, Division of Curriculum and Instruction, Bureau of Curriculum Innovation, 1970.

Excellent and useful pamphlet listing books for children and adults, museums in Massachusetts, other sources of information, and publishers' addresses. The editors examined hundreds of items and found most to be of poor quality. The annotations indicate both positive and negative features of each entry.

Carlson, Ruth Kearney. *Multi-Ethnic Literature for Children and Adolescents.* Illus. Louise Noack Gray and Ernest Jaco. Dubuque, Iowa: William C. Brown, 1972.

This excellent reference contains two chapters on the Native American. One chapter discusses poetry and folklore, with the poetry section of particular interest and value. The other concerns contemporary problems and attitudes. One of the most valuable features of this book is the suggestions given for working with children to help them expand their awareness of the Native American.

Council on Interracial Books for Children. *Chronicles of American Indian Protest.* Greenwich, Conn.: Fawcett World, 1971. Pb.

Excellent primary source materials to balance the white perspective of history books concerning the Native American.

Deloria, Vine, Jr. *Custer Died for Your Sins.* New York: Macmillan, 1969.

An excellent and unique discussion of the conditions of the American Indian. Controversial, personal, and impressive. Deloria is former Executive Director of the National Congress of American Indians. He is a Standing Rock Sioux. His opinions and interpretations of current and past events compel the reader to raise many questions.

Dusold, Lenore, "A Study of the Portrayal of the American Indian in Selected Children's Fiction," unpublished Master's Report, Palmer Graduate Library School, Long Island University, Brookville, N.Y., 1970.

Examines a number of children's books, analyzing them for prejudice toward the Native American. Establishes criteria such as rejecting assimilation as a goal, combatting stereotypes, and valuing of the culture. Applauds the current goals of self-determination through tribal power and nationalism. Bibliography and discussion of the books is included.

Fisher, Laura, "All Chiefs, No Indians: What Children's Books Say About American Indians." *Elementary English,* Vol. 51, No. 2 (Feburary 1974), 185–89.

An excellent analysis of the clichés, stereotypes, and distortions presented in children's books that deal with Native Americans. Fisher recommends a number of books that she judges to be better than most in fostering healthy attitudes in the reader.

Griese, Arnold A. "Ann Nolan Clark — Building Bridges of Cultural Understanding," *Elementary English,* Vol. 49, No. 5 (May 1972) 648–58.

A description of Ann Nolan Clark and her work. Pays particular attention to her literary style and to her contribution to young Native Americans' self-image.

Griffin, Louise (ed.). *Multi-Ethnic Books for Young Children: Annotated Bibliography for Parents and Teachers.* Washington, D.C.: National Association for the Education of Young Children (published jointly with ERIC), 1970.

More than 150 entries are children's books about the Eskimo and American Indian. The comments are addressed to teachers in terms of the classroom usage of the books. Not enough attempt is made to evaluate the quality or authenticity of the works. Many useful sources are cited.

Henry, Jeanette (ed.). *Index to Literature on the American Indian.* 1970, 1971, 1972, 1973 (separate volumes). San Francisco: Indian Historian Press, 1974.

Lists an enormous quantity of periodicals, texts, and books published about the American Indian. Produced by Indians under the direction of the all-Indian American Indian Historical Society. Has a section on juvenile literature, and a special supplementary index to the young people's periodical, *The Weewish Tree.* None of the entries is annotated, unfortunately, but the vast amount of material listed is invaluable.

Hirchfelder, Arlene (ed.). *American Indian and Eskimo Authors: A Comprehensive Bibliography.* New York: Association on American Indian Affairs, 1973.

Introduction by Mary Gloyne Byler points out the gains made because of changes in non-American Indian attitudes. Bibliography is annotated helpfully and is extensive. Children's books are not included in this list, although some of the entries also appear in *American Indian Authors for Young Readers.*

Icolari, Dan (ed.). *Reference Encyclopedia of the American Indian,* second edition, Vol. II. *Who's Who.* New York: Todd Publications, 1974.

Listing of prominent American Indians, and non-Indians active in fields to which the subject of the American Indian is related. Could be even more useful if a subject listing were made (that is, authors, businessmen, educators, illustrators, and the like.) It would also be helpful if the annotations made it clear which people are Native Americans and which are not.

Keating, Charlotte Matthews. *Building Bridges of Understanding Between Cultures.* Tucson, Ariz.: Palo Verde Publishing Company, 1971.

Includes a chapter on Indians and Eskimos. Keating provides an annotated bibliography for preschool and primary levels, for upper elementary levels, and for junior high and high school. Her annotations are very personalized and extensive.

Klein, Barry T. (ed.). *Reference Encyclopedia of the American Indian,* second edition, Vol. I. New York: Todd Publications, 1973.

A very thorough listing of government agencies, museums, libraries, associations, courses, government publications, magazines and periodicals, and other resources on the Indians of North America. Several thousand entries are included in the extensive bibliography. An invaluable resource.

Mickinock, Rey. "The Plight of the Native American," pp. 102-6 in *Issues in Children's Book Selection*. New York: R. R. Bowker, 1973. (Reprinted from September 1971 *School Library Journal*.)

Author, a member of the Ojibway Nation, discusses the inaccuracies and misconceptions printed in many children's books. He recommends several books for their accuracy and usefulness. He also clears up a number of false images some books have presented.

Monjo, F. N. "Monjo's Manifest Destiny: Authors Can Claim Any Territory in Literature," *School Library Journal*, Vol. 20, No. 6 (May 1974), 36-37. Monjo responds in this article to Byler's criticism of his book *Indian Summer*. Concedes that the Native American has been maligned in literature and promises to seek further advice, but defends the author's right to write about any topic of interest "so long as they're truthful, and try to write well."

National Conference of Christians and Jews. *Books for Brotherhood*. 1973. (43 West 57th Street, New York. N.Y. 10019) 1973.

Some of the books in this annotated bibliography deal with Native Americans. The list contains books published between 1971 and 1972 and is regularly updated. Both adult and children's books are included.

Newman, Jeffry, "Indian Association Attacks Lies in Children's Literature," Interracial Books for Children. *Bulletin*, Vol. 2, No. 3 (Summer 1969). Decries the lack of accuracy about Native Americans, especially in children's books. Presents list of criteria for evaluating books on Native Americans.

Steiner, Stan. *The New Indians*. New York: Harper & Row, 1968.

A report of the contemporary progress of American Indian protest. Steiner is a supporter of Vine Deloria, Jr. He speaks as an advocate of the "new Indians." The book is informative and provocative.

Stensland, Anna Lee. *Literature by and about the American Indian, An Annotated Bibliography for Junion & Senior High Students*. Urbana, Ill.: National Council of Teachers of English, 1973.

Although most of the books described here are for readers older than twelve years of age, mature youngsters as well as teachers, librarians, and parents will find the information very useful. The bibliography part of the book contains Stensland's opinions, which seem pertinent and well founded. A Study Guide to nine selections is provided, serving as a useful format for working with other books. Short biographies of Native American authors add to the book's value.

Vogel, Virgil J. *The Indian in American History*. Chicago: Integrated Education Association, 1968. (343 S. Dearborn St., Chicago, Ill. 60604.) (ERIC Dec No. 033 783.)

Obliteration, defamation, disembodiment, and disparagement are the four ways the author discloses have been used to malign the Native American. Bibliography includes useful sources of information.

Wolfe, Ann G. *About 100 Books . . . a Gateway to Better Intergroup Understanding*. New York: American Jewish Committee, Institute of Human Relations, 1972.
Includes books published between 1969 and 1972. Although several hundred books were examined, the one hundred best were selected. Six of the entries are related to Native Americans.

NATIVE AMERICAN PUBLISHERS

ABC (AMERICANS BEFORE COLUMBUS). National Indian Youth Council, 3102 Central, S.E.,Albuquerque, N. Mex. 87106
ABC (AMERICANS BEFORE COLUMBUS). National Indian Youth Council, P.O. Box 118, Schurz, Nev. 89427
AMERICAN INDIAN HISTORICAL SOCIETY. 1451 Masonic Ave., San Francisco, Calif. 94117
CHEROKEE EXAMINER. Jim Heilman, Optimystical Omnibus, 5673 Buchanan St., Los Angeles, Calif. 90042
CITY SMOKE SIGNALS. Sioux City American Indian Centre, 1114 W. 6th St., Sioux City, Iowa 51103
FORT APACHE SCOUT. P.O. Box 898, Whiteriver, Ariz. 85941
INDIAN AFFAIRS. 432 Park Ave., S., New York, N.Y. 10016
INDIAN HISTORIAN PRESS. 1451 Masonic Ave., San Francisco, Calif. 94117
INDIAN VOICES. University of Chicago, 1126 E. 59th St., Chicago, Ill. 60637
NATIVE NEVADAN. 1995 E. 2nd St., Reno, Nev. 89502
NAVAJO CURRICULUM CENTER PRESS. O'SULLIVAN, WOODSIDE & COMPANY, 2218 E. Magnolia, Phoenix, Ariz. 75034
THE NAVAJO TIMES. P.O. Box 428, Window Rock, Ariz. 86515
THE NISHNAWBE NEWS. Rm. 214, Kaye Hall, Northern Michigan University, Marquette, Mich. 49855
ROSEBUD SIOUX HERALD. Box 435, Roosevelt Town. N.Y. 13683
THE SENTINEL. National Congress of American Indians, 1346 Connecticut Ave. N.W., Washington, D.C. 20036
WARPATH. P.O. Box 26149, San Francisco, Calif. 94126

Bibliography

Allen, Terry. *The Whispering Wind: Poetry by Young American Indians.* Garden City, N.Y.: Doubleday, 1972. (Ages 10–up.)
Fourteen Native American poets' works. Poets are described in introductory remarks before each section of poetry. Not all the poetry is directly about the experience of being a Native American, but much of it is. The quality is excellent.

Annixter, Jane and Paul. *White Shell Horse.* New York: Holiday House, 1971. (Ages 12–up.)
Agapito maintains his faith and inherits his uncle's powers of foreseeing. He embodies the Navajo virtues and values and, in the end, returns with his people to their homeland. They manage to use weapons other than warfare to cope with the Whites.

Baker, Betty. *At the Center of the World.* Illus. Murray Tinkelman. New York: Macmillan, 1973. (Ages 8–11.)
These tales, based on Papago and Pima myths, are very well retold by the author. The illustrations are also very well done. All are old creation myths; they describe Coyote as the child of the sun and the moon.

————. *Killer-of-Death.* Illus. John Kaufmann. New York: Harper & Row, 1963. (Ages 12–up.)
Story of how the Apache (meaning "enemy") came to accept that as their name. Details of tribal customs included here. Killer-of-Death is the hero. His tribe is all but wiped out by the Whites' treachery. As a result of this, his feud with a fellow brave is eradicated, and he becomes a fierce enemy of all Whites. In the end he recognizes the need to acquire knowledge to continue to exist in a white man's world. One of the few books to describe the Whites' practice of scalping Native Americans, even the children.

Bales, Carol Ann. *Kevin Cloud: Chippewa Boy in the City.* Chicago: Reilly and Lee, 1972. (Ages 5–8.)
Introduction tells of the effects of the destruction of the Chippewa by the Whites. Father is gone. Kevin lives with his extended family in a section of Chicago called Uptown. Book could use more editing, but story is interesting. Photos are excellent. General mood is rather hopeless, but family is loving and remembers old stories and customs.

Barnouw, Victor. *Dream of the Blue Heron.* Illus. Lynd Ward. New York: Delacorte Press, 1966. Pb. Dell. (Ages 9–11.)
Wabus is a Chippewa boy who is caught in a struggle between his

274

grandfather, who wants to continue with the old ways, and his father, who admires and wants to practice white ways. In the end, Wabus decides to be a lawyer and to speak for his people. Well-written but somewhat double-edged story.

Baron, Virginia Olsen (ed.). *Here I Am.* Illus. Emily Arnold McCully. New York: Dutton, 1969. (Ages 6-up.)
A number of poems by Native Americans are included in this anthology of poems written by young people in some of America's minority groups. Poems are of uneven quality, but are all very expressive.

Bealer, Alex W. *Only the Names Remain, the Cherokees and the Trail of Tears.* Illus. William Sauts Bock. Boston: Little, Brown, 1972. (Ages 9-11.)
Author, though not a Native American, has been interested and involved in Native American affairs since his boyhood. This book tells of the history of the Cherokee nation since the white man came to America. It tells of their strength and of their tragedy. Clearly demonstrates the illegal and immoral behavior of the Whites as individuals and as institutions.

Belting, Natalia. *Our Fathers Had Powerful Sons.* Illus. Laszlo Kubinyi. New York: Dutton, 1974. (Ages 9-up.)
A collection of songs from many Native American groups. Somewhat romantically illustrated but a well-constructed book.

Benchley, Nathaniel. *Only Earth and Sky Last Forever.* New York: Harper & Row, 1972. (Ages 12-up.)
A well-constructed novel of the Cheyenne and Sioux and their battle against the white man for survival. The story revolves around Dark Elk and his desire to make a name for himself as a warrior so as to win the right to marry Lashuka, the young woman he loves. Joining Crazy Horse, he takes part in the battle in which Custer is killed. In the end, the future is dismal for everyone. The story is gripping, but the reader should seek out additional sources for authenticity and a clearer picture of the historical events.

Bierhorst, John (ed.). *The Fire Plume: Legends of the American Indians.* Illus. Aland E. Cober. New York: Dial Press, 1969. (Ages 9-12.)
Tales from the Algonquin tribes. Well told, dramatic, useful.

———— (adaptor). *Songs of the Chippewa.* Illus. Joe Servello. New York: Farrar, Straus & Giroux, 1974. (All ages.)
A beautiful book. Well researched, and carefully presented.

Biesterveld, Betty. *Six Days from Sunday.* Illus. George Armstrong. Chicago: Rand McNally, 1973. (Ages 12-up.)

The author, who has lived among the Navajo, writes of them respectfully and with affection. Willie Little Horse is anxious about going to school. He really does not want to leave home. The family is understanding of his feelings but determined that he will go. Much is discussed about the value of the old ways compared to new ways. An optimistic book.

Bluenose, Philip, and Carpenter, Walter S. *Knots on a Counting Rope.* Illus. Joe Smith. New York: Holt, Rinehart and Winston, 1964. (Ages 7-10.)
The grandfather tells his young grandson the story of his name and about the counting rope as an allegory of life. He keeps tying knots on the rope as he goes through life. When there is no more room for knots, life is over and death will come. Lovely illustrations.

Borland, Hal. *When the Legends Die.* Philadelphia: Lippincott, 1963. Pb. Bantam. (Ages 12-up.)
For older readers — a hard, ugly look at the life of one Ute Indian. Tom Black Bull was orphaned young and grew up tough. At the end of the story, he determines to learn more about himself and his people.

Brown, Dee. *Wounded Knee: An Indian History of the American West* (adapted for young readers by Amy Ehrlich from Brown's *Bury My Heart at Wounded Knee*). New York: Holt, Rinehart and Winston, 1974. (Ages 11-up.)
An accounting of the many broken promises of the United States government to the Native Americans. Angering and shameful behavior on the part of the Whites. Powerful book.

Bulla, Clyde Robert. *Squanto, Friend of the Pilgrims.* Illus. Peter Burchard. New York: Crowell, 1954. (Ages 7-10.)
This very interesting story is about Squanto, a Patuxet Indian, who goes with Charles Robbins in the early seventeenth century to England. He has many adventures including being put on display, captured and sold as a slave, and returning home only to find his tribe wiped out by illness. Becoming a friend to the Pilgrims, he helps them to survive. The text is written in a somewhat condescending manner, indicating that Native Americans are very childlike. White ways are seen to be superior to American Indian ways. No indication is given that the settlers will eventually destroy the Indians.

Carlson, Vada, and Witherspoon, Gary. *Black Mountain Boy: A Story of the Boyhood of John Honie.* Illus. Andrew Tsinajinnie. Chinle, Ariz.: Navajo Curriculum Center, 1968. (Ages 10-up.)

Told in the first person by John Honie, a Navajo medicine man. Navajo values come through clearly in his account of his boyhood. Excellent for positive self-image.

Clark, Ann Nolan. *Circle of Seasons.* Illus. W. T. Mars. New York: Farrar, Straus & Giroux, 1970. (Ages 8–11.)
The author has been a teacher in schools for Native American children and has written many books about American Indians. This book tells about the Pueblo Indians and their observance of the different seasonal ceremonies, including Christian ones. It is told in a somewhat patronizing style, particularly when, in describing Thanksgiving, the author describes the "Old Ones," who disapprove of the children's veneration of the Pilgrims. She says "White ways may be good, but they are difficult to comprehend and to accept." No other hint is given that there is any conflict or problem among the Pueblos.

Clifford, Eth. *The Year of the Three-Legged Deer.* Boston: Houghton Mifflin, 1971. Pb. Dell. (Ages 8–up.)
1819–1820 is the year described in this book, which is set in Indianapolis. The story is about the family of Jesse Benton, white trader, his Lenni Lenape Indian wife, and their two children. During this year many events take place, including the trials and convictions of three white men who murdered some Delaware Indians; the death of Chilili, the young daughter; and the removal of the Delaware Nation beyond the Mississippi River. Jesse's wife and son leave him to go with the Lenni Lenape. This is a sad, thought-provoking book.

Clymer. Eleanor. *The Spider, the Cave, and the Pottery Bowl.* Illus. Ingrid Fetz. New York: Atheneum, 1971. (Ages 8–12.)
Kate and her younger brother Johnny stay with their grandmother during the summer, finding good clay for her so that she can continue to make her pottery. Unfortunately, the grandmother is depicted as passive and helpless, but the story, in general, is sympathetic and interesting.

Coatsworth, Elizabeth. *The Cave.* Illus. Allan Houser. New York: Viking, 1958. (Ages 7–10.)
Beautiful and authentic story of a Navajo boy and his special understanding of the task of a shepherd.

Collier, Peter. *When Shall They Rest?: The Cherokees' Long Struggle with America.* New York: Holt, Rinehart and Winston, 1973. Pb. Dell. (Ages 12–up.)
A factual telling of the history of the Cherokees, up to today. The

author acquaints the reader not only with the shameful past history of U.S. treatment of the Cherokees, but also with the problems foisted upon the Cherokees today.

Cone, Molly. *Number Four*. Boston: Houghton Mifflin, 1972. (Ages 12–up.)
The story tells of Benjamin and his recognition of wanting to acknowledge his Indian heritage. His attempts to influence the school principal to help Indian students fail. In the end, he dies. The reader is left to hope that his death will awaken some understanding on the part of the townspeople. Not a very strong or clear book, but a noble attempt.

Courlander, Harold. *People of the Short Blue Corn, Tales and Legends of the Hopi Indians*. Illus. Enrico Arno. New York: Harcourt Brace Jovanovich, 1970. (Ages 9–11.)
Introduction tells nothing of the contemporary history of the Hopi. The tales are very complex and not very clearly told. Not as well done as the author's African tales.

Crary, Margaret. *Susette la Flesche: Voice of the Omaha Indians*. New York: Hawthorn, 1973. (Ages 12–up.)
Susette la Flesche was a remarkable woman who fought long and hard for her people, the Omaha Indians. Well educated, she gave speeches all over the country. She and her friends helped win the battle with Congress for the Omaha to return to their own land. The author indicates that the Omaha believed the white way was the right way and that Susette la Flesche encouraged them in this belief. The reader would have to read more to find the whole story.

Curry, Jane Louise. *Down from the Lonely Mountain*. Illus. Enrico Arno. New York: Harcourt, Brace & World, 1965. (Ages 9–11.)
California Indian tales. Excellent for reading aloud.

Dalgliesh, Alice. *The Courage of Sarah Noble*. Illus. Leonard Weisgard. New York: Scribner's, 1954. (Ages 6–9.) (Newbery Honor Book.)
Classic of Connecticut settlers who were friendly to the Native Americans. Sarah is the young white girl who is the heroine of the story. Her father leaves her with a kind neighboring Native American family. No real issues are raised in the story; while it is probably useful that the Native Americans are seen as kind and helpful, the tone is somewhat patronizing.

Distad, Audree. *Dakota Sons*. Illus. Tony Chen. New York: Harper & Row, 1972. (Ages 8–11.)
Tad, a white boy, makes friends with Ronnie, a Lakota Sioux.

Despite the prejudice of some of the townspeople and some of the other young people, their friendship flourishes.

Dodge, Nanabah Chee. *Morning Arrow.* Illus. Jeffrey Lunge. New York: Lothrop, Lee and Shepard, 1975. (Ages 6-10.)
A warm story of a young Navajo boy and his old grandmother. The story is slightly marred by the author's habit of changing tenses during the narration. But the effect is that of loving devotion and survival.

Dolch, Edward W. and Marguerite L. *Pueblo Stories in Basic Vocabulary.* Illus. Robert S. Kerr. Champaign, Ill.: Garrard, 1956. (Ages 6-11.)
Simply told stories of the Pueblo Indians. Some of them are over-simplified, but, on the whole, they are interesting. Illustrations are not very good. Value of the book lies in its simple vocabulary; young children can read it on their own. Somewhat flawed by the tribes' not being individually named. Other books in this series not as good.

Embry, Margaret. *My Name Is Lion.* Illus. Ned Glattauer. New York: Holiday House, 1970. (Ages 9-11.)
The author has lived in New Mexico and has taught in a BIA School. In this very negative story, the only good character is the white school teacher. The Navajo are depicted as surly, lazy drunkards, and the school does not seem to bear much relationship to the students' needs.

Fife, Dale. *Ride the Crooked Wind.* Illus. Richard Cuffari. New York: Coward, McCann & Geoghegan, 1973. (Ages 10-up.)
Po has lived with his grandmother since the death of his parents. When his grandmother is hospitalized with tuberculosis, he is sent to the Indian Boarding School. He believes in the traditional ways of the Paiute, and has learned them well. The story tells how he begins to bend somewhat because of his competent, successful uncle. This book, valuing the traditions, suggests ways that Native Americans can retain their pride in the old ways and utilize the new.

Georgakas, Dan. *Red Shadows.* Garden City, N.Y.: Doubleday (Zenith Books), 1973. (Ages 11-up.)
Sympathetic, but uneven account of the period from 1600 to 1900 of American Indians across the country.

Gridley, Marion E. *American Indian Woman,* New York: Hawthorne, 1974. (Ages 12-up.)
Author has written many books about Native Americans but seems very maternalistic in her writing. She glosses over the removal of the

Native Americans to Indian Territory; she is totally progovernment, and proassimilation. Many of the women that she describes are deemed admirable by her because they aided the Whites. In some cases they betrayed their own people to do so. Most of the women married white husbands and lived (or live) in white fashion. Included is Nancy Ward, who introduced the practice of keeping black slaves to the Cherokee. Nowhere is this practice censored by the author.

————. *Indian Tribes of America.* Illus. Lone Wolf. Northbrook, Ill.: Hubbard Press, 1973. (Ages 11–up.)
A useful reference for children to help differentiate among the different tribes and to appreciate their special qualities. The author conveys a sense of the contributions that each tribe has made and of the heritage behind each tribe.

Hassrick, Royal B. *The Colorful Story of North American Indians.* London: Octopus Books, 1974. (Ages 11–up.)
A lavishly illustrated account of Native Americans across the United States. Author is a Commissioner of the Indian Arts and Crafts Board. Too many of the illustrations show battles or bloody scenes with Indians acting savagely. The author seems, at times, to be disrespectful of his subject. He claims that "Custer has been vindicated at this massacre at Wounded Knee." The book is full of interesting facts and beautiful photographs and paintings, but the attitude of the author mars the effect, although his intentions are positive.

Hays, Wilma Pitchford. *Little Yellow Fur.* Illus. Richard Cuffari. New York: Coward, McCann & Geoghegan, 1973. (Ages 7–10.)
A well-intentioned story, based on the author's own childhood experience. But it is told from a white perspective, and with a condescending, though sympathetic attitude. Story tells of a little white blond girl who lives with her pioneer family on what was once Sioux land.

Heide, Florence Parry. *The Key.* Illus. Ati Forberg. New York: Atheneum, 1972. (Ages 10–12.)
Three stories about different people. The first one, "Wild Bird," is about a young Native American who lives with his grandfather in a small room in the city. They are very poor. The grandfather tries to instill in the boy a knowledge and valuing of his heritage. The story indicates that he may be doomed to failure.

Henderson, Nancy, and Dewey, Jane. *Circle of Life: The Miccosukee Indian Way.* Photographs by David Pickens. New York: Messner, 1974. (Ages 8–10.)

A close look at modern Miccosukee life. The book also describes the past history and customs of the tribe. The tribe now has control over government funds and programs. This means that now the Miccosukee people can control their own education and culture. They can teach and practice their own ways. They can also manage their own economic affairs. The book is respectfully written, and holds out hope of survival and dignity for Native Americans.

Hillerman, Tony. *The Boy Who Made Dragonfly*. Illus. Laszlo Kubinyi. New York: Harper & Row, 1972. (Ages 10–up.)
A folk tale, originated somewhere around the fifteenth century. It tells of the Zuni ancient ways. The virtues extolled here are charity, obedience and reverence, as well as loyalty to one's people. A well-told tale.

Hirsch, S. Carl. *Famous American Indians of the Plains*. Drawings by Lorence Bjorklund. Chicago: Rand McNally, 1973. (Ages 12–up.)
The book is lavishly illustrated with paintings by famous artists, as well as the drawings by Bjorklund. Tells with respect of the accomplishments, customs, and circumstances of the Plains Indians.

Hodges, Margaret. *The Fire Bringer: A Paiute Indian Legend*. Illus. Peter Parnell. Boston: Little, Brown, 1972. (Ages 7–up.)
Beautifully told and illustrated story of how the coyote and a Paiute boy brought fire to people.

Hoff, Syd. *Little Chief*. (An "I Can Read" Book.) New York: Harper & Brothers, 1961. (Ages 5–8.)
An example of the negative kinds of books that children have had. Little Chief, who wants children to play with, meets some pioneer children who say they have found him. When he saves them from a stampeding herd of buffalo, in gratitude the people from the wagon train decide to stay and settle. This is supposedlya happy reward for Little Chief.

Jones, Hettie. *Coyote Tales*. Illus. Louis Mofsie. New York: Holt, Rinehart and Winston, 1974. (Ages 8–12.)
Coyote is a recurrent character in Native American tales, which are similar in many ways to the African tales of Spider. Illustrations (by a Native American illustrator) are better than the style of the fairly well-told tales.

Jones, Hettie (ed.). *The Trees Stand Shining: Poetry of the North American Indian*. Illus. Robert Andrew Parker. New York: Dial Press, 1971. (Ages 6–up.)
Chants, songs, and poems of Native Americans across the country. Beautifully illustrated.

Keegan, Marcia. *The Taos Indians and Their Sacred Blue Lake.* New York: Messner, 1972. (Ages 8–11.)
Photos and captions (written by Taos Indians) are interesting and excellent. Story is somewhat nonexistent but states that the Taos Indians, in 1971, had the Blue Lake region returned to them by the United States government. The photos and captions carry the book.

Kirk, Ruth. *David, Young Chief of the Quileutes: An American Indian Today.* New York: Harcourt, Brace & World, 1967. (Ages 8–10.)
Describes contemporary lives of Quileute Indians in the state of Washington. David Hudson, eleven years old, is designated as their chief. The book is illustrated with photographs by the author. The text is of a surface nature but interesting.

Lampman, Evelyn Sibley. *Rattlesnake Cave.* Illus. Pamela Johnson. New York: Atheneum, 1974. (Ages 9–12.)
A fast-moving adventure story that has a white boy as the hero, but one who shows respect for Native American customs and beliefs. Hero is not a conventional stereotype.

———. *White Captives.* New York: Atheneum, 1975. (Ages 9–12.)
Based on a true story, this book tells of the lives of two Mormon girls when they were taken captive by Tonto Apaches and later were sold as slaves to the Mohave Indians. The customs of the Native Americans are clearly described. The author conveys the points of view of both the white girls and the Indians.

———. *The Year of Small Shadow.* New York: Harcourt Brace Jovanovich, 1971. (Ages 10–12.)
Small Shadow is brought to Daniel Foster, a white lawyer, to be his son for a year. Small Shadow's father is in jail for stealing a horse. The young Native American behaves perfectly: he is obedient, eager to please, and docile. He overcomes everyone's hostility when he manages to get rid of what the town considers to be a menacing Indian. The author is well meaning, and in the end, Small Shadow returns to his father and his tribe; but in general, the white perspective mars the story.

Lewis, Richard (ed.). *Out of the Earth I Sing.* New York: Norton, 1968. (All ages.)
Illustrations are powerful and remarkable photographs of original art work by the people who are represented by the poetry. Many Native American songs, chants, and poems are included.

Lockett, Sharon. *No Moccasins Today.* New York: Thomas Nelson, 1970. (Ages 10–13.)
Jay Williams, a senior in high school, lives on the Chuala Indian

Reservation in the state of Washington. He learns to appreciate his Native American heritage during the course of this story. Cooperation among the people is demonstrated, as well as their dignity and their prospects of independent economic survival. A useful, though overly simplified book.

McConkey, Lois. *Sea and Cedar: How The Northwest Coast Indians Lived.* Illus. Douglas Tait. Seattle: Madrona Press, 1973. (Ages 10–up.)
Written in the past tense; tells of the traditional customs of the Northwest Coast Indian group. Customs described respectfully. White man's interference told of at the end. Excellent illustrations.

McDermott, Gerald. *Arrow to the Sun.* New York: Viking, 1974. (Ages 5–8.) (Caldecott Award.)
Adaptation of a Pueblo Indian tale. Very stylized illustrations. The story is similar to other hero tales in which the father is a deity and the son must prove himself to be worthy.

McGovern, Ann. . . . *If You Lived with the Sioux Indians.* Illus. Bob Levering. New York: Four Winds Press, 1974. Pb. Scholastic. (Ages 7–9.)
Questions and answers about the habits and customs of the Sioux in the first half of the nineteenth century. Told somewhat condescendingly, but it is a well-intentioned attempt to acquaint readers with the customs and to change some attitudes about Native Americans.

Marriott, Alice. *Winter Telling Stories.* Illus. Richard Cuffari. New York: Crowell, 1947 and 1969. (Ages 9–12.)
Kiowa Indian stories about Saynday, who "got lots of things in our world started and going." These tales are of the good deeds and also of the mischief of Saynday. Author is an anthropologist who specializes in studying the Native American.

Marriott, Alice, and Rachlin, Carol K. *American Indian Mythology.* New York: Crowell, 1968. Pb. Apollo. (All ages.)
Contains many myths from various tribes. Retold by authors who heard them from Native American storytellers. Authors are anthropologists; collection is excellent. Introduction is long, aimed at adult readers, and somewhat condescending.

Martin, Fran. *Raven-Who-Sets-Things-Right, Indian Tales of the Northwest Coast.* Illus. Dorothy McEntee. New York: Harper & Row, 1975. (Ages 10–up.)
A retelling of stories originally transmitted by native storytellers of the Pacific Northwest coastal Indians. The Raven stories are interesting and carry a flavor of the people in this telling.

Matson, Emerson N. *Legends of the Great Chiefs.* Nashville: Thomas Nelson, 1972. (Ages 10–up.)
Format of the book is that great chiefs are described; then one or two tales handed down by that chief's tribe are told. The short biographies are not really adequate, and most of the tales end with somewhat obscure points. An interesting book to use as a comparison with others.

————. *Longhouse Legends.* Illus. Lorence Bjorklund. Camden, N.J.: Thomas Nelson, 1968. (Ages 10–up.)
Well-told, interesting tales of the Pacific Northwest Indians.

Meltzer, Milton. *Hunted Like a Wolf: The Story of the Seminole War.* New York: Farrar, Straus & Giroux, 1972. Pb. Dell. (Ages 12–up.)
Interesting and informative account of the Seminoles of Florida, their relationship with black people, and their resistance to white encroachment in their land. Here again the treachery of the United States government is made clear.

Miles, Miska. *Annie and the Old One.* Illus. Peter Parnell. Boston: Little, Brown, 1971. (Ages 6–8.) (Newbery Honor Book.)
A Navajo girl futilely tries to prevent her grandmother's death, which is predicted when her mother finishes weaving a rug. But in the end, she accepts death as a necessary part of life. The customs of the Navajo are described in the process of the story; the illustrations are beautifully done, and the text is respectful of Navajo ways.

Monjo, F. N. *Indian Summer.* Illus. Anita Lobel. New York: Harper & Row, 1968. (Ages 5–8.)
A very negative portrayal of Native Americans, supposedly told from the pioneer point of view. Sterotype of cowardly, stupid savages.

O'Dell, Scott. *Island of the Blue Dolphins.* Boston: Houghton Mifflin, 1960. Pb. Dell. (Ages 12–up.) (Newbery Medal, ALA Notable.)
This story, a modern classic of courage and survival, is based on a true story. Karana is abandoned on an island after all her people have left and her brother has been killed. She manages to survive for many years and is rescued, at last, by missionaries.

————. *Sing Down the Moon.* Boston: Houghton Mifflin, 1970. Pb. Dell. (Ages 10–up.) (Newbery Honor Book.)
Describes, in a somewhat softened manner, the Long Walk of the Navajo. The main character, a young Navajo woman, is remarkable in her courage and strength. The story focuses on the character of the young woman rather than on the hardships of the Navajos. Some customs are described in this very well-written book.

Parker, Arthur C. *Skunny Wundy: Seneca Indian Tales.* New edition of 1926 version. Illus. George Armstrong. Chicago: Albert Whitman, 1970. (Ages 8–up.)
Author, a Seneca Indian, was an anthropologist and museum director. The stories are somewhat reminiscent of the Anansi tales of Africa. Skunny Wundy is a magical, clever character. ("Mighty hunters" are called Skunny Wundy; good storytellers are called Skunny Wundy.) These are animal tales, well told, and convey the special qualities that the Iroquois believed the animals had.

Perrine, Mary. *Salt Boy.* Illus. Leonard Weisgard. Boston: Houghton Mifflin, 1968. Pb. also. (Ages 4–9.)
Salt Boy is a young Navajo boy who wants his father to teach him how to rope a horse. His father promises to do so when Salt Boy becomes more responsible about caring for his mother's sheep. Salt Boy rescues a lamb and earns his roping lesson. The Navajo valuing of sheep is clearly conveyed here.

Porter, C. Fayne. *The Day They Hanged the Sioux, and Other Stories from Our Indian Heritage.* Philadelphia: Chilton, 1964. Pb. Scholastic. (Ages 12–up.)
Nine stories of outstanding Native Americans who worked for their people. An appendix includes some selected folklore told to the author by contemporary young Native Americans. The entire book helps to give a perspective of history different from the usual white-oriented text.

Raskin, Joseph and Edith. *Indian Tales.* Illus. Helen Siegl. New York: Random House, 1969. (Ages 8–10.)
Very well-told stories. Illustrations add to appeal of text. Respectful recounting, mostly of animal tales.

Richter, Conrad. *The Light in the Forest.* New York: Knopf, 1953. Pb. Bantam. (Ages 12–up.)
For older readers. The story of True Son who is captured and raised by Tuscarawas. He is forced to return to his white family but cannot exist there. Nor can he become part of the Native American tribe again. In the end, he is alone and without a future. Unlike other stories written by Whites, the attempt at an other-than-white perspective is successful.

Rushmore, Helen, and Hunt, Wolf Robe. *The Dancing Horses of Acoma and Other Acoma Indian Stories.* Illus. Wolf Robe Hunt. Cleveland: World, 1963. (Ages 12–up.)
Stories recounted to author by her illustrator, Wolf Robe Hunt. Most of them are well told, and clear, even though there are many com-

plicated details. Some of the tales include the magic characters Spider Woman and Spider Boy. Author is respectful of the old traditions. Illustrations are excellent.

Sandoz, Mari. *These Were the Sioux*. Illus. Amos Bad Heart Bull and Kills Two. New York: Hastings House, 1961. Pb. Dell. (Ages 10-up.)
A factual but personal description of the customs and beliefs of the Sioux. The author lives near the Sioux. The account is somewhat idealized but interesting.

Scheer, George F. *Cherokee Animal Tales*. Illus. Robert Frankenberg. New York: Holiday House, 1968. (Ages 8-10.)
These well-told tales include mythic explanations of natural phenomena. Of particular value is the history of the Cherokee, which the author provides in a respectful style.

Sleator, William. *The Angry Moon*. Illus. Blair Lent. Boston: Little, Brown, 1970. (Ages 5-8.) (Caldecott Honor Book.)
A retelling of a Tlingit Indian story. Tlingit motifs form the inspiration for the exciting illustrations. In this story the moon is the villain, capturing a young girl. Lupan, her friend, rescues her with the aid of the magical Old Grandmother.

Sneve, Virginia Driving Hawk. *Betrayed*. New York: Holiday House, 1974. (Ages 10-up.)
The story tells how a member of the Teton tribe rescues some white captives from the Santee. No group is portrayed as villainous. The action is not very exciting, and the book's point is somewhat obscure.

———. *High Elk's Treasure*. Illus. Oren Lyons. New York: Holiday House, 1972. (Ages 9-up.)
Fictionalized history. Dramatic account of contemporary Lakota Sioux family and their adventures. Some history comes out in the telling of the story, which conveys a sense of pride in being Native American but also indicates some of the problems.

———. *Jimmy Yellow Hawk*. Illus. Oren Lyons. New York: Holiday House, 1972. (Ages 12-up.) (Council on Interracial Books for Children Award.)
Adventures of a young modern Sioux Indian who lives on a reservation in South Dakota. Conveys a sense of the mixture of old ways and new.

———. *When Thunders Spoke*. Illus. Oren Lyons. New York: Holiday House, 1974. (Ages 12-up.)

Norman Two Bull, who lives with his parents in the Dakota reservation, changes his ideas in this story about the old ways and new ways. There is conflict in the family concerning how to live in modern times as a Native American. In the end, the reader feels that Norman, still respecting the old ways, will try to use whatever new ways are appropriate for his success. Excellent illustrations; well-written text.

Syme, Ronald. *Geronimo, the Fighting Apache.* Illus. Ben F. Stahl. New York: Morrow, 1975. (Ages 8–12.)
This biography, sympathetic to Geronimo and the Apache, is drawn from many documents. Quotes from Geronimo and others alive at the time convey a sense of authenticity to the book.

Tamarin, Alfred. *We Have Not Vanished.* Chicago: Follett, 1974. (Ages 12–up.)
Informative, useful book describing the Native Americans still living on the East Coast of the United States from Maine to Florida. The history, political structure, and customs are briefly described.

Whitney, Alex. *Stiff Ears: Animal Folktales of the North American Indians.* New York: Walck, 1974. (Ages 7–10.)
Brief folk tales from the Hopi, Chippewa, Iroquois, Chinook, Pawnee, and Cherokee. Each tale teaches a lesson. Not very well told but interesting. Author provides reader with a short explanatory introduction to each story.

Williams, Barbara. *The Secret Name.* New York: Harcourt Brace Jovanovich, 1972.(Ages 8–12.)
A white family takes in a young Navajo girl to make a home for her while she is going to school. The eldest brother has a Navajo friend, who tries to instruct the rest of the family in how to treat the girl. The author indicates that white ways are infinitely superior to Indian ways. She attempts to be fair, but the effect is condescending.

Wolf, Bernard. *Tinker and the Medicine Men.* New York: Random House, 1973. (Ages 9–12.)
Tinker is six years old. The book pictures his way of life as part of the Navajo Nation. His father is a medicine man, using both traditional and peyote practices. In addition to describing the family relationship and Navajo conditions, the author leads the reader through a peyote ceremony. The photographs aid greatly in the telling. The author is obviously respectful and admiring of the Navajo way of life in Monument Valley.

Wondriska, William. *The Stop.* New York: Holt, Rinehart and Winston, 1972. (Ages 6–9.)
The story is about a little boy who stays in Monument Valley with an injured colt, while his brother goes to get his father and uncles. He stays to care for the colt, even though he is frightened. The illustrations show no humans or animals. They are paintings of the valley at different times of day and night. People and their stories are insignificant next to the magnificence of this valley, which is part of the Navajo reservation.

Yellow Robe, Rosebud. *An Album of the American Indian.* New York: Franklin Watts, 1969. (Ages 9–11.)
Illustrated with paintings, drawings, and photos. Authentic detail. Native American culture, history, and viewpoint.

NOTES and ADDITIONS

9

The Female

WHAT WAS BEGUN more than one hundred years ago as women's battle for the vote has broadened today into a quest for equality of opportunity and respect for both men and women. More and more people of all classes have become conscious of the feminist movement and of the issues involved in it. Men, too, have added their voices and their energy, recognizing that liberation from stereotypic and self-destructive roles is essential for everyone, not only for women.

Media such as television, radio, motion pictures, magazines, newspapers, comic strips, adult books, and children's books continue to produce a number of traditionally stereotyped programs, situations, and characters. These media, however, also reflect the growing awareness of the transition in sex-role definitions and behaviors. The trend is a positive one, signifying the concerns of an increasingly independent and enlightened public.

Many research studies by psychologists, teachers, and professionals in affiliated areas have confirmed the abuses of the stereotypes of sex roles. One significant study by Broverman et al. (see References) concludes that clinical psychologists have regularly defined anything but conventional sex-role behavior as abnormal. This definition extends to characteristics beyond behavior and indicates that male characteristics are valued far above female. The authors of the article contend that "abstract notions of health will tend to be more influenced by the greater social value of masculine stereotypic characteristics than by the lesser valued feminine stereotypic characteristics" (p. 1). The study goes on to

▶ **Try This**

Recognizing that each of us is at a different level from everyone else in our attitudes toward masculine and feminine characteristics and roles, complete the following chart to inform yourself more completely about your own position. Be honest with yourself; no one else need see this. The purpose of this self-test is to help you recognize and articulate your own attitudes so that you can examine the areas that are likely to influence you in your work with children. If you are uncomfortable with some of your responses, use this information to determine what your next step will be.

Attribute	admirable in				usually found in			
	Men	Women	Both	Neither	Men	Women	Both	Neither
Intelligence								
Health								
Compassion								
Strength								
Good Grooming								
Ambition								
Aggression								
Acquiescence								
Loquacity								
Sexual Appeal								
Flirtatiousness								
Obedience								
Tenacity								
Silence								
Good Manners								
Strong Emotions								
Self-control								
Quick Temper								

demonstrate that the concept of the healthy adult and the healthy male are congruent, while the concept of the healthy female differs from that of the healthy adult. Aggression, independence, objectivity, leadership, sense of adventure, ambition, self-confidence, and logic are among those valued male characteristics that are considered unhealthy for women to exhibit.

The assigned female characteristics of being talkative, tactful, gentle, religious, neat, vain, quiet, and dependent on others for security are considered to be signs of emotional problems in males and in the generalized category of "adult" when evidenced to any great extent. The authors of the study suggest that clinicians examine their own biases in order to serve their clients well. They conclude: "The cause of mental health may be better served if both men and women are encouraged toward maximum realization of individual potential rather than to an adjustment to existing restrictive sex roles" (p. 7).

The psychologists have not caused the problem. They are reflecting the attitudes that society has consistently held about men and women who deviate from the expected norm. We are moving slowly from this position, but any change is still a battle that we must wage with care. The gains that have been made are in the direction of women's moving toward men's positions. That is, women wear clothes styled like men's, take jobs that have traditionally been reserved to men, and adopt some "male" behaviors, such as greater independence, admission of ambition, and carefully controlled assertiveness. The women's movement has educated the general public considerably.

A number of important social problems and questions must be confronted, however. A great gap still remains between the new attitudes and behaviors that demonstrate them. Men, men's tasks, male characteristics, and male behaviors generally remain those valued over corresponding female categories. Men who take on women's tasks tend to be looked at askance. Men who are gentle, passive, self-effacing, religious, and emotional open themselves to criticism. Though few people question the desire of women to climb to the level of male esteem, they wonder why any man would consent to give up his superior position. Their doubts are understandable. Certain men are apprehensive about their ability to remain independent and secure without the measuring rod of the "inferior" women beneath them. To some minds, there are, in addition, questions about the effect equal job opportunity will have on the economy; about the future of the family with so many mothers working; about the rising divorce rate, which is at times attributed to the newfound independence and opportunities for women.

Recognition and discussion of these problems should lead to self-analysis. Once people become aware of their preconceptions and of their fears, they can then begin to deal with today's realities. We are a society in transition — in which women and men can choose their behavior, and in which they can maintain the traditional mode, move dramatically beyond it, or adopt some middle ground. It is important that everyone have a sense of the options available to them so that they may choose consciously and productively.

People's roles are linked with their personality characteristics. Just as male traits are valued above female, so, too, male roles are the more favored ones. Housekeeping, child nurturing, nursing, serving as a stewardess, and other traditionally assigned jobs for women are regarded as inferior to positions conventionally reserved for men. A doctor is more valued than a nurse, a pilot more than a stewardess, an athlete more than a cheerleader. Until recently, young girls were limited in their thinking of positions of authority as viable career options. Female lawyers, police, physicians, and pilots are still considered to be the exception and, indeed, the "strange ones" in some areas. Many of the women holding these jobs feel they are unusual, as well. An anecdote circulating among many women's groups concerns the attitudes of these females toward themselves: the riddle was told at a party of a man and his son who were involved in a tragic automobile accident, in which the father was killed and the son was rushed to the hospital for emergency surgery. When the surgeon who was performing the operation looked down at the child, the surgeon exclaimed, "My God, that's my son!" The question is, how could that be? None of the people at the party could come up with the right answer. They guessed that the surgeon was mistaken or that it was a long-lost son, and that the dead man was the boy's stepfather. Although the people at the party were all physicians and surgeons, both male and female, not one of them guessed that the surgeon was the boy's mother! Similarly, when children in school are queried as to their occupational aspirations, most girls continue to select those jobs that are designated as conventionally available to females, while most boys select those assigned to conventional adult males, despite the fact that their parents might be employed in unstereotypic positions.

There are, of course, those occupations that are considered to be lower-class jobs, which, nevertheless, are reserved for men. Ditch-digging (at least here in the United States), heavy janitorial work, professional gardening, street-cleaning, and garbage-collecting, even dish-washing, are considered to be in the male domain when they are performed for payment. Some of these job areas are slowly but surely being invaded by females, in approximately the same proportions and with the same public reaction of shock as in the more highly prestigious areas. We see female toll collectors, road workers, truck and bus drivers, and gasoline station attendants. On the other hand, we are also beginning to notice more male nursery-school teachers, telephone operators, and nurses. The number of males taking hitherto female assignments is not as great as the movement in the other direction, but it is there and is discernible.

▶ Try This

Draw up a list of occupations that you believe are primarily the responsibility of men. Draw up a similar list of occupations for women. Rank them as to prestige, salary level, and interest. Presenting the list, without the sex designation, to an elementary school class, have the students mark which jobs they feel are available to them. Compare the sex of the students with your designated list; discuss the results with the students.

One of the dangers of any movement is that it will go too far and become too extreme in its direction. Most advocates of women's rights are careful to say that women should feel comfortable if they have decided not to join the paid labor force. If women choose to remain as full-time housekeepers and mothers, that choice is supported. But information and encouragement about all available career and leisure-time options should be communicated to everyone. Similarly, constructive personality qualities should be accepted as reasonable and normal without regard to gender. Males and females should feel free to behave as they choose without other people's constraints being forced upon them, as long as they are within legal and ethical boundaries. Society, however, has exerted such a strong influence on sex-role behavior that sometimes it is difficult to say whether a certain role is a person's true option or whether that person has simply been socialized into thinking that it is. Today's educators, counselors, and leaders in general have the responsibility of presenting models and providing materials that expand people's repertoires.

Language has been used as an effective tool for both imprisonment in, and release from, sex-role constraints. A *spinster* is generally an object of pity and derision; a *bachelor* is to be envied. Educators and administrators are referred to as *he*; teachers are *she*. The universal pronoun, until recently, has been *he*. *Man* has stood for person, and we have no pronouns in the singular form that represent both males and females. Some attempts have been made to create new pronouns, but it is this author's opinion that the pronoun *they* will soon come to be both singular and plural, representing both sexes. The use of *person*, rather than *man*, is fairly widespread if somewhat awkward. *Fireperson, mailper-*

son, *chairperson*, and others will probably be replaced with short forms of the terms or with different names entirely — fire fighter, letter carrier or postal worker, and chair, or head.

Books for children have been active culprits in limiting choices and maintaining discrimination. Most traditional books show females dressed in skirts or dresses even when they are engaged in activities inappropriate for this sort of costume. Illustrations also have conventionally placed females in passive observer roles, while males have been pictured as active. Studies have demonstrated time and time again that illustrations confirm the subordinate, less valued role for the female, while stressing the active, adventuresome, admirable role for the male. (See annotated References for specific examples.) Often a happy ending for a story occurs when a tomboy reforms and becomes a proper young lady. When a heroine is permitted to retain her active qualities, it is usually made clear to the reader that she is the notable exception and that all the other girls in the story are "normal"; that is, interested in dolls and clothing, passive, obedient, graceful, and conventionally pretty.

Publishers of children's readers have consciously maintained this situation up to now because they have tried to appeal to boys' interests. Their contention has been that, since most of the children who are in need of remedial reading are boys, boys should have stories that will especially appeal to them. They then reason that since people should enjoy reading about themselves in a positive light, the majority of the characters should be boys. They have not been concerned with girls because they subscribe to the belief that girls will read anything but that boys stay away from stories that have girls as the main characters. This phenomenon does hold true to a certain degree. Some boys have been taught to be embarrassed if they enjoy fairy tales and sentimental stories. Girls do read a variety of books, but boys enjoy books that have such active female characters as Pippi Longstocking, Charlotte and Fern in E. B. White's *Charlotte's Web*, Mary and Laura in the Laura Ingalls Wilder series, and Alice in Carroll's *Alice in Wonderland*. Both boys and girls enjoy reading well-constructed stories. They enjoy relating to heroes and heroines who are well balanced in terms of their action and their inventiveness. Boys who have been socialized to believe that reading is primarily a girl's activity suffer no matter what the reading material is.

Publishers have now recognized that sexist bias harms everyone, both girls and boys, women and men. Many publishers of children's texts have designed guidelines that they circulate to authors and artists guiding them in writing nonsexist, nonracist books. Some of these are listed in References at the end of this chapter. It would be useful for readers to adapt and adopt those that seem most pertinent.

Suggested Criteria

Wherever possible, characters should be individuals, consistent with their own personalities within the context of their situations. Thus, males and females can be portrayed in negative fashion, provided they appear in an individualized setting rather than in a stereotypic fashion. Care should be taken that the negative characteristics are not generalized to include all people of that character's category.

The same kind of sensitivity should be displayed toward females as a group as for any ethnic minority; that is, the same attention should be paid to avoiding common stereotypes of occupations, reaction, or behavior.

Occupations should be gender-free. Women and men should be pictured doing similar tasks and with roughly the same distribution of responsibility and prestige.

Parents should be shown both in their roles as parents and in their other occupations. Fathers and mothers should be responsible for care of the children, house, and decisions about their lives.

Attributes such as mechanical competence or grace should not be restricted by sex. Achievements should be judged equally, not through a filter of sex-role difference. A woman should not be complimented for throwing a ball well "for a girl." Nor should a man be praised for taking care of a house "as well as a woman could."

Competition between males and females should be discouraged. Cooperation should be encouraged. Competition should not be the mode of relating.

Clothing should be functional and differentiated. Males and females should be dressed in clothing appropriate to their activities and economic situation and consistent with their personalities.

Females need not always be weaker, shorter, or more delicate than males. A normal mixture is useful.

Wherever possible, illustrations showing real people in real situations should be used to convey the message.

Both males and females should be independent when appropriate and dependent upon each other when that is in context. Males and females should each be logical or emotional, depending on the situation.

Above all, both males and females should be treated with dignity and respect for their individual characteristics.

Language that indicates bias should be avoided. The McGraw-Hill Book Company provides thorough recommendations regarding the use of language. The suggestions include a number of situations in which care should be exercised in the use of language and provide excellent examples of appropriate terms. Following are excerpts from the guidelines:

McGraw-Hill Guidelines for Equal Treatment of the Sexes*

In references to humanity at large, language should operate to include women and girls. Terms that tend to exclude females should be avoided whenever possible.

> The word *man* has long been used not only to denote a person of male gender, but also generically to denote humanity at large. To many people today, however, the word *man* has become so closely associated with the first meaning (a male human being) that they consider it no longer broad enough to be applied to any person or to human beings as a whole. In deference to this position, alternative expressions should be used in place of *man* (or derivative constructions used generically to signify humanity at large) whenever such substitutions can be made without producing an awkward or artificial construction. In cases where *man*-words must be used, special efforts should be made to ensure that pictures and other devices make explicit that such references include women.

Here are some possible substitutions for *man*-words:

no	*yes*
mankind	humanity, human beings, human race, people
primitive man	primitive people or peoples; primitive human beings; primitive men and women
man's achievements	human achievements
If a man drove 50 miles at 60 mph . . .	If a person (or driver) drove 50 miles at 60 mph . . .
the best man for the job	the best person (or candidate) for the job
manmade	artificial; synthetic, manufactured; constructed; of human origin
grow to manhood	grow to adulthood; grow to manhood or womanhood

> The English language lacks a generic singular pronoun signifying *he* or *she*, and therefore it has been customary and gramatically sanctioned to use masculine pronouns in expressions such as "one . . . *he*," "anyone . . . *he*," and "each child opens *his* book." Nevertheless, avoid when possible the pronouns *he*, *him*, and *his* in reference to the hypothetical person or humanity in general.

* Adapted and reprinted by permission of McGraw-Hill Book Company.

Various alternatives may be considered:

1. Reword to eliminate unnecessary gender pronouns.
2. Recast into the plural.
3. Replace the masculine pronoun with *one, you, he or she, her or his*, as appropriate. (Use *he or she* and its variations sparingly to avoid clumsy prose.)
4. Alternate male and female expressions and examples.
5. To avoid severe problems of repetition or inept wording, it may sometimes be best to use the generic *he* freely, but to add, in the preface and as often as necessary in the text, emphatic statements to the effect that the masculine pronouns are being used for succinctness and are intended to refer to both females and males.

These guidelines can only suggest a few solutions to difficult problems of rewording. The proper solution in any given passage must depend on the context and on the author's intention. For example, it would be wrong to pluralize in contexts stressing a one-to-one relationship, as between teacher and child. In such cases, either using the expression *he or she* or alternating *he* and *she*, as appropriate, will be acceptable.

Occupational terms ending in *man* should be replaced whenever possible by terms that can include members of either sex unless they refer to a particular person.

Different pronouns should not be linked with certain work or occupations on the assumption that the worker is always (or usually) female or male. Instead either pluralize or use *he or she* and *she or he*.

Males should not always be first in order of mention. Instead, alternate the order, sometimes using: *women and men, gentlemen and ladies, she or he, her or his.*

Language that assumes all readers are male should be avoided.

The language used to designate and describe females and males should treat the sexes equally.

Parallel language should be used for women and men.

no	*yes*
college men and co-eds	students

Note that *lady* and *gentlemen, wife* and *husband,* and *mother* and *father* are role words. *Ladies* should be used for women only when men are being referred to as *gentlemen.* Similarly, women should be called *wives* and *mothers* only when men are referred to as *husbands* and *fathers*. Like a male shopper, a woman in a grocery store should be called a *customer*, not a *housewife*.

Women should be identified by their own names (e.g., Indira Gandhi). They should not be referred to in terms of their roles as wife, mother, sister, or daughter unless it is in these roles that they are significant in context. Nor should they be identified in terms of their marital relationships (Mrs. Gandhi) unless this brief form is stylistically more convenient (than, say Prime Minister Gandhi) or is paired up with similar references to men.

A woman should be referred to by name in the same way that a man is. Both should be called by their full names, by first or last name only, or by title.

Unnecessary reference to or emphasis on a woman's marital status should be avoided. Whether married or not, a women may be referred to by the name by which she chooses to be known, whether her name is her original name or her married name.

Whenever possible, a term should be used that includes both sexes. Unnecessary references to gender should be avoided.

Terms for women should maintain the same dignity accorded to terms for men.

no	yes
the fair sex; the weaker sex	*women*
the distaff side	*the female side or line*
the girls or the ladies (when adult females are meant)	*the women*
girl, as in: I'll have my *girl* check that.	I'll have my *secretary* (or my *assistant*) check that. (Or use the person's name.)
lady used as a modifier, as in *lady* lawyer	*lawyer* (A woman may be identified simply through the choice of pronouns, as in: *The lawyer made her summation to the jury.* Try to avoid gender modifiers altogether. When you *must* modify, use *woman* or *female*, as in: *a course on women writers, or the airline's first female pilot.*)

no	yes
the little woman; the better half; the ball and chain	*wife*
female-gender word forms, such as *authoress, poetess, Jewess*	*author, poet, Jew*
female-gender or diminutive word forms, such as *suffragette, usherette, aviatrix*	*suffragist, usher, aviator* (or *pilot*)
libber (a put-down)	*feminist; liberationist*
sweet young thing	*young woman; girl*
co-ed (as a noun)	*student*
(*Note:* Logically, *co-ed* should refer to any student at a co-educational college or university. Since it does not, it is a sexist term.)	
housewife	*homemaker* for a person who works at home, or rephrase with a more precise or more inclusive term
The sound of the drilling disturbed the housewives in the neighborhood.	The sound of the drilling disturbed everyone within earshot (or everyone in the neighborhood).
Housewives are feeling the pinch of higher prices.	Consumers (customers or shoppers) are feeling the pinch of higher prices.
career girl or career woman	name the women's profession: *attorney Ellen Smith; Maria Sanchez, a journalist* or editor or business executive or doctor or lawyer or agent
cleaning woman, cleaning lady, or *maid*	*housekeeper; house* or *office cleaner*

Women should be treated as part of the rule, not as the exception.

Generic terms, such as doctor and nurse, should be assumed to include both men and women, and modified titles such as "woman doctor" or "male nurse," should be avoided. Work should never be stereotyped as "woman's work" or as "a man-sized job." Writers should avoid showing a "gee-whiz" attitude toward women who perform competently; ("Though a woman, she ran the business as well as any man" or "Though a woman, she ran the business efficiently.")

Women should be spoken of as participants in the action, not as possessions of the men. Terms such as *pioneer, farmer,* and *settler* should not be used as though they applied only to adult males.

Clearly, the use of language plays an important part in communicating equal valuing of both sexes. Most publishers are keenly aware of the need for authors to consider their words carefully. Those people who fear that the feminist movement is too extreme quarrel with the suggestions for language reform and care. They dislike the term *Ms.* and prefer to maintain the traditional use of the male universal pronouns. They argue that people should understand that *he* is meant to include both males and females. But most proponents of the language guidelines as exemplified by McGraw-Hill argue persuasively that, although the intent to represent all people may indeed be there, until our society includes equal treatment of the sexes as a regular practice, females will be excluded not only in word but in deed as well.

▶ Try This

Examine an article in today's newspaper or in any current magazine, and/or three children's books of your choice. Using *only* the language criteria, tape a piece of masking tape over each word that does not meet the nonsexist standard (for example, if *congressman* is used as the universal term to include male and female senators and representatives, place a piece of tape over that word).

Write an appropriate nonsexist word on the masking tape to replace the offender. Try this with children, too. They can do it.

One must recognize that a story existing only as a didactic device is not a lasting or even very effective story. The talent of an author to present a gripping plot, a vivid character, or a moving description supersedes the appropriate use of pronouns. Unfortunately, a number of books are currently being produced with little to commend them other than their good intentions. Some of these noble attempts will be described later on in this chapter. Others will simply be ignored; there are enough examples of both good writing and good intent to exclude most work that exhibits poor literary quality.

Women's groups and publishers have compiled many bibliographies to help us provide children with entertaining, enlightening materials that, at best, challenge the traditional constraints of sex-role behavior and that, at least, are moving toward a nonsexist stance. Every day new books, articles, and other information are published with this intent. Teachers, counselors, parents, and librarians have undertaken the responsibility of guiding young people to a better sense of the options that a nonsexist society makes available to them. The young audiences are seen as the most accepting of the new trend and the most likely to influence the course of future events.

It is for this reason that children's literature should help in recognition of different points of view about this and other changing mores in our society. Books should be a reflection of our lives, our past, and our future trends. They should present a diversity of life patterns and a range of opinions. And, as a matter of fact, they do. Although too many books retain the conventional patterns and attitudes, there are a number of recent books that encourage young readers to adopt different ideas of sex-role responsibility. Some books remain critical of the new trend but present the idea to the reader; some books simply reflect the variety of behaviors to be seen today.

Discussion of Children's Books

FOLK AND FAIRY TALES

It is logical to expect that, since folk and fairy tales rely so strongly on patterns and tradition, all of these stories would reflect a heavily sex-role stereotyped format. Most of them do. The typical hero is strong, brave and active, highly extroverted, nonintellectual, and willing to take great physical risks. It is usually the male who initiates action and controls the situation. Conversely, the heroine is weak, demure, passive, in need of rescuing, somewhat pensive (although never bright), and, above all, obedient. The heroine seldom is in control of her own destiny. Her greatest reward is to become the bride of her prince-rescuer and to serve him happily ever after. Sometimes there are females in these tales who are not constrained by the burden of being the heroine. They, such as servant girls, witches, fairy godmothers, and wicked stepsisters, can be powerful, intelligent, average in looks, or even ugly, strong and disobedient.

Although Alison Lurie (see annotated References) believes that these strong females are supportive of the women's liberation movement, most other critics believe that fairy tales and folk tales, particularly those nineteenth-century collections of the Grimm brothers and those of

Lang, now help to perpetuate the restrictive sex-role stereotypes. Rosemary Minard edited *Womenfolk and Fairy Tales* because of her concern for maintaining a literary diet well balanced with fantasy for her children, while at the same time helping them to form positive self-images, suitable for contemporary times. Her collection includes African, Irish, Scandinavian, Japanese, Chinese, and other stories. They range from "East of the Sun and West of the Moon" and Walter de la Mare's "Mollie Whuppie," which have heroines who perform daring and clever deeds and who marry the prince, to "The Stolen Bairn and the Sidh," which has as its heroine a mother who rescues her child from the fairies, and "The Chinese Red Riding Hoods," who trick the wicked wolf. The collection is an entertaining and excellent one. The stories conform to the expected patterns of folk tales, with three being the magic number and the youngest child usually being the one who accomplishes the daring deeds. The fantasy and imagination are stimulating to the reader. And the heroines are admirable. The males are not denigrated; they are, however, not so important in the stories as the females are. This is a useful and balancing book.

Some writers feel so strongly about the heretofore unbalanced treatment of women in fairy tales that they have gone to the other extreme and made the men victims. Jay Williams, in the admittedly humorous and charmingly illustrated book, *The Practical Princess*, has Princess Bedelia performing all kinds of clever acts. After brilliantly outwitting a snobbish and vicious dragon, she rescues the sleeping prince. Unfortunately, all of the males in the book are simpletons; further, they permit themselves to be ordered about and humiliated by her. The happy ending, for example, occurs when the prince agrees to shave his beard and cut his hair to please Princess Bedelia. Williams's later fairy tale, *Petronella*, is far more equitable in its treatment of males and females, although the prince is the clown character in the story; in fact, the hero is the sorcerer. The prince is depicted as foolish simply in order to overturn the myth of the perfect prince, not as discrimination against males.

Some writers are consciously inventing fairy tales that can be constructively read by contemporary children. Harriet Herman's *The Forest Princess* has this intention. Her princess, a magical creature who grows up alone in the forest, learns to take care of herself in many ways, such as constructing her own furniture and relating to wild animals. One day the prince of a nearby kingdom is tossed by a storm onto the beach near the forest. He and the princess spend some time together in the forest. After a while they both go to the prince's kingdom, where everything is different from the forest. She is made to conform to the expectations of the kingdom, which are very restrictive for females; but needless to say, she makes a great impact upon the entire kingdom. The story is not so heavy-handed as others with the same didactic intent, and the writing is good. The book is a worthwhile addition to a fairy tale library.

Richard A. Gardner has also created several tales with a didactic intent. Dr. Gardner's *Fairy Tales for Today's Children* are written in a light, smooth fashion, with excellent lessons to impart. His hero prince refuses to perform the meaningless heroic acts that the princess demands. And she recognizes that his criticism of her commands connotes courage, strength, and beauty of intellect. She apologizes to him, and, after spending a great deal of time getting to know each other better, they marry. Gardner's "Hans and Greta" describes both children as equally intelligent and courageous. They return home after vanquishing the witch, knowing that they cannot change their stepmother, but agreeing to use their own natural qualities to try to get along with her when she is in good moods and to try to avoid her when she is in bad moods. "The Ugly Duck" does not turn into a swan but learns to cope with his different appearance. "Cinderelma" never meets a fairy godmother, but goes to the ball entirely because of her initiative. After agreeing to marry the prince, she visits with him at his castle and they mutually decide that they are not suited for each other. She eventually starts her own business and marries a man who shares her interests. The fantasy in Dr. Gardner's stories is not so rich as that in traditional fairy tales, but the lessons are explicit. They are taught humorously, but their point is clear. The messages are worthwhile, and perhaps counteract the myths of romantic, unreflective love at first sight and happily-ever-after weddings.

Jane Yolen, an author who has written many contemporary fairy tales with a classical quality about them, attempts to teach no lessons. Her aim is to stretch the imagination and to communicate a sense of universality. Her language is poetic; her plots, complex. But she usually manages, within the context of the fairy tale, to create characters who are active, intense, thoughtful, and complete whether they are male or female. Her heroines are unusual. In the collection *The Girl Who Cried Flowers and Other Tales*, women are the central figures in three of the stories. In the story "Silent Bianca" the heroine's words emerge frozen from her mouth; she cannot be heard until her words thaw. As she is noted for her wisdom, her words are valued; people must, thus, take the time to listen. The prince asks her to marry him because of her beauty, her powerful intellect, and her silence. She acquiesces gracefully to his proposal, and the reader has the sense of a shared rule to follow. A second tale is contrary to tradition in that the need to satisfy others is what destroys Olivia, the girl whose tears turn into flowers. Olivia is exploited by all of the people in her community, who care only about the free source of flowers that she provides them. When, after her marriage, she is forbidden by her husband ever again to weep, her former friends desert her. Her inappropriate virtue, total obedience to others, causes her to die. The third heroine, the most active of the three, has, as her chief characteristic, an insatiable curiosity about the future. After she accepts the task of becoming the Weaver of Tomorrow, her curiosity is sated, but she has chosen a lonely life. The allusions to the Devil make the reader suspect that she has been influenced by evil; nevertheless, she takes control of her fate. Her ending is not conventional.

These women are unique in their qualities, as they are in Yolen's other stories. In *The Emperor and the Kite*, Djeow Seow uses ingenuity and courage to rescue her father, the Emperor. In *The Girl Who Loved the Wind*, Danina manages to escape from the sheltered, safe world that her father has designed for her. In *The Magic Three of Solatia*, Sianna becomes the wise and just ruler of her country. She also demonstrates bravery, inventiveness, intelligence, compassion, and the ability to be a wonderful mother. She is a dutiful but independent daughter. Her qualities are extraordinary, but she is a believable and admirable woman. Among her teachings are that it is acceptable and useful for people, even men, to cry, that tenderness should not be reserved to female behavior, and that every act has its consequence that must be considered before the action is undertaken. She is truly a model to be emulated. But even with all of the lessons to be learned, the stories retain their entertaining quality. The morals do not intrude upon the reader's enjoyment of the magic of the tales.

Any collection of fairy or folk tales has lessons to teach and morals to impart. Young readers should be helped to recognize what they may be absorbing. They should learn to consider consciously the messages being communicated; for example, one activity that students can use with any fairy tale is to note who initiates the activity. It is a male or a female? What would happen in any of these tales if the initiator's sex were changed? Another activity could be to list those qualities considered admirable in females and those considered admirable in males in specific stories, and to discuss how this consideration matches with contemporary times. Another possible approach might be to reconstruct the society that constitutes the setting of the tale in order to see what changes the readers would render in the society to make the tale more acceptable.

CLASSICS

Classics are stories that have withstood the test of time and remain popular over a long period of years. Most people also ascribe to classics a certain literary quality and a sense of universal appeal. This second characteristic is not true of all acknowledged classics; *Little Women*, for example, is generally considered to be a "girls' book." Some stories, such as *Charlotte's Web,* are thought of as modern classics because it looks as if their popularity will endure for a long time. Most classics are products and reflections of their time but manage to supersede the temporal; they indicate to the reader a sense of timelessness, at least in some elements of the plot and characterization and probably in the values that they impart to the reader.

Frances Hodgson Burnett's *The Secret Garden* contains a number of interesting characters in addition to the heroine, who is bold, assertive, capable of initiating her own behavior, and independent. The boys in the story are equally unusual for their time. One of them is, at first, weak, spoiled, and dependent. Another is kind, gentle, and wise beyond his years, with a capacity for loving and nurturing that is admired by everyone else in the book. Both boys and girls enjoy reading this unusual and beautiful book despite the fact that its main character is a girl.

Little Women, by Louisa May Alcott, also contains several unusual characters, Marmee and Jo in particular. Jo is one of literature's exemplars of the active young women. Most of the values transmitted by this book are concerned with people's relationships to each other as respected individuals. There is also much emphasis on the responsibility of each human being to care about and for every other person. But boys do not usually like to be seen reading this book; its title and its reputation classify it "for girls only." Perhaps at some time in the future this will no longer be the case, and boys will be permitted to enjoy it without fear of embarrassment.

Other classics with females as the major characters include *Caddie Woodlawn*, by Brink, and *The Courage of Sarah Noble*, by Dalgliesh. In both books the heroines are daughters in pioneer families. Boys seem willing to read both of these books, perhaps because of their historical topics, perhaps because of their active male characters. But these books, and those in *The Little House* series by Wilder, although they contain female figures who are somewhat different from the expected type, also consistently reaffirm the conventional position of male superiority, strength, and wisdom.

Classics, folk tales, and fairy tales should be discussed with regard to the differences existing now in contrast to their era. Often the books will contain assertions that are no longer valid, but were perhaps appropriate for the time. In Sorensen's *Miracles on Maple Hill*, for example, Marly, the inquisitive, assertive, sensitive, active heroine, comments about her brother and other boys: "They seemed afraid they'd stop being boys altogether if they couldn't be first at everything."

A useful class activity would be to seek out quotes from books such as these. After the quotes are located, the next step could be to delete them entirely from the story to see if the plot is in any way damaged.

Another useful study could involve students' selecting classics and commenting on what, in their opinion, made each book a classic. Then they could produce some suggested changes to make these classics contemporary in social terms. Debates could be arranged on whether or not the classics should be amended. The entire works of specific authors, such as Alcott, Burnett, and Sorensen could be examined for evidence of consistent attitudes toward males and females. "Best Balanced Character" bulletin boards could be constructed, with space for opposition opinions made available. The main purpose of all of these activities is to have students compare contemporary expectations with historical treatment of males and females in books acknowledged to be of high quality.

NONFICTION

Readers would do well to consult any of the numerous histories of real women and factual discussions designed to counteract the one-sided stereotypic presentations of the past. Some of these books, such as Norma Klein's *Girls Can Be Anything*, are directed toward the very young reader who has already been limited by some preconceptions. In this book, Marina and Adam are friends who enjoy playing together. Marina constantly seeks accurate information from her parents to contradict Adam's commands. He tells her, for example, that she must be a nurse and he the doctor. Marina's parents consistently reinforce the idea that she can be anything when she grows up and certainly that she can be anything in fantasy play. The two children eventually work out an excellent arrangement, sharing equally the high-status pretend roles and the auxiliary ones without regard to gender. Although the book's message does not yet accurately reflect reality (we as yet have no female Presidents of the United States), the statement of possibility is important, and the expectation of eventual reality must be imparted to young readers.

There are already too many books on the market like the notorious *I'm Glad I'm a Boy! I'm Glad I'm a Girl!* by Whitney Darrow, Jr. This book has been used as a horrible example in numerous articles written about the sorry state of affairs in books depicting sex-role expectations for young children. It can, of course, be used as an excellent discussion starter because it is so extremely sexist. It describes what toys boys play with and what toys girls enjoy. It states that "Boys are strong. Girls are graceful." One of the most hooted-at pronouncements in the book is "Boys fix things. Girls need things fixed." If all such books were as explicitly and obviously outdated, (although this book has a 1970 copyright date), there would not be as much of a problem as there is. It is the books that are subtle in their sexism that are more powerful. They either overlook females in hitherto all-male situations, or they hint that females who fill the formerly male positions are unusual at best and peculiar in general. Even such well-intentioned books as Vestly's *Hello Aurora* — describing a family situation in which the mother works outside the home and the father takes care of the children and housework — mars its message by the degree of hostility and derision with which the family is treated by almost everyone in the book. In its defensiveness, the book seems to transmit the message that something is wrong with the arrangement.

Another book that has an excellent intent is Joel Rothman's *I Can Be Anything You Can Be*. Although the idea is to indicate that girls can do anything that boys can, and can aspire to the same careers, the action is that of competition. The implication is that females had better be more able in their jobs than men or they will not be permitted to retain them. Much more beneficial is Eve Merriam's *Boys and Girls, Girls and Boys*, which emphasizes mutual respect and cooperation as well as equality. Another very useful book is Harlow Rockwell's *My Doctor*, which describes what goes on during a visit to the doctor's office for a checkup. The primary intent of the book is to remove a child's fear of visiting the doctor by a clear and specific picture of what the child can expect. But the doctor in this book is a woman. And one of the parents in the waiting room is a male. Here is a book that unobtrusively gives the message of approval for these roles.

Some of the most convincing and positive books that have the intention of encouraging readers to build an acceptance of new roles for both males and females are those that describe real people already doing real things that defy the stereotype. These books are particularly effective when they utilize photographs as their illustrations. Some of these books include the entire *What Can She Be?* series, which includes descriptions of an architect, a lawyer, a newscaster, and others. All are women; all are successful; all have full, admirable lives. The series, by Gloria and Esther Goldreich, is well written and well photographed. It takes into consideration all sorts of social circumstances, problems, and issues. It is designed for a wide age range but can be used even beyond the upper age limit of ten years suggested by the publishers.

There are many excellent histories of the women's movement: Dale Carlson's *Girls Are Equal Too*, Elaine Landau's *Feminism in America*, Janet Harris's *A Single Standard*, and Ruth Warren's *A Pictorial History of Women in America* are a few such. For those readers, mostly older children, who enjoy simply reading this category of book, these histories (or, as they are coming to be known, "herstories") are valuable, fascinating, and illuminating. Teachers would do well to encourage students to use these books as references instead of the standard historical texts and encyclopedias in current use. Famous women ought to be included as part of the regular social studies curriculum rather than in a separate category. Wherever possible, the female point of view should be included in a discussion of any historical period or event. Female artists, authors, and scientists should be studied as routinely as their male counterparts are, not as anomalies but as representatives of their profession. Students should be encouraged to do extensive research to update their assigned texts. Sections of mimeographed additions should be appended to the standard texts, correcting and filling in where there have been omissions. Biographies should become part of the accepted compilation of texts used in studying history.

BIOGRAPHIES

A visit to any library or bookstore will produce evidence that biographies of males far outnumber biographies of females, out of all proportion to the numbers of famous people of either sex. But there has been an increasing number of books that young people can read about women who have made important contributions to the world. Most of the recent biographies deal with women who have been concerned with the feminist cause. But others, such as biographies of poets and queens, have also appeared.

In reading a biography it is essential that the student recognize the biographer's bias. Because of the difficulty in determining what is truth and what is romanticized when one reads about an admired character, it is useful to try to acquire more than one book about any given person. In reading of Sarah Emma Edmundson, who disguised herself as a male for several years during the Civil War and served as a soldier and as a spy, there are numerous disputes about what really happened and what she was really like. There is even a difference of opinion about her name. If one were to read the book *Emma Edmonds, Nurse and Spy*, by Talmadge and Gilmore, one could assume that the heroine not only hated being a woman but also that she had no regard for any women. The reader might also be puzzled by the lack of insight provided into Emma's character, thoughts, and motivations. The authors of the biography refer to Emma as "he" during the time that she masquerades as Frank Thompson. They provide few details of her life in the army, expecting the reader to be satisfied with vague explanations of separate pup tents and cursory physical examinations.

But the book *Girl Soldier and Spy: Sarah Emma Edmundson*, by Mary Hoehling, develops Sarah's character and permits the reader to share her feelings. Of course, the character's emotions are no more than informed speculation on the part of the author, but the account of the research that she did for the book is impressive. She went beyond written records to seek out family members and people who knew of

Sarah, both in her male and female identities. During the course of the book, Hoehling never lets the reader forget that the main character is a woman. Sarah retains those qualities that she had as an attractive young woman even when she is pretending to be a man. True, she wants to prove to her father that she can be as good as a boy, but the reader does not feel she is resentful of her womanhood. In *Emma Edmonds* she seems to be a strange creature, out of place in this world, always wishing to be a man. In *Girl Soldier and Spy* there are excellent reasons for her actions, and she is in control of her situation. She is a pitiful figure in one book, an admirable one in the other.

An interesting project for students would be to research this and any other little-known character and to come up with their own version of the character's life. Reading both books could lead students to debate the believability of either. Most notable people have several biographies written about them; it would not be difficult to search out more than one about each person considered. This could be a useful activity for a group of students: Assembling as many different versions of a subject's life as they could find, each would read more than one and compare notes. Criteria can be set up for judging the accuracy of a book. In those cases in which there seems to be general agreement about the details of a character's life, they could decide which of the biographies is the most appealing or most useful or best written.

Harriet Tubman is one woman about whom a number of books have been written, all of which are in accord about the details of her remarkable life. The points of view are generally consistent — that Harriet was a brave, successful, unusual woman. The methods of presentation, however, vary from straightforward telling of the story to acquainting the reader with the horrors of slavery. Jacob Lawrence's *Harriet and the Promised Land* relies on the power of the illustrations to convey the difficulty of Harriet's task and the strength that she needed to endure. Lawrence's book is a controversial one because some critics believe that the illustrations are too harsh for children. Some critics even believe that the illustrations are demeaning of black people although the artist is, himself, black. Readers should be made aware of the controversy so that they will be encouraged to judge for themselves how they feel about the pictures. It is also a good idea to encourage students to recognize that they must read factual work as well as fiction with a critical mind.

Other black women who helped the cause of black people and who were courageous and strong have had biographies written about them. Sojourner Truth, Juliette Derricotte, Maggie Mitchell Walker, Ida Wells Barnett, Septima Poinsette Clark, Charlotte Forten, Shirley Chisholm, and others can be found on the biography shelves. Most of the authors are respectful of their topic and knowledgeable about their heroines. Polly Longsworth, for example, has written a well-constructed fictionalized autobiography of Charlotte Forten. The book makes the point that the abolitionist and women's libration movements are compatible and similar.

Not only black women are the subjects of biographies. Amelia Earhart, Florence Nightingale, Eleanor Roosevelt, Emily Dickinson, Edna St. Vincent Millay, Chris Evert, Maria Tallchief, Elizabeth Blackwell, and numerous others in every field of endeavor can be found described in books. Most of these women defied social convention and family pressure in order to accomplish what they did. Most of them endured ridicule and abuse, but persevered. *Nellie Bly, Reporter,* by Nina Brown Baker, describes the challenging and socially effective reporting done by this woman. The book also bemoans the fact that Nellie Bly is probably better remembered for her stunt of going around the world alone in fewer than eight days than she is for her work in cleaning up insane asylums, prisons, and other abusive institutions. Nellie Bly had a life in which fame, prosperity, poverty, and adversity were all ingredients. Whatever she achieved was on her own initiative and only after struggling against opposition.

Margaret Sanger, Pioneer of Birth Control, by Lader and Meltzer, also describes a woman who had to endure tremendous opposition. But Sanger was a determined woman. She was soundly criticized for her controversial views about marriage and for her ideas of appropriate behavior for women, but her work far outlasted her notoriety and continues to have far-reaching consequences for the world in general. This biography, like many of the others, makes no pretense that its subject is uncontroversial or flawless. It demonstrates that personal contentment is not necessary for public good. It also describes people who dare to be different because of principle, not whim.

GIRLS AS MAIN CHARACTERS

Many works of fiction have, as their main characters, girls who dare to be different. Sometimes, as with the young women in O'Dell's *Island of the Blue Dolphins* and George's *Julie of the Wolves,* this difference spells survival. In both books the young women, alone in the wilderness, must cope with their environment in order to remain alive. In both cases the heroines face their situations with courage and intelligence. Julie must also cope with problems of a personal societal nature throughout the book. Her spiritual survival becomes an issue. For Karana, the physical is the challenge. Readers who wonder if the books would be as effective if the main characters were male may change the gender of the characters to see if this affects the story. A poll can be conducted to see how many male readers would prefer that these main characters be male.

Other tales of survival with female protagonists should also be read with this question in mind. Howard's *The Ostrich Chase* is the story of a young woman who refuses to be bound by the traditions of her tribe. Her elderly grandmother, aiding her in her rebellion, almost loses her life in the process. Khuana, however, manages to surmount the problems and to retain her womanly qualities as well. Maude, the heroine of Lofts's *The Maude Reed Tale* overcomes social pressure that is as strong as any physical blocks. She manages to change her mother's expectations of her and to do what she wants with her life despite the fact that she lives in the Middle Ages, a time when the social system was cast in stone.

But these women are rarities. They are the striking examples set against the more conforming females. Even books such as *Queenie Peavy*, by Burch, and *Pippi Longstocking*, by Lindgren, make it clear that the strong-willed, intelligent, self-managing, disobedient heroines are anomalies beyond the norm. How comfortable are young girls with using these females as models? How admirable and believable do young males find them to be? Both of the heroines described above are extremely lonely and somewhat unhappy young women, despite their bravado. They, like Fitzhugh's *Harriet the Spy*, crave friends and want others to like and accept them. The adventures that they have and the ideas they act upon are humorous and clever. But what child would want to be in their situation? These supergirls do not lead enviable lives although their exploits are fun to read about.

Perhaps a more constructive female model is to be found in the character of Beth Lambert in Bette Greene's *Philip Hall Likes Me: I Reckon Maybe*. Although competition between males and females is a primary issue intruding on the book, Beth emerges as a very admirable character to be emulated and respected by readers. Beth, who is very bright, can do everything very well. At first she permits her liking for Philip Hall to inhibit her from doing her best; she doesn't want to "show him up." But her good sense wins out when she realizes that she has a responsibility to herself to do her very best.

The main character of Vera and Bill Cleaver's *Ellen Grae* is another bright, sensitive, and appealing character. In each of the three books in which she appears, she maintains her own integrity and strength. But again, both she and Beth are outstanding, clearly different from all of the other girls in the stories. They are the exceptions. It is difficult to build a consistent positive image of females if all the bright, capable ones are seen to be different from the rest. Nevertheless, these heroines are good to have; we simply need more of them. We also should learn to expect to find as many competent females as males in stories. Our expectations are sure to influence authors. If students are made aware of this necessity, they can begin to write letters to favorite authors, suggesting that more females be used as equals and compatriots of males. Authors enjoy reading fan mail and may respond to their readers' suggestions.

WOMEN IN CHILDREN'S BOOKS

Rarely the main characters in children's books, women usually appear incidentally as mothers or teachers or adult foils for the plot. When they are the main characters, they are usually laughable and somewhat ridiculous. Certainly that is the case with Peggy Parish's *Amelia Bedelia*. All the stories are hilarious. They are all built on puns; Amelia Bedelia takes everything literally and her behavior is accordingly bizarre. In one story, for example, when she is asked to dress a chicken for dinner, she obediently put clothes on the chicken. The only reason that the other characters in the book tolerate her is because she is such an excellent baker and cook who makes everything right by feeding the family. She is totally exploited and demeaned by the other characters. But there is no denying that these plays on words are very popular with children and are indeed very funny. It is too bad that humaneness loses out to humor. Perhaps children can change the stories so that other people are kinder to Amelia. They can suggest other ways of making the funny plays on words happen in a different context, or perhaps they can transform Amelia to a nonhuman robot. Bringing the problem to their attention will at least make them aware of it; they they can decide on a course of action.

Ellen MacGregor's *Miss Pickerell* series also uses a very humorous woman as its protagonist. She is a very intelligent, if eccentric person who has fabulous adventures. She is much brighter than most of the males in the books. Her eccentricities are harmless and her appearance is unthreatening. She is an exceptional person. Herein lies the problem: she is really a fantasy. But like Mary Poppins, who also has her faults, it is good to encounter a remarkable female character.

Amelia Bedelia, Mary Poppins, and Miss Pickerell are unmarried and childless. Mothers are never protagonists. Although the mother in *A Wrinkle in Time*, by Madeleine L'Engle, is beautiful and brilliant, she is surprisingly passive in the face of her husband's mysterious disappearance. But the fact that she works in her laboratory is useful in a contemporary book. Working mothers generally have to put up with much criticism in fiction; their children are often seen to suffer from their lack of time and interest. Kerr's *Dinky Hocker Shoots Smack* and Perl's *That Crazy April* are examples of books in which the children resent their mother's involvement outside the house and in which the mothers do not seem to be able to handle the situation well. But the mothers in *Evan's Corner*, by Elizabeth Starr Hill; *Mushy Eggs*, by Florence Adams;

and *Mom, the Wolf Man and Me*, by Norma Klein, manage to work at their jobs and to maintain a nurturing role with their children.

Contrary to reality, not many fictional mothers have paid jobs. The role of the mother in most children's books is still that of the house-keeper, cook, and comforter. This role reaches its climax in the book *The Mother Market*, by Nancy Brelis, in which the children seek a suitable mother. The qualities that they want are those of the good and faithful servant, although it is never expressed in quite those terms. The happy ending is that they find their own true and ideal mother who will dedicate herself to their happiness. In *The Night Daddy*, by Maria Gripe, the mother copes well with her job and her parental responsibilities by working at night and hiring a young man to baby-sit while she is gone. Not much is made of the mother's work in most of the books that do mention mothers and their jobs. But two charming and useful books, Eve Merriam's *Mommies at Work* and Joe Lasker's *Mothers Can Do Anything*, picture mothers in all sorts of roles in addition to their mothering ones. Again, the Goldreich series — particularly those that picture the women at home with their families as well as outside the home at work — are worthwhile books to have and to refer to.

Activities in which children are asked to describe the work that their mothers and fathers do and then to try to find matching characters in books may reveal that parents' jobs are rarely described. The students may then write job descriptions for parents in the stories that exclude them. Again, some letters to favorite authors may help. Another activity related to books of fiction could have children describe the characteristics of ideal parents. They could then locate books that contain parents matching these descriptions and books that conflict with, or differ from, the descriptions. They then can be encouraged to aim for a rethinking and expanding of their descriptions and of those qualities that they consider to be ideal.

Another exercise could have the students describe ideal characteristics for boys and for girls, again matching characters in literature. They can compare their lists with each other, with the books, and even categorize the descriptions according to age levels. Older women, particularly grandmothers, are emerging as sometimes interesting and unique individuals. Udry's *Mary Jo's Grandmother* presents a woman who is independent and capable, while the grandmother in Klein's *Naomi in the Middle* is a tennis-playing, somewhat brusque individual who unashamedly confesses to an antipathy toward infants.

This chapter has devoted itself to a consideration of the treatment of females in children's books. The feminist movement contends that human liberation is the goal. It would, therefore, be useful also to consider the treatment of males in children's books. Young readers as well as concerned adults can apply to males the same criteria suggested for females, as males have been victimized by stereotypic expectations almost as severely in some senses as females. Readers should observe how young male characters are treated and expected to act. They should reflect on the literary role of the father and should watch for the imposition of a competitive system in which males are required to win. They should note which stories are free of these restrictions and recommend them to each other. They should mount letter-writing campaigns to publishers and authors.

Slowly but surely, books and the media are reflecting society's direction. Active critical reading and responding will help speed the process.

REFERENCES

Ahlum, Carol, and Fralley, Jacqueline M. *Feminist Resources for Schools and Colleges, A Guide to Curricular Materials.* Old Westbury, N.Y: Feminist Press, 1973.
> An excellent and complete compilation of resources. The Clearinghouse on Women's Studies directed this project. The annotated bibliography includes lists of books and articles on sexism in education, materials for the elementary school teacher. The children's books listed are not annotated, but all other entries are. Multimedia are also included. The cost of this twenty-page pamphlet was $1.25 in 1973. It may have since risen, but it is a very worthwhile resource.

Allyn and Bacon, Inc. *Sensitivity Guidelines for Artists.*
> Specific in terms of avoidance of stereotype. Very useful for purposes of analysis.

Benefic Press. *Checklist for Female-Male Roles in Books.*
> Brief, but fair to both sexes.

Bernstein, Joanne. "The Changing Roles of Females in Books for Young Children," *The Reading Teacher*, Vol. 27, No. 6 (March 1974), 545–49.
> Deplores the relatively small quantity of books in which females are the main characters and are viewed positively. Suggests that boys would benefit in many ways from reading such books. Describes several books in which girls are active, valued characters.

Boston Community to Improve the Status of Women. *Education Task Force Report*, December, 1971.
> List of articles and addresses of resources on sexism.

Brookline Public Schools. "Report on the Sex-Role Stereotyping Commission, 1974." (Robert I. Sperber, Superintendent of Schools, Brookline, Mass. 02146.)
> Provides guidelines for evaluating written materials. Also serves as a model for what school systems can do to combat sexism in the schools.

Broverman, Inge K.; Broverman, Donald M.; Clarkson, Frank E.; Rosenkrantz, Paul S.; and Vogel, Susan R. "Sex-Role Stereotypes and Clinical Judgments of Mental Health," *Journal of Consulting and Clinical Psychology*, Vol. 34, No. 1 (February 1970), 1-7.

Important and revealing report of a study conducted with clinical psychologists, demonstrating that male characteristics are viewed as positive for adults, and female characteristics are not. Further, the study concludes that unstereotypic sex-role behavior is viewed as abnormal.

Cohen, Martha. *Stop Sex Role Stereotypes in Elementary Education, A Handbook for Parents and Teachers.* Hartford, Conn.: Connecticut Public Interest Research Group, 1974.

The pamphlet contains discussions of sex-role stereotyping, and suggestions for helping children recognize and deal with it. An excellent set of criteria is offered for examining texts and trade books. Descriptions of materials, strategies, and workshops useful for educating people to combat sex-role stereotyping are presented. Fairly extensive annotated bibliography of children's books, films, and materials for teachers and parents is included. The list of addresses of key publishers and organizations adds a bonus to this invaluable pamphlet.

Cooper, Susan. "Womenfolk and Fairy Tales," *New York Times Book Review*, April 13, 1975, p. 6.

Cooper reviews Rosemary Minard's book *Womenfolk and Fairy Tales* unfavorably. She disagrees with the author's premise that girls and boys need admirable heroines. She considers this to be "an adult neurosis foisted upon children." She believes that readers identify with all characters, male and female, and that "an anthology based on a feminist approach is fettered by self-consciousness."

DeGroot, Roseann M. "A Comparison of the Parental Image Found in Selected Children's Books of the Nineteen-Thirties with those of the Nineteen-Sixties," unpublished Master's Report, Palmer Graduate Library School, Long Island University, Brookville, N.Y. 1970.

This paper describes the changing role of the father as well as that of the mother. Talks of the problem of the absentee parent and surrogate parents. Lists characteristics and checks whether either or both parents exhibit them.

Donlan, Dan. "The Negative Image of Women in Children's Literature," *Elementary English*, Vol. 49, No. 4 (April 16, 1972), 604-11.

Donlan quotes from nursery rhymes and fairy tales to demonstrate how women have been portrayed as weak or wicked or stereotypically stupid. The article has some interesting arguments. The ending is unfortunate, poking fun at W.I.T.C.H., a women's liberation organization.

Feminists on Children's Literature. "A Feminist Look at Children's Books," *School Library Journal*, Vol. 18, No. 5 (January 1971), 19-24. Reprinted in *Children's Books, Views and Values*, edited by Fritz J. Luecke. Xerox Educational Publications, 1973.

Finds an extreme imbalance in language and in number of female characters compared to male. Divides books into categories: "sexist," "cop-outs," "positive images," and "especially for girls." Particularly focuses on Newbery Award winners, but includes others as well. Hopes eventually to omit the last category entirely.

Feminists on Children's Media. *Little Miss Muffet Fights Back, Recommended Non-Sexist Books About Girls for Young Readers*, 1971.

This annotated listing was one of the first of its kind. It presents brief but descriptive annotations of children's books judged to be nonsexist. The criteria for judging are not listed. Some of the books are not as adequately described as others, but this is a good basic beginning for readers interested in accumulating books with a positive image of females.

Fisher, Elizabeth. "Children's Books: The Second Sex, Junior Division," *New York Times Book Review*, Part II, May 24, 1970, pp. 6+. Reprinted in *And Jill Came Tumbling After*, ed. Stacey et al. (New York: Dell, 1974), pp. 116-22. Also a KNOW reprint.

Analyzes certain picture books for sexist indoctrination. Provides the reader with a productive point of view when considering children's books.

Frasher, Ramona, and Walker, Annabelle. "Sex Roles in Early Reading Textbooks," *The Reading Teacher*, Vol. 25, No. 8 (May 1972), 741-49.

Analyzes four leading reading series published in 1962, 1966, 1968, and 1970 for their treatment of male and female characters. Concludes that women are presented in a distorted fashion. Mothers in particular are represented as inferior. The authors recommend that more research be done and that publishers change their texts to better reflect society's values.

Frazier, Nancy, and Sadker, Myra. *Sexism in School and Society*. New York: Harper & Row, 1973. Pb.

A very useful reference for raising awareness, particularly for educators. While there is no specific analysis or mention of children's books, the implications for evaluation of materials are clearly indicated in this text. Unfortunately, it has no index, but the suggested activities, sources, and discussion make the text worthwhile.

Gersoni-Stavn, Diane. "Feminist Criticism: An Overview," *School Library Journal*, Vol. 20, No. 5 (January 1974), 22.

Reviews the negative stereotyping of girls in children's books. Cautions critics to engage in humanistic criticism that supports both males and females. Also pleads for maintenance of aesthetic standards. Gives excellent advice to readers and critics. A very thoughtful, constructive article.

―――. "Reducing the 'Miss Muffet' Syndrome: An Annotated Bibliography," *School Library Journal*, Vol. 18, No. 5 (January 1972), 32-35.

Reviews the progress that books have made in depicting females. Although many more females now appear in books, much still needs to happen in describing "everyday" females. There is also a notable lack of excellence in biographies for younger and middle-grade children. Approximately forty books for younger intermediate and older children are described positively in their treatment of female characters.

―――. "The Skirts in Fiction About Boys: A Maxi Mess," *School Library Journal*, Vol. 17, No. 5. (January 1971), 66-70.

Criticizes the treatment of girlfriends and mothers of male heroes in fiction for preteens. Most of the books discussed are very popular with boys. Cites a few notable exceptions but demonstrates, with numerous examples, that females are depicted negatively in too many popular books.

Ginn and Company. *Treatment of Minority Groups and Women*, 1975.

Provides criteria for art and design as well as content. Includes extensive list of extremely useful concerns and criteria. Contains suggestions for settings as well as different sorts of people.

Greenleaf, Phyllis Taube. *Liberating Young Children from Sex Roles.* Somerville, Mass.: New England Free Press, 1972.

A discussion of teachers' experiences with preschool children in trying to liberate them from sex-role stereotypes. Practical suggestions and a realistic look at the problems involved in changing stereotypic attitudes and behavior make this a very useful pamphlet.

Hagan, Elizabeth, and the Central New Jersey Chapter of National Organization for Women. "Sex Role Stereotyping in Elementary School Readers." Princeton, N.J.: Women on Words and Images, 1970.

Concludes that elementary school texts are not taking seriously the expectations and potential of girl students. Fifteen reading series were examined, from primer to sixth-grade level. The observations provide a useful framework for others who would like to replicate the study.

Heide, Wilma Scott. "On Women, Men, Children, and Librarians," *School Library Journal*, Vol. 20, No. 5 (January 1974), 17–21.

Defines sexism and sexist behavior. Urges librarians to actively include feminist literature, displays, and programs in libraries.

Heyn, Leah. "Children's Books," *Women: A Journal of Liberation,* Vol. 1, No. 1 (Fall 1969), 22–25.

Discusses the influence of books on a child's development and education. Decries the secondary role of women in children's books. Hopes for less sex channeling in the future, particularly in career placement. The article critiques a number of books but provides no bibliography.

Houghton Mifflin Company. *Avoiding Stereotypes.*

Presents a position statement on minorities and women. Also has compiled annotated bibliographies of its publications dealing with these populations.

Howe, Florence. "Educating Women: No More Sugar and Spice," *Saturday Review* (October 16, 1971), 76–77.

Criticizes the extensive sex-role stereotyping in children's trade books and texts, both fiction and nonfiction. Hopes for far-reaching reform in curriculum as well as evidence of greater sensitivity in texts and literature.

Interracial Books for Children. *Bulletin.* "10 Quick Ways to Analyze Books for Racism and Sexism," Vol. 5, No. 3 (1974), 1.

Criteria to use when examining children's books. Incisive and useful.

Jones, Bartlett C. "A New Cache of Liberated Children's Literature — In Some Old Standbys," *Wilson Library Bulletin*, Vol. 49, No. 1 (September 1974), 52–56.

Criticizes feminist complaints and research in children's literature. Locates many classics in which he claims females have a very positive image. Suggests extensive research be done to see if literature does have an effect on self-image and identity. Concludes that the situation is not at all desperate for female image in children's books.

Key, Mary Ritchie. "The Role of Male and Female in Children's Books — Dispelling All Doubt," *Wilson Library Bulletin,* Vol. 46, No. 2 (October 1971), 167-76.

Presents a summary of numerous studies on sexism and children's books. Concludes that stereotyping is rampant. Sees hope in the emergence of new attitudes and behaviors in recent books for children.

Kram, Judith. "How to Combat Sexism in Textbooks," Interracial Books for Children. *Bulletin,* Vol. 6, No. 1 (1975), 3-8.

Suggests activities and strategies for changing the texts used in a public school system. Letter-writing campaigns and other procedures are recommended. Specific helpful resources are listed.

Lanes, Selma. "On Feminism and Children's Books," *School Library Journal,* Vol. 20, No. 5 (January 1974), 23.

Urges differentiation between art and propaganda. Criticizes books that display male or female characteristics rather than universal human behavior. But Lanes agrees with the cause of feminism and welcomes healthy propaganda. She cautions against an unbalanced preoccupation with propagandistic literature in a total reading diet.

Lewis, Susan. "Exploding the Fairy Princess Myth," *Scholastic Teacher,* Vol. 99, No. 3 (November 1971), 6-12.

Criticizes texts, books, counselors, and educators for accepting the fairy princess stereotype. Offers "A Chauvinistic Index for Educators" (p. 11). Also provides a list of resources for women's studies.

Lieberman, Marcia R. "Some Day My Prince Will Come: Female Acculturation Through the Fairy Tale," *College English,* Vol. 34, No. 3 (December 1972), 383-95.

Analyzes the Lang versions of fairy tales and demonstrates the negative effects of these on women. Beauty and passivity are presented as the most important female qualities in these tales; marriage is a female's greatest reward. The author argues powerfully that fairy tales inculcate stereotypic sex-role behaviors into child readers.

Loercher, Donna. *Girls and Boys Together.* Whitestone, N.Y.: Feminist Book Mart, 1974.

An annotated bibliography listing nonracist and nonsexist books for children. The list is divided into four categories: young readers (7-up), young adults (12-up), and special items. Unfortunately, the publishers are not listed, which makes the books difficult to find if they are not ordered through this catalog. The date of publication is also omitted. The entries are well annotated, however, and the bibliography can be a useful reference.

Luckenbill, W. Bernard. "Fathers in Adolescent Books," *School Library Journal,* Vol. 20, No. 6 (February 1974), 26-30.

Fifty books for adolescents are examined. Most fathers and mothers are narrowly stereotyped. But author warns against overly contrived, didactic presentations.

Lurie, Alison. "Fairy Tale Liberation," *New York Review of Books*, Vol. 15, No. 11 (December 1970), 42–44.

The author argues that folk and fairy tales help prepare children for women's liberation, since so many of the characters are women and so many women are strong. She then goes on to suggest collections of tales.

McGraw-Hill Book Company. *Guidelines for Equal Treatment of the Sexes in McGraw-Hill Book Company Publications.*

The guidelines are concerned with eliminating stereotypes for both males and females in McGraw-Hill publications. Vocabulary is directly dealt with; examples of positive and negative language are given. The guidelines are very specific and very helpful.

Moberg, Verne. *A Child's Right to Equal Reading.* Washington, D.C.: National Education Association, 1972.

Specific instructions on how to conduct community workshops to recognize and combat sexism in children's books.

Moran, Barbara K. "Women's Rights Address Book," *Woman's Day*, October 1972, 25.

A very valuable list of more than sixty national groups and agencies, with a concise description of what each agency offers.

Nadesan, Ardell. "Mother Goose: Sexist?" *Elementary English*, Vol. 51, No. 3 (March 1974), 375–78.

Expresses no opinion, but invites readers to draw their own conclusions from the quotes and excerpts included in the article. Most of the findings support the conclusion that males are better treated than females are.

Nilsen, Alleen Pace. "Women in Children's Literature," *College English*, Vol. 32, No. 8 (May 1971), 918–26.

Critiques Caldecott Award winners from 1951 to 1970. Suggests several causes of unfairness toward females in children's books. Recommends that good books be written with interesting, strong females so that both boys and girls will want to read them.

Oliver, Linda. "Women in Aprons: The Female Stereotype in Children's Readers," *Elementary School Journal*, Vol. 74, No. 5 (February 1974), 253–59.

After pointing out the stereotypes in children's readers, Oliver recommends guidelines for the treatment of women. She then goes on to criticize several stories, specifically providing a framework for other readers to do the same.

Pogrebin, Letty Cottin. "Down With Sexist Upbringing," *Ms.* Preview Issue, Spring 1972, 18.

This article, which includes the annotated bibliography "A Basic Library for Liberated Children," tells in a personal, powerful style of the negative effects of sexism in children's books and TV shows. The author criticizes books from nursery rhymes to texts. She provides her own list of approved books for the reader.

————. "Girls' Liberation," *New York Times Book Review*, Section 7, Part III, May 6, 1973, pp. 4+.

A witty and challenging article pointing out the sexism in science books, calendars, and psychologically oriented books, such as Joan Fassler's works. Pogrebin raises provocative questions for readers to consider.

Prida, Dolores, and Ribner, Susan. "Feminists Look at 100 Books: The Portrayal of Women in Children's Books on Puerto Rican Themes," Interracial Books for Children. *Bulletin*, Vol. 4, Nos. 1 and 2 (Spring 1972).

Commentary, analysis, and annotated bibliography of children's books containing Spanish-speaking female characters. The same damaging stereotypes adhere to Puerto Rican female characters as to their Anglo counterparts, perhaps with greater intensity.

Reeder, Kik. "Pippi Longstocking — Feminist or Anti-Feminist?" Interracial Books for Children. *Bulletin*, Vol. 5, No. 4 (1974), 1.

Reveals the racism and sexism in the *Pippi* books. Criticizes Pippi because she is not a real girl; she is "a boy in disguise" (p. 2). All the other female characters in the series behave like "real girls." Pippi behaves in a sexist-stereotypic fashion toward other girls.

Schram, Barbara A. "Misgivings About — The Giving Tree," Interracial Books for Children. *Bulletin*, Vol. 5, No. 5 (1974), 1, 8.

Criticizes this very popular book because of its dominant male-subordinate female, master–slave romanticization. Makes some excellent arguments.

Scott, Foresman and Company. *Guidelines for Improving the Image of Women in Textbooks.*

Provides examples of negative presentations and positive sample ways to correct them. Pertains primarily to textbooks, but could be useful as well for trade books.

Shargel, Susan, and Kane, Irene.. *We Can Change It.* San Francisco: Change for Children, 1974.

Annotated bibliography of ninety-three nonsexist, nonracist children's books. Also lists publishers and alternative publishers' addresses. Includes some ideas for using these books in the classroom.

Stacey, Judith; Béreaud, Susan; and Daniels, Joan (eds.). *And Jill Came Tumbling After, Sexism in American Education.* New York: Dell, 1974.

An informative anthology of articles on sexism in education from nursery school through college. The only articles on children's books are Elizabeth Fisher's and Women on Words and Images' (annotated separately in these References). But the other articles serve as a background for study.

Stewig, John, and Higgs, Margaret. "Girls Grow Up to Be Mommies: A Study of Sexism in Children's Literature," *Library Journal*, Vol. 98, No. 2 (January 15, 1973), 236–41.

Criticizes some carelessly mounted research and praises some that is excellent. Confirms the conclusions that women "play a subordinate, home-related role" in picture books.

Tibbetts, Sylvia-Lee. "Sex Differences in Children's Reading Preferences," *The Reading Teacher*, Vol. 28, No. 3 (December 1974), 279-81.

Examines the acknowledged assumption that girls will read anything, but boys will read only these books pertaining to boys and their interests. Concludes that this bias is societally imposed rather than an inherent sex characteristic. Females and things female are considered inferior and therefore are rejected. Thus a societal change is in order, rather than publishers' conforming to current malpractice.

Weitzman, Lenore J.; Eifler, Deborah; Hokada, Elizabeth; and Ross, Catherine. "Sex Role Socialization in Picture Books for Pre-School Children," *American Journal of Sociology,* Vol. 77, No. 6 (May 1972), 1125–50.

The Caldecott Award winners in particular are examined in light of their influence on acceptance of sex-role stereotyping. Other award winners and popular books for children are also analyzed. Illuminating article, evidencing careful research.

Women on Words and Images. *Dick and Jane as Victims, Sex Stereotyping in Children's Readers.* Princeton, N.J.: National Organization for Women, 1972.

One hundred thirty-four readers from fourteen different publishers were analyzed. This well-written, well-researched, well-documented study presents a powerful case for change in textbooks. The same recommendations can be carried over to all books for children. An extremely useful reference.

FEMINIST ORGANIZATIONS AND PUBLISHERS

BETHANY PRESS. 2640 Pine Blvd., P.O. Box 179, St. Louis, Mo. 63116

CHANGE FOR CHILDREN. 2588 Mission St., Rm. 226, San Francisco, Calif. 94110

CONNECTICUT PUBLIC INTEREST RESEARCH GROUP. P.O. Box 1571, Hartford, Conn. 06101

FEMINIST BOOK MART. 162-11 Ninth Ave., Whitestone, N.Y. 11357

FEMINIST PRESS. SUNY College at Old Westbury, P.O. Box 334, Old Westbury, N.Y. 11568

FEMINISTS ON CHILDREN'S MEDIA. P.O. Box 4315, Grand Central Station, New York, N.Y. 10017

KNOW PRESS. P.O. Box 86031, Pittsburgh, Pa. 15221

LOLLIPOP POWER, INC. P.O. Box 1171, Chapel Hill, N.C. 27514

NATIONAL FOUNDATION FOR THE IMPROVEMENT OF EDUCATION RESOURCE CENTER ON SEX ROLES IN EDUCATION. Suite 918, 1156 15th St., N.W., Washington, D.C. 20005

NATIONAL ORGANIZATION FOR WOMEN (local branches in each state). Central Office, 1957 E. 73rd St., Chicago, Ill. 60649

NATIONAL ORGANIZATION FOR WOMEN. Central New Jersey Chapter, R.D. 4, 25 Cleveland Lane, Princeton, N.J. 08540

NEW ENGLAND FREE PRESS. 60 Union Square, Somerville, Mass. 02143

NEW SEED PUBLISHING COMPANY. P.O. Box 3016, Stanford, Calif. 94305

WOMEN ON WORDS AND IMAGES. P.O. Box 2163, Princeton, N.J. 08540

Bibliography

Adams, Florence. *Mushy Eggs.* Illus. Marilyn Hirsh. New York: Putnam's, 1973. (Ages 4–8.)
The women in this story are admirable and have several dimensions. The housekeeper–baby-sitter has her own friends and family, and the boys' mother copes well with her computer job and the boys. They all seem none the worse for wear.

Adamson, Joy. *Elsa.* New York: Pantheon Books, 1961. (Ages 6–up.)
True story of a strong, sensitive woman, her husband, and their lioness friend, Elsa. Easy to read with beautiful photographs of Elsa.

Alcott, Louisa May. *Little Women.* Boston: Little, Brown, 1868. Pb. Macmillan. (All ages.)
Portraits of four sisters in a loving family, each with an individual personality and a different vision of her future life. A classic. Jo is one of the sources of the literary image of the active female.

Allinson, Beverly. *Mitzi's Magic Garden.* Illus. George Buckett. Champaign, Ill.: Garrard, 1971. (Age 6.)
Mitzi busily plants a garden, gets wonderful results, and benevolently gives away what grows.

Andre, Evelyn M. *Things We Like to Do.* New York: Abingdon Press, 1968. (Ages 5–8.)
A large picture book depicting children of both sexes in various activities that are fun to do: play with friends, bake a cake, play with dolls.

Ayars, James Sterling. *Happy Birthday, Mom!* Eau Claire, Wis.: E. M. Hale, 1963. (Ages 6–9.)
A book that reinforces the stereotype of girls as silly and emotional through a story about a girl's birthday present to her mother. Also a sexist portrayal of family life.

Babbitt, Natalie. *Phoebe's Revolt.* New York: Farrar, Straus & Giroux, 1968. (Ages 6–9.)
Set in the Victorian era. A girl decides she does not want to wear ruffles and frills and likes her father's clothes instead. Finding that her father's clothes are not right, either, she finally finds a comfortable compromise. Somewhat of a cop-out but useful nevertheless.

Baker, Elizabeth. *Tammy Camps Out.* Illus. Beth and Joe Krush. Boston: Houghton Mifflin, 1958. Pb. also. (Ages 8–12.)
Tammy goes camping with her brother and her father and is teased for being silly and incompetent, until a landslide occurs and she must blaze a trail and seek help.

Baker, Nina Brown. *Nellie Bly, Reporter.* Illus. W. Blickinstoff. New York: Henry Holt, 1956. Pb. Scholastic. (Ages 8-12.)
An interesting biography of a determined and intelligent woman. Contains telling commentary about early twentieth-century America.

Baldwin, Anne Norris. *Sunflowers for Tina.* Illus. Ann Grifalconi. New York: Four Winds Press, 1970. Pb. Scholastic. (Ages 5-8.)
Tina, a black child living in the city, craves a garden. Her brother shows her sunflowers growing in a vacant lot, and that makes her happy. She, in turn, dances a sunflower dance for her grandmother, making the old woman happy. The lot of the female in this book is not, in general, a pleasant one.

Black, Algernon D. *The Woman of the Wood.* Illus. Evaline Ness. New York: Holt, Rinehart, and Winston, 1973. (Ages 3-8.)
Three men on a journey carve a woman out of wood, make her clothes, and teach her to speak. They each want to own her, but a wise old man tells them that she belongs to herself and only she can choose whom and what she wants. Although the moral is useful, the presentation is flawed by the one-dimensional characteristics of the woman and the transformation of the old man into a handsome young one.

Blaine, Marge. *The Terrible Thing That Happened at Our House.* Illus. John C. Wallner. New York: Parents' Magazine Press, 1975. (Ages 4-8.)
When a young girl's mother resumes her career, the child feels as if her world has fallen apart. She is intolerant of the new arrangements that the family makes. Resenting her parents' new roles, she wants her old, comfortable life back again. After a confrontation, the family together decide on a course of action satisfactory to all. The solution is a good one, but the tone of the book is negative.

Blassingame, Wyatt. *Combat Nurses of World War II.* Illus. Gil Walker. New York: Random House (Landmark Books), 1967. (Ages 9-up.)
A historical recounting of the teamwork among those who were involved in the battles of World War II. Free of sentimentality and of the exploitation found in some depictions of war-related events.

Bonsall, Crosby. *And I Mean It, Stanley.* New York: Harper & Row, 1974. (Ages 5-8.)
The friendship of an active, imaginative little girl, who builds contraptions in a junk yard, and a giant dog named Stanley.

———. *The Case of the Scaredy Cats.* New York: Harper & Row, 1971. (Ages 5-8.)

A group of boys make plans to get rid of the girls who have invaded their clubhouse, but the plan backfires. Unfortunately, this book encourages competition between the sexes.

Brelis, Nancy. *The Mother Market* (formerly *The Mummy Market*). Illus. Ben Shecter. New York: Harper & Row, 1966. Pb. also. (Ages 10–up.)
Elizabeth, Jenny, and David hate their housekeeper, who cares only about keeping house. They go the Mummy Market to choose a mother. They bring home a succession of unsuitable mothers until they finally locate one who is perfect, and who turns out to be their very own long-lost, formerly enchanted mother. Although there are several female characters in this book who are individuals, and interesting, the dominant feeling conveyed is the stereotypic sex-role expectation.

Brink, Carol Ryrie. *Caddie Woodlawn*. Illus. Trina Schart Hyman. New York: Macmillan, 1935. Pb. also. (Ages 9–12.) (Newbery Medal.)
A frontier story of the lively childhood adventures of Caddie and her brothers in the 1860s. Although Caddie's adventurous and active qualities are admired, the reader recognizes that she is expected to grow into a "conventional" woman.

Brownmiller, Susan. *Shirley Chisholm*. Garden City, N.Y.: Doubleday, 1970. Pb. Archway. (Ages 9–11.)
A biography of Shirley Chisholm, the first black woman to become a U.S. Representative. The book provides an insight into the business of American politics.

Buckley, Helen E. *Grandmother and I*. New York: Lothrop, Lee and Shepard, 1961. (Ages 4–8.)
A story of the uses of all different people's laps — Daddy's lap for playing cowboy, Mommy's for hair combing, and Grandmother's for curling up to sleep. Stereotypic roles for males and females. Books of this sort help cement the stereotypes and need careful assistance in their reading.

Buckmaster, Henrietta. *Women Who Shaped History*. New York: Macmillan, 1966. Pb. Collier Books. (Ages 10–up.)
An excellent compilation of short biographies of six women who were important contributors to our country's development. Well written, well balanced, and well selected.

Budd, Lillian. *Calico Row*. Chicago: Albert Whitman, 1965. (Ages 5–8.)
A friendship story of a boy and a girl working together to find the most wonderful thing on Calico Row, where they live.

Burch, Robert. *Queenie Peavy*. Illus. Jerry Lazare. New York: Viking, 1966. (Ages 9-12.)
Queenie is a strong, intelligent, capable thirteen-year-old. Her self-motivation and determination help her to overcome her father's negative influence and the teasing that she endures because he is in the penitentiary. She does things that only boys are usually thought of as doing, is frequently in trouble, and almost gets into serious trouble. But in the end, the support of many adults and her own intelligence win out. The book is somewhat overly sweet, but Queenie's character provides a useful image for women in this kind of book.

Burnett, Frances Hodgson. *The Secret Garden*. Philadelphia: Lippincott, 1911. Pb. Dell. (Ages 9-14.)
A bold, assertive girl comes to live in a new place, discovers a secret garden, a new friend, and how to care about others.

Burt, Olive. *Black Women of Valor*. Illus. Paul Frame. New York: Messner, 1974. (Ages 9-11.) (Newbery Medal.)
Tells the stories of four black women who demonstrated their courage and ability: Juliette Derricotte, Maggie Mitchell Walker, Ida Wells Barnett, Septima Poinsette Clark. The book also contains a long list of other black women of valor. Valuable addition to information about black history. One would wish, however, that the author had not so facilely referred to each of the women by her first name.

Byars, Betsy. *The Summer of the Swans*. New York: Viking, 1972. Pb. Avon. (Ages 10-12.)
Somewhat stereotypic story of Sara, an unhappy adolescent girl who becomes friends with a helpful boy named Joe. Sara needs Joe's help to find her younger brother. The "happy" ending is that Sara and Joe will date.

Caines, Jeannette. *Abby*. Illus. Steven Kellogg. New York: Harper & Row, 1973. (Ages 3-8.)
Abby is Kevin's little adopted sister. He loves her; but sometimes, when he gets annoyed, he upsets Abby by saying that he does not like girls. The mother is seen reading and studying. Abby is active and clever.

Carlson, Dale. *Girls Are Equal Too, The Women's Movement for Teenagers*. New York: Atheneum, 1973. (Ages 11-up.)
This book raises strong issues and presents clear arguments reflecting the feminist position. Good sections on women's rights and job inequality and on the history of women's rights.

Cleary, Beverly. *Ellen Tebbits* and *Henry Huggins.* New York: Morrow, 1951 and 1950. (Ages 9–11.)
Comical stories about a girl who meets a friend in ballet class, and a boy who brings home a dog that he finds on a bus. Both books enforce the stereotypes that boys and girls do and like completely different things, with boys being valued over girls.

————. *Ramona the Pest.* New York: Morrow, 1968. (Ages 9–11.)
Everyone calls curious, lively Ramona a "pest," but she has a different image of herself during her first few months of kindergarten. Overturns the image of the typical little girl.

Cleaver, Vera and Bill. *Delpha Green & Company.* Philadelphia: Lippincott, 1972. (Ages 10–up.)
Delpha accepts the responsibility for the world's welfare. A very self-reliant person, she manages to cope very well with seemingly unsurmountable family problems, but the focus on astrology weakens the book. And the happy capitulation of almost the entire town is somewhat difficult to believe.

————. *Ellen Grae.* Illus. Ellen Raskin. Philadelphia: Lippincott, 1967. (Ages 9–11.)
Ellen Grae is an unusual heroine. She is imaginative beyond belief, and is, in fact, not usually believed by the other characters in the book. A nonconformist in many ways, much to the dismay of her parents and other adults, she is, however, sensitive and appealing.

————. *Lady Ellen Grae.* Illus. Ellen Raskin. Philadelphia: Lippincott, 1968. (Ages 9–11.)
Another very well-written story by the Cleavers. Ellen Grae is the imaginative, sensitive, loving, bright heroine, who manages, despite her eccentricities, to endear herself to everyone. In this book, her parents decide that she should learn "ladylike" ways. The parody on stereotypic feminine characteristics is somewhat broad, but the demonstration that individual differences are far more acceptable than mindless conformity helps the reader to overlook the flaws.

————. *Me Too.* Philadelphia: Lippincott, 1973. (Ages 12–up.)
Lydia tries to teach her retarded twin, Lorna. Devoting an entire summer to her sister's education, she endures the hostility of neighbors and the desertion of a friend. She is clever, energetic, introspective, nasty at times, and a clear individual. She is free of sex-role stereotypes. She finally accepts the fact that her sister will remain retarded and that there is little that she can do for her.

————. *Where the Lilies Bloom.* Illus. Jim Spanfeller. Philadelphia: Lippincott, 1969. Pb. New American Library. (Ages 9–up.) (National Book
Award Finalist.)
Set in Appalachia. A fourteen-year-old girl cares for her family after
the sickness and death of their father, whom they bury and pretend
is still alive. Her strength is impressive but is insufficient without the
help of her siblings and outside circumstances.

————. *The Whys and Wherefores of Littabelle Lee.* New York: Atheneum,
1973. (Ages 12–up.)
An independent, determined young woman overcomes the hardships of her rural mountain life. Her aunt does not conform to the
feminine stereotype until she decides to discontinue her doctoring
and settles down to be cared for by the man she loves. Each character, however, is an individual.

Clifton, Lucille. *Don't You Remember?* Illus. Evaline Ness. New York:
Dutton, 1973. (Ages 3–7.)
Desire Mary Tate, black, four years old, and very lively, considers
herself to have the best memory in her family. She has three elder
brothers, one of whom has taken a year off from school to care for
her. Her parents both work, and her ambition is to grow up and
work at the plant, "just like Daddy." Division of labor because it
must get done, not because of sex role.

————. *Good, Says Jerome.* New York: Dutton, 1973. (Ages 3–7.)
Jerome, frightened by many things, asks his sister for the answers.
She usually has good comforting answers for him and helps him
deal with many aspects of life. Jerome is not punished or derided for
his feelings; he is permitted to display them and to be reassured.

Coatsworth, Elizabeth. *The Princess and the Lion.* New York: Pantheon,
1963. (Ages 8–12.)
A folk tale in which the princess does the rescuing, assisted by a
royal lion and a royal donkey. Yet, despite her courage and her
cleverness, she must remain on the "servant" level of the king's
women, while her brother becomes king.

Cohen, Miriam. *The New Teacher.* New York: Macmillan, 1972. Pb. also.
(Ages 3–6.)
A group of boys and girls at a racially mixed city school get a new
teacher and decide that they like her. The activities of the children
are not determined by sex. The book is not a literary classic, but does
provide a good model for nonsexist activities.

Colby, C. B. *Police: Skill and Science Combat Crime.* New York: Coward, McCann, 1971. (Ages 9–up.)
This book describes the workings of a police organization, but women are shown only directing traffic and in office work. In reality, women are involved in several other aspects of police work not indicated in this book.

Colman, Hila. *Diary of a Frantic Kid Sister.* New York: Crown, 1973. (Ages 8–11.)
Written in a narrative/diary form, this is the sensitive story of an eleven-year-old girl's relationships with her mother and her elder sister, all of whom are having difficulty coping with their roles.

Coombs, Patricia. *Molly Mullett.* New York: Lothrop, Lee and Shepard, 1975. (Ages 6–10.)
Although the heroine of this story is female, she is the only female in the book who is not totally downtrodden. And even she needs the help of a blackbird in order to succeed. Her father never learns to appreciate her. A very sexist book.

Credle, Ellis. *Down, Down the Mountain.* New York: Nelson, 1934. (Ages 5–8.)
Two West Virginia mountain children grow and sell turnips to buy themselves shoes. In this story there is no distinction between men's and women's work, unusual for a story which takes place so long ago.

Dalgliesh, Alice. *The Courage of Sarah Noble.* Illus. Leonard Weisgard. New York: Scribner's, 1954. (Ages 6–9.)
A girl travels into the wilderness in 1707 with her father. She lives with the Indians while her father returns for the rest of the family. She exhibits patience and adaptability but is not particularly different from the stereotype.

Danish, Barbara. *The Dragon and the Doctor.* Old Westbury, N.Y.: Feminist Press, 1971. Pb. (Ages 3–8.)
A story with consciously changed sex roles (doctor is female, nurse is male) about a dragon with a sick tail, who is very grateful to the doctor for her help. Too labored and obvious to be effective.

Darrow, Whitney, Jr. *I'm Glad I'm a Boy! I'm Glad I'm a Girl!* New York: Simon and Schuster, 1970. (Ages 4–7.)
A perpetuation of the stereotypic roles of males and females: "Boys are doctors; girls are nurses." This book need not be summarily discarded; it can be used to start lively discussions.

DeRegniers, Beatrice, and Gilman, Esther. *The Little Girl and Her Mother*. New York: Vanguard, 1963. (Ages 7–up.)
This book deals with the relationship between a girl and her mother, but presents being a mother and doing housework as the only alternative for the girl's future life. The mother is a particularly dull person, with no apparent interests outside of her house.

Dolin, Arnold. *Great American Heroines*. Illus. Rafaello Busoni. New York: Lion Press, 1960. (Ages 12–up.)
The biographies of many American women, including Helen Keller, Pocahontas, Mary Lyon, Harriet Beecher Stowe, Susan Anthony, and Amelia Earhart. Sacrifice and hardship are stressed in these descriptions, somewhat overshadowing the women's own characteristics.

Eichler, Margaret. *Martin's Father*. Chapel Hill, N.C.: Lollipop Power, 1971. Pb. (Ages 3–7.)
Martin and his father go through a typical day together. There is no mother, and the two males perform what is conventionally considered to be women's work. This would have been an even more effective book if a mother had been present, working alongside Martin and his father.

Eisenberg, Eleanor. *The Pretty House That Found Happiness*. Illus. Betsy Warren. Austin, Tex.: Steck-Vaughn Company, 1964. (Ages 4–9.)
Although the author has the excellent intention of causing adopted children to feel welcome and wanted, she constructs a situation in which boys are expected to be active and girls passive. The father plays with his son and is strong, while the mother does laundry and waters plants.

Engebrecht, P. A. *Under the Haystack*. New York: Thomas Nelson, 1973. (Ages 11–up.)
When deserted by her mother and stepfather, Sandy, a thirteen-year-old girl courageously manages to take care of her sisters and the farm where they live. She must work hard, defend herself, and cope with great responsibility.

Erwin, Betty K. *Who Is Victoria?* Illus. Kathleen Anderson. Boston: Little, Brown, 1973. (Ages 9–11.)
Victoria, a poltergeist, is the lively spirit of an elderly spinster librarian. The setting is rural Wisconsin in the 1930s, the events and effects of the Depression forming part of the story. Margaret Evans wants to be a doctor; she is a very active girl, but her mother, who has a degree in mathematics, is content to remain at home and cook and clean. Her husband, a physician, is happy with the arrange-

ment. Victoria comes into everyone's lives, fulfills her lifelong dreams of action, and disappears when the librarian dies. At the end of the book, nothing and no one is changed. Except for the independence and aspirations of Margaret, this is a thin book.

Ets, Marie Hall. *Play With Me.* New York: Viking, 1955. Pb. also. (Ages 3-6.)
When a girl is noisy, she cannot get anyone to play with her, but she is rewarded for sitting quietly — for then all wild creatures come to her side. The atypical girl is again punished until she conforms. Too bad the main character here is not a boy.

Faber, Doris. *Lucretia Mott: Foe to Slavery.* Champaign, Ill.: Garrard, 1971. (Ages 8-12.)
The biography of a Quaker woman who spent her life fighting for voting and educational rights for women and Blacks.

Fassler, Joan. *All Alone with Daddy.* New York: Behavioral Publications, 1969. (Ages 3-8.)
Seems to encourage little girls to be "just-like-mommy and to grow-up-and-marry-somebody-just-like-daddy." Its counterpart, *Man of the House,* permits the little boy to be a surrogate husband. Although the books try to provide comfort to children going through the throes of the oedipal complex, readers who do not subscribe to a Freudian point of view will find much to criticize.

Felton, Harold W. *Mumbet, the Story of Elizabeth Freeman.* Illus. Donn Albright. New York: Dodd, Mead, 1970. (Ages 9-12.)
A fairly elementary and not very detailed description of the life of one of the first women to gain her freedom by using the power of the law.

Field, Rachel. *Hitty, Her First Hundred Years.* Illus. Dorothy Lathrop. New York: Macmillan, 1937. (Ages 9-11.)
Hitty is a passive doll who has countless adventures for which she is not responsible, and is rescued time and again. This classic, although presenting a female as the heroine, maintains the stereotype.

Fitzhugh, Louise. *Harriet the Spy.* New York: Harper & Row, 1964. Pb. Dell. (Ages 9-12.)
An amusing, brash portrayal of a sometimes stubborn eleven-year-old girl who wants to be a spy and bluntly writes down all her observations of family and community life in her secret notebook. Harriet is clever, inventive, and not very sensitive to other people's feelings. The other children in the book are also not stereotyped.

Gardner, Richard A. *Dr. Gardner's Fairy Tales for Today's Children*. Illus. A. Lowenheim. Englewood Cliffs, N.J.: Prentice-Hall, 1974. (Ages 8–up.)
Four fairy tales loosely adapted from classical versions. The characters behave in rational, constructive fashion rather than adhering to traditional patterns. The stories are fun.

Gauch, Patricia Lee. *This Time, Tempe Wick?* Illus. Margot Tomes. New York: Coward, McCann & Geoghegan, 1974. (Ages 7–11.)
Temperance Wick, a bold unselfish girl, defies rebellious American soldiers in order to protect her mother, horse, and house during the Revolutionary War.

George, Jean Craighead. *Julie of the Wolves*. Illus. John Schoenherr. New York: Harper & Row, 1972. (Ages 12–up.) (Newbery Medal and National Book Award.)
An Eskimo girl runs away from an unhappy situation. Living in the frozen wilderness, she courageously makes friends with the wolves and learns their ways of survival. She must face problems not only of individual survival but also of the changing ways of her people.

Goffstein, M. B. *Goldie the Dollmaker*. New York: Farrar, Straus & Giroux, 1969. (Ages 5–8.)
Goldie is an artist who lives in the forest making dolls. She is lonely for someone who understands her feelings about her work, but her confidence in these feelings is reaffirmed by the end of the book.

Gold, Sharlya. *Amelia Quackenbush*. New York: Seabury Press, 1973. (Ages 9–12.)
Amelia dislikes her name, is uneasy about her family, and is not very comfortable with herself. Although the book attempts to present a feminist point of view, it is never suggested that the mother go to work. The happy ending is that the mother will read less and cook more. Students could easily generate much more practical solutions to the family's problems, thus making the book a useful one.

Goldreich, Gloria and Esther. *What Can She Be? An Architect*. Photographs by Robert Ipcar. New York: Lothrop, Lee & Shepard, 1974. (Ages 4–10.)
Part of the "What Can She Be?" series, this book maintains the quality of the others. The information is well presented; the photographs are clear. This book does not, incidentally, include as many women in professions as the others do, but it is, nevertheless, a useful addition to any library.

—————. *What Can She Be? A Lawyer.* Photographs by Robert Ipcar. New York: Lothrop, Lee & Shepard, 1973. (Ages 4–10.)
Part of the series devoted to describing women in professions formerly considered to be for men only. This book describes how Ellen Green manages to be a lawyer, wife, and mother. Ms. Green has a varied clientele and is shown to be an able attorney, as well as a competent, happy, well-adjusted woman. An excellent, well-conceived book.

—————. *What Can She Be? A Newscaster.* Photographs by Robert Ipcar. New York: Lothrop, Lee & Shepard, 1973. (Ages 5–10.)
A straightforward book about a woman who works as a TV and radio newscaster and also has a good family life.

Goodyear, Carmen. *The Sheep Book.* Chapel Hill, N.C.: Lollipop Power, 1972. (Ages 3–7.)
Describes the cycle of raising sheep for their wool, which then becomes yarn and eventually a garment. The illustrations by the author are appropriate to the text. The farmer is a woman. The message of the text is didactic without being oppressive.

Graves, Robert. *Two Wise Children.* Illus. Ralph Pinto. New York: Harlan Quist, 1966. (Ages 8–up.)
The friendship of Bill Brain and Avis Deed grows stronger after each experiences and then loses the magic power to be able to do or to know anything beyond the ordinary. Their friendship is unusual because of the intrusion of the supernatural.

Gray, Genevieve. *I Know a Bus Driver.* Illus. C. Dougherty. New York: Putnam's, 1972. (Ages 6–9.)
This is one book of a series that attempts to familiarize children with their community workers, but it stereotypes "male" and "female" jobs at the same time. (All workers in the book are men, except the telephone receptionist, who is a woman.)

Greene, Bette. *Philip Hall Likes Me: I Reckon Maybe.* Illus. Charles Lilly. New York: Dial Press, 1974. (Ages 9–12.) (Newbery Honor Book.)
Beth Lambert is black, eleven years old, and extraordinarily bright and competent. She is a lively, ambitious, successful young woman, who wants to be a veterinarian, and the reader knows that she will succeed. The major flaw in this book is that Beth and Philip, the boy to whom she is attracted, must always compete with each other. Competition is stressed between the boys and the girls. Though it works out "happily" in the end, the idea of one-upmanship mars the otherwise flavorful and excellent book.

Greene, Constance. *Leo the Lioness.* New York: Viking, 1970. (Ages 12–up.)
The story of a fourteen-year-old girl growing up with her boy-crazy friends, Jen and Nina. Portrayed here are many types of boys and girls and their relationships to themselves and to one another.

————. *A Girl Called Al.* Illus. Byron Barton. New York: Viking, 1969. Pb. also. (Ages 11–up.)
Alexandra wants to be called Al. Not interested in being a conformist, she wants to do carpentry rather than cooking; but the school will not permit it. An elderly janitor who cooks, and is proud of his waxed floor, teaches her carpentry. Very sensitive and easily hurt, she is constantly searching for a father, since her own parents are divorced. The "happy ending" indicates that Al will become a conventionally attractive young woman and will be able to attract men.

Greenfield, Howard. *Gertrude Stein, a Biography.* New York: Crown, 1973. (Ages 12–up.)
A frank and clearly written biography of the controversial woman. Her personal life is described and explained, as well as her public accomplishments.

Gripe, Maria. *The Night Daddy.* Illus. Harold Gripe. New York: Delacorte Press, 1971. Pb. Dell. (Ages 8–11.)
An unusual story about the relationship between a young girl and her adult male baby-sitter who stays nights while her mother works. The story takes place in Sweden; it is not yet realistic for the United States.

Handforth, Thomas. *Mei Li.* Garden City, N.Y.: Doubleday, 1938. (Ages 5–8.) (Caldecott Award.)
Mei Li, a Chinese girl, goes to a big circus, has many experiences, and gains some self-pride.

Harris, Janet. *A Single Standard.* New York: McGraw-Hill, 1971. (Ages 10–up.)
Although this book contains a historical approach to the feminist movement, it stresses the sociological and psychological implications more than the history. The book relates to every aspect of women's lives.

Haskins, James. *Fighting Shirley Chisholm.* New York: Dial Press, 1975. (Ages 12–up.)
The dynamic black representative is described here in excellent detail. Haskins's book is very frank and inclusive.

Henriod, Lorraine. *Marie Curie.* Illus. Fermin Rocher. New York: Putnam's, 1970. (Ages 7-10.)
A "beginning to read" biography dispelling the myth that radium was discovered accidentally. In simple but clear language it points out the care and study that Marie Curie devoted to her profession.

Herman, Harriet. *The Forest Princess.* Illus. Carde Petersen Duinell. Berkeley, Calif.: Over the Rainbow Press, 1974. Pb. (All ages.)
A modern-day fairy tale in which a princess wakes a sleeping prince with a kiss and then enchants him with her independence and self-assurance.

Heyn, Leah. *Challenge to Become a Doctor: The Story of Elizabeth Blackwell.* Old Westbury, N.Y.: Feminist Press, 1971. (Ages 9-13.)
The biography of the struggle of a determined woman to become a doctor despite the discrimination evident in the all-male profession. Blackwell, in fact, became the first woman physician.

Heyward, Dubose, and Zarssoni, Marjory. *The Country Bunny and the Little Gold Shoes.* Boston: Houghton Mifflin, 1939. Pb. also. (Ages 5-8.)
A story about a rabbit who is a mother and a strong, proud Easter Bunny at the same time. While she is out delivering Easter eggs, her little bunnies, boys and girls alike, are taking care of the house. Note the early copyright date.

Hill, Elizabeth Starr. *Evan's Corner.* Illus. Nancy Grossman. New York: Holt, Rinehart and Winston, 1967. (Ages 4-8.)
Evan's mother is busy with work and family. His elder sister and father also help with the care of the children. The family is poor but manages well.

Hochman, Sandra. *The Magic Convention.* Illus. Ben Shecter. Garden City, N.Y.: Doubleday, 1971. (Ages 8-up.)
A girl goes to a professional magician's convention, sees an exciting performance by a woman magician, and decides more than ever that she wants to be a magician.

Hochschild, Arlie Russell. *Colleen the Question Girl.* Illus. Gail Ashby. Old Westbury, N.Y.: Feminist Press, 1974. Pb. (Ages 5-10.)
Colleen is an intelligent young girl who questions everyone about serious and confusing topics — race, discrimination, wealth, and status.

Hoehling, Mary. *Girl Soldier and Spy: Sarah Emma Edmundson.* New York: Messner, 1959. (Ages 10-up.)

A well-written account of this unusual woman. The author always refers to her heroine as a woman, and it is as a woman that Sarah accomplishes her adventures. Her qualities are womanly, even when she is pretending to be a man. The author values women and presents the story so that readers may do so as well.

Holman, Felice. *Victoria's Castle*. Illus. Lillian Hoban. New York: Norton, 1966. (All ages.)
Victoria is an only child with a wild imagination, with which she builds a castle and a fantasy world filled with unusual animals.

Hopkins, Lee Bennett. *Girls Can Too!* Illus. Emily McCully. New York: Franklin Watts, 1972. (Ages 5–8.)
A book of positive poems about what different girls can do, think, and feel. The only flaw in the book is the inclusion of poems encouraging competition between the sexes.

Horvath, Betty. *Be Nice to Josephine*. Illus. Pat Grant. New York: Franklin Watts, 1970. (Ages 5–8.)
Charlie unwillingly gives up his baseball game to take his cousin Josephine fishing, and finds that, despite himself, he has a good time. But he ruins his good behavior by succumbing to his friends' teasing.

———. *Not Enough Indians*. New York: Franklin Watts, 1971. (Ages 9–11.)
Problems arise among a group of six boys and one girl playing Indians one afternoon. Not only are they racist, they are also sexist.

Howard, Moses L. *The Ostrich Chase*. Illus. Barbara Seuling. New York: Holt, Rinehart and Winston, 1974. (Ages 10–14.)
Khuana, a young woman of the Bushman tribe, violates tradition by learning to hunt and to build fires. Because of these skills, she is able to save her grandmother's life and to conquer the desert. She nevertheless remains interested in womanly things as well. She is an admirable character.

Hunt, Irene. *Up a Road Slowly*. Chicago: Follett, 1966. Pb. Grosset and Dunlap. (Ages 12–up.) (Newbery Medal.)
Julie goes to live with a strict aunt when her mother dies. Julie learns to admire her aunt enough to want to stay with her instead of returning to live with her remarried father. Mixed messages about the role of women are communicated in this book.

Hunter, Kristin. *The Soul Brothers and Sister Lou*. New York: Scribner's, 1968. Pb. Avon. (Ages 12–up.) (Council on Interracial Books for Children Award.)

Detailed portrayal of a group of black teen-agers, both boys and girls, growing up in Harlem. Lou is bright, active, and ambitious. There are other, less admirable characters, and the effect is, in general, not that of the liberated female.

Jacobs, Helen Hull. *The Tennis Machine.* New York: Scribner's, 1972. (Ages 10–up.)
Story of a thirteen-year-old tennis champion who is trying to break away from her dominating father in order to think and to act on her own. She is only partially successful by the end of the book.

Jewell, Nancy. *Try and Catch Me.* Illus. Leonard Weisgard. New York: Harper & Row, 1972. (Ages 4–8.)
An active girl is self-sufficient and energetic. As she goes about her play, a boy teases her and seems to disapprove of what she is doing. But in the end, he approaches her and invites her to join him in a swim. The competition somewhat mars the story, but both the boy and the girl are described in positive ways.

Johnson, Elizabeth. *Break a Magic Circle.* Boston: Little, Brown, 1971. (Ages 8–11.)
A boy breaks a magic circle of mushrooms and is enchanted. He is saved, though, and the magic circle fixed, with the help of a girl and her little brother.

Jordan, June. *Fannie Lou Hamer.* Illus. Albert Williams. New York: Crowell, 1972. (Ages 6–10.)
A well-told biography of a brave black woman who fought for the rights of black people and who began a cooperative in Mississippi.

Katz, Bobbi. *Nothing But a Dog.* Illus. Esther Gilman. Old Westbury, N.Y.: Feminist Press, 1972. (Ages 4–8.)
Very active girl wants a dog. She is pictured wearing all kinds of clothing (even including dresses) and engaging in all kinds of activities. In the end she gets her dog, but the book essentially has no plot. It presents the image of the girl in a nonstereotypic manner.

Kaufman, Joe. *Busy People.* New York: Golden Press, 1973. (Ages 5–7.)
A book about community life and careers that includes women and men, Blacks and Whites, in nonstereotyped roles.

Keats, Ezra Jack. *A Letter to Amy.* New York: Harper & Row, 1968. (Ages 5–8.)
Peter writes a letter to Amy to invite her to his birthday party. Through a misunderstanding, Peter hurts Amy's feelings, but she comes to his party and all ends happily. Peter's other guests are all boys. They tease Peter about Amy, but Peter remains unperturbed. The book subtly reinforces the notion that girls are inferior.

Keller, Gail Faithfull. *Jane Addams.* Illus. Frank Aloise. New York: Crowell, 1971. (Ages 7–9.)
A clear description of the work and personality of Jane Addams. Simply, but in useful detail, her life is well narrated.

Kerr, M. E. *Dinky Hocker Shoots Smack.* New York: Harper & Row, 1972. Pb. Dell. (Ages 12–up.)
A book dealing with many unique, individual adolescents not accepted by the adult community, and centering on Dinky, an overweight girl who is neglected by her community-oriented parents.

Kingman, Lee. *Georgina and the Dragon.* Illus. Leonard Shortall. Boston. Houghton Mifflin, 1972. (Ages 7–10.)
Georgina Gooch is determined to live up to her suffragist great-grandmother's tradition. She crusades for equal rights and manages to raise the level of consciousness of her whole neighborhood. She is fun — her energy and intelligence are outstanding. An excellent book.

Klein, Norma. *Girls Can Be Anything.* Illus. Roy Doty. New York: Dutton, 1973. (Ages 3–6.)
Marina's friend Adam tells her she has to be the nurse or the stewardess when they play. But Marina's parents tell her she can be anything, even the doctor, the pilot, or U.S. President. Marina tells this to Adam, and they change the way they play their games.

———. *It's Not What You Expect.* New York: Pantheon Books, 1973. Pb. Avon. (Ages 12–up.)
Oliver and Carla, fourteen-year-old twins, can find little to divert themselves from the pains of their parents' separation; so, for the summer, they decide to open a gourmet French restaurant. In general, males and females are not stereotyped.

———. *Mom, the Wolf Man and Me.* New York: Pantheon Books, 1972. Pb. Avon. (Ages 10–up.)
Brett, an illegitimate child, and her mother live together happily and discuss serious issues openly. When her mother makes friends with a man and eventually marries him, Brett is able to accept this change after an uneasy time.

———. *Naomi in the Middle.* Illus. Leigh Grant. New York: Dial Press, 1974. (Ages 7–10.)
Most of the characters in this book are female; all are individuals. They are pictured wearing comfortable clothes and doing activities of all sorts. The grandmother is an interesting character in her own

right. She is not very fond of infants, preferring "more complicated" older children. The shop teacher is female. And so is Alice, Bobo's pet rat.

————. *A Train for Jane.* Illus. Miriam Schottland. Old Westbury, N.Y.: Feminist Press, 1974. (Ages 6–10.)
A verse-story telling how, despite all efforts of persuasion by her parents, Jane insists on a train for a Christmas present. It is fine for other girls to want "girls'" toys but she loves her train.

Konigsburg, E. L. *About the B'nai Bagels.* New York: Atheneum, 1969. Pb. also. (Ages 8–12.)
Though Mark is the main character in this story, his mother is also central. She is unhappy because her elder son is acting out his independence. The father suggests patience, a psychiatrist, or a new interest. It is evident the entire family believes that woman's place is in the kitchen. Even when the mother manages the Little League baseball team, she takes orders and advice from her son and husband. She is loved, but not respected in the same way as the males are. Women are primarily sex objects or cooks in this book.

————. *From the Mixed-Up Files of Mrs. Basil E. Frankweiler.* New York: Atheneum, 1967. Pb. also. (Ages 8–12.) (Newbery Medal.)
Claudia and Jamie run away from home and hide in the Metropolitan Museum of Art, where they get involved in a mystery centered around a work of art formerly owned by Mrs. Basil E. Frankweiler. Both Claudia and Mrs. Frankweiler are strong females with individual personalities.

————. *Jennifer, Hecate, Macbeth, William McKinley and Me, Elizabeth.* New York: Atheneum, 1967. Pb. also. (Ages 9–12.) (Newbery Honor Book.)
Elizabeth and Jennifer are friends. At first their friendship is based on the supposed practice of witchcraft, but both girls are outcasts, partly because they do not dress and behave as the other girls do. Jennifer is excluded also because she is black. The author values these two girls over the others, but adults would do well to guide readers to recognize the racist and sexist behavior of the other characters.

Krasilovsky, Phyllis. *The Very Little Girl* and *The Very Little Boy.* Garden City, N.Y.: Doubleday, 1953. Pb. also. (Ages 5–8.)
Two books dealing with the problems of being small and with growing up. However, the books use sex-stereotyped settings and actions for the girl and the boy.

Krauss, Ruth. *I'll Be You and You Be Me.* Illus. Maurice Sendak. Lenox, Mass.: Bookstore Press, 1973. Pb. also. (Ages 8–up.) (*N.Y. Times* Best Illustrated Children's Books of the Year.)
Warm ideas, in poetry form, about friendship between boys and girls.

Lader, Lawrence, and Meltzer, Milton. *Margaret Sanger, Pioneer of Birth Control.* New York: Crowell, 1969. Pb. Dell. (Ages 12–up.)
A biography of Margaret Sanger, a strong determined woman who fought to make birth control a right for all women, especially the poor. She was strong enough to maintain her own individuality.

Landau, Elaine. *Women, Women, Feminism in America.* New York: Messner, 1970. (Ages 12–up.)
Presenting a strong case for equality of the sexes, the author describes many instances of discrimination as the basis for her argument. She also tells of countries, such as Israel and Sweden, where great advances in the cause of equality have been made. A well-written, persuasive book.

Larrick, Nancy, and Merriam, Eve (eds.). *Male and Female Under 18.* New York: Avon Books, 1973. (Ages 8–up.) Pb.
Comments and poems contributed by girls and boys, aged eight to eighteen, reflecting how they feel about their sex roles. The responses range from strong support of tradition to militant anger.

Lasker, Joe. *Mothers Can Do Anything.* Chicago: Albert Whitman, 1972. (Ages 3–8.)
This book demonstrates the variety of jobs that mothers can hold, including scientist, linesman, artist, and lion-tamer. The illustrations are fun, and the message is an important one.

Lawrence, Jacob. *Harriet and the Promised Land.* New York: Simon and Schuster, 1968. (Ages 6–10.) (*N.Y. Times* Best Illustrated Children's Books of the Year.)
In verse and colorful pictures, this book describes the courageous black woman, Harriet Tubman, who escaped from slavery and helped many others to escape also. Her life was difficult and unconventional, as she persevered in her heroic actions despite grave danger.

L'Engle, Madeleine. *A Wrinkle in Time.* New York: Farrar, Straus, 1962. Pb. Dell. (Ages 12–up.) (Newbery Medal.)
Meg is the heroine of this science-fiction adventure about two children who travel into space with three wise, magical creatures to find their scientist-father. Their mother, too, is brilliant and a scientist.

————. *The Young Unicorns.* New York: Farrar, Straus, 1968. (Ages 12-up.)
An elaborate mystery set in New York with a blind musician, Emily, and a scientific whiz, Sue, as heroines of the story.

Levinson, Irene. *Peter Learns to Crochet.* Illus. Ketra Sutherland. Stanford, Calif.: New Seed Press, 1973. Pb. (Ages 5-8.)
Peter wants to learn to crochet but has trouble finding someone to teach him, until he asks his teacher, Mr. Alvarado. Somewhat artificial, but not unbelievable.

Levitin, Sonia. *Rita, the Weekend Rat.* Illus. Leonard Shortall. New York: Atheneum, 1971. (Ages 8-12.)
Cynthia is a second grader who hates being a girl. She has a rat named Rita, whom she cares for on the weekends. She begins to reconcile herself to being a girl, by the end of the book, but does not stop being active or taking care of Rita and her baby rats.

Levy, Elizabeth. *Nice Little Girls.* Illus. Mordicai Gerstein. New York: Delacorte Press, 1974. (Ages 5-8.)
Jackie, a girl who wants to be a boy, is teased by her classmates, scolded by her teacher, but listened to and reassured by her parents. Finally, another girl in class wants to become friends with Jackie, and she is no longer an outcast. Somewhat mixed messages are conveyed in this book.

Lexau, Joan. *The Trouble with Terry.* Illus. Irene Murray. New York: Dial Press, 1962. Pb. Scholastic. (Ages 8-12.) (Wel-Met Award.)
Terry is a tomboy. Her mother, troubled about this, wants Terry to be more ladylike. Terry and her brother are friends, and she is accepted by her brother's friends. The book does not make great strides toward liberation, but it takes a few steps.

Lindgren, Astrid. *Pippi Longstocking.* Illus. Louis Glanzman. New York: Viking, 1950. Pb. also. (Ages 9-11.)
Pippi is a lively, independent heroine who lives, without parents, in a magical, adventurous world, which amazes her two friends next door. She stands out as painfully different and somewhat lonely.

Lofts, Norah. *The Maude Reed Tale.* Illus. Anne and Janet Grahame Johnstone. Nashville: Thomas Nelson, 1972. Pb. Dell. (Ages 10-up.)
The setting is the Middle Ages. Maude, about twelve years old, has a twin brother, who runs away from home to be a minstrel. Maude wants to be a wool merchant. The conflicts of personal and societal values, besides the cleverness of the heroine, make the book a vital one. The writing is of excellent quality.

Longsworth, Polly. *Emily Dickinson: Her Letter to the World*. New York: Crowell, 1965. (Ages 10–up.)
A nicely constructed biography of Emily Dickinson. Her recluse behavior is accepted as a logical result of her way of life, rather than being presented as a mystery.

———. *I, Charlotte Forten, Black and Free*. New York: Crowell, 1970. (Ages 10–12.)
Charlotte Forten serves as the narrator of this fictionalized autobiography. Her life was an eventful, rich one. She meets and works against slavery with many famous people. The book describes other abolitionists, such as the Grimke sisters and William Lloyd Garrison, and tells the stories of such notable Blacks as Frederick Douglass, James Forten, and William Wells Brown, among others.
The fight for women's rights is seen as a parallel and compatible one with abolition.

Lystad, Mary. *Jennifer Takes Over P.S. 94*. Illus. Ray Cruz. New York: Putnam's, 1972. (Ages 3–8.)
Jennifer imagines how she would run the school, while sitting on the "punish bench" for kicking a girl who hit her first.

McCloskey, Robert. *One Morning in Maine*. New York: Viking, 1952. (Ages 5–8.)
Two sisters spend a lovely day with their father digging clams and going to the mainland by motorboat. Although life is not stereotyped for the little girls, it seems to be for the parents.

McGinley, Phyllis. *A Girl and Her Room*. Illus. Ati Forbey, New York: Franklin Watts, 1963. (Ages 5–8.)
Changes in a girl's room are followed as the girl grows from birth to early womanhood. Too sweet, too simple.

———. *Lucy McLockett*. Illus. Helen Stone. Philadelphia: Lippincott, 1958. (Ages 5–8.)
A fairly liberated story for its time. Although the expectation is that Lucy will be well-behaved and demure, she is permitted to climb trees, play active games with boys, and ride a bicycle. All of this is counterbalanced by her other activities, which are predominantly female-role-linked; but the book is not ruined by its flaws. Lucy emerges as a very lively girl. An updating of the illustrations would go a long way in alleviating the sexist message.

———. *Sugar and Spice, The ABC of Being a Girl*. Illus. Colleen Browning. New York: Franklin Watts, 1959. (Ages 5–8.)
This book is about the "lovely things" a girl does, beginning with A and ending with Z. It is a classic example of the gentle persuasion of

sex stereotyping. The girl is always wearing a dress. Her dolls are constantly with her. She is loving, gentle, obedient.

MacGregor, Ellen. *Miss Pickerell Goes to Mars.* Illus. Paul Galdone. New York: McGraw-Hill, 1951. Pb. Scholastic. (Ages 9–11.)
Miss Pickerell is an old woman who travels from one exciting adventure to another, all over the universe. She is much brighter than most of the males, and accomplishes more than most people. There is a long series of Miss Pickerell books, each with a new adventure.

Mann, Peggy. *Amelia Earhart, First Lady of Flight.* Illus. Kiyo Komoda. New York: Coward, McCann, 1970. (Ages 10–12.)
A biography of the first woman to become a well-known aviator. Earhart is one of the women most written about.

Martin, Patricia Miles. *Dolley Madison.* Illus. Unada Gliewe. New York: Putnam's, 1967. (Ages 6–10.)
A "beginning-to-read" biography, the book somewhat oversimplifies the details of Dolley Madison's life. It also implies that her son, Payne, was loving and attentive, when history indicates that he caused her great problems.

Mathis, Sharon Bell. *Listen for the Fig Tree.* New York: Viking, 1974. Pb. Avon. (Ages 12–up.)
Muffin Johnson, sixteen years old and blind, is extraordinarily competent. She manages her mother and all of the details of housekeeping. She sews and shops and has excellent relationships with people. Her mother is weak, and almost destroyed over the death of the father. The male characters in this story are not stereotyped, but Muffin is too super to be believed. The only chink in her armor surfaces when someone attempts to rape her. She also relies too strongly on the opinion of Ernie, whom she plans to marry. Her devotion and feelings about her black heritage are a strong part of the book.

————. *Sidewalk Story.* Illus. Leo Carty. New York: Viking, 1971. Pb. Avon. (Ages 9–11.) (Council on Interracial Books for Children Award.)
Lilly Etta Allen is the nine-year-old protagonist. By her refusal to accept an unfair situation, she manages to help her friend Tanya overcome eviction. Lilly Etta enlists the aid of the newspapers and also acts on her own to protect her friend's possessions.

Matsumo, Masako. *Chie and the Sports Day.* Illus. Kazue Mizumara. Cleveland: World, 1965. (Ages 8–11.)
Chie's older brother Ichiro and his friends disdain playing with girls. Chie's mother permits her to help prepare food for the Sports Day.

The mother will cut short an important meeting to be able to attend. Fortuitously, at sports day, Ichiro needs a little girl to run the three-legged race. Chie and Ichiro come in first. No father is evident, but the mother seems to lead a balanced life, although it is clear that "boys are superior to girls."

Meltzer, Milton. *Tongue of Flame. The Life of Lydia Maria Child.* New York: Crowell, 1965. Pb. Dell. (Ages 12–up.)
A well-written account of the life and times of Lydia Maria Child, who fought for such causes as abolition, women's rights, and rights of Native Americans. This book is one of the excellent series of biographies entitled "Women of America."

Merriam, Eve. *Boys and Girls, Girls and Boys.* New York: Holt, Rinehart & Winston, 1972. Pb. also. (Ages 3–8.)
An unpretentious book showing children, boys and girls alike, exploring, being active and enjoying life.

———. *Mommies at Work.* New York: Knopf, 1961. Pb. Scholastic. (Ages 5–7.)
A book showing all the things that mothers can do outside the house — a very broad and varied range, all compatible with being a mother.

Miller, Arthur. *Jane's Blanket.* New York: Viking, 1972. (Ages 5–8.)
A little girl grows and her security blanket shrinks in size. She eventually relinquishes the blanket to some birds.

Minard, Rosemary. (ed.) *Womenfolk and Fairy Tales.* Illus. Suzanna Klein. Boston: Houghton Mifflin, 1975. (Ages 7–10.)
Females are the major characters in all of the stories in this book. They are not all unstereotypic, but they do, in general, exhibit such qualities as intelligence, courage, and ingenuity. The introduction is a valuable addition to the tales themselves.

Mizumura, Kazue. *If I Were a Mother.* New York: Crowell, 1968. (Ages 4–7.)
A look at many different animal mothers for clues as to what a human mother would do.

Mosel, Arlene. *The Funny Little Woman.* New York: Dutton, 1972. (All ages.) (Caldecott Medal and Children's Book Showcase.)
This story is about a woman who is very content making dumplings and who laughs all the time — habits that get her into and out of trouble.

Myers, Walter. *The Dragon Takes a Wife.* Illus. Ann Grifalconi. New York: Xerox Education Publications, 1972. (Ages 7–9.)

Harry, the dragon, takes lessons from Mabel Mae, the good fairy, so that he can vanquish a knight. He does so, marries Mabel Mae, gets a good job at the post office, and never fights again.

Nash, Ogden. *A Boy Is a Boy*. Illus. Arthur Shilstone. New York: Franklin Watts, 1960. (Ages 9–11.)
A puppy is looking for his master, a little boy, and meets a host of animals who ask him to describe the creature called "boy" that the puppy wants to find. Terribly stereotypic descriptions.

Nathan, Dorothy. *Women of Courage*. Illus. Carolyn Cather. New York: Random House, 1964. (Ages 10–up.)
Biographies of five brave women: Susan B. Anthony, women's rights crusader, Jane Addams, social reformer who worked for the poor, Mary McLeod Bethune, educator of black children, Amelia Earhart, daring aviator, and Margaret Mead, anthropologist searching for the "secrets of human nature."

Neilson, Winthrop and Francis. *Seven Women: Great Painters*. Philadelphia: Chilton, 1969. (Ages 12–up.)
Serious critique of seven famous painters, from Angelica Kauffman to Georgia O'Keefe.

Ness, Evaline (compiler and illustrator). *Amelia Mixed the Mustard and Other Poems*. New York: Scribner's, 1975. (All ages.)
A collection of poems dedicated to all females. Each one of the poems has a heroine at its center. The mood is light; the poems are well selected.

Ness, Evaline. *Do You Have the Time, Lydia?* New York: Dutton, 1971. (Ages 5–8.)
Lydia and her brother live with their father, who is a florist. Lydia is a little dynamo. Her only problem is that she fails to complete most of what she begins. She is, however, sensitive to the feelings of others; and when she recognizes that her actions are irresponsible, she determines to change her ways — not to be less active, but to see her projects through to completion. The doctor and other characters in the book are Blacks; Lydia and her family are Whites.

———. *Sam Bangs and Moonshine*. New York: Holt, Rinehart and Winston, 1966. (Ages 3–7.)
Sam (Samantha) lives with her father near the ocean and has a very vivid imagination, which her father calls "moonshine." When a potential calamity is narrowly averted, Sam learns the difference between reality and "moonshine." Sam and her father have an excellent relationship. Respecting and accepting her special qual-

ities, he does not impair her individual nature. He also helps her to become better adjusted to her mother's death.

Noble, Iris. *Emmeline and Her Daughters: The Pankhurst Suffragettes.* New York: Messner, 1974. (Ages 12–up.)
Detailed story of the British Pankhurst family. The mother and three daughters were ardent and active fighters for women's rights.

Norton, Mary. *The Borrowers.* New York: Harcourt Brace Jovanovich, 1953. Pb. also. (Ages 8–up.)
The first of a series of books about little people called Borrowers who live under the floors and in the walls of human's houses. In this book, Arietty, an adventurous female, is taken out by her father to learn how to borrow — something usually done only by males.

O'Dell, Scott. *Island of the Blue Dolphins.* Boston: Houghton Mifflin, 1960. Pb. Dell. (Ages 10–up.) (Newbery Medal, ALA Notable.)
Karana, a young Native American girl, is alone on her home island after her tribe has left and her brother has been killed by wild dogs. She manages her own survival courageously for many years until, at last, she is rescued by missionaries.

————. *Sing Down the Moon.* Boston: Houghton Mifflin, 1970. Pb. Dell. (Ages 7–up.) (Newbery Honor Book.)
A courageous young Navajo woman experiences all sorts of dangers: she is kidnapped by Spaniards, endures the Long Walk to Fort Sumner, and manages to return, with her husband and child, to their original home. The story focuses on the character of the young woman rather than on the hardships of the Navajos.

Ortiz, Victoria. *Sojourner Truth, A Self-Made Woman.* Philadelphia: Lippincott, 1974. (Ages 12–up.)
In reading the story of this remarkable black woman, much history is learned. The link between the feminist and abolitionist movement is described. Sojourner Truth, a pioneer for the cause of black civil rights, vigorously fought for her people until her death.

Parish, Peggy. *Amelia Bedelia.* Illus. Fritz Siebel. New York: Harper & Row, 1963. Pb. Scholastic. (Ages 5–8.)
A humorous story about a maid who takes all her orders literally and almost ruins the household. She is an object rather than a person. She usually is forgiven all of her clumsiness when she bakes something delicious.

Paustovsky, Konstantin. *The Magic Ringlet.* Translated by Thomas Whitney. Reading, Mass.: Addison-Wesley, 1971. (Ages 6–10.)
A young Russian girl lives with her sick grandfather. She is given a

magic ring that will bring her happiness and her grandfather health, but she loses it — and persistently tries to find it in a snowy forest.

Peck, Ellen. *How to Get a Teen-Age Boy and What to Do with Him When You Get Him.* New York: Bernard Geis, 1969. Pb. Avon. (Ages 12–up.)
A practical guide on how to attract a teen-age boy and be a "successful" teen-age girl, with specific clues as to what shampoo to use and how to put on makeup.

Penny, Grace Jackson. *Moki.* Boston: Houghton Mifflin, 1960. Pb. Avon. (Ages 8–12.)
Moki, a ten-year-old Cheyenne girl is dissatisfied doing "women's work," but she is put down every time that she tries to assert herself. This does not stop her, though. In the end she is awarded an honor rarely given to women.

Perl, Lila. *That Crazy April.* New York: Seabury Press, 1974. (Ages 9–12.)
Eleven-year-old Cress's mother is very much involved in the women's movement. Her father cheerfully participates in the maintenance of the house, and supports his wife's interests. Cress resents her mother's activities. In the end she realizes that she will develop her own interests and personality and will learn to survive on her own terms. The book is not a potential classic, but it raises interesting questions.

Pfeffer, Susan Beth. *The Beauty Queen.* Garden City, N.Y.: Doubleday, 1974. (Ages 12–up.)
A girl is coerced by her mother to enter the local beauty contest. She wins the titles of Miss Great Oakes and Miss Harrison County. After much thought, she realizes that being a beauty queen has no real meaning for her; she rejects her titles and the values they represent.

Phillips, Lynn. *Exactly Like Me.* Chapel Hill, N.C.: Lollipop Power, 1972. (Ages 3–8.)
A young girl will not permit herself to be boxed in by stereotypes. The writing in this little book leaves much to be desired, but the message is a useful one.

Reavin, Sam. *Hurray for Captain Jane!* Illus. Emily Arnold McCully. New York: Parents' Magazine Press, 1971. (Ages 5–8.) (Children's Book Showcase.)
Jane, the protagonist, goes on a fantasy ocean voyage while she is taking a bath. The captain of the ship, she saves the ship from crashing into an iceberg. When she awakens from her fantasy, she plans to pilot a plane for her next adventure.

Reit, Seymour, and Goldman, Louis. *A Week in Hagar's World: Israel.* London: Macmillan, 1969. (Ages 5–8.)

A week in the life of a little Jewish girl who lives in a Kibbutz in Israel, illustrated beautifully by photographs. The nonsexist aspects of Kibbutz life are displayed.

Rich, Gibson. *Firegirl*. Illus. Charlotte Purrington Farley. Old Westbury, N.Y.: Feminist Press, 1972. (Ages 8–12.)
A girl has ambition to become a fire fighter and learns all about what it takes to realize this goal.

Rizzo, Ann. *The Strange Hocket Family*. Old Westbury, N.Y.: Feminist Press, 1974. (Ages 6–10.)
A self-conscious story in which male and female roles are absolutely reversed, and the "normal" stereotype is made to look peculiar.

Rockwell, Harlow. *My Doctor*. New York: Macmillan, 1973. (Ages 3–7.)
Description of a regular medical checkup, and the doctor is a woman. The description is matter-of-fact; the message is not intrusive.

Rodgers, Mary. *Freaky Friday*. New York: Harper & Row, 1972. Pb. also. (Ages 10–up.)
A girl magically turns into her mother for a day and sees herself from a new perspective.

Rothman, Joel. *I Can Be Anything You Can Be*. New York: Scroll Press, 1973. (Ages 5–9.)
This book is an open-ended argument between a girl and a boy revolving around the taunt "I can be anything you can be." It is unfortunate that the action revolves around a competition.

Rubinger, Michael. *I Know an Astronaut*. Illus. Joel Snyder. New York: Putnam's, 1972. (Ages 6–9.)
Uncle Bill, an astronaut, takes his nephew Tommy to the Space Center for a tour and a simulated trip to the moon. Women are excluded completely in this book — they are not even pictured in the Space Center.

Sachs, Marilyn. *Peter and Veronica*. Illus. Louis Glanzman. Garden City, N.Y.: Doubleday, 1969. Pb. Dell. (Ages 8–12.)
Peter and Veronica are good friends despite their differences of sex, religion, and social acceptability and despite pressures exerted by parents and peers. They finally realize that good friendship can sometimes be very painful. Veronica is strong, pugnacious, and awkward. She begins to change in physical appearance but does not want that to affect her relationship with people.

Sarah, Becky. *Fanshen the Magic Bear*. Illus. Dana Smith. Stanford, Calif.: New Seed Press, 1973. (Ages 6–10.)

Laura is the rent collector for a very rich, lazy, unkind king. She does not like her job and knows that people cannot afford to pay their rent; she is helped to change this by Fanshen the Magic Bear. A thin, not very well presented story.

Sawyer, Ruth. *Roller Skates.* Illus. V. Angelo. New York: Viking, 1936. Pb. Dell. (Ages 9–12.) (Newbery Medal.)
Lucinda is the lively, bouncy heroine of this story. The episodes take place in very upper-class old New York. Lucinda is unusual for her time but beautifully in tune with today.

Scoppetone, Sandra, and Fitzhugh, Louise. *Suzuki Beane.* Illus. Louise Fitzhugh. Garden City, N.Y.: Doubleday, 1961. (Ages 7–10.)
Supposedly the story of two children, one from a "beatnik" family, the other from a "square" family. The two children are not really valued by their families. The solution that Suzuki and Henry arrive at is the happy ending in the book, but dangerous for real life — they run away together. The language is supposedly that of the "beatnik" crowd. A glossary is provided for the uninitiated reader. Words such as *swing, split, shuck,* and *hang-up* are defined.

Scott, Ann Herbert. *Sam.* Illus. Symeon Shimin. New York: McGraw-Hill, 1967. (Ages 3–8.)
Sam wants to play, but his mother, father, sister and brother all send him away — they are too busy. When Sam begins to cry, they all realize the cause of his unhappiness. Mother finds a task for him: she helps him learn how to bake a raspberry tart. Beautiful illustrations. Loving, aware family. Child permitted to cry, not criticized. Nonsexist task for him.

Seed, Suzanne. *Saturday's Child — 36 Women Talk About Their Jobs.* Chicago: J. Philip O'Hara, 1973. Pb. Bantam. (Ages 11–up.)
Thirty-six women who have had successful careers in architecture, theatre, law, carpentry, science, and so on, talk about their training, how they chose their jobs, and how their jobs affect their families.

Segal, Lore. *Tell Me a Mitzi.* Illus. Harriet Pincus. New York: Farrar, Straus & Giroux, 1970. (Ages 5–8.)
The three stories describe a contemporary Jewish family living in New York City. The males are subtly valued over the females in these stories, although that is not the intention of the author. Mitzi is a competent child, but Jacob is even more so for his age. Mitzi's mother almost never takes off her apron, and does nothing but housework. Mitzi's father participates in the house and also takes the children for outings. The relationship is a loving one except that the family expects the mother to ignore her own illness and to care

for them. Luckily the grandmother is available to nurse them when they are all ill. Too many stereotypes mar the essentially positive message of the story.

Sharmat, Marjorie Weinman. *Gladys Told Me to Meet Her Here.* Illus. Edward Frascino. New York: Harper & Row, 1970. (Ages 3–8.)
Irving is the narrator. He and Gladys are best friends. He arrives first for a meeting with Gladys and is concerned because she is late. Gladys is obviously an active, alert child. She and Irving have a friendship that is not based on sex roles. The story could have been narrated by a girl; the events could stay the same. Except for one negative reference to nurses, this is a nonsexist book.

Shulevitz, Uri. *Rain Rain Rivers.* New York: Farrar, Straus & Giroux, 1969. (Ages 5–8.)
The author-illustrator poetically describes the positive effects of rain. The central character is an active and responsible girl. A boy could also have been this central character. The fact that it is a girl creates a positive basis for young readers' sex-role redefinition.

Simon, Norma. *I Know What I Like.* Illus. Dora Leder. Chicago: Albert Whitman, 1971. (Ages 3–7.)
Integrated pictures. Children like all kinds of different things; unfortunately, boys and girls are pictured in somewhat stereotypic situations.

Simon, Seymour. *A Tree on Your Street.* Illus. Betty Fraser. New York: Holiday House, 1973. (Ages 6–9.)
A group of children, both boys and girls, studying the trees in their neighborhood, learn about the leaves, the bark, the variety of trees, and the animals that live in trees.

Sorensen, Virginia. *Miracles on Maple Hill.* Illus. B. and J. Krush. New York: Harcourt, Brace, 1956. Pb. also. (Ages 9–12.) (Newbery Medal.)
Marly and her family move to Maple Hill. Although Marly is an active, lively heroine, the characters have very sex-stereotyped expectations and behaviors. The story is a conventional but well-written one, demonstrating how the simple qualities and simple life are the best.

————. *Plain Girl.* Illus. C. Geer. New York: Harcourt, Brace, 1956. Pb. Scholastic. (Ages 9–11.) (Wel-Met Award.)
Esther is a member of an Amish family. The story revolves around the conflict between the teachings of her group and the rest of the world. Esther is a strong heroine because she struggles to think for herself and to make decisions about how she will behave.

Speare, Elizabeth George. *The Witch of Blackbird Pond.* Boston: Houghton Mifflin, 1958. Pb. Dell. (Ages 12–up.) (Newbery Medal.)
Kit Tyler, orphaned as a young teen-ager, decides to leave her native island of Barbados to live with her maternal aunt, Puritan uncle, and two female cousins. Kit's upbringing has been aristocratic, and she has unquestioningly owned slaves. She has also been educated and encouraged to lead an active life. The role of the female in Colonial days, as well as the impact of politics and religion, is dramatically described in this book. The women in it are individuals, as are all the characters. Although the characterizations are not stereotypic, the males emerge as stronger and more highly valued. Nevertheless the book is excellent.

Steiner, Charlotte. *Tomboy's Doll.* New York: Lothrop, Lee and Shepard, 1969. (Ages 6–up.)
Tommy, whose real name is Marie Louise, is a tomboy. Her mother hopes to change Tommy's behavior by giving her a doll. At first Tommy uses the doll very creatively as a scarecrow and shuttlecock, among others. But the "happy" ending consists of Tommy's bowing to convention, and permitting her true feminine nature to emerge. A *very* sexist book.

Sukowiecki, Sandra Lucas. *Joshua's Day.* Illus. Patricia Reilly Vevitrall. Chapel Hill, N.C.: Lollipop Power, 1972. (Ages 3–6.)
Contemporary story of a single working mother and her son's experience in a city day-care center.

Supraner, Robyn. *Think About It, You Might Learn Something.* Illus. Sandy Kossin. Boston: Houghton Mifflin, 1973. (Ages 8–12.)
Written as a personal journal. Jennifer presents episodes of her life and her private thoughts about what it is like to be a preadolescent daughter, sister, relative, and friend.

Talmadge, Marian, and Gilmore, Iris. *Emma Edmonds, Nurse and Spy.* New York: Putnam's, 1970. (Ages 10–12.)
The authors describe the heroine as if she were a transvestite. Women are not valued. The story seems to revolve around Emma's lifelong efforts to be a man. It is a surprise when she marries, and there are severel other inadequately explained events. Not nearly so useful a book as Hoehling's biography of the same person.

Taves, Isabella. *Not Bad for a Girl.* New York: M. Evans, 1972. (Ages 10–up.)
The true story of a little girl who prefers to play baseball than to play with dolls. Though the coaches object, her father takes her side.

Taylor, Mark. *Jennie Jenkins.* Illus. Glen Rounds. Boston: Little, Brown, 1975. (Ages 6–10.)

Jennie is described as an unusual girl. She is honest, hard-working, and disdains "normal" feminine behavior. The other females are "typical." Although the book is patterned from the folk-song "Jennie Jenkins" and attempts broad humor, the message communicated is one of derision of women. No such message is intended, but the humor is misplaced.

Terris, Susan. *Amanda the Panda and the Redhead.* Illus. Emily McCully. Garden City, N.Y.: Doubleday, 1975. (Ages 3-8.)
The family functions in an equitable, unself-conscious manner. Father and mother both cook, clean, and nurture children. Clothing of mother, teacher, and children is comfortable.

Thane, Elswyth. *Dolley Madison: Her Life and Times.* New York: Macmillan, 1970. (Ages 12-up.)
An interesting description, not only of Dolley Madison, but also of the times she lived in and of several of the famous people she knew. Many details of life during the early development of America are described. Although not a complete description of the era, it should interest serious students sufficiently to lead them to further reading.

Thayer, Jane. *Quiet on Account of Dinosaur.* New York: Morrow, 1965. (Ages 5-8.)
A girl loves studying dinosaurs and grows up to be a scientist, museum director, and dinosaur-expert.

Thomas, Marlo; Steinem, Gloria; and Pogrebin, Letty Cottin. *Free to Be You and Me.* New York: McGraw-Hill, 1974. Pb. also. (All ages.)
Collection of stories, poems, and songs dealing with people's potential to become whatever they want to become.

Travers, P. L. *Mary Poppins.* Illus. Mary Shepard. New York: Harcourt, Brace, and World, 1934. (Ages 9-11.)
The story of four children and their new nanny, Mary Poppins, who has magical powers and takes them on all sorts of fantastic adventures. The Banks household is sexist, and some of the episodes clearly display a "white man's burden" attitude. But Mary Poppins is decidedly not a stereotypic female.

Udry, Janice May. *Mary Jo's Grandmother.* Illus. Eleanor Mill. Chicago: Albert Whitman, 1970. (Ages 5-8.)
One snowy Christmas, Mary Jo visits her old but independent grandmother, who lives alone in the country. When her grandmother has an accident, Mary Jo gets help. Both Mary Jo and her grandmother are capable females.

Ungerer, Tomi. *No Kiss for Mother.* New York: Harper & Row, 1973. (Ages 6-12.)

Piper resents his doting mother's constant concern, help, and kissing. He finally yells at her for showing affection to him in front of his friends. She responds by striking him. Piper realizes his mother's concern and buys her flowers, which she receives, resisting an appreciative embrace. Too bad that she capitulates, and encourages her son in his unfeeling sex-stereotype.

Vestly, Anne-Cath. *Hello Aurora.* Illus. Leonard Kessler. Translated by Eileen Amos; adapted by Jane Fairfax. New York: Crowell, 1974. (Ages 7-10.)
A very didactic but charming story about a Norwegian family. Mother is a lawyer. Father, who is studying for his doctorate, stays home with Aurora, the young daughter, and Socrates, the baby. The father is not tremendously adept, but he and Aurora manage fairly well. The neighbors disapprove of the arrangement, and Aurora is uncomfortable; but the reader is totally drawn into the situation. Many values are stated in the book. The parents are too good; the world is too one-sidedly different from them — but the book is useful, nevertheless.

Waber, Bernard. *Ira Sleeps Over.* Boston: Houghton Mifflin, 1972. Pb. Scholastic. (Ages 4-8.) (Children's Book Showcase.)
Ira does not bring his teddy bear when he goes to sleep at his friend's house. He finds out when he gets there that his friend has a teddy bear, too. Nicely supportive of children and their feelings.

———. *Nobody's Perfect.* Boston: Houghton Mifflin, 1971. (Ages 5-8.)
A series of small humorous incidents involving friendship between girls and boys.

Wagner, Jane. *J.T.* Illus. G. Parks, Jr. New York: Van Nostrand Reinhold, 1969. Pb. Dell. (Ages 8-12.)
J.T. is a boy growing up in Harlem with his mother. Through his attachment for a scrawny cat, J.T. expresses his feelings and sensitivity for all the people in his life. He hates fighting and craves affection.

Warren, Ruth. *A Pictorial History of Women in America.* New York: Crown, 1975. (Ages 10-up.)
A useful overview of the role of women in America's development. The book focuses on the women rather than the historical context. Many women are included. The text is interesting and well written.

Weisner, William. *Turnabout.* New York: Seabury Press, 1972. (Ages 6-10.)
Old Norwegian folk tale about a husband and wife who trade jobs. Husband botches everything, while the wife does well, and the

husband promises never again to say he works harder. If both people were competent, the story would be better. This book is sexist because it degrades men.

Werth, Kurt, and Watts, Mabel. *Molly and the Giant.* New York: Parents' Magazine Press, 1973. (Ages 5–8.)
Molly outwits a giant and is brave and clever enough to get herself and her sisters married to three princes in this modern tale. Perhaps some day there will be a different happy ending.

White, E. B. *Charlotte's Web.* Illus. Garth Williams. New York: Harper & Row, 1952. Pb. Dell. (Ages 3–8.) (Newbery Honor Book.)
Charlotte, a clever and witty spider, saves the life of her "true friend" Wilbur, the pig, in this story of a deep friendship. Fern, the human female protagonist, changes from a girl interested in animals to a girl interested in boys — one of the only flaws in this beautiful book.

Wilder, Laura Ingalls. *Little House in the Big Woods* and *Little House on the Prairie.* Illus. Helen Sewell. New York: Harper & Row, 1932 and 1935. (Ages 6–11.)
The first two books in a series about a little girl growing up with her family and leading an interesting frontier life. The women, who actually lived, are accurately portrayed. Although victims of their time, they display courage and strength.

Williams, Jay. *Petronella.* Illus. Friso Menstra. New York: Parents' Magazine Press, 1973. (Ages 5–8.)
Petronella, the youngest of three children, sets off to seek her fortune and rescue a prince. She finds a prince, but it turns out he is really just a parasite dependent on the enchanter at whose house he is staying. Petronella ends up marrying the wise, kind enchanter rather than the nitwit prince.

———. *The Practical Princess.* Illus. Friso Menstra. New York: Parents' Magazine Press, 1969. (Ages 5–8.)
A turnabout fairy tale: Princess Bedelia is intelligent, brave, active, kills a dragon, and rescues an enchanted prince from a wicked sorcerer. All the men in this story are incompetent and ignorant. This is a sexist story because it humiliates and downgrades men.

Wood, James Playsted. *Emily Elizabeth Dickinson.* Nashville: Thomas Nelson, 1972. (Ages 11–up.)
A personalized biography of the poet, emphasizing the mystery of Emily's choosing to remain, for the last years of her life, inside her house. The description of Amherst during the nineteenth century adds flavor to the book.

Yolen, Jane. *The Emperor and the Kite.* Illus. Ed Young. Cleveland: World, 1967. (Ages 5-8.) (Caldecott Honor Book.)
Loyal Djeow Seow rescues her father, the Emperor, who has been captured by evil men and locked in a high tower. Written in a poetic style, it is a story of a girl's love, courage, and ingenuity.

———. *The Girl Who Cried Flowers and Other Tales.* Illus. D. Palladini. New York: Crowell, 1974. (Ages 8-11.) (National Book Award Finalist.)
Three of these five tales have female protagonists. They are far from traditional: one contains a wise and frostily silent queen; one has a woman who takes upon herself the burden of designing the world's fate; one is destroyed by her desire to please.

———. *The Girl Who Loved the Wind.* Illus. Ed Young. New York: Crowell, 1972. (Ages 5-8.) (Children's Book Showcase.)
Danina is kept from the outside world by her father, who wants to protect her from all sad things. But despite the garden wall, Danina hears the wind's voice and eventually accepts the wind's challenge to discover the world for herself.

———. *The Magic Three of Solatia.* Illus. Julia Noonan. New York: Crowell, 1974. (Ages 10-up.)
Sianna is a wise and strong and active heroine. The reader sees her grow from childhood into womanhood, retaining all of these qualities. These imaginative stories sustain a poetic and folkloric quality that is very satisfying.

———. *Pirates in Petticoats.* Illus. Leonard Vosburgh. New York: David McKay, 1963. (Ages 10-up.)
An engagingly written series of descriptions of female pirates. Interesting from a historical view. The book is in need of some updating but is, nevertheless, worth reading.

Young, Eleanor R. *Mothers, Mothers, Mothers.* Illus. Nancy Fuller. Minneapolis: T. S. Denison, 1971. (Ages 5-8.)
An attempt at conveying a universal and multiethnic image of mothers. Unfortunately, it confirms stereotypes, and ignores the father altogether.

Zolotow, Charlotte. *The Summer Night.* Illus. Ben Shecter. New York: Harper & Row, 1974. (Ages 4-8.)
When a little girl cannot sleep, her father tries all kinds of remedies for her sleeplessness and finally accompanies her on a walk. The father is tender and understanding. The reader assumes that the mother is absent because of death, divorce, or temporary reasons. It

would have been far more effective as a nonsexist book if the mother had been at home and the father had still behaved in this way.

————. *William's Doll.* Illus. William Pene duBois. New York: Harper & Row, 1972. (Ages 3–8.)

William likes to do "male" things, such as sports and trains, but he also wants a doll. His father, brother, and friends (male) are perturbed by this. No mother is included in the story. Grandmother comes to his rescue by getting him a doll and explaining that he can practice for the time when he becomes a father himself. This book will serve as the basis for much discussion.

NOTES and ADDITIONS

10

Using Children's Books in a Reading Program

TEACHING CHILDREN to read can be the most reward-ing of all teaching experiences. To see the "aha" of discovery as they make the connection between the written symbols and language as they know it is worth all the planning and time that the teacher must expend. This initial linking of the written symbol with meaningful language is called "decod-ing." Many workable, effective systems and approaches are available for helping children acquire decoding ability. No single approach is the best; all are potentially successful.

The more advanced skills of reading are introduced and reinforced either at the same time that decoding skills are acquired or after students are somewhat comfortable and facile at recognizing the written symbols. These more advanced skills include comprehension, recall of detail, recall of sequence, ascertaining the author's intent, evaluating information, appreciating style, classifying, telling the difference between opinion and fact, and inference. A good reader also appreciates a variety of kinds of books. There are many subcategories and levels of these more advanced skills, but most educators agree that these critical thinking/reading skills form the essential basis of an education.

When reading is taught in a conventional manner, three "ability" groups are probably formed at the beginning of the semester, each group using a different level book from the same publisher's series, each group progressing at a given pace, answering the same questions, using the same vocabulary, and filling in the same workbook pages. The procedure is essentially the same for every reading period. All the groups do reading at the same time. The teacher divides his or her time equally among all the groups each day. While the teacher works with one group, the other two groups are occupied with workbooks or with answering the questions predetermined by the teacher's manual for that text, or with performing the exercises recommended by the same manual. At the end of a unit, the publisher often provides a test to see whether or not the children have successfully completed that section of the text. If the students do not pass the test, they generally repeat all of the reading that they have just completed. Sometimes they must move to the lower group when they fail the test, because they cannot be placed in a special group and obviously cannot keep up with the group in which they were originally placed. Or else, if a number of children have failed the test, those children who have passed it must either wait until their group-mates catch up with them again or, less frequently, leap to the more advanced group.

The standard procedure for a reading lesson in such a program includes guided silent reading. The children read an assigned portion of an assigned story in order to answer assigned questions. For those children who complete both the reading and the questions before the teacher is ready for them, there may be extra work in the form of more questions; or they may play a game, do their homework, or be permitted to read books other than their texts. The implication is, that after their "real" work, they may do extra, less educational activities.

The assumptions underlying this conventional approach include a reliance upon the expertise of a publisher's staff to diagnose and prescribe for the reading needs of any given group of children. It is also assumed that the stories in the books are appropriate for all the children using the texts. The stories are usually read in the sequence in which they occur in the book, leading to the expectation that a collection of stories must be read in order. While timing is not specifically prescribed, all the children are expected to complete at least one full book — ideally the one on their grade level — during the semester.

Indifference or outright dislike of a story can cause a child to read it badly. A story that is unappealing to a child can lead to that child's being perceived as a poor reader. Sometimes the fact that the child has been called away from an attractive activity to "do reading" leads to a poor performance of that particular reading lesson.

In some conventional approaches, comprehension skills are generally equated with simple recall and with locational skills. When a question is asked about a reader's opinion, there is usually an expected right answer. Rarely is there a question in the manual that does not have a correct answer supplied to the teacher; open-ended questions are not regularly included. Children are discouraged from expressing their real opinions about anything because they risk being chastised or penalized for a wrong or unexpected answer. A criticism or an expressed dislike of a story is sometimes viewed as an attack upon the whole reading program rather than as an exercise of critical reading skills. In this way these well-intentioned texts can discourage the very skills that they purport to teach.

Word attack skills are sometimes handled in a fashion that blocks their acquisition. Most publishers' series rely on a particular sequence and style of word analysis, some advocating a strongly phonic approach, some devoting their attention to a patterning or linguistic approach. Others recommend a combination of sight word memorization, phonics, structural analysis, and context clues. All these techniques are useful for certain children at some point, but the prescribed sequence and required focus is sometimes totally inappropriate for a substantial number of children.

Conforming to the expectations of any given series can create problems — the child who cannot keep up with the rest of the class, or the children who become discipline problems because of their reading difficulties. Concerned teachers try to form more and more ability groups composed of children who do not fit into any of the three established groups. They become increasingly more frustrated by the illogic of treating every child in the same fashion despite each child's obvious differences.

In any given classroom, if only one series is used and if it is used in a rigid, narrowly structured fashion, it too often occurs that children learn to dislike, and to be bored by, reading. They also learn to view reading as a time of day and a set of unpleasant practices rather than as a process, a convenience, and a possible source of pleasure. They become dependent upon directions from the teacher rather than upon themselves as independent readers. Many classroom teachers, also bored by the procedure, recognize that the children are not acquiring the skills appropriate to good reading. But the readers have good stories in them; they can comfortably be used as resources and options for children to select, in the same way that library books are. The skills can be learned from them when they are self-selected by the children.

▶ Try This

Select three different sets of materials, each published by a different publisher. The three sets should each represent a different approach to word attack (phonic, linguistic, whole word, eclectic, or others). Select one teacher's manual and accompanying child's text for each of the three approaches, each aiming at the same grade level. Use the following questions as a guideline for examining the texts. The purpose of this exercise is to demonstrate that there is more than one single correct way to teach skills. It is also to help you analyze the procedures for teaching reading.

1. What does the manual say is the purpose of the series? (You can usually find the intent in the first chapter of the teacher's edition.)

2. Search for evidence in the lesson plans that the publisher is accomplishing the stated purpose. How well do you believe they have done it?

3. What are the skills stressed in this series?

4. How do the lessons accomplish the teaching of the skills?

5. How comfortable is the format of the teacher's manual? How specific are the instructions to the teacher? How convenient is the organization for you? How easy is it for you to locate the skills expectations and the recommendations for teaching them?

6. How does the publisher recommend that the series be geared to individual differences?

7. What kind of content does the book present? Are there several authors, or one? How varied are the literary forms? Are there poems, plays, folk tales, biography, fiction, etc.?

8. How varied are the characters in the stories? What kinds of representations are there of lower classes, rural and urban children, minority cultures, unusual life styles, and foreign cultures?

9. How well does the text handle racism, sexism, violence, war, and other important social issues?

10. Compare the three series that you have examined in terms of your opinion of their advantages and disadvantages.

Publishers have begun in recent years to recognize and acknowledge the competence of the classroom teacher. They also are recognizing the importance of using a diversity of materials. These publishers are, therefore, producing programs that use many different books rather than rely on the basic text. Some of the more widely used of these new series are the Scholastic and Random House Individualized programs, and the James Moffett *Interaction* series, published by Houghton Mifflin. These series encourage teacher intervention and management, and student self-evaluation and management. It is becoming more and more accepted that an effective reading program must be personalized and individualized.

Principles of This Reading Program

Two principles govern an effective individualized or personalized reading program. *Self-selection* and *self-evaluation* are necessary ingredients of any approach that aims to meet the skills and interest needs of the students. Self-selection involves the students' selecting whatever reading they wish to use to help themselves learn to read better. The students are first made aware that the program is aimed at a constant growth in reading ability and that they are each responsible for aiding in that process. The fact that they choose their own reading materials insures that they are interested. Their responses to the reading that they have selected are encouraged, taking the form of critical and analytic evaluation. If a student dislikes a book, the opinion is seen as valid and, therefore, to be respected. Not an attack on the system, it is, rather, an indication that the system is working.

Choice of reading material implies a different book for almost every child; it therefore follows that there is no expectation of uniformity of rate. Each child, reading at a separate pace, finishes a different number of books at any given time from the other children. Since the pages are of different length and format, it is difficult, if not impossible, to compete with other children in terms of speed of reading. The learning of reading, therefore, becomes a question of individual interest rather than of group conformity.

All kinds of skills come into use when the students must exercise their own judgment about the reading material that they will use. Of course, the teacher remains the final arbiter and is usually an influence on the child, but the goal is to have the children assume the greatest responsibility possible. The students in this sort of program recognize that reading is necessary, not only as a school goal but as a life tool as well.

SELF-SELECTION

Each child selects what he or she wishes to use to learn to read better. One of the potential discomforts for teachers in a program in which the students and teachers engage in a learning partnership is that teachers feel the need to have read everything first. They wonder how else they will know if the student is giving the "right" answer to a comprehension question. After the experience of having had a manual supply them with all of the correct answers, it is sometimes difficult to move immediately to a system that has no visible keys to the answers. They soon recognize, however, that the questions they ask invite a process to be displayed; the answer can be right even if the details are wrong. For example, when a teacher asks a child to tell about the story, and the plot sounds coherent, sequenced, and logical, the teacher can assess that the child has no problems in sequencing or in retelling a story. Then, perhaps, another child reading the same story relates an entirely different accounting of the plot. A logical activity would then be for the teacher to have the two children come together to talk about what they have read. The teacher may be motivated to read the book as a result of the discrepancy, and a three-way conversation can ensue. A group of additional children may become interested in the story, with several interesting conversations as the result. Even if one of the original readers of the story had at first totally misunderstood it, the potential learning is far more valuable than the initial right answer. After all, if a person is asked to summarize a story, it is the procedure of recalling the story, assessing the situations, and culling from this what the major theme is — according to the understanding of the reader — that is evidence of important skills acquisition. Any reasonable answer demonstrating this process can be accepted and discussed. There are many ideas contained within any work of any complexity. And if the answer that the child gives does not sound reasonable, the teacher can always ask the student to elaborate.

▶ Try This

Go to a children's library and ask three children to relate to you the plots of books they have recently completed. Read the books; then compare the children's answers with the ones that you would have given.

One of the values of this sort of program includes the learning that children can take part in with each other. They can stimulate interest, raise questions, and interact in a lively fashion. How often in a conventional reading program does this kind of discussion take place? Further, the questions and ideas raised by the books published for children today are far more challenging than the questions suggested by the designers of the teachers' manuals. Teachers would do well to encourage the sort of thinking these books foster.

Another question raised by the practice of permitting children to select their own reading is that of accumulating enough materials so that children will have sufficient reading materials to choose from. This is one of the most easily accomplished aspects of the program. One of the means of initiating the change is to call the children together to ask what sorts of reading materials they can suggest that will be useful in the classroom to help teach them to read better. The children will volunteer such suggestions as magazines, library books, newspapers, catalogs, comic books, cereal boxes, signs, telephone books, instructions for games, paperback books, and all sorts of other books, such as cookbooks, manuals, social studies texts, reference books, and others. All these suggestions are useful and can be very productive in a reading program. But the bulk of the reading will probably be done with books that the children can select from the library, from their collections at home, or from the numerous paperback book clubs available to school children. Even in communities that have a very low economic level, the libraries can supply a sufficient variety in order to meet the needs of the children. Regular trips to the library can yield six books per child. This provides enough of a supply to satisfy the children's reading appetites.

Teachers initiating the individualized program worry about the students' appropriate acquisition of skills. They wonder how they can manage to mount a skills program without the benefit of a manual. The first task of a teacher, in this case, is to compile a list of skills, which can be gleaned from manuals, from texts aimed at the teaching of reading, from curriculum guides, or from the lists circulated by the publishers. Once this list has been secured, the teacher can duplicate the list for all of the children; then, as the skills are encountered and acquired, the teacher and the children check them off. Since skills can be acquired with any reading matter, there are no established sequences or specific vocabularies necessary. Thus children can practice word attack, comprehension, and oral interpretation skills using materials that they enjoy and at their own pace.

The key competence for the teacher to develop here is that of informal diagnosis. The teacher must learn to listen to a child read, observe the general reading behavior of the child, and make diagnoses. Then the teacher and child together can suggest prescriptions to satisfy the child's reading needs. The informal reading inventory familiar to many teachers is useful in this program: it involves a simple set of procedures. After the child selects any passage of approximately one hundred words, the teacher listens to the child read the passage aloud. During the reading, the teacher records the errors that the child makes. After the reading, the teacher and the child together look at the errors to compile a list of the strengths and needs the child has exhibited. Then, together they work out a program for responding to the reading needs.* (For those teachers who are uneasy about their competence in this area, this author has included in References several specific "how-to" resources.) Teachers should become comfortable about postponing direct instruction until several children exhibit the same need.

▶ Try This

Armed with a portable tape-recorder, find a child (a visit to the children's library or a classroom should prove fruitful). Ask the child to select a book and to choose a passage of approximately one hundred words. Tape-record the child's reading of this passage. After the child has finished, both of you read the passage again while listening to the tape. Then analyze the reading: mark the errors; note the strengths; list the needs. Ask the child what next steps may be feasible. Make some suggestions yourself. Decide what questions may be useful to determine the meaning of the story.

One of the temptations a teacher should resist in this sort of program is to ask the child to select a more difficult book if there seems to be no problem in word recognition. *There is no such thing as a book that is too easy!* It is up to the teacher to help the child practice the more complex reading skills if there seems to be no immediate need for word analysis practice. Skills of comprehension, oral performance, writing, and interpretation may be recommended. But the book itself is not too easy. How many of us as adults always read something that is mechanically difficult for us to manage? The mechanical aspects of reading are important, of course, but they are not the only skills needed.

However, there *is* such a thing as a book that is too difficult. If a child selects a book that is too arduous mechanically, the frustration encountered will impede any learning. Children should, therefore, be taught how to assess whether or not a book will be frustrating for them. If they look at a passage of one hundred words in any book they plan to select, and count on the fingers of one hand the errors they make when reading this passage silently, they can be taught to recognize that a book is likely

---

* Eldon E. Ekwall. *Locating and Correcting Reading Difficulties* (Columbus: Merrill, 1970), is an excellent paperback source to consult for aid in this process.

to be too hard if they make more errors than the fingers on one hand. If they encounter five or fewer errors, the book will probably be manageable. If they count more than five errors, they should be strongly encouraged to reject the book for the time being and to select another, more readable book.

SELF-EVALUATION

From the start, when a child is doing self-selection for a reading program and participating in the diagnostic procedure, that child is also doing self-evaluation. In a good individualized program, the child is aware of the necessity for self-evaluation. The children must be informed about reading skills, the questions raised in books, and the procedures useful for carrying out a program responding to reading needs. Children in this program have the responsibility of maintaining some records of their progress. They usually have some say in what sorts of records they will keep, what form they will take, and how the records will be used. The children not only help to evaluate their own progress, they also work with each other, sharing their reading and their reactions with each other and with the teacher. It is this taking of responsibility that is one of the most important features of the program.

Implementing the Program

The teacher would do well to gather the entire class together and involve the children in each new step. The accumulation of materials should be done only after the children have suggested what materials would be appropriate. The teacher should also lead the children in a discussion of the purposes of reading. Once the class knows that the reading program will be tailored to their ideas and needs, they participate in it actively and enthusiastically. Engaging in discussions about the books they are reading, they recommend books to each other. The organization of the program can vary; but it is useful if certain activities, such as teacher/ student conferences, small-group instruction, and sharing, are built in.

KINDS OF GROUPS

An individualized reading program involves more kinds of groupings than does a conventional one. There is no need, however, for any permanent groups. The reasons for grouping are varied in this program. Sometimes a temporary group is formed because it has been established that all the children in this particular group share a next step. The teacher and the children may decide that it would be useful to practice initial consonant blends. Or a group may meet together because they have all been reading stories about war, for example, and would like to compare their reading. Perhaps a group will meet in order to write, practice, and present a play on a book that all have read. Another may meet regularly to design and to paint a mural depicting a segment of a story that they all have read and wish to share with the rest of the class.

The teacher may feel that it is sometimes necessary to call together the entire class. Perhaps methods of book selection will be the topic of discussion, or the whole class may have exhibited the need for a session on record-keeping and its uses. Or the whole class may want to view a presentation that a small group has prepared. It is also likely that one or two children may want to perform some sort of reading in front of the entire group. The decisions are made jointly by the teacher and children.

The kinds of groupings include not only small instructional groups, interest groups, whole class groups, teacher-led groups, and child-led groups, but also the grouping of one child and reading material, one child teaching another, two children sharing an activity, and teacher and one child. Each of the groups is formed for a specific reason and lasts only as long as there is necessity for that particular structure. The teacher and one child usually meet together for a regularly scheduled conference, generally for the purpose of diagnosis. It is less efficient to teach one child when there is the likelihood that other children are ready for the same next step. Therefore, it is useful for the teacher and student to assess what next step may be appropriate and then, in subsequent conferences, to locate other children who are also ready. In this way, the conference serves as the primary diagnostic situation. The child comes to the conference with his or her records in hand; together, the teacher and child review the child's progress. Perhaps the teacher will have the child read aloud, or they may discuss the book. A recommendation for further work should come from the conference.

SCHEDULING

The children can participate actively in the management of a schedule by signing up for activities, by suggesting activities, by reminding each other of the time, and by maintaining the writing of the schedule. The schedule, which varies daily, is usually posted on a bulletin board or on the chalkboard. Sometimes it may be comfortable for the schedule to be somewhat set; for example, the class may decide to have reading every day from 9:30 to 11:00. Then they may want to divide that time into a half-hour for conferences, a half-hour for small-group instruction, and a half-hour for sharing. The conferences probably will require no more than five to ten minutes each if they are confined to diagnosis. The small groups will probably need ten to fifteen minutes of instruction each, and the sharing could include several presentations to the entire class. Another possible arrangement could include a general schedule posted for the entire day, with children and teacher inserting activities and signing up for times that are flexible and arranged on a day-to-day basis. However the schedule is managed, the purpose is to respond most closely to the needs of the children. The sharing time can also continue informally throughout the day. Discussions of issues, arguments, and mutual recommendations become general practices.

ROOM ARRANGEMENT

Once the teacher and the children have brought in all of the materials that they wish to use for the reading program, they can plan together how to arrange it in the room. Any sort of room is appropriate for this kind of program. A self-contained or open space, large or small room can be arranged conveniently to house the materials of an individualized reading approach. The children can establish the system as a permanent one or can change it every month. When the children are in charge, they care more about the maintenance of the area. What sort of arrangement they make is not important as long as the other children can locate materials; it is helpful if they post some chart indicating the arrangement. Sometimes the children place the books in order of size; sometimes they arrange them by color. More often, they choose to place them in order of difficulty or in interest categories. The process of categorizing is a valuable one no matter what the ultimate arrangement is. The students acquire a knowledge of the books available and expand their own reading interests in the process.

RECORD-KEEPING

Both the teacher and the children should maintain and use records. Records should serve as reporting devices to parents and interested observers, but they can also be used as reminders for the participants and as evaluative devices for the program. Records need not be uniform; they can vary throughout the semester according to the interests and needs of the participants. Each should be given the opportunity to decide what to include in her or his record. Most people want to include the date, the name of the reading, and some comments, while others want more specific indications of strengths, needs, and activities accomplished. Students usually find it interesting to keep a section of their records for special vocabulary work; they also may want to include a section on favorite books or characters or ideas. Whatever their records look like, they should be used whenever they have a conference with the teacher. Both teacher and children could attach a list of the reading skills as suggested by a manual, and they could regularly check off the skills accomplished during the week before.

Activities

The activities suitable for an individualized reading program are varied. The children read independently after having selected books that they are interested in. They maintain records, participate in diagnosis, engage in small-group instruction, help to teach some small groups, and share their reading with their classmates in as many interesting ways as they can think of. Some ideas for sharing books are as follows:

Opaque Projector	The illustrations or original drawings may be flashed on the wall and used as a background while parts of the story are narrated.
Original Poem	May be written to laud or describe a character in the book.
Outline of the Story	Choices in the area are a five-sentence outline; a series of ideas, an arrangement of questions or pictures in sequence, or movie scenes. These activities can be aided by the use of mural, movie rolls, slides, or posters.
Panel Discussion or Debates	Useful for evaluating plot, characters, and solutions, and for accepting and valuing differences of opinion.
Pantomime	The character is shown in action. The audience is urged to take part by telling what action is being performed and by whom.
Picture Album	If a student has difficulty in drawing, she or he may take pictures from magazines to show impressions of characters or scenes.
Puppets	Incidents may be portrayed, characters impersonated, or the story reported.
Exhibits or Collections	May be used with books that are of informational nature. Or books that are concerned with a particular issue may be

	placed on display, with comments written by students.
Bulletin Boards	Reviews, three-dimensional displays, eye-catching titles may attract students' attention, leading them to read.
(Simulated) Interview with the Author	If two students have read the same books, one can answer questions as the author, while the other poses as an interviewer. Or real authors may be invited.
Souvenirs	Any items that are connected with the topic or period dealt with in the book are an aid to reporting.
Photographs	Student-taken photographs of situations or scenes to illustrate the story can be used to arouse interest and to personalize the book.
Tableau	It is effective in presenting a story in which action is important. A series of "frozen" actions can convey many messages.
This Is Your Life	Personal events from the life of a character in the book can be interestingly reviewed in this manner. The author can also be the subject of this sort of presentation.
Twenty Questions	The sharer answers *yes* or *no* to the questions of the group. The children can try, in twenty questions, to guess the character's identity or the title of the book or the topic it deals with.
Vocabulary Lists	This technique may be employed for books that present entertaining dialogue, unusual terminology, or simply colorful words.
Posters	May be used to advertise the book, the characters, or the theme.
Portraits	A portrait of a favorite character may be drawn and framed. The author's description may be used as a guide. A gallery of portraits may be set up.

Book for a Day	The entire class or a group of children may wish to dress as characters in a book. They can portray the characters not only in dress but in actions and typical speech habits as well.
Making Slides	Incidents of stories may be shown on student-made slides. As the slides are shown, accompanying parts may be read or explanations given. The oral parts may be taped for more effectiveness.
Reading Log	Notes, pictures, and impressions that are related to the story or stories that a child has read may be organized creatively in a notebook or log. It is up to the child to develop it in a unique way.
Letters	Children may write letters to one of the characters in the book telling them of some particular incident. These letters can be mailed to the author.
	Appreciation letters or letters of inquiry can be written to the author, publisher, or illustrator.
Predictions	Students read a part of a book, then try to predict what will happen: how a problem will be solved or the kind of ending the author may write. They then complete their reading and compare endings with the author's. (You may like the students' solutions better than the authors'!)
Poems	The student writes a comment, summary, or impression of the book in the form of a limerick or poem.
Title Changes	Students write other titles for the book, make new dust jackets for each new title, and display them with the original on a bulletin board.
Story Changes	Students add a chapter to the story or rewrite the first or last chapter. They can also add new characters, present and solve new problems, or change key incidents.

Tests	Students write a brief test on the book. Five to ten questions are sufficient. Duplicate the tests, and let each child who reads the book take the test "for fun."
T.V. Games	Games based upon "What's My Line?", "I've Got a Secret," "Concentration," etc. Groups of students enjoy this and can write very entertaining commercials to amuse the audience.
Book Jackets	A child can design a jacket to reflect the message of the book.
Crossword Puzzle	A crossword puzzle using new words learned in a story can be constructed.
Mobiles	A mobile can be made with a coat-hanger and pictures of scenes in the book. They could be the child's own work or from magazines.
Map or Diagram	Books about treasure hunts and mystery lend themselves especially to this type of sharing.
Movie Roll	The child can take a roll of paper and draw a series of events from a book. These pictures can be shown individually through an opening in a box. It should look like a T.V. screen and can be of any size.
Book Salesman	A child tries to "sell" a book to another child or group of children. This is a good exercise in being persuasive and in analyzing people's interests.
Diorama	This is a three-dimensional representation of a scene. It is usually made in a box such as a shoe box. The figures and scenery are placed inside.
Headlines or Caption for a Newspaper Account	They should be short and to the point. The chapter titles can be changed to headlines or may be used to transform the story into a newspaper account.
Dramatization	Radio or television skit — this could be done by an individual or a group. It could

	be combined with murals, puppets, shadow-plays.
Appropriate Music for Story Theme	Many famous pieces of music have been inspired by children's stories, especially fairy tales. Children can select music which they feel reflects the mood of whatever they are reading. By creating a multi-arts experience themselves, they are in effect enhancing their own appreciation of both reading and music.
Dolls Dressed Like Characters	A child can make costumes for small dolls to represent a character.
Arrangement of Bookshelf of Similar Books	This can be done by an individual or by a group who has read the same book. Posters and pictures can be added.
Mural	This can be a group or class activity. The scene can be drawn or pasted on mural paper, or it can be done on a board with colored chalk.
Blurbs	These should be interest-arousers and not reveal too much of the plot. A collection of these can form a bulletin board display to serve as motivation for the class.
Autobiography	The student rewrites or tells the story from the viewpoint of one of the characters.
Oral Reading	The student reads aloud an interesting portion of the book. This helps develop oral reading proficiency as well as interest in the book.
Character Analysis	Which characters would the student like to have as a friend? Who has behaved most admirably? etc., etc.
New Information	The student reports any new words, concepts, information, attitudes learned from the reading.
Library Acquisitions	A group of students who have read a book give opinions on whether or not the book should be purchased for the classroom or school library.

A child who enjoys, and is interested in, reading books becomes a better reader. Children can usually influence and motivate each other more effectively than adults can; they will probably add other ideas to the list given above. Inventive teachers can adapt these ideas to their own class interests and abilities and invariably add many more.

This sort of approach to the teaching of reading attends to the goals of a wholesome, constructive educational process. In addition, it supports the lively exchange of opinions generated by the reading of varied books and engenders the reading and thinking habit for life.

REFERENCES

Abbott, Jerry L. "Fifteen Reasons Why Personalized Reading Instruction Does Not Work," *Elementary English*, Vol. 49, No. 1 (January 1972).
Urges readers to try a personalized program and demonstrates that it can and does work.

Aukerman, Robert C. *Approaches to Beginning Reading*. New York: Wiley, 1971.
An encyclopedia of beginning reading approaches. This book describes the published and informal methods and materials of teaching beginning reading. Materials are described; research is summarized; methodology is presented. An excellent reference.

Baily, A. V., and Housekeeper, G. "Does Individualized Reading Affect Other Subject Areas?" *Elementary English*, Vol. 49, No. 1 (January 1972), 37-43.
Bases research on a questionnaire aimed at getting teachers' day-by-day observations. Results summarized — the question the title asks is answered "yes — favorably."

Brogan, Peggy, and Fox, Lorene K. *Helping Children Read: A Practical Approach to Individualized Reading*. New York: Holt, Rinehart and Winston, 1961.
An excellent and practical text. Includes instructions on how to manage an individualized reading program from first grade through eighth. Useful for incorporating skills, management, and methodology.

Carlson, Ruth Kearney. *Literature for Children: Enrichment Ideas*. Dubuque, Iowa: William C. Brown, 1970.
Contains hundreds of activities that can be done with children to extend the impact of books.

Darrow, Helen F., and Howes, Virgil M. *Approaches to Individualized Reading*. New York: Appleton-Century-Crofts, 1960.
An excellent overview of the different approaches to individualized reading. Includes record-keeping techniques.

Decker, Isabelle M. *100 Novel Ways with Book Reports*. New York: Citation Press, 1969.
Includes a hundred ideas, complete with instructions, materials

needed, suggestions to the teacher, for sharing books. Also has bibliographies of writing aids, book lists, critical books.

Dolch, E. W. "Getting Started with Individualized Reading," *Elementary English,* Vol. 37, No. 2 (February 1960), 105–12.
Step-by-step procedures. Useful bibliography.

Duker, Sam. *Individualized Reading.* Springfield, Ill: Charles C. Thomas, 1971.
An extensive annotated bibliography of many aspects of individualized reading.

Ekwall, Eldon E. *Locating and Correcting Reading Difficulties.* Columbus: Merrill, 1970. Pb.
Presents an excellent format for diagnosing children's reading needs in an informal setting. Suggests several options for activities to help children overcome their reading difficulties. Describes the process of reading.

Fader, Daniel N., and McNeil, Elton B. *Hooked On Books.* New York: Berkley, 1968. Pb.
A forceful presentation of the value of teaching reading through the use of trade books, and, in this case, paperbacks. Fader's style of writing is entertaining and informative. Older students are the clients here, but the principles apply to any age level.

Harris, Larry A., and Smith, Carl B. (eds.). *Individualizing Reading Instruction, A Reader.* New York: Holt, Rinehart and Winston, 1972. Pb.
Many articles by experts in the field describing different aspects of reading instruction. All phases of instruction are included.

Howes, Virgil M. *Individualization of Instruction: A Teaching Strategy.* New York: Macmillan, 1970.
Clearly written, useful techniques for individualizing instruction.

Kohl, Herbert. *Reading, How To.* New York: Dutton, 1973. Pb. Bantam.
A very clearly written account of how to teach reading in an open classroom. The philosophy and methodology of an open classroom are well described.

Miller, Wilma H. "Organizing a First Grade Classroom for Individualized Reading Instruction," *The Reading Teacher,* Vol. 24, No. 8 (May 1971), 748–52.
A nicely organized and practical article suggesting specific ideas for implementing individualized reading in the first grade.

New York City Board of Education. *A Practical Guide to Individualized Reading,* publication no. 40, New York City Board of Education, Bureau of Educational Research, 1960. (110 Livingston St. Brooklyn, N.Y. 11201.)
Exactly what the title says — an invaluable guide on how to establish and maintain an individualized reading program.

Povey, Gail, and Fryer, Jeanne. *Personalized Reading.* Encino, Calif.: International Center for Educational Development, 1972.
Practical introduction to the methodology of individualized reading. Games, techniques, record-keeping ideas, and an open philosophy are conveyed.

Reasoner, Charles F. *Releasing Children to Literature.* New York: Dell, 1968. Pb.

Interesting and open-ended ideas for encouraging critical reading. This book specifically pertains to the Dell Yearling books, but the activities are imaginative and pertinent to any books. Thirty specific books are included, many of which are concerned with topics such as death, siblings, females, and war.

―――. *Where the Readers Are.* New York: Dell, 1972. Pb.

Another invaluable teachers' guide to imaginative and stimulating activities to accompany the reading of books. Reasoner specifically discusses thirty-four Dell Yearling books, but the ideas extend far beyond the particular books.

Sartain, Harry W. "What Are the Advantages and Disadvantages of Individualized Instruction?" International Reading Association Conference *Proceedings,* Vol. 13, Part 2 (1969), 328–56.

An excellent analysis of individualized reading, with advice for turning disadvantages into advantages.

Veatch, Jeannette. *How to Teach Reading with Children's Books.* New York: Bureau of Publications, Teachers College, Columbia University, 1964.

An excellent book describing in great detail how to manage an individualized reading program.

―――. *Reading in the Elementary School.* New York: Ronald Press, 1966.

The most comprehensive text of its kind. All phases of individualized reading are discussed and explained. Many activities, practical suggestions, and information are included.

Wiberg, John L., and Trost, Marion. "A Comparison Between the Content of First Grade Primers and the Free Choice Library Selections Made by First Grade Students," *Elementary English,* Vol. 47, No. 6 (October 1970), 792–98.

Demonstrates that there is a marked disparity between the content of primers and the books that children select from the library.

Yeager, Allan. *Using Picture Books with Children.* New York: Holt, Rinehart and Winston, 1973.

This is a guide to Holt's Owlet books. Yeager recommends using picture books with children of all ages and suggests how to adapt activities.

APPENDIX A

Publishers' Addresses

ABC (AMERICANS BEFORE COLUMBUS). National Indian Youth Council, 3102 Central, S. E., Albuquerque, N. Mex. 87106
ABC (AMERICANS BEFORE COLUMBUS). National Indian Youth Council, P.O. Box 118, Schurz, Nev. 89427
ABELARD-SCHUMAN LTD. 257 Park Ave., S., New York, N.Y. 10010
ABINGDON PRESS. 201 Eighth Ave., S., Nashville, Tenn. 10010
ADDISON-WESLEY PUBLISHING CO., INC. Jacob Way, Reading, Mass. 01867
AFRO-AM PUBLISHING CO. 1727 S. Indiana Ave., Chicago, Ill. 60616
ALLYN AND BACON, INC. 470 Atlantic Ave., Boston, Mass. 02210
AMERICAN ASSOCIATION OF SEX EDUCATION AND COUNSELORS. 815 15th St., N.W., Washington, D.C. 20005
AMERICAN COUNCIL ON EDUCATION. 1 Dupont Circle, N.W., Washington, D.C. 20036
AMERICAN FEDERATION OF TEACHERS (AFT). 1012 14th St., N.W., Washington, D.C. 20005

AMERICAN INSTITUTE OF FAMILY RELATIONS. 5287 Sunset Blvd., Los Angeles, Calif. 90027

AMERICAN JEWISH COMMITTEE. Institute of Human Relations, 165 East 56th St., New York, N.Y. 10022

AMERICAN LIBRARY ASSOCIATION. 50 E. Huron St., Chicago, Ill. 60611

AMERICAN MEDICAL ASSOCIATION. 535 N. Dearborn St., Chicago, Ill. 60610

AMURU PRESS, INC. 161 Madison Ave., New York, N.Y. 10016

APPLETON-CENTURY-CROFTS, INC. 440 Park Ave., S., New York, N.Y. 10016

ARCHWAY. 1 W. 39th St., New York, N.Y. 10018

ASSOCIATION FOR THE STUDY OF AFRO-AMERICAN LIFE AND HISTORY, INC. 1401 14th St., N.W., Washington, D.C. 20005

ASSOCIATION ON AMERICAN INDIAN AFFAIRS, INC. 432 Park Ave., S., New York, N.Y. 10016

ASTOR HONOR, INC. 67 Southfield Ave., Stamford, Conn. 06904

ATHENEUM PUBLISHERS. 122 East 42nd St., New York, N.Y. 10017

AVON BOOK DIVISION. The Hearst Corporation, 959 Eighth Ave., New York, N.Y. 10019

BANTAM BOOKS, INC. 666 Fifth Ave., New York, N.Y. 10019

THE BEACON PRESS. 25 Beacon St., Boston, Mass. 02108

BEHAVIORAL PUBLICATIONS, INC. 72 Fifth Ave., New York, N.Y. 10011

BENEFIC PRESS. 10300 W. Roosevelt Rd., Westchester, Ill. 60153

BERKLEY PUBLISHING CORPORATION. 200 Madison Ave., New York, N.Y. 10016

BETHANY PRESS. 2640 Pine Blvd., P.O. Box 179, St. Louis, Mo. 63166

BOOKSTORE PRESS. 39 Housatonic St., Lenox, Mass. 01240

R. R. BOWKER CO. 1180 Ave. of the Americas, New York, N.Y. 10036

BRADBURY PRESS. 12 Overhill Rd., Scarsdale, N.Y. 10583

BROADSIDE PRESS. 12651 Old Mill Pl., Detroit, Mich. 48238

WILLIAM C. BROWN, PUBLISHERS. 135 S. Locust St., Dubuque, Iowa 52001

BUREAU OF PUBLICATIONS. Teachers College, Columbia University, New York, N.Y. 10025

CHANGE FOR CHILDREN. 2588 Mission St., Rm. 226, San Francisco, Calif. 94110

CHEROKEE EXAMINER. Optimystical Omnibus, 5673 Buchanan St., Los Angeles, Calif. 90042

CHILD STUDY ASSOCIATION OF AMERICA. 9 E. 89th St., New York, N.Y. 10028

CHILDRENS PRESS, INC. 1224 W. Van Buren St., Chicago, Ill. 60607

CHILTON BOOK COMPANY. 401 Walnut St., Philadelphia, Pa. 19106

CITATION PRESS. 50 West 44th St., New York, N.Y. 10036

CITY SMOKE SIGNALS. Sioux City American Indian Centre, 1114 W. 6th St., Sioux City, Iowa 51103

COLLIER BOOKS. 866 Third Ave., New York, N.Y. 10022

COMBINED BLACK PUBLISHERS. 7848 S. Ellis Ave., Chicago, Ill. 60619

CONNECTICUT PUBLIC INTEREST RESEARCH GROUP. P.O. Box 1571, Hartford, Conn. 06101

COUNCIL ON INTERRACIAL BOOKS. 1841 Broadway, New York, N.Y. 10023

COWARD, MCCANN & GEOGHEGAN, INC. 200 Madison Ave., New York, N.Y. 10016

COWLES BOOK COMPANY, INC. 488 Madison Ave., New York, N.Y. 10022

THOMAS Y. CROWELL COMPANY. 666 Fifth Ave., S., New York, N.Y. 10003

CROWN PUBLISHERS. 419 Park Ave., S., New York, N.Y. 10016
THE JOHN DAY COMPANY. 666 Fifth Ave., New York, N.Y. 10010
DELACOURTE PRESS. 750 Third Ave., New York, N.Y. 10017
DELL PUBLISHING COMPANY. 750 Third Ave., New York, N.Y. 10017
T. S. DENISON & CO., INC. 5100 W. 82nd St., Minneapolis, Minn. 55437
THE DIAL PRESS. 750 Third Ave., New York, N.Y. 10017
DODD, MEAD & COMPANY, INC. 79 Madison Ave., New York, N.Y. 10003
DOUBLEDAY AND COMPANY, INC. 501 Franklin Ave., Garden City, N.Y.
    11531
DRUM AND SPEAR PRESS. 1902 Belmont Road, N.W., Washington, D.C. 20009
E. P. DUTTON & COMPANY, INC. 201 Park Ave., S., New York, N.Y. 10003
PAUL S. ERIKSSON, INC. 119 W. 57th St., New York, N.Y. 10019
EUTU PUBLISHING CO. P.O. Box 471, Amherst, Mass. 01002
EVANS AND COMPANY. 216 East 49th St., New York, N.Y. 10017
FAMILY PLANNING AND POPULATION INFORMATION CENTER. 7600 Strom Ave.,
    Syracuse, N.Y. 13210
FARRAR, STRAUS & GIROUX. 19 Union Square, W., New York, N.Y. 10003
FAWCETT WORLD LIBRARY. Fawcett Place, Greenwich, Conn. 06830
FEMINIST BOOK MART. 162-11 Ninth Ave., Whitestone, N.Y. 11357
FEMINIST PRESS. SUNY College at Old Westbury, P.O. Box 334, Old Westbury,
    N.Y. 11568
FEMINISTS ON CHILDREN'S MEDIA. P.O. Box 4315, Grand Central Station, New
    York, N.Y. 10017
FITZGERALD PUBLISHING CO. P.O. Box 264, St. Albans, N.Y. 11412
FOLLETT PUBLISHING COMPANY. 201 N. Wells St., Chicago, Ill. 60606
FORT APACHE SCOUT. P.O. Box 898, Whiteriver, Ariz. 85941
FOUNDATION FOR CHANGE. 1619 Broadway, New York, N.Y. 10019
FOUR WINDS PRESS. 50 W. 44th St., New York, N.Y. 10035
GARRARD PUBLISHING COMPANY. 1607 N. Market St., Champaign, Ill. 61802
BERNARD GEIS ASSOCIATES, INC. 128 E. 56th St., New York, N.Y. 10022
GINN AND COMPANY. 191 Spring St., Lexington, Mass. 02173
GOLDEN PRESS, INC. 850 Third Ave., New York, N.Y. 10022
GOODYEAR PUBLISHING COMPANY. Pacific Palisades, Calif. 90272
GROSSET AND DUNLAP, INC. 51 Madison Ave., New York, N.Y. 10010
GROVE PRESS, INC. 53 E. 11th St., New York, N.Y. 10013
E. M. HALE & COMPANY. 1201 S. Hastings Way, Eau Claire, Wis. 54701
EMERSON HALL PUBLISHERS, INC. 209 W. 97th St., New York, N.Y. 10025
HANOVER HOUSE (DOUBLEDAY AND CO., INC.) 501 Franklin Ave., Garden City,
    N.Y. 11531
HARCOURT BRACE JOVANOVICH. 757 Third Ave., New York, N.Y. 10017
HARLIN QUIST BOOKS (DELL). 750 Third Ave., New York, N.Y. 10017
HARPER & ROW PUBLISHERS, INC. 49 E. 33rd St., New York, N.Y. 10016
HARVEY HOUSE (E. M. HALE & Co.) 1201 S. Hasting's Way, Eau Claire, Wis.
    54701
HAWTHORN BOOKS, INC. 260 Madison Ave., New York, N.Y. 10016
HILL AND WANG, INC. 72 Fifth Ave., New York, N.Y. 10010
HOLIDAY HOUSE. 18 E. 56th St., New York, N.Y. 10022
HOLT, RINEHART & WINSTON, INC. 383 Madison Ave., New York, N.Y. 10017

HOUGHTON MIFFLIN COMPANY. 2 Park St., Boston, Mass. 02107

HUBBARD PRESS. P.O. Box 442, 2855 Shermer Rd., Northbrook, Ill. 60062

INDEPENDENT PUBLISHERS GROUP. c/o David White, Inc., 60 E. 55th St., New York, N.Y. 10022

INDIAN AFFAIRS. 432 Park Ave., S., New York, N.Y. 10016

INDIAN HISTORIAN PRESS. 1451 Masonic Ave., San Francisco, Calif. 94117

INDIAN VOICES. University of Chicago, 1126 E. 59th St., Chicago, Ill. 60637

INSTITUTE OF POSITIVE EDUCATION. 7848 S. Ellis Ave., Chicago, Ill. 60619

INTERNATIONAL CENTER FOR EDUCATIONAL DEVELOPMENT. 16161 Ventura Blvd., Encino, Calif. 91316

INTERNATIONAL READING ASSOCIATION. 800 Barksdale Rd., Newark, Del. 19711

JOHNSON PUBLISHING CO. Book Division, 820 S. Michigan Ave., Chicago, Ill. 60605

P. J. KENEDY AND SONS. 866 Third Ave., New York, N.Y. 10022

ALFRED A. KNOPF, INC. 201 E. 50th St., New York, N.Y. 10022

KNOW PRESS. P.O. Box 86031, Pittsburgh, Pa. 15221

LERNER PUBLICATIONS CO. 241 First Ave., N., Minneapolis, Minn. 55401

LION PRESS. Sayre Publishing Co., Inc., 52 Park Ave., New York, N.Y. 10016

J. B. LIPPINCOTT COMPANY. E. Washington Square, Philadelphia, Pa. 19105

LITTLE, BROWN AND COMPANY, INC. 34 Beacon St., Boston, Mass. 02106

LOLLIPOP POWER, INC. P.O. Box 1171, Chapel Hill, N.C. 27514

LONGMANS, GREEN AND COMPANY, INC. 750 Third Ave., New York, N.Y. 10017

LOTHROP, LEE AND SHEPARD. Division of William Morrow, 105 Madison Ave., New York, N.Y. 10016

McGRAW-HILL BOOK COMPANY. Princeton Rd., Hightstown, N.J. 08520

McINTOSH & OTIS. 18 E. 41st St., New York, N.Y. 10017

DAVID McKAY COMPANY, INC. 750 Third Ave., New York, N.Y. 10017

MACMILLAN PUBLISHING COMPANY. 866 Third Ave., New York, N.Y. 10022

MACRAE SMITH. 225 South 15th St., Philadelphia, Pa. 19102

MADRONA PRESS, INC. 113 Madrona Place, E., Seattle, Wash. 98112

CHARLES E. MERRILL PUBLISHING COMPANY. 1300 Alum Creek Dr., Columbus, Ohio 43216

JULIAN MESSNER, INC. DIVISION OF SIMON AND SCHUSTER, INC., 1 West 39th St., New York, N.Y. 10018

WILLIAM MORROW & COMPANY, INC. 105 Madison Ave., New York, N.Y. 10016

N.A.A.C.P. 1790 Broadway, New York, N.Y. 10019

NATIONAL ASSOCIATION FOR THE EDUCATION OF YOUNG CHILDREN. 1834 Connecticut Ave., N.W., Washington, D.C. 20009

NATIONAL CONFERENCE OF CHRISTIANS AND JEWS. 43 W. 57th St., New York, N.Y. 10019

NATIONAL COUNCIL OF TEACHERS OF ENGLISH. 1111 Kenyon Rd., Urbana, Ill. 61801

NATIONAL EDUCATION ASSOCIATION. 1202 16th St., N.W., Washington, D.C. 20036

NATIONAL FOUNDATION FOR THE IMPROVEMENT OF EDUCATION RESOURCE CENTER ON SEX ROLES IN EDUCATION. Suite 918, 1156 15th St., N.W., Washington, D.C. 20005

NATIONAL ORGANIZATION FOR WOMEN (local branches in each state). Central Office, 1957 E. 73rd St., Chicago, Ill. 60649

NATIONAL ORGANIZATION FOR WOMEN. Central New Jersey Chapter, R.D. 4, 25 Cleveland Lane, Princeton, N.J. 08540

NATIVE NEVADAN. 1995 E. 2nd St., Reno, Nev. 89502

NAVAJO CURRICULUM CENTER PRESS. O'Sullivan, Woodside, & Company, 2218 E. Magnolia, Phoenix, Ariz. 75034

THE NAVAJO TIMES. P.O. Box 428, Window Rock, Ariz. 86515

THOMAS NELSON, INC. 30 E. 42nd St., New York, N.Y. 10017

THOMAS NELSON & SONS. Copewood & Davis St., Camden, N.J. 08103

NELSON-HALL CO. 325 W. Jackson Blvd., Chicago, Ill. 60606

NEW DAY PRESS. c/o Karamu House, 2355 E. 89 St., Cleveland, Ohio 44106

NEW ENGLAND FREE PRESS. 60 Union Square, Somerville, Mass. 02143

NEW SEED PUBLISHING CO. P.O. Box 3016, Stanford, Calif. 94305

NEW YORK CITY BOARD OF EDUCATION. Publications Office, 110 Livingston St., Brooklyn, N.Y. 11201

THE NISHNAWBE NEWS. R. 214, Kaye Hall, Northern Michigan University, Marquette, Mich. 49885

W. W. NORTON & CO., INC. 500 Fifth Ave., New York, N.Y. 10036

OCTOPUS BOOKS LIMITED. 59 Grosvenor St., London, England, E1X 9DA

ODYSSEY PRESS. 4300 W. 62nd St., Indianapolis, Ind. 46268

OFFICE OF EDUCATION. U.S. Dept. of Health, Education and Welfare, Washington, D.C. 20202

J. PHILIP O'HARA PUBLICATIONS INC. 20 E. Huron, Chicago, Ill. 60611

OVER THE RAINBOW PRESS. P.O. Box 7072, Berkeley, Calif. 94707

OXFORD UNIVERSITY PRESS, INC. 200 Madison Ave.. N.Y., N.Y. 10016

MAX PADELL, INC. 72-34 Yellowstone Blvd., Forest Hills, N.Y. 11375

PALO VERDE PUBLISHING CO., INC. 609 N. Fourth Ave., Tucson, Ariz. 85705

PANTHEON BOOKS, INC. 201 E. 50th St., New York, N.Y. 10022

PARENTS' MAGAZINE PRESS. 52 Vanderbilt Ave., New York, N.Y. 10017

S. G. PHILLIPS. 305 W. 86th St., New York, N.Y. 10024

PHILOSOPHICAL LIBRARY, INC. 15 E. 40th St., New York, N.Y. 10016

PLATT & MUNK PUBLICATIONS. 1055 Bronx River Ave., Bronx, N.Y. 10472

POCKET BOOKS, INC. 1 W. 39th St., New York, N.Y. 10018

PRENTICE-HALL, INC. Englewood Cliffs, N.J. 07632

G. P. PUTNAM'S SONS. 200 Madison Ave., New York, N.Y. 10016

RAND, MCNALLY AND COMPANY. Box 7600, Chicago, Ill. 60680

RANDOM HOUSE, INC. 201 E. 50th St., New York, N.Y. 10022

REILLY AND LEE BOOKS. Dist. by Henry Regnery Company, 114 W. Illinois St., Chicago, Ill. 60610

JULIAN RICHARDSON ASSOCIATES. 540 McAllister St., San Francisco, Calif. 94102

RITCHIE WARD PRESS. 474 S. Arroya Blvd., Pasadena, Calif. 91105

THE RONALD PRESS COMPANY. 79 Madison Ave., New York, N.Y. 10016

ROSEBUD SIOUX HERALD. Box 435, Roosevelt Town, N.Y. 13683

ST. MARTIN'S PRESS, INC. 175 Fifth Ave., New York, N.Y. 10010

SCARECROW PRESS. 52 Liberty St., P.O. Box 656, Metuchen, N.J. 08840

SCHOLASTIC BOOK SERVICES. 50 W. 44th St., New York, N.Y. 10036

ABELARD-SCHUMAN. 666 Fifth Ave., New York, N.Y. 10019
SCIENCE HOUSE. 59 Fourth Ave., New York, N.Y. 10003
SCIENCE RESEARCH ASSOCIATES, INC. 1540 Page Mill Rd., Palo Alto, Calif. 94304
SCOTT, FORESMAN, & CO. 1900 E. Lake Ave., Glenview, Ill., 60025
WILLIAM R. SCOTT, INC. 333 Ave. of the Americas, New York, N.Y. 10014
CHARLES SCRIBNER'S SONS. 597 Fifth Ave., New York, N.Y. 10017
SCROLL PRESS. 22 E. 84th St., New York, N.Y. 10028
SEABURY PRESS. 815 Second Ave., New York, N.Y. 10017
THE SENTINEL. National Congress of American Indians, 1346 Connecticut Ave.,
    N.W., Washington, D.C. 20036
SIECUS. 1855 Broadway, New York, N.Y. 10023
SIMON AND SCHUSTER, INC. 630 Fifth Ave., New York, N.Y. 10020
STECK-VAUGHN CO. P.O. Box 2028, Austin, Tex. 78767
STIPES PUBLISHING COMPANY. 10–12 Chester St., Champaign, Ill. 61820
LYLE STUART, INC. 120 Enterprise Ave., Secaucus, N.J. 07094
THE THIRD PRESS: JOSEPH OKPAKU PUBLISHING CO., INC. 444 Central Park W.,
    New York, N.Y. 10025
THIRD WORLD PRESS. 7850 S. Ellis Ave., Chicago, Ill. 60619
CHARLES C. THOMAS PUBLISHER. 301–327 E. Lawrence Ave., Springfield, Ill.
    62717
TIME-LIFE BOOKS. Time and Life Bldg., Rockefeller Center, New York, N.Y.
    10020
HOWARD TIMMONS COMPANY. Capetown, South Africa
TODD PUBLICATIONS. 11 Third St., Rye, N.Y. 10580
U.S. COMMITTEE FOR UNICEF. 331 E. 38th St., New York, N.Y. 10016
D. VAN NOSTRAND CO. 120 Alexander St., Princeton, N.J. 08540
VAN NOSTRAND REINHOLD CO. 450 W. 33rd St., New York, N.Y. 10001
VANGUARD PRESS. 424 Madison Ave., New York, N.Y. 10017
THE VIKING PRESS, INC. 625 Madison Ave., New York, N.Y. 10022
WADSWORTH PUBLISHING CO., INC. 10 Davis Drive, Belmont, Calif. 94002
HENRY Z. WALCK, INC. 19 Union Square, W., New York, N.Y. 10003
WALKER AND COMPANY. 720 Fifth Ave., New York, N.Y. 10019
WARPATH. P.O. Box 26149, San Francisco, Calif. 94126
FRANKLIN WATTS, INC. 730 Fifth Ave., New York, N.Y. 10019
DAVID WHITE, INC. 60 East 55th St., New York, N.Y. 10021
ALBERT WHITMAN & COMPANY. 560 W. Lake St., Chicago, Ill. 60605
JOHN WILEY & SONS, INC. 605 Third Ave., New York, N.Y. 10016
H. W. WILSON CO. 950 University Ave., Bronx, N.Y. 10451
WINDMILL BOOKS. Simon and Schuster, Inc., 630 Fifth Ave., New York, N.Y.
    10020
THE WESTMINSTER PRESS. Witherspoon Building, Philadelphia, Pa. 19107
WOMEN ON WORDS AND IMAGES. P.O. Box 2163, Princeton, N.J. 08540
THE WORLD PUBLISHING COMPANY. 110 E. 59th St., New York, N.Y. 10022
THE WRITER, INC. 8 Arlington St., Boston, Mass. 02116
XEROX EDUCATIONAL PUBLICATIONS. 245 Long Hill Rd., Middletown, Conn.
    06457
YOUNG SCOTT BOOKS. Addison-Wesley Publishing Company, Reading, Mass.
    01867

Selected List of Children's Book Awards

Randolph J. Caldecott Medal

Determined each year by a special committee of the American Library Association Children's Services Division, this award is given to the illustrator of the picture book judged to be the most distinguished of the previous year. The book must be published in the United States, and the illustrator must be a citizen or resident of the United States.

1938 *Animals of the Bible,* by Helen Dean Fish, illus. Dorothy P. Lathrop
Honor Books: *Seven Simeons,* by Boris Artzybasheff
Four and Twenty Blackbirds, by Helen Dean Fish, illus. Robert Lawson

1939 *Mei Li,* by Thomas Handforth
Honor Books: *The Forest Pool,* by Laura Adams Armer
Wee Gillis, by Munro Leaf, illus. Robert Lawson

Snow White and the Seven Dwarfs, by Wanda Gág
Barkis, by Clare Newberry
Andy and the Lion, by James Daugherty

1940 *Abraham Lincoln,* by Ingri and Edgar d'Aulaire
Honor Books: *Cock-a-Doodle Doo,* by Berta and Elmer Hader
Madeline, by Ludwig Bemelmans
The Ageless Story, by Lauren Ford

1941 *They Were Strong and Good,* by Robert Lawson
Honor Book: *April's Kittens,* by Clare Newberry

1942 *Make Way for Ducklings,* by Robert McCloskey
Honor Books: *An American ABC,* by Maud and Miska Petersham
In My Mother's House, by Ann Nolan Clark
Paddle-To-The-Sea, by Holling C. Holling
Nothing At All, by Wanda Gág

1943 *The Little House,* by Virginia Lee Burton
Honor Books: *Dash and Dart,* by Mary and Conrad Buff
Marshmallow, by Clare Newberry

1944 *Many Moons,* by James Thurber, illus. Louis Slobodkin
Honor Books: *Small Rain: Verses from the Bible,* selected by Jessie Orton
Jones, illus. Elizabeth Orton Jones
Pierre Pigeon, by Lee Kingman, illus. Arnold E. Bare
The Mighty Hunter, by Berta and Elmer Hader
A Child's Good Night Book, by Margaret Wise Brown, illus.
Jean Charlot
Good Luck Horse, by Chin-Yi Chan, illus. Plao Chan

1945 *Prayer for a Child,* by Rachel Field, illus. Elizabeth Orton Jones
Honor Books: *Mother Goose,* illus. Tasha Tudor
In the Forest, by Marie Hall Ets
Yonie Wondernose, by Marguerite de Angeli
The Christmas Anna Angel, by Ruth Sawyer, illus. Kate
Seredy

1946 *The Rooster Crows,* illus. Maud and Miska Petersham
Honor Books: *Little Lost Lamb,* by Golden MacDonald, illus. Leonard
Weisgard
Sing Mother Goose, by Opal Wheeler, illus. Marjorie Torrey
My Mother Is the Most Beautiful Woman in the World, by
Becky Reyher, illus. Ruth Gannett
You Can Write Chinese, by Kurt Wiese

1947 *The Little Island,* by Golden MacDonald, illus. Leonard Weisgard
Honor Books: *Rain Drop Splash,* by Alvin Tresselt, illus. Leonard Weis-
gard
Boats on the River, by Marjorie Flack, illus. Jay Hyde Bar-
num
Timothy Turtle, by Al Graham, illus. Tony Palazzo
Pedro, The Angel of Alvera Street, by Leo Politi
Sing in Praise: A Collection of the Best Loved Hymns, by Opal
Wheeler, illus. Marjorie Torrey

1948 *White Snow, Bright Snow,* by Alvin Tresselt, illus. Roger Duvoisin
       Honor Books: *Stone Soup,* by Marcia Brown
                   McElligot's Pool, by Dr. Seuss
                   Bambino the Clown, by George Schreiber
                   Roger and the Fox, by Lavinia Davis, illus. Hildegard
                   Woodward
                   Song of Robin Hood, ed. Anne Malcolmson, illus. Virginia
                   Lee Burton

1949 *The Big Snow,* by Berta and Elmer Hader
       Honor Books: *Blueberries for Sal,* by Robert McCloskey
                   All Around the Town, by Phyllis McGinley, illus. Helen
                   Stone
                   Juanita, by Leo Politi
                   Fish in the Air, by Kurt Wiese

1950 *Song of the Swallows,* by Leo Politi
       Honor Books: *America's Ethan Allen,* by Stewart Holbrook, illus. Lynd
                   Ward
                   The Wild Birthday Cake, by Lavinia Davis, illus. Hildegard
                   Woodward
                   The Happy Day, by Ruth Krauss, illus. Marc Simont
                   Bartholomew and the Oobleck, by Dr. Seuss
                   Henry Fisherman, by Marcia Brown

1951 *The Egg Tree,* by Katherine Milhous
       Honor Books: *Dick Whittington and His Cat,* by Marcia Brown
                   The Two Reds, by Will, illus. Nicolas
                   If I Ran the Zoo, by Dr. Seuss
                   The Most Wonderful Doll in the World, by Phyllis McGinley,
                   illus. Helen Stone
                   T-Bone the Baby Sitter, by Clare Newberry

1952 *Finders Keepers* by Will, illus. Nicolas
       Honor Books: *Mr. T. W. Anthony Woo,* by Marie Hall Ets
                   Skipper John's Cook, by Marcia Brown
                   All Falling Down, by Gene Zion, illus. Margaret Bloy
                   Graham
                   Bear Party, by William Pène duBois
                   Feather Mountain, by Elizabeth Olds

1953 *The Biggest Bear,* by Lynd Ward
       Honor Books: *Puss in Boots,* by Charles Perrault, illus. and trans. Marcia
                   Brown
                   One Morning in Maine, by Robert McCloskey
                   Ape in a Cape, by Fritz Eichenberg
                   The Storm Book, by Charlotte Zolotow, illus. Margaret Bloy
                   Graham
                   Five Little Monkeys, by Juliet Kepes

1954 *Madeline's Rescue,* by Ludwig Bemelmans
       Honor Books: *Journey Cake, Ho!,* by Ruth Sawyer, illus. Robert McClos-
                   key

When Will the World Be Mine?, by Mariam Schlein, illus. Jean Charlot

The Steadfast Tin Soldier, by Hans Christian Andersen, illus. Marcia Brown

A Very Special House, by Ruth Krauss, illus. Maurice Sendak

Green Eyes, by A. Birnbaum

1955   *Cinderella, or the Little Glass Slipper*, by Charles Perrault, trans. and illus. Marcia Brown

Honor Books: *Book of Nursery and Mother Goose Rhymes*, illus. Marguerite de Angeli

Wheel on the Chimney, by Margaret Wise Brown, illus. Tibor Gergely

The Thanksgiving Story, by Alice Dalgliesh, illus. Helen Sewell

1956   *Frog Went A-Courtin'*, ed. John Langstaff, illus. Feodor Rojankovsky

Honor Books: *Play With Me*, by Marie Hall Ets

Crow Boy, by Taro Yashima

1957   *A Tree Is Nice*, by Janice May Udry, illus. Marc Simont

Honor Books: *Mr. Penny's Race Horse*, by Marie Hall Ets

1 is One, by Tasha Tudor

Anatole, by Eve Titus, illus. Paul Galdone

Gillespie and the Guards, by Benjamin Elkin, illus. James Daugherty

Lion, by William Pène duBois

1958   *Time of Wonder*, by Robert McCloskey

Honor Books: *Fly High, Fly Low*, by Don Freeman

Anatole and the Cat, by Eve Titus, illus. Paul Galdone

1959   *Chanticleer and the Fox*, adapted from Chaucer, illus. Barbara Cooney

Honor Books: *The House That Jack Built*, by Antonio Frasconi

What Do You Say, Dear?, by Sesyle Joslin, illus. Maurice Sendak

Umbrella, by Taro Yashima

1960   *Nine Days to Christmas*, by Marie Hall Ets and Aurora Labastida, illus. Marie Hall Ets

Honor Books: *Houses From the Sea*, by Alice E. Goudey, illus. Adrienne Adams

The Moon Jumpers, by Janice May Udry, illus. Maurice Sendak

1961   *Baboushka and the Three Kings*, by Ruth Robbins, illus. Nicholas Sidjakov

Honor Book: *Inch By Inch*, by Leo Lionni

1962   *Once a Mouse*, by Marcia Brown

Honor Books: *The Fox Went Out On a Chilly Night*, illus. Peter Spier

Little Bear's Visit, by Else Holmelund Minarik, illus. Maurice Sendak

The Day We Saw the Sun Come Up, by Alice E. Goudey, illus. Adrienne Adams

1963   *The Snowy Day*, by Ezra Jack Keats
       Honor Books: *The Sun Is a Golden Earring*, by Natalia M. Belting, illus.
                    Bernarda Bryson
                    Mr. Rabbit and the Lovely Present, by Charlotte Zolotow,
                    illus. Maurice Sendak

1964   *Where the Wild Things Are*, by Maurice Sendak
       Honor Books: *Swimmy*, by Leo Lionni
                    All in the Morning Early by Sorche Nic Leodhas, illus.
                    Evaline Ness
                    Mother Goose and Nursery Rhymes, illus. Philip Reed

1965   *May I Bring a Friend?*, by Beatrice Schenk de Regniers, illus. Beni
       Montresor
       Honor Books: *Rain Makes Applesauce*, by Julian Scheer, illus. Marvin
                    Bileck
                    The Wave, by Margaret Hodges, illus. Blair Lent
                    A Pocketful of Cricket, by Rebecca Caudill, illus. Evaline
                    Ness

1966   *Always Room for One More*, by Sorche Nic Leodhas, illus. Nonny Hogro-
       gian
       Honor Books: *Hide and Seek Fog*, by Alvin Tresselt, illus. Roger Duvoisin
                    Just Me, by Marie Hall Ets
                    Tom Tit Tot, by Evaline Ness

1967   *Sam, Bangs and Moonshine*, by Evaline Ness
       Honor Book: *One Wide River to Cross*, by Barbara Emberley, illus. Ed
                   Emberley

1968   *Drummer Hoff*, by Barbara Emberley, illus. Ed Emberley
       Honor Books: *Frederick*, by Leo Lionni
                    Seashore Story, by Taro Yashima
                    The Emperor and the Kite, by Jane Yolen, illus. Ed Young

1969   *The Fool of the World and the Flying Ship*, by Arthur Ransome, illus. Uri
       Shulevitz
       Honor Book: *Why the Sun and the Moon Live in the Sky*, by Elphinstone
                   Dayrell, illus. Blair Lent

1970   *Sylvester and the Magic Pebble*, by William Steig
       Honor Books: *Goggles*, by Ezra Jack Keats
                    Alexander and the Wind-up Mouse, by Leo Lionni
                    Pop Corn & Ma Goodness, by Edna Mitchell Preston, illus.
                    Robert Andrew Parker
                    Thy Friend, Obadiah, by Brinton Turkle
                    The Judge, by Harve Zemach, illus. Margot Zemach

1971   *A Story — A Story*, by Gail E. Haley
       Honor Books: *The Angry Moon*, by William Sleator, illus. Blair Lent
                    Frog and Toad Are Friends, by Arnold Lobel
                    In the Night Kitchen, by Maurice Sendak

1972   *One Fine Day*, by Nonny Hogrogian
       Honor Books: *Hildilid's Night*, by Cheli Durán Ryan, illus. Arnold Lobel

If All the Seas Were One Sea, by Janina Domanska
Moja Means One, by Muriel Feelings, illus. Tom Feelings

1973   The Funny Little Women, retold by Arlene Mosel, illus. Blair Lent
Honor Books: Anasi the Spider, adapted and illus. Gerald McDermott
Hosie's Alphabet, by Hosea, Tobias, and Lisa Baskin, illus.
Leonard Baskin
Snow White and the Seven Dwarfs, trans. Randall Jarrell,
illus. Nancy Ekholm Burkert
When Clay Sings, by Byrd Baylor, illus. Tom Bahti

1974   Duffy and the Devil, retold by Harve Zemach, illus. Margot Zemach
Honor Books: Three Jovial Huntsmen: A Mother Goose Rhyme, adapted and
illus. Susan Jeffers
Cathedral: The Story of Its Construction, written and illus.
David Macaulay

1975   Arrow to the Sun, A Pueblo Indian Tale, by Gerald McDermott
Honor Book: Jambo Means Hello, Swahili Alphabet Book, by Muriel Feelings,
illus. Tom Feelings

Child Study Association of America/Wel-Met Children's Book Award

Awarded each year by the Child Study Association, this award is given to a book
published in the preceding year that relates to problems and realities in children's lives.

1944   Keystone Kids, by John R. Tunis

1945   The House, by Marjorie Allee

1946   The Moved-Outers, by Florence Crannel Means

1947   Heart of Danger, by Howard Pease

1948   Judy's Journey, by Lois Lenski

1949   The Big Wave, by Pearl Buck

1950   Paul Tiber, by Maria Gleit

1951   The United Nations and Youth, by Eleanor Roosevelt and Helen Ferris

1952   No Award

1953   Twenty and Ten, by Claire Huchet Bishop
Jareb, by Miriam Powell

1954   In a Mirror, by Mary Stolz

1955   High Road Home, by William Corbin
The Ordeal of the Young Hunter, by Jonreed Lauritzen

1956   Crow Boy, by Taro Yashima
Plain Girl, by Virginia Sorensen

1957   The House of Sixty Fathers, by Meindert DeJong

1958   Shadow Across the Campus, by Helen R. Sattley

1959   *South Town*, by Lorenz Graham

1960   *Jennifer*, by Zoa Sherburne

1961   *Janine*, by Robin McKown

1962   *The Road to Agra*, by Aimee Sommerfelt
       The Girl From Puerto Rico, by Hila Colman

1963   *The Trouble with Terry*, by Joan Lexau

1964   *The Rock and the Willow*, by Mildred Lee
       The Peaceable Revolution, by Betty Schechter

1965   *The High Pastures*, by Ruth Harnden

1966   *The Empty Schoolhouse*, by Natalie S. Carlson

1967   *Queenie Peavy*, by Robert Burch
       Curious George Goes to the Hospital, by Margaret and H. A. Rey

1968   *The Contender*, by Robert Lipsyte

1969   *What It's All About*, by Vadim Frolov
       Where Is Daddy? The Story of a Divorce, by Beth Goff

1970   *The Empty Moat*, by Margaretha Shemin

1971   *Migrant Girl*, by Carli Laklan
       Rock Star, by James Lincoln Collier

1972   *John Henry McCoy*, by Lillie D. Chaffin
       The Pair of Shoes, by Aline Glasgow

1973   *A Sound of Chariots*, by Mollie Hunter

1974   *A Taste of Blackberries*, by Doris Buchanan Smith

1975   *Luke Was There*, by Eleanor Clymer

Council on Interracial Books for Children Award

Awarded each year by the Council to minority authors whose unpublished manuscripts are judged to be outstanding.

1968   *Where Does the Day Go?* by Walter N. Myers
       The Soul Brothers and Sister Lou, by Kristin Hunter

1969   *ABC: The Story of the Alphabet*, by Virginia Cox
       Sidewalk Story, by Sharon Bell Mathis
       Letters from Uncle David: Underground Hero, by Margot S. Webb

1970   *Jimmy Yellow Hawk*, by Virginia Driving Hawk Sneve
       Sneakers, by Ray Anthony Shepard
       I Am Magic, by Juan Valenzuela

1971–1972   *Morning Song*, by Minfong Ho
            The Rock Cried Out, by Florenz Webbe Maxwell
            The Unusual Puerto Rican, by Theodore Laquer-Franceschi

1973   *Morning Arrow,* by Nanabah Chee Dodge
       Grandfather's Bridge, by Michele P. Robinson
       Eyak, by Dorothy Tomiye Okamoto
       Song of the Trees, by Mildred D. Taylor
       El Pito De Plata De Pito, by Jack Agueros

1974   *Simba, Midnight (The Stallion of the Night) and Mweusi,* by Aishah S.
          Abdullah
       My Father Hijacked a Plane, by Abelardo B. Delgado
       Yari, by Antonia A. Hernandez

National Book Award, Children's Book Category

Awarded each year by a specially selected panel of judges — generally consisting of children's book authors — this award is given to a book published the preceding year in the United States, written by an American citizen. The book is judged for its literary excellence.

1969   *Journey From Peppermint Street,* by Meindert DeJong
       Finalists: *Constance,* by Patricia Clapp
                 The Endless Steppe, by Esther Hautzig
                 The High King, by Lloyd Alexander
                 Langston Hughes, by Milton Meltzer

1970   *A Day of Pleasure: Stories of a Boy Growing Up in Warsaw,* by Isaac Bashevis
          Singer
       Finalists: *Pop Corn & Ma Goodness,* by Edna Mitchell Preston
                 Sylvester and the Magic Pebble, by William Steig
                 Where the Lilies Bloom, by Vera and Bill Cleaver
                 The Young United States, by Edwin Tunis

1971   *The Marvelous Misadventures of Sebastian,* by Lloyd Alexander
       Finalists: *Blowfish Live in the Sea,* by Paula Fox
                 Frog and Toad Are Friends, by Arnold Lobel
                 Grover, by Vera and Bill Cleaver
                 Trumpet of the Swan, by E. B. White

1972   *The Slightly Irregular Fire Engine,* by Donald Barthelme
       Finalists: *Amos and Boris,* by William Steig
                 The Art and Industry of Sandcastles, by Jan Adkins
                 The Bears' House, by Marilyn Sachs
                 Father Fox's Pennyrhymes, by Clyde Watson
                 Hildilid's Night, by Cheli Durán Ryan
                 His Own Where, by June Jordan
                 Mrs. Frisby and the Rats of NIMH, by Robert C. O'Brien
                 The Planet of Junior Brown, by Virginia Hamilton
                 The Tombs of Atuan, by Ursula K. LeGuin
                 Wild in the World, by John Donovan

1973   *The Farthest Shore,* by Ursula K. LeGuin
       Finalists: *Children of Vietnam,* by Betty Jean Lifton and Thomas C. Fox
                 Dominic, by William Steig
                 The House of Wings, by Betsy Byars

The Impossible People, by Georgess McHargue
Julie of the Wolves, by Jean Craighead George
Long Journey Home, by Julius Lester
Trolls, by Ingri and Edgar Parin d'Aulaire
The Witches of Worm, by Zilpha Keatley Snyder

1974 *The Court of the Stone Children,* by Eleanor Cameron
Finalists: *Duffy and the Devil,* by Harve Zemach
A Figure of Speech, by Norma Fox Mazer
Guests in the Promised Land, by Kristin Hunter
A Hero Ain't Nothin' But a Sandwich, by Alice Childress
Poor Richard in France, by F. N. Monjo
A Proud Taste for Scarlet and Miniver, by E. L. Konigsburg
Summer of My German Soldier, by Bette Greene
The Treasure Is the Rose, by Julia Cunningham
The Whys and Wherefores of Littabelle Lee, by Vera and Bill Cleaver

1975 *M. C. Higgins, the Great,* by Virginia Hamilton
Finalists: *My Brother Sam Is Dead,* by James Lincoln Collier and Christopher Collier
The Devil's Storybook, by Natalie Babbitt
Doctor in the Zoo, by Bruce Buchenholz
The Edge of Next Year, by Mary Stolz
The Girl Who Cried Flowers and Other Tales, by Jane Yolen
Joi Bangla! The Children of Bangladesh, by Jason and Ettagale Laure
Remember the Days: A Short History of the Jewish American, by Milton Meltzer
I Tell a Lie Every So Often, by Bruce Clements
Wings, by Adrienne Richard
World of Our Fathers: The Jews of Eastern Europe, by Milton Meltzer

John Newbery Medal

The most coveted children's book award, this prize is given annually to the book judged by a special committee selected by the American Library Association Children's Services Division to be the most outstanding work of children's literature published during the preceding year. The award is given only to those authors who are American citizens, and the book must be published in the United States.

1922 *The Story of Mankind,* by Hendrik Willem van Loon
Honor Books: *The Great Quest,* by Charles Hawes
Cedric the Forester, by Bernard Marshall
The Old Tobacco Shop, by William Bowen
The Golden Fleece and the Heroes Who Lived Before Achilles, by Padraic Colum
Windy Hill, by Cornelia Meigs

1923   *The Voyages of Doctor Dolittle,* by Hugh Lofting

1924   *The Dark Frigate,* by Charles Hawes

1925   *Tales From Silver Lands,* by Charles Finger
       Honor Books: *Nicholas,* by Anne Carroll Moore
                    Dream Coach, by Anne Parrish

1926   *Shen of the Sea,* by Arthur Bowie Chrisman
       Honor Book: *Voyagers,* by Padraic Colum

1927   *Smoky, The Cowhorse,* by Will James

1928   *Gayneck, the Story of a Pigeon,* by Dhan Gopal Mukerji
       Honor Books: *The Wonder Smith and His Son,* by Ella Young
                    Downright Dencey, by Caroline Snedeker

1929   *The Trumpeter of Krakow,* by Eric P. Kelly
       Honor Books: *Pigtail of Ah Lee Ben Loo,* by John Bennett
                    Millions of Cats, by Wanda Gág
                    The Boy Who Was, by Grace Hallock
                    Clearing Weather, by Cornelia Meigs
                    Runaway Papoose, by Grace Moon
                    Tod of the Fens, by Elinor Whitney

1930   *Hitty, Her First Hundred Years,* by Rachel Field
       Honor Books: *Daughter of the Seine,* by Jeanette Eaton
                    Pran of Albania, by Elizabeth Miller
                    Jumping-Off Place, by Marian Hurd McNeely
                    Tangle-Coated Horse and Other Tales, by Ella Young
                    Vaino, by Julia Davis Adams
                    Little Blacknose, by Hildegarde Swift

1931   *The Cat Who Went to Heaven,* by Elizabeth Coatsworth
       Honor Books: *Floating Island,* by Anne Parrish
                    The Dark Star of Itza, by Alida Malkus
                    Queer Person, by Ralph Hubbard
                    Mountains Are Free, by Julia Davis Adams
                    Spice and the Devil's Cave, by Agnes Hewes
                    Meggy Macintosh, by Elizabeth Janet Gray
                    Garram the Hunter, by Herbert Best
                    Ood-le-uk the Wanderer, by Alice Lide and Margaret Johan-
                    sen

1932   *Waterless Mountain,* by Laura Adams Armer
       Honor Books: *The Fairy Circus,* by Dorothy P. Lathrop
                    Calico Bush, by Rachel Field
                    Boy of the South Seas, by Eunice Tietjens
                    Out of the Flame, by Eloise Lownsbery
                    Jane's Island, by Marjorie Allee
                    Truce of the Wolf and Other Tales of Old Italy, by Mary Gould
                    Davis

1933   *Young Fu of the Upper Yangtze,* by Elizabeth Lewis
       Honor Books: *Swift Rivers,* by Cornelia Meigs

The Railroad to Freedom, by Hildegarde Swift
Children of the Soil, by Nora Burglon

1934 *Invincible Louisa,* by Cornelia Meigs
Honor Books: *The Forgotten Daughter,* by Caroline Snedeker
Swords of Steel, by Elsie Singmaster
ABC Bunny, by Wanda Gág
Winged Girl of Knossos, by Erik Berry
New Land, by Sarah Schmidt
Big Tree of Bunlahy, by Padraic Colum
Glory of the Seas, by Agnes Hewes
Apprentice of Florence, by Anne Kyle

1935 *Dobry,* by Monica Shannon
Honor Books: *Pageant of Chinese History,* by Elizabeth Seeger
Davy Crockett, by Constance Rourke
Day on Skates, by Hilda Van Stockum

1936 *Caddie Woodlawn,* by Carol Ryrie Brink
Honor Books: *Honk, the Moose,* by Phil Stong
The Good Master, by Kate Seredy
Young Walter Scott, by Elizabeth Janet Gray
All Sail Set, by Armstrong Sperry

1937 *Roller Skates,* by Ruth Sawyer
Honor Books: *Phoebe Fairchild: Her Book,* by Lois Lenski
Whistler's Van, by Idwal Jones
Golden Basket, by Ludwig Bemelmans
Winterbound, by Margery Bianco
Audubon, by Constance Rourke
The Codfish Musket, by Agnes Hewes

1938 *The White Stag,* by Kate Seredy
Honor Books: *Pecos Bill,* by James Cloyd Bowman
Bright Island, by Mabel Robinson
On the Banks of Plum Creek, by Laura Ingalls Wilder

1939 *Thimble Summer,* by Elizabeth Enright
Honor Books: *Nino,* by Valenti Angelo
Mr. Popper's Penguins, by Richard and Florence Atwater
Hello the Boat!, by Phyllis Crawford
Leader by Destiny: George Washington, Man and Patriot, by
Jeanette Eaton
Penn, by Elizabeth Janet Gray

1940 *Daniel Boone,* by James Daugherty
Honor Books: *The Singing Tree,* by Kate Seredy
Runner of the Mountain Tops, by Mabel Robinson
By the Shores of Silver Lake, by Laura Ingalls Wilder
Boy with a Pack, by Stephen W. Meader

1941 *Call It Courage,* by Armstrong Sperry
Honor Books: *Blue Willow,* by Doris Gates
Young Mac of Fort Vancouver, by Mary Jane Carr

The Long Winter, by Laura Ingalls Wilder
Nansen, by Anna Gertrude Hall

1942 *The Matchlock Gun*, by Walter D. Edmonds
Honor Books: *Little Town on the Prairie*, by Laura Ingalls Wilder
George Washington's World, by Genevieve Foster
Indian Captive: The Story of Mary Jemison, by Lois Lenski
Down Ryton Water, by Eva Roe Gaggin

1943 *Adam of the Road*, by Elizabeth Janet Gray
Honor Books: *The Middle Moffat*, by Eleanor Estes
Have You Seen Tom Thumb?, by Mabel Leigh Hunt

1944 *Johnny Tremain*, by Esther Forbes
Honor Books: *These Happy Golden Years*, by Laura Ingalls Wilder
Fog Magic, by Julia Sauer
Rufus M., by Eleanor Estes
Mountain Born, by Elizabeth Yates

1945 *Rabbit Hill*, by Robert Lawson
Honor Books: *The Hundred Dresses*, by Eleanor Estes
The Silver Pencil, by Alice Dalgliesh
Abraham Lincoln's World, by Genevieve Foster
Lone Journey: The Life of Roger Williams, by Jeanette Eaton

1946 *Strawberry Girl*, by Lois Lenski
Honor Books: *Justin Morgan Had a Horse*, by Marguerite Henry
The Moved-Outers, by Florence Crannell Means
Bhimsa, The Dancing Bear, by Christine Weston
New Found World, by Katherine Shippen

1947 *Miss Hickory*, by Carolyn Sherwin Bailey
Honor Books: *Wonderful Year*, by Nancy Barnes
Big Tree, by Mary and Conrad Buff
The Heavenly Tenants, by William Maxwell
The Avion My Uncle Flew, by Cyrus Fisher
The Hidden Treasure of Glaston, by Eleanore Jewett

1948 *The Twenty-One Balloons*, by William Pène duBois
Honor Books: *Pancakes–Paris*, by Claire Huchet Bishop
Li Lun, Lad of Courage, by Carolyn Treffinger
The Quaint and Curious Quest of Johnny Longfoot, by
Catherine Besterman
The Cow-Tail Switch, And Other West African Stories, by
Harold Courlander
Misty of Chincoteague, by Marguerite Henry

1949 *King of the Wind*, by Marguerite Henry
Honor Books: *Seabird*, by Holling C. Holling
Daughter of the Mountains, by Louise Rankin
My Father's Dragon, by Ruth S. Gannett
Story of the Negro, by Arna Bontemps

1950 *The Door in the Wall*, by Marguerite de Angeli
Honor Books: *Tree of Freedom*, by Rebecca Caudill

The Blue Cat of Castle Town, by Catherine Coblentz
Kildee House, by Rutherford Montgomery
George Washington, by Genevieve Foster
Song of the Pines, by Walter and Marion Havighurst

1951   Amos Fortune, Free Man, by Elizabeth Yates
Honor Books: Better Known as Johnny Appleseed, by Mabel Leigh Hunt
Gandhi, Fighter Without a Sword, by Jeanette Eaton
Abraham Lincoln, Friend of the People, by Clara Ingram Judson
The Story of Appleby Capple, by Anne Parrish

1952   Ginger Pye, by Eleanor Estes
Honor Books: Americans Before Columbus, by Elizabeth Baity
Minn of the Mississippi, by Holling C. Holling
The Defender, by Nicholas Kalashnikoff
The Light at Tern Rocks, by Julia Sauer
The Apple and the Arrow, by Mary and Conrad Buff

1953   Secret of the Andes, by Ann Nolan Clark
Honor Books: Charlotte's Web, by E. B. White
Moccasin Trail, by Eloise McGraw
Red Sails to Capri, by Ann Weil
The Bears on Hemlock Mountain, by Alice Dalgliesh
Birthdays of Freedom, Vol. 1, by Genevieve Foster

1954   . . . And Now Miguel, by Joseph Krumgold
Honor Books: All Alone, by Claire Huchet Bishop
Shadrach, by Meindert DeJong
Hurry Home Candy, by Meindert DeJong
Theodore Roosevelt, Fighting Patriot, by Clara Ingram Judson
Magic Maize, by Mary and Conrad Buff

1955   The Wheel on the School, by Meindert DeJong
Honor Books: Courage of Sarah Noble, by Alice Dalgliesh
Banner in the Sky, by James Ullman

1956   Carry On, Mr. Bowditch, by Jean Lee Latham
Honor Books: The Secret River, by Marjorie Kinnan Rawlings
The Golden Name Day, by Jennie Lindquist
Men, Microscopes, and Living Things, by Katherine Shippen

1957   Miracles on Maple Hill, by Virginia Sorensen
Honor Books: Old Yeller, by Fred Gipson
The House of Sixty Fathers, by Meindert DeJong
Mr. Justice Holmes, by Clara Ingram Judson
The Corn Grows Ripe, by Dorothy Rhoads
Black Fox of Lorne, by Marguerite de Angeli

1958   Rifles for Watie, by Harold Keith
Honor Books: The Horsecatcher, by Mari Sandoz
Gone-Away Lake, by Elizabeth Enright
The Great Wheel, by Robert Lawson
Tom Paine, Freedom's Apostle, by Leo Gurko

1959 *The Witch of Blackbird Pond,* by Elizabeth George Speare
      Honor Books: *The Family Under the Bridge,* by Natalie S. Carlson
                   Along Came a Dog, by Meindert DeJong
                   Chucaro: Wild Pony of the Pampa, by Francis Kalnay
                   The Perilous Road, by William O. Steele

1960 *Onion John,* by Joseph Krumgold
      Honor Books: *My Side of the Mountain,* by Jean George
                   America Is Born, by Gerald W. Johnson
                   The Gammage Cup, by Carol Kendall

1961 *Island of the Blue Dolphins,* by Scott O'Dell
      Honor Books: *America Moves Forward,* by Gerald W. Johnson
                   Old Ramon, by Jack Schaefer
                   The Cricket in Times Square, by George Seldon

1962 *The Bronze Bow,* by Elizabeth George Speare
      Honor Books: *Frontier Living,* by Edwin Tunis
                   The Golden Goblet, by Eloise McGraw
                   Belling the Tiger, by Mary Stolz

1963 *A Wrinkle in Time,* by Madeleine L'Engle
      Honor Books: *Thistle and Thyme,* by Sorche Nic Leodhas
                   Men of Athens, by Olivia Coolidge

1964 *It's Like This, Cat,* by Emily Cheney Neville
      Honor Books: *Rascal,* by Sterling North
                   The Loner, by Ester Wier

1965 *Shadow of a Bull,* by Maia Wojciechowska
      Honor Book: *Across Five Aprils,* by Irene Hunt

1966 *I, Juan De Pareja,* by Elizabeth Borten de Treviño
      Honor Books: *The Black Cauldron,* by Lloyd Alexander
                   The Animal Family, by Randall Jarrell
                   The Noonday Friends, by Mary Stolz

1967 *Up a Road Slowly,* by Irene Hunt
      Honor Books: *The King's Fifth,* by Scott O'Dell
                   Zlateh the Goat and Other Stories, by Isaac Bashevis Singer
                   The Jazz Man, by Mary H. Weik

1968 *From the Mixed-Up Files of Mrs. Basil E. Frankweiler,* by E. L. Konigsburg
      Honor Books: *Jennifer, Hecate, Macbeth, William McKinley, and Me,
                   Elizabeth,* by E. L. Konigsburg
                   The Black Pearl, by Scott O'Dell
                   The Fearsome Inn, by Isaac Bashevis Singer
                   The Egypt Game, by Zilpha Keatley Snyder

1969 *The High King,* by Lloyd Alexander
      Honor Books: *To Be a Slave,* by Julius Lester
                   When Shlemiel Went to Warsaw and Other Stories, by Isaac
                   Bashevis Singer

1970 *Sounder,* by William H. Armstrong
      Honor Books: *Our Eddie,* by Sulamith Ish-Kishor

The Many Ways of Seeing: An Introduction to the Pleasures of Art, by Janet Gaylord Moore

Journey Outside, by Mary Q. Steele

1971   *Summer of the Swans,* by Betsy Byars

Honor Books: *Knee-Knock Rise,* by Natalie Babbitt

Enchantress from the Stars, by Sylvia Louise Engdahl

Sing Down the Moon, by Scott O'Dell

1972   *Mrs. Frisby and the Rats of NIMH,* by Robert C. O'Brien

Honor Books: *Annie and the Old One,* by Miska Miles

The Headless Cupid, by Zilpha Keatley Snyder

Incident at Hawk's Hill, by Allan W. Eckert

The Planet of Junior Brown, by Virginia Hamilton

The Tombs of Atuan, by Ursula K. LeGuin

1973   *Julie of the Wolves,* by Jean Craighead George

Honor Books: *Frog and Toad Together,* by Arnold Lobel

The Upstairs Room, by Johanna Reiss

The Witches of Worm, by Zilpha Keatley Snyder

1974   *The Slave Dancer,* by Paula Fox

Honor Book: *The Dark Is Rising,* by Susan Cooper

1975   *M. C. Higgins, the Great,* by Virginia Hamilton

Honor Books: *My Brother Sam Is Dead,* by James Lincoln Collier and Christopher Collier

The Perilous Gard, by Elizabeth Marie Pope

Phillip Hall Likes Me. I Reckon Maybe, by Bette Greene

Figgs & Phantoms, by Ellen Raskin

For other children's book awards see *Awards and Prizes,* a paperback published by the Children's Book Council, 175 Fifth Ave., New York, N.Y. 10010.

APPENDIX *C*

Other References for Children's Literature

Anderson, William, and Groff, Patrick. *A New Look at Children's Literature*. Belmont, Calif.: Wadsworth, 1972.

Provides a methodology for literary analysis of children's stories. Also examines and discusses the different types of children's literature. Presents a stimulating and intelligent set of recommendations for teaching literature to children. Contains an annotated bibliography of children's books corresponding to the different types of books examined in the text. Interesting and informative book.

Arbuthnot, May Hill, and Sutherland, Zena. *Children and Books*, 4th edition. Glenview, Ill.: Scott, Foresman, and Company, 1972.

Revised considerably from the 1964 edition, this valuable reference provides discussions of books based on a genre approach. One chapter takes surface recognition of issues. The appendixes provide the reader with book-selection aids, references, publishers' addresses, children's book awards, and a pronunciation guide. The book also recommends criteria for judging children's books. This text is one of the most comprehensive references published in the field of children's literature.

Benedict, Stewart H. *A Teacher's Guide to Contemporary Teeenage Fiction.* New York: Dell, 1973. Pb.

A practical teaching guide to Dell Laurel and Laurel-Leaf editions. Unfortunately, the suggested questions are closed-ended, even when they ostensibly ask opinion questions. The summaries and many of the suggested activities are interesting and useful. Fifteen books are included in this inexpensive paperback.

Brooks, Peter (ed.). *The Child's Part.* Boston: Beacon Press, 1969.

Provides a scholarly and historical approach to children's literature. Focuses on French critics and sources but concerns itself with children's literature in general.

Cameron, Eleanor. *The Green and Burning Tree.* Boston: Little, Brown, 1969. Pb. also.

A collection of essays written by the author about children's books. Sensitive analyses of the feelings and intentions of authors. The book includes discussions of fantasy, as well as on how to write for children.

Carlsen, G. Robert. *Books and the Teenage Reader.* New York: Harper & Row, 1967. Pb. Bantam.

Useful discussion of literary genres for readers age twelve and up. But extremely out-of-date. Does not acknowledge any of the social issues handled by contemporary books. Bibliographies are briefly annotated.

Carlson, Ruth Kearney. *Emerging Humanity, Multi-Ethnic Literature for Children and Adolescents.* Dubuque, Iowa: William C. Brown, 1972.

Descriptions and suggestions for using children's books containing characters of different ethnic and cultural backgrounds. Very practical and classroom-oriented.

———. *Enrichment Ideas.* Dubuque, Iowa: William C. Brown, 1970.

Each chapter contains a brief discussion of the topic, the history of language, vocabulary expansion, poetry, and books using loneliness as a theme. Selected references are listed, but not annotated. Hundreds of activities are described for children to do as an extension of their reading about and studying the above topics. A treasure chest of a book.

Catterson, Jane H. (ed.). *Children and Literature.* Newark, Del.: International Reading Association, 1970. Pb.

Articles representing an overview of children's literature. Includes theory as well as practice for classroom teachers.

Chambers, Dewey W. *Children's Literature in the Curriculum.* Chicago: Rand, McNally, 1971.

Somewhat limited attempt to introduce children's books into all of the curriculum areas in the elementary school.

Cianciolo, Patricia Jean (ed.). *Picture Books for Children.* Chicago: American Library Association, 1973.

An excellent resource and guide. The annotations of the books are useful and informational. The categories overlap somewhat, but the book is, in general, easy to use.

Cullinan, Bernice E. *Literature for Children: Its Discipline and Content.* Dubuque, Iowa: William C. Brown, 1971.
Advocates that critical reading of literature be taught to elementary school children. Presents literary analyses of children's narrative fiction. Suggests activities for teachers and students to extend their critical abilities further.

Egoff, Sheila; Stubbs, G. T.; and Ashley, L. F. (eds.). *Only Connect, Readings on Children's Literature.* Toronto: Oxford University Press, 1969.
A highly literate and stimulating collection of essays critically analyzing and discussing different aspects of children's literature.

Georgiou, Constantine. *Children and Their Literature.* Englewood Cliffs, N.J.: Prentice-Hall, 1969.
This book presents a genre approach to the study of children's literature. Its uniqueness lies in the lushness of its illustrations and its focus on the aesthetic quality of books. The extra-wide blocks of text are difficult to read, but the text itself is interesting. Not enough books are described for a text that aims at being used as a reference.

Gillespie, Margaret C. *History and Trends.* Dubuque, Iowa: William C. Brown, 1970.
A fascinating and thorough account of the history of children's literature, including several little-known names and interesting bits of information. Little attention is paid to contemporary times, but the book as a whole is entertaining and informative.

Haviland, Virginia. *Children's Literature, A Guide to Reference Sources.* Washington, D.C.: Library of Congress, 1966. *First Supplement,* 1972.
Two books containing an enormous number of annotated references covering the entire field of children's literature. The format is somewhat difficult to use. There are some important references omitted, but the two volumes are extensive resources.

Hopkins, Lee Bennett. *Books Are by People.* New York: Citation Press, 1969. Pb. Scholastic.
Interesting accounts of authors and illustrators of children's books. Hopkins interviewed one hundred and four people for this book. The information is presented in a personal, informal style. *More Books by More People,* by the same author, published in 1974, adds sixty-five additional authors and illustrators to the list. The interviews in the second book are longer and contain longer comments by the people interviewed.

Huck, Charlotte S., and Kuhn, Doris Young. *Children's Literature in the Elementary School.* New York: Holt, Rinehart and Winston, 1968.
Soon to be revised, this edition of the text is, nevertheless, valuable, extensive, and informative. Although the book emphasizes a genre and historical approach to children's literature, it also includes a substantial section on practical and creative methods for the classroom. Descriptions of children's books are sensitively and interestingly written. An awareness is expressed of the issues in children's books.

Issues in Children's Book Selection, A School Library Journal/Library Journal Anthology. New York: R. R. Bowker, 1973.
A collection of articles presenting perspectives on selecting children's books. Such topics as censorship, moral values, sex, self-image, and feminism are briefly but usefully presented. All of the articles are reprinted from the *School Library Journal.*

Larrick, Nancy, *A Parent's Guide to Children's Reading*, 4th edition. New York: Bantam Books, 1975. Pb.
Extensive, practical information and advice for parents and other concerned adults on how to encourage children to read. Many books are annotates in useful. contemporary categories.

————. *A Teacher's Guide to Children's Books.* Columbus: Merrill, 1963. Pb. also.
Excellent advice and practical suggestions for using children's books in the elementary school classroom. Some books are briefly described, but the emphasis is on their use.

Lickteig, Mary J. *An Introduction to Children's Literature.* Columbus: Merrill, 1975.
An overview of all of children's literature. Every topic is lightly touched on with indications for further study. The biographies, unfortunately, are not annotated. The author maintains an objectivity about all the topics and all the books. The appendixes and suggested references are useful. The author also contributes some practical suggestions for working with children.

Lonsdale, Bernard J., and Mackintosh, Helen. *Children Experience Literature.* New York: Random House, 1973.
Combines a genre approach with a practical, classroom approach. Includes a chapter on literature and personal growth. Somewhat uncritical but useful reference.

Luecke, Fritz J. (ed.). *Children's Books, Views and Values.* Middletown, Conn.: Xerox Education Publications, 1973. Pb.
Eight excellent articles reprinted from several scholarly journals concerning issues in children's literature. Issues included are death, violence, feminism, and multiethnic books.

Meeker, Alice M. *Enjoying Literature with Children.* New York: Odyssey Press, 1969. Pb.
Practical but somewhat traditional ideas for incorporating children's books into the elementary school curriculum.

National Council of Teachers of English. *High Interest–Easy Reading.* New York: Citation Press, 1972.
Concise and personalized annotations of many books in a number of different categories. This helpful list is aimed at students who need to have their interest awakened to reading.

Pilgrim, Geneva Hanna, and McAllister, Mariana K. *Books, Young People and Reading Guidance,* 2nd edition. New York: Harper & Row, 1968.
Discusses books in light of their guidance function for young people. Includes a consideration of the different reasons why people read.

Reasoner, Charles F. *Releasing Children to Literature.* New York: Dell, 1968. Pb.
Interesting and open-ended ideas for encouraging critical reading. This

book specifically pertains to the Dell Yearling books, but the activities are imaginative and pertinent to any books. Thirty specific books are included, many of which are concerned with topics such as death, siblings, females, and war.

————. *Where the Readers Are.* New York: Dell, 1972. Pb.
Another invaluable teachers' guide to imaginative and stimulating activities to accompany the reading of books. Reasoner specifically discusses thirty-four Dell Yearling books, but the ideas extend far beyond the particular books.

Reid, Virginia M. (ed.). *Reading Ladders for Human Relations,* 5th edition. Washington, D.C.: American Council on Education, 1972. Pb.
Excellent resource for books and how to extend their use with young readers. This book includes many themes pertaining to personal and emotional guidance. Creating a positive self-image and coping with change are among these themes.

Robinson, Evelyn R. (ed.). *Readings About Children's Literature.* New York: David McKay, 1966.
A book of readings relating to a genre and pedagogic approach to children's literature. The articles are interesting and provide different perspectives on books for children.

Sebesta, Sam Leaton, and Iverson, William J. *Literature for Thursday's Child.* Chicago: Science Research Associates, 1975.
A somewhat confusing mixture of a critical, genre, and practical approach to children's literature. The illustrations are lavish and enjoyable. The book is difficult to use.

Smith, Dora V. *Fifty Years of Children's Books.* Champaign, Ill.: National Council of Teachers of English, 1963. Pb.
A beautifully written, extremely informative, though traditional book on the history of children's literature. No mention is made of any contemporary issues.

Smith, James A. *Creative Teaching of Reading and Literature in the Elementary School.* Boston: Allyn and Bacon, 1970. Pb.
Lesson plans, suggestions, and a discussion of the philosophy of creative teaching make this book a very useful one for teachers.

Smith, James Steel. *A Critical Approach to Children's Literature.* New York: McGraw-Hill, 1967.
A scholarly literary approach to children's books. The author presents a methodology for critical analysis of children's literature.

Smith, Lillian H. *The Unreluctant Years.* New York: Viking, 1971. Pb.
A highly literate series of discussions of the different genres of children's literature. Smith presents her critical approach.

Strang, Ruth; Phelps, Ethylyne; and Withrow, Dorothy. *Gateways to Readable Books,* 4th edition. New York: H. W. Wilson, 1966.
An annotated bibliography of over one thousand entries classified into areas of interest to reluctant readers. Most of the books contain high interest but are at a fairly simple reading level.

Viguers, Ruth Hill. *Margin for Surprise*. Boston: Little, Brown, 1964.
Essays reflecting on the author's love of books and her respect for their impact on children. Viguers presents her opinions, her recollections, and her observations.

Whitehead, Robert. *Children's Literature: Strategies of Teaching*. Englewood Cliffs, N.J.: Prentice-Hall, 1968. Pb.
Hundreds of practical ideas for using books in the classroom. No mention is made of the impact or issues involved in books, but the intent is to provide a cookbook of ideas for activities.

Yolen, Jane. *Writing Books for Children*. Boston: The Writer, 1973.
Yolen advocates that books for children be written so that the writer and reader can "take joy." The book includes an awareness of the social issues involved in books but also advises authors to refrain from heavy didacticism. A well-written, interesting book.

Zaccaria, Joseph S., and Moses, Harold A. *Facilitating Human Development Through Reading; The Use of Bibliotherapy in Teaching and Counseling*. Champaign, Ill.: Stipes, 1968. Pb.
An extensive annotated bibliography follows a theoretical section on how to use books in a therapeutic manner with young readers.

Author / Illustrator Index

Aardema, Verna 196, 217
Abbott, Jerry L. 374
Abbott, Sarah 80, 96
Abdul, Raoul 217
Abdullah, Aishah S. 390
Abel, Midge 269
Adams, Adrienne 386
Adams, Florence 54, 59, 313, 323
Adams, Julia Davis 392
Adamson, Joy 323
Adkins, Jan 390
Adoff, Arnold 192, 217
Agee, James 96
Agle, Nan Hayden 59
Agueros, Jack 390
Ahlum, Carol 315
Albright, Donn 331
Alcock, Gudrun 218
Alcott, Louisa May 96, 306, 307, 323
Alexander, Lloyd 390, 396
Alexander, Martha 17, 25, 64, 110, 184, 190, 218
Alexander, Rae Pace 208, 218
Aliki 139, 231
Allee, Marjorie 388, 392
Allen, Terry 96, 274
Allinson, Beverly 323
Aloise, Frank 338
Ambrus, Victor 136

Ames, Louise Bates 23
Amos, Bad Heart Bull 286
Amos, Eileen 353
Andersen, Hans Christian 90, 386
Anderson, Kathleen 330
Anderson, Lonzo 25, 218
Anderson, William 398
Andre, Evelyn M. 323
Andrews, Benny 217
Andry, Andrew C. 16, 25, 153, 161
Angelo, Valenti 349, 393
Anglund, Joan Walsh 75
Annixter, Jane 264, 274
Annixter, Paul 264, 274
Arbuthnot, May Hill 398
Arkhurst, Joyce Cooper 196, 219
Armer, Laura Adams 383, 392
Armstrong, George 275, 285
Armstrong, William 92, 96, 204, 205, 214, 219, 396
Arenstein, Misha 129
Arnett, Kathleen 219
Arno, Enrico 226, 278
Arnstein, Helene S. 16, 25, 93
Arouni 236
Arty, L. C. 229
Artzybasheff, Boris 383
Arundel, Honor 51, 59, 86, 96, 157, 161
Asch, Frank 16, 26

Ashby, Gail 335
Ashley, L. F. 400
Asinof, Eliot 96, 127, 131
Atwater, Richard 393
Auckerman, Robert C. 374
Ayars, James Sterling 323

Babbitt, Natalie 323, 391, 397
Bacchus, Joan 229
Bach, Alice 19, 26
Baez, Joan 136
Bahti, Tom 388
Bailey, Carolyn Sherwin 394
Baily, A. V. 374
Baity, Elizabeth 395
Baker, Augusta 209, 214
Baker, Betty 121, 263, 264, 274
Baker, Elizabeth 131
Baker, Nina Brown 311, 324
Baldwin, Anne Norris 96, 219, 324
Bales, Carol Ann 266, 274
Bambara, Toni Cade 220
Bamy, Jan 140
Bare, Arnold E. 384
Barkley, James 219
Barnes, Nancy 394
Barnett, Moneta 32, 102, 232
Barnouw, Victor 259, 268
Barnum, Jay Hyde 384
Baron, Virginia Olsen 220, 275

Barthelme, Donald   390
Bartoli, Jennifer   97
Barton, Byron   62, 334
Baskin, Hosea   388
Baskin, Leonard   388
Baskin, Lisa   388
Baskin, Tobias   388
Baskin, Wade   160
Bateman, Patricia   167
Bawden, Nina   59
Baxter, Katherine   209
Baylor, Byrd   388
Bealer, Alex W.   265, 275
Beatty, Patricia   91, 96
Beck, Armin   209
Beck, Katy   209
Beckman, Gunnel   86, 97
Beim, Jerrold   26, 193, 220
Beim, Lorraine   193, 220
Belting, Natalia M.   275, 387
Bemelmans, Ludwig   384, 385, 393
Benchley, Nathaniel   121, 131, 265, 275
Bendick, Jeanne   161
Benedict, Stewart H.   399
Bennett, Jay   97
Bennett, John   392
Bereaud, Susan   321
Berger, Terry   59, 196, 220
Bernstein, Dan   110
Bernstein, Joanne E.   209, 315
Berry, Erik   393
Best, Herbert   392
Besterman, Catherine   394
Bewley, Sheila   169
Bhang, Samuel, Jr.   235
Bianco, Margery   393
Bible, Charles   230
Bierhorst, John   97, 275
Biesterveld, Betty   268, 275
Bileck, Marvin   387
Bingham, Jane   209
Birnbaum, A.   386
Birtha, Jessie   209
Bishop, Claire Hucket   388, 394, 395
Biskin, Donald   8
Bjorklund, Lorence F.   223, 281, 284
Black, Algernon D.   324
Blaine, Marge   324
Blassingame, Wyatt   324
Bleeker, Sonia   73, 95
Blevuad, Erik   109
Blickenstaff, Wayne   36, 324
Block, William A.   150, 158
Bloom, Harold   136
Blue, Rose   50, 60, 82, 98, 191, 220, 221

Bluenose, Philip   98, 276
Blume, Judy   26, 60, 156, 157, 161
Blustein, Ellen   230
Bock, William Sauts   275
Bogan, Louise   131
Bolognese, Don   241
Bolton, Carole   85, 98
Bond, Jean Cary   194, 221
Bonsall, Crosby   26, 120, 131, 324
Bontemps, Arna   98, 221, 394
Booth, Cordelia   221
Borack, Barbara   98
Borland, Hal   267, 276
Bostick, Christina   129
Bothwell, Jean   222
Bouchard, Lois Kalb   27
Bowen, William   391
Bowman, James Cloyd   393
Boyd, William   249, 391
Branfield, John   19, 27
Breasted, Mary   158
Brelis, Nancy   314, 325
Brenner, Fred   243
Brewer, Joan   158
Brink, Carol Ryrie   306, 325, 393
Britton, Jean E.   209
Broderick, Dorothy M.   176, 209
Brogan, Peggy   374
Brooks, Jerome   60, 98
Brooks, Peter   399
Broverman, Donald M.   291
Broverman, Inge K.   315
Brown, Dee   255, 265, 269, 276
Brown, James Jr.   230
Brown, Marcia   385, 386
Brown, Margaret Wise   78, 99, 384
Brown, Myra Berry   17, 27
Brown, Turner Jr.   222
Browning, Colleen   342
Brownmiller, Susan   325
Bruckner, Karl   99, 131
Bryan, Ashley   222
Bryson, Bernarda   387
Buchenholz, Bruce   391
Buck, Pearl S.   86, 95, 99, 127, 132, 153, 161, 388
Buckett, George   323
Buckley, Helen E.   97, 325
Buckmaster, Henrietta   325
Budd, Lillian   325
Buff, Conrad   384, 394, 395
Buff, Mary   384, 395
Bull, Amos Bad Heart   286
Bulla, Clyde Robert   276
Burch, Robert   97, 312, 326, 389
Burchard, Peter   222, 245, 276

Burglon, Nora   393
Burkert, Nancy Ekholm   388
Burland, C. A.   132
Burnett, Frances Hodgson   306, 307, 326
Burnette, Robert   254, 269
Burr, Dane   217
Burt, Olive   222, 223, 326
Burton, Virginia Lee   384, 385
Busoni, Rafaello   330
Butler, Francelia   93
Butterworth, W. E.   132
Byars, Betsy   20, 27, 326, 390, 397
Byler, Mary Gloyne   259, 263, 268, 269

Cacciola, Tina   170
Caines, Jeannette   27, 192, 223, 326
Calderone, Mary S.   159
Cameron, Eleanor   4, 8, 391, 399
Cane, Suzanne S.   270
Carlsen, G. Robert   399
Carlson, Dale   308, 326
Carlson, Natalie Savage   18, 27, 199, 223, 389, 396
Carlson, Ruth Kearney   210, 270, 374, 399
Carlson, Vada   276
Carpenter, Frances   196, 223
Carpenter, Mia   164
Carpenter, Walter S.   98, 276
Carr, Albert   128, 132
Carr, Mary Jane   393
Carr, Robin   93
Carroll, Lewis   295
Carty, Lee   243, 246
Carty, Leo   107, 343
Cather, Carolyn   345
Catterson, Jane H.   399
Caudill, Rebecca   387, 394
Chaffin, Lillie D.   389
Chalmers, Mary   40
Chambers, Bradford   223
Chambers, Dewey W.   399
Chan, Chin-yi   384
Chan, Plao   384
Charles, Milton   226
Charlip, Remy   99
Charlot, Jean   384, 386
Chastain, Madye Lee   226
Chatfield, Carol A.   270
Chen, Tony   278
Child Study Association of America   28, 159
Childress, Alice   391
Chorao, Kay   38, 60
Chrisman, Arthur Bowie   392
Cianciolo, Patricia Jean   9, 399

Citron, Abraham F.   210
Clapp, Ouida H.   210
Clapp, Patricia   390
Clark, Ann Nolan   265, 277,
    384, 395
Clark, Leonard   122, 132
Clarkson, Frank L.   315
Cleary, Beverly   19, 28, 327
Cleaver, Bill & Vera   21, 60, 86,
    87, 99, 312, 327, 328, 390
Clements, Bruce   391
Clifford, Eth   277
Clifford, Mary Louise   224
Clifton, Lucille   21, 29, 162,
    167, 188, 192, 199, 224,
    225, 328
Clymer, Eleanor   21, 29, 61,
    259, 277, 389
Coalson, Glo   39
Coatsworth, Elizabeth   86, 99,
    277, 328, 392
Cobble, Alice Wembi   225
Cober, Aland E.   97, 275
Coblentz, Catherine   395
Coburn, John B.   79, 100
CoConis, Ted   27
Cohen, Martha   316
Cohen, Miriam   328
Cohen, Vivian   163
Cole, Sheila R.   93, 329
Coles, Robert   225
Collier, Christopher   123, 132,
    391, 397
Collier, James Lincoln   123,
    132, 389, 391, 397
Collier, Peter   265, 277
Collins, Judy   136
Colman, Hila   18, 29, 226, 329,
    389
Colum, Padraic   391, 392, 393
Compere, Janet   241
Cone, Molly   278
Conger, John Janeway   23
Coolidge, Olivia   396
Coombs, Patricia   329
Cooney, Barbara   386
Cooper, Susan   316, 397
Copley, Heather   132
Corbin, William   388
Corcoran, Barbara   22, 29
Corcos, Lucille   188, 226
Cornelius, Paul   210
Courlander, Harold   196, 226,
    278, 394
Coutant, Helen   101
Cowan, Lore   126, 132
Cowley, Joy   117, 133
Cox, Mahala   9
Cox, Virginia   389

Crain, Henrietta   94
Crampton, Patricia   62
Crary, Margaret   278
Crawford, Phyllis   393
Credle, Ellis   329
Crichlow, Ernest   193, 220, 247
Crosby, Alexander L.   127, 132
Cruz, Ray   34, 166, 237, 342
Cuffari, Richard   33, 34, 64,
    103, 164, 166, 237, 279,
    280, 283
Cullinan, Bernice E.   400
Cunningham, Julia   391
Curry, Jane Louise   391

Dabcovich, Lydia   29
Dahl, Roald   4, 5, 9, 91, 226
Dalgliesh, Alice   263, 278, 306,
    329, 386, 394, 395
Dalke, Susan Sallade   102
Dalrymple, DeWayne   243
Daniels, Joan   321
Danish, Barbara   329
Darrow, Helen F.   374
Darrow, Whitney, Jr.   307, 329
Daugherty, James   384, 386, 393
d'Aulaire, Edgar   384, 391
d'Aulaire, Ingri   384
Davies, Hilary   154, 163
Davis, Dorritt   20, 30
Davis, Lavina   385
Davis, Mary Gould   392
Davis, Mavis Wormley   210
Day, Beth   162
Dayrell, Elphinstone   387
DeAngeli, Marguerite   227, 284,
    386, 394, 395
Deasy, Michael   188, 227
Decker, Isabelle M.   374
deGroat, Diane   61, 65
DeGroot, Roseann M.   316
DeJong, Meindert   133, 388,
    390, 395, 396
de la Mare, Walter   303
Delgado, Abelardo B.   390
Deloria, Vine Jr.   254, 255, 270
del Solar, Charlotte   159
Denby, Robert V.   210
dePaola, Tomi   79, 100
deRegniers, Beatrice Schenk
    330, 387
Desbarats, Peter   193, 227
DeSchweinitz, Karl   162
Despert, J. Louise   57
de Treviño, Elizabeth Borton
    227, 296
Dewey, Jane   266, 280
di Grazia, Thomas   25, 27, 248
Dillon, Diane   104

Dillon, Leo   104
Dinh, Vo   100
Distad, Audree   267, 278
Dixon, Paige   22, 30, 100
Dobrin, Arnold   78, 100
Dodge, Nanatah Chee   279, 290
Dolch, Edward W.   279, 375
Dolch, Marguerite L.   279
Dolin, Arnold   330
Domanska, Janine   388
Donald, M.   315
Donelson, Kenneth L.   9
Donlan, Dan   316
Donovan, John   52, 61, 92, 100,
    101, 156, 162, 390
Doty, Roy   26, 338
Dougherty, C.   333
Douglas, Stephanie   29, 225
Douglass, Joseph H.   210
Drescher, Joan E.   96
du Bois, William Pène   385, 394
Duinell, Carde Peterson   335
Duker, Sam   375
Duncan, Lois   18, 30
Dunning, Stephen   133
Dusold, Lenore   270
Duvoisin, Roger   385, 387

Eaton, Jeannette   392, 393, 394
Ebert, Len   245
Eckert, Allan W.   397
Edmonds, Michael   238
Edmonds, Walter D.   133, 394
Egoff, Sheila   400
Ehrlich, Amy   265
Eichenberg, Fritz   385
Eichler, Margaret   61, 330
Eifler, Deborah   322
Eisenberg, Eleanor   330
Ekwall, Eldon E.   365, 375
Elkin, Benjamin   386
Ellentuck, Shan   30
Ellis, Anne W.   23
Emberley, Barbara   119, 133,
    387
Emberley, Ed   119, 133, 387
Embry, Margaret   279
Engdahl, Sylvia Louise   397
Engebrecht, P. A.   21, 30, 330
Enright, Elizabeth   393, 395
Epstein, Beryl   20, 30
Erwin, Betty K.   330
Escourido, Joseph   223
Estes, Eleanor   30, 394, 395
Ets, Marie Hall   331, 384, 385,
    386, 387
Evans, Eva Knox   154, 162
Evans, Mari   227
Eyerly, Jeannette   61, 101, 162

Faber, Doris 331
Fader, Daniel N. 375
Fairfax, Jane 353
Farley, Carol 101
Farley, Charlotte Purrington
348
Fassler, Joan 79, 101, 194,
227, 331
Fax, Elton 196, 217, 231
Feelings, Muriel 228, 388
Feelings, Tom 221, 228, 229,
240, 388
Feingold, Maxine 159
Felton, Harold 331
Fenner, Phyllis, R. 134
Ferris, Helen 388
Fetz, Ingrid 169, 277
Field, Rachel 331, 384, 392
Fife, Dale 228, 268, 279
Finger, Charles 392
Fish, Helen Dean 134, 383
Fisher, Aileen 134, 163
Fisher, Cyrus 394
Fisher, Elizabeth 317
Fisher, Laura 270
Fitzgerald, Bertram A., Jr. 228
Fitzhugh, Louise 30, 119, 120,
134, 163, 312, 331, 349
Flack, Marjorie 384
Fleischhaver-Hardt, Helga
154, 163
Fletcher, Sydney 134
Folsom, Franklin 229
Forberg, Ati 102
Forbes, Esther 123, 134, 394
Forbey, Ati 280, 342
Ford, George 234
Ford, Lauren 384
Foreman, Michael 134
Forman, James 225
Foster, Genevieve 394, 395
Fox, Lorene K. 374
Fox, Paula 204, 208, 229,
390, 397
Fox, Thomas C. 128, 137, 390
Fralley, Jacqueline M. 35
Frame, Paul 222, 326
Franceschi, Theodore Laquer
389
Frank, Anne 86, 123, 135
Frank, Dick 40, 108
Frank, Josette 158
Frankenberg, Robert 286
Frascino, Edward 350
Frasconi, Antonio 386
Fraser, Betty 187, 350
Fraser, Kathleen 229
Frasher, Ramona 317
Frazier, Nancy 317
Freedman, Florence 198, 229

Freeman, Don 386
Friedman, Aileen 31
Friedman, Roberta 160
Friesel, Uwe 135
Fritz, Jean 198, 229
Frolov, Vadim 389
Fry, Rosalind 169
Fryer, Jeanne 375
Fuller, Nancy 355

Gag, Wanda 384, 392, 393
Gaggin, Eva Roe 394
Galdone, Paul 246, 386
Gaillard, T. L., Jr. 129
Gannett, Ruth S. 384, 394
Gardner, Richard A., M.D. 56,
60, 61-62, 304, 332
Gast, David K. 211
Gates, Doris 393
Gauch, Patricia Lee 135, 332
Geer, C. 350
Gendron, Lionel 163
Georgakas, Dan 279
George, Jean Craighead 84,
101, 311, 332, 391, 396,
397
Georgiou, Constantine 400
Gergely, Tibor 386
Gerhardt, Lillian, N. 129, 159
Gerson, Mary-Joan 17
Gersoni-Staun, Diane 317
Gerstein, Mordicai 341
Gillespie, Margaret C. 400
Gilman, Esther 330, 337
Gilmore, Iris 309, 351
Giovanni, Nikki 230
Gipson, Fred 102, 395
Gladstone, Gard 39
Glancy, Barbara J. 211
Glanzman, Louis, S. 39, 66, 248,
341, 348
Glasgow, Aline 389
Glasser, Barbara 230
Glattauer, Ted 279
Gleit, Maria 388
Gliewe, Unada 343
Goff, Beth 48, 62, 389
Goffstein, M. B. 332
Gold, Sharlya 31, 332
Goldman, Louis 347
Goldreich, Esther 332, 333
Goldreich, Gloria 332, 333
Goodyear, Carmen 333
Gordon, Judith 153, 163
Gordon, Sol 153, 163
Goudey, Alice E. 386
Graham, Al 384
Graham, Lorenz 211, 230, 384,
389
Graham, Margaret Bloy 385

Grahame, Anne & Janet 341
Grannis, Chandler B. 159
Granstrom, Jane 211
Grant, Leigh 34, 167, 338
Grant, Pat 336
Graves, Robert 333
Gray, Elizabeth Janet 392, 393,
394
Gray, Genevieve 31, 230, 231,
333
Gray, Louis Noack 210, 270
Green, Phyllis 102
Greenburg, Polly 188, 231
Greene, Bette 125, 135, 231,
312, 333, 391, 397
Greene, Constance C. 62, 334
Greenfeld, Howard 334
Greenfield, Eloise 17, 18, 23,
31, 102, 192, 231
Greenleaf, Phyllis Taube 318
Gregory, Horace 135
Grew, J. C. 129
Gridley, Marion E. 259, 279,
280
Griese, Arnold A. 270
Grifalconi, Ann 25, 27, 96,
218, 219, 224, 236, 250, 324
Griffin, Louise 211, 271
Grimm Brothers 91, 302
Gripe, Harold 62, 334
Gripe, Maria 55, 62, 314, 334
Groff, Patrick 398
Grollman, Earl A. 57, 72, 74,
75, 94
Grossman, Nancy 227, 234,
335
Groth, John 110
Gruenberg, Sidonie Matsner 23,
164
Guirma, Frederic 232
Gunther, John 102
Gurko, Leo 395
Guttmacher, Alan 159
Guy, Rosa 232

Habenstreit, Barbara 135
Hader, Berta 384, 385
Hader, Elmer 384, 385
Hagan, Elizabeth 318
Haley, B. 57
Haley, Gail E. 233, 387
Hall, Anna Gertrude 394
Hall, Donald 135
Hall, Elvajean 9
Hallas, Doris 225
Hallock, Grace 392
Hamilton, Virginia 193, 233,
390, 391, 397
Hampshire, Michael 28, 167
Hampton, Blake 161

Handforth, Thomas   334, 383
Hansen, Soren   155, 164
Hardy, Thomas   122
Harman, Humphrey   234
Harnden, Ruth   95, 380
Harris, Audrey   102
Harris, Janet   308, 334
Harris, Larry A.   375
Haskins, James   234, 334
Hassrick, Royal B.   280
Hautzig, Esther   390
Havighurst, Marion   395
Havighurst, Walter   395
Haviland, Virginia   400
Hawes, Charles   391, 392
Haynes, Betsy   234
Hays, Wilma Pitchford   264, 280
Heide, Florence Parry   102, 266, 280
Heide, Wilma Scott   318
Hellberg, Hans-Eric   62
Henderson, Nancy   266, 280
Henriod, Lorraine   335
Henry, Jeanette   271
Henry, Marguerite   394
Herman, Charlotte   164
Herman, Harriet   303, 334
Hermanson, Dennis   108
Hernandez, Antonia A.   390
Herzog, George   196, 226
Hettlinger, Richard F.   164
Hewes, Agnes   392, 393
Heyn, Leah   318, 335
Heyward, Dubose   335
Higgs, Margaret   321
Hill, Elizabeth Starr   32, 187-188, 234, 313, 335
Hillerman, Tony   281
Hilu, Virginia   159
Himlet, Ronald   36, 167
Hinton, S. E.   102
Hipshman, Helen   229
Hirsch, Marilyn   59, 323
Hirsch, S. Carl   266, 281
Hirschfelder, Arlene   271
Hitte, Kathryn   186, 235
Ho, Minfong   389
Hoban, Lillian   32, 336
Hoban, Russell   17, 32
Hochman, Sandra   335
Hochschild, Arlie Russell   335
Hodges, Bruce E., M.D.   164
Hodges, Margaret   263, 281, 387
Hoehling, Mary   136, 309, 335
Hoexter, Corinne   235
Hoff, Syd   102, 263, 281
Hoffman, Phyllis   194, 235
Hogrogian, Nonny   234, 322, 387

Hokada, Elizabeth   322
Holbrook, Stewart   385
Hold, Fibben   104
Holland, Isabelle   32, 62-63, 103, 156, 164
Holland, John   235
Holland, Viki   33
Hollander, John   136
Holling, Holling C.   384, 394, 395
Hollingsworth, Alvin   217
Holm, Anne   136
Holman, Felice   336
Holmes, Margaret C.   270
Holt, Deloris   199, 235
Hoover, Ross   165
Hopkins, Lee Bennett   129, 236, 237, 336, 400
Horvath, Betty   236, 336
Hosoe, Eikoh   137
Hoskisson, Kenneth   8
Housekeeper, G.   374
Houser, Allan   277
Howard, Moses L.   236, 312, 336
Howard, Rob   97, 162
Howard, Vanessa   236
Howe, Florence   318
Howe, Julia Ward   128
Howell, Ruth   236
Howes, Virgil M.   374, 375
Hoyt, Howard   94
Hubbard, Ralph   392
Huck, Charlotte S.   400
Hughes, Langston   236, 237
Hughes, Shirley   38
Hunt, Irene   95, 124, 136, 336, 396
Hunt, Mabel Leigh   394, 395
Hunt, Wolf Robe   285
Hunter, Kristin   33, 237, 336, 389, 391
Hunter, Mollie   103, 389
Hurd, Clement   165
Hurd, Edith   165
Hutchins, Pat   33
Hyman, Trina Schart   325

Icolari, Dan   271
Ignatowicz, Nina   143
Ilg, Frances L.   23
Ipcar, Robert   332, 333
Isaac, Barbara Kohn   137
Ish-Kishor, Sulamith   396
Iverson, William J.   402
Iwasaki, Chihiro   165

Jaco, Ernest   210, 270
Jackson, Edgar N.   72, 73, 94
Jackson, Ezra   229

Jackson, Florence   237
Jacobs, Helen Hull   337
James, Harold   220
James, Will   392
Jarrell, Mary   17, 33
Jarrell, Randall   388, 396
Jeffers, Susan   388
Jenkins, Esther C.   211
Jensen, Gordon   165
Jensen, Jesper   155, 164
Jeschler, Susan   162, 225
Jewell, Nancy   337
Jewett, Eleanore   394
Johansen, Margaret   392
Johnson, Annabel   63
Johnson, Bonnie   230
Johnson, Corinne B.   165
Johnson, E. Harper   242
Johnson, Edgar   63
Johnson, Elizabeth   337
Johnson, Eric W.   156, 165
Johnson, Gerald W.   396
Johnson, John E.   138
Johnson, Pamela   282
Jones, Adrienne   33, 237
Jones, Bartlett C.   318
Jones, Cordelia   136
Jones, Elizabeth Orton   385
Jones, Hettie   281
Jones, Idwal   393
Jones, Jessie Orton   384
Jordan, June   9, 20, 34, 191, 199, 237, 337, 390
Joslin, Sesyle   386
Judson, Clara Ingram   395

Kagan, Jerome   23
Kalashnikoff, Nicholas   395
Kalnay, Francis   396
Kane, Irene   214, 321
Kantrowitz, Mildred   78, 103
Katz, Bobbi   337
Kaufman, Joe   337
Kaufman, Michael   238
Kaufmann, John   223, 274
Keating, Charlotte Matthews   10, 212, 271
Keats, Ezra Jack   17, 34, 184, 185, 186, 191, 192, 214, 238, 239, 337, 387
Keegan, Marcia   282
Keith, Eros   229, 233
Keith, Harold   395
Keller, Gail Faithfull   338
Kellogg, Steven   26, 27, 31, 36, 136, 223, 326
Kelly, Eric P.   392
Kendall, Carol   396
Keniston, Kenneth   10
Kepes, Juliet   385

Kerckfoff, Richard 212
Kerr, Judith 126, 137
Kerr, M. E. 63, 338
Kerr, Robert S. 279, 313
Kessler, Leonard 353
Key, Mary Ritchie 319
Kiddell-Monroe, Joan 219
Kills Two 286
Kindred, Wendy 63
Kingman, Lee 338, 384
Kircher, Clara J. 23
Kirk, Ruth 282
Kirn, Ann 239
Klein, Barry T. 271
Klein, Carole 57
Klein, Norma 17, 18, 20, 34, 63, 64, 157, 166, 314, 338
Klein, Stanley 103, 307
Klein, Suzanna 344
Kluetmeier, Heinz 59
Knight, Clayton 137
Knudsen, Per Holm 158, 167
Kohl, Herbert 375
Kohn, Bernice 118, 137
Komoda, Kiyo 343
Konigsburg, E. L. 35, 239, 339, 391, 396
Kossin, Sandy 351
Kram, Judith 319
Kranz, Stewart 101, 227
Krasilovsky, Phyllis 339
Kratka, Suzanne C. 16, 25
Kraus, Robert 35, 197, 240
Krauss, Ruth 340, 385, 386
Krementz, Jill 189, 239
Krumgold, Joseph 395, 396
Krush, Beth 40, 41, 323
Krush, Joe 40, 41, 323, 350
Kubinyi, Laszlo 275, 281
Kubler-Ross, Elizabeth 94
Kuhn, Doris Young 400
Kushun, Carla 169
Kyle, Anne 393

Labastida, Aurora 386
Lader, Lawrence 311, 340
Laklan, Carli 389
Lampman, Evelyn Sibley 267, 282
Landau, Elaine 308, 340
Lane, Joan T. 130, 319
Lanes, Selma G. 212
Lang, Andrew 303
Langone, John 74, 94
Langstaff, John 386
Lantz, Paul 133
Larrick, Nancy 175, 212, 215, 239, 340, 401
Larue, H. S. 221
Lasker, Joe 35, 246, 314, 340

Latham, Jean Lee 395
Lathrop, Dorothy 331, 383, 392
Latimer, Bettye I. 185, 212
Laure, Jason & Ettagale 391
Lauritzen, Jonreed 388
Lawrence, Jacob 197, 240, 310, 340
Lawson, Robert 383, 384, 394, 395
Lazare, Jerry 36, 104, 326
Leaf, Munro 383
Leder, Dora 246, 350
Lee, Mildred 92, 103
Lee, Virginia 79, 103
LeGuin, Ursula K. 390, 397
Leichman, Seymour 137
L'Engle, Madeleine 85, 95, 103, 313, 340, 366
Lenski, Lois 388, 393, 394
Lent, Blair 286, 387, 388
Lester, Julius 23, 199, 206, 208, 212, 218, 240, 391, 396
Leuder, Edward 133
Levering, Bob 283
Levine, Milton I., M.D. 167
Levinson, Irene 341
Levitin, Sonia 341
Levy, Elizabeth 187, 341
Levy, Miriam 229
Lewin, Ted 60, 98, 231
Lewis, C. S. 122-23, 104, 137
Lewis, Elizabeth 392
Lewis, Richard 240, 282
Lewis, Susan 319
Lexau, Joan M. 20, 35, 56, 64, 190, 241, 341, 389
Lieberman, Marcia 319
Lickteig, Mary J. 401
Lide, Alice 392
Lifton, Betty Jean 128, 137, 390
Liley, Margaret 162
Lilly, Charles 231, 244, 333
Lindgren, Astrid 312, 341
Lindquist, Jennie 395
Lionni, Leo 386, 387
Lipke, Jean 167
Lipsyte, Robert 389
Little, Jean 36, 85, 104
Littledale, Freya 104
Livingston, Myra C. 10
Lobel, Anita 98, 116, 138, 284
Lobel, Arnold 41, 387, 390, 397
Locke, Linda A. 94
Lockett, Sharon 282
Loercher, Donna 319
Lofting, Hugh 202, 241, 392
Lofts, Norah 312, 341
Lone Wolf 280

Longfellow, Henry Wadsworth 127
Longsworth, Polly 242, 310, 342
Lonsdale, Bernard J. 401
Lopshire, Robert 120, 131, 138
Love, Sharron 20, 36
Lowenheim, Alfred 61, 62, 332
Lownsbery, Eloise 392
Lowry, Heath W. 10
Luecke, Fritz J. 316, 401
Lukenbill, W. Bernard 319
Lundgren, Max 104
Lunge, Jeffrey 279
Luric, Alison 302, 320
Lynch, Lorenzo 102
Lyons, Oren 268, 286
Lystad, Mary 342

MacCann, Donnarae 213
MacDonald, Golden 385
MacGregor, Ellen 313, 343
McAllister, Mariana K. 401
McAlpine, Julie Carlson 130
McCannon, Dindga 250
McCloskey, Robert 342, 384, 385
McConkey, Lois 283
McCully, Emily Arnold 27, 41, 103, 217, 220, 235, 275, 336, 347, 353
McDermott, Gerald 283, 388
McEntee, Dorothy 283
McGinley, Phyllis 342, 384
McGovern, Ann 194, 197, 242, 262, 283
McGowan, Tom 138
McGraw, Eloise 395, 396
McHargue, Georgess 391
McIntosh, Millicent 159
McKay, David 109
McKown, Robin 389
Macaulay, David 388
Macken, Walter 36
Mackintosh, Helen 401
Maginnis, Beverly 61
Malcolmson, Anne 385
Malkus, Alida 392
Mallet, Anne 36
Mann, Peggy 49, 64, 167, 343
Manushkin, Fran 36, 167
Marriott, Alice 283
Mars, W. T. 277
Marshall, Bernard 391
Marshall, Catherine 242
Martin, Fran 283
Martin, Frederic 99
Martin, Patricia Miles 343

Martin, Stefan   104
Mason, Miriam E.   36
Mathis, Sharon Bell   37, 104, 213, 242, 243, 343, 389
Matson, Emerson N.   262, 284
Matsuno, Masaka   37, 343
Maxwell, Florenz Webbe   389
Maxwell, William   394
May, Julian   167, 168
Mayle, Peter   155, 158, 168
Mazer, Harry   64-65
Mazer, Norma Fox   37, 54, 65, 88, 104, 391
Meader, Stephen W.   393
Means, Florence Crannel   388, 394
Meigs, Cornelia   391, 392, 393
Meeker, Alice M.   401
Mele, John   110
Meltzer, Milton   284, 311, 340, 344, 390, 391
Mendoza, George   104, 188, 243
Menstra, Friso   354
Mercer, Joan Bodger   160
Merghan, Don   168
Merriam, Eve   308, 314, 340, 344
Merrill, Jean   104, 138
Messer, Ronald K.   243
Mickinock, Rey   258, 272
Miles, Miska   79, 105, 284, 397
Milhous, Katherine   385
Mill, Eleanor   67, 108, 249, 352
Millay, Edna St. Vincent   87
Miller, Arthur   344
Miller, Don   224, 234, 249
Miller, Elizabeth   392
Miller, Mitchell   142
Miller, Wilma H.   375
Minard, Rosemary (ed.)   303, 316, 344
Minarik, Holmelund Else   386
Mindey, Carol   58
Minnesota Council on Family Relations   160
Mizumura, Kazue   37, 96, 343
Moberg, Verne   320
Mocniak, George   96
Moffett, James   362
Mofsie, Louis   281
Monjo, F. N.   138, 143, 198, 243, 263, 272, 284, 391
Montgomery, Rutherford   395
Montresor, Beni   387
Moon, Elzia   31
Moon, Grace   392
Moore, Anne Carroll   392
Moore, Janet Gaylord   397
Moore, Thomas   128
Moran, Barbara   320

Morris, Barbara   95
Morton, Marion   107
Mosel, Arlene   344, 388
Moses, Harold A.   403
Moss, Judith   95
Mukerji, Dhan Gopal   392
Murakin, Tak   168
Murgatroyd, Madeline   243
Murray, Irene   35, 341
Murray, Michele   338
Mussen, Paul Henry   23
Myers, Bernice   116, 138, 389
Myers, Walter Dean   244, 344

Nadisan, Ardell   320
Nagenda, John   244
Nash, Ogden   139, 345
Nathan, Dorothy   345
Neilson, Francis   345
Neilson, Winthrop   345
Neisser, Edith G.   23
Ness, Evaline   20, 29, 37, 105, 192, 224, 225, 324, 328, 345, 387
Neufeld, John   37, 160, 168, 244
Neville, Emily Cheney   396
Newberry, Clare   384, 385
Newfield, Marcia   65
Newland, Mary Reed   168
Newman, Jeffry   272
NicLeodhas, Sorche   105, 387, 396
Nicolas   385
Nilsen, Alleen Pace   95, 320
Nilsson, Hennert   162
Noble, Iris   346
Noonan, Julia   355
Norris, Gunilla   65
North, Sterling   396
Norton, Mary   346

O'Brien, Robert C.   390, 397
O'Dell, Scott   21, 37, 85, 105, 264, 284, 311, 346, 396, 397
Odenwald, Robert P.   168
Okamoto, Dorothy Torniye   390
Olds, Elizabeth   385
Oliver, Linda   320
Oppenheim, Joanne   116, 139
Ordbrown, Joyce   243
Orgel, Doris   19, 38, 105
Ortiz, Victoria   244, 346

Palazzo, Tony   384
Palladini, D.   355
Paquet, Basil T.   140
Parish, Peggy   38, 313, 346
Parker, Arthur C.   262, 285
Parker, Robert Andrew   281, 387

Parks, Carole A.   213
Parks, David   236
Parks, Gordon, Jr.   67, 249, 353
Parnell, Peter   105, 281, 284
Parrish, Anne   392, 395
Patchen, Kenneth   127, 139
Paustovsky, Konstantin   346
Payson, Dale   38, 105
Pease, Howard   388
Peck, Ellen   347
Penny, Grace Jackson   347
Perl, Lila   347
Perl, Susan   62, 313
Perrault, Charles   385, 386
Perrine, Mary   285
Perron, Robert   227
Perry, Jean M.   10
Petersham, Maud   384
Petersham, Miska   384
Peterson, Christian C.   270
Pevsner, Stella   65
Pfeffer, Susan Beth   347
Phelps, Ethylyne   402
Phillips, Lynn   347
Pickens, David   280
Pilgrim, Geneva Hanna   401
Pincus, Harriet   40, 349
Pinkney, Jerry   219, 227, 248, 250
Pinney, Doris   169
Pintauro, Joseph   105
Pinto, Ralph   240, 333
Platt, Kin   65-66, 105
Pogrebin, Letty Cottin   320, 352
Politi, Leo   384, 385
Pomeroy, Wardell   156, 168
Ponderhughes, J.   236
Pope, Elizabeth M.   397
Portal, Colette   169
Porter, C. Fayne   285
Porter, E. Jane   10
Porter, George   28
Porter, Pat Grant   38
Povey, Gail   375
Powell, Miriam   388
Powers, G. Pat   160
Powers, R. M.   242
Prather, Ray   233
Prempeh, Albert Kofi   196, 226
Preston, Edna Mitchell   387, 390
Prida, Dolores   321
Prince, Lenora E.   250
Pugh, Clifton   107
Puner, Helen W.   24

Quarles, Benjamin   229
Queen, Gertrude Davidson   58

Rabin, Gil   106
Rachlin, Carol K.   283

Randall, Florence Engel   244
Rankin, Louise   327
Ransome, Arthur   387
Raskin, Edith   285
Raskin, Ellen   60, 394, 397
Raskin, Joseph   285
Rawlings, Marjorie Kinnan   395
Reasoner, Charles F.   376, 401, 402
Reavin, Sam   347
Reed, Philip   387
Reeder, Kirk   321
Reid, Virginia M.   213, 402
Reiss, Johanna   126, 139, 397
Reit, Seymour   347
Remarque, Erick Maria   139
Rey, Margaret & H. A.   389
Reyher, Becky   384
Rhoads, Dorothy   395
Rhodin, Eric   106
Ribner, Susan   321
Rich, Gibson   348
Richard, Adrienne   391
Richter, Conrad   285
Richter, Hans P.   139
Riggs, Corrinne W.   10
Ringi, Kjell   118, 140
Riswald, Gilbert   63
Rizzo, Ann   348
Robbins, Ruth   386
Roberts, Margaret   140
Roberts, Wallace   164
Robertson, Don   228
Robins, Arthur   168
Robinson, Charles   59, 106, 107, 109
Robinson, Evelyn R.   402
Robinson, Jean   89, 106
Robinson, Mabel   393
Robinson, Michele P.   290
Rocher, Fermin   97, 236, 335
Rockwell, Anne   143
Rockwell, Harlow   308, 348
Rodgers, Mary   348
Rojankovsky, Feodor   386
Rollins, Charlemae   213
Rollock, Barbara   213
Romano, Clare   245
Romero, Lee   238
Roosevelt, Eleanor   388
Rosen, Winifred   38
Rosenkrantz, Paul S.   315
Ross, Catherine   322
Ross, Eulalie Steinmetz   75
Ross, John   245
Roth, Roslyn   130
Rothman, Joel   308, 348
Rothman, Larry   140
Rounds, Glen   351
Rourke, Constance   393

Rubinger, Michael   348
Rudolph, Marguerite   169
Rushmore, Helen   285
Ryan, Cheli Durian   140, 387, 390

Sachs, Marilyn   19, 22, 38, 66, 140, 348, 390
Sadher, Myra   317
Sagarin, David   239
Saint-Exupery, Antonie   106
Salten, Felix   106
Samson, Joan   16, 39
Sandin, Joan   62
Sandoz, Mari   286, 395
Sarah, Becky   348
Sartain, Harry W.   376
Sattley, Helen R.   388
Sauer, Julia   394, 395
Sawyer, Ruth   349, 384, 385, 393
Schaefer, Jack   396
Schecter, Betty   389
Scheer, George F.   262, 286
Scheer, Julian   387
Schepp, Steven   153, 161
Schick, Eleanor   17, 39, 66, 245
Schindelman, Joseph   226
Schlein, Miriam   39, 386
Schlesinger, Benjamin   58
Schmidt, Nancy J.   214
Schmidt, Sarah   393
Schnur, Gloria L.   24
Schoenherr, John   101, 332
Schottland, Miriam   339
Schraff, A. E.   245
Schram, Barbara A.   321
Schreiber, George   385
Schulte, Emerita Schroer   10
Schwartz, Albert V.   203, 214
Scoppetone, Sandra   119, 120, 134, 349
Scott, Ann Herbert   17, 39, 245, 349
Sebesta, Sam Leaton   402
Sechrist, Elizabeth Hough   140
Seed, Suzanne   349
Seeger, Elizabeth   393
Seeger, Pete   128
Segal, Lore   40, 349
Seldon, George   396
Seligmann, Jean H.   167
Sendak, Maurice   133, 142, 340, 386, 387
Seow, Djeow   305
Seredy, Kate   140, 384, 393
Servello, Joe   275
Seuss, Dr.   385
Seuling, Barbara   236, 336
Sewell, Helen   354, 386

Shannon, Monica   393
Shargel, Susan   214, 321
Sharmat, Marjorie Weinman   40, 350
Shearer, John   245
Shecter, Ben   42, 67, 80, 98, 106, 143, 325, 335, 355
Sheffield, Margaret   158, 169
Shemin, Margaretha   389
Shepard, John P.   11
Shepard, Mary   249
Shepard, Ray Anthony   185, 214, 245, 389
Sherburne, Zoa   389
Shilstone, Arthur   345
Shimin, Symeon   31, 33, 39, 163, 164, 231, 234, 245, 349
Shippen, Katherine   394, 395
Shortall, Leonard   338, 341
Shotwell, Louisa   245
Showers, Kay   169
Showers, Paul   154, 169, 195, 246
Shulevitz, Uri   107, 350, 387
Sidjakov, Nicholas   386
Siebel, Fritz   346
Siegl, Helen   285
Silvey, Anita   211
Simon, Norma   195, 246, 350
Simon, Seymour   350
Simont, Marc   385
Singer, Isaac Bashevis   390, 396
Singmaster, Elsie   39
Sitea, Linda   67
Siveat, Lynn   101
Skorpen, Liesel Moak   82, 107
Sleator, William   286, 387
Slobodkin, Louis   30, 384
Slote, Alfred   86, 107
Smith, Alvin   110
Smith, Carl B.   375
Smith, Dana   348
Smith, Dora V.   402
Smith, Doris Buchanan   79, 107, 389
Smith, Frank   163
Smith, Hugh   133
Smith, Ivan   107
Smith, James A.   402
Smith, James Steel   402
Smith, Joe   98, 276
Smith, Lillian H.   402
Smith, William Jay   131
Smyth, M. Jane   25
Snedeker, Caroline   392, 393
Sneve, Virginia Driving Hawk   259, 268, 286, 389
Snyder, Joel   348
Snyder, Zilpha Keatley   391, 396, 397

Solbert, Ronni 138, 246
Sommerfelt, Aimee 389
Sonneborn, Ruth A. 107, 190, 191, 246
Sorel, Edward 133
Sorensen, Virginia 40, 306, 307, 350, 388, 395
Soundburg, Helga 107
Sowell, Floyd 230
Spanfeller, Jim 99, 328
Speare, Elizabeth George 351, 396
Speare, M. E. 141, 396
Sperry, Armstrong 393
Spier, Peter 386
Stacey, Judith 321
Stahl, Ben F. 140, 287
Stanek, Muriel 56, 67, 160
Stanley, Henry M. 197, 217
Stawicki, Christine 397
Steele, Mary Q. 397
Steele, William O. 141, 396
Steichen, Edward 141
Steig, William 108, 141, 387, 390
Stein, Lucille 58
Stein, Sara Bennett 16, 40, 108, 153, 169
Steinem, Gloria 352
Steiner, Charlotte 351
Steiner, Stan 254, 272
Steinzer, Bernard 58
Stensland, Anna Lee 272
Steptoe, John 20, 21, 23, 31, 40, 152, 170, 185-187, 191, 214, 224, 231, 232, 246, 247
Sterling, Dorothy 201, 247
Stevens, Carla 154, 170
Stevens, Leonard 170
Stevenson, James 100
Stewig, John 321
Stolz, Mary 50, 67, 89, 108, 248, 388, 391, 396
Stone, Helen 342, 385
Stong, Phil 393
Strain, Frances 170
Strandquest, Dominique Michele 108
Strang, Ruth 402
Strong, Arline 236
Stubbs, G. T. 400
Stubley, Trevor 224
Stull, Edith G. 80, 108
Suba, Susan 167
Sucksdorff, Astrid Bergman 170
Sugarman, Tracy 26, 38
Suhl, Isabelle 203, 214
Suhl, Yuri 141
Sullivan, Stephanie Carlson 130
Sukowiecki, Sandra Lucas 351

Supraner, Robyn 351
Sutherland, Ketra 341
Sutherland, Zena 398
Swenson, Evelyn J. 95
Swift, Hildegarde 393
Syme, Ronald 287
Szasz, Suzanne 162
Szekeres, Cyndy 235

Tait, Douglas 283
Talbot, Charlene Joy 41
Talbot, Toby 108
Talmadge, Marian 309, 351
Tamarin, Alfred 266, 287
Tate, Joan 97
Taves, Isabella 351
Taylor, Francis 229
Taylor, Mark 351
Taylor, Mildred D. 248
Taylor, Sydney 41, 390
Taylor, Theodore 203, 214, 248
Terris, Susan 41, 352
Thane, Elswyth 352
Thayer, Jane 352
Thomas, Ianthe 187, 248
Thomas, Marlo 352
Thompson, Judith 214
Thum, Marcella 248
Thurber, James 384
Tibbets, Alfred B. 141
Tibbetts, Sylvia-Lee 321
Tiegreen, Alan 28
Tietjens, Eunice 392
Titus, Eve 386
Toman, Walter 13, 24
Tomes, Margot 135, 332
Topolski, Feliks 221
Torrey, Marjorie 384
Travers, P. L. 202, 249, 352
Treffinger, Carolyn 394
Trella, Sherry Crane 212
Tremblay, Jack 163
Tresselt, Alvin 384, 385, 387
Tripp, Wallace 107
Trost, Marion 376
Tsinajinnie, Andrew 276
Tuder, Tasha 384, 386
Tunis, Edwin 390, 396
Tunis, John R. 141, 142, 388
Turkle, Brinton 224, 246, 387

Udry, Janice May 108, 120, 142, 191, 249, 314, 352, 386
Ullman, James 395
Unsworth, Richard 159
Ungerer, Tomi 352
Untermeyer, Louis 142
Unwin, Nora S. 251
Uslander, Arlene S. 160

Valenzuela, Juan 389
vanLoon, Hendrik Willem 391
VanStockum, Hilda 142, 393
Veatch, Jeanette 376
Vestly, Anne-Catherine 308, 353
Vevitrall, Patricia Reilly 351
Viguers, Ruth Hill 403
Viorst, Judith 41, 78, 109
Vogel, Ray 188, 249
Vogel, Susan R. 315
Vogel, Virgil J. 254, 272
Volavkova, Hana 122, 142
Vosburgh, Leonard 355

Waber, Bernard 353
Wagner, Jane 67, 249, 353
Wahl, Jan 142
Walker, Alice 249
Walker, Annabelle 317
Walker, Gil 324
Wallner, John C. 324
Walsh, Joan 142
Walter, Mildred Pitts 250
Walton, Jeanne 215
Warburg, Sandol Stoddard 79, 109
Ward, Lynd 99, 134, 229, 385
Warmfeld, Hope 242
Warren, Betsy 330, 353
Warren, Ruth 308, 353
Watson, Clyde 42, 390
Watson, Wendy 42
Watt, Lois B. 215
Watts, Mabel 354
Weaver, Robert 64, 241
Webb, Margot S. 389
Weik, Mary Hays 250, 396
Weil, Ann 395
Weil, Lisl 109
Weiner, Sandra 250
Weisgard, Leonard 30, 109, 278, 285, 329, 337, 384
Weisman, Ann 222
Weisner, William 353
Weitzman, Lenore J. 322
Welch, Elizabeth H. 130
Wells, Rosemary 42
Wersba, Barbara 160
Werth, Kurt 99, 161, 354
Weston, Christine 394
Wheeler, Opal 384
White, David Omar 222
White, E. B. 92, 109, 295, 354, 390, 395
White, Edgar 250
White, Eula T. 160
Whitehead, Robert 403
Whitehead, Ruth 109
Whitney, Alex 263, 287

Whitney, Elinor 392
Whitney, Phyllis 250
Whitney, Thomas 346
Whittier, John Greenleaf 142
Wiberg, John L. 376
Wier, Ester 109, 396
Wiese, Kurt 384, 385
Wiggin, Kate Douglas 90, 109
Wigglesworth, Emmett 220
Wilder, Laura Ingalls 295, 306, 354, 393, 394
Wilkon, Jozef 135
Will 385
Williams, Albert 337
Williams, Barbara 267, 287
Williams, Garth 109, 354
Williams, Jay 303, 354
Williams, Oscar 87
Wilson, Beth P. 250
Wilson, John 35, 217, 241
Windsor, Patricia 86, 110
Winthrop, Elizabeth 22, 42, 156, 170

Witherspoon, Gary 276
Withrow, Dorothy 402
Wojciechowska, Maia 86, 110, 376
Wolf, Anna W. M. 58, 73, 95
Wolf, Bernard 287
Wolfe, Ann G. 215, 272
Wolkstein, Diane 160
Wondriska, William 142, 288
Wood, James Playstead 354
Woodard, Gloria 212
Woods, George 212
Woodward, Gloria 213, 214
Wunderlich, Elaine 215
Wyse, Lois 110, 184

Yashima, Taro 386-388
Yates, Elizabeth 251, 394, 395
Yeager, Allan 376
Yellow Robe, Rosebud 288
Yolen, Jane 117, 143, 304, 355, 387, 391, 403
Young, Bernice Elizabeth 251

Young, Ed 355, 387
Young, Eleanor 355
Young, Ella 372
Young, Jacqueline Lee 215
Young, Jim 110
Young, Rodney L. 143

Zaccaria, Joseph S. 403
Zapleen, Simone 170
Zarssoni, Marjory 335
Zaturenska, Maria 135
Zemach, Harve 387, 388, 391
Zemach, Margot 387, 388
Zim, Herbert S. 73, 75
Ziman, Edmund, M.D. 24
Zimnik, Reiner 123, 143
Zindel, Paul 92, 110, 170
Zion, Gene 385
Zolotow, Charlotte 17, 42, 55, 67, 111, 120, 143, 355, 387, 388
Zuber, Barbara 221
Zwack, Jean M. 24

Title Index

Abby 27, 192, 223, 326
ABC Bunny 393
ABC: The Story of the Alphabet 389
The ABC's of Black History 119, 235
About the B'nai Bagels 339
About Dying 108
About 100 Books . . . A Gateway to Better Intergroup Understanding 215, 273
Abraham Lincoln 384
Abraham Lincoln, Friend of the People 395
Abraham Lincoln's World 394
Across Five Aprils 124-125, 136, 396
Across the Meadow 80, 81, 106
Adam of the Road 394
Adam's ABC's 228
Adam's World: San Francisco 187, 229
Admission to the Feast 86, 97
"Adventures in Blackland with Keats and Steptoe" 219
The Adventures of Spider: West African Folk Tales 196, 219
Africa: A List of Printed Materials for Children 185, 196, 211

African Herd Boy — A Story of the Masai 222
African Myths and Legends 219
African Wonder Tales 196, 223
The Ageless Story 384
An Album of the American Indian 288
Alexander and the Windup Mouse 387
Alice in Wonderland 295
All Alone 395
All Alone With Daddy 331
All Around the Town 385
"All Chiefs, No Indians: What Children's Books Say About American Indians" 270
All Falling Down 385
All in the Morning Early 387
All-of-a-Kind Family Downtown 41
All Quiet on the Western Front 139
All Sail Set 393
"All They Do Is Run Away" 209
All Us Come Across the Water 224
"The All-White World of Children's Books" 212
Almost Twins 38
The Almost Year 244

Along Came a Dog 396
Always Room for One More 387
Amanda the Panda and the Redhead 41, 352
Amanda's Choice 102
Amelia Bedelia 313, 346
Amelia Earhart, First Lady of Flight 343
Amelia Mixed the Mustard and Other Poems 345
Amelia Quackenbush 31, 332
America is Born 396
America Moves Forward 396
An American ABC 384
American Heroes All 141
American Indian and Eskimo Authors: A Comprehensive Bibliography 271
American Indian Authors for Young Readers: A Selected Bibliography 259, 268, 269, 271
"American Indian Life As Portrayed In Children's Literature" 269
American Indian Mythology 283
American Indian Women 259, 279
"The American Negro in Children's Literature" 215

American Negro Poetry 98, 221
Americans Before Columbus 395
America's Ethan Allen 385
Amos and Boris 390
Amos Fortune, Free Man 251, 395
Amy and Laura 19, 38
Amy and the New Baby 17, 27
Anansi the Spider 388
Anatole 386
Anatole and the Cat 386
And I Mean It, Stanley 324
And I Must Hurry for the Sea Is Coming In 188, 243
"And Jill Came Tumbling After, Sexism in American Education" 321
. . . And Now Miguel 395
Andy and the Lion 384
The Angry Moon 286, 387
The Animal Family 396
Animals of the Bible 383
"Ann Nolan Clark — Building Bridges of Cultural Understanding" 270
Anne and the Sand Dobbies 79, 100
Anne Frank: Diary of a Young Girl 123, 126, 134, 135
Annie and the Old One 79, 81, 105, 284, 397
"Annotated Bibliography of Integrated and Black Books for Children" 211
Ape in a Cape 385
The Apple and the Arrow 395
The Apple Strudel Soldier 138
The Apple War 116-17, 138
Apprentice of Florence 393
Approaches to Beginning Reading 374
Approaches to Individualized Reading 374
April's Kittens 384
Apt. 3 185, 238
Are You There God? It's Me, Margaret 156, 161
Arrow to the Sun 283
Arrow to the Sun, A Pueblo Indian Tale 388
The Art and Industry of Sandcastles 390
At the Center of the World 263, 274
Audobon 393
"An Author Speaks" 211
The Avion My Uncle Flew 294
Avoiding Stereotypes 318

Awards and Prizes 397
Away Is So Far 108

Baboushka and the Three Kings 386
A Baby Is Born 167
A Baby Sister for Frances 17, 32
A Baby Starts to Grow 154, 169
The Bad Island 141
Bambi 106
Bambino the Clown 385
Bang, Bang, You're Dead 119, 134
Banner in the Sky: The Story of a Boy and a Mountain 395
"Barbara Frietchie" 142
Barkis 384
Barkley 102
Bartholomew and the Oobleck 385
Bartholomew, We Love You 19, 38
"Basic Concepts of Death in Children's Literature" 94
"Battle Hymn of the Republic" 128
Be Nice to Josephine 336
Bear Party 385
The Bears' House 22, 39, 66, 390
The Bears on Hemlock Mountain 395
The Beauty of Birth 169
The Beauty Queen 347
The Beach Tree 99
Beeswax Catches A Thief 239
Before You Were A Baby 169
The Beginnings of Life: How Babies Are Born 154, 162
Behavior Patterns in Children's Books 23
Being Born 170
Belling the Tiger 396
Benjie 190, 241
Benjie On His Own 241
Betrayed 286
Better Known as Johnny Appleseed 395
Bhimsa, The Dancing Bear 394
Bibliotherapy: An Annotated Bibliography 10
The Big Book of Cowboys 134
Big Brother 35
Big Sister, and Little Sister 42
The Big Snow 385
Big Tree 394
Big Tree of Bunlaky 393
The Big Wave 86, 95, 97, 388

The Biggest Bear 385
Billy And Our New Baby 16, 25
Bimby 222
The Bird's Christmas Carol 90, 109
The Birth of Sunset's Kittens 154, 170
Birth: The Story of How You Came To Be 163
Birthday 21, 40, 246
Birthdays of Freedom, Vol. 1 395
Bisha of Burundi 224
The Black American in Books for Children: .Readings in Racism 213
"Black Americans In Children's Books" 215
"Black and White: An Exchange" 212
The Black BC's 199, 224
Black, Black, Beautiful Black 220
The Black Cauldron 396
Black Courage 245
Black Crusader, Frederick Douglass 235
The Black Experience in Children's Books 213
Black Fairy Tales 196, 220
Black Folktales 240
Black Fox of Lorne 395
Black Image: Education Copes With Color 211
"Black Images in Children's Literature: Revised Editions Needed" 210
Black Is 222
Black is Beautiful 194, 242
"Black is Bountiful" 212
Black Is Brown Is Tan 192, 217
The Black Man in America, 1932-1954 237
Black Misery 236
Black Mountain Boy: A Story of the Boyhood of John Honie 276
Black Out Loud 217
The Black Pearl 396
"Black Perspectives in Books for Children" 214
Black Pilgrimage 228
"Black Publishing for Black Children" 211
"Black Women Are Proud" 210
Black Women of Valor 222, 326

The Blanket Word 86, 96
Blowfish Live in the Sea 390
The Blue Cat of Castle Town 395
Blue Willow 393
Blueberries for Sal 385
Blue's Broken Heart 104
Bo and The Old Donkey 107
Boats on the River 384
Bongo Bradley 230
A Book for Jodan 65
Book of Nursery and Mother Goose Rhymes 386
Books and the Teenage Reader 399
Books Are By People 400
"Books by African Authors for Non-African Children" 214
Books for Brotherhood 213, 272
Books, Young People and Reading Guidance 401
The Borrowed House 142
The Borrowers 346
A Boy Is A Boy 345
Boy of the South Seas 392
The Boy Who Could Make Himself Disappear 65-66
The Boy Who Could Sing Pictures 137
The Boy Who Didn't Believe in Spring 188, 224
The Boy Who Made Dragonfly 281
The Boy Who Was 392
The Boy Who Wouldn't Talk 27
Boy With A Pack 393
The Boys and Girls Book About Divorce 56, 61-62
Boys and Girls, Girls and Boys 308, 344
Boys and Sex 156, 168
The Boy's Book of Verse: An Anthology 134
Brady 199, 229
Bright April 198, 227
Bright Island 393
Break a Magic Circle 337
The Bronze Bow 396
Brothers and Sisters 23
Brothers and Sisters Are Like That 28
Brown is a Beautiful Color 194, 221
Bubble Bath 36, 167
Building Bridges of Understanding Between Cultures 10, 212, 271
Bury My Heart At Wounded Knee 255, 269

Busy People 337
By the Shores of Silver Lake 393

Caddie Woodlawn 306, 325, 393
Calico Bush 392
Calico Row 325
"A Call for Help: Exploring The Black Experience in Children's Books" 211
Call It Courage 393
Carry On, Mr. Bowditch 395
The Case of the Scaredy Cats 324
The Castles of the Two Brothers 31
The Cat Who Went to Heaven 87, 99, 392
Cathedral: The Story of Its Construction 388
The Cave 277
The Cay 203, 214, 248
"The Cay: Racism Rewarded" 214
Cedric the Forester 391
Challenge to Become a Doctor: The Story of Elizabeth Blackwell 335
Changes 106
"The Changing Image of the Black in Children's Literature" 209
"The Changing Role of the Child in American Society as Reflected in Literature for Children" 10
"The Changing Roles of Females in Books for Young Children" 315
Chanticleer and the Fox 386
"The Charge of the Light Brigade" and other Story Poems* 142
Charlie and the Chocolate Factory 4-5, 8, 202, 226
"Charlie and the Chocolate Factory: A Reply" 9
Charlotte's Web 92, 109, 295, 306, 354, 395
Checklist for Female-Male Roles in Books 315
Cherokee Animal Tales 262, 286
Chie and the Sports Day 37, 343
Child Behavior 23
Child Development and Personality 23
Children and Books 398
Children and Literature 399

Children and Their Literature 400
Children Experience Literature 401
Children of Divorce 57
Children of the Resistance 126, 132
Children of the Soil 393
Children of Vietnam 128, 137, 390
"Children's Books" 318
"Children's Books and Racism" 212
Children's Books: Awards and Prizes 397
"Children's Books Relating to Death" 75
"Children's Books: The Second Sex, Junior Division" 317
Children's Books, Views and Values 316, 401
Children's Literature, A Guide to Reference Sources 400
First Supplement 400
"Children's Literature and Value Theory" 9
"Children's Literature — in Chaos, a Creative Weapon" 10
Children's Literature in the Curriculum 399
Children's Literature in the Elementary School 400
Children's Literature: Strategies of Teaching 403
A Child's Good Night Book 384
The Child's Part 399
A Child's Right to Equal Reading 320
The Chinese Red Riding Hoods 303
Chloris and the Creeps 53, 66, 105
The Christmas Anna Angel 384
Chronicles of American Indian Protest 270
Chronicles of Negro Protest 223
Chucaro: Wild Pony of the Pampa 396
Cinderella, or the Little Glass Slipper 386
Cinderelma 304
Circle of Life: The Miccosukee Indian Way 266, 280
Circle of Seasons 265, 277
City ABC's 188, 227
The City Book 188, 226
City in the Summer 245
City in the Winter 66

Clearing Weather   384, 392
Cock-a-Doodle Doo   384
The Codfish Musket   393
Colleen the Question Girl   335
The Colorful Story of North
   American Indians   280
Combat Nurses of World War II
   324
Combatting the Influence of
   Black Stereotypes in Chil-
   dren's Books   209
"A Comparative Analysis of the
   Depiction of War in Select-
   ing Juvenile Fiction Pub-
   lished prior to and since
   1960"   130
"A Comparison Between the
   Content of First Grade
   Primers and the Free Choice
   Library Selections Made By
   First Grade Students"   376
"A Comparison of the Parental
   Image Found in Selected
   Children's Books of the
   Nineteen-Thirties with those
   of the Nineteen-Sixties"
   316
Conception and Contraception
   167
Confessions of An Only Child
   17, 18, 34, 166
Conjure Tales by Charles W.
   Chestnutt   245
The Conjure Woman   245
Constance   390
The Contender   389
"A Content Analysis of Chil-
   dren's Contemporary Fic-
   tion Books that Pertain to
   Broken Homes and Steprela-
   tionships"   58
"A Content Analysis of Materi-
   als for the Early Sex Educa-
   tion of Children"   159
"A Content Analysis of Selected
   Fiction for Elementary
   School Children Depicting
   the Theme of Sibling Rela-
   tionships and Rivalries"   24
The Corn Grows Ripe   395
Council on Interracial Books for
   Children Bulletin   177, 178,
   202, 206, 210
The Country Bunny and the
   Little Gold Shoes   335
The Courage of Sarah Noble
   263, 278, 306, 329, 395
The Court of the Stone Children
   391
Cowslip   234

The Cow-Tail Switch, And Other
   West African Stories   196,
   226, 394
Coyote Tales   281
A Crack in the Pavement   236
Craig and Joan: Two Lives for
   Peace   96, 127, 131
The Crane   123, 143
The Creoles of Color of New
   Orleans   234
Crow Boy   386, 388
Creative Teaching of Reading
   and Literature in the Ele-
   mentary School   402
The Cricket in Times Square
   396
"Criteria in Selection of Black
   Literature for Children"
   215
A Critical Approach to Chil-
   dren's Literature   402
The Crystal Cabinet, An Invita-
   tion to Poetry   135
The Crystal Nights   138
Curious George Goes to the
   Hospital   389
Custer Died for Your Sins   254,
   270

Dakota Sons   267, 278
The Dancing Horses of Acoma
   and Other Acoma Indian
   Stories   285
Daniel Boone   393
The Dark Frigate   392
The Dark is Rising   397
The Dark Star of Itza   392
Dash and Dart   384
Daughter of the Mountains
   394
Daughter of the Seine   392
David He No Fear   230
David, Young Chief of the
   Quileutes: An American
   Indian Today   282
Davy Crockett   393
Dawn   107
"The Dawning of the Age of
   Aquarius in Multi-Ethnic
   Children's Literature"   211
The Day I Had To Play With My
   Sister   26
A Day of Pleasure: Stories of a
   Boy Growing Up in Warsaw
   390
Day on Skates   393
The Day of the Bomb   99, 131
The Day the Hurricane Happened
   25, 218

The Day They Hanged the
   Sioux, and Other Stories
   From Our Indian Heritage
   285
The Day We Saw the Sun Come
   Up   386
The Dead Bird   78, 99
Dead End School   225
"Death and Dying: Facts, Fic-
   tion, Folklore"   95
Death Be Not Proud   102
"Death as Presented in Chil-
   dren's Books"   93
"Death in Children's Litera-
   ture"   93, 95
A Death In the Family   96
Death Is a Noun, A View of the
   End of Life   74, 94
The Death of a Wombat   107
Deathman Do Not Follow Me
   97
The Defender   395
Delpha Green and Company
   28, 327
"A Descriptive Bibliography of
   Selected Children's Books
   That Treat Death's Effect
   on the Child Hero (With an
   Essay on Death as a Theme
   in Children's Books)   94
The Devil's Storybook   391
Diary of a Frantic Kid Sister
   18, 19, 29, 329
Dick and Jane as Victims, Sex
   Stereotyping in Children's
   Readers   322
Dick Whittington and His Cat
   385
Did the Sun Shine Before You
   Were Born?   153, 163
Dinky Hocker Shoots Smack
   313, 338
"Dirge Without Music"   87
The Divorced Mother   58
Do You Have the Time, Lydia?
   20, 37, 345
Dobry   393
Doctor in the Zoo   391
Doctor Dolittle   202, 203, 214
"Doctor Dolittle, The Great
   White Father"   203, 214
"Does Individualized Reading
   Affect Other Subject
   Areas?"   374
Dolley Madison   343, 352
Dominic   390
Don't Worry, Dear   194, 227
Don't You Remember?   21, 29,
   192, 224, 328
Don't You Turn Back   237

The Door in the Wall   394
Down, Down the Mountain
   329
*Down From the Lonely Moun-
   tain*   278
Down Ryton Water   394
Down the Rabbit Hole   212
"Down with Sexist Upbringing"
   320
Downright Dencey   392
*Dr. Gardner's Fairy Tales for
   Today's Children*   332
The Dragon and the Doctor
   329
The Dragon Takes a Wife   344
Dream Coach   392
Dream of the Blue Heron   259,
   268, 274
The Drinking Gourd   198, 248,
   263
The Drowning Boy   41
Drummer Hoff   119, 133-134,
   387
Drums and Trumpets   122, 132
Dry Victories   199, 237
Duck in the Gun   117, 133
Duffy and the Devil   388, 391

*East of the Sun, and West of the
   Moon*   303
Edgar Allan   37, 244
The Edge of Next Year   108,
   391
"Educating Women: No More
   Sugar and Spice"   318
Education Index   76
Education Task Force Report
   315
The Egg Tree   385
The Egypt Game   396
El Pito De Plata De Pito   390
Ellen Grae   60, 312, 327
Ellen Tebbits   327
Elsa   323
Elvira Everything   16, 26
*Emerging Humanity, Multi-
   Ethnic Literature for Chil-
   dren and Adolescents*   210,
   399
*Emily and the Klunky Baby and
   the Next-Door Dog*   56, 64
*Emily Dickinson: Her Letter to
   the World*   342
Emily Elizabeth Dickinson   354
Emma Edmonds Nurse and Spy
   309-310, 351
*Emmeline and Her Daughters:
   The Pankhurst Suffragettes*
   346

The Emperor and the Kite   305,
   355, 387
The Empty Moat   389
The Empty Schoolhouse   200,
   223, 389
Enchantress From the Stars
   397
End of the Game   226
The Endless Steppe   390
*Enjoying Literature With Chil-
   dren*   401
Enrichment Ideas   399
"Evaluative Criteria to Be Used
   as Guides by Writers of Chil-
   dren's Literature"   10
Evan's Corner   32, 187, 188,
   234, 313, 335
Everett Anderson's Year   224
Every Man Heart Lay Down
   230
Everybody Ought To Know
   139
"Everything You've Always
   Wanted to Know About Sex
   Education"   160
Exactly Like Me   347
Explaining Death to Children
   74, 94
Explaining Divorce to Children
   57
"Exploding the Fairy Princess
   Myth"   319
*Exploring Black America: A
   History and Guide*   248
Eyak   390

*Facilitating Human Development
   Through Reading: The Use
   of Bibliotherapy in Teaching
   and Counseling*   403
The Fairy Circus   392
"Fairy Tale Liberation"   320
Fairy Tales for Today's Children
   304
Family Constellation   24
A Family Failing   51, 53, 59
*Family Life Literature and
   Films*   160
The Family of Man   141
The Family Story in the 1960's
   23
The Family Under the Bridge
   396
*Famous American Indians of
   the Plains*   266, 281
Fannie Lou Hamer   337
Fansben the Magic Bear   348
The Farthest Shore   390
*Fast Sam, Cool Clyde and
   Stuff*   244

The Fastest Quitter in Town
   102
Father Fox's Pennyrbymes
   390
A Father Like That   55, 67
"Fathers in Adolescent Books"
   319
The Fearsome Inn   396
Feather Mountain   385
" 'Feeling Books' Develop Social
   and Personal Sensitivities"
   9
"Feminist Criticism: An Over-
   view"   317
"A Feminist Look at Children's
   Books"   316
*Feminist Resources for Schools
   and Colleges: A Guide to
   Curricular Materials*   315
"Feminists Look at 100 Books:
   The Portrayal of Women in
   Children's Books on Puerto
   Rican Themes"   321
"Fifteen Reasons Why Person-
   alized Reading Instruction
   Does Not Work"   374
Fifty Years of Children's Books
   402
Figgs & Phantoms   397
Fighting Shirley Chisholm   334
A Figure of Speech   37, 88, 89,
   104, 391
The Final Mystery   103
Finders Keepers   385
*The Fire Bringer, A Paiute In-
   dian Legend*   263, 281
*The Fire Plume: Legends of the
   American Indians*   97, 275
Firegirl   348
First Snow   100
First Will and Testament   139
Fish in the Air   385
Five Little Monkeys   385
The Flight of the Doves   36
Floating Island   392
Fly High, Fly Low   386
Fog   92, 103
Fog Magic   394
*The Fool of the World and the
   Flying Ship*   387
"For Young Readers: Introduc-
   ing Death"   94
The Forest Pool   383
The Forest Princess   303, 335
The Forgotten Daughter   393
Foundations for Change   210
Four and Twenty Blackbirds
   383
*The Fox Went Out On a Chilly
   Night*   386

"The Fractured Family in Adolescent Literature" 57
Freaky Friday 348
Freddy's Book 168
Frederick 139
Free To Be You and Me 352
Friedrich 387
A Friend Can Help 59
The Friends 232
Frog & Toad are Friends 387, 390
Frog and Toad Together 397
Frog Went a'Courtin' 386
From the Mixed-up Files of Mrs. Basil E. Frankweiler 35, 339, 396
Frontier Living 396
The Funny Little Woman 344, 388
The Funny Old Bag 109

Gabrielle and Selena 193, 194, 227
Gaelic Ghosts 105
The Gammage Cup 396
Gandhi, Fighter without a Sword 395
The Garden Is Doing Fine 101
Garram the Hunter 392
Gateways to Readable Books 402
Grayneck, the Story of a Pigeon 392
George Washington 395
George Washington's World 394
Georgina and the Dragon 338
Geronimo, The Fighting Apache 287
Gertrude Stein, a Biography 334
"Getting Started With Individualized Reading" 375
Ghosts and Spirits of Many Lands 104
Gillespie and the Guards 386
Ginger Pye 395
A Girl and Her Room 342
A Girl Called Al 62, 334
The Girl from Puerto Rico 389
The Girl Inside 101
A Girl Like Me 162
Girl Soldier and Spy: Sarah Emma Edmundson 136, 309-310, 335
The Girl Who Cried Flowers and Other Tales 304, 355, 391
The Girl Who Loved the Wind 305, 355
Girls and Boys Together 319

Girls and Sex 156, 168
Girls Are Equal Too, The Women's Movement for Teenagers 308, 326
Girls Are Girls and Boys Are Boys 163
Girls Can Be Anything 307, 338
Girls Can Too! 336
"Girls Grow Up to Be Mommies: A Study of Sexism in Children's Literature" 321
"Girls' Liberation" 320
Giving Away Suzanne 18, 30
Gladys Told Me to Meet Her Here 350
Glory of the Seas 393
Go and Hush the Baby 20, 27
The Gods and Heroes of War 132
Goggles 185, 238, 387
Golden Basket 393
The Golden Fleece and the Heroes Who Lived Before Achilles 391
The Golden Goblet 396
The Golden Journey: Poems for Young People 131
Golden Legacy 197, 198
The Golden Treasure of Poetry 142
The Golden Name Day 395
Goldie the Dollmaker 332
Gone-Away Lake 395
" 'Good Children' (our Own), 'Bad Children' (Other People's), And the Horrible Work Ethic" 10
The Good Greenwood 106
Good Luck Horse 384
The Good Master 393
Good Old James 100
Good, Says Jerome 29, 225, 328
"Good-bye Black Sambo" 213
Goodnight, Andrew, Goodnight, Craig 39
The Goose Girl 91
Grandfathers Are to Love 110, 184
Grandfather's Bridge 390
Grandma Didn't Wave Back 82, 98
Grandmother and I 325
Grandmothers Are to Love 184
Grandpa 98
Grandpa's Maria 62
Great American Heroines 330
The Great Excluded: Critical

Essays on Children's Literature 93
The Great Minu 250
The Great Quest 391
The Great Wheel 395
The Green and Burning Tree 399
Green Eyes 386
The Grizzly 63
Grover 87, 88, 99, 390
Growing Time 79, 80, 83, 109
Growing Up 162
Growing Up With Sex 164
Guests in the Promised Land 391
"A Guide to Sex Education Books: Dick Active, Jane Passive" 158
"Guidelines for Equal Treatment of the Sexes in McGraw-Hill Book Company Publications" 320
"Guidelines for Improving the Image of Women in Textbooks" 321
Guy Lenny 64-65

The Half Sisters 18, 19, 27
Hang Tough, Paul Mather 86, 107
Hans and Greta 304
Happy Birthday, Mom 323
The Happy Day 385
Harlem, The Story of a Changing Community 251
Harriet and the Promised Land 197, 240, 310, 340
Harriet the Spy 312, 331
Harvey's Hideout 32
The Hating Book 120, 143
Hat-Shaking Dance and Other Tales from the Gold Coast 196, 226
Have You Seen Tom Thumb? 394
The Headless Cupid 397
Heart of Danger 388
The Heavenly Tenants 394
Hello Aurora 308, 353
Hello the Boat! 393
Helping Brother and Sisters Get Along 24
Helping Children Read: A Practical Approach to Individualized Reading 374
Helping Your Child to Understand Death 73, 95
Henrietta, the Wild Woman of Borneo 38
Henry Huggins 327

"Here Come Processions" 122
Here Comes Tagalong 36
Here I Am 220, 275
A Hero Ain't Nothin' But a
    Sandwich 391
He's My Brother 35
Hi Cat 238
Hi, New Baby 16, 25
The Hidden Treasure of Glaston
    394
Hide and Seek Fog 387
High Elk's Treasure 268, 286
High Interest — Easy Reading
    401
The High King 390, 396
The High Pasture 95, 389
High Road Home 388
Hildilid's Night 387, 390
His Enemy His Friend 141
His Own Where 390
History and Trends 400
Hitty, Her First Hundred Years
    331, 392
Home From Far 36, 85, 104
A Home With Aunt Florry 41
Hongry Catch the Foolish Boy
    230
Honk, the Moose 393
Hooked on Books 375
Hooray for Jasper 236
The Horsecatcher 395
Hosie's Alphabet 388
The House 388
The House of Dies Drear 233
The House of Sixty Fathers
    133, 388, 395
The House of Wings 390
The House That Jack Built 386
Houses From the Sea 386
How Babies Are Born — The
    Story of Birth for Chil-
    dren 164
How Babies Are Made 153,
    161
How Do I Feel? 195, 246
How Many Blocks in the World?
    191, 220
How the Children Stopped the
    Wars 142
"How to Combat Sexism in
    Textbooks" 319
How to Get a Teen-Age Boy
    and What to Do With Him
    When You Get Him 347
How to Teach Reading With
    Children's Books 376
How We Are Born 167
How You Were Born 168
The Hundred Dresses 394
The Hundred Penny Box 104

Hunted Like a Wolf: The Story
    of the Seminole War 284
The Hunter I Might Have Been
    104
Hurray for Captain Jane 347
Hurry Home Candy 395

I Am Better Than You 120,
    121, 138
I Am Magic 389
I Am the Darker Brother 217
I Can Be Anything You Can Be
    308, 348
I, Charlotte Forten, Black and
    Free 242, 342
I, Juan de Pareja 227, 396
I Know A Bus Driver 333
I Know An Astronaut 348
I Know What I Like 195, 246,
    350
I Love Gram 107, 190, 246
I Love My Mother 110
I Never Saw Another Butterfly
    122, 142
I Tell a Lie Every So Often
    391
I, Trissy 54, 65
I Was There 139
I Wish I Had An Afro 245
I Won't Go Without A Father
    56, 67
I Wrote My Name On the Wall,
    Sidewalk Songs 246
If All the Seas Were One Sea
    388
If I Had My Way 17, 34, 166
If I Ran the Zoo 385
If I Were a Mother 344
If It Weren't For You 17, 42
If You Lived with the Sioux
    Indians 261, 283
I'll Be You and You Be Me
    340
I'll Fix Anthony 41
I'll Get There. It Better Be
    Worth the Trip 52, 61, 92,
    101, 156, 162
I'm Glad I'm a Boy! I'm Glad
    I'm a Girl! 307, 329
"The Image of American Indians
    Projected by Non-Indian
    Writers" 269
The Image of the Black in Chil-
    dren's Fiction 176, 209
The Impossible People 391
In a Mirror 388
In My Mother's House 384
In the Forest 384
In the Night Kitchen 387

Inch By Inch 386
Incident at Hawk's Hill 397
Index to Literature on the
    American Indian 271
"Indian Association Attacks Lies
    in Children's Literature"
    272
Indian Captive: The Story of
    Mary Jemison 394
The Indian in American History
    254, 272
Indian Summer 263, 272, 284
Indian Tales 285
Indian Tribes of America 280
"The Individual and War Resis-
    tance" 129
Individualization of Instruction:
    A Teaching Strategy 375
Individualized Reading 375
Individualized Reading Instruc-
    tion: A Reader 375
"Innocence Is a Cop-Out" 160
Integrated School Books 213
Interaction 362
"Interracial Children's Books:
    Problems and Progress"
    210
An Introduction to Children's
    Literature 401
Invincible Louisa 393
Ira Sleeps Over 353
Island of the Blue Dolphins 21,
    37, 85, 105, 284, 311, 396
Issues in Children's Book Selec-
    tion 401
It's Like This, Cat 396
It's Not the End of the World
    60
It's Not What You Expect 20,
    34, 63-64, 157, 166, 338
It's Wings that Make Birds Fly
    250

J. D. 227
J. T. 67, 249, 353
Jambo Means Hello, Swahili
    Alphabet Book 228, 388
James and the Giant Peach 91
Jane Addams 338
Jane's Blanket 344
Jane's Island 392
Janine 389
Jareb 388
The Jazz Man 250, 396
Jealousy in Children: A Guide
    for Parents 24
Jeanne D'Arc 134
Jennie Jenkins 351
Jennifer 389

Jennifer, Hecate, Macbeth,
  William McKinley, and Me,
  Elizabeth 239, 339, 396
Jennifer Takes Over P.S. 94
  342
Jimmy Yellow Hawk 268, 286,
  389
The Joan Baez Songbook 128,
  136
John Henry McCoy 389
John John Twilliger 142
"Johnny Has Gone For a
  Soldier" 128
Johnny Jack and His Begin-
  nings 153, 161
Johnny Tremain 123, 134, 394
Joi Bangla! The Children of
  Bangladesh 391
Joshua's Day 67, 351
Journey Cake, Ho! 385
Journey From Peppermint Street
  390
Journey Outside 397
Juanita 385
The Judge 387
The Judy Collins Songbook
  128, 136
Judy's Journey 388
Julie of the Wolves 84, 101,
  311, 332, 391, 397
Julie's Heritage 242
Jumping-Off Place 392
Just Me 387
Justin Morgan Had a Horse
  394

Kevin Cloud: Chippewa Boy in
  the City 266, 274
The Key 102, 266, 280
Keystone Kids 388
Kid Brother 26
Kildee House 395
Killer-of-Death 264, 274
"The Kinds of Books We Give
  Children: Whose Nonsense?"
  212
King of the Wind 394
The King's Fifth 396
A Kite for Bennie 230
The Knee Baby 17, 33
The Knee-High Man And Other
  Tales 240
Knee-Knock Rise 397
Knots on a Counting Rope 276

Lady Ellen Grae 60, 327
Lands End 89, 108
Langston Hughes 390
Langston Hughes, American
  Poet 249

"Language Arts — The Invisible
  Child" 210
The Last Battle 137
Laurie's New Brother 39
Leader By Destiny: George
  Washington, Man and
  Patriot 393
Leap Before You Look 50, 53,
  67
Legends of the Great Chiefs
  262, 284
Leo the Lioness 334
Let's be Enemies 120, 121,
  142
A Letter to Amy 238, 337
Letters From Uncle David: Un-
  derground Hero 389
Li Lun, Lad of Courage 394
Liberating Young Children from
  Sex Roles 318
Library Literature 76
Life and Death 73, 95
The Life and Death of a Brave
  Bull 86, 110
The Life and Legend of George
  McJunkin: Black Cowboy
  229
The Light in the Forest 285
The Light of Tern Rocks 395
Lillan 65
Lillie of Watts 250
Lion 386
The Lion, the Witch, and the
  Wardrobe 104
Listen for the Fig Tree 242,
  343
Listen, Rabbit 163
"Literature by and about
  Negroes for the Elementary
  Level" 272
"Literature by and about the
  American Indian: An An-
  notated Bibliography for
  Junior and Senior High
  Students" 272
Literature for Children: Enrich-
  ment Ideas 374
Literature for Children: Its Dis-
  cipline and Content 400
Literature for Disadvantaged
  Children 215
Literature for Thursday's Child
  402
Little Bear's Visit 386
Little Blacknose 392
Little Chief 263, 281
A Little Demonstration of Af-
  fection 22, 42, 156, 170
The Little Girl and Her Mother
  330

The Little House 306, 384
Little House in the Big Woods
  354
Little House on the Prairie 354
The Little Island 384
Little Lost Lamb 384
The Little Match Girl 90
The Little Mermaid 90
"Little Miss Muffet Fights Back,
  Recommended Books
  About Girls for Young
  Readers" 317
The Little Prince 106
The Little Red Schoolbook
  155, 164
Little Town on the Prairie 394
Little Women 90, 96, 305, 306,
  323
Little Yellow Fur 264, 280
Living Things and Their Young
  168
Locating and Correcting
  Reading Difficulties 365,
  375
The Lollipop Party 191, 246
Lone Journey: The Life of
  Roger Williams 394
The Loner 109, 396
Lonesome Boy 221
Long Journey Home, Stories
  from Black History 199,
  240, 391
The Long Secret 163
A Long Way to Whiskey Creek
  91, 97
The Long Winter 394
The Longest Weekend 158,
  161
Longhouse Legends 284
Look at Me 169
Look at Your Eyes 195, 246
Lordy, Aunt Hattie 248
Love and Sex Growing Up 165
Love and Sex in Plain Language
  156, 165
Lucky Wilma 63
Lucretia Mott: Foe to Slavery
  331
Lucy McLockett 342
Luke Was There 61, 389

McElligot's Pool 385
"McLuhan, Youth, and Litera-
  ture" 8
M.C. Higgins, the Great 233,
  391, 397
Madeline 384
Madeline's Rescue 385
The Magic Convention 335
A Magic Eye for Ida 60

Magic Maize 395
The Magic Moth 79, 83, 103
The Magic of Black Poetry 217
The Magic Ringlet 346
The Magic Three of Solatia
    305, 355
Make Way For Ducklings 384
Making Babies 153, 169
Malcom X 217
Male and Female Under 18
    340
Man and Woman 168
The Man Without A Face 32,
    62-63, 156, 164
Many Moons 384
The Many Ways of Seeing: An
    Introduction to the Pleasures
    of Art 397
Marchers for the Dream 199,
    223
Margaret Sanger, Pioneer of
    Birth Control 311, 340
Margin for Surprise 403
Marie Curie 335
Marshmallow 384
Martin's Father 61, 330
The Marvelous Misadventures of
    Sebastian 390
Mary Jane 201, 247
Mary Jo's Grandmother 108,
    249, 314, 352
Mary Poppins 202, 249, 352
The Matchlock Gun 133, 394
A Matter of Life and Death
    128, 132
Matthew, Mark, Luke and John
    127, 132
Matt's Grandfather 104
"The Maturation of the Junior
    Novel: From Gestation to
    the Pill" 160
The Maude Reed Tale 312, 341
Maxie 103
May I Bring A Friend 387
May I Cross Your Golden
    River? 22, 30, 100
Me Day 64, 241
Me Too 21, 28, 327
Meet the Austins 85, 95, 103
Maggy Macintosh 392
Mei Li 334, 383
Men Against War 135
Men, Microscopes, and Living
    Things 395
Men of Athens 396
"Men Who March Away" 122
"Mental Health Aspects of the
    Effects of Discrimination
    Upon Children" 210
The Middle Moffat 394

The Middle Sister 36
The Mighty Hunter 384
Migrant Girl 389
Millions of Cats 392
Mine's the Best 120, 131
Minn of the Mississippi 395
"Minorities in Fiction for
    Young Children" 209
The Minstrel and the Mountain
    117, 143
"Minstrel Boy" 128
Miracles on Maple Hill 40, 306,
    350, 395
"Misgivings About 'the Giving
    Tree' " 321
Miss Hickory 394
Miss Pickerell Goes to Mars
    343
Misty of Chincoteague 394
Mitch and Amy 19, 28
Mitzi's Magic Garden 323
Moccasin Trail 395
The Moffats 30
Moja Means One 388
Moki 347
Molly and the Giant 354
Molly Mullet 329
Molly Whuppie 303
Mom, the Wolf Man and Me
    157, 166, 314, 338
Mommies at Work 314, 344
Mommy, Where Do Babies
    Come From? 170
"A Monjo's Manifest Destiny:
    Authors Can Claim Any
    Territory in Literature"
    272
A Month of Sundays 50, 60
The Moon Jumpers 386
"Moral Development through
    Children's Literature" 8
More All-of-a-Kind Family 41
More Books by More People
    400
Morning Arrow 279, 390
Morning Song 389
The Most Wonderful Doll in the
    World 385
Mother Goose 384
Mother Goose and Nursery
    Rhymes 387
"Mother Goose: Sexist?" 320
The Mother Market 314, 325
The Mother Tree 109
The Mother Whale 165
Mothers Can Do Anything 314,
    340
Mothers, Mothers, Mothers
    355
Mountain Born 394

Mountains are Free 392
The Moved-Outers 388, 394
Mr. Justice Holmes 395
Mr. Penny's Race Horse 386
Mr. Popper's Penguins 393
Mr. Rabbit and the Lovely
    Present 387
Mr. T.W. Anthony Woo 385
Mrs. Frisby and the Rats of
    NIMH 390, 397
Mukasa 244
The Mulberry Music 105
Multi-Ethnic Books for Young
    Children: An Annotated
    Bibliography for Parents and
    Teachers 211, 271
"Multi-Ethnic Literature for
    Children and Adolescents"
    270
"Multi-Ethnic Literature: Prom-
    ises and Problems" 211
Mumbet, The Story of Elizabeth
    Freeman 331
Musby Eggs 54, 59, 313, 323
The Music Box 105
My Black Me: A Beginning
    Book of Black Poetry 217
My Brother Bernard 30
My Brother Sam Is Dead 123,
    132, 391, 397
My Brother Stevie 21, 29
My Dad Lives in a Downtown
    Hotel 49, 64
My Dark Companions and Their
    Strange Stories 197, 217
My Darling, My Hamburger
    170
My Doctor 308, 348
My Father Hijacked a Plane
    390
My Father's Dragon 394
My Grandpa Died Today 79,
    84, 101
My Grandson Lew 111
My Mother is the Most Beauti-
    ful Woman in the World
    384
My Name is Lion 279
My Side of the Mountain 396
My Special Best Words 20, 23,
    40, 152, 170
My Turtle Died Today 80, 108

Nana Upstairs and Nana Down-
    stairs 79, 81, 100
Nansen 394
Naomi in the Middle 18, 19,
    34, 167, 314, 338

"The Negative Image of Women in Children's Literature" 316

Negroes in the Early West 223

Nellie Bly, Reporter 311, 324

"Nervose of the Thought: War and Peace in Children's Books" 129

A New Baby Is Coming to My Home 165

"A New Cache of Liberated Children's Literature — In Some Old Standbys" 318

New Found World 394

The New Indians 254, 272

New Land 393

New Life: New Room 20, 34, 191, 237

A New Look at Children's Literature 398

The New Teacher 328

Nice Little Girls 341

Nicholas 392

The Night Daddy 55, 62, 314, 334

Nine Days to Christmas 386

Nino 393

No Kiss for Mother 352

No Mocassins Today 282

No Time for Glory: Stories of World War Two 134

Nobody Asked Me If I Wanted a Baby Sister 17, 25

Nobody's Family Is Going to Change 30

Nobody's Garden 136

Nobody's Perfect 352

Noisy Nora 42

Nonni 97

The Noonday Friends 396

North to Freedom 136

North Town 230

Not Bad for a Girl 351

Not Enough Indians 336

Nothing At All 384

Nothing But a Dog 337

"Nothing but the Facts-of-Life" 158

The Nubie 221

Number Four 278

Oh Lord, I Wish I Was a Buzzard 188, 231

Old Abe: The Eagle Hero 143

"Old and New Sexual Messages in Fairy Tales" 160

Old Arthur 82, 107

The Old Dog 80, 84, 96

Old Ramon 396

The Old Tobacco Shop 391

Old Yeller 102, 395

Omar at Christmas 250

Omoteji's Baby Brother 17, 31

On City Streets: An Anthology of Poetry 239

On Death and Dying 94

"On Feminism and Children's Books" 319

On Mother's Lap 17, 39

On Our Way, Poems of Pride and Love 236

On the Banks of Plum Creek 393

On the Other Side of the River 116, 139

"On Women, Men, Children and Librarians" 318

Once a Mouse . . . 386

One Day for Peace 127, 133

One Fine Day 387

One Hundred Novel Ways with Book Reports 374

1 is One 386

One Morning in Maine 342, 385

The One-Parent Family 58

The One-Parent Family Perspectives and Annotated Bibliography 58

One Sad Day 118, 137

One Wide River to Cross 387

Onion John 396

Only Connect, Readings on Children's Literature 400

Only Earth and Sky Last Forever 265, 275

Only the Names Remain, the Cherokees and the Trail of Tears 265, 275

Ood-le-uk the Wanderer 392

The Ordeal of the Young Hunter 388

Orders to Vietnam: A Novel of Helicopter Warfare 132

"Organizing a First Grade Classroom for Individualized Reading Instruction" 375

The Ostrich Chase 236, 312, 336

The Other City 118, 249

Our Eddie 396

Our Fathers Had Powerful Songs 275

Out of the Earth I Sing 240, 282

Out of the Flame 392

The Outsiders 102

"Overdue" 213

Paddle-To-The-Sea 384

Pageant of Chinese History 393

The Pair of Shoes 389

Pancakes — Paris 394

A Parent's Guide to Children's Reading 401

Parents' Answer Book 159

The Parents' Guide to Everyday Problems of Boys and Girls 23

Paul Robeson, The Life and Times of a Free Black Man 233

Paul Tiber 388

Paz 140

"Peace, A Publishers for Peace Bibliography" 129

The Peaceable Revolution 389

Pecos Bill 393

Pedro, The Angel of Alvera Street 384

Peggy's New Brother 17, 39

Penn 393

People of the Dream 255

People of the Short Blue Corn, Tales and Legends of the Hopi Indians 278

The Perilous Gard 397

The Perilous Road 141, 396

Personal Problems of Children 9

Personalized Reading 375

Peter and Veronica 348

Peter Learns to Crochet 341

Peter's Chair 17, 34, 185, 192, 238

Petronella 303, 354

Philip Hall Likes Me, I Reckon Maybe 231, 312, 333, 397

Phoebe Fairchild: Her Book 393

Phoebe's Revolt 323

A Pictorial History of Women in America 308, 353

"The Pictorial Treatment of Afro-Americans in Books for Young Children" 209

Picture Books for Children 399

Pierre Pigeon 384

The Pig War 121, 131

Pigman 92, 110

Pigtail of Ah Lee Ben Loo 392

Pippi Longstocking 91, 312, 341

"Pippi Longstocking — Feminist or Anti-Feminist?" 321

Pirates in Petticoats 355

Plain Girl 350, 388

The Planet of Junior Brown 233, 390, 397

Play With Me 331, 386

"The Plight of the Native American" 272

The Pocket Book of Modern Verse 87

Pocket Book of Verse 141
A Pocket Full of Seeds 140
A Pocketful of Cricket 387
Poems for Red-Letter Days 140
A Poetry Sampler 135
Police: Skill and Science Combat
    Crime 329
Poor Richard in France 391
Popcorn and Ma Goodness 387,
    390
"Portrayal of the Black in
    Children's Literature" 209
Potatoes, Potatoes 116, 138
A Practical Guide to Individual-
    ized Reading Instruction 375
The Practical Princess 303, 354
Pran of Albania 392
Prayer for a Child 384
The Preacher's Kid 221
The Pretty House that Found
    Happiness 330
The Princess and the Lion 328
Princess of the Full Moon 232
A Proud Taste for Scarlet and
    Miniver 391
"Publishers can Play a Key Role
    in Sex Education" 159
Pueblo Stories in Basic Vocabu-
    lary 279
The Pushcart War 138
Puss in Boots 385

The Quaint and Curious Quest of
    Johnny Longfoot 394
Queenie Peavy 312, 326, 389
Queer Person 392
Quiet on Account of Dinosaur
    352
A Quiet Place 221

Rabbit Hill 394
The Railroad to Freedom 393
Rain Drop Splash 384
Rain Makes Applesauce 387
Rain Rain Rivers 350
Ramona the Brave 28
Ramona the Pest 327
Rascal 396
Rattlesnake Cave 282
Raven-Who-Sets-Things-Right,
    Indian Tales of the North-
    west Coast 282
Reading, How to 375
Reading in the Elementary
    School 376
Reading Ladders for Human
    Relations 10, 213, 402
Readings About Children's
    Literature 402

"Reality Reflected in Children's
    Literature" 9
Red Sails to Capri 395
Red Shadows 279
"Reducing the 'Miss Muffet'
    Syndrome: An Annotated
    Bibliography" 317
Reference Encyclopedia of the
    American Indian 271
"Reflections of Life Through
    Books" 10
Reflections on a Gift of Water-
    melon Pickle . . . And Other
    Modern Verses 133
Releasing Children to Literature
    376, 401
Remember the Days: A Short
    History of the Jewish
    American 391
"A Reply to Roald Dahl" 9
Report of the Sex-Role Stereo-
    typing Comm., 1974 315
"Resources in Educating for
    Conflict Resolution" 130
Return to Hiroshima 137
Reunion in December 85, 98
"Review of Peter Mayle's Where
    Did I Come From?" 159
"Reviews of She Came Bringing
    Me That Little Baby Girl,
    and My Special Best Words"
    23
Ride the Crooked Wind 268,
    279
Rifles for Watie 395
"Rightness of Whiteness" 210
Rita, the Weekend Rat 341
The Road to Agra 389
The Rock and the Willow 389
The Rock Cried Out 389
Rock Star 389
The Roe Deer 170
Roger and the Fox 385
"The Role of Male and Female
    in Children's Books —
    Dispelling all Doubt" 319
"The Role of the Book in
    Combatting Prejudice" 213
Roller Skates 349, 393
Rooftops and Alleys: Adventures
    With a City Kid 238
Roosevelt Grady 245
The Rooster Crows 384
Rufus M. 394
Runaway Papoose 392
Runaway Slave 197, 242
The Runaway Summer 59
Runner of the Mountain Tops
    393

Sabrina 218
Salt Boy 285
Sam 39, 245, 349
Sam, Bangs and Moonshine
    105, 345, 387
Sam the Minuteman 121, 131
Saturday's Child — 36 Women
    Talk About Their Jobs 349
Scat 78, 100
A Screaming Whisper 236
Sea and Cedar: How the North
    West Coast Indians Lived
    283
Seabird 394
Seashore Story 387
The Secret Garden 91, 306, 326
The Secret Life of T. K. Dearing
    89, 106
The Secret Name 267, 287
Secret of the Andes 395
The Secret River 395
The Secret World of the Baby
    162
Selected Books About the Afro-
    American for Very Young
    Children 209
Selected Media About the
    American Indian for Young
    Children 270
Send Wendell 31, 231
Sensitivity Guidelines for Artists
    315
Seven Simeons 383
The Seven Wishes of Joanna
    Peabody 231
Seven Women: Great Painters
    345
Seventy-five Recommended
    Teenage Books on War 130
"Sex Differences in Children's
    Reading Preferences" 321
Sex Education and the Schools
    148, 159
Sex Education: Issues and
    Directions 160
"Sex Is Not a Four-Letter
    Word" 160
"Sex Role Socialization in
    Picture Books for Pre-School
    Children" 322
"Sex-Role Stereotypes and
    Clinical Judgments of Mental
    Health" 315-316
"Sex Role Stereotyping in
    Elementary School Readers"
    318
"Sex Roles in Early-Reading
    Textbooks" 317
Sex: Telling It Straight 165

Sexism in School and Society 317

"Sexuality in Books for Children"   159, 160

Shadow Across the Campus 388

Shadow of a Bull   86, 110, 396

Shadrach   395

She Come Bringing Me That Little Baby Girl   17, 23, 31, 192, 231

The Sheep Book   333

Shen of the Sea   392

Shirley Chisholm   325

Show Me: A Picture Book of Sex for Children and Parents 154-155, 163

Shumway   243

Sidewalk Story   243, 343, 389

Silence Over Dunkerque   142

Silent Bianca   304

The Silver Pencil   394

Simba, Midnight (The Stallion of the Night) and Mwensi 390

Simon and the Game of Chance 97

Sing Down the Moon   264, 284, 346, 397

Sing in Praise: A Collection of the Best Loved Hymns   384

Sing Mother Goose   384

The Singing Tree   393

The Single Parent Experience 57

A Single Standard   308, 334

Sister   18, 19, 32, 102, 232

Six Days From Sunday   268, 275

Skipper John's Cook   385

The Skirts in Fiction About Boys: A Maxi Mess   317

Skunny Wundy: Seneca Indian Tales   262, 285

The Slave Dancer   204, 206, 209, 229, 397

The Slightly Irregular Fire Engine   390

Small Rain: Verses From the Bible   384

A Smart Kid Like You   65

The Smartest Bear and His Brother Oliver   19, 26

Smoky, The Cowhorse   392

Sneakers   389

Snow White and the Seven Dwarfs   384, 388

The Snowy Day   184, 239, 387

So, Nothing Is Forever   33, 237

Sojourner Truth, A Self-Made

Woman   244, 346

"Some Day My Prince Will Come: Female Acculturation Through the Fairy Tale"   319

Some of the Days of Everett Anderson   225

Someone Small   98

The Son of Someone Famous 63

Song of Robin Hood   385

Song of the Pines   395

Song of the Swallows   385

Song of the Trees   248, 390

Song of the Chippewa   275

The Soul Brothers and Sister Lou   33, 237, 336, 389

A Sound of Chariots   103, 389

Sounder   92, 96, 204, 206, 209, 214, 219, 396

"Sounder: A Black or a White Tale?"   214

Sourland   92, 96, 219

South Town   230, 389

Spice and the Devil's Cave 392

The Spider, the Cave and the Pottery Bowl   259, 277

Spin a Soft Black Song: Poems for Children   230

Squanto, Friend of the Pilgrims 276

Starting Out Right, Choosing Books About Black People for Young Children   185, 188, 192, 193, 194, 197, 198, 212, 218, 227

The Steadfast Tin Soldier   386

Steffie and Me   194, 235

Stephanie's Children   140

"The Stereotypic Family in Children's Literature"   24

Stevie   40, 185, 186, 247

Stiff Ears, Animal Folktales of the North American Indians 263, 287

The Stolen Bairn and the Sidh 303

Stone Soup   384

The Stop   288

Stop Sex Race Stereotypes in Elementary Education. A Handbook for Parents and Teachers   316

The Storm Book   385

A Story, A Story   233, 387

The Story Grandmother Told 184, 190, 218

The Story of Appleby Capple 395

The Story of Doctor Dolittle 241

The Story of Mankind   391

Story of the Negro   394

The Strange Hocket Family 348

The Stranger   140

Strawberry Girl   394

Striped Ice Cream   20, 35, 241

"A Study of the Portrayal of the American Indian in Selected Children's Fiction" 270

Subject Guide to Children's Books in Print   128, 197, 260

Sugar and Spice, the ABC of Being a Girl   342

The Summer Before   86, 110

The Summer Night   355

Summer of My German Soldier 125, 135, 391

The Summer of the Swans   27, 326, 397

The Sun is a Golden Earring 387

Sunflowers for Tina   96, 219, 324

The Sunshine Family and the Pony   21, 36

Susan's Magic   59

Susette LaFlesche, Voice of the Omaha Indians   278

Suzuki Beane   349

Sweet Pea: A Black Girl Growing Up in the Rural South   189, 239

Swift Rivers   392

Swimmy   387

Swords of Steel   393

Sylvester and the Magic Pebble 108, 387, 390

T for Tommy   241

Taking Sides   64

Tales and Stories for Black Folks   220

Tales from the Kraals   243

Tales from Silver Lands   392

Tales from the Story Hat   196, 212

Tales of a Fourth Grade Nothing 26

Tales of Mogho, African Stories from Upper Volta   232

Tales Told Near a Crocodile 234

Talking about Death   72, 94

Tammy Camps Out   323

Tangle-Coated Horse and Other Tales 392
The Taos Indians and Their Sacred Blue Lake 282
A Taste of Blackberries 79, 80, 83, 107, 389
T-Bone the Baby Sitter 385
A Teacher's Guide to Children's Books 401
A Teacher's Guide to Contemporary Teenage Fiction 399
"Teaching Race Relations in the Nursery School" 212
Teacup Full of Roses 37, 243
Tell Me a Mitzi 40, 349
Telling a Child About Death 72, 94,
"Ten Quick Ways to Analyze Books for Racism and Sexism" 178, 318
The Tennis Machine 337
The Tenth Good Thing About Barney 78, 79, 109
The Terrible Thing That Happened at Our House 324
The Thanksgiving Story 386
That Crazy April 313, 347
That New Baby 16, 39, 167
Then Again, Maybe I Won't 157, 161
Theodore Roosevelt, Fighting Patriot 395
These Happy Golden Years 394
These Were the Sioux 286
They Were Strong and Good 384
Thimble Summer 393
Things We Like to Do 323
Think About It, You Might Learn Something 351
This Street's For Me 236
This Time, Tempe Wick? 135, 332
Thistle and Thyme 396
"The Thought, Not Necessarily the Deed: Sex in Some of Today's Juvenile Novels" 160
Three Jovial Huntsmen: A Mother Goose Rhyme 388
The Three of Us 164
Thy Friend, Obadiah 387
Tim, the Peacemaker 135
Time-Ago Lost: More Tales of Jahdu 233
The Time-Ago Tales of Jahdu 234
Time of Wonder 386

The Times They Used To Be 157, 162, 225
Timothy Turtle 384
Tinker and the Medicine Man 287
Titch 33
To Be A Slave 206, 208, 240, 396
Tod of the Fens 392
"Today's Literature for Today's Children" 10
Tom Fox and the Apple Pie 42
Tom Paine, Freedom's Apostle 395
Tom Tit Tot 387
Tomboy's Doll 351
The Tombs of Atuan 390, 397
Tongue of Flame, The Life of Lydia Maria Child 344
The Tortured Americans 254, 269
A Train for Jane 339
Train Ride 186, 247
The Treasure is the Rose 391
"The Treatment of Characters in Popular Children's Fiction" 11
"The Treatment of Death in Children's Literature" 95
"Treatment of Minority Groups and Women" 318
A Tree is Nice 386
Tree of Freedom 394
A Tree on Your Street 350
The Trees Stand Shining: Poetry of the North American Indian 281
A Trick of Light 22, 29
Trolls 391
The Trouble With Terry 35, 341, 389
Truce of the Wolf and Other Tales of Old Italy 392
"True/False: Messages for the Black Child" 213
The True Story of How Babies are Made 158, 167
Trumpet of the Swan 390
The Trumpeter of Krakow 392
Try and Catch Me 337
Turn the Next Corner 218
Turnabout 353
Twenty and Ten 388
The Twenty-One Balloons 394
Two is a Team 193, 220
Two Knots on a Counting Rope 98
The Two Reds 385
Two Sisters and Some Hornets

20, 30
Two Tickets to Freedom 198, 229
Two Wise Children 333

The Ugly Duck 304
Umbrella 386
Uncle Mike's Boy 60, 98
Uncle Misha's Partisans 41
Uncle Remus Tales 197, 217, 219
Under the Haystack 21, 30, 330
The United Nations and Youth 388
The Unreluctant Years 402
The Unusual Puerto Rican 389
Up a Road Slowly 95, 336, 396
The Upstairs Room 126, 139, 397
Uptown 186, 247
Using Picture Books with Children 376

Vaino 392
The Very Little Boy 339
The Very Little Girl 339
A Very Special House 386
The Vicksburg Veteran 138
Victoria's Castle 336
The Voyages of Doctor Dolittle 392

Walk Home Tired, Billy Jenkins 187, 248
Walk Together Children, Black American Spirituals 222
War and Peas 134
"War in the Classroom" 129
Watching the New Baby 16, 39
Waterless Mountain 392
The Wave 387
The Way It Is: Fifteen Boys Describe Life in Their Neglected Urban Neighborhood 235
We Are Having a Baby 33
We Build Together 213
We Can Change It 214, 321
We Have Not Vanished 266, 287
We Were There at the Normandy Invasion 137
Wee Gillis 383
A Week in Hagar's World: Israel 347
The Weewish Tree 269

Wembi, The Singer of Stories
225
"What Are the Advantages and
Disadvantages of Individual-
ized Instruction?" 376
What Can She Be? A Lawyer
333
What Can She Be? A Newscaster
333
What Can She Be? An Architect
332
*What Can You Do Without A
Place to Play* 186, 235
"What Did You Write About
the War, Daddy?" 130
What Do You Say, Dear? 386
"*What is a Racist Book?*" 208
What Made You You? 161
What Mary Jo Shared 191, 249
What Mary Jo Wanted 191
*What to Tell Your Child About
Birth, Death . . .* 93
*What to Tell Your Child About
Sex* 159
"What your Child Really Wants
to Know About Sex and
Why" 9, 158
What's It All About 389
Wheel on the Chimney 386
The Wheel on the School 395
When Clay Sings 388
When Hitler Stole Pink Rabbit
126, 137
When Parents Divorce 58
*When Shall They Rest? The
Cherokees' Long Struggle
With America* 265, 277
*When Shlemiel Went to Warsaw
and Other Stories* 396
When the Legends Die 267,
276
*When the Whale Came to My
Town* 110
When Thunders Spoke 268, 286
When Violet Died 78, 79, 103
When Will the World Be Mine?
386
Where Did I Come From? 155,
158, 159, 168
Where Do Babies Come From?
158, 169
Where Does the Day Go? 389
"*Where Have All the Flowers
Gone*" 128
*Where is Daddy? The Story of a
Divorce* 48, 62, 389
Where the Lilies Bloom 21,

28, 86, 99, 328, 390
Where the Readers Are 376,
402
Where the Wild Things Are 387
*The Whispering Wind — Poetry
by Young American Indians*
96, 274
Whistle for Willie 185, 239
Whistler's Van 393
White Captives 282
White Shell Horse 264, 274
White Snow, Bright Snow 384
The White Stag 140, 393
Who is Victoria? 330
Who Look at Me 238
Whose Town? 230
Why Did He Die? 102
"*Why Good Interracial Books
Are Hard to Find*" 211
Why Me? 19, 27
*Why the Sun and the Moon Live
in the Sky* 387
*The Whys and Wherefores Of
Littabelle Lee* 86, 99, 328,
391
The Wicked Kings of Bloon
136
Wild Bird 266
The Wild Birthday Cake 385
Wild in the World 390
William's Doll 356
Willow Hill 250
Willy Is My Brother 38
*The Wind and the Rain: An
Anthology of Poems for
Young People* 136
Windy Hill 391
Winged Girl of Knossos 393
Wings 391
The Winner 118, 140
*Winning Hearts and Minds, War
Poems by Vietnam
Veterans* 140
Winterbound 393
Winter-Telling Stories 283
The Witch of Blackbird Pond
351, 396
The Witches of Worm 391,
397
The Woman of the Wood 324
*Woman, Woman! Feminism in
America* 340
Women of Courage 345
"Women in Aprons: The Female
Stereotype in Children's
Readers" 320
"Women in Children's Litera-

ture" 320
Women Who Shaped History
325
Womenfolk and Fairytales
303, 314, 316
"*Womenfolk and Fairytales*"
316
"Women's Rights Address
Book" 320
The Wonder Smith and His Son
392
The Wonderful Little Boy 97
*The Wonderful Story of How
You Were Born* 164
A Wonderful, Terrible Time
248
Wonderful Year 394
The World of Ellen March 61
*World of Our Fathers: The Jews
of Eastern Europe* 391
*Wounded Knee: An Indian
History of the American
West* 265, 276
A Wrinkle In Time 313, 340,
396
Writing Books for Children
403

Yari 390
The Year of Small Shadow
267, 282
*The Year of the Three-Legged
Deer* 277
Yonie Wondernose 384
You Can Write Chinese 384
Young and Black in America
218
"Young Children and Books
on Death" 95
*Young Fu of the Upper
Yangtze* 392
Young Mac of Fort Vancouver
393
"Young People: Victims of
Realism in Books and in
Life" 9
The Young Unicorns 341
The Young United States 390
Young Walter Scott 393
Youth and Sex 165

*Zachary's Divorce in Free to
Be You and Me* 66-67
Zawani Goes to Market 228
Zeely 234
*Zlateh the Goat and Other
Stories* 396

Subject Index

Activities for adults 13, 19, 47, 48, 70, 71, 76, 114, 115, 146, 147, 148, 175, 176, 177, 182, 190, 191, 258, 259, 260, 291, 294, 301, 313, 314, 361, 363, 365; see also Try This under Blacks, Death, Divorce, Females, Native Americans, Old Age, Reading, Sex, Siblings, War

Activities for students 17, 19, 21, 49, 50, 51, 54, 72, 77, 80, 82, 83, 86, 87, 89, 90, 91, 93, 115, 118, 119, 120, 122, 127, 129, 157, 158, 175, 188, 190, 194, 195, 196, 201, 244, 265, 267, 268, 294, 301, 305, 306, 307, 309, 310, 311, 312, 313, 314, 315, 332, 363, 369-373, 374, 376; see also Try This under Blacks, Death, Divorce, Females, Native Americans, Old Age, Reading, Sex, Siblings, War

Addams, Jane 338, 345

Addams, Jane, Book Award; see Awards

Adoption 27, 37, 50, 58, 192, 223, 244, 326, 330

Africa; see the Black in Africa

ALA Notable Books; see Awards

Allotment Act 257

Alternative Life Styles 13, 21, 24, 36, 40, 157, 166, 349

Anthony, Susan B. 330, 345

Articles of Confederation 256

Association of American Indian Affairs 259

Awards 383-397
 ALA Notable Books 105, 284, 346
 Jane Addams Book Award 203
 The Brooklyn Art Books for Children Citations 197, 240
 Randolph J. Caldecott Award 105, 119, 133, 185, 228, 233, 238, 239, 283, 286, 320, 322, 334, 344, 355, 383-388
 Child Study Association of America/Wel-Met Children's Book Award 35, 61, 62, 103, 107, 133, 341, 350, 388-389
 Children's Book Showcase 344, 347, 353, 355
 Council on Interracial Books for Children Award 33, 237, 243, 248, 286, 336, 343, 389-390

Follett Award 125
National Book Award
 Children's Book Category 38, 66, 124, 137, 233, 240, 328, 332, 355, 390-391
 John Newbery Medal 27, 35, 40, 85, 86, 87, 96, 99, 101, 102, 105, 109, 110, 123, 132, 133, 134, 136, 139, 140, 141, 204, 206, 219, 226, 227, 229, 231, 233, 239, 240, 250, 251, 278, 284, 316, 325, 326, 332, 333, 336, 339, 340, 346, 349, 350, 351, 354, 395-397
 New York Times Best Illustrated Children's Books of the Year 119, 197, 240, 250, 340
 Woodward School Annual Book Award 203

Baby Sitters 54, 55, 56, 57, 59, 62, 313, 314, 323, 334
Barnett, Ida Wells 310, 326
Bethune, Mary McLeod 345
Bibliotherapy 4 (defined), 9, 10, 14, 47
Biography; see Blacks, Female, Native Americans
Blacks 8, 172-251

activities for children on the
topic of   175, 188, 190,
194, 195, 196, 201, 244
in Africa   183, 196-197, 211,
212, 214, 217, 219, 220,
222, 223, 224, 225, 226,
228, 232, 233, 234, 236,
239, 240, 242, 243, 244,
250, 251
biographies of   197-198, 199,
217, 218, 221, 222, 223,
228, 229, 233, 235, 240,
242, 244, 245, 311, 326,
331, 337, 340, 342, 346
criteria for books containing
177, 182-183, 196, 204,
209, 212, 215
and desegregation   200, 201,
223, 225
family life   181, 184, 187,
189, 190-193, 217, 221,
224, 228, 230, 234, 235,
236, 238, 245
in folktales and fairytales
183, 195-197, 219, 220,
223, 225, 226, 230, 232,
233, 234, 239, 240, 243,
245
negative treatment in children's books   176, 179,
184, 196, 202-203, 209-
210, 211, 214, 223
poetry about   217, 218, 220,
221, 230, 236, 237, 238,
239, 240
self-image   175, 179, 183,
194-195, 200, 202, 210,
215, 220, 221, 223, 242
slave trade   206, 207, 229
slavery   124, 198, 199, 206,
207, 222, 226, 229, 230,
234, 245
stereotypes   177, 178, 189,
190, 191, 192, 201, 209,
212, 213, 218, 225, 242
urban dialect   186, 199, 231,
237, 244, 245
Try This on the topic of   175,
176, 177, 182, 190, 191
underground railroad   198,
199, 207, 208, 230, 233,
243
white authors writing about
196, 198, 200-201, 203-208
Blackwell, Elizabeth   311, 335
Block, William A.   150
Bly, Nellie   311, 324
Brooklyn Art Books for Children
Citations; see Awards
Brown, William Wells   242, 342

Bureau of Indian Affairs   256,
257, 258, 269, 279

Randolph J. Caldecott Medal;
see Awards
Calderone, Mary S.   147, 159
Chief Crazy Horse   265, 275
Chief Joseph   255
Child, Lydia Maria   344
Children's Book Award; see
Awards
Chisholm, Shirley   310, 325,
334
City, The; see also Ghettos;
Urban Life
New York   186, 244
San Francisco   187, 229
Clark, Septima Poinsette   310,
326
Classics   305-307
Colonists   253, 256
Columbus, Christopher   255
Communes   21, 36, 40
Council on Interracial Books for
Children   177, 178-182
Council on Interracial Books for
Children Award; see Awards
Craft, Ellen and William   198,
229
Criteria   3, 4, 10, 173, 174; see
also Blacks, Death, Divorce,
Females, Native Americans,
Old Age, Siblings, War
Critical Thinking Skills   80,
118, 120, 125, 128, 157,
173, 174, 206, 269, 309,
310, 315
Curie, Marie   335
Custer, General   254, 270, 280

Death   7, 69-111
activities for children on the
topic of   72, 77, 80, 86,
87, 90, 91, 93
advice to adults on   71-72,
73, 75, 79, 94, 108
of animals   78, 79, 80, 83,
84, 92, 98, 99, 100, 102,
103, 104-105, 106, 107,
108, 109, 110
attitudes toward   69, 70-71,
91, 93, 103, 106, 110, 111
criteria for books about   76-
77
funerals   78, 79, 97, 100,
103, 104, 105, 107, 109
immortality   79, 104
misconceptions concerning
71, 72, 73, 79, 81, 84, 105,
106

of old people   81, 84, 88, 97,
100, 101, 105, 108, 110,
111, 284
of parents   33, 73, 85, 86,
87, 88, 91, 92, 96, 97, 98,
99, 101, 102, 103, 105,
108, 109, 110, 328
of peers   79, 80, 83, 86, 92,
102, 106, 107, 109, 110,
389
one's own   86, 97, 100, 107
reactions to   83, 84-85, 86,
87, 101, 103, 105, 107, 110
religious practices and attitudes
toward   74, 75, 87, 90, 99,
100, 103, 104, 284
of siblings   22, 28, 30, 36,
37, 79, 83, 85, 87-88, 96,
98, 103, 243
by suicide   54, 87-88, 96, 99,
127, 105-106
Try This on the topic of   70,
71, 76
Derricotte, Juliette   310, 326
Desegregation   200, 201, 223,
225
Dickinson, Emily   311, 342
Divorce   6, 44-67
activities for children on the
topic of   49, 50, 51, 54
advice for coping with   49,
50, 54, 56, 57
aftermath   52, 53, 241
causes of   50-51, 53, 54, 57
criteria for books about   46-
47
reactions to   45-46, 53, 105
Try This on the topic of   47,
48
Douglass, Frederick   235, 242,
342

Earhart, Amelia   311, 330, 345
Edmonds, Emma; see
Edmundson, Sarah Emma
Edmundson, Sarah Emma   309-
310, 335-336, 351
Ellington, Duke   199
Evert, Chris   311

Fairy tales; see Folk tales
Females   8, 290-356
activities for children on the
topic of   294, 301, 305,
306, 307, 309, 310, 311,
312-313, 314, 315, 332
biographies of   134, 135,
136, 259, 309-311, 324,
325, 330, 331, 334, 335,
337, 338, 340, 342, 344,

345, 346, 352
characteristics attributed to
291-292, 293, 294, 296,
305, 306, 307, 315, 316,
344
criteria for books containing
295-302, 303, 308, 310,
315, 316, 317, 318, 319,
320, 321, 322
in folktales and fairy tales
302-305, 316, 319, 320,
328
occupations 293-294, 296,
298, 300, 307, 308, 311,
323, 329, 332, 333, 335,
340, 341, 344, 347, 348,
349, 352, 355
poetry about 336, 340, 345,
352
stereotypes 151, 290, 291,
292, 296, 302, 303-304,
306, 307, 315, 316, 317,
318, 319, 320, 321, 323,
325, 327, 329, 339, 342,
343, 345, 347, 348, 350,
353, 355
terminology 294, 296-301,
320
Try This on the topic of
291, 294, 301, 313-314
working mothers 50, 56,
292, 313-314, 323, 324,
328, 335, 340, 344, 351,
353
Feminist Movement 290, 292,
301, 302, 308, 309, 311,
314, 326, 338, 340, 342,
344, 346, 347, 353
Fitzgerald Publishing Company
197
Folk tales 176-177, 195-197,
302-305; see also Blacks,
Females, Native Americans
Follett Award; see Awards
Forten, Charlotte 242, 310,
311, 342
Forten, James 242, 342
Fortune, Amos 251, 395
Foster children 21, 29, 221
Foundations for Change 210
Francis, Milly Hadjo 259
Freeman, Elizabeth 331
Fulton, Wallace 148

Gannett, Deborah Sampson
199
Garrison, William Lloyd 242,
342
Geronimo 287
Ghettos 180, 186, 241; see

also City; Urban life
Grandparents 37, 62, 79, 81,
82, 84, 88, 89, 96, 97, 98,
99, 100, 101, 102, 104,
105, 106, 107, 108, 110,
111, 184, 190, 191, 218,
219, 236, 241, 246, 249,
266, 267, 277, 279, 280,
284, 312, 314, 324, 336,
338, 352

Hamer, Fannie Lou 337
Handicaps
blindness 242, 343
emotional problems 21, 22,
27, 29, 32-33, 39, 62-63,
65-66, 102, 156, 164-165,
233, 390, 397
illness 19, 27
obesity 233, 313, 338, 390,
397
retarded 21, 27, 35, 326,
327
Hitler, Adolph 126, 137, 142
Hughes, Langston 249, 390

Illustrations 15, 118, 119,
134, 151, 152, 185, 187,
188, 193, 196, 197, 199,
209, 242, 258-259, 262,
266, 295, 296, 308, 310
Information Center on Children's
Cultures 196, 211
Intermarriage 192, 217, 237

Jackson, Andrew 256
Jane Addams Peace Association
203
Jeanne D'Arc 134
Jews 40, 41, 122, 123, 125,
126, 134, 135, 137, 138,
139, 140, 141, 142, 347,
348, 349, 391, 397

Kauffman, Angelica 345
Keller, Helen 330
King, Martin Luther 199
Kissinger, Henry 117
Kohlberg, Lawrence 9

laFlesche, Suzette 278
Louisiana Purchase 256
Lyon, Mary 330

McDermott, John F. 49
McGraw-Hill Book Company
Guidelines for Equal Treat-
ment of the Sexes 297-301
McJunkin, George 229
Madison, Dolley 352

Malcolm X 199, 217
Marriage, attitudes toward 53
Marshall, John 256
Massachusetts Commission
Against Discrimination
209
Mead, Margaret 345
Millay, Edna St. Vincent 311
Minorities 173, 174, 175, 180,
181, 195, 202, 208, 209,
211, 213, 218
Mott, Lucretia 331
Myths 32, 132

NAACP 213
National Book Award Children's
Book Category; see Awards
National Conference of Chris-
tians and Jews 213
Native Americans 8, 253-288
Acoma 285
activities for children on the
topic of 265, 267, 268
Algonquin 262, 275
Apache 264, 282, 287
assimilation of 259, 267
attitudes toward 253-255,
260, 261, 269
authors 254, 259, 262, 268,
269, 282, 285
Battle of Little Big Horn; see
also Custer's Last Stand
biographies 259, 262, 278,
285, 287
Cherokee 256, 260, 265,
275, 277, 280, 286, 287
Cheyenne 265, 275, 375
Chief Crazy Horse 265
Chief Joseph 255
Chinook 287
Chippewa 266, 274, 287
Chuala 282
Colville Reservation 254
contemporary life 102, 254,
261, 263, 266-269, 278,
279, 282, 286, 287
criteria for books 260-262
Custer's Last Stand 258, 265
customs 253, 254, 258, 260,
261, 264, 265-266, 268,
277, 282, 283, 284, 285,
286, 287
Delaware 277
descriptive terms about 255-
256, 260-261, 262-263, 264
folklore 262, 270, 274, 281,
283, 285, 286, 287
Geronimo 287
government policy toward
256-258, 264, 265, 266,

269, 276, 278, 280,
Hopi 262, 278, 287
Iroquois 262, 282, 287
Kiowa 262, 283
Lenni Lenape 277
massacre at Wounded Knee
    255, 258, 265, 280
Miccosukee 266, 280-281
misrepresentation in children's
    books 189, 254, 258-259,
    263, 264, 276, 280, 281,
    284
Mohave 282
Navajo 105, 264, 265, 267,
    268, 274, 276, 277, 279,
    284, 285, 287, 288, 346
Nez-Perce 255
Ojibway 272
Omaha 278
Paiute 262, 263, 279, 281
Papago 262
Patuxet 276
Pawnee 287
Pima 262
Plains 266, 268
poetry 270, 274, 275, 281,
    282
Pueblo 265, 277, 279, 283
Quileute 282
reservation life 254, 284
self-determination policy
    254, 284
Seminoles 284
Seneca 262, 285
Sioux 254, 260, 261, 265,
    267, 268, 269, 270, 275,
    278, 280, 283, 286
stereotypes 280, 282, 284
termination policy 257, 266
Taos 282
Teton 286
Tlingit 286
Try This on the topic of
    258, 259, 260
Tuscarawa 285
Ute 267, 276
white authors writing about
    259, 261, 263, 264, 265-
    266, 267, 275, 280, 282,
    287
Zuni 262, 282
New York Times Best Illus-
    trated Children's Books; see
    Awards
John Newbery Medal; see
    Awards
Nightingale, Florence 311
Nino, Pedro Alonso 199
Northwest Territory Ordinance
    256

O'Keefe, Georgia 345
Old Age 7, 20, 30, 80-83, 88-
    89; see also grandparents
    activities for children on the
        topic of 82, 83, 89
    criteria for books about 82,
        88
    nursing homes 82, 88, 89,
        98, 104, 106
    problems of 81, 88, 96, 100,
        102, 104, 106, 107, 110
    reactions to 103, 104, 106,
        107, 110
    senility 41, 82, 89, 98, 104,
        105, 106, 108
    stereotypes of 81, 109
    Try This on the topic of 70

Open Family Series 16, 40,
    108, 169
Pankhurst, Emmeline and
    daughters 346
Parents 13, 14, 15, 21, 316
    Rejection by 21, 22, 28, 30,
        36, 39, 53, 56, 59, 64, 65,
        66, 241, 327, 330
    Single 20, 23, 37, 40, 44-67,
        92, 101, 105, 152, 156, 157,
        162, 166, 170, 314, 316,
        334, 336, 345
    Stepparents 36, 53, 54, 60,
        61-62, 64-65, 66, 105
Parents Without Partners 46,
    56
Pocahontas 330
Poetry
    about Blacks 217, 218, 220,
        221, 230, 236, 237, 238,
        239, 240
    about Death 102
    about Females 336, 340, 345,
        352
    Native Americans 270, 274
        275, 281, 282
    about War 122, 127-128,
        132, 133, 135, 136, 139,
        140, 141, 142
Poor People's March 199, 223
Pregnancy; see Sex

Quarles, Benjamin 199

Racism 5, 172-175, 201, 202,
    203-204, 226, 243
Reading 358-376
    activities for children on the
        topic of 363, 369-373,
        374, 376
    approaches 2, 3, 359, 361,
        374

diagnosis 359, 363, 364-365,
    367, 375
grouping for 359, 366-367
materials 359, 360, 361, 364,
    366, 368
record-keeping for 366, 368-
    369
self-evaluation for 362, 365,
    366
self-selection in 361, 362,
    363-366
skills 2, 6, 80, 358-359, 360,
    362, 364, 369
Try This on the topic of
    361, 363, 365
Realism 4, 9
Reference: see section on Ref-
    erences in each chapter
Robeson, Paul 233
Robbins, Charles 276
Roosevelt, Eleanor 311
Rural life 189-190, 239

Sanger, Margaret 311, 340
Sex 7, 145-170
    activities for children on the
        topic of 157, 158
    abortion 157, 163, 166, 170
    adolescence and 146, 148,
        155, 156, 157, 160, 161,
        162, 168
    attitudes about 145, 147,
        149, 150, 151, 152, 153,
        154, 155, 156, 157, 158
    criteria for books 147, 148,
        149, 151-152, 153, 154
    homosexuality 32, 33, 62,
        63, 147, 156, 162, 164,
        165, 168
    humor 151, 152, 155
    incest 22, 42, 156, 170
    intercourse 155, 156, 162,
        163, 166, 167, 168
    masturbation 147, 155, 156,
        168
    menstruation 156, 157, 162,
        163
    negative attitudes about 146,
        152, 153, 154, 155, 156,
        157, 158, 161, 162, 166,
        167, 168
    nocturnal emissions 157
    pornography 146
    pregnancy 17, 18, 19, 34,
        35, 157, 158, 162, 163,
        166, 167, 314, 338
    premarital 146, 156, 157,
        158, 160, 162, 163, 166,
        170

puberty   146, 155, 156, 157, 161, 162, 163, 164
reproduction   153, 154, 155, 160, 161, 162, 163, 164, 165, 166, 167, 168, 169, 170
sexuality and   147-148, 152, 155, 157, 158, 160, 167, 169, 170
stages of development   147, 150, 158, 159
stereotypes   152, 154, 167, 168
terminology   151, 153, 154, 155, 162, 163, 164, 169
Try This on the topic of   146-147, 148
Sex Information and Education Council (SIECUS)   147, 148, 159
Sexism   295, 307, 315, 317, 336
Sexist words, alternatives for   297-301
Siblings   6, 12-42, 323, 328, 329
    activities for children on the topic of   17, 19, 21
    birth order   13, 24
    cooperation and love   17, 20-21, 25, 27, 28, 29, 32, 40, 41, 104, 187, 188, 225
    criteria for books about   14-15
    eldest   18, 19, 20, 26
    middle child   13, 35, 36
    new baby   14, 15-18, 25, 27, 32, 33, 34, 39, 42, 166, 167, 192, 231-232, 238-239
    responsibility   21-22, 28, 30, 39, 109, 330
    rivalry   15, 16, 17, 18-20, 24, 26, 30, 32, 38, 41, 166
    Try This on the topic of   13, 19
    twins   19, 20, 21, 22, 26, 28,

29, 34, 36, 41, 85, 338, 341
    youngest child   13, 18, 19, 20, 29, 31, 33, 39, 42
Single Parents; *see* Parents, single
Slavery   124, 198, 199, 206, 207, 222, 226, 229, 234, 245, 310
Stein, Gertrude   334
Stereotypes; *see* Blacks, Females, Native Americans, Old Age, Sex
Stowe, Harriet Beecher   330
Suicide; *see* Death
Tallchief, Maria   311
Terezin Concentration Camp   122, 142
Truth, Sojourner   244, 310, 346
Try This; see Blacks, Death, Divorce, Females, Native Americans, Old Age, Reading, Sex, Siblings, War
Tubman, Harriet   197, 198, 199, 240, 242, 310, 340

Underground Railroad   198, 199, 207, 208, 230, 233, 243, 263
Urban life; *see also* City; Ghettos   185, 186, 188, 224, 235, 236, 239, 245, 266

Values clarification   2, 6, 9
Violence   119, 123, 126

Walker, Maggie Mitchell   310, 326
War   7, 113-143
    activities for children on the topic of   115, 118, 119, 120, 122, 127, 129
    adoption of war offspring   127
    allegories   115-119, 123-124,

134, 135, 136-137, 138, 140, 141, 142, 143
    American Civil   124-125, 128, 136, 138, 141, 143
    American Revolutionary   121, 123, 132, 332
    attitudes about   114, 121, 122, 124, 125, 126, 128, 129, 130, 131, 132, 133, 134, 135, 139, 142
    Biafran   114
    causes of   117, 126, 138
    criteria for books about   114-115
    First World War   139
    French Revolution   140
    Indochinese   113, 127, 128, 130, 131, 132, 133, 137
    Korean   127
    Middle Eastern   114
    patriotism and   128, 132
    Pig War   131
    propaganda   114, 127
    Second World War   114, 125-126, 131, 132, 133, 134, 135, 136, 137, 138, 139, 140, 141, 324
    Spanish American   128
    Try This on the topic of   114, 115
    Vietnamese; *see* Indochinese
Ward, Nancy   280
Wel-Met Award; *see* Awards (Child Study Association of American/Wel-Met)
W.I.T.C.H.   316
Women's International League for Peace and Freedom   203
Women's Movement; *see* Feminist Movement
Wordless books   118, 140
Woodward School Annual Book Award; *see* Awards
Working mothers; *see* Females

NOTES and ADDITIONS

NOTES and ADDITIONS

NOTES and ADDITIONS

NOTES and ADDITIONS

NOTES and ADDITIONS